THE EVANGELICAL FAITH

Other Books by Helmut Thielicke:

Between God and Satan

A Little Exercise for Young Theologians

Out of the Depths

The Silence of God

THE EVANGELICAL FAITH

HELMUT THIELICKE

Translated and Edited by
GEOFFREY W. BROMILEY

VOLUME ONE

PROLEGOMENA

THE RELATION OF THEOLOGY
TO MODERN THOUGHT FORMS

T. & T. CLARK LIMITED
36 GEORGE STREET, EDINBURGH

To
Wilfrid Laurier University
Waterloo, Ontario
in grateful appreciation
of the award of the LL.D. degree (*honoris causa*)

Copyright © 1974, Wm. B. Eerdmans Publishing Company

Translated from the German edition *Der Evangelischer Glaube* © 1968, Helmut Thielicke, J. C. B. Mohr (Paul Siebeck), Tübingen.

PRINTED IN THE U.S.A.
FOR
T. & T. CLARK LTD., EDINBURGH

0-567-02354-0

FIRST PRINTED. . . .1978

Editor's Preface

It is a particular pleasure to introduce this first volume of Helmut Thielicke's *Evangelical Faith* to the English-speaking world. Until the publication of an abridgement of his *Theological Ethics* Thielicke was mainly known in English for his powerful sermons. His real vocation, however, has been that of a theologian, and it is no secret that he has been disconcerted rather than flattered that his incidental activity should have become the basis of his reputation. The present work should help to correct the situation.

In contrast to the *Theological Ethics,* the *Evangelical Faith* is presented with a minimum of compression and no arbitrary rearrangements. If some of the material is less relevant to the non-European scene this does not reduce its value. It is indeed a salutary corrective to parochialism and enhances the significance of the book in terms of expansion of knowledge and insights. The few abridgements in the text and footnotes and in the concluding excursus involve no material excisions.

Written at the height of demythologization and death of God debates, the book might seem in a sense to be outmoded. But this is a superficial impression. These dated issues serve only as illustrations of the fundamental and very pertinent analysis that is Thielicke's main theme, and if anything they are enabled to function the more successfully as such by the new element of historical detachment. To make the transition to more recent forms of Thielicke's two types of theology is a simple and illuminating exercise.

The book is, of course, distinctively Lutheran in orientation. Nevertheless, it is not a Lutheran dogmatics in the narrower sense. The background and approach are more broadly ecumenical and a wider audience is in view. What is attempted is not the promotion of a sectional position. It is the helping of the whole church as it tries to find its way theologically in a new and perplexing age.

Geoffrey W. Bromiley

Pasadena, California

5

Contents

The Task

This first volume of a systematic theology will attempt clearance work in a cluttered situation. It will survey current debates from a defined standpoint, try to pin down terms like myth or death of God which are often bandied about far too freely, and seek to give them their true meaning. The attempt, then, is to get a grasp of modern theology, sounding out and preparing the ground on which to build.

The present intellectual and spiritual situation is marked by a distinctive dualism.

Secularization has posed the unavoidable question how it is that the emancipated world no longer understands, and refuses to listen to, the Christian message. Is it because of the outdated cosmology used by these statements? Is it because of the transcendence of a concept of God which must appear fantastic to a generation oriented to the world as it is? Or is it because the standpoint and horizon of human existence have changed so that the message answers questions that are no longer put (e.g., how one can find a gracious God) and leaves unanswered those that seem to be basic against a different horizon (e.g., how a new structure of society can be achieved, instead of being improvised or patched up, when the established structure is breaking down, or how freedom can be lived out in the confines of a world of management)?

As Christian proclamation has sought at great intellectual cost and not without love to enter into new questions and to bring contemporaries in different ages within its own horizons, it has expected that it would make itself intelligible and be heard afresh. Today, however, we have seen the alarming situation that, apart from an intellectual minority, most believers have thought they could discern a selling out of the essentials and they have reacted in panic, while secularists, represented by journalists, have seemed to enjoy the supposed squabbling and for the rest have regarded the new positions more as a confirmation of their familiar existentialism than as missionary invitation. In an almost unstoppable dialectic these modern conceptions of theology seem to be reactions to the dwindling readiness to listen and also pacemakers of the galloping consumption. They are both effects and also causes of the increasing deafness.

What has gone wrong? How have the signals been crossed? Or is this the legitimate and promised offense that pointed proclamation will always provoke and by which it may feel it is validated? Can the theologies that have specifically and with heightened voice turned to contemporaries feel confirmed in their expectation when they have obviously struck a nerve when the neighbor sees (i.e., the thing is set before him) and yet does not see, hears and yet does not hear (Matthew 13:13)?

These are the points at issue. They take us deeper than a mere diagnosis of the age. They touch on the essence of the Christian message itself. Any attempt at an answer compels us to confess what we mean by this message and what is our responsibility to it. The real battle begins already once we begin to ask what form the first skirmishing and reconnoitering will take.

This dogmatics, then, begins with a different kind of prolegomena from what we find at the beginning of most dogmatic systems. It is true that most of the conventional questions of fundamental principle will be dealt with. But they are all set in a framework that includes an analysis of the situation and attempts an orientation of modern theological thought within it.

For most readers there may be an element of piquancy in the fact that an author should take this course when he attacks his theological contemporaries and colleagues in this very regard. This prolegomena is directed specifically against a theology which is obsessed with analyses of so-called modern man, which always orients itself to contemporaries, which is concerned about their understanding, which becomes wholly dependent on the conditions of such understanding. By reason of preliminary hermeneutical questions it can never get to the point and it threatens to fall under the verdict that Wilhelm Busch passes on Platonic love, namely, that of being an eternal seeking without leaving any imprint. Are we for our part falling into the same trap? Are we not becoming preoccupied with analyses and explorations?

The Method

I have begun with this question in self-criticism and in so doing, to compare the less with the greater, I have come to methodological conclusions similar to those stated by Schleiermacher in his second letter to Friedrich Lücke. In that letter he dealt with the objection that his dangerous introduction to the *Christian Faith* had given the impression that for the sake of his contemporaries he had set up a pantheistic forecourt of general religion, as though, in modern terms, he had entered too fully into its self-understanding, so that the element of Christian dogmatics in his work was controlled in advance by a dubious sign. Schleiermacher replied with the argument that in principle he could just as well have put this general element, relevant to the contemporary situation, at the conclusion in the form of a retrospective survey; then, perhaps, it could even have taken on added warmth and appeared in a truly Christian light. He decided to follow the sequence adopted in order to orient the Christian faith to the intellectual consciousness of his day, as we might now put it. He insists, however, that he has always worked out this orientation in awareness and in the light of what he later expounds as the central concept of all dogmatics, as its basic text (John 1:14).

Without trying to follow Schleiermacher either in method or matter, the author finds himself formally in a similar position. He already has in view the building he wants to build. For decades, in lectures and seminars, he has made beginnings, broken off, and then started again. He could have begun the final building and then later, when it was erected, given the *post-festum* reason why he built it here and how many negotiations he had to conduct with neighbors and earlier builders on the site in order to secure it for the purpose.

This prolegomena, too, could have been an epilogue. But for practical reasons it has seemed more suitable to begin by showing contemporaries, bewildered by the many voices and the confusion of the position, how the unhappy situation has developed and what are the ways out of it. In a time that is so replete with theological postulates and preconceptions one can hardly begin building a system without considering existing encumbrances. Otherwise the reader would be constantly asking how such statements are possible and whether the author has failed to note the barriers and obstacles that modern consciousness perceives in this area. Hence the author is forced to freight the material statement of his dogmatics with various methodological considerations and contemporary safeguards.

It is as well, therefore, to clear the decks at the outset and to confess, polemically, one's own position in the intellectual and theological situation.

The related criticism does not mean that critical acts of destruction come first and then one can consider how the theological structure of thought may be erected on the leveled site. No, the selection and preparation of the site take place as there is already awareness of the architectural plan, and we shall make the survey from the pinnacles of the building as even now we see it in our thoughts. Thus the building is always present in the prolegomena, and the instructed reader can at least get a hint of its outlines from the preparatory activities. (This latent presence of the goal at which we aim through the foggy sea of our age forms incidentally the only *tertium comparationis* uniting this modest venture with the great Schleiermacher.)

The outline of the planned building is the more easily perceived in view of the fact that the author's *Theological Ethics,* especially the first volume, is already in large part a dogmatics and thus expresses already his normative intentions. This will also explain the many references to that work scattered across these pages. Only an ill-disposed reader will accuse the author of quoting himself so much because he regards his utterances as particularly illuminating or important. The real explanation is the simple one that most of the references to the *Theological Ethics* are made when in a varied complex of problems a thought can be touched on only briefly and the author wishes to convince the reader that he has examined it more thoroughly elsewhere and that the brief attention paid to it in this work is not due simply to superficiality.

Mediating Theology?

Since this prolegomena has to wrestle with extreme standpoints that come to public attention under the slogans "conservative" and "modern"— we shall make a serious effort to dismantle these—a theology of mediation may easily be suspected when the author adopts neither position and yet in spite of all his criticisms seeks to find more than mere darkness or error in both of them. His concern is to show why he thinks he sees in them intellectual (and often dubious) superstructures of the one Christian faith. Those who from the outset regard any attempt to find a comprehensive system as an angling for syntheses and a pasting over of antitheses will have little taste for analyses of this type.

One can truly speak of mediation only on two assumptions.

The first is when there is a pragmatic desire to hold opposing positions together. But the man for whom the truth and not the goal of holding together is the criterion by which he makes his decisions can never be a mediator for all the pain he feels at possible divisions, at a possible tearing apart of the body of Christ.

The second is when a more or less honest broker in a position of neutrality to the two parties and their dispute tries to reconcile the differences. In this sense again mediation is not the goal in this work. If neither of the positions is adopted, this is not due to the indifference of a broker but rather because a third position is adopted. A preface is not the best place to present the basis of this third position. The book itself must do that. This anticipatory note concerning the dubiousness of a mediating theology is simply meant to ward off criticism in advance.

The Title

I have decided to give this dogmatics a conventional title directly corresponding to its theme. The title, then, is not meant to be more than this. If I had taken the liberty of choosing a title expressing my special intention (which would have put me out of step and been rather too alien from the usual ones), I would have actualized an early favorite thought and called the work *Being in Truth*. But would the allusion to John 18:37 have been caught in this designation, which still seems to me to be so fine and relevant? Does not the noun "being" carry too much of an echo of Heidegger for modern ears?

Since, however, I find my real theological purpose most pregnantly described in that title, it is perhaps fitting that in the preface I should provide my abandonment of it (even though already announced) with a little obituary notice in which I briefly state the intention of the book that it had so precisely expressed.

Since God discloses himself to man and seeks to be his God, any statement about God is also a statement about his relation to man. To that degree man is there in every theological utterance and thus gives it an anthropological reference. The only question is how this reference is to be defined.

From the Enlightenment and especially from Schleiermacher onwards, and right up to our own times, this reference has been expressed in the postulate that God must come into the consciousness of man and that a theology has thus to be a location of God in the human scheme of understanding. Now it is true that there is no statement about God that does not stand in relation to an existing nexus of consciousness. If we want to speak connectedly of God we have to confess what this means for conscience, for hopes and fears, for questions and self-understanding. The term "doctrine of faith," which was current in the nineteenth century, related to this inclusion in the consciousness, to this reference to the believer, and it usually understood faith itself as a form of our self-understanding. (The book itself will discuss this in more detail.)

Although in virtue of his self-disclosure God cannot in fact be discussed without this reference to the human consciousness, this does not entail his enclosure within it. More precisely, faith is not to be defined as an element in this consciousness as though it could be exhibited therein, e.g., as a kind of religious consciousness or as the province of religion. This is impossible first because all the relations of meaning in human consciousness are transformed when a man begins to believe and secondly because man cannot understand himself so long as he does not know God and understand himself in relation to him.

Hence when I use the title *Evangelical Faith* I do not have in mind a doctrine of faith in the sense indicated. I am not thinking of faith insofar as it is or can be integrated into our consciousness. What I have in view is faith to the degree that it stands representative for him who is believed and for what is bound up with his benefits. The attack launched in this book against Cartesianism in modern theology ought to show that my primary interest is not in the subject of faith but in that in which faith believes and by which the subject is changed into a "new creature."

If, then, the book is about the relation between God and man and not about a purely transcendent God taken theistically in and for himself, I understand primarily by this relation an ontic rather than a noetic relation. Man "is" his relation to God. He is the one created by him, in flight from him, visited by him and justified.[1]

Thus Luther can describe as the subject[2] of theology the correlation between lost man and the redeeming God. For Calvin, too, the sum of theology

---

[1] Cf. Luther in *Enarratio Ps. 51* (1552), who relates the knowledge of God, divine and theological wisdom, to the justifying and saving God and man created, lost and sinful (WA, 40, II, 327, 11ff.).

[2] Subject is meant here in the sense of *hypokeímenon;* it refers both to the one who does theology and also to its theme.

is the knowledge of God and ourselves in this sense.[3] He who speaks of God can do so only in such a way that he speaks of God's relation to man.

This might tempt us to try to present theology as anthropology, but only in such a way that man always appears as he is defined by God and what is transcendent to him is always stated along with him. Now obviously the correlation of God and man will also be reflected in the consciousness; both Luther and Calvin speak of the knowledge (*cognitio*) of God and man. This reflection, however, is only the superstructure, the echo of that which ontically defines man's existence, the fact that he is lost and also saved.

In this sense the Johannine statement which was originally intended to be the title of this book, and which is still at least its lodestar, refers to the truth of a being or to a being in the truth, to that relation which sustains human existence. Whether thinking man—including theologically thinking man—arrives at the truth depends on whether before all theory or acts of thought he "is" in the truth.

The Venture of a System

In conclusion the author would like to discuss another matter.

In an age which publishes little more than collections of theological essays, and which is thus characterized as an age of questioning and transition, it might seem presumptuous to set forth here the first part of a complete dogmatic system. I can only confess quite simply that I am aware of the venture involved and also of my own inadequacy for it. Yet it has become my conviction that the basic questions that have arisen and that trouble us cannot be, if not mastered at least properly tackled, just by ordinary individual polemics but only by attempting a doctrinal totality. When problems affect the substance of Christian faith and touch on all its dimensions, then it is challenged as a whole and it must react accordingly.

Perhaps for the moment we are indeed in a position only to put individual stones in the mosaic, and I have every respect for theological colleagues whose important monographs help to do this so impressively. Yet I myself must make the venture of recapturing the total picture or at least of recalling it, of giving a reminder of its existence. I do not want to miss the woods for the trees. To those hard at work in the woods I will perhaps look like a passing hiker, possibly even a happy-go-lucky fellow who is looking around in all directions instead of concentrating on a particular growth (although this kind of journey can often be the most strenuous). I greet them all with friendship, gratitude, and respect, even if they may view me with a certain indignation, and I am aware that the more or less passable trails are due to their labors. If these foresters and their associates, however, are kind enough to spare the forest rambler a few glances, they will perhaps notice that he has had to take note of their work, for otherwise he would not be here and would never have reached this part of the forest. The rambler is simply seeking in all modesty to give a first report on what is going on in

---

[3] Cf. *Institutes* (1536); *Johannis Calvini opera selecta,* ed. P. Barth, I (Munich, 1926), p. 37.

this forest, on what he has seen in it, and on why he regards it, not as the aggregate of felled or stricken trees or trees standing alone, but rather as a vast and inviting forest.

Thanks

Finally thanks are expressed to all who have helped the author in this work, to his assistants Dr. K. D. Nörenberg and H. Kuhfuss, who have not only discussed all the problems with him but also taken on many technical tasks, including preparation of the indexes, and to his trusty friend and colleague Dr. Rainer Röhricht, with whom he has been associated for many years in a very vital and beautiful fellowship of common labor. The secretaries Miss L. Hinrichsen and Mrs. A. K. Ziegler also deserve credit for their valuable technical help.

Abbreviations

Apol. CA	Apology of the Confession of Augsburg
ATD	*Das Alte Testament Deutsch*
CA	Confession of Augsburg
CD	Karl Barth, *Church Dogmatics*, ed. G. W. Bromiley and T. F. Torrance (1936ff.)
Cl	Otto Clemen, *Luthers Werke in Auswahl* (1925ff.)
Denz.	Heinrich Denzinger, *Enchiridion Symbolorum*, Editio XXXIII
EA	*Dr. Martin Luthers sämmtliche Werke* (Erlangen, 1826-1857)
ETh	*Evangelisches Theologie, Monatsschrift*, ed. E. Wolf (Munich)
Form. Conc. Sol. decl.	*Solida declaratio* of the Formula of Concord; cf. LBK
GC	Luther's Larger Catechism
GV	Rudolf Bultmann, *Glauben und Verstehen*, I-IV (1933ff.); E.T. *Faith and Understanding*, I (1969)
Holl	Karl Holl, *Gesammelte Aufsätze zur Kirchengeschichte* I, 6th ed. (1932), II, III (1928)
Inst.	John Calvin, *Institutes of the Christian Religion* (the reference is to the last edition of 1559 unless otherwise indicated)
KD	*Kerygma und Dogma. Zeitschrift für theologische Forschung und kirchliche Lehre*, ed. W. Joest (Göttingen)
KM	*Kerygma und Mythos*, ed. H. W. Bartsch (1951ff.); E.T. 1953 (Vol. I)
LBK	*Die Bekenntnisschriften der evangelisch-lutherischen Kirche*, ed. Deutscher Evangelischer Kirchenausschuss, 3rd ed. (Göttingen, 1956)
LThK	*Lexikon für Theologie und Kirche*, ed. J. Höfer and K. Rahner (1957ff.)
RGG 2 and 3	*Die Religion in Geschichte und Gegenwart*, 2nd ed., ed. H. Gunkel and L. Zscharnack (Tübingen, 1927ff.); 3rd ed., ed. K. Galling (1957ff.)
SC	Luther's Small Catechism
Stud. gen.	*Studium generale. Zeitschrift für die Einheit der Wissenschaften . . .* (Heidelberg)
TDNT	*Theological Dictionary of the New Testament*, ed. G. Kittel and G. Friedrich, tr. G. W. Bromiley (1964ff.)
ThE	Helmut Thielicke, *Theologische Ethik* I-III (1951ff.); E.T. (altered and abridged) *Theological Ethics* (1966ff.)

ThEx	*Theologische Existenz heute*
ThLZ	*Theologische Literaturzeitung,* ed. K. Aland (Berlin)
WA	*D. Martin Luthers Werke.* Kritische Gesamtausgabe (Weimar, 1883ff.)
ZThK	*Zeitschrift für Theologie und Kirche,* ed. G. Ebeling (Tübingen)

Perhaps we have become antiquated—
We now need to read in more modern style.
                                        Goethe

What makes a theologian is living,
nay rather dying and damning,
not thinking, reading, or speculating.
                                        Luther

I think, therefore I am.
                Descartes

I am thought, therefore I am.
                Franz von Baader

He is—therefore I think.
  Johann Georg Hamann

Part One

THE STATE OF THEOLOGICAL DISCUSSION

Orientation of
Our Theological Thinking

I

Address to the Contemporary World

1. ADDRESS AS PART OF THE HISTORICITY OF THE MESSAGE

To do theology is to actualize Christian truth, or, better, to set it forth in its actuality and to understand it afresh thereby. To that extent theology is by nature, and not merely in its pedagogical implications, historical. It has nothing whatever to do with timeless truth. Hence there can be no timeless or supratemporal theology (*theologia perennis*).

In fact a written dogmatics never begins anew. It is always in a distinct tradition of thought. This implies certain conditions. It must wrestle with questions already posed. Thus no theology today can ignore the open and very delicate problem of the relation of revelation and history. For the documentation of revelation, the Bible, contains historical matter. To that extent it raises the question whether and how far the document is verifiable for a mind that is aware of being bound by specific criteria of historical truth.

As these questions must be tackled and prior solutions critically examined, there must be confrontation between Christian truth and the modern mind, the ruling structures of thought, the understanding of self and the world among contemporaries. For every word, including God's Word, implies a recipient, present-day man, contemporaries. This Word is historical not merely in the sense of being grounded in history but also as it is addressed to historical situations. Both the authors and the recipients of verbal messages are subject to the process of history.

The message, then, cannot be detached at either point. If an effort is made in this direction there arises the false notion of perennial theology characterized by an abstract conceptual system. Scholasticism and seventeenth-century orthodoxy are classical examples.

If, however, the temporality of Christian truth is taken seriously, two results follow.

First, the relation of the biblical authors to specific points in history means that their statements have to be seen in their historical determination, their contemporary reference; hence the intention behind them has to be distinguished from the means of expression placed at their disposal by current ideas, vocabulary, etc. This is one of the reasons—and perhaps the most conclusive—why the historical question is forced on theology.

But this raises the problem whether the active radius of the methods of historical inquiry is enough to bring to light the core of intention in the biblical message, to bring into being, therefore, a relation of immediacy between two spheres or phases which are poles apart. Since those methods are themselves controlled by the habit of the modern mind, the one who understands today is at issue as well as the one who wrote yesterday. At no point in theological reflection can one ignore these two historical references.

Second, the one who understands today is genuinely at issue when we realize that the word of proclamation is addressed to him, i.e., to "us," and thus seeks to encounter us. This encounter, however, presupposes the communication of two structures and hence a certain analogy between them, no matter how this may be defined. When there is complete absence of analogy, as between a man and a star, there can be no encounter. Where there are traces of an analogy, as between a man and his dog, there can be corresponding traces of encounter. Through Christian truth, however, there is an encounter that concerns man's existence, that touches his personal core, his heart, so that it applies to him unconditionally. A high degree of analogy is thus presupposed.

This analogy, then, must be defined. Such a definition must be guided by the question how far Christian truth radically concerns and strikes man, or, more precisely, modern man. To answer this question one must fix the horizon within which man asks, despairs, and founders, and yet also within which he thinks and hopes he can still prevail. There is no address unless this horizon is fixed and accepted.

To this extent there is in fact a correlation between the questions man puts and the Christian answer, and conversely a correlation between the questions Christian truth puts to man and his need to put these questions to himself.[1] It might well be that man himself has no questions, that he enfolds himself in the indifference of unquestioning vegetating. In this case the questions put to him by Christian truth involve a releasing of his own questions or counterquestions. (Note that the first correlation of question and answer in the Bible is God's question to Adam, not Adam's question to God [Genesis 3:9].)

In any case the hearer of the word of proclamation, and hence the contemporary, is always implicated when that word is set forth. He is thus implicated as well when theology steps in and unfolds the word reflectively. For theology can unfold the word only as it deals with an addressed word and very emphatically makes it known in its present significance, in its actuality "for me."

---

[1] In this respect Paul Tillich is on the right track with his principle of correlation (cf. *Systematic Theology*, I [1951], pp. 59ff., 203ff.) even though the second set of questions is far less prominent than the first in consequence of his ontological thought-schema. Cf. on Tillich the author's "Theologische Verkündigung in der modernen Welt," *Universitas* (1959), pp. 149ff.

To this end it is not enough to present faith alone as the content of the address, although Christian truth does appeal to faith. Only a very abstract correlation corresponding to perennial theology would describe a general address to faith. The real address can only be to "believing man" in his concreteness.

This is true already because faith by nature is always under assault. It exists in the Nevertheless. It is faith against something as well as faith in something. It is achieved only as the enduring of trial. But in many of their forms assault and trial are historically variable. To that extent they change with each new present. Although there is a sphere of primal and unchanging models of temptations (we can understand directly temptations such as those of Psalm 73), one may still say that the trials of the young Luther or Jerome are quite different from those of Jacobsen or Camus or the organization man of the modern age. Each of them demands a new point in preaching and a new thematic emphasis in theological reflection.

Since address, both that of preaching and also that of theological reflection on the basis of preaching, belongs constitutively to the word, one can understand why there is a history of preaching and theology and why no form of preaching nor theological system can claim timeless validity and simply be accepted by later generations. Even confessions cannot claim canonical validity for the form of their statements in the sense of conferring on themselves the structure of nonhistorical timelessness. As their address changes, i.e., as they must become actual for each new generation, they have to be interpreted. This new interpretation is a differentiation of their doctrinal intention from their historically conditioned form.[2]

Thus the history of theology is fundamentally no other than the history of its various attempts at address. And this history is the history of relevance for contemporaries.

The fact of this history yields the postulate that every theology must relate to the contemporary world, that it must be modern. But in relating to contemporaries theology cannot neglect the theological dialog which is in process. At essential points this dialog is undoubtedly a dialog about the substance of theology, e.g., the understanding of the Bible, controverted questions between confessions, Christ's person and work, justification, or eschatology.

Nevertheless, as the substance of theology is kept in view, we must also have an eye for the one to whom it applies, the one addressed. The reason why the contemporary recipient comes into play is not just because we have to ask: "How shall I put it to my children?" It is not just because we have to consider homiletical and catechetical techniques. The question of the How of transmission is secondary, vital though it is and difficult to answer. In contrast, regard for the one addressed is not secondary; it is basic and material. For if the matter of the word is to concern and strike me radically, the question who I am is an integral part of the material question.

Recent theological history also shows that the question who I am and how

---

[2] Cf. F. Brunstäd, *Theologie der luth. Bekenntnisschriften* (1951), pp. 9ff.

far the word of proclamation applies to me has been the main force behind every fresh theological inquiry. It was this question that forced upon Schleiermacher, Ritschl, Wilhelm Herrmann, Bultmann, and Bonhoeffer their new conceptions of the matter of theology.[3]

2. DISTINCTION BETWEEN ACTUALIZATION AND ACCOMMODATION

This observation leads on to the further insight that the formulation of theological teaching is not only with a view to the contemporary. It is also in terms of the contemporary. It is set in train by him. (The two aspects are obviously related, but the difference in nuance should be noted.) Every new need provokes new theological reflection and leads to new insights in the course of it. Thus a sense of guilt in an age like that of Luther can be a challenge to theology. The affliction of conscience deriving from this sense of guilt can no longer be relieved by an understanding of justification that is itself crippled by the legalism of the idea of merit. Indeed, this understanding of justification has itself provoked and confirmed the guilt-complex. Hence the doctrine of justification needs revision. The contemporary situation which found a spokesman in Luther thus had a constructive effect on theological thought and gave it what Lessing liked to call a historical "push" in the right direction.

Another age may be more troubled by anxiety than guilt. It stands under the threat of non-being. Its problem is a sense of finitude or of the absurdity of existence. This problem can then have its own constructive effect and release new theological aspects.

Whenever the need changes, or, better, its dominant accent shifts, we get a new form of challenge and of the resultant push.[4] Observation of these events brings to light certain structural constants that make it possible for us to establish a kind of typology of these historical pushes.

The changing need usually produces two recurrent and typical reactions to existing theology.

First, the younger contemporary may say that traditional theology is no longer relevant to him, that he does not find his own existential problems in it, and that he is thus compelled to say resignedly that he does not belong here. Thus after the First World War the shaken contemporary represented by Karl Barth could no longer recognize the disjointed world in the syntheses of Protestant culture and its theology. The contemporary's sense of misunderstanding and irrelevance constituted a challenge to theology which forced it to make corrections and to return afresh to its kerygmatic theme.

---

[3] The question whether the same may be said of Karl Barth is hard to answer, but for reasons I cannot go into here I am inclined to think that it can.

[4] ". . . when the time comes for this basic event (by which the authority of God's Word encounters the conscience), theology is challenged by the time to bear responsibility for the event coming at the right time." G. Ebeling, "Wort Gottes und kirchliche Lehre," *Konfession und Ökumene* (1964), p. 58.

Second, however, the contemporary in a different type of reaction may desire, whether pragmatically or out of an impulse of conservatism, not to give up the traditional force of Christianity. He thus refrains from resigned repudiation. But since he has to actualize the traditional matter in order to attain to a living relation with it, he simply cuts the ill-fitting garment to suit himself. Strictly speaking this is not really an actualization of traditional truth. It is an accommodation.

Actualization always consists in a new interpretation of truth, in its re-addressing, as it were. The truth itself remains intact. It means that the hearer is summoned and called "under the truth" in his own name and situation.

Accommodation, on the other hand, takes a different tack. It calls the truth "under me" and lets me be its norm. It is pragmatic to the extent that it assigns truth the function of being the means whereby I master life.

The Enlightenment, which liked the idea of accommodation, is for many reasons that cannot be discussed here no very good example of this pragmatic alienation of truth. The "German Christians" of Hitler's day might serve as an extreme but also a very exact model. They were trying to make Christianity a specific, made-to-measure religion which would exert no pressure and cause no offense. Here the contemporary did indeed make himself the measure of all things, including the truth, according to his own understanding of himself.

To distinguish the two reactions, recognizing the pertinence of the one (actualization) and the misappropriating of the other (accommodation), the distinction of outlook must be perceived. Phenomenologically and externally the two outlooks seem to be identical twins, i.e., variant forms of one and the same process of modernization. In reality, however, they are as opposite as two antithetical ethical attitudes, namely, loyalty and disloyalty.

3. GROWTH IN THEOLOGICAL KNOWLEDGE THROUGH RE-ADDRESS

The two reactions of contemporaries—resigned withdrawal: "This does not concern me," or manipulating accommodation—constitute a theological challenge and thus give a push; they are challenges in Toynbee's sense.

The first reaction, which rejects the relevance of traditional truth, forces on theology an actualization or reinterpretation of the message with the contemporary in view. Theology tries not to ignore this existential need and theme but rather to speak to it and to adopt it. This takes place through the act we have called address.

The second reaction, in which the contemporary accommodates the truth, also forces actualization on theology if it is to resist illegitimate accommodation. In this case actualization has a polemical edge. It finds a falsification of truth already there, and to that extent, in Hegelian terms, it must negate the negation. As Christian truth authoritatively strikes the contemporary conscience and takes on actuality for it, it necessarily shatters the false structure of accommodation and the self-deification housed in it. It becomes judgment. The polemic against the contemporary spirit of which we spoke is simply an attempt to pass on human autonomy the judgment implicit in Christian truth.

The Barmen Declaration of 1934 is a classical example of this polemical form of actualization. It was directed against the "German Christian" accommodation. It did not regard itself as a new confession adding to existing utterances of the church something that was missing. It construed itself as a reinterpretation of the Reformation confessions. It simply "explained" what had been transmitted to contemporaries and in a specific way pronounced on accommodation and self-deification the judgment already present in the ancient confessions.[5]

This polemical actualization as a form of statement may be seen also in the classical confessions themselves. In structure they first say "We confess and teach" and then go on to say "We reject." The rejection can be understood only in the light of the preceding affirmation, so that grammatically it might seem that the rejection has the form of a consecutive clause: "We confess . . . *so that* what follows is implicitly rejected. . . ."

What follows materially precedes chronologically, for a current error was the spur to theological reflection on what had to be confessed, so that the error was seen as a challenge. This challenge made the confession necessary, even the positive side. To that extent it promoted growth in theological knowledge.

Hence the necessary address to contemporaries who did not understand themselves aright and who misunderstood Christian truth constituted, and still constitutes, an impulse to the development of doctrine. It sets such insights in the clear light of reflection. The insights were already part of the legacy of teaching. (Otherwise the error could not have been perceived and there could have been no appeal to "the" Christian truth.) Thus far, however, they had been in a state of incubation. Only the challenge of contemporaries activated them. For this challenge necessitated argument. It demanded "a reason for the hope that is in you" (1 Peter 3:15). It made it necessary to seek out and express this reason and to develop doctrine in its name. It brought what was latent into the light of reflection.

Since theological truth is therewith historical; since it is provoked by the contemporary and his situation; since it is thus addressed to him, all theological work must begin by confronting its age, and not just its age in general, but also the way in which current theology has responded to its and our age. One has thus to ask: Which challenges has it replied to? Which has it overlooked? To what extent has it come under the control of these challenges by reacting in the form of accommodation and not just actualization?

This is the reason why we must begin, not by discussing the ongoing theological debate, but by defining our position in it vis-à-vis our theological

---

[5] Cf. H. Asmussen, *Dokumentenband* (Wuppertal-Barmen, 1934), pp. 11ff.

contemporaries. They too, as is now clear, are concerned about the relevance of their thinking. All of them are, not just those who are modern and even avant-garde, but also those who are called conservative. Even rigid fundamentalists are trying to be more elastic at least in the techniques of homiletical presentation to the contemporary world.

In some way, then, every theology lives and thinks in the correlation of challenge and response. Our question is how it so lives and thinks, and we have then to consider how we ourselves should live and think in this correlation. Our hope is that raising and discussing this question has already led us, and will lead us further, into the central domain of dogmatics. Insight into the historicity of Christian truth is already part of this.

II

Terminological Inadequacy of the Terms Modern and Conservative and Their Replacement with Cartesian and Non-Cartesian

Instead of speaking of modern and conservative theology, we shall refer simply, but materially more accurately, to the Cartesian and non-Cartesian structure of theological thought (abbreviated as Theology A and Theology B).

1. GENERAL HISTORY OF THE TERM MODERN

There is a general sense today (and has been for some time) that there is a modern theology and a conservative theology. The one may also be labelled progressive and the other reactionary. Any man setting forth a system of Christian truth must either let it be known to which side of the alternative he belongs or he must contest the alternative. Our own concern is to deny that it exists. This prolegomenon leads us into debate with contemporary theology and gives us occasion to characterize our own position polemically, which is not the worst form of characterization.

The alternative of modern and conservative is in fact misleading. Since the terms are mostly used loosely as slogans, they should first be defined more precisely. To this end we shall deal briefly with the word "modern."[1]

The late Latin adjective *modernus* is used early in the second millennium for the Nominalists who, as opposed to theological epistemology and its Platonic acceptance of the reality of universals, recognized only the existence of the individual. The builder of the first Gothic cathedral also called his work an *opus modernum* to distinguish it from *opera antiqua*. "Modern" can then be used almost as a term of opprobrium to decry departures from theological tradition. Thus the papal legate Simon de Brion described as *moderna curiositas* the progressive theological inquisitiveness he thought he found at the new university of Paris in 1253.

The term underwent modification in the course of time. Originally denot-

---

[1] Good material may be found in *Aspekte der Modernität* (1965), ed. H. Steffen; cf. esp. the essays by H. Anton (pp. 7ff.) and H. R. Jauss (pp. 150ff.).

ing the contrast between present-day thought and ancient philosophy (cf. the famous Quarrel of Ancients and Moderns in 1687), from the time of Sperander's *À la Mode-Sprach der Teutschen* in 1727, and then in the nineteenth century, it is used increasingly for polemical detachment from the immediate past. It thus denotes the *dernier cri*, as in Ortega y Gasset (*Revolt of the Masses* [E.T. 1932], pp. 35ff.), who finds in it the sense of being right up to date, progressive, and superior. It thus comes to express more clearly an element present in germ in the distinction from antiquity, namely, that of having achieved maturity instead of merely playing the pitiable role of following a tradition. From the time of the Enlightenment traditional truths are not just accepted but subjected to criteria supplied by one's own theoretical and practical consciousness. Each man is a "somebody"—the dignity of autonomy suggests this—and to that degree he swims against the stream of tradition. The stress is more and more on opposition to the immediate past, to what was regarded as true yesterday, and the reason for this is that there is a sense of the progress of science and perhaps of man himself, so that permanent self-correction and advance are necessary, and modern systems dissolve with increasing speed and become increasingly hectic. Undoubtedly there lies behind the term "modern" a specific understanding of man as come of age and of history as a progressive process.

The ideological character of the term, and its vacillation in meaning, raise doubts already as to its suitability for denoting a theological standpoint. This scepticism is deepened when we try to systematize the range of meaning that the term has today. This brings to light three basic aspects.

The first is its normative understanding. Ortega is representative here when he points out that the present or last standpoint is a norm by which to judge all that precede. This is because it is regarded as better and more advanced than all prior standpoints and opinions. Perhaps the implied belief in progress is induced by technology with its one-way-street of progress in which the new is better than the outmoded. But even if it is, the question still remains whether in other spheres of the human, mind as well as ethos, there might not also be regression and decadence. Do not lean periods usually follow great resurgences? This theme has been so well developed in the literature of culture, society, and artistic criticism that we need only allude to it here.

Second comes the analytic concept of the modern. The interest here is statistical rather than normative. It depicts the state of modern man. The classical example is Nietzsche, especially in his work *Vom Nutzen und Nachteil der Historie für das menschliche Leben* (1873/74). Modern man is here depicted as a kind of Sisyphus who carries around with him a monstrous burden of heavy stones of knowledge, who has not learned how to handle the past and tradition, and who is bowed down by the force of external materials so that his own vital powers are damaged and finally destroyed. People of this kind, living other men's lives rather than their own, are extinguished as subjects. They fall victim to the cold daemon of knowledge. They become "proud apes." We are ill with modernity. "Modern" here does not express what ought to be. It is a chronological description of our state, the state of latecomers who threaten to become *homunculi*. In contrast to the optimistic normative concept, this analytical concept is supremely pessimistic. And in view of the tension between the two views, one can only ask whether "modern" really has any meaning at all.

Third, there is a conservative concept (cf. R. Haas, "Wie modern sind die englischen Klassiker?" in *Neusprachliche Mitteilungen* [1966], 4, pp. 208ff.). At first glance the conservative concept of the modern seems to be a contradiction in terms, since the modern and the conservative are usually at odds. Yet we see a reason for it when we think of Kierkegaard's idea of repetition, namely, that part of the past is repeated in re-presentation and its contemporaneity is thus displayed. Thus Haas shows how modern English literature, which might be called classical in rank, adopts ancient mythological models. In contrast to theological demythologizing, these are right up to date and thus potentially modern. "The Esperanto of primal images is always understood." Poetry, which is linguistically shaped aetiology, remains modern just because it is so old, not in spite of it. Worth noting here is that Dante in his *Divine Comedy* (Paradise, Canto 17) refers to a point in which all ages are present. Here the term "modern" denotes presence, whether in relation to primal models of being or to past events which become contemporary and which I can repeat. The modern here is not a new thing opposing the past polemically and in self-conscious criticism. It takes up the past into itself. (In this sense one might find in Nietzsche, too, references to a legitimate and hence positive modernity.)

The term "modern" is thus so varied in sense that if used without differentiation it is meaningless. Hence it is as well to select one of the possible understandings and to state plainly what this is.

Before noting how modernity affects theology we shall point out at once that the third nuance does at least approximate the position represented here.

2. THEOLOGICAL CONCEPT OF MODERN

In theology "modern" came into use especially in the nineteenth century. It denotes here the concern to bring theological statements into harmony with the sense of truth as this had been transformed by historical and scientific study.

This formulation is intentionally broad. "Into harmony with" leaves open for the moment the question whether theology is simply to be in correspondence with the new understanding of truth, relating itself to the new questions and becoming answerable to their premises, or whether it should acknowledge the normative rank of the new understanding and accommodate itself to it.

In any case the word "modern" occurs increasingly in the titles of many theological books whether conservative or "positive" on the one side or liberal and accommodating on the other. Such works are especially common at the beginning of the present century. One may also note at this period the Roman Catholic condemnation of Modernism as a heresy.

Nowadays the word is used in almost stereotyped fashion for existentialist theology (Bultmann) and for schools which place the thematic stress of theological thought on the correspondence of revelation with the man of self-resting finitude and the post-religious generation (Tillich, Bonhoeffer). The aim of this thinking is certainly not to give the modern self-consciousness a dominant position and then to accommodate Christian truth to it as a function, though this charge is constantly made in popular attacks. The real point is to work out the possibilities of understanding Christian truth. To that extent the theme is one of appropriation. Hence these trends, and not these alone, take up themes with which theology has been incessantly concerned since Semler and Lessing.

The theme of appropriation brings contemporaries into play since it is they who are to appropriate. We are thus back at the problem of address, and hence also of understanding, of reinterpretation.

Since it is a matter of understanding, and this involves hermeneutics, the subject of understanding must be investigated, the conditions he brings with him, the needs which give rise to his questions, the self-understanding which determines their drift, and the scheme of thought within which he asks and with whose help he formulates the questions.

We shall leave open for the moment the question whether or how far this investigation might do what was not intended and invest the subject of understanding with a normative rank for what is understood. This must be discussed later. Here we may simply state that investigating the subject and presuppositions of understanding is the principle which controls all theologies of this type. But since this investigation, as we shall see, claims every living theologian apart from some in fundamentalist circles, and the only distinction is in the rank assigned to the investigation within the system, it is hardly appropriate to reserve the word "modern" for specific trends alone. Any adult theology is trying to be modern, for the word it has to expound and to unfold systematically contains within itself the element of address and ongoing reinterpretation. Hence we have to say, not without irony, that the modern is already old, at least two hundred years old.

It would thus be possible to attach the label "modern" to theological constellations that fall under the pluperfect of the eighteenth century or the perfect of the nineteenth century. (Indeed, much of what is supposedly modern may be found fairly exactly in Semler.) The confusion caused by the word perhaps reaches the height of absurdity when it is stated that the dialectical theology arose out of, and reacted against, that which regarded itself as modern and was decried as such. Thus Gogarten was a student of the "modern" Troeltsch, and Barth and Bultmann began as students of the "modern" Herrmann.[2] This dubious concept twists the sequence of generations and puts the modern on the scrap heap or takes the scrap and makes it the epitome of a new "latest thing." It is thus rather wryly that Paul Wernle already bewails

---

[2] Cf. *Anfänge der dialektischen Theologie* (Munich, 1966), p. XIII.

the outmoding of modern theology in 1915.[3] One is tempted to add to Jung's slogan that "the future has already begun" the further slogan that "the modern is already out of date." In fact Heinz Beckmann[4] points out that the attempts of modern theology to raise the question of God in the horizontal and secular dimension of fellow-humanity, as in Herbert Braun, have already been outmoded by present-day literature: "Christians can no longer answer in the vertical dimension. They have long since put their treasure in earthly barns. Whereas modern literature has almost completely lost any interest in what is called fellow-humanity, Christians increasingly orient themselves horizontally and hence they can no longer understand at all the decisive question of modern literature." As so often, that which thinks of itself as specifically modern in theology is following tracks that have long since been abandoned. Along these lines Harvey Cox accuses Bultmann's attempts at modernization of giving a nineteenth-century answer to a twentieth-century dilemma. Bultmann does not speak to modern man because he puts the mythical language of the Bible into that of yesterday's metaphysics (modern only in his own view) instead of into the vocabulary of today's post-metaphysical world.[5]

We thus propose to abandon the term modern, since it says both too much and too little. Instead we shall describe the trends which with erroneous exclusiveness are called modern as variations of Cartesian theology. This, too, brings out only one aspect, and it would be too much of a simplification if meant to characterize the totality of these complex theologies. To denote a specific aspect, however, the word Cartesian is valid. For Descartes (b. 1596) with his statement *Cogito, ergo sum* (I think, therefore I am) initiated all the movements which find their point of departure in the I as the subject of experience and understanding.

In Descartes, of course, the I is abstract (*res cogitans*) with no specific contours (in the contemporary sense). (The same applies to the transcendental ego of Kant.) Nevertheless, Descartes paves the way for making the relevance of the knowing self the center of thought. In the age of historicism this beginning very logically produces the further question who or what this I is and what are the conditions of its existence. In investigation of the I Descartes ushers in the first phase by affirming its existence; the question of the who or what constitutes the second phase.

This reflection on the I underlying the act of thought and belief causes the cleavage in intellectual history signified by the name Descartes. It entails the modern revolution to the extent that henceforth every object of thought, understanding, perception, and indeed will and belief, is related to the conditions contained for these acts in the subject that executes them. Kant works out the principle programmatically in his great *Critiques*. The I is always present now as an autonomous theme. In his explication of the principles of microphysics Heisenberg can even reduce this presence of the observing sub-

---

[3] K. Barth and E. Thurneysen, *Ein Briefwechsel* (Munich-Hamburg, 1966), p. 40; E.T. p. 36.

[4] *Godot oder Hiob. Glaubensfragen in der modernen Literatur* (1965), p. 24.

[5] Harvey Cox, *The Secular City* (1965), p. 252.

ject to the formula that we must always be aware of being participants in the drama of life and not just spectators, since the observer actively enters the field of observation with his probe. Man, then, always stands over against when he observes; he is always himself a theme (cf. Heisenberg's *The Physicist's Conception of Nature* [E.T. 1958], pp. 14-16, 24).

It is strange that while Descartes' theological contemporaries registered the earthquake caused by his philosophy they failed to locate its true epicenter, i.e., in awareness of the ego. Contemporary attacks were directed against Descartes' supposed atheism and his blasphemous attempt to make a method out of doubt. They showed systematically how all the *loci* of dogmatics are changed and damaged under the influence of his philosophy (cf. Peter van Mastricht's *Novitatum Cartesianarum Gangraena* of 1677). Also attacked were the results of Cartesian thought, but with no consideration of the questions that produced these results or of the subjective principle that made the questions necessary. Only in Christopher Wittig's *Consensus veritatis in Scriptura divina . . . revelatae cum veritate philosophica a Renato Descartes detecta* (Leiden, 1682) does one get slight hints that the importance of the new awareness of the ego was suspected. For if Wittig does not discuss the subjectivity of present-day believers, he does reflect on the ego of the authors of Scripture as this was conditioned by time, situation, and knowledge. These men were entangled in *praejudicium* (preconception), e.g., cosmological and scientific concepts. We moderns, who think in terms of other presuppositions, cannot share these primitive preconceptions. Hence we must look in the Bible for insights that express "pure truth" independently of such hypotheses.

Indirectly at least one sees here the difference between the subjective situation of the authors of Scripture and our own. There are also traces of the task of transposition thereby imposed. The way is thus prepared for that reflection on the I, its situation, preconceptions, and self-understanding, which Descartes initiated and which constantly gained in strength. (For the contemporary debate between Descartes and theology cf. the fine materials in E. Bizer, "Die reformierte Orthodoxie und der Cartesianismus," ZThK, 55 [1958], pp. 306-372.)

3. THEOLOGICAL CONCEPT OF CONSERVATIVE

The term "conservative" does not have such a varied history as the term "modern." But it is ill adapted to denote a mode of theological expression and it leads to no less distortion than its counterpart. This distortion consists in the fact that "conservative" is taken to imply a reactionary form of thought which simply transmits traditions in an authoritarian, immature, and mechanical way with no effort to come to grips with them or to appropriate them.

Now this type may be found occasionally, but it would be hard to produce any theologian of eminence on whom such a verdict could be passed. More common is the type that thinks theologically, and also preaches, in distinctive detachment from time and situation. This suggests the caricature of the conservative as one who ignores time, and especially his own time. Yet here again this is not so much a type of the conservative theologian as of the esoteric "ivory-tower" theologian who in his own dimension can be unconservative and even revolutionary, and will certainly be original.

To give an example, Hermann Friedrich Kohlbrügge (b. 1803), for many years pastor of the Dutch Reformed church in Elberfeld, was a theologian of this kind. H. K. Hesse says in his biography (*H. F. Kohlbrügge* [1935], pp. 384f.) : "It is remarkable how little the 'age' found an echo in this man." The economy blossomed in his day. The railway and the steamship were invented. Science and technology advanced with giant steps. "But all this hardly touched him. Not because he was not a vital and open man, but in spite of the fact that he carried a harp with many strings in his heart. These were not touched. He . . . ignored culture, even the culture of Protestantism, in his sermons. . . . He had to proclaim the word." (Cf. also K. Barth, *Protestant Theology in the Nineteenth Century* [E.T. 1973], pp. 634ff.) This man could preach a highly individual, not at all conservative, christocentric doctrine of justification, and the freedom of the Christian man, without regard for the incipient pressures of an industrial society. His friend and admirer, Daniel von der Heydt, was a captain of industry who by calling was close to the epicenter of the age. But he did not seem to find anything missing in his theological friend. Probably he too lived in two sharply differentiated dimensions.

At any rate, among leading conservative theologians we do not find mere reactionaries. It must also be pointed out that in origin the term "conservative" has nothing to do with reaction. When it became a slogan for opposition to the French Revolution it could not be synonymous with ossification since it championed the right of living history over against an artificial state constructed abstractly and proclaimed to be correct. It naturally seeks to preserve or reclaim what has come into being historically, not because it is subservient to the law of sloth, but because what has come into being has proved itself. This cannot be said unless the criteria of reason and conscience are claimed and the judgment thus displays maturity and commitment.[6]

Historically, then, it is illegitimate to apply the term "conservative" to a theologian simply to suggest that he has swallowed earlier theological ideas, e.g., those of Paul or the Reformation, naively and uncritically, possibly as a champion of verbal inspiration. In fact no responsible and eminent theologian today ignores historico-critical research and its questions, dismisses evolution with an "It is written," or sets forth a doctrine of revelation without facing historical relativism.

We are thus confronted with the strange fact that the two basic theological

---

[6] H. Barth, *Der konservative Gedanke* (1958); H. J. Schoeps, *Konservative Erneuerung* (1958).

types A (modern) and B (conservative) are both close to one another and also far apart.

They are close because both are in touch with the age. They take up its questions and assess the approaches and results of scientific research where this shows affinity to the theological sphere. They both inquire into this affinity, e.g., into the significance of the biological theory of evolution for belief in creation, or the application of historical method to salvation history, or the verifiability or unverifiability of the biblical records. It may be that the degrees of affinity or verifiability vary. Yet none of the concerns represented by Theology A is negated by Theology B.

If the closeness of the two may be easily seen, and the differences within them are differences of degree, the fundamental distinction between them is more difficult to pin down. Nevertheless it seems to exist. Everyone is aware of it. Even those who cannot or will not examine it theoretically see a choice here and decide for one theology or the other. What is this distinction? In dealing with this question we shall be plunged into the basic problems of theology itself.

III

Sketch of Cartesian Theology (Theology A) and Its Essential Problems

1. CONCENTRATION ON THE ACT OF UNDERSTANDING AND APPROPRIATION

Perhaps one might say first and generally that Theology A is marked by a dominant interest in the addressee of the message, the one to whom it is directed and who is to appropriate it. Since we have defined address as an essential feature of the message and have thus seen the contemporary as posited along with it, there can be no doubt but that this is a lawful interest which is not indeed the privilege of a particular school but has been integral to almost all vital theologies since the Enlightenment.

Nevertheless, one may question whether a theological system ought to begin with this question of the addressee. The orientation or first step might control all further developments. When interest in the receiving I is primary we shall call this the Cartesian approach. Its primary concern is the process of appropriation, or, more radically, the possibility of this process.

The urgency of this question is obvious once man has discovered himself in his adulthood, e.g., as a rational creature. For the sake of his dignity he can no longer submit blindly to authority and be merely the passive recipient of imparted truth. In his selfhood, his autonomy, he can no longer bypass himself or ignore himself. In asking what truth is, he must figure in the discussion in his responsibility for this truth as a partner. Since Kant discovered man's autonomy one can no longer accept a truth-claim or an imperative unless it has passed the censor of theoretical and practical reason.

The claim, however, is not to go uncontrolled merely for the sake of man's autonomous dignity. As Kant pointed out, God's dignity is also at stake. For God does not want to force us as a heteronomous tyrant. He does not want servile obedience. He wants filial obedience. He wants us to turn to him spontaneously. We can do this, however, only if we are vanquished or inwardly persuaded by the claim of the message.

When we grasp this aspect of the new approach, it is plain that the Christian tradition has not been shaken and unsettled from without by the rise of the adult self but that some elements in the tradition itself are brought to life thereby and given new emphasis. As the self-consciousness of the aduit self is particularly sensitive to any heteronomy and reacts against forced faith, it also releases new impulses, giving new life to the Pauline and Reformation antithesis to servile obedience and in philosophical reflection preparing the way for a new understanding of gospel as opposed to law and of the freedom of a Christian man.

Hence what we have called the Cartesian approach does not have to be an enemy of theological tradition; on the contrary, it can contribute new insights to it. To this extent the thesis of the adult I is part of this tradition; indeed, it is a product of it. The idea of autonomy, as noted, is simply a secular form of the idea of Christian freedom. Hence the Reformation dialectic of law and gospel is taken up in another way when the question of appropriation is stressed and the central problem is how the adult I can accept or appropriate the Christian message on its own responsibility and without compulsion. In fact, if a man is an individual (the *autos* behind autonomy), he has to ask this question.

It is unavoidable, then, that the *autos* should become a theme of theological importance, that the anthropological question should be given a new stress. The question is now relevant what points of contact the message finds in our prior understanding, in our needs, hopes, and existential queries; what concepts, e.g., in contemporary philosophy, are at our disposal in putting the message into another schema; what transpositions have to be made and whether these are possible. Another question that will play a role is whether the changed view of the world, the current view, will have an effect on the possibility of appropriation. For obviously we cannot ignore our post-Copernican cosmology when the message of the Bible comes to us clothed in other cosmologies. Otherwise we should be betraying the talent of maturity committed to us. We should be unlawfully renouncing the task of being a self-responsible criterion of truth.

If we accept this critical responsibility, the next task is to consider whether and how far the kerygma can be detached from those cosmologies, or, in other words, to what sphere the kerygma belongs, to the sphere of cosmological truth or to that of existential truth. More simply, the choice we have to make is whether the Bible is a textbook of cosmology so that the view of the world it transmits is binding—which is hardly possible in view of the progress made by physics and astronomy since antiquity—or whether we have here existential messages to my self-understanding which can be separated from the outmoded cosmological notions in which they are set.

A veritable maze of new problems is thus posed by the Cartesian approach. The feature common to all of them is that they center on the situation of the adult self who is summoned to appropriate the message. The question of understanding thus becomes more and more central until finally hermeneutics becomes a theological discipline of its own. I can appropriate only what I can understand and penetrate. The claim that I must understand is a protest against blind acceptance of a heteronomous truth-claim. Conversely, it is the proclamation of responsible adulthood.

But as understanding becomes the content of a claim, the Cartesian approach raises other questions. To ask about understanding is to ask about the conditions of understanding in the subject. The problem of analogy also arises. Since there can be appropriation only if there is some analogy between me, who must understand, and that which is to be understood, one must ask what affinity there is between the message and the presuppositions of my understanding. The anthropological question is again at issue. It must be said again that this new emphasis on the anthropological does not inject an alien element into the Christian tradition. For faith in God implies a statement about the man who believes. Since I can speak of God only as he discloses himself to me, only as he wills to be there for me as my God (Immanuel), we have to speak about man when we speak about God. We can know Christ only as we know his blessings (*beneficia*), as Melanchthon said already in the preface to his Loci (1521). But how can we speak of his blessings without speaking of him who experiences them, of man? The attempt to make a statement about God which will not contain any anthropology can only end in speculation about naked deity, God in himself, and thus cross the horizon of any possible theology.[1]

2. HISTORICAL EXAMPLES

It is important that we should illustrate this Cartesian approach with a brief survey of its development in the history of theology.

Unmistakable concentration on the anthropological concern may be seen linguistically when, especially in circles that distinguish themselves from conventional theology as new or modern, the term "doctrine of faith" comes to replace dogmatics. Obviously there can be no dogmatics which does not or cannot interpret dogma as the theme and content of faith. Nevertheless, one can detect a plain shift of interest when the believer who is called upon to appropriate dogma becomes the starting-point of theological thinking. "Doctrine of faith" is thus a programmatic term to the degree that the conditions of understanding and appropriation now become the normative theme of theology.

This is indeed the theme which usually forms the broad vestibule to dogmatic discussion. But it is more than a vestibule, for these introductory matters now become the most passionate theological controversies. The discussion is no longer dominated by eucharistic or christological debates but by these questions of appropriation, of the credibility of the message. The problem of the relation between revelation and reason, history, or existence is involved here. From reading Schleiermacher's *Letters to Lücke*[2] one can

---

[1] In this regard one must agree with Bultmann when he says that to speak about God we obviously have to speak about ourselves (GV, I, p. 28; E.T. p. 55); we simply speculate, i.e., talk about an idea of God, and not God himself, if we do not speak about man at the same time (p. 117; E.T. p. 148).

[2] Ed. H. Mulert (1908).

quickly see what will be, and still is, the heart of all theological controversies today. If one looks more closely, it is seen indeed that even when central dogmas are at issue the focus is still on the possible appropriation of the kerygma rather than its content. Thus, if we turn to chapters or monographs on the resurrection message, it is not as though the historical core of the message were suppressed, but we do not have to be especially sensitive to note that the real interest is in other problems and cross-opinions, namely, whether and how far the account that claims my faith is verifiable, whether and how far a historical event involving my sense of history can be a basis of faith and not just an idea of faith projected into history (Wilhelm Herrmann), whether and how far something narrated historically can apply to me unconditionally (Paul Tillich). Epigrammatically one might almost say that the kerygmatic content plays a role only insofar as these questions obviously imply it. The theological focus is on the questions. This is the dominant note. Hence calling dogmatics the doctrine of faith is a linguistic symbol.

We find it first in a work written by P. J. Spener in 1688. Although Spener's *Doctrine of Evangelical Faith* does not yet contain the basic critical questions and is thus only a pioneer, the focus of interest on the problem of appropriation is clear enough, though it has a pietistic rather than an epistemological slant. The pietistic interest means, however, that processes in the I (in the zone of anthropology), e.g., that of regeneration, have become independent theological themes. These are the condition on which the truth can come to me. Here is a clear departure from the orthodox theology of the schools with its confirmation of dogmas by rational deduction from principles. E. Hirsch is thus right when he says that Spener is in contrast "almost like a modern man in spite of his theological wig."[3] For all the pietistic schema within which he thinks, Spener is in fact modern and paves the way for Theology A to the extent that in his view "nothing is more dangerous for faith, nor favorable to the spread of atheism, than when a preacher makes statements which have no basis and thus provide no genuine certainty" (*op. cit.*, p. 105). Here one can detect the modern question of appropriation and its possibility even though rational criteria are not used and a basis is found in the new creation of a regenerate existence. As existence is brought to the truth it hears the voice (John 18:37) and is certain of it. Thus Spener is in fact the first theologian in the German church to try to do justice to subjectivity and individuality in the sphere of theological conviction.

In examining the friend-foe relation between "modern" theology and Pietism more attention should be paid to Spener. The ambivalence of the relation is based on the paradoxical union of closeness and distance between the two. The closeness is in the analogy of the formal schema in which they both move, putting the question of assurance and appropriation, directing attention to the structure of the subject, and thus adopting the Cartesian approach. The distance may be seen in the very different ways in which they put the

---

[3] *Geschichte der neueren evangelischen Theologie*, II (1951), p. 95.

question of the subject, for in Theology A general criteria of truth are sought that are present in the pre-Christian and secular consciousness, whereas in Pietism the criteria are sought in the regenerate existence that has already been addressed by the kerygma.

The classical doctrine of faith which puts the subject and the process of appropriation at the very heart and is thus a model for all that follow was then written by Schleiermacher (1st ed. 1821/22). Later examples that have become famous are those by A. Schweizer (1863ff., influenced by Schleiermacher), J. A. Dorner (1879), D. F. Strauss (1840), Philippi (3rd ed. 1883ff.), E. Troeltsch (1925), and H. Stephan (1941).[4]

Some emphases that especially characterize the Cartesian approach may be noted.

1. In theological history Lessing set up the first model of the new style of investigation when he attacked authoritarian faith, especially in his controversy with Pastor Goeze. How can "contingent truths of history," which are only partly verifiable, constitute an absolute basis of certainty? Only "necessary truths of reason" can do this, since these alone are in my mind and to the extent that they are transmitted from without can be appropriated by it. Hence miracles which are only told to me cannot be a basis of certainty.[5] To find the true basis of possible certainty, then, I must examine the structure of the subject. Only in this structure can I find the conditions for the possibility of absolute certainty. This certainty is possible only if the truth that claims me is analogous to what my structure of consciousness contains within it as the consciousness of truth. Since I am a rational being who is aware of being enlightened and mature, any truth-claim that reaches me can be received and appropriated by me only if it contains a rational truth. This means, however, that a truth which is only historically attested and not validated by reason is mere scrap. If, on the other hand, it is so validated, it can be detached from the history that attests it once it has been perceived. For religion is not true because the evangelists and apostles taught it; they taught it because it is true.[6] I thus have my own autonomous access to truth. Perhaps in the dull and immature stages of my development the truth will first come to me by way of history. But when I perceive it and have myself appropriated it, I am independent of the one who transmits it and stand on my own feet. When the historical education of the race ends, there will only be the pure and eternal gospel of reason.[7]

We maintain that in putting the question of possible certainty Lessing adopts the Cartesian approach insofar as he examines the structure of the

---

[4] On the usage cf. O. Ritschl, *Dogmengeschichte des Protestantismus,* I (1908), pp. 14ff.

[5] *Lessing's Theological Writings,* tr. H. Chadwick (London, 1956), pp. 51ff. (*On the Proof of the Spirit and of Power*).

[6] *Axiomata,* Witkowski ed., VII, p. 214.

[7] *The Education of the Human Race* 76 and 85 in *Lessing's Theological Writings,* tr. Chadwick, pp. 95f. Cf. H. Thielicke, *Offenbarung, Vernunft und Existenz, Studien zur Religionsphilosophie Lessings,* 5th ed. (1957).

conditions of absolute certainty immanent in the consciousness. But he can define these conditions only by first defining the existence of him who has the consciousness. The basic definition is that man's existence is that of a rational being. The process within which there is or never can be certainty is necessarily indicated therewith.

2. We find the same schema of thought, but with a different definition of man's existence, in Schleiermacher. Already in the *Reden über die Religion* (1799) he poses the question of possible certainty. To establish this for "cultured despisers," i.e., secular contemporaries, he must show the place of religion in general, or, better, he must show that general consciousness includes a religious structure. Only when he succeeds in doing this can he commend religious truths to his secular contemporaries, not as a religious dictate, but as something that is compatible with their given consciousness and can thus be assimilated by it. The religious experience already present in every consciousness, and simply needing to be brought to life, is contemplation and feeling of the "universum" (Second Address). What prophets and apostles have expressed verbally so that it reaches us by way of proclamation, what they report concerning miracles, revelations and inspirations, is simply a symbolical account of the primary experience, which can be reproduced because it is there in our consciousness too. The Holy Scriptures become a dogmatic dictate and indigestible alien body only when received as dead letters and not understood as symbols behind which one must seek the true meaning. For every sacred scripture is simply a mausoleum of religion, a monument that a great spirit was once there who is there no longer; not the man who believes in a sacred scripture has religion, but the man who does not need one and could make his own.

Here as in Lessing there is protest against a dead historical faith. What comes to us thus will always be heteronomous and to that extent will remain outside. I can only appropriate a truth that is made of the stuff of my own consciousness. This is the case with religious truth. Thus far I can reproduce it in myself.

Here again, as in Lessing, there is passing reference to history. That which in me is only in a state of slumber and incubation was fiery and vital in religious geniuses and prophets. As sparks of the great spirits fall into my consciousness, this is itself enkindled and awakened. Once this happens, my own religious autonomy arises. What I had first only in the form of a reproduction of the experience of others I can now produce alone and of myself; I could make my own sacred scripture.

If, then, we change the definition of human existence and speak of religious man instead of rational man, the schema of thought is just the same as in Lessing. Both Schleiermacher in the *Reden* and Lessing, too, adopt the Cartesian approach and inquire into the structure of human consciousness in order (a) to fix the place of religious truth in our consciousness and (b) to show that this truth can be assimilated by the consciousness. Only after passing through these stages of discussion can one establish the possibility of a reproduction and indeed an autonomous production of religious truth.

But we have here only variations on what we term appropriation and certainty.

In Schleiermacher's *Glaubenslehre* (E.T. *The Christian Faith* [1928] the same schema of thought is even clearer even though in a more complicated and dialectically more refined form. A general definition of consciousness is given in the introduction and thus an anthropological vestibule is provided as in the Cartesian approach. The general situation as regards consciousness is that we all have existentially a feeling of absolute dependence whose point of reference we call God (§ 4).

Note the (Cartesian) thrust of the argument. Schleiermacher does not begin with God's revelation which then imparts to me the feeling of being radically dependent on him. The exact opposite is the case. The existential feeling of absolute dependence is first there in my consciousness. Only then do I denote its source by the term God (§ 4). (Theological students often miss the point here.)

The *Letters to Lücke,* in which Schleiermacher interprets himself, show that he thinks this way of going about it applies only to his method and does not mean that his own existential pilgrimage led him from that general self-consciousness of dependence to the particular Christian revelation. "As though only a trace of an inner Christ (i.e., declared in the prior existential experience of absolute dependence) preceded the historical Christ for me," he can angrily reply to his opponents (p. 11). Nothing is further from his intention than to absorb what is distinctively Christian into general religious knowledge (p. 28), as in the *Reden.* Quite the reverse! As one who is in a state of piety, who has already been affected by the Christian revelation, he is simply inquiring into the conditions of self-understanding on whose basis this was possible.

His ontic pilgrimage is thus different from his noetic epistemology. In life he first becomes a Christian and enters a pious state by receiving Christ. From that vantage-point he then asks what conditions there had to be in his self-consciousness for this to happen, for him to be able to appropriate the Christian revelation. But once he puts all this in a system and gives noetic form to what he has experienced ontically, he has to reverse things, beginning with a general analysis of consciousness, showing thereby how the thought of God is contained within it (as the source of the feeling of absolute dependence), and then analyzing the individual doctrines in order to show how they are simply statements about our religious states, our self-consciousness, and the facts of inner anthropology. For Christian doctrines are conceptions of religious states verbally expressed (*The Christian Faith,* § 15). Thus sin is a term for hampering of free development of consciousness (§ 66). Redemption is to be understood as the setting aside of inability to set consciousness of God in relation to real life-factors (§ 11). Hence the state of redemption is simply an affiliation of the feeling of absolute dependence (§ 11). Revelation is the originality of a fact underlying a religious society to the extent that, conditioning the individual content of the pious affections found in the society, it cannot itself be understood in terms of any preceding historical nexus (§ 10). As in the *Reden,* revelation is thus a term for the originality of religious experience.

Schleiermacher is decisively misunderstood if his epistemological method is confused with the historical course of his faith and experience. (He complains of this misunderstanding to Lücke and would have had to complain of it often if he could have heard later expositions, including that of Emil Brunner.) But if the anthropological vestibule, the analysis of general self-consciousness, and the relevant locating of the Christian religion apply only to the subsequent reflection of the believer, to his later survey of conditions in the consciousness, nevertheless it is still typical, and denotes the Cartesian approach, that there is and can be this reflection. This is explicable only if one realizes that according to the general sense of the age Christian revelation is understood as something that man come of age cannot swallow. The only way to overcome this prejudice is to show where the claims can be admitted into our consciousness, and to show moreover that they already have bridgeheads there.

Here, too, the process of appropriation is the primary theme. Here already, perhaps for the first time, the crucial question of Cartesian theology comes to light, namely, whether it will be content simply to indicate the place of doctrines in our consciousness, whether it will not surreptitiously attempt something more and very different, whether it will not secretly make this consciousness the norm and criterion of what doctrines can be assimilated. Is Schleiermacher simply pointing out in neutral fashion a place in the consciousness? Or are not the doctrines changed in content to fit the consciousness, to make them digestible? Do they not undergo reduction when presented as the expression of a modification of the consciousness? Are they not starved and impoverished? Do they not lose much of their content? Are they not necessarily restricted to what can be formulated in an anthropology? Even more pertinently, is not the criterion of the truth of theological theses the degree to which they can be anthropologized? Can § 30 of *The Christian Faith* mean anything else but this when it states that the theses of Christian doctrine can be presented *either* as descriptions of human states *or* as concepts of divine qualities and modes of action *or* as statements about the nature of the world, all three being related? There is a plain shift of accent here compared to the christological affirmations of Melanchthon's *Loci* (1521). We are no longer told merely that the personal attributes of Christ, inasmuch as they are declared to us as blessings (*beneficia*), have an affinity to anthropology, so that a christological statement also has anthropological significance. Anthropology (human conditions), theology (divine qualities and modes of action), and cosmology (the nature of the world) are now interchangeable disciplines. A theological thesis that cannot be transferred into anthropology or cosmology without any loss of value can no longer claim theological rank. Does not this pave the way for the normativity of the anthropological analysis of existence? This is the question constantly raised by the Cartesian approach; it is the crucial question.

3. Bultmann's theology is the climax of the Cartesian inquiry into the

conditions of understanding that the believer brings with him, and also into the process of understanding and appropriation.

The slogan "existential interpretation" is an indication of this. Understanding is always oriented to a specific inquiry and goal.[8] This can be identical with the intention of the text so that this imparts the matter sought itself and directly.[9] But I may also investigate the text's cultural or psychological relations, which are not the point of its programmatic statement.[10] In this case we are dealing with its indirect content. Hence the goal of my inquiry may have very different aspects. The difference is grounded in my perspective, which makes it possible for me to approach the text from different angles. This is a first indication that what is at issue is the one who understands (as regards his perspective) in the act of understanding. This subject brings himself with him and is thus himself part of the theme of understanding.

This is particularly so in relation to kerygmatic texts which claim me in my decision. Here the claimed existence is the presupposition of possible understanding. The first statement to be made if one is to say how far this is a condition is that there must already be a living relation to the matter which is directly or indirectly expressed in the text and which controls the goal of the inquiry.[11] If, for example, I did not already know something about the uncertainty and ungovernability of my existence I could not grasp what the word "hope" means or how far it might apply to me. If I did not already know something about the self-alienation and inauthenticity of my existence I could not understand the meaning behind the word "sin." So it is with all other words as well.

Hence the text speaks of something to which I have a living relation. It is thus directed to a "pre-understanding" which I bring with me about every subject. Its theme already has an existing place in my consciousness. I can thus interpret it existentially, i.e., in terms of my living relation to it.

If this interpretation is not done naively but with intellectual strictness, it is possible only on the basis of existential analysis, i.e., as a methodical unfolding of the self-understanding posited with existence.[12] Thus methodical interpretation is possible only as I first develop that self-understanding in order to find the terminology that will direct my interpretation. This may be achieved, however, only in the secular deliberation that is the business of a philosophical analysis of existence.[13]

Hence this investigation of self- and pre-understanding is indispensable if one is to achieve the presupposition for methodical, in this case existential, interpretation. This investigation is a matter for secular philosophy, Martin Heidegger being Bultmann's authority here. Naturally the theologian might do the job himself. But in so doing he would only be doing what the philosopher does. He would be dealing with preliminary secular questions which are part of the irrevocable task of theology. For theology is impossible without

---

[8] GV, II, p. 216.   [9] GV, II, p. 227.   [10] Loc. cit.   [11] Loc. cit.
[12] KM, II, p. 193; E.T. p. 194.   [13] Ibid., p. 192; E.T. pp. 192f.

interpretation of the text underlying it. This will not disclose itself, however, without the directive terminology that makes it possible for me to give my inquiry a suitable orientation. This terminology is present already in my pre-Christian consciousness.

Again we have a variation of the consistent line of Theology A. The message is given a location in our consciousness. While Bultmann, unlike Schleiermacher or Dilthey,[14] deliberately avoids psychological categories, and while he could also be said to take a very different path from Lessing, who oddly seems to play no part for him, there is no doubt but that his formal schema of investigation is the same. The common question is that of appropriating the message and hence of the one who has to do the appropriating. It is a matter of the system of coordinates to which the content of faith must be related.

There thus arises a preliminary anthropological structure. Anthropology is an introduction to theology which cannot be skipped. The question of the content of my faith can be answered only when a reply has first been given to that of the conditions under which it can be appropriated. This "need for an introduction obviously arises only when one is no longer or not yet sure of the matter itself, when one has still to decide what one is trying to do and with what right and means one intends it, when agreement has still to be reached on the point and possibility of the task, when one no longer has such a grasp of the given factors, the axioms with which every discipline works, that there is confidence their truth can be demonstrated simply by the fact and the manner of working with them."[15]

Somewhat wryly we must allow that modern atheistic philosophy also sees more anxiety than living faith in the theological concern to mediate faith philosophically and to demonstrate the conditions of its possibility in the subject. Thus Francis Jeanson thinks the efforts of Roman Catholic theology (Daniélou and Tresmontant are specifically mentioned) to find a contact for revelation in the analogous human consciousness finally become bogged down in concepts of the subject. Efforts to support faith in this way necessarily avenge themselves since they contradict its nature (Jeanson, *La foi d'un incroyant* [1963]).

Demonstrating its uncertainty of faith is no real criticism of the approach, although Barth and Jeanson think so. It is simply to show why the accent has shifted from the matter itself to questions of method and from these again to anthropology. Here we must again keep before us, as Schleiermacher did, the question whether the way through the vestibule leads me into the spacious main building or whether, involuntarily and unintentionally, it hampers all further progress and enables me to get only a very partial view of the main building. As we have noted in relation to Schleiermacher, this is the decisive question that has to be put to the Cartesian approach.

4. A final example of this trend is Paul Tillich. Here one sees it in extreme

---

[14] GV, II, pp. 211ff.

[15] K. Barth, *Die christliche Dogmatik,* I (1927), p. 12.

form, as in his statement that the first step in creative philosophy is radical doubt.[16] Doubt is what relates the philosopher to the prophet and puts both in the same isolation as the Cartesian I experiences. This doubt is radical because it relates not merely to the traditions and symbols of the fellowship of faith but to all that one might call the natural view of the world, the presuppositions of everyday common sense. It is the fundamental doubt that is given with human existence itself, that makes it human existence. What is this doubt?

It comes to expression in the basic question of all philosophy: Why is there something and not nothing?[17] This questioning of all reality, including my own, releases the ontic shock that causes the chain reaction of philosophical questions. But how does this question arise?

Primarily because man is the being who can and must ask[18] inasmuch as he has to understand and project a goal. This self-consciousness is what lifts him above the level of unquestioning vegetating. The existential reason why the being called man can and must ask about himself, and hence put the question of being (why something and not nothing?), is to be found in his finitude. The significance of this for inquiry may be seen from two angles.

First, finitude means that we shall come to an end, that we are exposed to non-being. The manner in which we are aware of finitude is anxiety. This forms the productive ontological shock that releases the question of being. Second, the reason why the finite that is aware of itself must put the question of being may be seen from its opposite. That is to say, an infinite being would not have to put this question. He would be identical with being; he would be God. Again, a being not aware of its finitude cannot put it since it is unable to transcend itself and its limits.[19] Thus the question of being is constitutively linked to man's finitude and his awareness of it.

We are constantly exposed to the question that affects ourselves and our being. In this sense human existence is a continual process of question and answer. Hence the claim of revelation, kerygma, and the Christian tradition can only remain outside me with alien heteronomy if it is not interwoven into this process. Since revelation has the last word about man, it deals with the being about which man is asking in virtue of the ontological shock. In fact, all ideas of revelation may be set in this schema.

Sin is man's self-alienation from his authentic being; redemption is the positing of a new being, the restoration of lost participation.[20] Thus Tillich arrives at his famous principle of correlation, by which he expresses the relation of existence and revelation, of question and answer. God is the answer to the question implied in man's finitude.[21] This does not end the process of question and answer, for in face of the answer that comes from God man puts new questions;[22] the answer offers more than the question can contain, and the situation created by it also raises new questions.

---

16 *Ges. Werke*, V, p. 164.   17 *Ibid.*, p. 141.   18 *Ibid.*, p. 143.   19 *Ibid.*, p. 144.
20 Tillich in *Eranosjahrbuch* (1954), p. 257; cf. K. D. Nörenberg, *Analogia imaginis* (1966), pp. 193ff.
21 *Systematic Theology*, I, p. 64.   22 *Ibid.*, p. 61.

Thus the relation between question and answer is dialectical. It entails a circle that determines theological work. Theology formulates the questions implied in human existence and it formulates the answers present in the divine self-declaration under the direction of the questions that lie in human existence.[23] For example, if God is correlative to the threat of non-being, he is the infinite power of being. If anxiety is awareness of finitude, God is the infinite ground of confidence. In correlation with the riddle of historical existence, the kingdom of God is the meaning, fulfilment, and unity of history. In this way one can reach an understanding of the traditional symbols of Christianity that keeps their force and opens them up to the questions treated in existential analysis.[24]

We again see the Cartesian schema. Revelation and its symbols[25] can apply unconditionally to me only as they lose their heteronomous externality, are received by me, and within the process of question and answer are related to what has to do with the essence of human existence, namely, that it questions itself and its relation to being. Hence the Christian symbols have to be seen in their relation to this question. Only thus can they be appropriated and opened up to the questions treated in existential analysis.

This existential analysis, as in Lessing, Schleiermacher, and Bultmann, again becomes herewith a normative chapter of theology, an introduction or vestibule granting access to the main building and perspectives by which to see it. Thus the Cartesian I, or its self-awareness, stands at the commencement of theology and will not be ignored. Its cry is that it will show us how far what follows has unconditional relevance.

But this inquiry might take on more than the significance of orientation (in the sense of showing me what to look for, from what angle and to what end to investigate the biblical materials and Christian symbols). It might exercise a selective function (in the sense that the only significant aspects of the materials are those indicated by the question of existence, while the rest may be ignored). This is the decisive problem that always arises with Theology A, as our previous examples have shown.

3. DAWN OF THE NEW AGE: EMANCIPATION OF ADULT MAN

After considering some typical examples of Theology A, or Cartesian theology, we shall pause for a moment to consider the result of our deliberations.

We began (Chapter III. 2) by stating that one can speak of God only as one (also) speaks of man. The reason given was that I have God only as he discloses himself to me and wills to be there for me. Hence I speak of myself too when I speak of him. "The Word became flesh" sponsors this relation of God to human existence.

Since this relation is of the essence of the kerygma insofar as it is addressed to man, there is no stage of the Christian tradition at which it has not played

---

[23] *Loc. cit.*   [24] *Loc. cit.*
[25] On symbols in Tillich cf. Nörenberg, *Analogia imaginis*.

a role. Sometimes it has been thematic, sometimes implied and indirect, but it has never been suppressed, except in some docetic heresies. For to abandon address would be to rob the kerygma of its point and substance.

Nevertheless—and this is the question raised by our historical examples—even if address and the relation to human existence have always been there in fact, there has not until recently been a Cartesian theology.

In other words, before the dawn of what is ambivalently called "modern," theology has not focused on the believing and understanding I, on the conditions of credibility, or on the digestibility of the message. There have been vestibules of course. Thomism with its principle of analogy had to reflect on nature (and especially man) before going on to grace. Augustine already built a bridge between *humanitas* and *christianitas* with the help of some delicate engineering.[26] Lutheran orthodoxy also opened its systems with far-ranging discussions of general revelation in nature and history. But the significance and intentions were always different from those of Cartesian theology when this examines the possibility, presuppositions, and conditions under which the message is intelligible and relevant and can be appropriated by me. All previous discussions of this kind, however dubious in detail, stayed with the premise that the message is addressed and that one has thus to learn in its name where it will strike us. Hence the question of man's place, situation, and nature was guided and controlled by prior knowledge of the message. There was never any *analogia entis* constructed from below and beginning with the kind of secular existential analysis that Bultmann demands. Even if only implicitly, the *analogia entis* was always bound up with the *analogia fidei*.[27]

That has all changed now. The tradition of Theology A shows this. Here a general and pre-Christian self-understanding of man is a separate theme which must be dealt with before the theological agenda is tackled. This theology has standing orders that come first, and we know how these affect the further course of things. Since these matters concern man's general situation, since they are pre-theological (although of great theological relevance), the implied existential analysis can be left to secular philosophy; Bultmann, Tillich, and their predecessors all have philosophical sponsors. Even when the theologians do the analysis on their own, like Schleiermacher, they stress the fact that they have no privileges as believers but are in solidarity with men of the world, even those who despise the faith. The whole point of Schleiermacher's apologetic is to bring to light this solidarity and to make its own secular self-consciousness plain to these men without the aid of a revelation.

The urgent question thus arises how this new thing has arisen which

---

26 Cf. W. von Loewenich, *Von Augustin zu Luther* (1959), pp. 9ff.

27 Cf. G. Söhngen, "Analogia entis oder analogia fidei?" *Die Einheit in der Theologie* (1952), pp. 235ff.; F. Flückiger, "Analogia entis und analogia fidei," Stud. gen. (1955), 2, pp. 678ff.; E. Przywara, "Analogia entis in analogia fidei," *Antwort, K. Barth zum 70. Geburtstag* (1956), pp. 266ff. Cf. ThE, II, 2, § 3839ff.; E.T. II, p. 544.

earlier theology did not know and which has thus contributed to the describing of Theology A as "modern."

The answer surely is that man has learned to see himself as adult and
this has made him his own theme. For he can now put the question of existence even if there is no God.[28] Once he gets the idea he can comprehend
humanity apart from God and must respect its autonomous dignity as an
end in itself, there is no going back. This means that he can no longer ignore
himself or deny himself as a criterion of what comes to him as a truth-
claim or ethical imperative, what meets him as a divine dogma or commandment. Otherwise he would be unfaithful to the dignity of humanity. And in
ignoring himself and bowing to authoritarian claims, would he not also
defame the dignity of divine revelation itself? Would not this be degraded
if accorded only the role of a tyrannical dictate and refused the confidence
that it could persuade us, i.e., overcome us with its own evidence? There
are hints enough in Kant that he respects autonomy in the name of God's
own dignity and wants to protect God from the role of a heteronomous
tyrant.

If, knowing he has come of age, man cannot ignore himself without sinking
back into guilty immaturity and allowing servile fear to be the impulse of
faith, then all the questions arise that we have seen in our survey of
Theology A. One has to ask: How can I—I who am somebody, the *autos*
behind autonomy—appropriate the Christian message? Existential analyses
have then to be made to establish the elements in my existence or situation
that go to meet the message or refuse it, no matter whether these elements
be found in the theoretical structure of consciousness (Lessing), feeling
(Schleiermacher), or the structure of finite and necessarily self-questioning
existence (Bultmann and Tillich).[29]

A series of further questions is then released. Maturity is not just manifested in the fact that I ask about myself and seek understanding thereby.
It also finds expression in the fact that my intellectual conscience is not
wounded by having to recognize that it is tied to certain scientific axioms,
methods, concepts, and insights. Even in the consciousness of those who
cannot test them in detail these foundations and results of science gain the
rank of convictions and thus impinge on their autonomy. In this sense one
may say that the scientific view of the world and the historical sense with its
problem of verifiability and historical relativity have achieved self-evident
status in our collective consciousness.

But then at once the problem arises how I can appropriate a kerygma that
comes to me within an ancient cosmology and an understanding of history
vastly different from modern historicism. It is obviously incompatible with
the self-understanding of autonomous adulthood simply to adopt that antiquated and outdated thinking and to do violence to one's intellectual con-

---

[28] To use the phrase of G. Grotius (*etsi non esset Deus*) in his work on international
law.
[29] Cf. the analysis of subjectivity in M. Heidegger, *Holzwege,* p. 225.

science thereby. If one is not to regard the kerygma as antiquated too, the further question then arises whether and how far it may be differentiated from the cosmological and mythical forms in which it is expressed. Is everything connected with the cosmology or the ancient terminology (e.g., Gnostic) only a cipher that does not belong to and can thus be detached from the matter itself? More concretely, is there still an ascension even though heaven is not to be sought up above but in the depths of being?

Only a superficial person could pretend that this task of differentiation is easy even when the possibility of it is affirmed in principle. For instance, is the message of Christ's resurrection only a mythical way of talking to help bring out its significance, so that what is said in storylike form about the third day does not belong to the matter itself but only to the "concepts" of faith (W. Herrmann) that are not binding on me but are to be replaced with my own commentary? Does not my intellectual conscience, which knows the limits of historical verifiability, point to this solution? Or do the statements of the first witnesses sound suspicious in the light of this solution when they find the significance of the resurrection in the initiation of a new aeon, so that for them everything depends on the fact that it happened, on its facticity?

However that may be—and we cannot decide it here—it is clear how many questions crowd in upon us, all unleashed by the one fact that man has discovered and can no longer ignore himself in his adulthood. This is why there have to be large vestibules in which existential analyses are made, questions of appropriation are discussed, and the structure of the kerygma must be investigated in relation to its digestible contents and modes of expression that cannot be adopted but have to be translated into modern terms. This is why there is such an expansion of introductory questions, as is most strikingly shown by the blossoming of hermeneutics (the science of the structure and processes of understanding) into a new theological discipline. Man is now preoccupied with himself, his authenticity and alienation, his existential character and categories of understanding. He focuses on the envelope which carries the address and the sender's name. He turns it around suspiciously and asks with what right he can get a letter from this sender. What has he in mind in thus writing to me? What connection is there between us to explain this and to hold out hope that the letter will contain something relevant and helpful? He, the recipient, must examine what is in his house even if it is only a letter. He knows the sender by hearsay (he has prior understanding to what region he might belong, in what neighborhood of being he is to be sought). So, as we hope, he finally opens the letter, and yet even in reading it he does not cease to think about himself, and with good reason if the letter is filled with news that applies to him.

The analogy is imperfect, but even in caricature it brings out a true aspect of what it illustrates. This is the element of prior deliberation. Even the incidental and exaggerated idea that the letter might not be opened is not entirely wide of the mark. Inquiry into the act and possibility of faith hardly leaves time for the content of faith. Intensive preoccupation with the question of method blinds us to what methodologically purified perception should show us. "They are continually sharpening knives and no longer have anything to cut" (Karl Rahner).

4. CRUCIAL POINT IN THEOLOGY A: DOMINATION OF EXISTENTIAL ANALYSIS

The monstrous growth of preliminary questions is no real argument against the content-relation expressed here. It might be just a procedural error, a wrong distribution of the work load, and a well-meaning admonition could be enough to correct it. It might also be that a new inquiry—and the problems posed by adulthood are genuinely new—releases the same kind of passionate concentration that anything new usually does. Radical criticism could hardly be based on this. But is this really the situation? Are we not confronted with a material problem, namely, whether the starting of theological thinking with existential analysis, with reflection on the self-understanding of man in general and of modern man in particular, not only makes access possible to the content of theology but also prejudices what one will later have to say about this content?

This is the question posed by our historical examples, and we must now try to answer it. The question is—and it is the crucial issue in modern theology—whether in a very lofty, profound, and unintentional way the kerygma is put under man's control, so that in the last analysis theology is reduced to a mere chapter in anthropology.

If theology begins with an explication of the man who experiences himself as a hearer of the message, might it not itself become a phase in this explication when the kerygma has given its additional impulse to it? Certain confessional groups today which were formed after the mass gathering at Dortmund in 1966, and which are establishing positions against this theological front, are motivated by a feeling that this might be so.[30]

Now this observation should not be misconstrued. The confessional movement is not being introduced as a star witness for the criticism the author himself will make. It cannot be this because, although it has probably put its finger on the real weakness, namely, that theology is here changed into anthropology, it tries to deal with it in a reactionary way, namely, by suppressing the problem of appropriation raised by man's adulthood.

This charge is not made lightly, especially as the author concedes that these groups have seized on the crucial point in Theology A, even if more by way of intuition than analysis. And if one or other of their members should read this book, he would be grateful if the charge is seen as an expression, not of aloofness, but rather of the desire that there should be readiness to listen and to engage in self-criticism lest false fronts should be set up and fellowship should be disrupted where perhaps it could continue, or arise again.

The movement—and this is the charge—is avoiding the test implicit in the problem. But faith which refuses rather than undergoes the test degenerates

---

[30] Cf. W. Künneth, *Die Welt,* No. 252 (1967), p. III.

into servile obedience. It does not win for itself what it has inherited from the past, for pain and doubt and questioning are needed to do this. It simply transmits it without having a share in what is in the packet. It guards the ashes but does not tend the flame. It is untrue to the tradition by making it a mere passive tradition. This faith comes under the reproof of Alexander Schweizer (d. 1888): "Once the fathers confessed their faith; today many Christians are concerned only to believe their confessions."

Today faith demands that the questions of Theology A be faced. If other answers are sought, as in this book, we shall have to wring them out of the questions, or wrestle with the questions and force modifications on them by argument.

Hence we are not adducing the confessional movement as a star witness. We mention it for two reasons, first because it has at least seized on the sore point in Cartesian theology, and second, because one can see from the breadth of the movement that the destiny of Christian truth is at issue and not just an internal matter of theology.

5. SUMMARY AND PROSPECT

The sum of what we have been saying may be formulated as follows.

First, Theology A with its question of appropriation is addressing a problem which has been inescapably posed by the adulthood of man and the emancipation of existence and reason from the days of the Enlightenment.

Second, in pursuit of this inquiry a tragic entanglement of thought occurs, since the arguments needed to throw light on the presuppositions of an understanding of revelation with the help of existential analysis unintentionally become means to determine in advance what revelation must be according to the nature and form of communication if the predicate of intelligibility is to apply to it.

Third, since intelligibility is requisite if there is to be revelation, communication, or message (used here as synonyms), the conditions of it are also the limits of what is binding for me in the claims of revelation. (There is an exact analogy here to Kant's idea of transcendental apperception in virtue of which it can be predicted, on the basis of phenomenal forms and categories, what can be the content of a possible experience and to that extent what can be binding as experience.)

Fourth, a tragic change arises out of this, for what was originally meant to establish the possibility of appropriation, and was thus far a confession of openness to the kerygma, threatens to turn into its opposite, closing itself to the kerygma to the degree that only some kerygmatic contents can slip through the net of the prior conditions. If we impose conditions for receiving messages we put them under our own control, and openly or secretly we are thus editing them.

Fifth, none of the types of the theology being discussed aims deliberately to bring the kerygma under its own control. (Reimarus is perhaps the only theologian who set out to do this and was intent on destroying Christian truth; this is why we did not include him under Theology A.) But a certain autonomy set in train by the premises of this theology regulates the kerygma in spite of the original intention and protestations to the contrary.

Sixth, there is an element of the tragic in this entanglement to the extent that (1) the argument itself takes over and escapes from the control of the one who is using it, and (2) it no longer allows to be maintained what ought to be maintained according to the original intention, namely, that the prior existential analysis should not affect what I am prepared to receive in the kerygma.

Often, then, an astonishing discrepancy develops between what is personally confessed and what can be expressed intellectually. The degree of disparity will vary with different thinkers (and may be investigated in their sermons). It is hardly perceptible in Bultmann, in whom one will find nuances but not material differences. In Schleiermacher, however, it is very marked. From many personal conversations I sense the same in Tillich. But this is not our present concern.

What we have summed up under these six heads we shall now illustrate by one example. In principle we might have used for this purpose all the examples already adduced, or another thinker not in that series. For reasons of space we shall limit ourselves to one typical example and for reasons of topicality we shall select the theology of Bultmann. The outlines of the debate will apply to other representatives of Theology A, and even in this one case we shall be able to touch only on certain central points in our criticism.

6. DEBATE WITH A REPRESENTATIVE

a. Analysis

We shall begin with a thesis of Bultmann which establishes the controlling character of self-understanding (and hence of the Cartesian approach). This is that an understanding or interpretation should always be oriented to a specific inquiry or goal. I understand Isaiah when my inquiry is directed to the matter which determined and controlled him. I do not (properly) understand him if I investigate his psychological presuppositions or use him as a source for the history of the religion and culture of Israel. I can do this, but if as a historian I thus relate him as a source to ends of my own I can hardly claim to understand him. I am more like the wardrobe expert who has to get the costumes right in a play but who, unlike many historians who seem to have motes in their eyes at this point, does not venture to think that he understands a period merely because he can produce the right uniforms.

True understanding arises only with a specific orientation to what is the issue for the one I seek to understand. In kerygmatic texts this means that I cannot understand them in terms of the psychological or historical presuppositions of the author, e.g., Isaiah. The author is impressed into service and governed by that about which he speaks. This matter is what I really have to investigate if I am to understand him. But if this controlling subject, e.g., Paul's theme of guilt and justification, is irrelevant to me and I have no living relation to it, then I am in no position to understand who the author is and what his concern is. I cannot claim the key to his existence and I miss the real issue even if I am an acknowledged expert in New Testament Greek. For Paul exists under that theme. This existence has a theme.

The man who interprets Paul psychologically, as has happened, will not get at the theme. He will explain what Paul seems to be in terms of the psychical context, but this, complex though it may be in detail, is governed by the material subject of Paul's proclamation. Similar hermeneutical misunderstandings arise when non-Christian psychiatrists treat Christians for religious complexes. If they have no access or living relation to the theme of faith to which a Christian relates in his existence they are unable to distinguish what is legitimately governed by faith and what may be assigned to a pathological condition. Everything which a Christian believes and which, e.g., oppresses him with a sense of guilt will be understood as neurosis. The sickness cannot be understood because the man who has it is not understood. There is no relation to the theme of faith in orientation to which the Christian exists and which is defective in his zones of sickness. Faith is the goal in terms of which he should be examined. Only thus can what is authentic be distinguished from pathological alienation in the existence of believers and understanding or diagnosis be achieved. (It is the merit of Victor Frankl to have worked out insights of this kind in his logotherapy.)

We can accept what Bultmann says in relation to history and psychology. The positive part of his hermeneutics, however, is more dubious. He argues that if understanding is always oriented to a goal, it is never presuppositionless. More precisely, it is always directed by a pre-understanding of what it is seeking in the text. Only on the basis of such a pre-understanding are inquiry and interpretation possible at all.[31] But what does it mean to have a pre-understanding?

The concept has two meanings. It means (a) what I already know about the kerygmatic theme. Thus I bring to Paul's doctrine of sin a pre-understanding in the sense that I know the difference between good and bad or authentic and alienated existence. The totality of what the natural man brings along these lines Bultmann finds representatively in Heidegger. Only because I have this pre-understanding can Paul's themes ring a bell for me. Only for this reason can they be the goal of my investigation. Only for this reason can I appropriate them. Otherwise they would be like oriental music. The pre-understanding which, e.g., philosophy has in its acquaintance with man's guilt, is then corrected and restructured into a new understanding by the kerygma. At this level one finds in Bultmann a good chunk of the humanist, historico-psychological tradition which can easily be traced back biographically to his teachers.

The concept then has a second meaning (b) which is not so well known or so frequently mentioned in general discussion, which is much more complicated, but which also has more important implications for his theology.

---

[31] ZThK, 47 (1950), p. 51.

From this angle pre-understanding always relates to a specific way in which man evaluates himself. He may view himself as lost, as having fallen away from authenticity. Philosophy as well as theology can speak of this lostness of the natural man, of his being disordered. Thus Heidegger's philosophy calls man back from lostness to himself.[32] Man also knows his finitude. He knows he is subject to death. He thus knows he is a victim of anxiety. Being in the world is unsettling for him. Pre-understanding is thus a type of self-understanding. This in turn is a kind of self-evaluation. These deliberations lead, as we have seen, to the general existential analysis that precedes this theology.

Now what is the role of this self-understanding when it encounters revelation, the kerygma? This can be put very simply: it is transvaluated. Dying and rising again with Christ, the man who naturally sees himself as finite and subject to judgment has the experience of receiving a new future and can evaluate himself as one who is ordered to *zoé* (life). He thus acquires a new self-understanding.

We see here that the natural self-understanding is only conditionally ready for change. It inquires of the kerygma what impulses for transformation are contained in it. Only thus far is man concerned. What is not pertinent to his self-understanding, what cannot then be interpreted anthropologically, must remain inactual. Certain predetermined conditions must be fulfilled if a saying or account in the NT is to qualify as binding kerygma. Understanding reports of events as acts of God presupposes a pre-understanding of what can be an act of God.[33] Such an act, for example, cannot be demonstrated objectively. Hence the historical character of the kerygma, e.g., the facticity of the cross and resurrection, is relatively inactual and irrelevant for self-understanding. All this is necessarily assigned to the sphere of an illegitimate objectification of God, i.e., of miracle and myth. Salvation events do not need facticity to transform my self-understanding. Any doctrine of salvation, or even Plato, can do it.

Bultmann does, of course, make a more precise distinction. He does not abandon historicity as such. But the autonomous and normative power of the concept of "pre-understanding" permits him only a slender history that goes little beyond the historical character of a figure like Plato. Thus Christ's resurrection is not a historical fact in the outside world. It is a visionary reflection in the psyche of the disciples evoked by encounter with him who walks on earth.

Sometimes Bultmann has used comparison with a dream to make it clear that this reflection does not imply that the resurrection was not historical or took place only in the disciples' psyche. As he puts it, "When I dream of a friend, the dream image I have for the moment is not the reflection of a real state. But I produce the dream about my friend only because I have really met him. The dream is a commentary on a real encounter. Similarly the resurrection 'dream' of the disciples is a reaction to their experience of Jesus

---

[32] KM, I, p. 37; E.T. p. 27. [33] ZThK, 47 (1950), p. 66.

Christ. The vision interprets the figure of Jesus as one who is superior to death."[34]

In other words, the pre-understanding is not just a chronological "pre" which I bring with me to the kerygma. It also has the material force of a postulate and works on what may be validated as kerygma. It is like a sieve through which the contents of the kerygma are filtered. But there can pass through this sieve only what is valid truth, what can become the content of a self-understanding, and what—this is the main point—can be seen in connection with the existing self-understanding, so that it is also demonstrable. Consciousness, not history, is what takes place in Bultmann. Thus the pre-understanding takes on the rank of a criterion and norm, of a criterion that works secretly and subjectively.

Bultmann, then, is not interested in whether NT facts like Christmas, Easter, or Pentecost are real facts or whether they are myths or perhaps commentaries on facts in mythological form, like the Easter stories. The thought-content of historical events and also that of myth can equally affect the understanding of my existence. Hence I do not lose Christ if I describe as myth every story that objectifies God. The story is not thereby eliminated. It can be existentially just as fruitful as an interpreted story which is related to its thought-content. This leads us to our main objection to Bultmann's principles of hermeneutics. The principle of pre-understanding is a normative principle which operates as a criterion imposed on the Bible from without.

Now the pre-understanding does not have or have to have by nature a heteronomous character alien to Scripture. It assumes that the investigation of man conducted by secular existential analysis, and his diagnosis as one who is estranged from authentic being, is the matter that constitutes the theme of the biblical texts. Only thus can the postulate arise that I must seek the goal of the texts which is "prefigured" in my pre-understanding as it is "figured" in the texts themselves and which thus implies the analogy between the texts and myself that is basic to all understanding. We are thus well aware that Bultmann does not accept the idea that he is importing an alien principle into the texts on the basis of his pre-understanding, and is then making it heteronomous.

Nevertheless there can be no mistaking the fact that the analogy does not work out at all as expected. The concentration on prior existential analysis, the exclusive listening to the voice of one's own existence prior to the text, surreptitiously gives rise to a very programmatic, sharply delineated, and rigid self-understanding which also becomes an arbitrary schema. Even if this schema is worked out originally on the assumption that it fits the intention of the text and thus makes possible an analogous understanding, the upshot shows that it does not do what was hoped. It cannot fulfil expectations because the autonomy of existential analysis brings with it emancipation of the resultant self-understanding. The ineluctability of this may be suspected from the very fact that Bultmann can delegate this analysis to philosophers

---

[34] From a mimeographed work published during the war.

who do it out of their own secular consciousness without so much as glancing at the NT.[35] This delegation means that we have the independent and large vestibule of anthropology in which the future developments of theological thinking are predetermined.

At this point we see the limit of Bultmann's thesis that the orientation of a text is to be investigated. This always presupposes that the orientation is to an existential theme in my self-understanding. Although Bultmann understands the kerygma as the decisive question, he does not take seriously into account the possibility that the biblical text is questioning me, or, better, that it is tossing aside all my questions and teaching me how to ask the right questions (cf. the counter-questions of Jesus in the NT). He is not taking seriously into account the possibility that in regard to the kerygma more takes place in heaven than in my *nous* which forms the self-understanding. He does not reckon with the fact that what is much more important than my dying and rising again with Christ is that Christ died and rose again in fact and apart from me, that the salvation history of the years A.D. 1-30, that in other words—and every word is being weighed carefully and formulated precisely here—that facticity outside me, has ontic priority over the later fulfilment of dying and rising again in me.

Bultmann, then, is not objective but prejudiced by his self-understanding when it comes to saying what is needed to qualify for the title of kerygma.

This element of prejudice consists in the question whether and how far a text can be interpreted existentially, i.e., become the content of a possible self-understanding. Fairness to Bultmann demands that we point out that in his program and intention he does not want to be prejudiced, but this happens necessarily and involuntarily on the basis of the autonomous effect of his approach. He himself has stated emphatically that our mode of inquiry should not be allowed to prejudice us about the contents of the subject nor to anticipate particular exegetical results.[36] He is prepared to argue that the pre-understanding must be critically tested in our interpretation of the text, that it must be set at risk, that it must itself be questioned, and the claim of the text heard, as the text is questioned.[37] Our attack, then, is not on Bultmann's intention but on the schema of thought which prevents its realization.

This distinction is important since it has a bearing on the problem of heresy. We must obviously hesitate to stigmatize someone as a heretic—and Bultmann has often been called this—when his theology has to be opposed only because it cannot maintain a basic openness to the text or a basic readiness to let its premises be corrected thereby. The charge of heresy should surely refer to doctrinal intention and not just to doctrinal form as this is grounded in a specific schema of thought.

Opposition to Bultmann cannot begin with his postulate that a text must

---

[35] Bultmann does not think it can in fact be done apart from the NT, since there would be no modern philosophy without the NT, Luther, and Kierkegaard (KM, I, p. 35; E.T. p. 26), but he then seems to contradict himself in the very next sentence by saying that modern philosophy is not materially shaped by its historical origin.
[36] KM, II, p. 191; E.T. p. 191.   [37] GV, II, p. 228.

be examined in terms of its specific goal. I have to approach a text in this way if I am to have any hermeneutical criterion and am not to follow a theory of inspiration that forces me to accept everything as God's Word or kerygma just because it is there. For example, how can I see my way through the esoteric jungle of Revelation without critical hermeneutical principles of this kind? One has only to look at the sects to see what happens when such principles are disregarded. Critical principles of interpretation are in fact needed. Our question to Bultmann, however, is how far he has taken the principles from the text itself, how far he has taken seriously its own understanding of itself as a historical record (cf. the way Bultmann dismisses the NT miracle stories as theologically irrelevant), and how far he has imported his principles from without by way of the concept of pre-understanding and modern cosmology, with the result that he is comparatively indifferent to the question whether the kerygmatic contents (e.g., the crucifixion and resurrection) are real or mythical.

In a thinker of Bultmann's stature, who has pondered each of his theses deeply, this question can be discussed endlessly. Even if we could develop our counter-thesis more explicitly than is possible here, no definitive result could be attained. In every theological controversy, however, a point is reached where one has to say to the other side that the thrust of your thinking seems to point in a specific direction, dehistoricizing in the case of Bultmann, or, to take another example, the treatment of grace as a human attribute in Roman Catholicism. You may mount all kinds of rearguard or flanking movements with the help of massive arguments, but my assessment cannot be shaken. Even a little experience in controversy will back up the fact that this point does come. A purely intellectual encounter in question and answer form can go on forever and never reach a decision. This is one reason why doctrinal decisions are not made in the framework of theological discussion but take the form of confession and anathema, using theological arguments and provoking theological controversies, but not being themselves the product of theological argumentation.

Bultmann questions the text, but does not really let the text question him in regard to his own premises, e.g., the modern world-picture which always comes up as the heart of his demythologizing. He consistently links revelation to natural understanding. If we are right, the final secret or difficulty of Bultmann's theology is that he has no doctrine of the Holy Spirit. Only when this doctrine is properly worked out does one have to reckon with the thought that the word does not just ring a bell in an existing pre-understanding but it creates its own hearers, so that there is a new creation.[38]

Only as I let the text question me and call me in question do I take the historical subject seriously. Otherwise I am in danger of taking only myself and my presuppositions seriously. Bultmann takes with dangerous seriousness the presuppositions and principles of the nineteenth century that are

---

[38] Cf. on this C. H. Ratschow, *Der angefochtene Glaube,* 2nd ed. (1960), pp. 140ff.

operative in him.[39] This brings us face to face with the problem of what Bultmann calls the hermeneutical principle.

We may best begin with the question whether a hermeneutical principle is possible. Will not an expository principle of this kind autonomously forsake the function of a servant for that of a master that controls the text? Epigrammatically one might say that I already know what the text will or can say to me because I can deduce it from the hermeneutical principle at my disposal.

Does not this difficulty exist even when, as with the material principle of the Reformation, the hermeneutical criterion is taken from the text itself? Is not the fulness of the text cramped thereby? Does not the text continually challenge and correct hermeneutical criteria?

For our part, we incline to the view that there is no hermeneutical principle in the strict sense but only in the form of a "heuristic interim." Naturally, to understand a text, I have to have a set of questions or a standpoint from which to view it. There is an analogy here to a scientific experiment, which is made on certain assumptions. But these assumptions may have to be corrected by the result of the experiment. Thus Luther's thesis may be right when he says that the OT is to be interpreted from the standpoint of whether or how far it presents Christ. But if some parts of the OT do not fit this, the interpreter must be ready to let his standpoint be altered by the text itself and to accept new insights. This is what we mean when we say that there can be no fixed and immutable hermeneutical principle, whether brought to the text or taken from it. There can be only a principle which is always open to change. The tragedy of the schema of thought at issue is that while Bultmann acknowledges the reformability of the hermeneutical principle he is hampered by his own premises from putting it into practice.

A further criticism to be made is that what Bultmann calls his hermeneutical principle has an astonishing affinity to the thought-categories of the Enlightenment, especially Lessing and Semler.

For the former the kerygma is a nonfixable x which can be determined only in accommodation to contemporary recipients. This means that exposition is historical as well as the kerygma. It is tied to the situation of the expositor. A hermeneutical principle thus arises which the orthodox doctrine of inspiration could never produce. Semler puts the same question as Lessing: In what relation are the biblical texts to be interpreted? Simplified—and Semler is in fact more complex than this—his answer is that exposition must relate to the rational truth concealed in the Bible. This is not very different from Bultmann's self-understanding of the author. Along the lines of Lessing one might add that this self-understanding needs to be released,

---

[39] A remarkable difference between "modern" theology and the "modern" Liberalism opposed by positive theology in the nineteenth century is that whereas the latter was accused of "presuppositionless scholarship" instead of starting with the premise of "revelation in the historical Jesus" (M. Kähler, *Dogmatische Zeitfragen,* I [1898], p. 85), we now accuse the former of latent presuppositions that control its theological thinking.

to be given a push, by revelation. In the form of rational truth it has in some sense a historical base, as in Bultmann.

Now it is true that Bultmann understands (or means to understand) the content of self-understanding rather differently from Lessing.

He will not admit autarchous rational truth to be the content of self-understanding. But this is not, perhaps, because Bultmann's self-understanding, in distinction from Lessing's rational truth, is historically related, i.e., constitutively and constantly posited by the historical truth of the kerygma. In our view the constant appearance of historicity in Bultmann's thought is due to the fact that the plane of existential philosophy on which he moves has no place for rational truth. On this plane (e.g., in Heidegger, Jaspers, Marcel, and Sartre) truth is always unbound truth, truth becoming free. Hence it is always historical. It is released by situations and men. It exists only for the moment. In this sense truth is historical in Bultmann. It is set free by the kerygma and in constant dialog with it.

In appearance, then, faith and understanding are constitutively bound to the history of Christ. In reality, however, the kerygma in that unleashing of existential truth has basically the rank merely of another mode of encounter claiming me and releasing truth in me. As against Bultmann, then, we believe there is greater affinity between him and Lessing than a first glance might suggest. The apparent difference is for the most part a difference of expression. The one expresses himself within the schema of rationalism, the other within that of existentialism.

b. Critical Evaluation

In view of what has been said, the crucial questions that must be put to Bultmann may be summarized as follows.

1. Can an event be called a historical fact only when the tools of historical research can prove that it happened or when it can be put on the level of what can be fixed historically? Such a proof or concession is impossible in principle if we accept the criteria of historical truth set up by Ernst Troeltsch (causality, immanence, and analogy). When Bultmann treats only what takes place in this world as historical, he is implicitly following those criteria. Hence he cannot accept as historical the normative events that took place between Christmas and Pentecost. The question is, however, whether we can call the accounts of these events myths or legends or whether we should learn from these events what is historical in the most strict and proper sense.[40] Might it not be, as we shall argue later, that we learn only from the resurrection what history, God's action in the world, really is, so that we are not to subject the resurrection to the standard of what we previously understand by history?

Is not Bultmann working out a prior understanding of what history has to be and applying it to everything that advances a claim to historicity instead of being ready to let his view be enlarged by certain contents of history

---

[40] Cf. Richard R. Niebuhr, *The Resurrection and Historical Reason* (1957).

when these prove to be the center that gives history its true meaning?

Does not our pre-understanding of what deserves to be called historical need constant revision and replacement like the hermeneutical principle?

2. Can one describe a statement of the kerygma as theologically binding only if it seems to be a possible self-understanding of Christian existence? It may be conceded that all the facts of biblical salvation history as summed up in the Apostles' Creed have an affinity to human existence. They aim at this. Theologically, then, they cannot be dealt with in isolation. They become a theme of theology only as they are understood as God's history on and with man. Yet one should stress the fact that primarily and permanently this is a history *on* man (alien righteousness) and only derivatively a history *in* man. If the ontological distinction between Christ's person and work as *in se* and *pro me* cannot be upheld, the distinction should not be abandoned in principle. It maintains Christ's person over against man's and thus prevents it from becoming the mere content of pious Christian self-consciousness, whereby, as Barth puts it, the kerygma is reduced to statements about man's inner life. Since Bultmann thinks the kerygma exists only where it can be the content of a possible self-understanding, he is guilty of such reduction, finding a theological statement only where this can become an anthropology of a specific kind. In salvation history, however, more takes place in heaven and outside me than in the *nous* that constitutes self-understanding.[41] Bultmann's thinking plainly stands in the tradition of consciousness theology (Schleiermacher, Ritschl, Herrmann) in this regard.

Thus G. Bornkamm strikes a sensitive spot in this theology when he shows very fully that Paul is not interested at all in a new self-consciousness and that the attempt to interpret him along these lines thus entails a reduction of his theology to mere anthropology. What Paul is trying to do is to proclaim a new history and existence in which I am taken up into Christ's history.[42] More specifically this means, not adoption of Christ's history into my self-understanding, but my adoption into Christ's history by implantation into the continuity of the salvation event.

Naturally this does not mean that we are just to reverse what Bultmann does. We cannot do this, since that implantation into history does not exclude my consciousness or self-understanding. I am adopted only as I believe in Christ. Belief, however, involves my consciousness and hence affects my self-understanding. Nevertheless a difference of emphasis is manifest. By nature faith is not characterized by its element of consciousness but by the *extra se* to which it relates, namely, the history of Christ into which we are adopted.[43]

---

[41] Cf. CA, I, on the distinction between *extra* and *intra me* in relation to the person and work of both Christ and the Holy Spirit.

[42] "Mythos und Evangelium," ThEx, N.F. 26, p. 25.

[43] To avoid the idea of faith as itself a work Luther expresses the same thought by calling the subject of faith a "mathematical point" rather than an area where faith can be located or whence it can be derived (WA, 40, II, 527, 9; 40, III, 572, 23; 40, I, 21, 12, etc.).

Parenthetically one might ask whether Bultmann's disparagement of the OT (cf. GV, II, p. 186; *Geschichte und Eschatologie* [1958], p. 29) is not connected with the fact that his schema of consciousness theology does not let him think in terms of adoption into Christ's history and pre-history (cf. on this W. Pannenberg, "Heilsgeschehen und Geschichte," KD [1959], 3, pp. 223ff.). But we cannot go into this here and merely suggest it to the reader for his own consideration.

3. Since the NT kerygma is "addressed," the question of the recipient and his situation is implied, and hence also that of the sphere to which the kerygma goes. This question carries with it the further one where we are to seek orientation in this sphere. The NT witnesses gave their own answer by referring to the OT. Here is the preparatory history of promise to which the NT message is annexed as fulfilment and new eschatological promise (Romans 9-11). The analogy which must link the message with him who receives it lies in the typological preparation for the NT in the OT.[44] Historical continuity provides it. This continuity persists even when the structural analogy seems to be broken or interrupted insofar as a gulf opens up between promise and fulfilment and typology can no longer give adequate expression to the continuity between OT and NT. This crisis arises when the fulfilment of prophecies is different from what those who received them expected. The fulfilment adds a new and surplus factor (cf. the "how much more" of Romans 5:17) which is not felt to be a break with the prophecy, however, but is interpreted in terms of it, so that the thought of prophecy and fulfilment, and the implied continuity, persists. Gerhard von Rad has this continuity between Christ's history and pre-history in view when he says that our knowledge of Christ would be incomplete without the witness of the OT: "Christ is proffered to us only in the double witness of the chorus of expectation and recollection."[45]

Decisive in the present context is that the sphere into which the NT kerygma comes, the existence to which it is addressed, is delineated by the OT. The historical continuity of OT and NT is the analogy that is always presupposed when it is a matter of linking those who are to understand to what they are to understand. As we are adopted into the history and pre-history of Christ, as we are set in the continuity of promise and fulfilment, creation and redemption, OT and NT, we are summoned to the place into which the NT kerygma seeks to come. As the message is addressed, this place is always presupposed by it. Bultmann is well aware that there has to be this place. But he does not seek it in the OT history of promise, or even in the sketch of human existence in Genesis 1-11—man's created, fallen, and yet preserved existence.[46]

He seeks it in man's pre-understanding, in existential analysis rather than Christ's history and pre-history. If it is sought in Christ's history and pre-

---

[44] L. Goppelt, *Typos* (1939).
[45] "Typologische Auslegung des AT," ETh (1952), p. 33.
[46] Cf. the author's *How the World Began* (E.T. 1961).

history, the vestibule of the place of understanding is determined by the kerygma itself and is seen in terms of the analogy of faith. If it is sought in pre-understanding, and existential analysis is needed, it is built independently of the kerygma to which it is supposed to lead. The path and goal of understanding are slanted accordingly by the orientation of the pre-understanding.

Two insights result.

First, a decisive influence is exerted on one's whole theology by where one seeks the place to which the NT kerygma is spoken and where one gets information on the nature and structure of this place, in the OT or in existential analysis.

Second, existential analysis and the OT are thus rivals (if not alternatives). Insofar as a general pre-understanding is sought, interest in the OT wanes and it is theologically disparaged. The opposite is equally true. Since the Cartesian approach of Theology A wants to establish the vestibule of theology by existential analysis, one finds in it a consistent depreciation of the OT. Its very presence in the canon is an embarrassment which, e.g., Schleiermacher as a preacher avoids only by artifice.

Since address is part of the kerygma, the question of the place where it is spoken is unavoidable. It is a crucial theological question. Every theological system has a vestibule in this sense. The only question is where the plan comes from. This will affect the structure as a whole. Here at the outset, before the main questions are tackled, a decision is made about the role of the OT in all theological thinking.

But not only the OT is at stake. Many other decisions depend on how we understand it, including our understanding of the canon and of history and historicity in general. Once we realize this, it is clear that the Cartesian approach of Theology A is the crucial question in it and that with the answer to this question prior decisions are made of incalculable range and significance.

IV

Key Hermeneutical Question in Theology A
Problem of the Form and Content of
Statements as Seen in the Significance of
Mythical Statements for Theology

1. LINGUISTIC AND MATERIAL CONFUSION REGARDING THE TERM MYTH[1]

In Theology A the form of theological statements plays a twofold role.

First, these statements can be kerygmatic content only insofar as they can be put in familiar language. Since contemporary philosophy usually fixes the vocabulary in which the current understanding of existence is expressed, it is especially inclined to use the terminology fashioned by philosophy. The act of understanding thus takes place as traditional terms are translated into the vocabulary of modern thought.

Thus far Theology A simply does what every theology must do. The issue is how the translation is done, namely, how far contemporary terms are simply used and how far they assume a normative function. We have referred to this already.

Second, Theology A has a further interest in the mode of expression. As we have seen, it presupposes man's adulthood. Modern science has helped to bring this about by giving man an enlightened view of the world. Part of the intellectual honesty of adult man is that in the area of faith he will accept no truth-claim that conflicts with scientific knowledge. But this brings about tension with the biblical tradition since the message was originally proclaimed in the forms of the ancient view of the world. Thus, in the Genesis creation stories pre-Copernican cosmology is employed. This leads on to the question (already noted) how far the outmoded forms of statement can be distin-

---

[1] Bibliography: R. Bultmann, "NT und Mythologie," KM, I (1951), pp. 15ff.; E.T. "New Testament and Mythology," KM (1953), pp. 1ff.; J. J. Bachofen, *Der Mythus von Orient und Occident* (ed. M. Schroeter, 1926); E. Auerbach, *Mimesis, Dargestellte Wirklichkeit in der abendländischen Literatur* (1946); N. Berdyaev, *The Meaning of History* (1949); P. Tillich, RGG², IV, pp. 363ff.; G. Stählin, TDNT, IV, pp. 363ff.; G. Stählin, TDNT, IV, pp. 762ff.; C. Hartlich, W. Sachs, *Der Ursprung des Mythosbegriffs in der modernen Bibelwissenschaft* (1952); H. Thielicke, "Die Frage der Entmythologisierung," KM, I, 159ff.; E.T. pp. 138ff.

guished from the contents stated. This distinction does not mean elimination of the forms but the need to interpret the texts expressed in them.[2] If in the act of interpretation the invalid and outmoded form is not to be abandoned, however, it must still be separated from the permanently valid kerygmatic content.

This may all sound very plausible and is certainly very familiar in general outline, but problems soon arise in detail. The constant question is: What is mere form and what is true content? We may again take the resurrection as an example. Is the resurrection of Christ on the third day a historical fact, even if not verifiable? Or is it just a mode of expression from a cosmology that does not yet contain the modern idea of a closed nexus of nature and history, so that transcendental interventions like the raising of the dead offer no difficulty? If the latter interpretation of Easter is accepted, if the Easter fact is reduced to a mere manner of speaking, one arrives at Bultmann's version of Easter theology, namely, that it simply expresses the meaning of the cross.[3] In this case the account of a supposed fact is just a way of expressing something else. Far-reaching theological decisions obviously depend on whether one opts for kerygmatic content or mere form.[4]

The question of myth arises here. For myth is a form of expression. When it speaks of the origin of the world, of heaven, of Olympus, of the gods, of what transcends the horizon of our experience, then, Bultmann thinks, its statements are not meant directly. Cosmologically it is not trying to give an objective picture of the world [5] or information about its origin. The immediate objects of its pronouncements are simply an indication of its real concern, namely, how man understands himself in his world. Thus it is to be interpreted, not cosmologically but anthropologically, or, better, existentially.[6]

This interpretation strips away the symbol and translates what is said there indirectly into the clear terms of modern vocabulary and cosmology. The fact that myth speaks symbolically is connected with the world-view from which it takes its modes of expression. The ancient world is not the objectifiable world of experience known to modern science. It is a world open on every side. The boundaries between transcendence and immanence are fluid if they exist at all. This world and the world to come are interchangeable. In myth, then, man thinks he experiences certain powers as the basis and limit of his world and his own action and suffering, and conceptually he integrates these powers into the circle of the known world, its objects and forces. He speaks of that which belongs to the other world in terms of this world, and of the gods in terms of men.[7]

The mythological vocabulary used by the NT is taken especially from later Jewish apocalyptic and the Gnostic redemption myth.[8] Since the

---

[2] KM, I, pp. 21ff.; E.T. pp. 9ff.   [3] KM, I, p. 44; E.T. p. 38.

[4] We have greatly simplified the alternatives here, for even if the resurrection is accepted as a fact the influence of the ancient view of the world has still to be investigated. One must still ask what is fact in the story and what is legend. Have the angels the same factuality as the empty tomb?

[5] KM, I, p. 22; E.T. p. 10.   [6] *Loc. cit.*   [7] *Loc. cit.*   [8] KM, I, p. 26; E.T. p. 15.

means of expression are historically conditioned in this way, the contents require demythologization.

This ugly and negative word, which popular thought avidly seized upon, denotes little more than the process of interpretation. From a historically and cosmologically conditioned statement I have to extract what is really meant, the self-understanding behind the form. I have also to transpose this true sense into the cosmology and vocabulary of my own age.

One may easily see that in demythologization all the problems arise which we have illustrated by the example of the resurrection, and especially the question of what is to be assigned to the form and what to the content.[9]

It is part of the style of myth, we are told, to depict the other world in terms of this world and to put the transcendent in the circle of normal objective experience. But what about Christmas? Ignoring the trappings and looking only at the core of the message, we find that the core itself says that the Word was made flesh, that God thus comes into our world, that he does so incognito and hence the miracle cannot be demonstrated objectively and scientifically, and yet that in this concealment he really is in the manger at Bethlehem, that the whole point is God's coming down in our history. Now this might be called mythological symbolism, the expressing of the other world in terms of this world, or of God in human terms. If so, John's *Logos sarx egeneto* ("the Word was made flesh") is simply a form of expression. This form has to be penetrated and interpreted and will point us in a different direction like the Easter kerygma. Or else—this is the alternative—we find the whole point of the gospel in the fact that God comes down in human form and in love accepts solidarity with us. But then we are construing the incarnation of the Word as content and not just form. Which of the two views is right? We shall have to discuss this later in the dogmatics proper. For the moment we are simply elucidating the problem.[10]

The debate stirred up by Bultmann's proposed demythologizing has been so coarsened by thesis and antithesis, proclamation and counter-confession, that the only alternatives seem to be simple affirmation or rejection. In their views of one another the two sides have taken refuge in stereotypes. On the one side is the ancient foe wreaking subtle destruction and on the other an ossified conservatism which is disloyal to what is artificially conserved, since it deprives it of all possibility of being up to date. The two movements do not

---

[9] Wilhelm Herrmann, who used the terms "basis of faith" and "concept of faith," was the first to raise this question programmatically. As he saw it, some facts (e.g., the inner life of Jesus) are the basis of faith, while other things that are stated as facts are simply self-reflections of faith, e.g., the divine sonship, the vicarious significance of Christ's passion, the resurrection, etc. Cf. *Gesammelte Aufsätze*, ed. F. W. Schmidt (1923), p. 293.

[10] Barth shows a fine grasp of this problem when he speaks of man seeking the infinite who is finite as such, the one who, as he is there, is here, the God who as God is man (*Das Wort Gottes und die Theologie* [1929], p. 161; E.T. *The Word of God and The Word of Man* [1928], p. 191). Cf. also H. Iwand, *Nachgel. Werke*, I (1962), pp. 184ff.

just fight under the slogans of modern and conservative (or reactionary) but accuse one another of sinning against the kerygma. The demythologizers say: You attack the kerygma by making it a dead thing. The conservatives reply: You are making a complete break and reducing theology to existentialist philosophy.

We have spoken of an unhappy coarsening, but in fact an anthropological constriction seems unavoidable when Bultmann assesses what is kerygmatically binding by whether and how far it fits the pre-understanding provided by existential analysis, and then assigns the nondigestible remnants to the sphere of a historically conditioned mode of expression or mythological thought-schema.

On the other hand, apart from some fundamentalists who are better Christians than theologians, there are few conservative theologians who would contest the presence of mythical elements, and hence of temporally conditioned forms of expression, in Holy Scripture. What OT commentary does not make some comparison between the flood story and the Gilgamesh epic? Who can deny that there are allusions to Gnostic speculation in Paul's comparison between Adam and Christ, or that Revelation borrows from the apocalyptic mythology of later Jewish eschatology? Is there then too big a difference at this point? Are not the two parties closely related in many matters? Nevertheless, they feel that they are in opposition in spite of affinities in detailed analysis. What is the reason for this apparent contradiction?

The most barren and useless attempt to define the mutual "hostility" would be to say that the one side is "too" conservative in its effort to keep traditional doctrine intact, i.e., without interpretative selection, whereas the other is "too" critical or radical in the way it degrades essential content to the level of mere mode of expression. When controversy becomes purely quantitative: "There is too strong or weak an emphasis," or "This goes too far or not far enough," one can be certain that the basic issues are not clear. Either the antitheses can be stated qualitatively (and not just quantitatively) or they are no true antitheses.[11]

If we apply this insight to the debate between Theology A and Theology B the question arises whether there is a qualitative distinction and where it is to be located, or whether the whole thing is a sham fight in view of the fact that both sides accept the mythical form.

In fact there seem to be two qualitative antitheses in this controversy.

We have already discussed the first, namely, that Theology A by starting with existential analysis prejudges what can be accepted as possible kerygmatic content. We recall Bultmann's decisive principle that the understanding

---

[11] Even Martin Kähler in a fine essay "Die moderne Theologie und die Kirche," *Dogmatische Zeitfragen*, I (1898), p. 80, resorts to quantitative distinction when he says that there is only a difference of degree and not of kind between modern theology and positive (i.e., conservative) theology, since we are all modern in our approach to scholarship and theology or the way we speak figuratively of supersensory things.

of accounts of events as God's action presupposes a pre-understanding of what can be called God's action.[12]

The second qualitative antithesis, to which we must now turn, arises through the apparent lack of clarity on both sides as to what is meant by mythical ways of speaking or indeed by myth in general. Since this term has played a vital role since the Enlightenment, and especially in the nineteenth and twentieth centuries, this lack of clarity has muddied the debate and helped to put the two sides at cross purposes.[13] First, then, we shall attempt a linguistic clarification and then we shall show the possible qualitative antithesis at the heart of banal quantitative distinctions.

Perhaps it might be demonstrated in this way that the NT itself is engaged in self-liberation from myth. But then the question immediately arises: From what myth? This question cannot be answered unless one distinguishes between different modes of the mythical and does not lump them all together under the one word. If this experiment succeeds and demythologization is perceived in the NT itself, then we shall get instructions for the legitimate demythologization to be practiced today. The NT itself will indicate both the manner and also the limit of such operations. They must be done in accordance with the NT and not one-sidedly controlled by existential analysis and its pre-judgment.

2. UNDERSTANDINGS OF MYTH

a. Myth as a Way of Apprehending Being. The Category of Depth

(1) Mythicizing as a Transcending of Logos

We begin by asking whether it is adequate to regard myth simply as a way of putting what belongs to the other world in our own categories (Bultmann), so that the postulate of demythologization commits us to a host of prior decisions on what is to be taken as content and what is to be taken as form. Might it not be that these decisions are based on a misunderstanding of myth?

Definitions are needed if we are to get a grasp of modern usage.[14]

A preliminary observation might be made on certain hermeneutical difficulties that beset all modern definitions and interpretations of myth. As we shall see, modern man (even as scholar) has reservations about myth. This is no less so when he is open and sensitive to the world of myth. He cannot accept a mythical narrative naively and directly. He cannot believe it. To him it is a symbolical statement and to that extent it cannot be regarded as authentic (cf. Cassirer and Lévy-Bruhl; cf. also K. Kerényi, *Umgang mit dem Göttlichen,* 2nd ed. [1961], p. 41).

---

[12] ZThK (1950), 1, p. 66.

[13] Cf. D. F. Strauss and others (Hartlich and Sachs, *op. cit.*).

[14] Only with uneasiness do we accept Bultmann's word demythologizing instead of the more correct demythicizing. There is the same distinction between myth and mythology as between transcendent and transcendental or Bultmann's beloved existential and existentialist.

Two objections have been brought against this modern view of myth. First, for those who live in the mythical world myth expresses primarily and directly what it narrates, so that it is not meant symbolically (Malinowski, *Myth in Primitive Psychology* [1925]). In this world men relate naively to myth, whereas symbolical interpretation implies a broken relation. Second, symbolical interpretation regards myth as a mere form, whereas in fact it has kerygmatic content. Symbolical interpretation with its illusion that myth is a mere manner of expression erroneously thinks that mythical and nonmythical man can hold the same convictions but state them differently. Modern man puts in demythicized form the same content or self-understanding as was once held by mythical man. Kerényi argues against this that what has altered, and could alter, is the content and not just the mode of thought (*op. cit.,* p. 32).

This point is important and means that we are not to jump too easily to a symbolical contemporaneity of contents. Nor can myth be set aside merely by substituting another form for the mythical manner of expression. The content changes when myth is abandoned.

Yet this historical argument is not wholly adequate. If it were the only criterion of our relation to myth, the relation would be merely negative. We should no longer believe the stories; our orientation to existence would be quite different. There would thus be no point in interpreting myth at all; we could only recite it as something alien. But is there really any product of the human spirit that defies and even forbids interpretation? Would not this break human solidarity? This solidarity is grounded especially in the assumption that certain factors in human life remain constant (e.g., knowledge of finitude, anxiety, or hope). To interpret myth is simply to set it in relation to common questions and to see it in the light of these constant factors. Hence we can and must investigate its understanding of man and the world and interpret it symbolically.

What a scholar like Kerényi says is still important. It shows us that we can never grasp myth adequately by this mode of interpretation. We are making a symbol of what was real content for those who believed in myth. In doing this—and we are forced to do it—we are differentiating form and content in a way that was alien to antiquity.

The interpreter takes myth differently from mythical man. His relation to it is broken. Symbolical interpretation is strictly improper. Only when we realize this and remember it, as interpretation usually fails to do, can we investigate the understanding of man and the world expressed in myth. With this reservation and this awareness we shall now survey modern definitions of myth.

Nicholas Berdyaev in his *The Meaning of History* (1949) regards myth as a reconstruction of life embracing the essence of all historical occurrence and thus including a dimension that is closed to objectifying thought with its focus on the foreground (p. 22). We cannot, he says, comprehend purely objective history (*loc. cit.*). This is not because of a need for mystification that peers into the background. It is simply because the subject of the history is included in it and hence has to feel and unlock the historical (p. 23). To plumb the depths of the ages is to plumb the depths of self (p. 23). For this reason history cannot be known from without but only from within (p. 25), i.e., by anamnesis of the basis, goal, and meaning of one's own existence.

Thus knowledge of history includes a non-objective element which is not to be found in external reality but without which external reality will remain obscure and impenetrable. Since my own existence has absolute meaning, this meaning, this inner spiritual reality, is the true source of historical knowledge (p. 44). This thought is possible, however, only if the absolute meaning, the divine life itself in a very deep and mysterious sense, is history, a historical drama, a historical mystery play (p. 45). On this view what we call time in our earthly historical process is seen to be an inner period of eternity itself (p. 64), so that time and eternity are not totally different and incommensurable spheres (p. 65). Hence in history, through the sick and evil time which consumes and destroys, turning life into a cemetery so that the new life of sons may arise over the dead bones of their forgotten fathers, true time is brought into being . . . noumenal and not phenomenal time, which upholds the interconnection and in which is no breach between present and future (p. 74).

Myth makes statements about this true time by making us aware of the true relation between time and eternity. This relation cannot be inferred from external phenomena. It can be read off only from the existence of the observer (insofar as he is more than a mere spectator). Hence myth cannot portray reality in the sense of modern historicism. It can only proceed symbolically, showing that history is a likeness and opening it to its background. It thus uses a form of statement that transcends the objectively verifiable and yet is true—far more so than the banal "correctness" which confines itself to the partial, objectifiable aspect of reality.

The mythical mode of expression is not governed, then, by a naiveté which thinks it can put the other world into the category of events in this world. It is controlled by the overwhelming force of experienced reality, which mocks at objective comprehensibility and thus opens up the objective symbolically to that which presses in upon it. To man who has this mythical experience of reality it is the modern historicist who seems naive since he is a mere spectator and his shallow intuition regards as primitive fantasy what in fact represents true realities.[15]

Leopold Ziegler's interpretation of myth is basically similar.[16] As he sees it, what we have called modern naiveté is caught in a false alternative posed by narrow habits of thought, namely, that we must choose between poetic myth and historical narration (p. 337). This is no true dilemma. Myth presents the meaning and total aspect of reality. It involves historical interpretation and not just research.

---

[15] Cf. Gerhard Nebel's acute study *Das Ereignis des Schönen* (1953).
[16] *Überlieferung* (1936).

Hence a historical occurrence is not brought into question or even eliminated when it is hieratically or mythically stylized in traditional depiction. This stylization, which intermingles gods and men or the primal and eschatological, is no alternative to facticity. It simply discloses the hidden core of meaning in the facts. Thus a certain style of historical writing can give historical significance to single incidents only by way of myth. Only when it integrates it with the background of sacred history does it undergird its intrinsically indifferent and silent and insipid chronology with meaning (*loc. cit.*). Thus the Greek words myth and history come together at a deep level in common meaning; both denote history as it is narrated, reported, and investigated (p. 338).

If Berdyaev and Ziegler derive the mythical form from the quality of reality itself, Bachofen derives it from the many associations which it can evoke and which make it superior to abstract unilinear thinking. Using the word "symbol" for what we call the "mythical symbol," he says that this evokes intuition while abstract speech can only explain. It affects all aspects of the human spirit in contrast to speech. It has roots in the depths of the soul, whereas speech only ruffles the surface. It is directed inwards, speech outwards. It alone can combine the most varied things into a single impression. Speech puts them in a series and presents them only partially to the mind when a single glance is needed to grasp them in totality. Words make the infinite finite, whereas symbols conduct the spirit of the finite and becoming world into the kingdom of the infinite world of being (*Der Mythos . . .* , p. 337). It is striking that Bachofen charges speech with doing what myth does for Bultmann, namely, making the infinite finite.

Precisely what myth expresses by the category of depth may be seen again in Auerbach's figurative interpretation of biblical stories. Thus the story of Peter's denial seems to be only about a police action and its consequences,[17] about everyday people. This would be farce or comedy in other ancient literature. But behind the everyday guise is a basic event. Peter exemplifies conflict and a situation of decision. An action on earth, irrespective of its concrete here-and-now reality, signifies not only itself but something else as well,[18] which relates to eternal and not just to temporal destiny. Only in virtue of this can the everyday enjoy literary status.

The story of the offering of Isaac has a similar background quality. It is not told as Homer would tell it. Homer's narrative has no background. What he tells is always the present and this fills the stage.[19] But the paltry information on time and place in the Isaac story is only the necessary symbol enwrapping the immanent event and pointing beyond itself. The acts are part of a totality and are tensely directed to a goal. This totality is the world and its history.[20] Thus the horizontal and causal link is broken. The here and now is no part of an earthly series (or is not concerned to be this); it is also what

---

[17] *Mimesis*, pp. 47ff.; E.T. 1953, pp. 41ff.   [18] *Ibid.*, p. 495; E.T. p. 490.
[19] *Ibid.*, pp. 9ff.; E.T. pp. 5ff.   [20] *Ibid.*, pp. 19f.; E.T. p. 14.

has been and what will be in the future. Strictly, for God, it is eternal, beyond time, perfect already in the fragmentary earthly event.[21]

Figurative interpretation shares with mythical form the transcending of the objective. Like myth, it has reality in view, the only true reality, reality as God sees it. This reality may contradict objective reality (as in myths about the gods) or it may harmonize with it to the extent that it keeps everyday reality but gives it the rank only of a symbol, so that it is relativized in rela-tion to the more powerful background. The common feature in myth and figurative meaning is that both are open to the background, to the depth of being, and they thus share the resultant concept of reality.

If myth is understood in this sense as a transcending of the merely objec-tive and hence partial aspect of reality, as a statement about a higher power that presses in and resists the clutch of objectifying conceptuality, the ques-tion arises whether demythologization is not unrealistic insofar as it accepts only a partial aspect of reality. To be sure, this reduction is not by way of historical objectification. Existential interpretation differs from this. In so doing it even comes close to the origin of myth in two respects. First, it starts at the point where Berdyaev finds the origin of myth, namely, in the non-objective self-experiencing of existence and not in the external phenom-enon. Second, it is against the objectifying misunderstanding of myth. This takes place when what myth reports is treated as an event in the historic foreground, is not construed in terms of its depth, and is thus accepted merely as a banal anthropomorphism.

In spite of its attack on objectification, however, the existential interpre-tation transposes myth into a conceptually comprehensible self-understand-ing. It thus divests it of its symbolism (to use Bachofen's word) and makes it into speech. In this concern to grasp the contents of myth conceptually—even though the concepts are those of existential philosophy rather than objectifying metaphysics—can one not detect the same constriction as we noted earlier in another respect when speaking of the anthropological strait-jacket? Should we not rather say that the mythical mode of expression can-not be abandoned if a specific dimension of reality is to be spoken of, so that the alternative of mythical or historical is inappropriate, just as it might well be inappropriate to retain (or remove) the mythical in the name of an exis-tential rather than a historicist understanding, forcing it into the concepts of this understanding?[22]

(2) Remythicizing as a Transcending of Logos

If the protest expressed in the final question be accepted, one may surmise

---

[21] *Ibid.*, p. 77; E.T. pp. 64f.

[22] For "to retain" here Thielicke uses the Hegelian "aufheben," which can also mean "to eliminate." The idea is that of being kept in another form; cf. H. Naumann, *Germanischer Schicksalsmythos* (1934), who relates the myth of the Midgard ser-pent to the ontology of Heidegger in terms of a similar transposition.

that an age that has gone through the phase from myth to logos,[23] and has thus attempted demythicization, will have to undertake remythicizing if it is still open to, or rediscovers, the depth of being. It will thus produce a myth of second degree. It will have to do this because it is faced with the same problems as gave rise to myth in the first place.

We do in fact find the process of remythicizing. Plato is the classical example.

Plato has the Greek Enlightenment behind him. He no longer believes naively in the gods like Homer.[24] Yet he still sets philosophy against the background of the Apollo myth (Krüger, *op. cit.,* p. 31), for in his account Socrates bases his mission on an oracle of Delphic Apollo (Apology, 21a). The saying of the Pythia that he is the wisest of all men is fulfilled in his thinking (Phaedon, 21d, 23b).

Plato takes this step into myth even though he realizes that there is tension between mythical self-forgetfulness and philosophical self-awareness. The former is passion and being seized, while the latter is self-critical deliberation. Yet the two are not wholly antithetical, as might be suggested by the modern idea of the sovereign subject which resists self-forgetfulness and alien control. Plato does in fact fight the self-forgetfulness of myth, but not because he contends for man's sovereign autonomy (Krüger, *op. cit.,* p. 32). He accepts rapture, but asks the post-mythical question by what we are snatched away. He affirms passion as conscious rapture by the power of a desire that liberates us from the world; he denies it as a source of self-forgetfulness (*ibid.,* p. 32). But since superior being is present in that desire, the concept with its objective reference, the mere logos, is not adequate to express its reality. The pure truth about the soul and the world is too high for the logos by which we ought to know it (*ibid.,* p. 56). It cannot be put in the terminology of logos. The new resort to myth is an expression of humility, of the need for help.

We have here a new turn in the relation to myth. Previously the need was to interpret its meaning, to put its symbols in the language of logos (unless, of course, it was contemptuously rejected).[25] But now a conceptual interpretation of reality is already present and mythical forms are required to express it.

The difference between this new resort to myth and pre-philosophical naiveté is that the attitude to myth is now one of irony rather than belief. Myth is permanently relativized when viewed only as a needed form. A "game" is played with interchangeable symbols that can be fitted to the required end and hence have no power of their own. Yet it is a serious game, for only in this way can expression be given to the superior force that evokes awe and dread and that escapes conceptualization.

---

[23] Cf. W. Nestle, *Vom Mythos zum Logos,* 2nd ed. (1942); G. Krüger, *Einsicht und Leidenschaft. Das Wesen des platonischen Denkens* (1939).

[24] Cf. W. F. Otto, *Die Götter Griechenlands,* 2nd ed. (1934), pp. 226ff., E.T. *The Homeric Gods* (1954); W. Jaeger, *Paideia,* II (1944), pp. 237ff., E.T. 1945, pp. 212f.

[25] Cf. the allegorical interpretation of myth in Thaegenes (Nestle, *op. cit.,* pp. 128ff.) and in contrast its rejection in Ionian philosophy.

Demythicizing and remythicizing are distinctly interfused in Plato. His demythicizing does not replace myth with interpretation as though the symbols were a dispensable form and concepts could be substituted for them. The old myths are liquidated, including their contents, which cannot be reinterpreted. The demythicizing is radical. But the experience of being which remains calls for a new form of mythical expression. Remythicizing is demanded.

This process differs completely from the demythologizing of Theology A. Nevertheless one may see in it two elements which are significant for the present-day relation to myth and which thus call for consideration.

The first is that not every myth is the same. Nor do myths differ merely in form and intention, which is too self-evident to require discussion. There is a basic and qualitative distinction between the modes of mythical expression.

Myth can have a kerygmatic content. This is liquidated by Plato. He does not draw his experience of being from myths and their interpretation.

One also finds myths without core or kerygma. These are possible forms of expression but have no content of their own. They are purely instrumental, a mere means to impart something drawn from very different sources.

This is all very relevant to the modern debate and will have to be taken up again later. It raises the question whether there might not be a dekerygmatizing of myth in the NT, i.e., an employment of mythical forms without any mythical contents.

The second element, which is also pertinent, is that the mythical form of expression has an indelible or indestructible character. Like Plato, and in a different way the NT, we too are unable to get along without it. Remythicizing is demanded unless we are dangerously to restrict our powers of expression.

In fact the process of remythicizing is in full swing in the poets. To convey their experience of being these offer continual variations on the theme of myth. They are convinced that the Esperanto of primal images will always be understood. Poetry is linguistically informed aetiology which is modern for every generation, not in spite of the fact that it is so old, but just because it is so old.[26]

Thus many mythical elements may be seen in R. M. Rilke, Gottfried Benn, Ernst Jünger, and Gerhard Nebel. But the greatest resurgence even of classical myth is in English literature, where one might mention James Joyce, T. S. Eliot, D. H. Lawrence, C. Fry, T. Williams, O'Neill, Golding, Durrell, Auden, and Updike with their use of such themes as Ulysses, the Eumenides, Orpheus, the Phoenix, Paradise Lost, the shield of Achilles, and the Centaur. Psychoanalysis, too, uses myth. It could even be asked whether science does not follow the mythical principle of expressing the invisible in terms of the visible, e.g., in the model of the atom.

---

[26] R. Haas, "Wie modern sind die englischen Klassiker?" *Neusprachliche Mitteilungen,* 4 (1966), pp. 208ff.

In view of this obvious return to mythical symbolism the question arises whether a theology preoccupied with demythologization, with interpretation of the significant elements in mythical statements, is really modern enough. Have not the contemporaries for the sake of whose supposed rationality this enterprise has been undertaken already moved on a good deal farther ahead? It is hard not to give an impression of irony when one asks whether the theology of demythologization, instead of moving with real culture, has not involuntarily saddled itself with popular culture.[27] At any rate, it seems that, except in theology, we are already in the stage of remythicizing exemplified in Plato. And like Plato no one is simply refurbishing the old myths or reviving their contents. (Sartre and Anouilh make something quite different out of Orestes and Antigone.) On the other hand, none of the most eloquent poets can dispense with mythical symbols that go beyond the partial, objective aspect of reality, the dimension of logos, and can communicate direct experience of being. We raise once again the question whether the movement from primary to secondary myth might not be of great theological pertinence.

b. Myth as a Statement about Transcendence. On the Theological Understanding of Myth

In our description of the various types of myth we have so far left out one important member. The examples we have taken and interpreted from Berdyaev, Ziegler, Auerbach, and Krüger all relate to man's direct experience of being, especially in the form of an understanding of history. In mythical statements man found the total aspect of being that transcends objective experience. He came to know its depth. Whether he took this from myth or experienced it as he himself was seized by being and then expressed it ironically in myth (like Plato), what determined the mythical form was always the experienced depth or background of being.

In biblical revelation, however, we find a basic modification of this experience that is not without influence on the employment of mythical speech. The experience is not now grounded in one's own encounter with being, or, better, in the fact that thought lets itself be claimed by being to state the truth of being, especially the truth that man is its watcher or herdsman.[28] Rather this experience of being is grounded in a word which comes to man and by and in which God discloses himself. Man does not unlock being, nor does being unlock itself to him as though immanent in him. In free and voluntary address, in gracious resolve, God calls man in his Word, presents himself (Exodus 20:2), reveals himself (1 Corinthians 2:1f.), comes, and dwells among those whom he calls (Ezekiel 43:7; John 1:14). This initiation by God of a history with man we call revelation. Since it is based on an initiative in the heart of God, revelation is qualitatively different from the disclosure of being in the form of immanence or from coming into being in the form of existence.[29]

---

27 Cf. Schleiermacher's *Second Letter to Lücke,* p. 37.
28 M. Heidegger, *Über den Humanismus* (1949), pp. 5, 29.   29 *Ibid.,* p. 29.

The question logically arises, then, how far the event of divine self-declaration can be put in any other form than that of myth. The transcendent has no vocabulary of its own. Speaking in tongues (1 Corinthians 14:2ff.)[30] is perhaps direct expression, but it is not communication unless interpreters translate it back into speech, and this means that it has to be expressed in an unsuitable medium. For speech, like rational concepts, works against the horizon of immanent experience.[31] It thus involves brokenness and indirectness for anything transcendent it seeks to express. In Tillich's sense it can only be symbolical.[32] The symbol is not strict, since it means something different from what it is. A banner is made of cloth but the cloth points beyond itself. Similarly words that belong by nature to our world have a symbolical meaning when they refer to something not of this world. Concepts are stretched similarly. They have to express what they are not able to express. They are like the cloth pointing to something else.

But they have to be stretched in this way, since what encounters us—the meeting with revelation—has to be communicated. This can be done only as the means at hand are used. Speech is the means at hand.

But speech is demanded for another reason. God's self-disclosure takes place in such a way that God has a history with us.[33] This means that he enters our history, dwells among us, has the Word made flesh. In the terms used above, this means that God gives up his transcendence, sets himself against the horizon of our history, and in solidarity with our historical existence "is tempted like as we are" (Hebrews 4:15f.). Making himself present, God comes into our world and experience.

He is still, of course, an object of faith. He remains under the veil of the cross. He comes in alien form, incognito. Objectifying analysis cannot grasp him. Yet he is still in our world. Even for the historicist, and hence for our speech, there are traces of his presence, even if they cannot be read properly. The historian can establish the existence and influence of Jesus of Nazareth. But what he means as Kyrios, what he is in this significance, transcends what can be established objectively.

God's self-disclosure, in virtue of which he is present in our history, has thus a distinctive ambivalence. It has direct force on the one side and indirect on the other. To deny the indirect side, to see Jesus only directly, is to make of him the "Jesus of history" and to fall into the Ebionite heresy. To deny the direct side and to make him a pure symbol is to dehistoricize revelation, to make Christ the bearer of an idea, and thus to fall into the docetic heresy. Every Christology will have within it something of this ambivalence of direct

---

[30] Cf. the author's *Between Heaven and Earth* (E.T. 1965).

[31] On the complicated problem of speech cf. R. H. Müller-Schwefe, *Die Sprache und das Wort* (1966), pp. 95ff., 110ff.

[32] K. D. Nörenberg, *Analogia imaginis* (1966).

[33] The Hebrew word *dabar* means event as well as word. It may thus be compared to our word history, which means both what is said (narrated history) and also what took place (experienced history); cf. Jeremiah 1:12; Ezekiel 12:25, 28 (H. W. Wolff, "Das Geschichtsverständnis der alttestamentlichen Prophetie," ETh [1960], 5, p. 220).

and indirect statement, as we shall show later when dealing with the theme.

In relation to myth our present concern is with the element of indirectness. In all statements about God's self-disclosure, his coming into our history, there will be a certain symbolism insofar as our terms have to mean something that does not fit their immanent content. The change of concepts that has to take place in biblical usage can best be shown by individual illustrations. In the present context a few general indications may be given.

When John's Gospel uses "Logos" it is adopting a Stoic term and thus employing existing vocabulary. In so doing it is claiming the preparation which took place linguistically as philosophers made use of the word.[34] On the other hand John's idea of the Word that is consubstantial with the Father cannot be expressed by the Stoic concept. When the word is used of Christ it undergoes a shift of sense. Christ is not defined by what the Stoics meant when they used the term. The very opposite is the case. The real nature of Logos is defined by what Christ is as the eternal Word.

One can test this out by seeing how the reverse process took place in the early Apologists (Justin Martyr or Tatian). Here the "Logos" of Greek philosophy is taken over unaltered and Christ is defined by the concept. He is thus the fulfilment of secular wisdom rather than its contradiction (1 Corinthians 1:18ff.; 2:14). The Logos concept is the bridge on which the philosopher meets the Christian message, not finding in it something different that transcends wisdom, but rather recognizing himself in it.

As with John's "Logos," so it is with other words. Christology adopts the existing vocabulary and uses such concepts as Messiah, Son of Man, or High Priest. But once these words are impressed into service, their meaning changes. They are defined by that, or by him, who thus employs them.

Naturally the change in meaning is not total. If it were, the terms could be used at random and filled with any content. This is not so. They have from the outset some affinity to the content in whose service they are put. Thus the word "Logos" undoubtedly has in its normal use an element that strains toward the content it is given in John.

One might describe the affinity and change by saying that when the words enter the NT they are baptized; a new creation is made of them; the "old" of their former content has passed away. Yet in spite of this surrender of identity as a new creation, their former existence continues as in baptism. This is an indication that the choice of words for what has to be expressed in revelation is not haphazard. Even if they are only symbolical and "improper," they have special qualifications for the new function allotted to them.

In this sense symbols, too, are not arbitrary. They may not be strict, since they point away from themselves to something else. But even in their original stage of meaning they are candidates with special qualifications for the new job they are given.

The dialectic of change and continuity here is particularly well expressed

---

[34] J. Maritain, *An Essay on Christian Philosophy* (1955), pp. 20f.

by the word baptism. As in life itself, there can even be relapse of the baptized terms back into the original paganism. This takes place when the former content is revived, as with Logos in the Apologists. Most Christian terms have suffered this fate. A vivid modern instance is the understanding of spirit as reason or as the human spirit in general.

One might even say that this regression is the stylistic law that produces heresies or antichrists. Paganism seldom invades Christianity in the form of blatant antithesis. Familiar Christian words are usually enlisted as supporters who can smuggle the new spirit into Ilion in a Trojan horse. Hence the first steps are seldom recognized for what they are. Only when the horse is inside the walls of Troy does the hatch open and Agamemnon, Menelaus, and the rest spring out to turn the Trojan flank.

There are theologians today who use Christian terms to say the opposite of what they have hitherto denoted. D. F. Strauss is an early example. For him Christ is the idea of humanity. Hence the doctrine of the two natures means that mankind is the child of the visible mother and the invisible father, of nature and spirit. Mankind is also the one that dies, rises again, and ascends into heaven as it progresses from a state of nature to developing spiritual life (*Leben Jesu,* 4th ed. [1840], § 151, II, pp. 709ff.; E. T. *Life of Jesus* [1892 ed.], § 151, pp. 779ff.).

This is a relapse of terms from their baptism. And as the appearance of apostates does not change, so words do not placard their backsliding. The change takes place under the cover of an abiding form. This structural peculiarity of incipient movements of relapse is the reason why the spirits must be distinguished (1 Corinthians 12:10) to detect error. Because of the continuity, objective analysis can achieve little. True and false prophets are so alike in statement and appearance that this kind of analysis is hardly possible (Karl Barth, CD, II, 2, pp. 393ff.).

We argue, then, that human terms are claimed and set in service by God's revelation. Under the presupposition of the ambivalence noted, they now denote something different from their proper content. To that extent they are "improper" and symbolical.

This leads Tillich, for what seem to be obvious reasons, to speak of a mythical form when it is a question of declaring revelation. Myth does indeed share with symbol the ability to express the knowledge of being that transcends objective experience with means that are taken from the stock of immanent ideas and normal concepts. For myth is a symbol, constructed of elements of reality, for the unconditioned and transcendent that is at issue in the religious act.[35] Since it is constructed out of the elements of reality but follows a plan determined by the unconditioned that is at issue, its content cannot be discovered by mere analysis of the elements. They are simply symbolical. Their point is not in themselves. They point outside themselves. Hence myth is misunderstood if it is stripped of its symbolism and

---

[35] RGG², IV, 364. Cf. also the essay "Religiöser Symbolismus," *Die Frage nach dem Unbedingten, Gesammelte Werke,* V, pp. 187ff.

taken directly. Tillich finds this misunderstanding even in the mythical stage itself. Mythical man misunderstands myth when he objectifies the divine which myth presents symbolically. The pious Christian can make the same mistake when he takes, e.g., the eschatological statements of Revelation directly and treats them as descriptions of a future in this world.[36]

The question already put to Bultmann arises again at this point. Is the statement that myth contains an objectification of the divine reversible? Does objectification always denote the presence of myth, of symbolical indirectness? If so, the incarnation is only a mythical "cipher" for the idea of presence. It is a way of indicating that God is there. It does not denote God's existence in a single man, an individual. For, as D. F. Strauss might say, the idea, when it realizes itself, does not lavish its fulness on one example and begrudge it to others; it loves to bestow its riches on many examples, i.e., it manifests itself collectively, so that the subject of the predicates that the church confers on Christ is not an individual (Jesus Christ) but an idea (that of humanity).[37] Kierkegaard was protesting against this Hegelianism when he found the paradox of the incarnation, the supreme condescension of God, precisely in the fact that God does not stop at an idea but becomes a man, lavishing his fulness on one example, accepting an extreme incognito, the scandalous opposite of what reason has always understood by God.[38]

Is, then, the fact that the elements of reality are unsuitable for the unconditioned which is at issue in the religious act due to the inadequacy of mythical and symbolical language as such? Do we have here what Zwingli would call *alloiosis,* a figure and its defectiveness? Or is the problem ontic rather than verbal, namely, the inadequacy that God himself accepts, the supreme incognito or self-alienation which in loving condescension he adopts when he enters into solidarity with us, exposes himself to the pressures of history, and is tempted like as we are (Hebrews 4:15)? This is the question that has to be put to Tillich as well as Bultmann.

We have already hinted at an answer by mentioning that the statements of the NT are characterized by an ambivalence of directness and symbolic indirectness. They are direct insofar as they record events, God's presence and mighty acts in history. They are symbolic and indirect insofar as what they signify, the quality of salvation history inherent in them, cannot be read off directly but in the form of events is found only as sign and indication. Only when one accepts this ambivalence can one guard the paradox of the incarnation, of the infinite become finite, against the misunderstanding that this is only figure and not fact. Only thus can a dike be established against the dissolving of history in the idea of a self-representation of humanity as in the left-wing Hegelian D. F. Strauss. Only thus can one finally lay a foundation for what Bultmann says at the end of his essay "New Testa-

---

[36] The mythical objectification of the divine in space, time, and humanity is contested by prophetic religion, transcended by mystical religion, and regarded as unworthy and nonsensical by philosophical religion (*Gesammelte Werke,* V, p. 189).

[37] *Leben Jesu, loc. cit.*

[38] *Training in Christianity* (1944), pp. 26ff., 127.

ment and Mythology," namely, that God's transcendence is not reduced to immanence, as in myth, but that we have instead the paradox of the presence of the transcendent God in history.[39]

But can this "presence" really break the hold of mythical *alloiosis,* can it denote Kierkegaard's presence in an individual and thus prevent slippage into a mere idea, if the framework of the historically possible is imposed, if the understanding of records of events as God's work presupposes a pre-understanding of what God's work can be? In that final thesis does not Bultmann say more than his theological prolegomena have prepared us for? What reply can he give if it is objected that he is contradicting his own pre-suppositions? Schniewind is surely right when he both provides a different basis for the statement and also revises it, arguing that what Bultmann should have said is that the proclamation "the Word was made flesh" means the presence of the transcendent God in history, but to opponents this seems to reduce the transcendence of God to immanence.[40] Opponents are bound to see it thus, for the paradox of presence in an individual is to them a scandal. To claim that a man who was forsaken by God and despised by men is salvation resists all proof, whether of signs or of wisdom, even the wisdom that can interpret myth.[41]

Myth, then, is a legitimate mode of expression to the extent that by symbolical indirectness it gives expression to the fact that what sustains our reality cannot be adequately expressed by the vocabulary of this reality. The question arises, however, whether the incarnation (*Deus vere homo*) is to be regarded as a mythical "cipher" and hence, as in Strauss, as the clothing of an idea. Analysis of myth itself, as is now clear, cannot show that it is not. No point of Christian truth can be protected against confusion with mythical speech, just as Christ himself cannot be protected against confusion with a mere rabbi, enthusiast, or founder of religion. This confusion is only secondarily caused by our structure of thought, which is oriented to the world and can handle what is not of this world only brokenly and symbolically. Primarily the confusion is ontic; its basis is in God's gracious acceptance of solidarity with man. God's love causes him to come in human form (Philippians 2:7) and hence to become interchangeable and defenseless. This nondemonstrability or planned defenselessness of God means among other things that his coming into history can be interpreted as mythical *alloiosis.* If nevertheless faith confesses the real presence of God in history, this is not because it can prove that we have here more than mythical *alloiosis.* What compels faith to acknowledge the presence of God is rather the testimony of the Holy Spirit which smites it by the Word that has set up tent among us (John 1:14). This supra-mythical element can still be expressed only in mythical symbols, in this case that of tabernacling.

The instance just given brings us face to face with the distinctive inter-twining of the mythical and the supra-mythical.

The incarnation as such is supra-mythical. It can be confused with myth

---

[39] KM, I, p. 48; E.T. p. 44.   [40] KM, I, p. 109; E.T. p. 86.   [41] *Loc. cit.*

and God's condescension can even be adduced as a theological argument for this. But it does not really point away from itself to something else (Strauss' idea), as myth does. Quite nonmythically and nonsymbolically it points to itself. Yet this basic saying is still surrounded by symbols, among which many would reckon not merely the metaphor of setting up tent but also legendary embellishments in the stories of Christmas, Easter, and the Ascension, at any rate to the extent that these are meant to express in our terms the miracles of transcendent coming that is the subject of faith.

The intertwining of supra-mythical facticity and ongoing mythical symbols demands a concluding statement. The NT is supra-mythical inasmuch as it proclaims as reality what belongs to the structure of mythical speech (the incarnation). In so doing it goes beyond myth. It thus demythologizes, yet not in such a way as to set forth the signification of mythical statements, but rather by claiming a reality behind the mythical ciphers. On the other hand, it also uses many mythical figures of speech. This apparently confused handling of myth calls for clarification and suggests that myth can have different and even heterogeneous meanings in the NT. In fact this can be demonstrated. We shall thus consider the NT use of myth in the next section.

V

The Crux: Kerygmatic and Disarmed Myth

1. TIME AND WORLD-ORDER AS MYTHICAL FORCES

Failure to distinguish between the two different types of myth seems to us to be the reason for the confusion and even paralysis that has led to the demythologizing debate. Our present thesis is that the Bible itself carries out a permanent act of demythicizing and that it does so in exemplary fashion. This means that theology can do likewise only if it seeks to understand the biblical kerygma as this understands itself.

If we are to be able to assess the way in which the Bible attacks myth, wrestles with it, and also uses it, we shall have to analyze what it means by myth in thus attacking and using it. Such analysis leads us to the distinction just made, namely, between kerygmatic myth and disarmed myth, i.e., myth that is reduced to mere *alloiosis* or symbolism.

We take the term *alloiosis* from Zwingli, who used it in the eucharistic debate with Luther. Zwingli was challenging the Lutheran doctrine of the communication of attributes, i.e., of the divine and human attributes in Christ. When it is said, for instance, that Christ suffered, or did a miracle, it is to be noted that he suffered as man and did the miracle as God. To take the natures seriously they must be differentiated, and not, as in Luther, confounded. For a miracle-working man is no man, and a suffering God no God. If in spite of this the Bible says that Christ is the subject of such heterogeneous acts, this is a figure of speech, *alloiosis*. The confusion is only in words, not in reality; it is important in Christology to distinguish between mode of expression and the true reality expressed (cf. G. Thomasius, *Christi Person und Werk,* II [1857], pp. 307ff.). The idea of *alloiosis* seems to us to be especially valuable when used for myth as this is impressed into service as simply a mode of expression. One also sees at this point that the problem of the figure of speech is not just a modern problem in theology.

Kerygmatic myth as we understand it is myth in its original and proper form as found in Babylonian and Greek antiquity. This myth contains anthropological, cosmological, and theological statements. If myths present the genesis of the world in terms of a process of becoming in which the gods are also implicated in the form of conflicts and mutual slaughter, this only shows that they are not really transcendent (as the Creator-God of the Bible is). The point is that destiny rules the world.[1] This carries with it an understanding of man, since man is surrendered to this trans-subjective fate that is there from the outset. Myth, then, contains a kerygma in thus saying something about the nature and origin of the world. This world that surrounds man is his destiny; he is part of it.

The kerygmatic element in myth may be seen in a structural feature found in almost all classical myths, namely, their understanding of time as circular, self-returning, spheric, or spheroid.[2] Cyclic time is represented by the year with its recurrent seasons. The infinitude of the world is thus characterized by the cycle with its constant return and unending repetition.

In the Greek world, being tied to this line which is without beginning or end is felt to be a curse and enslavement. Thus the yearning for redemption is directed to liberation from the cycle and therewith the overcoming of time itself. Thinking that is rooted in myth finds it absurd in the extreme to think of redemption in time or a redeemer coming into time. The Greek idea of salvation is spatially controlled by the antithesis of this world and the next, not temporally controlled by the antithesis of now and then.[3] Similar ideas may be found in the myths of India.[4]

The very structure of myth, with its use of the category of cyclic time, already implies as such a kerygmatic statement. To that extent the understanding of time is not a purely formal one which permits the gospel to be drawn into it and thus proclaimed in mythical mode (this mode). The basic model of mythical statement, its category of time, is incompatible with the basic model of the gospel statement, namely, that the Word was made flesh, that God came into time, that there is such a thing as the time of salvation (*kairos*) or salvation history. Having this point, the gospel is a protest from the very outset, not just against the individual statements of myth, but against the structure of mythical statement itself, and also against the understanding of the world and self that is manifested in this structural expression. The opposition of the gospel to myth is not only expressed in the thesis that God came into time but also continued logically in the structure of time determined thereby. This structure is marked by two elements that set it in antithesis to myth.

First, time is no longer fleeting but unconditioned. God makes time the *kairos*, the acceptable time (2 Corinthians 6:2), the place of the mighty

---

[1] Cf. F. G. Jünger, *Griechische Mythen* (1947), p. 18; W. Baetke, *Art und Glaube der Germanen* (1934), p. 59. Cf. ThE, I, 3, § 1330ff.

[2] Cf. L. Ziegler, *Überlieferung* (1936), pp. 337ff.; G. Delling, *Das Zeitverständnis des NT* (1940); O. Cullmann, *Christ and Time* (1949), pp. 51ff.; G. Stählin, TDNT, IV, pp. 769ff.; G. van der Leeuw, *Phänomenologie der Religion* (1933), pp. 362ff.; E.T. *Religion in Essence and Manifestation* (1963), pp. 384ff.

[3] O. Cullmann, *op. cit.*, p. 52.

[4] Cf. A. Bertholet, E. Lehmann (ed.), *Lehrbuch der Religionsgeschichte*, II (1925), pp. 94ff.

works of God (Acts 2:11), in which he "lavishes himself" in time (Luther), giving my moment of life the stamp of eternity by relating it to those acts and making it the time of unrestricted decision. Here and now the issue is temporal and eternal salvation, for "we have Moses and the prophets" (Luke 16:29).

Second, time, having this goal of salvation, rushes on to its end. It moves forward from prophecy to fulfilment, from faith to sight, that God may be all in all (1 Corinthians 15:28).[5] Time is now linear, moving irreversibly to the set goal. Apocalyptic, for all its odd features, brings out the decided structural antithesis to myth with its logical development of the time schema and its doctrine of God's coming in time. Surrender of this means increased susceptibility to myth.

Yet one must be careful here. Myth has hints of linear time as well as circular time. There is the "little year" of life as well as the "great year" of the world cycle.[6] Myth, too, presents human life as a finite and irreversible span from birth to death. It learns this from the harsh reality of direct encounter with life. Is this little linear year an alien body in the mythical cycle? An anti-myth, as it were, in myth?

Not at all, for, first, the short stretch of individual life is woven into, and participates in, the cosmic cycle. So long as individual self-awareness and personality are not yet awakened,[7] the ending of the linear span of the little year cannot be felt as the loss of something unique but only as recurrence of the familiar process of birth and death as seen in nature in leaves or insects. Although the little year is finite, awareness of finitude as the coming to an end of something unique does not impinge on the mythical consciousness.

Then, second, this little year of human life comes from an unimaginable past and hastens toward an unforeseeable future.[8] To that degree it resembles the evil infinitude of natural numbers that are without beginning or end. For this reason the little year is not an island in the endless cyclical ocean, jutting out from it and alien to it. The individual life is itself oceanic; it shares the rhythm of waves and seasons. Strictly, then, it does not constitute history as distinct from natural time. We cannot use this term, because history is oriented to the finitude of individual life and personal self-awareness. Its background is linear time. Since this does not occur in myth, neither can there be a sense of history or of individual life. Only improperly can we equate the little year of myth with the idea of an individual life-history. Analogies to historical self-awareness have to be searched for in the world of myth, and even so they are conditioned and inadequate for all their indispensability as aids to understanding.

In sum, there is nothing unique or unconditional in the world of myth. The

---

[5] Cf. E. Käsemann, "Zum Thema der urchristlichen Apokalyptik," ZThK (1962), 3, pp. 257ff.; W. Pannenberg, *Christologie* (1964), pp. 78ff.; E.T. *Jesus: God and Man* (1968), pp. 66ff.

[6] Ziegler, *op. cit.*, pp. 343f.

[7] Cf. the author's *Tod und Leben* (1946), pp. 48ff.

[8] Ziegler, *loc. cit.*

individual is absorbed in the never-ending rhythm of the cyclic flow of events. As Goethe puts it in his *Grenzen der Menschheit,* the wave lifts us up and engulfs us, and we sink. Nothingness in face of the infinite in which I am swallowed up (if we can say "I" at all) erases the distinctness of what would regard itself as historically unique.

This nothingness can even be a threat at times to those who have found their way to historical self-awareness and differentiation from nature, namely, when they contemplate the spatial and temporal immeasurability of the starry heaven and are mythically conscious of being no more than a grain of dust in the cosmos. At such times the mythical sense is briefly recollected and threatens destruction where destruction is on this view impossible, since nothingness was the initial status. Only when they also remember the moral law, and the sense of personal freedom and uniqueness revives, is there emancipation from that engulfing infinitude and a sense of distance and differentiation from the stars.[9] Then the historical consciousness rejects the mythical consciousness.

Karl Heim (*Leitfaden der Dogmatik* [1923], pp. 3ff.) offers a theologically pertinent account of the mythical sense when he refers to the infinitude of the causal nexus within which scientific inquiry is pursued. As he points out, we traverse the infinite series but can never reach its goal and hence we can never wholly traverse it. This means that the causal explanation of the world is unable to answer the question of the why and wherefore of my life. It can only relate my situation to a prior one which certainly explains it but is itself inexplicable, and thus seems to be arbitrary (pp. 5f.). Heim, of course, does not speak of myth. He derives this empty infinitude from the answer of modern "post-mythical" science. Yet there is a formal analogy between it and the cyclical infinitude of myth. For Heim this dissolution in infinity is the mark of modern nihilism. Having lost the relation to the whole within which the causal series run their course, man has no place in this infinity. He is reduced to nothingness in face of the starry heaven.

This interpretation of empty infinity as a sign of nihilism is theologically relevant and fruitful. To be sure, it does not enable us to re-create the self-understanding of mythical man. For since this man had no sense of individuality or distance, his nothingness was not for him a painful banishment to the void (as we can easily suppose). It made possible instead the sense of being safely hidden or integrated in a trustworthy cosmos. In this sense the powers of Colossians 2:8ff. may be regarded as powers of order that can be worshipped and cultically placated if they are offended (Gogarten in ZThK [1953], 3, p. 348).

If Heim thinks the same phenomenon of infinity leads to insecurity and anxious nihilism, this is because the perspective has changed. The reference is to the man who in a post-mythical age still understands himself mythically. Through science, which ought to have freed him from myth for logos, he has paradoxically suffered a relapse into myth. "Suffered" may be

---

[9] Cf. Kant's *Critique of Practical Reason* (Liberal Arts Press, 1956), p. 166.

taken literally here, for in sinking back into myth he has not been able to recapture the naive security of mythical man. What upheld the latter is a burden to modern man. Hence the relapse is not total. He is still there himself. Having knowledge, he comes back to his original home different from what he was when he left.

To consider the change for a moment, and thus to go rather further than Heim, this modern man who is pushed back into empty infinitude by science is post-mythical insofar as he has become a person and attained to historical existence. He thus has the assurance of personal life, of unconditionality, of the infinite worth of personhood. But when, reflecting on this, he claims the forms of certainty that modern objectifying science puts at his disposal, he cannot establish his unconditionality. Everything is relative to conditions in the infinite causal series. Hence religious thinking is a shy stranger in the world of the sciences (K. Heim, *Das Weltbild der Zukunft* [1904], p. 259). The means that hold a monopoly for establishing things in the intellectual world cannot be used to establish individual existence. If only these means can be used, we are flung into the void. For historical man, aware now of personhood, cannot go back on personal self-certainty. Once this has come into being, it has an indelible character.

Modern man is thus plunged into an intolerable tension of certainties, into an antinomy of existence that brings depression. He no longer comprehends what he knows. Nor can he ignore it. He has to endure his post-mythical self-awareness as a person.[10] As post-mythical man he can no longer live mythically without being destroyed. There can be no return to a pre-historical state. Romantic fantasy may portray this as paradise but in truth it is a hell of nothingness for those who try to slip back past the angel of post-mythical knowledge. What would once offer security can now bring only destruction.

2. OVERCOMING OF MYTHICAL TIME BY HISTORICAL TIME

The Bible, and especially the NT, is poles apart from the world of myth. There is a structural antithesis even prior to the battle of content. The mythical mode of expression, being tied to a cyclical view of time, cannot introduce the point of the gospel into its schema. In curved time it is absurd that God should enter time, that the Word should be made flesh, that there should be qualified time (*kairos*). Thus the linear time of the Bible, the biblical understanding of history as an irreversible way from the fall to judgment, is a categorical protest against myth.

This radical antithesis between gospel and myth means that the understanding of God and that of human existence, which are interrelated as we have seen, are also very different in the two.

As regards the change in the understanding of God, the Bible formulates

---

[10] On this depression, which is not unlike the *acedia* of monasticism, cf. Kierkegaard's *Journals* for July 20, 1839; G. Bernanos, *The Diary of a Country Priest* (1937), p. 173; J. Sellmair, *Der Mensch in der Tragik,* 2nd ed. (1941); R. Guardini in his book *Hölderlin* (1939), pp. 318ff., 472ff.

the relation between God and the world in expressly anti-mythical terms. In myth the world is made of existent material, which has its own history, usually one of terror, as in Nordic saga. Through every variation the persistent note is that the gods and the world are embraced by a common nexus. In contrast, the God of Scripture creates the world out of nothing. He is thus apart from his creation. His creative action does not follow trends already immanent in existing material.[11]

This radically different relating of God to the world has implications for man's self-awareness. Mythical man interprets guilt as a result of the seeds of the curse already set in the world. Thus guilt is fate, pre-existing *anangke*. Tragedy with its equation of guilt and fate is a legitimate daughter of myth.[12] Where God creates out of nothing, however, man's guilt cannot be traced back to supra-personal trends already posited in the structure of the world. The attempt to do this results in accusing God, as Job did. There is no primal material to accuse. But man cannot be in the right against God (Job 40:2). Hence he must ascribe guilt to himself, and not to anyone or anything else.

In so doing, he stands opposed to the orderly course of the cosmos. He cannot derive himself from it (thus transforming guilt into fate). He cannot say like Adam: "The woman whom thou gavest to be with me" was the cause. Nor can the woman say: "It was the serpent." Nor, finally, can the serpent say: "Thou, God, didst put me in paradise, and so thou art the ultimate cause" (cf. Genesis 3). Man cannot invoke causal, cyclic, or other necessities to play down his distinctive personhood in the world. When God says: "Adam, where art thou?", calling him by name, Adam is set over against God and his world, including the woman and the serpent. He is alone. He can point to no cause. He is without the shelter of a mythical world to embrace him and to grant him the nothingness in which is no guilt.

This nonmythical view of God entails responsibility; man has to give an answer. The trees in the garden behind which Adam tries to hide (Genesis 3:8) symbolize the mythical cosmos which offers security and in which one may vanish. But it can no longer dissolve the person. God finds Adam. Detached from his world, having no background, he confronts the inquiring God in dreadful solitude. The mythical world is at an end.

Paul has classically described this transition from myth to the anti-mythical world of history in Galatians 4:1ff.: "I mean that the heir, as long as he is a child, is no better than a slave, though he is the owner of all the estate; but he is under guardians and trustees until the date set by the father. So with us; when we were children, we were slaves to the elemental spirits of the universe. But when the time had fully come, God sent forth his Son, born of woman, born under the law, to redeem those who were under the law, so that we might receive adoption as sons. And because you are sons, God has sent the Spirit of his Son into our hearts, crying, 'Abba! Father!' So

---

[11] Hence Hebrew uses the special word *bara'* as a technical term for God's creating to distinguish it from all human activity. Whereas man has to work with what is already there, God creates from nothing.

[12] Cf. ThE, III, Index "Tragik" and the discussion in ThE, I, § 748.

through God you are no longer a slave but a son, and if a son then an heir."

What the elements are in Galatians is greatly contested.[13] In general usage the reference is to the basic materials that determine the nature of the world and man. The stellar influences of astrology were also included in the second century. It might well be, however, that in Galatians the special reference was to the statutes of the Torah which governed the world and thus had for Jews the same determinative significance as mythical cosmic forces had for Gentiles. This is possibly why Paul chose the term. It embraces the polar antitheses of pre-Christian life as these found differing expression among both Jews and Gentiles. Common to cosmic forces and the statutes of the Torah is the fact that they hold man in the bondage of minority, so that his secret sonship and his status as heir remain latent.

This existence as a minor is outdated and done away the moment faith and immediacy to God are made possible by the coming of Christ. The man who, acknowledged by God, acknowledges him in return (Galatians 4:9; 1 Corinthians 13:12), is freed from bondage to the elements, the law, or anything else, and is called to freedom (Galatians 4:13). He now has the heir's control over what formerly controlled him. The believer is subject to him who created out of nothing (Romans 4:17) and in face of whom what is, is of little account. How, then, can he fall back out of this allotted sovereignty into the bondage of nothingness (Galatians 5:7ff.)? This has been done away; enslaving forces, whether of myth or Torah, have been overcome. Historical existence has replaced mythical existence. With it we achieve the status of the heir who has reached his majority.

This adulthood of post-mythical, historical man is surely misunderstood if it is equated with the modern idea of autonomy. The distinction is that in adulthood man has not achieved control in his own power; he has been empowered. Adulthood is not a domestic *coup d'état* by which the father is expropriated. It is institution to the rights of sonship at the time appointed by the father. The son is still a son and does not emancipate himself. He still receives, and has to give account for what is entrusted to him.

Since adulthood is based on an act of empowering, it is determined by the upward relation to God. The modern sense of autonomy has in contrast a downward relation, finding its basis in a sense of human dignity which, not based on empowering, achieves awareness only in superiority to the non-human, nonpersonal world, the world of animals and things. Not without pathos, it stands aloof from it. What is the starry heaven compared to the moral law that gives me freedom! That which is infinitely superior quantitatively is in truth the stamped possession of human existence, which has the privilege of controlling itself in contrast to all the things that are under the control of necessity, of natural causality, of elementary forces.[14]

---

[13] Cf. G. Delling in TDNT, VII, pp. 666ff.; L. Goppelt, "Die Herrschaft Christi," *Lutherische Rundschau* (1967), pp. 21ff.

[14] On the distinction between the upward and the downward relation cf. the pregnant passage in Kierkegaard's *Sickness Unto Death* (1946), p. 127; cf. ThE, I, §

The parable of the Prodigal Son shows what happens when adulthood forgets the source of its authority and degenerates into autonomy. The prodigal is first a recipient. He is given the signs of adulthood when the father divides the inheritance and grants him control of his own share. But he then emancipates himself and uses this share apart from the father. What is at first a received freedom still related to the father becomes pure autonomy and leads him into profound perversion. What he ought to control, what was given him as an inheritance, now gains power over him. The impulses stirred by all kinds of situations in the world begin to rule him. His inheritance slips away from him. The world becomes a far country. Instead of being a sphere of self-development it exercises the power of limitation, tyranny, and exclusion. Finally the pigs' trough becomes a symbol of his utter relapse into bondage.

This is the same relapse as that which Paul speaks of in Galatians when he warns against fresh entanglement with statutes and elemental forces (Galatians 4:10). It is the same as the relapse from history into myth, from the situation of the adult heir to the servitude of one who is under tutors and governors, yet not now as one who awaits the hour of freedom fixed by his father, but as one who has used his adulthood paradoxically to go back a stage while imagining that his progress and emancipation take him even further than sonship.

This descent is man's fate once he uses his adulthood only as a sign of autonomy without considering that it is a conferred and entrusted autonomy and that it consists only in responsibility to him who has conferred and entrusted it. Given freedom cannot become caprice. It cannot be a neutral thing with no values. It must be handled with gratitude to the one who has given it. This is why such freedom can never be license to sin (Romans 6:1, 15) without being snuffed out or degenerating again to bondage, as with the prodigal. We have freedom only as paradoxically we have become the servants of God (Romans 6:16).

It is also an act of higher homeopathy that we escape bondage to being only by submitting to a higher authority. In this way we die to sin and to all that comes between God and us (Romans 6:2). When we are dead to something it no longer has any power over us. Baptism is a sign that we belong to Christ's death and resurrection and thus slip out of the clutch of being (Romans 6:3f.). How, then, can we use our freedom in opposition to him who has conferred it on us? How can we with the help of this freedom turn again to the powers that have been vanquished and enthrone them afresh? God forbid (Romans 6:15)!

Freedom to misuse is in the strict sense perversion, a fall into the impossible (Galatians 5:4). For sin, wherein we fall victim to being, to the powers, is not a possibility that freedom can choose if it is to be true to itself (Galatians 5:13). It is true to itself only when it is always conscious of its

---

459ff. Since adulthood comes when God is the norm who establishes the boundary between minority and majority (Galatians 4:2), it is a reception, not a status posited by autogenous consciousness.

debt to him that granted it, so that it is a committed rather than an uncommitted freedom, committed to him who gave it its authority. This commitment, however, finds only two expressions and these are basically identical, namely, that we live to God in a new life, and that we are dead to all else, escaping its grip and thus achieving real freedom (Romans 6:3f.).

Hence the way from myth to history,[15] from minority existence under cosmic forces to the freedom of divine sonship, is irreversible. The message of adult existence as sons is a programmatic rejection of myth. We are baptized into Christ's death and hence we have died to myth. Myth is dead for us insofar and so long as we claim the death of Christ. For Christ's death is what faith appeals to when it says "Abba, Father." In this death faith believes in him who quickens the dead and calls things that are not as though they were (Romans 4:17). In the commitment to him who summons being out of nothing, what is loses its power. Hence myth, which lives by the power of what is, is also disarmed.

3. SURVEY OF DEFEATED MYTH: THE LORD, GODS, AND NOTHINGNESS

Since man through faith dies to myth and its powers, one may ask what this past and defused world looks like when surveyed in retrospect. For man naturally looks back on what he has escaped. He retains his identity. The disarming of myth took place in him. This "he" is not just the individual; it is mankind. Calling to God's people and transfer from mythical time to historical time were enacted in the race as a whole. There are, however, analogies to the transfer in individual life. Conscious decision for Christ, *metanoia,* includes renunciation of past allegiances. What was formerly gain is now refuse (Philippians 3:8). It has been revalued. This transvaluation of all values, this disarming of what was formerly held to be strong, causes the believer to reflect on the difference between the once and the now, since it is on him in his identity that God has acted (cf. Paul's reflection on his own past in Acts 7:58ff.; 8:1ff.; 22:19ff.; 1 Corinthians 15:9; Galatians 1:13ff.).

What does myth look like when surveyed thus in terms of historical existence, of faith?

Naturally it does not look the same to the believer as to mythical man himself. The latter is still under the powers. The message of their defusing has not yet reached him. The Bible does not in Enlightenment fashion, as in Reimarus or Feuerbach, dismiss myth as unreal projection. It sees in it the manifestation of real forces. Intellectually the man of antiquity cannot just deny existence to the gods under whom he once stood. Instead he sees them in their demonic quality. He thus revalues them. The gods are now demons (cf. 1 Corinthians 10:20). They are vain things, not just nothing (Jeremiah 10:8; 16:19; Isaiah 41:29, etc.).

---

[15] If this phrase suggests that we are adopting a thesis of Gogarten, later criticism (cf. Chapter XV. 3) should dispel the notion.

To find out what myth looks like to faith, we shall take some examples and ask what quality the gods have for faith. If they are disarmed rather than declared non-existent, their genuine power is recognized. Power can attach only to a substratum of reality that exercises it. This poses the question of the ontological quality of the gods. If for faith they are not nothing, what are they?[16]

The OT attack on pagan gods and idolatry brings out the ambivalence that is their characteristic. They can win power and yet they are empty. Yahweh is the first and the last, and besides him is no god (Isaiah 44:6). Yet in a way that accepts the existence of the gods he can be compared with them and extolled as incomparably superior (Exodus 15:11; 18:11; Psalm 72:18ff.; 86:8; 93:3; 96:4).

To understand the ambivalence of these sayings we shall consider some other aspects of the gods.

Man makes his own gods (Jeremiah 16:19f.); this is why they can only be empty and useless. Their weakness is obvious (2 Kings 18:33ff.). If man, instead of seeing himself as a creature, becomes the creator of his gods, he sins against himself as well as God. Thus those who made the golden calf (Exodus 32:4) "changed their glory into the similitude of an ox that eateth grass" (Psalm 106:19f.). The folly of this can be explained only by blind desire (cf. Jeremiah 2:24). What is at hand, be it wood or stone, is blindly seized on and made into gods (Jeremiah 2:24-28). In serious need, of course, soberness can replace their frenzy and cause them to cry to the true God: "Arise, and save us" (v. 27).

But this only shows the depth of the perversion. God is simply used as an aid in trouble, while what is in truth no more than a means (the wood out of which idols are made) is given the status of an end. One sees here the hopelessness of idolatry. The misused God will not hear (Jeremiah 2:19) and idols are silent (2:28). If we commit the sin of leaving God, the living fountain, and hewing out leaky cisterns (Jeremiah 2:13), we need not be surprised if we go thirsty.

References to the silence of the gods are legion. The work of men's hands —an ironical phrase—cannot be a refuge in the uncertain future toward which we move. In contrast, what comfort there is in the assurance that God sets and proclaims our destiny so that we move toward a future that is part of his plan (Isaiah 44:6-20, esp. 7f.)! Perhaps we have been deceived by idols for a time, but at the very latest in God's eschatological self-mani-

---

[16] On this whole question cf. Karl Barth, *Romans* (1950), pp. 240ff.; CD, I, 2, pp. 297f., 325ff., II, 2, pp. 511f.; D. Bonhoeffer, *Letters and Papers from Prison* (E.T., 1971 ed.), pp. 279ff.; E. Benz, *Ideen zu einer Theologie der Religionsgeschichte* (1960); H. Vossberg, *Luthers Kritik aller Religion* (1922); W. Holsten, *Christentum und nichtchristliche Religion nach der Auffassung Luthers* (1932); W. F. Otto, *Die Götter Griechenlands,* 2nd ed. (1934); E.T. *The Homeric Gods* (1954); G. van der Leeuw, *Der Mensch und die Religion* (1941); G. Nebel, *Weltangst und Götterzorn* (1951).

festation the difference between Creator and creature will be plain and the idol will perish as merely an absolutized creature.

To return to the question of the ambivalence of the being and non-being of the gods, of the power and folly of idolatry, we must now expound the statement that the gods are made by men's hands and are thus—in their modern form as ideas—the product of men's minds (Isaiah 44:12-15). This origin of the gods, this feature that they are creature rather than Creator, is the reason for their impotence, their non-deity. This diagnosis seems almost to anticipate Feuerbach. But this is not so. For Feuerbach argues that since the gods are mere projections of fear and hope they are non-existent, pure fantasy. Even in moments of extreme irony, however, the Bible never says this. The gods are empty, but they are. Idolatry is illusion, but the god gets a grip on us. What is the point of these tension-laden statements on the ontology of the gods?

One typical feature of the thesis that the gods are made by men is unmistakable. As products of men's hands or minds the gods can have no reality independent of man. They are just a part of his reality. They are human, all too human. Indeed, we must go further, for man does not just deify his own reality but here takes something under him, that ought to be an instrument, and makes it something which is over him and which is furnished with power over him. This is the height of perversion. The cedar from which he makes his idols (Isaiah 44:14f.) might well serve to warm him or to bake his bread. But he makes this instrument his god, this means an end (44:17). All this is folly, with no rhyme or reason in it (44:19).

Yet we must not miss the undertone that it is not folly in the Enlightenment sense that man falls victim to an illusion of the senses, to a victory of sense impressions over the controlling authority of reason. The different way of counteracting it shows that this is a different folly.

When the Enlightenment deals with folly it has only to point out the error and thus to restore control to reason. But this is not the therapy that the prophets recommend for idolatry (possibly because reason too can be darkened [Romans 1:21f.; 1 Corinthians 1:21]). Only as I claim the living fountain can I see how unsatisfactory is the cistern that I have hewed out myself (Jeremiah 2:13). The gods can be overcome only by God.

The illusion to which I fall victim in idolatry is not, then, an epistemological phenomenon or noetic error that critical alertness can correct. The self-deception of treating the perishable as eternal and the creaturely as divine has a theological root, namely, in an act of rebellion whereby I misuse creaturely means, so that the illusion is unavoidable.

Paul at the beginning of Romans describes with classical lucidity the process that leads to the self-deception, to the confusion of Creator and creature (Romans 1:18ff.).[17] Because man does not magnify God and is not thankful to him (v. 21), because he does not see himself in his creatureli-

---

[17] For a fuller exposition cf. the author's *Theologie der Anfechtung* (1949), pp. 14ff.

ness, the Creator-creature relation becomes confused in his thinking and blinding ensues (vv. 23ff.).

This blinding has an epistemologically relevant aspect. It means that the order of being is seen and assessed incorrectly. The truth is changed into a lie (v. 25). This causes perversion of the orders (vv. 26ff.), not just by misuse against better knowledge, but also by reason of the disintegration of knowledge through perversion. The revolt affects reason too. Hence it is not just that man recognizes God's majesty in his thoughts but will not acknowledge it in act, i.e., make the practical conclusions from his mental awareness. For Paul, the very opposite is true. Because we do not acknowledge God's majesty, refusing him praise and thanksgiving, we do not know him. To return to the metaphor of Jeremiah, if we do not know the eternal fountain, we cannot even see that our cisterns are leaky. To lose God as the standard is to lose all awareness of the nonsense of idols, of the folly and madness of the sacral inflation of the creaturely.[18] In this sense the ungodly are fools (Psalm 14:1; 53:1).

This folly, which has its basis in a flaw in existence, cannot in view of its existential origin be overcome merely by enlightenment, by epistemological manipulation, but only by dealing with the flaw that causes the folly. Only when one goes into the sanctuary in an existential act (Psalm 73:17) is there healing for the folly of regarding God as non-existent, absent, or ineffectual and of deifying the creature in his place.

We thus hold it to be decisive that epistemological folly has its basis in an existential state. The blindness of reason that leads it to confuse all rankings rests on a blinding of existence itself. Only, then, for him who is under God can the spheres of creation be properly ranked and the relation of Creator and creature, of end and means, be corrected.

At this stage it seems that the emptiness of the gods is easy to demonstrate biblically but their real power is not so cogently attested. For thus far belief in the gods has not been seen as affected by their reality but rather as a result of the folly that comes when God is rejected and everything is confused. The gods, then, do not affect me from without; they are "expressionistically" produced by me and my consciousness. We seem very close to Feuerbach's explanation of religion. How can this thesis be connected with the further thesis that the gods are not just "idea," a projection of consciousness, but that they represent real powers? The two theses together constitute the ambivalence of what the Bible says about idols. Where, then, is this second aspect, the real power of the gods? Where is the reality that even the NT is aware of when Paul refers to "gods many, and lords many," to what "are called gods" (cf. 1 Corinthians 8:5; 10:19f.)?

The quotation from Paul can help us in this matter. It brings out the full ambivalence. It ranges from the plain declaration that there is no such thing

---

[18] This is the starting-point for a theological criticism of reason (cf. ThE, II, 1, § 1321ff.; B. Lohse, *Ratio und Fides . . . in der Theologie Luthers* [1958]; J. Maritain, *An Essay on Christian Philosophy* [1955]).

as an idol[19] to the equally firm statement that there are gods many and lords many. How can we reconcile the two?

The statements occur in a discussion of the question whether the Christian may eat meat that has been dedicated to pagan gods.[20] In brief, Paul's position is as follows. In principle there can be no objection, since we have only one God, the Father of Jesus Christ (8:6). To that extent there are for us no other gods. No sacrifices can be made to beings that do not exist and have no significance for us. Hence the meat offered to them is only meat for us. It has no sacral implication. It is simply a means of nourishment. In principle eating idol meat is an *adiaphoron,* a matter of indifference.

If nevertheless Paul asks the Corinthians to refrain from eating it, this is for different reasons. Christians might participate whose spiritual understanding is undeveloped so that they do not yet see that idols are unreal. Their situation is thus very different from that of mature Christians who can eat without scruples. Since the immature still regard idols as realities, by eating they would be deciding against Christ, not accepting him as the only Lord. Hence those for whom Christ died might be destroyed (8:11). For they would be coming under the power of demons and letting ungodly forces come between them and the one Lord (10:18-22). In simple terms, the reasons why Christians should abstain from idol meats are not theological (there can be no theological reasons in view of the unreality of idols). They are ethical reasons which demand regard for weak and spiritually immature brethren.

The difference between the theological and ethical aspects reflects the ambivalence of what is said about the gods.

Theologically, since there is only one God, the gods are a negligible quantity. Ethically, however, their nothingness can suddenly become a real power which can captivate the weaker brother, who is not yet rendered immune by faith, if he comes under their influence (8:10ff.). Perhaps one might put it this way. Whereas God calls things that are not as though they were (Romans 4:17), unbelief calls what is not as though it were. It enables the idol's nothingness to become a demonic power (1 Corinthians 10:20). Its nothingness is intrinsically an occasion for achieving freedom over it (10:23, 29). The moment, however, that God is no longer the one and only Lord for me, I am deprived of my freedom by what is outside God. This takes his place as a demonic *alter ego.* I come under the sway of a power that is nothing in itself but is something for me. It is because the mature Christian cannot let this happen that he must freely abstain from anything that might rob another of his freedom (10:24, 33).

The demonic power which thus arises out of nothingness may again be described in antithetical analogy to God. I can make statements about God

---

[19] The very word "idol" (*eidolon*) expresses unreality (cf. A. Schlatter, *Paulus* [1934], p. 253; F. Büchsel in TDNT, II, pp. 375ff.).
[20] For a fuller discussion cf. ThE, II, 1, § 1303ff.

only as I confess what he is for me.[21] Similarly my statement about the idol depends on what it is for me, either nothingness, that which God has assigned to non-being, or something, and consequently a demonic power. Just as I cannot speak about God in himself but only about God with us (Immanuel), so I cannot speak about idols in themselves but only about what they are for me. If they are something and not nothing for me, they *are* something. They exist. Life is breathed into them. They can look and speak, as represented in images. They lodge in the crack between me and God, spread out from there, and finally cover an endless plain, so that God disappears behind the horizon.[22]

Now a general ontology that might speak about the being or non-being of God or the gods does not exist. Attempts to create it as in the proofs of God[23] are not merely epistemologically debatable but in them God is usually the pale and unreal construct of thought, the "God of the philosophers" (Pascal), whose intrinsic being is maintained but who is not for me. What is now a theological commonplace regarding statements about God himself and his intrinsic being relates just as pertinently to statements about idols. Here again nothing can be said about being or non-being as such but only about what the idol is for me. If, however, it is something for me (the weaker brother in Paul), it *is,* i.e., it takes on ontic quality and thus has more than psychological relevance. Nothingness can be called into being. It can become a power that captures me even though it was I who brought it into being, who thus accomplished the demonic counterpart of the divine creation out of nothing. This is the quickening that Nietzsche had in view when he said that if we look too long into the abyss, the abyss looks into us.[24] The abyss is emptiness, nothingness. As emptiness, without content, it cannot be an object of my gaze. Yet I concern myself with it. I look at it. And it gains power over me. From being an object of my gaze it becomes a subject that looks at me, that hypnotizes me, so that suddenly something is that really is not.

This strict non-being of idols, with this *de facto* being something, being for me, expresses exactly the ambivalence of what the Bible says about the gods. Within God's sphere of power, i.e., faith, in which God is the only one for us (1 Corinthians 8:6; Colossians 1:16f.), the gods are disarmed and cast into the nothingness of non-being. They have no more being or significance for us. Eating sacrificed meat is thus a taking of food with no

---

[21] Cf. Luther's exposition of the first two commandments in GC, where he relates faith to both God and false gods, true faith to the former and false faith to the latter.
[22] Although the confusion of Creator and creature in idolatry is the basic theme of all paganism, the manifestations in Paul and the prophets are comparatively primitive. We find other forms in Apollo and Dionysus (as presented by W. F. Otto), and further differentiation would be necessary in a full-scale analysis. Although the gods of the main religions are more than demonic powers, since they are interpretations of being of profound significance, they still raise the question whether Creator and creature, time and eternity, are not confused in them. This is what we had in mind in our discussion of the domination of cyclic time in myth.
[23] For reasons that cannot be given here Anselm's proof is an exception.
[24] *Beyond Good and Evil* (E.T. 1909), p. 97.

sacral or pseudo-sacral quality. Outside faith, however, the gods assume and exercise demonic force and attraction. It may be I who summon them up, as the sorcerer's apprentice does the waters, but once they are summoned up, once they are called out of nothing into being, they have a history with me that I did not plan and that I can no longer control. They now play with me and lead me where I do not want to go. They now become the abyss, which is indeed empty but which has a fascinating stare.

The explanation of the ambivalent statements about the gods is, then, that when I look back in faith on the defused world of myth the gods are empty, and yet I know that this is not so for those who reject God as the one source and the one light. For them the gods are powers. All the folly which assigns predicates of divine majesty to the transitory, all the blindness which causes me to confuse Creator and creature, cannot alter the fact that demonic forces are at work here.

We have now completed our retrospective survey of myth. At the heart of it was the question: What does disarmed myth look like from the standpoint of faith? How does faith interpret the gods, their being and their power? The results of our discussion may be summed up as follows.

As regards the being and power of the gods we can only speak with the ambivalence we have been considering. If this is taken to mean that one can say (however cautiously or restrictedly) that there are gods, this thesis can appeal to Scripture, but only with the admission that the assertion is irrelevant and also very rare (because it is irrelevant) in the NT.[25] The Bible has no general ontological statement about the intrinsic being of the gods. Typically it uses the term only relationally; except in relation nothing can be said about the being or non-being of the gods.

The first relation is that of the gods to God. In comparison with the one true God the gods are impotent, vain, and unprofitable (cf. Isaiah 44:8; 2 Kings 18:33ff.; Jeremiah 16:19f.).

The second relation is that of the gods to what is created. Unlike the Creator, they are not outside creation; they are entangled in it, in part as the material of the creaturely world. Their implication in what is created and perishable may be seen in the deification of the creaturely and the confusion of Creator and creature in idolatry. As Paul brings out in Romans 1:18ff., this can apply even to the most religious and sublimely philosophical variations of the perversion as well as to crude and trivial forms like fetishism (Isaiah 2:25ff.; Exodus 32:1ff.) or the primitive and stupid confusion referred to in Philippians 3:19: "Whose god is their belly."

The third relation is that of the gods to man. This may take two different forms.

If God is my only Lord, the gods are disarmed and hence they are nonexistent. If God is not my Lord, either because I do not yet know him and am outside the covenant, or because, as a weaker brother, I accept him only

---

[25] Cf. 1 Corinthians 8:5f.; 10:20 and on these H. Lietzmann, *Römerbrief,* 2nd ed. (1923), pp. 38, 39f.

partially, and my spiritual life is still immature, then there are ethically un-redeemed spheres[26] to which God's lordship has not yet extended, and here the beaten gods can fight a rearguard action and set up pockets of resistance where nothingness can win power over me and come to existence.[27]

This means, then, that nothing can be said about the gods as such; we can speak only of what they are for me. What they are for me is oriented, how-ever, to what God is for me and what I am for him. This rules out any neutral ontological statement about their being in general. It also rules out any ontological use of the concept of nothing in relation to them; we cannot simply say that they do not exist. For this reason we prefer to speak of their "nothingness" in an effort to bring out the personal aspect, as in the rela-tion between God and the gods. Regard must be had to this process when we try to make sense of the fact that nothingness can get power over me and thus come into being. This inevitably takes place when I do not acknowledge the process of negating, when I do not in faith accept all the depths and im-plications of the sovereignty of God. If the gods secure power over me and thus come into being in this way, it is not because they are anything in themselves but because God is not God for me, because I have conscious or unconscious reservations in relation to him, so that unredeemed areas arise and persist.

A fourth and final point here is that the gods cannot be overcome in En-lightenment fashion. This would demand perception of their non-being. This is impossible, however, since there is no such non-being. If I simply regard the gods as nothing on epistemological grounds, I have not understood their secret. Hence I cannot stop them winning power over me in another way. Thus, while I concentrate assiduously and critically on the religious field they slip behind me unnoticed and master the categories and criteria I am using, playing the role of Feuerbach's absolute reason or of idea. Reason employed without God becomes an absolutized force, takes on the godlike function of a world spirit, and produces views of things that sacrally exalt the creaturely.[28] If atheism is there at the end of this road,[29] this simply shows that the gods do not remain faithful when God is abandoned. The age of secondary substitute religions[30] then commences.

Surveying myth from the perspective of faith brings out the potentiality of the gods for being. Many forces are unleashed when God is not the one

---

[26] ThE, I, § 642, 689f.; E.T. I, pp. 130, 146.

[27] To prevent misunderstanding I should point out that my doctrine of the nothing-ness of the gods is not the same as Barth's nothingness of evil in CD, III, 3, pp. 349ff. In relation to Barth cf. ThE, I, § 596aff.; E.T. I, pp. 108ff.; G. Wingren, *Die Me-thodenfragen der Theologie* (1957), pp. 47ff.; R. Prenter, ThLZ (1946), pp. 161ff.; G. Gloege, *Heilsgeschehen und Welt* (1965), pp. 117ff.; G. C. Berkouwer, *The Triumph of Grace in the Theology of Karl Barth* (1956), pp. 60ff.

[28] Cf. R. Garaudy, *Gott ist tot. Das System und die Methode Hegels* (1965), pp. 422-430.

[29] *Ibid.*, p. 430.

[30] To adapt H. Freyer's phrase "secondary systems" (*Theorie des gegenwärtigen Zeit-alters*, 2nd ed. [1956], pp. 83f.; ThE, III, § 85).

supreme God for me. When he is, however, the gods lose all claim and are banished into nothingness.

4. EMPLOYMENT OF DISARMED MYTH IN THE LANGUAGE OF THE BIBLE

We can now understand two features in the attitude of both OT and NT to the world of myth.

The first is that of aloofness. The message (kerygma) of myth is refuted either in express polemic or implicitly by the message of the one God and Father of Jesus Christ. This aloofness extends to the structural basis of mythical statements, as illustrated in the negation of the mythical view of time.

The second and accompanying feature is that the disarming of myth and the evident reduction of the gods to nothingness confer freedom in relation to myth. What no longer controls me can be freely used. It can form figurative and conceptual material. Employment of myth as a means of expression indicates new sovereignty over a territory that has become an ungoverned no-man's-land and can thus be colonized. To change the metaphor, the statues of the gods have been broken to pieces and can be made into new mosaics. This freedom arises only where the material used has become neutral and no longer has autonomous content. This use excludes syncretism by combining the mythical material and the Christian message. There can be no religious promiscuity when the material employed as a mode of expression has lost its religious quality. Myth becomes an instrument when defused. "All things are lawful" (1 Corinthians 6:12; 10:23). The only limit is when myth has not entirely cast off its kerygmatic element and has thus retained a little of its power, as among weaker brethren.

It must be insisted, however, that this double attitude of aloofness and freedom can be appreciated, and its hermeneutical significance evaluated, only where there is the decisive differentiation that we have tried to achieve, namely, the differentiation between kerygmatic and sacrally freighted myth on the one side and on the other the disarmed myth that has degenerated into an empty form. Failure to make this basic distinction, or to make it clearly enough, is the fateful encumbrance of a hermeneutics which describes itself in terms of demythologization.

In fact both OT and NT display freedom in the employment of mythical materials even though Israel—a veritable marvel among oriental peoples— is cold toward myth[31] and makes only sparing use of it. When we do find it, the content is fundamentally changed and "what is borrowed is historicised, or better, baptised, i.e., integrated into the sphere of God's kingdom."[32] Some especially striking examples of this might be given.

Two things immunize Israel against the mythical world. The first is that the Lord of "creation out of nothing" is delivered from the close entangle-

---

[31] Gunkel in RGG[2], IV, 381.
[32] G. Stählin in TDNT, IV, p. 792.

ment of deity in nature (Gunkel) which is characteristic of myth. The second is that strict monotheism rules out stories of the gods in which there must be at least two gods (RGG², IV, 383). It is thus evident that when mythical images are used in the expression of Israel's faith they should be given an entirely new function.

The symbol of the sun, which is important in all myths, offers a good example. As in Babylonian myth, the sun can be a splendid hero coming forth to run his course (Psalm 19:5). Or—another mythical theme—it can outshine the morning star and plunge it into the depths (Isaiah 14:12ff.). Nevertheless the sun is not a numinous force as in myth. The lights in the firmament have only a conferred light (Genesis 1:14). When they are called lamps, this is intentionally degrading (von Rad, *Das erste Buch Mose,* ATD, 2, p. 42; E.T. *Genesis* [1961], p. 53). Most emphatically the stars were created only after the *Fiat lux* of Genesis 1:3. Hence they do not make light. They simply bear it. It already existed apart from them and before them (*ibid.,* p. 43). They are latecomers in creation, arriving only on the fourth day. This is a protest against the numinous power accorded to them in Babylonian myth, where Marduk, having vanquished chaos, makes the stars first, and grants them influence in the world (Zimmerli, "1 Moses 1-11," *Prophezei,* 2nd ed. [1957], pp. 57f.). What it meant to make this protest in an astrologically impregnated atmosphere may be seen from the constant threat of myth to the heart of Yahweh belief during the later monarchy (2 Kings 23:11f.). The importance of the protest may also be seen from the warnings against this threat and the prophetic contempt for such reversions (Deuteronomy 4:19; Job 31:26f.; Isaiah 47:13).

The rainbow, another mythical symbol, was originally the bow of the god of war and thunder, as in India and among the Finns and pre-Islamic Arabs. The bow was hung in the clouds, or set aside, as a sign of clemency. In an astonishing analogy Yahweh can be called a man of war (Exodus 15:3) and the image of the bow can also be used (Habakkuk 3:9). Nevertheless one can hardly miss the profound change in sense. This consists in the linking of covenant word and sign (Zimmerli, *op. cit.,* p. 350). The reference now is not to the shifting whims of a god whose anger is appeased but might break out again at any moment. God is now giving his covenant word of peace, guaranteeing that it will endure, and sealing it with a ratifying sign. The rainbow is not, then, a pointer to God's present mood. It loses all significatory value apart from the word. The word embraces it and constitutes it a sign. It is subordinate to the word and hence is dumb without it (cf. Genesis 9:12ff.).

The more strictly anthropological statements of the OT also put the mythical elements in new contexts that are quite different from the original reference. Thus in myth marriages between sons of God and daughters of men lead to the birth of Titanic supermen (Gunkel, *op. cit.,* p. 383). But in Genesis 6:1-4, where monotheism for once allows reference to the sons of God, the symbol has a very different point. It denotes infringement of the divinely set boundary between heaven and earth, an act that anticipates the arrogance of the generation which thought it could build a tower reaching from earth to heaven (Zimmerli, "Das Menschenbild des AT," ThEx, N.F. 14 [1949], p. 11).

The mythical understanding of the relation between the divine and the human is also completely recast. In ancient Babylonia Marduk slays the dragon of chaos and makes men of his blood so that they receive a share in Titanic life (Ungnad, *Die Religion der Babylonier und Assyrer* [1921], pp. 47-55). In the OT, however, there is a gulf between the Creator and creaturely man. Man has no ontic relation to God. The idea of creation out of nothing rules this out. Man is related by the impartation of God's Spirit (Genesis 2:7) and the Word that calls him (2:16f.). There is a violent protest against myth here even to the point of scorning to use mythical elements. The difference is so sharp that Babylonian material is unserviceable (cf. ThE, I, § 774ff.; E.T. I, pp. 554ff.).

Adoption of the idea of a realm of shades beyond the grave is particularly interesting and significant as regards the defusing of myth. Having no place in the faith of the OT, this idea had necessarily lost its point. In myth it denotes contact with the world of the dead and the life—however tenuous—of the deceased. But such contact is forbidden in the OT, and the fact that the only reference to the prohibition is in 1 Samuel 28 shows how irrelevant the whole question was.

The reason why such links with the dead are impossible is that the time between birth and the grave is ordained as man's time of salvation (cf. Luke 16:27-31). The dead can no longer meditate on God (Psalm 6:5; 31:10; 88:11ff.). Thus a mythical idea like that of contact with the dead might still linger on, but it is cut off from its source and is doomed to perish. As a withered bough is still there in a tree, but has no sap and hence has no further part to play, so it is with ideas that are present but devoid of theological meaning (Zimmerli, *op. cit.,* p. 17). Thus a mythical image might be used instrumentally, with no control over its own use, or it might die even as a symbol when there is no further possible use for it.

These are the two basic forms in which disarmed myth can play a limited role in statements of faith. The seed of myth can still come to life again, so that myth revives. This happens in the measure that faith declines, or, in weaker brethren, is not yet mature. The nothingness or power of the gods will depend on what, if anything, I let the one God be for me.

The NT, as we have already seen, presses on further in the same direction. Defused mythical elements can be used like meat sacrificed to idols. They can almost be toyed with.

Thus the three-decker universe can linger on as the spatial schema of myth, and Enlightenment old and new will never tire of referring to this outdated notion. In reality, as the spatial concepts of Hebrews show, it has been authoritatively shattered. While still there in the background, it does not dominate the statements of faith any longer. Thus in Hebrews 4:14 Christ strides through heaven and in 7:26 he is higher than all heavens. In Christ the spatial framework is broken as well as the temporal framework (J.

Schniewind, KM, pp. 89, 96f.). Neither framework is dominant any more. Neither forces the new message into itself. Both are simply material for expression.

The same applies in eschatology. Revelation is full of mythical images. Yet eschatology is not a mythology of the end of the world nor a mythological expression of timelessness (KM, p. 97). What it is can be learned only from the word and work of Jesus (*loc. cit.*). This is what controls the images and imbues them with meaning. They have no power of their own.

As regards the NT and myth, it is not without significance that when the word "myth" is used (normally in the plural), it does not refer to non-Christian religions but has other meanings. Thus it might denote heretical divergence from sound doctrine (2 Timothy 4:3f.; 1 Timothy 4:6f.), or alien teachings such as preoccupation with genealogies (1 Timothy 1:3f.), or the allegorical interpretation of Haggadic or Halakic sayings (Titus 1:13f.), or artificial and fantastic speculations (2 Peter 1:16; cf. G. Stählin, TDNT, IV, pp. 786ff.).

Finally we may refer to the way the fathers understood this defusing of myth, the church's self-demythologizing.

Patristic ecclesiology employs many mythical images. Thus the mystery of the moon plays a great role, e.g., in Augustine, Theophilus of Antioch, and Tertullian. In a world full of belief in astrology, lunar symbolism is used to describe the church, and the phases of the moon are related to it, since, as Augustine says, they present an understandable comparison for the plain man. But when the moon is used in this way it is taken from the sphere of myth and it undergoes a radical change in significance. As Ernst Wolf puts it (*Peregrinatio,* II [1965], pp. 140f.), the true Selene (the moon church) does not grow old. It does not die. It is ever young. It lives in virtue of Christ's resurrection. The significant thing in the metaphor is not the waxing and waning of the moon (the important cosmic rhythm of myth). If resurrection implies death, we think of death only in relation to resurrection, and it is thus vanquished.

As in the biblical model, myth loses its point here. The autonomy of its own imagery is set aside. It has become neutral material which is put to another use. Christ's resurrection sheds a different light on rising and perishing from that cast by the rhythm of the constellations.

We have now arrived at some significant conclusions for the present discussion.

The disarming of myth by faith in the God of all gods (Exodus 18:11; Psalm 95:3; 96:5; 97:7; Daniel 2:47, etc.) allows free employment of mythical materials. These are neutralized when used to express the OT or NT message. A new mosaic is made of them that differs completely from the original mythical statement. We find a formal similarity in the way that modern poetry employs myth but infuses into it new content (IV.2b).

This conclusion is hermeneutically important. If it is true, we cannot derive the intention of the biblical statement from a study of the origin of the materials used. The original content does little to fix the meaning of a text, just as a theory of human descent can do little to determine the nature of man. Both man and a literary text are to be expounded in terms of their orientation, not their biological or material derivation.

The expositor, then, must accept and observe the writer's relativizing of the material, of mythical elements adopted as modes of expression. Strack and Billerbeck (*Kommentar zum NT aus Talmud und Midrasch,* 2nd ed. [1956]) can argue that for almost every word of Jesus there is a model in the Rabbinic tradition. But the model has been reconstructed, or, to adopt an earlier image, baptized. Hence it is absurd to try to learn from the Rabbis what a saying of Jesus means, or from Gnostics what the Adam-Christ relation means in Paul (1 Corinthians 15:45), or from the Stoics what the Logos means in John (John 1:1), or from later Jewish apocalyptic what eschatological expectation means in Thessalonians (1 Thessalonians 5:1ff.; 2 Thessalonians 2:1ff.). The only point in consulting these sources is to see what change there has been with assimilation to the Gospel. An illustration of this change, this baptism, may be found in the new function the Logos concept is given in the Prologue to John. For John does not define Christ in terms of the Logos (as the early Apologists did). On the contrary, it is the nature and figure of Christ that determines what the Logos is.

At all events, biblical texts, like all others, can be interpreted only in relation to their goal (*telos*). Means of expression that are taken from various places are relativized according to this. But a crucial difficulty can hardly be overlooked here.

In specific instances it is often hard to say where the boundary lies between relativized materials on the one side and the *telos* on the other. An example already quoted may be recalled.

Bultmann thinks that mythical statements are characterized by a distinctive structure, namely, that they bring the transcendent down into the present, that the gods are implicated in this-worldly episodes and struggles, that the nonworldly is spoken of in worldly terms and the gods in human terms.[33] How, then, are we to interpret the Christmas story, the gospel of the incarnation? Is this just a typically mythical form which makes the divine human and puts the transcendent in history? Or is it the account of a real event, which may have analogies to mythical forms and which may even use some mythical symbols, but which is quite different from myth, telling of an event that is a change in aeons, and thus defusing myth, making it outmoded, putting it among the old things that have passed away (2 Corinthians 5:17)?

A basic theological decision is made when this boundary between myth and a binding message is drawn. There is brought to light here whether and how far myth is disarmed and put to work, whether and how far it may be more than a mere mode of statement, whether and how far it may have normative rank. The choice is not made possible merely by the insight that myth might have the function of a mere form of expression. Even if we see this— and what serious theology does not?—the question still remains: What be-

---

[33] KM, p. 10.

longs to the mode of expression and what belongs to the authoritative content? Is the incarnation a reality (even though perhaps with mythical embellishment)? Is it an event? Or is it merely the description of something significant, of an idea, just as myth has a meaning, and is it to be interpreted in terms of this meaning?[34]

Thus analysis of myth, of the distinction between original myth and disarmed myth, can certainly be an aid to theological interpretation, but as such it cannot help us over the hurdle of decision. A real decision has to be made. It must rest on reflection, but reflection alone cannot make it. At the central point we have now reached it can be made only as the message in the texts, e.g., in the Christmas story, overcomes me, only as a decision is thus made about me, only as the figure of Jesus Christ as Lord and Savior gains control over me. Only then will God's coming down into history, and the solidarity of his love, be manifest as an event which shatters the mythical world, employs the broken remnants as material, and allows us to see in the analogous humanity of the gods only at best the expression of a yearning that is here fulfilled in a new and unexpected way.

If this is so, if everything depends on the texts bearing self-witness to me in this sense, or, rather, on the Christ who is proclaimed in them winning control of me as Lord and Redeemer, then the decision demanded of me is not one I can take alone. As stated, it cannot be made merely in virtue of my insight into the new function of disarmed myth. For it depends on whether Christ reveals himself to me as Lord and Savior and on the sphere of theological statements delineated thereby. In other words, it depends on what is decided about me, whether I am called and chosen (Matthew 20:16; 22:14).

How else can we express my own lack of sovereignty in this regard? At issue is what the doctrine of the Holy Spirit has always maintained, namely, that faith is a miracle I cannot perform. It has to be given to me. Knowledge of God is grounded wholly in a happening which I cannot control, by which God discloses himself to me, and in virtue of which I can have a share in his self-knowledge (1 Corinthians 2:10f.; 13:12b).

If, then, I can understand the biblical message only in relation to him at whom it looks, a necessary pre-condition is that the interpreter has the same outlook as the text. To make this possible, the truth and the figure of Christ, which are identical,[35] must be revealed to the one for whom the text is to be disclosed. This means that no premises won outside faith, e.g., the insight that philosophical or mythical materials have been overcome and can now be employed as mere forms, can grant me leave to come at the texts from

---

[34] Bultmann never gets to grips with this question, while H. Raschke, *Das Christus-mysterium. Wiedergeburt des Christentums aus dem Geiste der Gnosis* (1954), gives an extreme answer in which the Gnostic Redeemer myth and the corresponding Logos speculation are our sources for apprehension of the gospel.

[35] John 14:6; 18:37f. Cf. the author's "Wahrheit und Verstehen" in H. R. Müller-Schwefe, *Was ist Wahrheit?* (1965), pp. 9ff., esp. 15f.; L. Goppelt, "Wahrheit als Befreiung," *op. cit.*, pp. 82ff.

outside. The text itself must disclose itself on the basis of presuppositions that it implies.

These presuppositions consist in the object of its gaze, the divine truth disclosed in word and deed (Acts 2:11) and fulfilled in the incarnation of the Word.[36] This self-disclosure again points to the lack of control which the testimony of the Holy Spirit has in view when it denies that God's Word can be disclosed from without with the aid of specific hermeneutical procedures and when instead it regards this disclosure as something that must first be done on man, as a gift of grace alone.

The resultant dialectic, namely, that what I have to understand is a presupposition of my being able to understand it, constitutes the hermeneutical circle which has always confronted theological epistemology. This dialectic is too sublime to let us say simply that we have here supernatural revelations in face of which man can only twiddle his thumbs in passive submission to fate or predestination. It demands, indeed, strenuous research and thought. It calls for a use of all the rules of interpretation. It does not let us set aside the question what material is used in the biblical kerygma, how it is used, and where finally the boundary lies between form and intention.

Only when these working rules are respected will the text itself be respected. The dialectic enclosed in the concept of the Spirit's testimony simply adds that these rules do not give access to the inner text, so that a man does not become righteous, or do justice to the text, merely by doing the work of interpretation. It expresses instead the fact that the means have point only when they serve a sovereign presupposition which is imparted as a gift. Only when heard does the message demand more exact and objective hearing of a more scientific kind.

The attempt to achieve the sense by method alone without an imparted presupposition, and thereby to wrest control over it, is a hermeneutical variation on the righteousness of works. "By grace alone" must be asserted in face of it. But as the faith given by grace, even though not achieved by works, still demands works, obedience, and methodical actualization (Romans 6:4, 11),[37] so the faith to which the Word discloses itself, even though not achieved with the help of hermeneutical methods, still demands that these methods be used when it has arisen.

In other words, while faith does not attain its object with the help of these methods, it encircles the achieved object with their help. It tries to refine its thinking, to make it more precise, and to lift up its certainty into the sphere of consciousness. The assurance of faith cannot be achieved by using specific methods. But when it is conferred by grace it becomes the object of intellectual clarification (and even historical analysis), is related

---

[36] On the continuity of the Testaments in this regard cf. K. Koch, "Der hebräische Wahrheitsbegriff im griechischen Sprachraum," and H. J. Kraus, "Wahrheit in der Geschichte" in *Was ist Wahrheit?*, pp. 47ff. and pp. 35ff.

[37] Cf. the discussion of indicative and imperative in ThE, I, § 314ff.; E.T. I, pp. 154ff.

to expanding dimensions of existence (thought, emotion, volition), and is seen to have more and more implications.

Along these lines sanctification is the process in which faith takes over all areas of life and sees its relevance to them. It thus opposes spiritual departmentalizing, as when the heart recognizes God but the extremities are starved of blood and thus remain numb. A good illustration is when various spheres, e.g., sex, economics, etc., are untouched by faith, pursue an autonomous course, and are not, then, objects of the new obedience (cf. ThE, III, Index, s.v. "Sanctification").

If, however, the basic condition is not fulfilled and faith does not look in the same direction as the Word in which it believes, then the Bible itself becomes the objectification of religious consciousness and therewith a document which mythically speaks of the other world in terms of this one and of the transcendent in terms of the secular. Nor can any religious insight, not even the insight that myth is a mere symbol, a relativized means of expression, make any difference in this situation.[38] In the last analysis, then, discussion of the question of demythologization goes beyond hermeneutics and methodology and is a debate about faith itself.

5. SUMMARY AND EPILOGUE

a. Results

We may now look back and consider the first goal we have achieved.

The chapter on the disarming of myth and its reduction to a mere mode of statement was the final section in our critical presentation of Cartesian theology (Theology A). We had to discuss myth because both theology and proclamation must measure up to the modern view of the world, or, more cautiously, must not require rejection of this view and force faith into a sacrifice of the intellect. The argument that the Bible contains outdated pre-Copernican cosmology and is also full of mythical elements seems to raise doubts as to the suitability of its statements for appropriation by the modern mind. Hence the problem demands clarification. This clarification is even more urgently needed to the degree that especially Theology A develops its approach from the modern mind and thus makes the matter of appropriation a central issue. In so doing it inevitably focuses on the difference in form between the pre-modern or mythical proclamation of the Bible and the type of proclamation demanded by modern science and self-awareness.

We have intentionally said that Theology A focuses on this. We do not say that it differs from other schools by being the only one to raise the question. No serious theology of the present age does not deal with the theme and is not "modern" in this sense. The difference between Theology A and other theologies (falsely labelled "conservative") lies in the degree of concentra-

---

[38] As Schniewind rightly observes, the Bible can only be understood as myth where there is no faith (KM, p. 90); constant examples of this may be seen from Porphyry on (cf. G. Stählin, TDNT, IV, pp. 791, 12ff.).

tion on the issue. In Theology A this question is the secret center of the whole theological enterprise.

It has achieved visibility by focusing on this important issue. Most of the controversies of the last generations, and especially of our own, are thematically determined by it. Demythologizing is only one variation. The fact that such violent debates have been unleashed by this variation is only partly due to its flaunting and ugly catchword. The real reason is that it appeals to the modern mind for which an ancient message is an unacceptable decree and which wants to decide its own commitments. This is why myth and demythologizing have become the theme of debate and have had to be discussed in the present volume.

To do justice to Theology A, to appreciate its true character as we have tried to do, we must understand its initial impulse. What it is attempting is to bridge the centuries. Its concern is with the credibility of faith, with the possibility of its appropriation.

This question has both an anthropological and a theological dimension.

1. The anthropological dimension is that man's adulthood and dignity require that his self-understanding be respected. This can be done only if the kerygma addressed to him corresponds to his questions and is significant for him as an answer to them (cf. Tillich's principle of correlation). Failing this, the kerygma is an authoritarian demand which seeks acceptance even though irrelevant. It thus treats him like a child.

His requirement that the kerygma must show its relevance as an answer to his own questions might be called the existential side of the anthropological dimension.

There is a theoretical side too. Modern man knows certain things, e.g., in the scientific and historical spheres. To some extent he has a fairly reliable scientific view of the world at his disposal. This means that he cannot believe contrary to his historical, physical, and philosophical knowledge. If he were to do so, it would lead to a conflict of truth and cleavage of consciousness. If, with the semi-educated, he cannot simply reject the kerygma in the name of modern science, he has to consider whether and how far what does not correspond to this science is really the heart of the kerygma which faith cannot surrender, or whether and how far it relates only to conditioned forms of expression and ideas that are interchangeable and can be put into modern forms of expression and ideas. Only in the second instance, which is the premise of Theology A, can the kerygma be appropriated and accepted as credible in a new and changed situation.

2. The approach of Theology A, as we have seen, has a theological as well as an anthropological side, although in fact this is not so important and claims less space in the discussion. God's deity is venerated in praise and thanksgiving (Romans 1:21) only when man submits to him with all he is and has. This means that there can be no areas in his life that are without God and exempt from his commandments and the freedom he confers. Hence God cannot be relegated to a religious department. This is done, however, if I grant him only contemplation and feeling (as in Schleier-

macher's Second Speech), give free rein to historical, scientific, and philosophical reason, and orient it simply to immanent reality (cf. the discussion
of autonomy in ThE, II, 2, § 1102ff., 1197, 423-886; E.T. II, pp. 172-174,
186, 71ff.). Just because reason is reciprocally related to existence (ThE, II,
1, § 1321-68), withholding reason from God means withholding existence
too, so that the question arises whether only the emotions are baptized and
reason is still pagan.

Hence the gospel is as little prepared to let reason escape and go its own
way as it is to degenerate into a mere decree or law for reason. If the dignity
of adult man is at stake in the one case, that of God's honor is at stake in
the other.

If the message of God and his mighty acts applies to the whole man, however, a twofold question arises. First, how far does this message affect man in
all the dimensions of his existence, in thought, emotion, and volition? Second, how far does it accord with the axioms and results of his rational knowledge (e.g., science), so that it can be appropriated in every dimension without exception?

This twofold question creates a chain reaction.

It raises the counter-question of the subject who must do the appropriating, of his self-understanding in regard to the questions to which the answers
of the kerygma must correspond, and of the criteria of his understanding of
truth by which every truth-claim must be measured.

But the moment the question of self-understanding arises and demands
serious theological consideration, it seems to us that we arrive at the crucial
question whose treatment and answering will influence the future course of
theology and give rise to the distinction between Theology A and Theology B.
Our investigation has made it clear that the question of self-understanding
does not itself cause the rift, since most theologies find a place for it, Karl
Barth being the great exception. What causes division is the rank accorded
to it in the total theological system. In other words, the real question is
whether and how far man's self-understanding is prepared to let itself be revalued and relativized when brought to the kerygma, or whether and how
far it is determined to assert itself as the normative criterion of the truth
addressed to it.

We have seen, of course, that the alternative is latent rather than programmatic. Thus we may accuse Theology A of taking the second path and making the self-understanding normative, but it does not do this intentionally; it
claims to be doing the very opposite.[39] As we have also seen, however, to
start with the self-understanding, with existential self-interpretation, is to
initiate an ineluctable movement whereby the existential approach takes on
normative significance and prejudges what can be accepted as an answer—
the answer of the kerygma—to its question. What matters is what is significant for me. Expectation of what is significant for me is determined by a

---

[39] Cf. the statements of Bultmann to this effect assembled in W. Schmithals, *Die
Theologie R. Bultmanns*, 2nd ed. (1967), pp. 237f.; E.T. *Introduction to the Theology of Rudolf Bultmann* (1968), pp. 233f.

pre-understanding which forms a constant framework into which the contents of the kerygma must be fitted. This framework itself cannot be revised.

This constant starting with the self-understanding, which takes cognizance only of what is significant and not of what is factual, is the thing that leads us to speak of the Cartesian approach of Theology A.

b. Disciples and Descendants of Theology A

The complex thought of Bultmann, which tries to safeguard itself against possible deductions, contains many hidden or implied points that are brought to light by his disciples. Thus the search for the significant which is inaugurated by the Cartesian approach, or, better, the concentration on this search, leads to a crisis in the relation to history, although, for the reason given, this is still latent in Bultmann himself.

For two reasons history itself is too big and alien to be adopted as significant. First, it is contingent, and second, it contains the past. Both aspects are in tension with the significant. For the significant, like Lessing's truth of reason, is necessary rather than contingent; hence it can be grasped by reason. Furthermore the significant is present rather than past. It applies to me; it belongs to my time.

Bultmann obviously sees the threatened breach in his relation to history. He tries to maintain contact, not letting the kerygma evaporate into a timeless idea, but remaining in dialog with history.[40]

To keep in touch with history in at least one dimension Bultmann makes a distinction which is not made by secular historians and which finds no parallel in other languages, namely, the distinction between "geschichtlich" ("historic") and "historisch" ("historical") (Kähler). There is, of course, some point to this distinction if by "Geschichte" we mean the personal element of encounter, decision, resolve, trust, or mutual evaluation, and by "Historie" the causal nexus of human events as this may be discerned in the remoter past.

Along these lines the former can indeed be significant and even contemporary, i.e., if the decisions about which we are told or to which we are summoned can be my own decisions and can thus bring about solidarity between the present and the past. In contrast the latter in its sheer "pastness" or "givenness" has no relevance to me at all.

This is where significance can part company with the facticity to which it was originally linked. The significant event that I die and rise again with Christ (2 Corinthians 4:11; 2 Timothy 2:11) was originally connected, according to Paul's definite statement (1 Corinthians 15:3ff.), with the fact of Christ's resurrection on the third day. But if only the co-dying and co-rising again is now of historical relevance, while the original event of Christ's resurrection belongs to the historical past and has no ultimate significance for me, then this might well be explained as a myth or legend or projection, not merely in respect to its embellishments, but in respect to its very core and center.

---

[40] In criticism cf. my essay in KM, pp. 147ff.

In this case the past, the basic facticity, is declared to be a matter of indifference in the name of the historically significant, and it is thus sucked into the present of the self whose consciousness itself normatively decides what can be accepted as present.

While this is all more implicit than explicit in Bultmann, it is stated with almost brutal logic by some of his pupils. Thus S. M. Ogden[41] says that the NT speaks of the cross as an eschatological event which never becomes an event of the past but lives on as the present in preaching and sacrament (Romans 6:3; 1 Corinthians 11:26; 2 Corinthians 6:2) and in the life of believers (2 Corinthians 4:10f.; Galatians 5:24; Philippians 3:10), as though we were not redeemed some 1900 years ago, or could have redemption in faith now apart from this past event. How can Ogden ignore all past statements or relegate them to the indifference of "Historie"? This is to turn the basic sayings upside down. The consequences are as follows.

Since the Easter event does not count as a past event, it cannot as such be a basis for faith in Christ. In the decision of Easter faith we simply have a renewal of the first decision which the disciples made in Galilee when they resolved to follow Jesus. Easter is just faith history, or a stage in this history. It no longer explains why there is an object of faith, namely, the risen Lord. And if faith is not constituted by its object any more, but by what it effects in the believer as its subject, by the authentic existence it brings about as identity with myself, then there can be no avoiding the next step, i.e., that of stating openly that other men in other times and places have achieved this authentic existence in other ways quite apart from faith in the risen Christ. Feeling that he can get along without the resurrection, and understand faith apart from Easter, Ogden finally reaches the point where he can forego Jesus himself.[42]

At this point the Cartesian crisis in the relation to history becomes an open surrender of history. When theology focuses so exclusively on man's self-consciousness and proclaims so exclusively what in the resultant pre-judgment he can regard as significant for him, the past and the contingent are banished to the realm of the irrelevant. All that is left is the present. And this present is the present of the Cartesian I.

Another extreme result of the Cartesian approach which one may see in Bultmann's disciples must now be considered. It is the impossibility on this view of any concept or practice of prayer. How this extraordinary gap arises is easy enough to see. If self-consciousness, oriented to the significant, holds at a distance anything that transcends this horizon, the true representative of transcendence, God, cannot be subjected to the self-consciousness, and is thus an embarrassment. The problem of irrelevance already seen in relation to the past and contingent elements in history, which had to be rejected, reaches a crisis at this point in relation to transcendence itself. If the consciousness will not receive from God, if it will not let itself be changed and

---

[41] *Christ without Myth* (1961).
[42] Cf. P. M. van Buren, *The Secular Meaning of the Gospel* (1963), p. 73.

renewed by him, if it gives precedence to itself and its categories over everything that claims to enter it and to be understood by it, then God's transcendence is an insuperable difficulty for this consciousness.

A drastic sign of this is prayer. When the reality of God, which transcends
consciousness, is not accepted, prayer is not addressed to anyone and it is
thus pointless. From being a dialog it becomes a meditative monolog. This
deduction is drawn by Herbert Braun and Paul M. van Buren, more cautiously by the former and more radically by the latter.

Braun does not abandon prayer in principle, but modern consciousness
involves for him a restructuring of prayer which abolishes in practice its
original meaning as confident and answered address to God.[43]

He first points out that intercession is not peculiar to Christianity but is
common to all religions, so that a critical treatment of it does not affect
the heart of Christianity. This argument is typical of the whole essay.

If prayer is understood phenomenologically as an act of the praying subject (set in words and accompanied by the emotions of fear and hope), then
Christian and pagan prayer are again reduced to the same level with no
distinctive features. The Cartesian *res cogitans* is no more unique or distinctive than the *res orans*.

Specifically Christian prayer is characterized only by the one to whom I
speak and in whose name I speak (John 14:13f.; 15:16; 16:23). The one
to whom I cry and to whom I appeal determines the theme of my prayer,
is the basis of its hope, confers its confidence, and denotes its content. If I
ignore this determinative factor my prayer necessarily loses all its contours
and becomes a mere specimen in the history of religion.

The fact that Braun starts with the historical analogy is enough to show
how far he puts God out of mind and retains the consciousness alone. The
assumption that God "is," that he is of this particular nature, and that I can
thus speak to him, is for him a theistic premise which, transcending the consciousness, can hardly be accepted by modern man.

This involves a change in the view of prayer. We now trust in purposeful
and rationally directed measures, like the work of the doctor. Prayer has the
function of an accompaniment. We do not expect, as previous generations
did, that a transcendent God will intervene directly. Instead, we see God at
work in the immanent causes which do not break the cosmic continuum.

Braun points out in this connection that the highest form of prayer in
the NT is that in which I pray that God's will may be done (Matthew 6:10b;
Luke 22:42), so that there is no dialogic tension between my will and his.
It need hardly be pointed out how wide of the mark this exegesis is.

The prayer "Thy will be done" is in fact the end of the dialog, of the
tension between my will and God's. I first speak as a child to his father.
I can thus be myself with all my valid or foolish wishes, fears, and hopes.

---

[43] H. Braun, "Gottes Existenz und meine Geschichtlichkeit im NT," *Zeit und Geschichte, Bultmann zum 80. Geburtstag* (1964), pp. 417f. Braun is replying here to
the objections of H. Gollwitzer, *Die Existenz Gottes im Bekenntnis des Glaubens*
(1963); E.T. *The Existence of God as Confessed by Faith* (1965).

But finally I surrender all that I am and want to the higher will of God. Finally! If no intermediate stage is present or needs to be overcome, then "Thy will be done" is either the expression of surrender to destiny, to pagan fatalism, or it is a meditative monolog on what is demanded, God being the norm or criterion. There is no real address, no hearing and answering. It is certainly out of line to think that the NT supports the view that prayer is a monolog of this type.

Even crasser is the degeneration of prayer into a mere monolog in van Buren.[44] Here the restructuring is again based on the idea that the modern mind is the criterion of what may be accepted as prayer. The Cartesian approach is plain to see. For while prayer was earlier thought to be speaking with God, modern secularism leaves us in the dark. We cannot assume that there is someone with whom to speak in prayer.[45] A secular understanding of prayer is thus to be sought in another direction.[46]

To postulate that someone is there is to count on it that God "is," and that he hears those who pray, so that there is some point in praying. But since this assumption is incompatible with the empirical premises of the secular mind, van Buren rejects it. If he does not take the logical course of scrapping prayer altogether, but tries to find an acceptable meaning for it, this can only mean that he wants to transpose the processes of consciousness of the NT man of prayer into those of modern man. Here again prayer is seen as immanent to the consciousness and it thus loses its real point, that of address to the God who is a "given" for all consciousness.

What is this restructured consciousness of the man who prays today?

It may be seen clearly from the change in the view of intercession. Intercession for our neighbors is reflection on their need in the light of the gospel.[47] This can be just as serious as earlier fasting and praying. It involves visiting our neighbors, discussing their situation with them, and seeing what can be done to help. One should note, however, that when van Buren says this he does not mean that intercession which does not lead to practical help is hypocrisy. This idea is still bound to the traditional view. What van Buren means is that this help takes the place of prayer. Intercession begins when we consider the situation in a Christian perspective and it then leads to appropriate action. This is what is meant by reflecting on it. With a newspaper in one hand and the Bible in the other the Christian tries to read the newspaper in the light of the Bible and can perhaps say that the Bible has opened his eyes to some aspects of the newspaper.[48] Prayers of thanksgiving are similarly expressions of the consciousness; they express the joy of a man at finding a certain measure of freedom.[49]

If few men pray today, according to van Buren, this is not because the relation to God has been disrupted either by our defection from him or by his withdrawal from us (Léon Bloy). This would involve the postulate of a

---

[44] *Op. cit.,* pp. 188ff.
[45] For the radical departure from the OT in this respect cf. H. J. Kraus, "Der lebendige Gott," ETh (1967), 4, pp. 169ff.
[46] Van Buren, *op. cit.,* p. 188.   [47] *Ibid.*   [48] *Ibid.,* p. 189.   [49] *Ibid.,* p. 190.

"someone" and it would also explain prayerlessness in terms of premises that no longer obtain today. Modern prayerlessness is due to the fact that the traditional language of prayer implies notions which are in conflict with the empirical stance of modern man. Thus prayer seems to him to be a flight from reality.[50] There will be a return to prayer only when prayer is reinterpreted and integrated into the empirical (Cartesian) schema of consciousness. This will come about when prayer is seen as reflection and the corresponding action.

The time when prayer meant knocking on a door that would then open (Matthew 7:8; Luke 11:10) has gone. The hour has come when God is a door that is permanently closed,[51] when transcendence is silent, when the empirical consciousness posits its own frequencies as absolute. All that is left is the God of Spinoza with whom there can be no personal relationship. If to the angry irony of the prophets the mark of the idol seemed to be that it was dumb, that it could neither hear nor answer, and if this is what made it inferior to the living God, the dumbness of the gods seems to have come again. But it now seems to include the dumbness of God. Plainly the death of God is already imminent.

The disturbing thing is to hear this, not from secularists, but from representatives of faith. Here again, although now in extreme form, we see the arrogant autonomy of certain movements of theological thought today.

Monolithic commitment to contemporary recipients of the message (for which the one who proclaims it is also contemporary!) leads at once to the dominion of the contemporary and his consciousness. This is a total perversion. And if the reader will not view it as cheap comfort, we may make the final point that God is so much God that he can understand and accept as prayer even that which was not meant as such.

---

[50] *Ibid.*
[51] G. Bernanos, *The Diary of a Country Priest* (1937), p. 23; cf. pp. 93f.

VI

Theology B: Counter-question and Question

1. PROBLEM OF CONSERVATIVE AND NON-CARTESIAN THOUGHT

We began by considering the distinction between "modern" and "conservative" theology. This we rejected. "Modern" is not a good term for linguistic reasons and so we replaced it with "Cartesian" (Theology A) as an indication that theologians of this school take the consciousness as their starting-point.

The word "conservative" is also a poor one to denote a theological movement. To be sure, it contains two elements that are well adapted to express theological intentions. These will be worked out later. Nevertheless, we should not accept the term, first because it is already freighted in theology to the extent that it has been equated with restoration or reaction, and thus carries with it the sense of what is past and dead and done with,[1] and second because it is hard to define exactly. It is a polemical word. It does not so much describe a positive position as a way of reacting. In general it opposes upheaval and is an antonym of revolution.[2] In view of the negative sense of "conservative" we have thus thought it better to use the word "non-Cartesian." This is a new term with no awkward overtones.

Nevertheless, we may learn from some aspects of the concept of "conservative" which are theologically relevant and which relate to the way theology usually reacts polemically.

First, in contrast to the common use of "conservative" for rigid adherence to the past, the word has from the very outset a decidedly historical reference, as may be seen from conservative interactions with the ideas of the French Revolution. Whereas the Revolution was trying to construct an abstractly rational state with synthetic means, the opposition appealed to the logic of historical growth and organic continuity. The living quality of history was

---

[1] Cf. O. H. v. d. Gablentz, "Reaktion und Restauration," *Festschrift für H. Herzfeld* (1958), pp. 55ff.

[2] In this regard it might be used synonymously with evolution or reformation (cf. A. Kuyper, *Calvinism: Six Stone-Lectures* [1898ff.], and the German title *Reformation wider Revolution* [1904]).

thus maintained (*conservare*) against the attack of pragmatic construction.

This does not have to mean the upholding of existing or outdated structures, the embalming of what is dead. A living relation to history such as we find in the protest against ideological construction will always see present action in openness to historical possibility. Hence it will not tie it to the past but will find it open to the future.

Thus theologians who call themselves "conservative" or "positive," or who are disparagingly called this,[3] are not just engaged, consciously at any rate, in the work of restoration. They, too, deal with current questions and expose the Christian understanding of truth to the fire of philosophical epistemology. In what theologians of the nineteenth century of whatever school did Kant's Copernican revolution leave no trace? And what theology of whatever school in the latter half of the twentieth century does not include some discussion of existentialism or historico-critical research, no matter how good or bad, how honest or slippery, how serious or trivial this discussion might be? This in itself is enough to show that the conservative concern to do justice to history takes up the present, including the speaker himself, into the historical process and hence into the living organism of occurrence. In this light the common idea that "modern" and "conservative" are mutually exclusive is already seen to be defective.

Second, the thrust of this conservative defense of history necessarily leads to a contrasting of the concrete with all *a priori* constructions of what ought to be as these are usually found in the ideological programs of revolution. The conservative man, said Heinrich Leo in 1864,[4] is characterized by the fact that he does not let himself be blinded by the shadows of abstraction but perceives that all attempts to subordinate life to abstraction lead to the very opposite, to a caricature of what was originally intended.

Theology describes that which in its own field leads to this caricature as "heresy." Heresies usually arise when one principle is torn away from the total organism of teaching and given one-sided dominion.[5] What reminds us of a caricature is the ensuing confusion. One or other member of the body of doctrine develops elephantiasis. In fact, what is usually placarded as modern in theology constantly involves this absolutizing of a particular point, in this case not necessarily an individual doctrine but perhaps a principle (e.g., in hermeneutics), or the historicity of revelation, or the significance of the self-consciousness. The fate of such absolutizings and abstractions has already been noted.

The conservative interest in the concrete has found programmatic expression especially in the political arena. Thus A. Bergsträsser claims that it is the basic intention of conservative thought to view the totality of existence

---

[3] Cf. the typical title of the work of T. Kaftan, *Moderne Theologie des alten Glaubens* (1905).

[4] Cf. H. J. Schoeps, *Konservative Erneuerung* (1958), p. 7.

[5] Cf. J. Brosch, *Das Wesen der Häresie* (1936), pp. 16ff., 85ff.; L. Goppelt, "Kirche und Häresie nach Paulus," *Denkschrift für W. Elert* (1955), pp. 9ff.; E. Wolf in RGG[3], III, 13.

in life and society as an organic nexus instead of understanding it one-sidedly in terms of economics or power politics.[6] Hence the whole is again advocated over against the part, whereas the abstract articulation of principles plays off the part against the whole and can thus lead to untruth if the part comes to be regarded as the truth. Formally, then, conservative thinking has an anti-heretical thrust.

This does not mean idealization of the conservative. This is ruled out by the fact that appeal to the totality of the organic nexus cannot itself be an extraction, a romantic bubble. The conservative can easily fall into the very error which it opposes if it makes of itself a principle and becomes "conservatism," as in the romantic cult with its principle of legitimacy.

If we disregard this perversion, the thrust of the conservative is toward the historically concrete. This actualism may be seen in theologians who are usually castigated, or extolled, as "conservative." It is found especially in preachers (along with the weaker products of a mere orthodoxy that is just attempting repristination). In contrast to some of the great conservative preachers, "modern" theologians of the schools, who are desperately trying to address their contemporaries in radical fashion, often fail because of their abstraction and lack of concrete imagination and association. The fact that the definite conservative is often much more concrete than the one who emphatically does not want to be a conservative is probably connected with the conservative relation to history, and especially with its recognition that the speaker, too, is exposed to the historical process.

Yet we should also keep in mind the various distortions into which the conservative need for actualism might fall.

Conservatism as an absolutizing of the conservative can indeed lead to rigidity and to a reactionary attachment to the past. In this case the reference to the present which the relation to actuality produces is negated. In theology, this happens when the kerygma simply becomes the historical past and traditional teaching is preserved without the slightest change. Since proclamation of what concerns us unconditionally still must become contemporary with us (otherwise it would be of no relevance), and the reactionary does not have this present-day reference, a pedagogic substitute is often adopted in order to achieve actuality, e.g., quotation of headlines or modern poets, use of slogans or jazz rhythms, which simply deck out the corpse in such a way as to suggest that it is still alive. The more definite the reaction the more violent is the effort to find an artificial modernity, although the hearers are not deceived for long.[7] The best examples are perhaps to be seen in some forms of American Fundamentalism, which is pseudo-conservative to the extent that materially it evades contemporary questioning of its theology but formally it abounds in associations with the life of the age.

Third, conservative thought avoids generalizations on what is conservative. It is thus open to the specific. This openness is again grounded in the

---

[6] RGG³, III, 1782.
[7] Cf. my book *Leiden an der Kirche*, 2nd ed. (1966), pp. 60ff.

conservative relation to history. For history, as distinct from nature, is the sphere of individuation, of what cannot be subsumed under a general principle.[8] Thus schematization is forbidden. Conserving is different in each people, just as each people is different (Heinrich Leo, *loc. cit.*). Hence what is to be defined as valid and imperative is also drawn into the process of history. The decision is an open one; it has to be continually taken afresh.

Understanding himself thus, the conservative avoids ossification. He is elastic. For the peoples and nations which the politically conservative has in view are individual and immune from rigid schematization. The epochs are also individual, bringing new questions and hence necessitating revisions. In theology this means that the old truth comes to each new age and takes individual form in relation to it. Its claim to be designed specifically for this age, to be a gospel for it, implies a kind of individualizing in time.

If there can be degeneration here too, it applies less to this individualizing in time. Here the conservative thrust and the underlying sense of continuity protect it from setting a given age apart, from extolling its modernity, from detaching it from the flow of history. The conservative degeneration of the specific may be seen more in the tendency to absolutize the individuality of one's own people, state, or social and personal forms of life. This can happen even though one does not want to export it to others but rather to preserve it as one's own collective or personal individuality. In this case absolutization finds expression in a sense of superiority, in pride at one's own privileged existence. The snobbery in this attitude is that one's own caste or class or nationality or race is invested with excellencies and others are accorded an inferior status. The conservative continually manifests this kind of distortion and the sense of the individual can easily contain an element of hubris.

The theologically conservative may suffer the same distortion. Here the arrogant overestimation of one's own individuality can be seen in the cocksureness with which the absoluteness of Christianity (i.e., of the individuality of one's own religion) is advocated. There is no questioning of one's own rights, e.g., the rights of mission, which ought to be done before one is authorized to proclaim that Christ is the First and the Last, the Absolute. Absoluteness is accepted as a pre-judgment and advocated without any critical testing. Acceptance of pre-judgments without submitting them to one's own judgment and putting them through the fire of questioning is reactionary and retrogressive. The possibility of the reactionary accompanies the habit of mind of the conservative like a shadow.

Fourth, the conservative is characterized not merely by a relation to history, to the concrete, and to the specific, but also by a reproductive attitude to the past. This calls for a more penetrating investigation which we shall now attempt.

---

[8] H. Rickert, *Die Grenzen der naturwissenschaftlichen Begriffsbildung. Eine logische Einleitung in die historischen Wissenschaften,* 5th ed. (1929), p. 227.

2. TEMPORALITY OF TRUTH (RE-PRESENTING AND FORGETTING)

As we have seen, the conservative tries to maintain tradition but in such a way that there is critical and contemporaneous appropriation. Hence the conservative adoption of tradition contains not merely an element of continuity but also one of variability. As distinct from mere restoration the conservative is thus elastic. His appropriation of tradition in freedom and according to the norm of present-day existence thus has the character of reproduction.[9]

The concept of reproduction is especially fruitful in this discussion since it implies one's own productivity—passive acceptance of tradition is negated—and at the same time it has in view the making present of the past, so that continuity with it is not broken by the introduction of something that is discontinuously new. The concept of reproduction also forces us to consider the relation of the old and the new, of the past and the present, and of speaker and hearer. Rather more sharply, the question might be put as follows: Does the concept of reproduction negate what is new and hence deny openness to the future? What place does it leave for new things, for progress, in the history of theology? Advocates of the conservative are well equipped to serve as partners in a radical discussion of this issue even though we are asking for more than a mere analysis of the conservative would demand. The idea of reproduction to which our discussion has led opens up all the important problems.

The confessions suggest themselves at once as a model. For they reproduce traditional truth. The element of "re" is that their concern is with the truth present in revelation and kept by the fathers. The element of "production" is that this truth is not stated in mere repetition and quotation but is formulated and "re-addressed" in relation to new questions and challenges. This may be seen in the very structure of confessional statements with their thesis ("We confess . . .") and antithesis ("We reject . . ."). Although the antithesis always comes second and positive statement takes precedence, it is the antithesis that makes a new presentation of the ancient truth acutely necessary. It is the provocation or challenge, whether of Anabaptists who by their doctrine of the Spirit make the confession speak about the "Word" which alone has the Spirit,[10] or of Donatists who goad the church into saying that its basis is not the sanctity of its members but the justification of sinners.[11]

The structure of all theological utterance is like that of the confessions. For, as we have seen in Chapter I, it is provoked by the present situation. In distinction from the confessions, however, it does not have to deal with an error that is being opposed to the truth. Existential questions of anxiety,

---

[9] Cf. Goethe's *Kampagne in Frankreich,* Cotta, X, p. 440.
[10] CA, V; LBK, I, 58.   [11] CA, VIII; LBK, I, 61.

finitude, or theodicy may arise, or Christian truth may be challenged by the truths of science and history.[12]

This confessional or theological debate between Christian truth and the opposing or challenging theses of the new age brings to light the dialectic between old and new which no theological statement can avoid.

The theological statement has a conservative aspect to the extent that it considers the faith of the fathers and includes itself in a tradition. This reference to the past is intensified by the fact that the faith of the fathers relates to a past event, the mighty acts of God (Acts 2:11), especially in concluding the covenant. The reference back both to the acts of God that are "given" for faith and also to the faith of the fathers which is "given" for our faith provides decisive comfort in every test that might be posed by the apparent injustice of the divine rule or by contemporary challenges, whether in the form of heretical divergence or of more general defection. The one who goes under in this test would be denying God and rejecting and betraying the saving work of Yahweh among the members of his people. The cloud of witnesses (Hebrews 12:1) surrounding the sufferer must not be forgotten. It stands surety for the confession (Psalm 73:15).[13]

Yet the conservative glance backward cannot be content with mere quotation. It works itself out in re-presentation, or, better, in making the witness of ancient faith contemporary to the present generation. This means interpretation. Interpretation raises the question of direction.[14] This is shaped by the present situation of the questioner, and especially by the test to which he is exposed and which makes him "pay heed to the word" (cf. Isaiah 28:19).

Thus the struggle caused by heresy may compel the traditional confession to answer a dubious aberration, so that it is actualized or made contemporary thereby. New applications are brought to light which were previously hidden; new dimensions are disclosed. Only when we practice throwing the discus can we see the point of the special muscular development portrayed in ancient statues. Previously one might very well fail to note it. Similarly the challenge of heresy can make us see elements in the confession which we missed earlier. They suddenly become a "word" for our own time. In this sense the Barmen Declaration of 1934 developed as in a dark room the negative of the earlier confessions in such a way that they were seen to oppose racism, totalitarianism, and a hybrid ideology of providence. The same actualizing takes place when we take the basic question of the Reformation confessions: "How can I find a gracious God?" and see in it such variants as those of modern secularism, e.g.: "Where is God?" "Does He really exist at all?" Interpreted thus, the confession is summoned out of the past into the present.

This is why there will always be new confessions. They will not be new

---

[12] Cf. again Tillich's principle of correlation (*Systematic Theology,* I, pp. 59ff., 203ff.).

[13] H. J. Kraus, *Psalmen* (1960), I, p. 507.

[14] Cf. Bultmann in KM, p. 191.

because they revoke the older ones but because they invoke them. They will not be revolutionary then. They will not set aside the past. They will seek continuity with it and bear witness to the identity of revealed truth. This witness is possible only as they are constantly new and perhaps strange in their newness, so that at first the old truth is not recognized in them. If it is, this might be a bad sign. For direct appropriation, e.g., by quotation, can easily take the form of clichés which may rob the old truth of its point, namely, that it is the truth which reaches out to me, which is unconditionally relevant to me, and which claims my present. The clichés of mere quotation would make the truth outmoded, and what is outmoded entails no commitment.

This can lead to the most outrageous ideas, e.g., that Christ rose again but it makes no difference to me and reaches me only as a set of formulae. The mode and form of statement push what is proclaimed into the distance of the past if witness is not also given to the significance of Christ's resurrection for me today, of its significance for the self-reposing immanence of secular man, for his enclosure in finitude, for his mortality.

A past which is conserved traditionalistically is an alteration rather than a preservation of the past.[15] The fidelity of unchanged repetition is a sham fidelity. To repeat Luther's sayings about government unaltered in a democratic age instead of adjusting them to the new situation is to be false to Luther. To apply his two-kingdom doctrine without interpretation to totalitarianism is to distort it out of recognition for all the "literal" appeal to it.[16]

Real fidelity is achieved when the old truth is related to the questions that agitate modern man, when its beam is focused on his present-day situation, and when it is stated in terms taken from his own vocabulary, especially that of philosophy (from Hegel to Heidegger) in educated circles.

The resultant strangeness of the old truth might seem to affect its identity but in fact it preserves it. For this identity is that of a truth that applies directly to, and is contemporary with, every present. This carries with it a constant need to transpose it, to put it in new terms. The apparent strangeness, which often jolts the indolence and noncommitment of the well versed, is simply a variation on the strangeness that the old truth has always had. The parables of Jesus were shockingly strange when first uttered. The shock is all the greater when what is unfamiliar (and what can be more unfamiliar than news of the grace of God visiting us?) comes in the familiar form of everyday speech.

It is because the old truth must be set in each new present that we have theological history and not timeless, once-for-all, perennial theology. As the saving facts to which faith relates are history, so too is self-renewing faith itself, and also the resultant reflection which explains the correspondence between what is believed and the self-understanding of every age. The fact that there is a history of theology, dogma, and the confessions points to the dialec-

---

[15] G. Ebeling, *Die Geschichtlichkeit der Kirche und ihrer Verkündigung* (1954), p. 37.
[16] Cf. ThE, II, 2, § 20ff.; E.T. II, pp. 7ff.; ThE, II, 1, § 2036ff.

tic in theology itself between the old and the new, between fixity and progress, between continuity and variability in theological truth.

The ambivalence in theological truth is related to a deeper ambivalence in the human subjectivity that appropriates it. This is what adds human confusion to eternal truth and makes of theological history, not a straightforward process of appropriation, but a confusing jungle. The ambivalence of human subjectivity might be described as follows.

On the one hand the question of correspondence between old truth and the present situation brings increase in theological knowledge. As we have seen, the fulness of the dimensions in which old truth is disclosed is produced thereby. When we have the courage to question, to be dissatisfied, to think with the heart we have and not just the one we should have,[17] when we ask in terms of the present situation and the way things now are, then that fulness of truth opens up before us. Dissatisfaction and attack make ventures necessary. They make us think dangerously and take risks. The one who merely recites securely does not know these. He sticks to the wording but is far from the reality, enslaved to a security that is alien to faith. As Kierkegaard might put it, the man who has this type of security clings to objectivity and is not an existential thinker; he avoids commitment.

One of the risks that are incurred with dissatisfaction and attack—and this is the other aspect of the ambivalence of subjectivity—is that inquiry will obscure rather than enlighten. Bringing truth up to date is a reflection or imitation of the incarnation (ThE, I, § 1322ff.). It leads us in two directions.

First—and we have noted this already in Theology A—it helps to predetermine the answer that is expected from old truth. We are not going to discuss again the possibility that an unexpected answer might be ruled out and that the questioner might thus be involuntarily ensnared in a monolog. Our present concern is with another aspect of this process of pre-conception, namely, that my inquiry performs a task of selection and thus causes me to forget, to overlook, or to push back into darkness, broad areas of the old truth which are not within my investigation. In other words, my approach acts like a spotlight which illumines only a specific portion of the whole.

It may be, of course, that this portion serves as an example. In this case the whole may be seen in it as in a microcosm. Luther's spotlight was like this. His principle of "by faith alone" could not have all God's acts, from creation to the last things, as its theme. And his related hermeneutical principle that the OT is God's Word only insofar as it presents Christ could not comprehend every dimension of the OT. The implied selectivity inevitably meant sectionalizing, simplification, and blurred perspective. Nevertheless, what was selected served as a good example. Only one point in the landscape was lit up, yet this was a decisive point from which the other parts, or at least the paths leading to them, might be discerned.

That Luther made such a good choice may well be connected with the fact that his leading question was taken from the kerygma itself, so that it was

---

[17] K. Rahner, *Schriften zur Theologie,* I (1954), p. 174; E.T. *Theological Investigations,* I (1961), p. 153.

biblical and could easily lead to the center. If this is so, one might conjecture that the illumined sections are the more restricted, and the dark areas the more extensive, the more definitely the hermeneutical inquiry is controlled by views which are imported into the old truth from the present-day situation, self-understanding, or vocabulary. To the degree that this happens the old truth is not just overwhelmed with questions; it is subjected to criteria which are alien to it or which contain only peripheral aspects.

A casuistical interpretation of the Bible can lead into this kind of blind alley since its sole interest is in the directions that the Bible can give for conduct. Now the Bible does not offer a code of this type. Its directions are given from the standpoint of the "new obedience" as an actualization of faith. Hence Scripture is overwhelmed when we try to extract from it whether nuclear war is permissible or women's liberation is justifiable. The point of the Bible is obscured if we put to it questions it does not itself ask.

The same problem arises in theology. Schleiermacher was no doubt asking legitimate questions of appropriation and re-presentation against the background of an objectifying orthodoxy. He also had good reasons for trying to link Christian truth with the self-consciousness by way of the feeling of absolute dependence, and for defining the place of appropriation accordingly. Finally, his investigation did bring to light some aspects of Christian truth, e.g., its character as commitment. All the same, when we ask what parts of the faith may be known by the self-consciousness and may then serve as a stimulus to piety, are we not according relevance only to some sections, and even to these only from a specific and partial angle? Is not sin, for example, reduced to a mere "sense of sin" instead of an ontic mark of human existence, so that it is only that which hampers the development of self-consciousness (*The Christian Faith,* § 66)? Does not the divine sonship of Christ become Christ's consciousness of God instead of God's being in Christ, so that the God-consciousness in Christ's self-consciousness is the one constant element that governs every moment (§ 94)? And what about eschatology, whose theme is remote from the present? Can one avoid the well-known "eschatological lacuna" in this regard?[18]

The question that is put to old truth from every present does indeed aim at re-presentation. To some degree it even achieves this. But it pays a price which may be very high. This kind of illumining also involves obscuring. The recollection is accompanied by a forgetting, a letting slip from sight. With the nearness brought by the question there also comes a distance of perspective which blurs the contours and may even erase them.

Hence the history of theology is a history of obfuscation as well as clarification. It is a history of intentional suppressions and unintentional repressions. This means that it is also a history of the constant retrieving and rediscovering of what is lost. But each discovery or rediscovery is made at the cost of new forgetting.

We have to realize this if we are to guard against the error that the his-

---

[18] E. Brunner, *Die Mystik und das Wort,* 2nd ed. (1928).

tory of theology is one of continuous growth in truth. In almost equal measure it is a history of forgetting the truth. Theology is undertaken by sinners and thus needs forgiveness as sinners themselves do. Even at best our work is in vain. Thought, including theological thought, is part of this work. Like all our work, it can go forward only as justified work.

The consideration that the question put to the old truth results in distance as well as presence, that it distorts by giving prominence to what is suggested by the question and pushing the rest into the background, has given rise to the idea that the true subject of faith is the church rather than the individual—the total church in both space and time. For the more individual the hermeneutical question is—individual in respect to the limited situation as well as the personality of the questioner—the greater is the distortion.

Thus the confessions have always been valuable as representing the consensus of the whole church. This consensus was at one time expressed by a representative assembly confessing on behalf of the entire body. (Vatican II is something of a parallel today.) Nor did this assembly merely represent the total church of its own day (which would be a part only temporally). It represented the church of all ages, the church of the patriarchs, prophets, and apostles, the church of the entire tradition. To that extent the church is in fact the true subject of faith, its keeper, the guardian of the treasure, whereas even the most learned theologian has at his direct disposal only sections and perspectives of the full body of teaching, enjoying the totality only indirectly by way of the church.

For the individual it would be hubris rather than conformity to the truth if he were to seek the whole. The only way he could have it would be by recitation and repetition, and in this case he would not really have it. Truly to have it and to share it one must apply it unconditionally and hence one must investigate it; one must be dissatisfied in Rahner's sense.

This entails sectional abbreviation. No one is able to receive in full existentially. Each needs supplementation by others, even if this take the form, not of smooth coordination, but of tensions and even mutual misunderstanding. At any rate, the theologian cannot be a soloist. He must be corrected by others, and especially by the whole church. His questions must be accompanied by other questions and counter-questions if they are not to end up in sterile monolog.

In Roman Catholicism the idea that the whole church is the subject of faith leads to the concept of implicit faith. Expounding the faith in the form of reflection is a task for the church as a whole.[19] Behind this thought, which was developed at the high point of Scholasticism, there clearly stands the thesis that the teaching office enjoys primacy, that the institutional church plays a mediatorial role, and that dogma has the significance of law.

Yet one can also descry elements that are close to what we have said about the particular horizon of individual theology. Hence evangelical debate with the concept is always worthwhile. The decisive point in such debate is

---

[19] A. Ritschl, *Fides implicita* (1890).

that we have the totality in faith (for what is more "total" than faith in the justification of the wicked? What more can Christology or eschatology contain?) but that reflection falls short of this. Thus we can be alongside Schleiermacher in the one church of believers even though we must take issue with his thought, with his faith in the form of reflection. This is why the Christian brotherhood can embrace opposing theological schools.

To this extent the Christian is always ahead of the theologian. He is so also because theology is never more than an inquiry into the basis of the Christianity that is already there. Faith in the justification of the wicked is true in both heaven and earth. It can be excelled and transcended only by eschatological vision. But theology in its subsequent reflection is restricted to sectors, and it is quickly dissolved by the next generation, the contemporary, or a later period in one's own life.

We are speaking of the temporal nature of theological truth and we have seen that this involves distance as well as contemporaneity, obfuscation as well as illumination. This ambivalence of subjectivity finds expression at another point too.

Second, re-presentation and actualization can be achieved only as the old truth is put in current terms. Since the philosophy of the day usually supplies these—at least at the reflective level if not at that of popular expression—it is easy to see why theology is related linguistically to philosophy, why it speaks the language of a Hegel or a Heidegger. If the principle holds good that a man has understood and appropriated only what he can put in his own words, this transposition is a sign of understanding. For our own words are used here. The singular phenomenon that what is said in our own words sounds strange to the familiar tradition and can cause a shock, is evidence of true re-presentation.

The linguistic medium of the contemporary age into which the old truth is put in this way does, of course, undergo a change when thus used. We must not forget this. It is like the alteration that we have seen in defused myth. We said of this that it is baptized when adopted into the Christian kerygma. It acquires a new meaning. The same applies to linguistic terms when they are impressed into service. They have only a diaconal role and they must shed their ideological content, which, of course, they do have.

Thus the term "kingdom of God," which Kant employed in his Utopian eschatology, cannot be adopted unchanged even by so Kantian a theologian as Albrecht Ritschl. It has to be de-ideologized. Whereas for Kant it denotes the uniting of men by the laws of virtue, for Ritschl it is the organization of humanity by action out of the motive of love (*Rechtfertigung und Versöhnung,* 3rd ed. [1889], III, pp. 11f.; E.T. *The Christian Doctrine of Justification and Reconciliation* [1902], pp. 511f.). The very parallelism here brings the difference of nuance into prominence. Similarly "being" does not mean the same thing in Tillich as in Heidegger. The process of dying to which theologically used and baptized terms are subjected is an old and persistent one. We can see it in the NT itself, especially in relation to the word "logos." In the Johannine Prologue the Hellenistic and Gnostic elements are distilled out of this term and the content of the figure of Jesus of Nazareth fills the empty vessel (R. Bultmann, *Evangelium des Johannes* [1941], pp. 9ff.; E.T. *The Gospel of John* [1971], pp. 24ff.).

But this process of de-ideologization can be reversed. In this regard we again have an analogy to the disarmed myth which is now no more than a means of expression.

As myth can regain its original force, so the original content of speech can come to life again. The basis is also the same as in the revitalization of myth. The weaker brother cannot accept the impotence of nothingness. He lets it be a force that can win power over the weak. The weaker brother is not here a man of lower intellectual level but a man who suffers from an ultimate weakness which can afflict even those of fine intellect. The early Apologists are an example.

In John the term "logos," having been emptied of its previous content, was defined by what Jesus Christ is. In the Apologists, however, Christ is defined by the "logos" and becomes universal reason in the Stoic sense. This happens because an apologetic interest begins to control things. The apologetic means revolts, as it were. Christ is placarded as the fulfilment of Greek philosophy. He is made plausible, with no further break or offense, to Hellenistic rationality. He has to be put in the system of coordinates of this rationality and accorded supreme value in it. The "logos," which is claimed only fragmentarily by philosophers, is equated fully with Christ. A complete congruence of significance and content is thus achieved. "Logos" is no longer a servant but a controlling norm. It is thus remythologized.

This regeneration of the original ideological content necessarily entails a degeneration of the message. This is robbed of its individuality and forced into a schema. It is defined by this schema. This is why Ritschl's theology is so Kantian, Biedermann's so Hegelian, and Bultmann's so Heideggerian. It is not just that the vocabulary evokes these associations. We find here the same process as in the Apologists. The schema employed mounts a revolt and usurps dominion over the matter it is supposed to express.

With clear allusion to Tillich's attempt to put old truth in modern terms, Emil Brunner says that in all such transpositions into the language of philosophy the spirit is adopted of what is meant to be regarded merely as an empty form. It is obviously not perceived that the meaning of the Bible is completely changed when it is interpreted abstractly in this way. The divine world of Scripture becomes Plato's world of ideas, the ontology of timeless being, the absolute . . . which has no counterpart but is the eternal basis of all things and also their non-being. The epitome of spiritualizing is that the symbolism of personalism and temporal event is replaced with that of the impersonal and timeless (*Dogmatics,* III [1962], Part IV, 8, pp. 401ff.). Tillich, of course, is aware of the possibility of the remythologizing of language and he does not think that he has surrendered the Christian message by using a vocabulary that is intentionally different from that of the Bible and the church. He argues that there is no point in developing a theological system without such reformulation, since this alone makes appropriation and re-presentation possible (*Systematic Theology,* II [1957], Preface, p. viii).

From our own standpoint we might criticize Brunner on the ground that he regards the change of substance as an inevitable result of linguistic transposition. Our own view is that in fact it depends on whether our listening to the text in faith maintains its power over the new formulation or whether the means revolts successfully and we thus have a reawakening of the ancient gods, i.e., remythologization.[20] Along these lines we may describe linguistic re-presentation as both an opportunity and also a temptation.

Thus we have to ask Tillich how far he has avoided the temptation which he ably diagnoses or whether his ontology has not in fact influenced materially what it is designed to state.[21]

Pausing to survey our deliberations thus far, we note that what is at issue is the term "reproduction," which is suggested by the idea of conserving. This term indicates a distinctive dialectical relation to the past, to old truth. On the one hand this is to be accepted. Truth confessed today is to be displayed in its identity with the old truth. The continuity of the tradition is thus to be maintained. Yet this acceptance does not imply rigid and unchanged quotation. The old truth has to be made present. Its content must be correlated with the questions and self-understanding of the age. Current speech has also to be used. A productive element is thus at work. Both aspects of this "production" have dangerous features. The correlation to current questions and self-understanding, while it brings the old truth into the present age, can carry with it a forgetting and a consequent distortion of perspective. The use of contemporary vocabulary makes possible a regeneration of ideological content, a linguistic remythologization, which subjects the kerygma to foreign rule.

Notwithstanding the dangers inherent in reproduction, every theology has a conservative aspect to the degree that it looks back and asks concerning old truth. The problem is that this might be a mere aspect which is limited and relativized by the dangerous elements in what is conservative, so that falsification ensues. Rigid conservation can lead to this as well as flexible conservative renewal.

This is why, even though we respect conservative elements, we prefer not to give the term "conservative" any normative rank, but to use instead the label "non-Cartesian." This best expresses the approach we have in view, namely, that while the present situation and its questions have to be considered, they must not become a normative principle nor must they be allowed to prejudice the answer; they must be constantly recast and transcended in encounter with the the text.

---

[20] The poet Hölderlin explores this in his hymn *Der Einzige*. The attempt to set Christ among the Olympian gods, to integrate him into the schema of numinous powers, does not succeed, and the poet is broken by the failure. Cf. R. Guardini, *Hölderlin* (1939), pp. 516ff.

[21] Cf. the author's essay on Tillich, "Der Spannungsbogen," *Festgabe zum 75. Geburtstag* (1961), pp. 22f.; U. Neuenschwander, "Vom Gebrauch neuer Begriffe in der Theologie," *ibid.,* pp. 63ff.

The conservative aspect of theology, its looking back to old truth, raises two problems. First, what is the reason for this constant looking back? Second, in what respect can one speak of anything new that is brought to light in the course of the history of theology? Both questions lead us to the meaning and significance of the Holy Spirit.

VII

Theological Starting-Point in the Doctrine of the Holy Spirit

The question as to old truth has a "spiritual" basis.

If faith and the resultant theological reflection look back, as we have seen, to what the fathers believed, if they try to grasp and re-present a tradition, this is not due to the conservative mentality of those who believe, think, and confess thus. (The simple fact that being conservative is a mentality is enough to disbar the term.) The explanation is the very opposite. Looking back at the essence of the gospel is required. It is grounded in the thing itself, not the person. It thus gives rise to a certain conservative mentality.

Looking back is grounded in the thing itself to the extent that faith and its reflection on what has happened once and for all relate to the great acts of God which are the data of faith (cf. *ephápax* in Romans 6:10; Hebrews 7:27; 9:12; 10:10). While it is true that the faith given to me is a saving event which takes place now, an act of the grace of God upon me, this saving act is not of the same rank as what took place then, as God's conclusions of the covenant, as the crucifixion and resurrection of Christ. Faith is only a subsequent act by which what took place then is appropriated to me now. Faith is simply a ratification of the covenant for me. This ratification today, however, is grounded in the existing covenant. If I today die and rise again with Christ (2 Corinthians 4:11; 2 Timothy 2:11), this presupposes that Christ has already died and risen again. Hence faith is relativized. It has no specific weight of its own.

This is why Luther liked to compare the subject of faith to a mathematical point (WA, 40, II, 527, 9). Faith is not to be regarded as a psychological process and hence as a work. It is defined exclusively by the one in whom it believes and to whom it relates itself.

The self-understanding and egocentricity of Cartesian theology threaten to banish this relativization of faith to forgetfulness by treating the present act of faith as equal to the past event on which it rests and even by making it the true content of the saving event. In spite of every safeguard it often seems that what is discussed is not the relation between the Christ-event of the past and its present actualization in faith but rather faith as itself the real point of the salvation event. Along these lines the work *Für und wider die Theologie Bultmanns* (2nd ed. [1952], p. 32) can even state that faith is the same work of God in me today as his work done once and for all in Christ for me yesterday, so that there is the closest possible union between faith and the salvation event (a supposed insight of the Reformation). Here one may hardly detect any relativization of faith. The priority of the past event is not maintained. Faith is given its own significance. It is now more and other than the subsequent response to God's assurance in the covenant that he will be gracious to me.

While Schniewind says that faith does not draw attention to itself (KM, I, p. 97; E.T. p. 72), but depends on encounter with a unique event, in many trends within Cartesian theology faith achieves a rank of its own. Even linguistically it is a subject and almost a personified hypostasis. In Ebeling and Fuchs it often seems to be a figure in salvation history which cooperates in the achievement of salvation. Thus Ebeling says that if faith is referred to Jesus, then Jesus is referred to faith (G. Ebeling, *Das Wesen des christlichen Glaubens* [1959], p. 50; E.T. *The Nature of Faith* [1961], pp. 45f.). Although he modifies this, the structure of his teaching shows that all christological and dogmatic statements are ultimately controlled by faith, and the decisive christological principle is that Jesus as the witness to faith becomes the basis of faith (*Word and Faith* [E.T. 1963], pp. 301f.). Fuchs goes even further and has fewer safeguards than Ebeling. Thus faith participates in the resurrection of the crucified by publicly recognizing Jesus as Lord; Christ is risen when this confession is an expression of love (ZThK [1962], 1, pp. 42f.). Faith, then, is not subsequent to the event. It helps to bring it to pass, cooperating in the resurrection.

Are we pressing the point unduly if we say that on this view the past event is nothing without faith? But if we are right, then what Fuchs says is the direct opposite of Luther's doctrine of participation in the Lord's Supper even by the unworthy. The doctrine, which was aimed against Zwingli, argues that when the Word is preached and the sacrament is administered something always happens. Reception in faith is not what makes it an event; it is this whether with faith or without it. Faith plays a part only to the degree that it decides whether what happens is for blessing and not for condemnation, as with unbelief (cf. Form. Conc. Sol. decl., VII, 123). The point of the doctrine is thus to safeguard the fact that Christ's sacramental presence for me is not dependent on my faith (P. Althaus, *Die christliche Wahrheit*, II [1948], p. 393). Faith does not cooperate in the event. The event is a given factor; it takes place on me and to me.

This is the element in the thing itself, in the gospel, which forces us to look back at what happened then. To put it simply, we were saved nineteen hundred years ago.[1]

---

[1] As pointed out, rather unexpectedly, by P. M. van Buren, *The Secular Meaning of the Gospel* (1963), p. 169.

The function of protecting the givenness of the event when it is being actualized, of not allowing it to become pure present, of seeing to it that salvation history is always there before me, is a function discharged by the Holy Spirit. No matter what the Holy Spirit discloses to me, no matter into what truth he leads me (John 16:13), it will always be true that he will take the things of Christ (John 16:14), referring back to what took place in Christ's history, so that it is for me a given which establishes my faith without itself being established by this faith.

Even if this is not the place to develop a full doctrine of the Holy Spirit, the testimony of the Spirit is significant at this point in various ways. For this testimony obviously has something to say about the relations of "then" and "now," about the Christ-event and faith, about the relation of my self-understanding to what takes place to me and what is a given for me, in short, about the problem of appropriation and re-presentation.

The relevant aspects of the doctrine of the Holy Spirit in this regard are as follows.

1. Negatively, this reference back to the saving event finds expression in the fact that we do not make Jesus Christ our Lord in our own reason or strength. We cannot produce faith of ourselves. This is the work of the Holy Spirit (SC; LBK, 511, 6). This means, however, that the historical Jesus of Nazareth, through the Holy Spirit,[2] makes himself contemporary with us.[3] The natural man (*psychikós ánthrōpos*) does not perceive the things of the Spirit of God (1 Corinthians 2:14). Hence he cannot produce the present which eventuates in faith. Nor can he reproduce the past in such a way that it is present for him and Christ becomes his (contemporary) Lord. In contrast, although it does not sound too well, one should rather say that Christ can reproduce himself and bring himself out of the past into the present.

This is the point of the Spirit's testimony. It means that the evidence of what we believe in is provided, not by faith, but by what we believe in itself, i.e., the given fact of the Christ-event. The Lord makes himself evident and hence he makes faith possible. Faith does not make the Lord evident. The Lord himself is the Spirit (2 Corinthians 3:17f.). He cannot be controlled, then, by the natural man.

The natural man cannot achieve re-presentation on his own initiative, i.e., by methodology or hermeneutical effort. The presence of the Lord in faith is a sovereign gift. Without this gift we have only a dead past and historical distance. The testimony of the Spirit is thus a protest against our own endeavor, preparation, thought, or work (CA, V; LBK, 58). Neither the preacher's planting and watering nor the hearer's running and willing can help if the Spirit does not himself achieve the re-presentation (Sol. decl., II, 55; LBK, 893, 55).

---

[2] This is the point of the *filioque,* which found a place in theology from the time of Tertullian and which was then adopted into the Nicene Creed in the West (LBK, 27).

[3] The Holy Spirit brings true "presence" (Form. Conc. Sol. decl., II; LBK, 8).

It is thus a mistake to try to bridge the gap to the given history with presuppositions of our own or subjective analysis. To do this is to expect to find possibilities of re-presentation. But concern about methodology, if it comes first and dominates the scene, is simply an expression of active preparation and is thus a latent protest against the monopoly of the Holy Spirit.

The doctrine of the Holy Spirit is for its part a protest against the Cartesian approach in theology, against beginning with existential analysis and preliminary hermeneutical questions. Hence we may well ask whether this is not the reason why the doctrine of the Holy Spirit seems to be so strangely awkward in Theology A, finding no real place in this type of theology.

The Augsburg Confession makes this point when it says that the Spirit is not a movement in creatures (CA, II, 6). The doctrine of the Holy Spirit does not invite introspection, the self-contemplation of the creaturely I. Instead, it directs attention away from the self.

The trinitarian description of the Spirit as a "person" is significant in this regard. Standing over against the human ego, the Spirit is God in person. He does not come into me in such a way as to be a movement within me. He remains an object of the prayer: "Come, Holy Ghost."

Some NT passages, if taken in isolation, might suggest that the Spirit is an inherent quality, e.g., Romans 8:4; 1 Corinthians 6:11; 1 John 3:9; 2 Peter 1:4. He seems here to be imparted to man almost as an indelible character. But we also find complementary statements in which the Spirit is more without than within, thus barring the way to any idea of his being simply a working or indeed a work in us. He is the one who works on us. We can safely speak of his work in us if the primacy of this "on us" is established (cf. G. Dehn, "Der neue Mensch," *Theologia viatorum* [1939], pp. 67ff., esp. 92ff.). This externality of the Holy Spirit will be even more plainly established under the next heading.

2. The Spirit's testimony does not just point us away from the self and its pre-conditions and activities. It also has the positive function of directing us to the self-evidence of the Word and of him to whom it bears witness. The Spirit orients us to Christ. He does not let us be bound to ourselves, i.e., to our carnality (Romans 8:9). For the Holy Spirit (*sphragízein*) is the seal of that which Christ signifies as a promise for the advance and consummation of the event of salvation (Ephesians 1:13; 4:30). Thus the Spirit points us away from ourselves to the past and the coming event of which Christ is initiator, content, and finisher.

How the Spirit refers us to this event that takes place outside the human psyche we are told by the Johannine Christ: "If I go not away, the Paraclete will not come unto you; but if I depart, I will send him unto you" (John 16:7). This means that the Spirit can be given only when certain events—the crucifixion and resurrection—have taken place which he will disclose to us. The "all truth" (*alétheia páse*) into which he will lead us is not truth that goes beyond the promised and enacted events. It is truth which unfolds these events and applies them to me (John 3:27; James 1:17).

This work of the Spirit in pointing us away from self and "in me" to what takes place "on and to me" finds expression in certain NT metaphors which seem at first to locate the work of the Spirit in human subjectivity. One might quote, for example, the comparison of the body to a temple in 1 Corinthians 6:19. Exegesis might easily conclude from this that the Spirit is the center of our entelechy, i.e., that which fulfils us from within, the impelling core of the spiritual organism. But in fact the Spirit here is more like the eternal light burning in the temple. He points us to something outside, to what has taken place on and to us. We are redeemed at great cost (1 Corinthians 6:20). The dignity ascribed to us as a temple rests on the reference to him whose possession the temple is. We cannot be the temple of Christ and the temple of Belial at the same time (2 Corinthians 6:16) because the references are in conflict. The temple does not point to itself but away from itself.

This metaphor has often commended itself as an illustration of the very differently slanted humanism (cf. W. von Humboldt) which makes the development of the human entelechy the real meaning of existence. Here the human temple is developed with architectonic symmetry and proportion. But instead of a sanctuary it becomes a museum. It has significance in itself, not in its external reference. Similarly the dignity of the human here is found aesthetically in its structure. But the dignity of the human in which the Holy Spirit dwells as his temple is defined by a dignity that is not its own (*dignitas aliena*).

This alien dignity shines forth the brighter when our own values are dubious and our humanist status is not so lofty. Thus it is by means of the weaker brethren that Paul shows that we are not to get too far ahead or to offend in relation to them. Christ died for them too. They too were bought with a price. They thus have a share in the dignity that makes them sacred (Romans 14:15; 1 Corinthians 8:11).

Christian humanism—if one may use the term—should not be concerned, then, with reason and conscience and similar marks of distinction from the animal kingdom. It should teach us to look at what is outside, at the dignity that is not our own, at what has taken place on and to us, and hence at what is a given factor for us.[4] When we are called the temple of the Holy Spirit, this external reference is in view. At issue is what is without, not within.

Lutheranism formulated this relation of the Spirit to the given and external event or word with a force that is not so easily matched in the Reformed statements. (This is because Lutheranism had to take issue more seriously with the sectarians.) The Schmalcaldic Articles say very definitely that only by and with the outward and prevenient word are grace and the Spirit imparted to anyone.[5] The work of the Spirit is to relate to us what this word tells us of the great acts of God, the forgiveness of sins, the resurrection of

---

[4] In all such questions as euthanasia and abortion this factor of our alien dignity always arises for Christians, and it cannot be regarded as a variable or changeable functional value. The crux of the debate between Christian and Marxist anthropology lies precisely at this point (cf. ThE, Index, "dignitas aliena").

[5] Art. VIII; LBK, 453, 3.

the body, and the life everlasting.[6] Only when we believe, then, can we receive him as the one who transforms us and kindles fervent love within us.[7]

When we say this, of course, we have to add what it is that we believe as thus disclosed and set at work within us by the Spirit. The Apology of the Confession of Augsburg offers here the memorable statement that we believe in God as a lovable object.[8] The human heart could not love the God of the law who simply commands and judges. Fervent love would be ruled out in such a case. This love is not something that has to be attained. It reflects subjectively what we experience transsubjectively as it happens outside us and to us, namely, that God is lovable.[9]

But how is God lovable?

God can be for me a lovable object only as this is attested to me, not as a mere assertion, but as a narrative of his self-demonstration as such, namely, in his mighty acts from the deliverance out of bondage in Egypt and through the wilderness to the warnings and promises of the prophets and finally the new covenant in the coming of Jesus Christ. The name of God that is proclaimed is also the name of his acts, of what has happened to us. God is there for us as we remember and look back upon the history which he has caused to happen to us and in which he has included us.

It is evident now how the Holy Spirit achieves re-presentation. He evokes faith, kindles fervent love, and opens up immediate access to God by illuminating the mighty acts of God as a nexus into which I am taken up and whose earlier stages are of contemporary or existential significance to me, so that in the simpler and more expressive language of Scripture I am pricked in the heart (Acts 2:37).

Peter's sermon in Acts offers an excellent illustration (Acts 2:14-36). He recalls what has happened. But the Spirit of Pentecost overcomes historical distance. He takes up those who are listening into the events. What the prophets foretold, what has now been fulfilled in the resurrection of Christ, is for the whole house of Israel (v. 36). It applies to "today," to "you." God can be seen in it as a lovable object. The natural man may have no organ to receive it (1 Corinthians 2:14). He can only remain at a historical distance. He can only relativize. But the Holy Spirit discloses it to you. Love, confidence, and faith are thus imparted. Loving is not a subjective faculty; otherwise it would be under the law. Love is a reflection, the subjective side, of the fact that God encounters me as one who is worthy of love, and his history is for me a manifestation of this love.

Formally, there is a similarity here to the righteousness of God as an active righteousness in Luther's sense (cf. Schrenk in TDNT, II, 198ff.; H. Iwand, *Glaubensgerechtigkeit* [1941], pp. 55ff.). Understood thus, righteousness is not disinterestedly distributive, handing out rewards and punishments.

---

[6] GC, Art. 3; LBK, 654, 41.

[7] Cf. Luther's "Come, Holy Ghost" in *The Lutheran Hymnal*, No. 224; Apol. CA, LBK, 185, 127.

[8] LBK, 186, 129.

[9] The author requests that the terminology used here not be related to the familiar controversy concerning the subject-object schema.

It confers on man the possibility of being righteous before God, of sharing in God's own righteousness. We are righteous before him when we are in conformity with him. We are not in conformity with him, however, by our own works or efforts. These would give us claims and thus put us in a legal relation. They would make us partners with God. But this would not do justice to his Godhead. It would be a transgression of human creatureliness. I do justice to God and attain to conformity with his will only when I enter into what he wills to be for me, namely, a gracious God. I do so only when I trust his self-declaration as such, only when I have faith in him.

As, then, the righteousness of faith corresponds to God's righteousness, so love of God corresponds to God as lovable object. In both cases (the love of God and the righteousness of God) the genitive can be both subjective and objective. The very grammar thus shows that this is a relation of complementarity. I can view the same love and righteousness from the divine perspective and also from the human perspective. They point to one another. This is possible only because they describe a relation and not the state of an isolated person, whether God or man. Loving and being righteous imply relation. I come into relation with God as I accept him for what he wills to be and has shown himself to be in his mighty acts, namely, the one who loves me and has come to me in grace.

This is why the Holy Spirit works primarily, not through what is done in man so that he is "full of the Holy Spirit" (Acts 2:4; 4:8, 31; 6:3, 5; 7:55; 11:24; Ephesians 5:18), but through what is done on and to him, so that he is really "full" of the Holy Spirit. In other words, the Holy Spirit directs the one whom he enlightens away from himself to a history which is outside him even though it includes him, and to a word which is again outside him, so that it is an external word. If the Holy Spirit also works within to call and enlighten and sanctify, this is because the strange thing that comes from without also becomes proper to man (cf. Iwand, *op. cit.,* pp. 56ff.). There are two reasons for this.

The first is that God does not hold back but pours out generously. He wills to be there for me. But if he wills this so unreservedly, then "I am" means only what he is for me (Luther, WA, 54, 186).

The second is related to the first. "I am" can no longer denote my isolated and self-grounded entelechy. It tells of what God is for me and hence of what I am in consequence. It expresses a relation. I am the one who is brought under God's covenant and visited by God in judgment and grace.[10] This is what Luther has in mind when he says that God and we are in the same righteousness, as God also creates with the same word and we are what he creates, so that we are in him and his being is our being (WA, 5, 144).

The "I am" is thus a mode of God's being, not pantheistically, but in such a way that my being is determined by what God addresses to me. Christ is an exemplar of my existence.[11] A bold complementarity can thus be expressed:

---

[10] W. Zimmerli, *Das Menschenbild des Alten Testaments* (1949), pp. 8ff.

[11] For references cf. E. Wolf in *Jesus Christus im Zeugnis der Heiligen Schrift* (1936), pp. 214ff.

Christ is my sin and I am his righteousness.[12] The "I am" is a statement about being in relation, for in every dimension of life I am characterized by what God is for me. I am created, fallen, and visited. I am judged and blessed.[13] The I is thus determined from without by what is done on it, by what God is for it.

When things are viewed thus, it is impossible to begin with a self-understanding or pre-understanding. For this would mean excluding the I from that relation and seeing it as a prior entity. Who I really am I learn only from the word that proclaims to me God's condescension, his covenant, and his mighty acts. The Holy Spirit who discloses this word to me does not point me to myself but away from myself to the events by which I am what I am.

This is why the debate whether the Holy Spirit is a person or a power, a lord who encounters me or a force that works in me, is pointless. Whether we refer to him in one way or the other is connected with the complementarity of all theologico-anthropological statements, and these in turn are based on the relation which determines human existence.

In the same light one can also see why the Holy Spirit has a conservative aspect (not to be confused, as we have noted, with conservatism). He has this because he refers us to the external word and therewith to the history of God with us to which it bears witness. He summons as witness what God has done to the fathers, the patriarchs, prophets and apostles, and what they have testified to in the word, and handed down as a word to our own time. The Holy Spirit effects the *actualization* of the past. He makes it present as something that took place for me. He includes me in the history attested here. But it is an actualization of the *past*. He reminds me of what took place. He thus bears witness to the author of these events, the God of Abraham, Isaac and Jacob, and the Father of Jesus Christ.

In thus making God's history contemporary, though not reducing it to timeless ideas, the Holy Spirit honors all times, past as well as future, recollected as well as promised. Hence when Pascal says: "The God of Abraham, Isaac, and Jacob, not of the philosophers and scholars," he has in view the God who comes into history, the subject of mighty acts, not God as a timeless idea. Similarly one might say of the Holy Spirit that he is not the spirit of the philosophers and scholars, but the Spirit who leads into history and who brings history to us.

Thus *nous* and *pneuma,* the wisdom of the world and the historical manifestation of divine wisdom (1 Corinthians 1:18ff.), are always at odds with one another. The wisdom of the world (the rational spirit) contemplates itself and conducts its inquiry according to its own axioms and immanent principles, so that its picture of ultimate reality—whether called God or not—is formed according to these premises. The Holy Spirit, however, has in view the historical events by which God defines me as what I am, so that as I

---

[12] Cf. P. Althaus, *Die Theologie Martin Luthers* (1962), pp. 180 and 199; E.T. 1966, pp. 203f., 227f.
[13] Cf. G. Jacob, *Der Gewissensbegriff in der Theologie Luthers* (1929).

must believe these events, so I have the definition of myself only in faith. Not God alone, but man defined by God too, is the object of faith.

It was the conflict with the sectarians that led Lutheranism in particular to stress this link between the Spirit and history, along with the word that bears witness to it. Negatively this is a safeguard against the supposed spiritual revelations of enthusiasm, which, being direct, are not grounded in the external word, and are thus only contemporary and do not include recollection as well. We will append only a few of the many possible quotations from Luther to back up our thesis.

Spirit and letter (2 Corinthians 3:6f.) are not to be viewed as antithetical; the Spirit writes "the letters on our hearts" (WA, 47, 184). "God will not give anyone the Spirit apart from the word and the preaching office" (17, 135). The Holy Spirit kindles faith and illumines the heart, but "not without the outward office or the outward use of the sacraments" (43, 187). One cannot boast of the Spirit without having "the open and outward word." For "the Holy Spirit has set his wisdom, counsel, and all secrets in the word and revealed them in Scripture." A spirit that looses itself from these is not from God, but "from hell" (36, 501).

VIII

The Holy Spirit as He Who Creates Anew and Yet Also Links to the Old

The New Place of Self-Understanding

1. PROBLEM OF CONTINUITY

We must consider at once an objection. This objection is an urgent one in relation to Cartesian theology. Against our thesis that the Holy Spirit does not let us begin with the axioms of our own self-understanding but turns our gaze on what has happened historically, this theology can advance a weighty argument which might be given the form of the following counter-questions.

How *can* I look outwards to let myself be defined by what takes place and to receive my self-understanding therefrom? This sounds as though I were a *tabula rasa,* a blank page to be filled only by the external word, the Word of God, while itself remaining passive. But this is surely an illusion. I am "someone" even before confrontation with that word. I have a definite self-understanding. I am of age. I am not a blank sheet. The Holy Spirit cannot ignore this, unless he avoids certain facts about me and is completely unrealistic. Are not my adulthood and my very humanity disregarded if it is assumed that the Holy Spirit causes me to be defined exclusively from without? Is not the external word degraded to a mere dictum if it no longer convicts me (convicting implies criteria), if it no longer calls me to conversion (conversion implies already being on a way), but simply fills an unresisting vacuum? If man is a vacuum and the Holy Spirit is the substance that fills it, we had better speak of physics rather than theology. A personal relation between God and man is impossible on this level. If this level is to be avoided, if the Word of God, the kerygma, is to encounter a concrete man with a specific self-understanding, then theological relevance must be ascribed to what is already there for the kerygma. It cannot be dismissed as belonging to the spirit of philosophy. Only as I take it seriously do I respect the claim of the kerygma that it can be appropriated by me, i.e., that it can enter into a specific relation to my self-understanding. Without this appropriation the kerygma remains outside or else it forces its way in as law, and is no true gospel. But the fact that it is gospel, that it tells of God's self-declaration as a lovable object, is the heart of the doctrine of the Spirit, of the non-Cartesian

138

theology, that we are championing. A self-contradiction thus seems to arise. The spontaneity with which I accept God as a lovable object is endangered if the Holy Spirit ignores man's prior self, treats the process of appropriation as irrelevant, and puts enforced belief in the place of spontaneous faith. This perverts everything and indeed turns it into its opposite.

We have tried to express here all the essential arguments that arise out of our study of Theology A. Obviously we are at the very heart and center of the debate. It will thus reward us to give due weight to the counter-questions.

Undoubtedly these objections would be right if we had actually said that the Holy Spirit ignores altogether the data of natural existence, directs our gaze only outwards (in a nondialectical sense), and relentlessly confronts us with the proffered revelation. Even Barth, however, would never want his statement that the word creates its own hearers (by the Spirit) to be taken so one-sidedly and nondialectically.

We have thus to consider how it is that the Holy Spirit, in effecting a new creation (2 Corinthians 5:17; Galatians 6:15), does not ignore the given realities of the old creation or the natural man, but claims them and integrates them into the new creation. In so doing we may formulate our thesis as follows. While the prior self-understanding of man is not ignored in the Spirit's work and remains a theological theme, it is not accorded the same rank as in Cartesian theology. It is not the starting-point of theology in the form of existential analysis. It is the object of a retrospective glance and is thus a secondary theme.

The problem that concerns us has been discussed in modern theology under the title of the problem of a point of contact.[1] The question is whether and how far there are elements in our natural consciousness (or conscience) which make God's Word intelligible to us, which go to meet it, and which are thus the presupposition of possible appropriation of it. This raises the further question of the analogy between revelation and nature, the problem of analogy of being. It thus gives rise not merely to the controversy between Theology A and Theology B[2] but also to that between Reformation and Thomistic theology.[3]

In this context we cannot go into the problem of analogy nor discuss the debate between Barth and Brunner in detail. We shall thus concentrate on the question of the point of contact to the degree that this impinges on the operation of the Holy Spirit as presented above.

In dealing with this question we shall study two models. The first is a

---

[1] Cf. the famous debate between Barth and Brunner in *Natural Theology* (1946).

[2] In this regard the Barth-Brunner debate is not a good example, since Brunner is not a typical representative of Theology A. Nevertheless, the points raised there are a good illustration of the encounter in many ways.

[3] In fact the Barth-Brunner debate has made the problem of analogy a subject of discussion interconfessionally as well as within Protestantism (cf. H. G. Pöhlmann, *Analogia entis und fidei* [1965]; H. Diem, *Theologie als kirchliche Wissenschaft* [1951], pp. 28ff.; G. Söhngen, *Die Einheit in der Theologie* [1952], pp. 235ff.).

philosophical one, that of the relation between the categorical imperative and the divine commandment. The second is a biblical one, the story of the Prodigal Son (cf. ThE, I, § 1605ff.).

2. PHILOSOPHICAL MODEL: THE COMMANDMENTS OF GOD AND THE CATEGORICAL IMPERATIVE

In his doctrine of the categorical imperative Kant not only discusses the philosophical problem of autonomy[4] but also unintentionally makes a contribution to the theological doctrine of the law. Without expressly referring to it he adopts Paul's teaching that the law kills. It kills because it comes to me as an external command, so that it forces me instead of leading to spontaneous obedience. In this heteronomous function the law can only lead to protest (Romans 7:11). It forces me into self-assertion. According to Paul its goal of bringing me into harmony with God's will can be achieved only if it makes love possible for me. Love is spontaneity. In love I enjoy totality, whereas the law divides me into an assenting self and an opposing self (7:7ff.). But love as the fulfilment of the law cannot be achieved by the law itself. As noted, if I am to love, God must come to me as the object of love.

Along the same lines as Paul, Kant bases his ethics of autonomy on the thought that no claim of any kind, whether command or revelation, can legitimately hold me unless it is approved by the criteria of my own ethical consciousness and is appropriated with the help of this approval. This condition must be observed if the dignity of my autonomy is not to be violated (which is anthropologically impossible) and the divine author of the law is not to be the epitome of tyrannical legalism and therefore of heteronomy (which is theologically impossible).

Thus Kant is dealing with the present issue. The self-understanding of the natural man, who thinks of himself autonomously, cannot be ignored if both the one who is claimed and that which claims are not to be subjected to tensions that will distort both. Obviously the Holy Spirit will not disregard these important realities. But if not, then we are face to face once more with the question whether we should not begin with existential analysis in the manner of Theology A, learning about the subjective conditions on which we can accept the claim. Does not Kant lead us back to the Cartesian starting-point?

This we must examine. The examination will show what weight or worth the question of the self-understanding of the natural man has when he is set under the claim of the Holy Spirit, i.e., when he is pointed away from self to the external word and comes to see that the natural man knows nothing of this word or Spirit, that the old man must die and become a new creature if he is to attain to understanding in this realm.

If, however, the Holy Spirit puts us to death and thus seems to create a *tabula rasa,* how can he make contact with anything? How can he treat any-

---

[4] Cf. the author's *Das Verhältnis zwischen dem Ethischen und dem Ästhetischen* (1932).

thing as existent, and take it seriously as such? This is the crux of the matter. With it we turn to what Kant says about the structure of the ethical consciousness in the (theologically) old or natural man.

The structure of the natural conscience in virtue of which man is a subject and is responsible, having to give an answer, finds classical formulation in the categorical imperative. "Act in such a way that the maxims of your will can always be accepted as the principle of general legislation" (*Critique of Practical Reason*, I, § 7). We have intentionally said that conscience in the absolute finds classical formulation in this imperative. This has to be said because conscience is not referred here to a specific national or divine law. It is defined simply as a supreme court in man that seeks maxims that are worthy to be regarded as a general law and can thus be adopted by the conscience "with a good conscience" as the norm of the will. When conscience is described in this open fashion, with no specific content, the reference is to its intrinsic form.

Two points are important here. (1) Conscience bends only to a law which has the highest worth the human mind can think of, namely, that of universal validity. This means that the categorical imperative is ready for a law which stands above personal opinion or the fluctuating voices of purely subjective moral instincts. These might express the tainted remnant of opportunistic inclination and uncontrolled self-will. They must first be tested by the criterion of general validity, by the principle which is above all selfishness or individualism. A ray of man's divine likeness thus seems to shine in this world of the categorical imperative, for man himself is here the subject, the autonomous subject, the final criterion of the universal law, the author of the law. In this subjectivity or autonomy he experiences, as Kant says, the basis of his self-regard, of his dignity.

(2) Even more important perhaps is the further fact that the categorical imperative must accept a law into the will if it is to meet that rigorous demand, whether it be the heroic ethic of Nietzsche or the radical requirements of the Sermon on the Mount in Tolstoy. Here if anywhere it is an urgent question whether this uncompromising readiness for a final demand on and against man can serve as a point of contact for the law of God. Of what more radical and selfless readiness can we conceive even theoretically? Is not this man's supreme openness, his greatest receptivity? Is not the conscience, illumined by that imperative, one long waiting or questing for the unconditional command, one long readiness for obedience? How can God, the author of the law, have more open doors if he will only see it and seek entry here and introduce his command as a maxim into the will at this point? Is not the imperative the one legitimate place for an encounter between God's address and man's listening to the extent that this takes the form of a word spoken and heard, a word heard as a claim, so that it has to be lived out and practiced?

We shall come close to an answer to these questions if we recall the metaphysical basis of the categorical imperative: You ought and therefore you can (*ibid.*, § 6).

Heidegger, too, can say that in the conscience existence summons itself to its most authentic possibility of being.[5] An "ought" which demands what is impossible in principle, reaching out beyond the arc of possible human action, is nonsensical. It cannot be achieved. It cannot be the content of what is possible for me. Hence it cannot claim to be an "ought." Man's primal ethical instinct counts upon a relation between "ought" and "can." It is thus evident that the imperative cannot ask of man what is beyond the unchangeable realities of his constitution and character. It can claim him only within this framework, within what he can achieve.[6] The imperative cannot challenge man as such, i.e., in his totality, along with his constitution. It can challenge him only insofar as he makes imperfect use of his constitution. Man himself, in his constitution and character, is the ethically indifferent presupposition of any ethics. His own place is thus secure.

The theological bearing of this comes to light when it is God's unconditional command that raises a claim to be accepted as a maxim into man's conscience, i.e., the categorical imperative. For God's command in its radical form—the command of love for both neighbor and enemy, the command not to covet (Matthew 5:43 par.; Luke 6:27, 35; Matthew 5:28) —certainly advances a claim to universal validity, but it does so in such a way as to question man himself in the very form of his existence, including his constitution and character. Indeed, it challenges the present aeon and all its structural laws.

We have to realize that if we fulfill this command, if we love our neighbor as ourselves, if we love our enemies, if we cease to covet, our whole history will come to a halt and we shall sink into the immobility of nonproductivity and starvation. For, to keep alive, this history needs the impelling forces of opposition, rivalry, oppression, passion, and conflict, so that fulfilment of the command is ruled out in principle by it.

For this reason the command, e.g., in the Sermon on the Mount, is God's assault on the present aeon with its laws and also on the total man to the degree that he is a representative of this aeon, to the degree that he *is,* i.e., in his given constitution, character, and structure, and not just in the sphere of his mobilized forces, of his capacity on the basis of his constitution.

I ought but I cannot. I cannot because I am what I am. This is the upshot of that assault. Man can alter himself only in his acts, not in his nature. The "I am" has determinative force for the "I will." This is why works cannot save. The "I will" cannot change the "I am." Good works do not make a good man, but a good man does good works, as Luther puts it.[7] Behind his works man is still the same man. Over this he has no control. Hence he has either to despair of God's total claim or to reject himself.

Does this mean, then, that the Holy Spirit, when he refers us to the external

---

[5] *Being and Time,* pp. 318f.

[6] Cf. the author's *Geschichte und Existenz,* 2nd ed. (1964), pp. 66ff.

[7] Thus the point in Luther's *De servo arbitrio* (*On the Bondage of the Will*) is that man is bound by the necessity of his own nature (cf. WA, 18, 634f., 709; E.T. pp. 102, 203f.).

word, transcends the conditions under which natural man exists? Are these conditions ignored? Do we not have the precise situation described by Theology A in its objections?

The problem is now somewhat clearer. We have stated that if there is in us a point of contact for God's revelation it will be found in the waiting, questing, and receptive conscience as described in the categorical imperative. Yet we have also seen that here, too, a chasm opens up with no bridge across it from man to God. For natural man in the grip of his autonomy lives in the illusion that if he ought he can. He cannot accept God's radical and unconditional law into his conscience because he is unable to hear and to recognize it as law, claim, attack. To demand that man and his world should be changed absolutely, that man should cease to be himself, that he should transcend the laws of life and existence, seems to make no sense at all—and sense is the chief maxim in this ethical view of things.

The "ought" which claims us in the law of God attacks the very basis of existence instead of limiting itself to the radius of ethical action within the framework of existence and on its basis. Hence it cannot be brought into harmony with man's self-understanding. Since it does not correspond to the ethical axiom "You ought and therefore you can," he cannot regard it as a command or an ought at all, and he cannot appropriate it as such.

A different explanation has thus to be found. Thus the divine command of love and the implied assault upon our whole world and our total existence might be viewed as the expression of universal pessimism or (as in Tolstoy) of a pacifism which is directed against the militant laws of reality. For, since man's natural ethos is indissolubly bound up with the illusion "You ought and therefore you can," and since this illusion is paradoxically made the criterion of all ethical reality, man in terms of himself and his own ethical maxims can never recognize God's law as ethical reality or a valid "ought," but necessarily has to dismiss it as illusion, as pessimistic illusion. For him it is thus unrealistic ideology, e.g., humanity expressed in ethical categories as pessimistic, pacifist, or some other humanity. Man's ethical self-understanding suffers here the fate of confusing illusion and reality. One might almost say that it suffers the fate of retrogression into a mythical world-view. When it finds a constitutive factor in man's disposition, in that which limits ontically the radius of his will, it adopts the mythical concept of cosmic matter as distinct from the belief in creation out of nothing. When this given matter qualifies my will and acts, zones of responsibility are changed into ethically neutral zones.

Yet everything depends on man's allowing the incursion of God's reality through the claim of the divine law to lead him to the very opposite view, namely, that the reality of the "You ought and therefore you can," and with it every other reality which is the basis on which he so confidently builds, is in fact an illusion. The illusion is that man is a subject who commands, and that he is thus at the center of his world, since it is he who draws its limits, making his own nature, the structure of the existence of the old man, the norm of all that can come to him as a claim or statement about his supposed possibilities.

When man protests against God's summons, therefore, he does so, not in the name of his reality, but in the name of the illusion he thinks is his reality. That he thinks he is fighting in the opposite direction, namely, against the fate of an unconditional demand and in the name of his own reality and aeon, is the sublime deception in the sin of illusion.

We have now achieved an important insight. The reality of man, e.g., his ethical reality, cannot be a systematic point of contact because it is a perverted and mythicized reality rather than the true one, because it is an illusion, and because it always isolates man. Only when God's prior reality is first disclosed to man does he learn to know his own reality.

This leads us to a first decisive conclusion. A given point of contact for revelation in the reality of man is impossible, since this reality arises only in faith, in revelation already enacted, and before that it can only be illusion in the sense described.

But this is not the end of the matter. It is still clear that God's law, or, more generally, God's claim, is addressed to the conscience of the natural man. This means again that it is addressed to man who by nature, by innate conscience, already has knowledge of an "ought," of obligation, of, e.g., the categorical imperative (cf. Romans 2:14f.). This is how man may be brought under obligation to God's law. And this still holds good even though the natural conscience and its categorical imperative are based on the "You ought and therefore you can," so that conscience builds a wall of partition between itself and God's law. Precisely for this reason contact between God's law and conscience cannot take place directly but only by way of a break. We shall now try to elucidate this.

If God as the author of the law makes contact with the natural "ought," if he compels the categorical imperative to adopt the command as a maxim of the human will, he does so only by challenging the natural "ought" and its illusion "You ought and therefore you can." The conscience is disquieted by God's law, not because it is aware of not having done, or having been able to do, all that it should, but because it begins to fear that it might be living in illusion and untruth, that its values and calculations are unfounded, that it is moving in the wrong direction. The result of this disquietude may be seen when the rich young ruler comes running to Jesus and falls at his feet (Mark 10:17). The presuppositions of his conduct were wrong. The confidence that his conscientious life would merit eternal life was misplaced. The unrest which impelled him was not just that he had not achieved perfection in his fulfilment of the law. He was now convinced that this fulfilment was itself defective (v. 20).

This, then, is the fear, the secret disquietude, of the natural conscience when confronted with the demand of God the Lord. If it acknowledges this demand—and of course it can refuse to do so—the presuppositions of its very existence are questioned. The categorical imperative itself withers when it is summoned before the new and unheard-of content of the law of God.

For if it makes it the principle of general legislation, it transcends its own presuppositions, namely, the presuppositions of the "You ought and therefore you can." What seems to be gain to the categorical imperative is its undoing. God has crossed the boundary or horizon of its existence.

How he does this cannot be objectified, since the creative Spirit of God who brings it about cannot be integrated into the structure of the "old" existence. There is here no mere perfecting of what is there already. Who God is and what he does to me cuts right across my theories about him. These theories relate always to the fulfilment of given beginnings. But here the very foundations of my existence are opened up to new creation, to the Creator Spirit. This is something that has not entered the heart of man and cannot be grasped by the natural man (1 Corinthians 2:9, 14). It has no place on his list of categories.

It is now evident that we cannot speak of a constant point of contact which may be located in the reality of the natural man and which forms a steady continuum. The grace which gives rise to the new creature makes this creature wholly new by giving him a new and true reality. If we speak of a point of contact, this is an improper, though necessary, term. It is necessary because we cannot understand the judgment God executes in his law if we do not see this law as the great disrupting of the presupposed illusion of the "You ought and therefore you can" which thus serves as a contact. For the essence of this judgment is that it takes from man the illusion of ability in which he has taken refuge with his pretended "ought." The judgment thus presupposes the illusory relation of "ought" and "can" (as a point of contact). By transcending this relation it shows itself to be judgment and leads through the valley of despair to radical revisions and reorientations. Thus God's judgment is in some sense a summons, a "contact."

The very depths of the ambiguity of man's existence are exposed here.

On the one side man's existence is always a self-entrenching against God which tries to break off all contact. In this instance the means of entrenchment is the ethical illusion of "You ought and therefore you can." In this illusion man himself is the subject who commands; he is autonomous. Clearly this illusion is possible only in a certain attitude. This attitude—and here we come back to our starting-point and complete the circle—is one of refusing to acknowledge God, to praise him, or to be thankful to him but of trying instead to stand on one's own feet (Romans 1:18ff.). In the present context this involves the illusion of not recognizing God's law as reality but of seeking a refuge in the illusion of autonomy, of the "You ought and therefore you can," against the reality of theonomy, of "You ought but you cannot."

On the other side man's existence means that at the very point where he deludes himself in the arrogant assurance of "You ought and therefore you can," he experiences the pain of "You ought but you cannot." The other aspect, then, is that at the very point where he began to invent God as a postulate and myth, as the metaphysical author of the "ought," and where God seemed to be adjusting only too smoothly to man's ability and supposed existence, man experiences God's assault on this existence in untruth. He learns that in this reality of his, God can live only on the cross, that he has to die on this cross, on this reality, and that there is a resurrection beyond this world and against it.

The final secret of the contact, then, is that God makes contact with man at the point where man digs in against him, at the nerve of man's curving in upon himself. The contact is thus a new creation and a new birth, and as such it is a transcending of the actual point of contact.

The miracle of the divine contact—and as a miracle it escapes all systematizing—is that God makes contact with man's attitude even though this is one of rejection and self-emancipation and even though there is in man no place which is independent of this attitude and which might serve as a neutral antenna to catch God's voice.

God creates anew the man to whom he speaks and whom he lifts up to sonship. We can know this event only as a miracle. For the miracle is characterized, established, and made relevant, not by how it happens, but by the one who performs it.

"Contact" is always an improper term because it secretly suggests the "how." It is used only for clarification. It should be written with chalk on the board and then at once rubbed out again.

If some of us are inquisitive like Nicodemus, and ask "how" these things can be, then the only possible answer is the "fact" that God so loved the world (John 3:4, 9, 16).

3. BIBLICAL MODEL: THE PARABLE OF THE PRODIGAL SON

The same dialectic of contact that we have seen in the philosophical model will also be found in Jesus' parable of the Prodigal Son in Luke 15:11-24.

Here again we note first the son's self-identity with which the father makes contact. It is his ontic privilege as a son, his specific biological relation to the father, which can lead him to ask his father for his inheritance, and which can cause the father to agree. Similarly, his reacceptance by his father when he returns penitent and empty-handed from the far country is essentially based upon the fact that the father is dealing with his son. The son has remained his son for all the alienation. His identity is not lost. His self persists. The father's action is unintelligible unless one notes this almost banal fact, the fact that on the son's departure and return the father makes contact with this persistent identity of the son, with this biological quality. This is the presupposition of all that the father does.

We are not dealing here with a pantheistic world-principle of love which embraces all creatures, which is indifferent to good and evil, to staying at home or going away, and for which there is no distinction between sons and servants or even men and animals. No, it is the son who returns. The ontic quality with which the father makes contact is a definite one that cannot be lost. It is biological sonship.

It is surely not a mistake to see in this specific relation of sonship, without which the father's action and contact would be hard to comprehend, a symbol of man's divine likeness. For this is what marks man off from other creatures and confers privileges on him. Only into man is the divine breath of life breathed to give him a part in God himself (Genesis 2:16). Only man is addressed by God as "Thou" (Genesis 1:28; 2:16f.). Other creatures can be described in terms of "It" (cf. ThE, I, § 690-1174; E.T. I, pp. 47ff.). It is because man is a person in this sense, called to partnership with God and qualified as a "Thou," that—again in distinction from other creatures—he can fall and break up the partnership.

For the same reason he can also be redeemed. The visitations of God in judgment and grace, the redeeming work of Christ, apply to him and not to fish in the sea or birds in the air. For the presupposition of judgment and grace is that their recipient can be addressed. Judgment and grace "contact" his being as a person. They presuppose that he can speak and answer. Although we shall differ from Emil Brunner in many respects, he is surely right when he states the elementary and almost platitudinous truth that only human subjects and not sticks and stones (can) receive the Word of God and the Holy Spirit.[8]

The item of comparison between the divine likeness and the parable of the Prodigal Son is that man as a son and partner stands in a position of privileged identity in his relation to God and all God's dealings with him have this presupposition as their point of contact. This identity persists through every stage—at home, abroad, and on the return home. It is constant and cannot be lost. Even extreme alienation is possible only within this framework. The animal cannot fall. Man can. This is a mark of his dignity. This is why, even in the depths, he is still a king, though a king with a broken sceptre and stained purple (Pascal). His humanity has an indelible character. It is the same through every experience. It is thus a permanent point of contact for all that God does in grace and judgment, for all that the father of the parable does when he entrusts the son with his inheritance and grants him forgiveness on his return.

Nevertheless, the situation is completely falsified if we regard this identity as a fixture in relation to which the stages of the relation between God and man are simply variations. This would be to introduce the Cartesian I, which develops in several variations of self-understanding, which can be the I that emancipates and alienates itself and then comes back to itself. In this case the identity is one which plays the role of a substance and which thus causes whatever happens to it to bring about accidental modifications of itself. The human self is on this view the constant point of reference and all the stages of its history are no more than modes of its self-understanding. In terms of the categorical imperative, the moral I of Kant maintains its identity and even the divine commands that come to it are only maxims which are integrated into the constant schema of its normative consciousness. We

---

[8] *Natural Theology,* pp. 23, 30. Cf. also Pascal's saying to the effect that only man knows his own misery; he is miserable in that he is, but he is great in knowing it (*Pensées,* No. 202). Hence thought constitutes the greatness of man (No. 158).

have seen, however, that the true situation is very different. When the commands of God, e.g., in the form of the radical requirements of the Sermon on the Mount, are accepted into the moral self-consciousness, the vessel that receives them is broken.

We are thus confronted with the paradoxical fact that we have to speak of an abiding identity, for otherwise we could not express man's answerability, and yet we cannot regard this identity as a fixture compared with which all that happens to it is mere variation, for otherwise we would deny to God's Word its creative quality and make it a mere cause of variations in self-understanding, a phenomenon of the immanence of the ego.

We thus have to use the concept of man's identity. But we cannot grant it normative rank. It is at most a conceptual instrument which is used only conditionally and provisionally. It thus shares the same fate as all the concepts used in theology. These cannot retain their original sense unchanged. They have to go through a process of dying and becoming. When they usurp normative rank—as "logos" did in the early Apologists—there is an alien intrusion into the kerygma and it suffers philosophical distortion.

The paradoxical way in which the concept of identity is used may be seen in the parable of Jesus.

If identity were straightforward (or nonparadoxical) the returning son could simply appeal to it. He would just have to make it known that he was the son to be able to make all the implied claims. But he does not do this. He makes it clear that he has forfeited the title. Twice we read: "I am no more worthy to be called thy son."

This formulation states the problem very precisely. It does not mean that he has ceased to be the son ontically. This would be absurd. It means two things.

First, he has lost the right to be "called" the son (even though he be it a hundred times). Calling implies recognition. A title carries with it an obligation. To do justice to the title of son, a son must act in a specific way in relation to his father. The son here has lost the title from this standpoint. He has not met the obligation. He has in fact contradicted it. This is the paradox of his identity. He is the son and then again he is not. For what is a son who has lost the right to be so called? Can he be defined at all ontologically? Possibly as a potential son who has the chance of retrieving the title?

That this is not so is shown, second, by the confession of the returning prodigal: "I am not worthy. . . ." He admits here that he can no longer appeal to his ontic quality as a son. He has lost the title in this second sense. For the title does not merely express an obligation that the son has to meet by acting as such. It also implies a claim that the son can make to the extent that he should be treated as a son. He has forfeited this claim. In giving up any appeal to the title of son, he expresses the fact: "I am no longer a son for thee; I no longer exist for thee." The father for his part confirms this: "This my son was dead" (v. 24). This means: "He was dead for me."

What is he ontically, then, apart from this "for me" or "for thee"? What is he "in himself"? We are back at the same question: How can a son of this kind be defined ontologically? What is a son who no longer exists for his father, who has dropped out of the relation that constitutes his being as a son? What is the point of any attempt to establish identity apart from that relation, to limit it to purely biological descent?

Now obviously the biological identity of the son (or the divine likeness of man) is a presupposition of the enacting of the story of the father and the son, or of God and man. But it is of no material significance for what takes place if it does not explain what takes place. It can do this, however, only if the identity of the son is going through different phases, if at the first it stands in the light of consciousness, then grows weaker and darker in the far country, and finally achieves its fulness again at the end in the identity of "bios" and "logos." Along these lines the son might appeal to at least his potential identity. But in fact he cannot do this, as we have seen.

Nor can we speak of mere variations of identity in which the constant subject is subjected to his changing self-consciousness. The one who is dead as a son is not a potential son. The idea of an entelechy that shrivels and then unfolds again, but is always centered on itself, is rejected here. The prodigal is not centered on himself when he is unable to appeal to himself. The dead man cannot claim that regard should be had to the seeds of possible development in him. If he is dead, he remains dead or has to be raised again. Raising again is the miracle that snaps the link between the old existence and the new.

Hence it makes no sense here to point to continuity or persistent identity. Nicodemus' question: "How can these things be?" being the impossible question of continuity, is rebuffed here too. Between the old existence and the new stands the miracle of a divine act, of the act of raising again performed by the Spirit. Between the two stands the miracle of the divine compassion, of a new creation.

Because new creation or a new creature is at issue (2 Corinthians 5:17; Galatians 6:15), identity is not just confirmed or filled out with the content of a new consciousness. The father in the parable does not simply act on a claim to the title of son, which in fact is not even made. Something completely new takes place that cannot be explained at all by the entelechy of the old existence. The miracle of raising again is performed on this identity. This miracle is not a creation out of nothing, for it is performed on the old self that still keeps its identity. Yet there is no discernible continuity between the former "living soul" and the present "life-giving spirit" (1 Corinthians 15:45ff.; cf. Ephesians 2:1, 5; 5:14).

It is worth noting that the very same problems arise in acute form in attempts to express the mystery of Christ's resurrection. This is a miracle which observes the gap between the old and the new. On the one side the risen Lord shows who he was, revealing his identity and displaying the marks of the nails (John 20:27). On the other side the continuity between what was sown in corruption and what rises again in incorruption is not demonstrable (1 Corinthians 15:39ff., 42).[9]

I *am* the son and yet I am also someone else. This is the paradox we need here, since identity has to be stated but is not self-evident. The best example of the paradox is Paul's "I live, yet not I, but Christ liveth in me" (Galatians 2:20). I am the one, yet not I, for something has happened that transcends the term identity but at the same time makes it unavoidable. For I need it to express the fact that I am the one upon whom this miracle of raising again takes place, and that this and only this is the miracle. Where there is to be seen in me no possibility of becoming new, where I am dead with no claim or chance of appeal, God has activated his own possibilities and the miracle of his fatherly mercy has taken place.

When we say that the concept of identity has been transcended but is still unavoidable, our interpretation of the parable has led us to the same result as did our study of the point of contact in terms of the philosophical model. In the latter we had to use the concept of natural conscience, expressed in the categorical imperative, to envisage the encounter between God's claim and our consciousness. But we saw that the vessel was burst open by the new contents it had to receive. Conscience cannot adopt in continuous succession the norms of autonomy and the unconditional nature of God's demands. There can be here no sequence of self-consciousness on the same level. Hence conscience itself loses its continuity.[10]

Surveying our deliberations, we note that our earlier statement that man's identity consists in his responsibility or addressability, while still true, is obviously limited. It is dubiously ambivalent. It is so because the term addressability might suggest that there is in man himself a possibility of bridging the gap between the old and the new, that there are in him elements of regeneration which would lead in a very different direction from that of a new creation. It is also ambivalent because it might suggest that what takes place on and to man can be subordinated to the interpretative schema of addressable man.

Either way we should have serious misunderstanding. God's creative Word does not belong to the schema of addressability. It transcends man's capacity for word. It creates all things new. God's Word creates its own hearer. It is seen by no eye, heard by no ear, neither does it enter man's heart (1 Corinthians 2:9f.). Between the old man and this Word there is no bridge or continuity. This Word cannot be integrated into something already there. It creates.

Nevertheless we have to refer to what is there if we are to bear witness to the miracle that God raises from the dead. Death is what forces the idea of

---

[9] On the significance of identity and continuity in the theology of the resurrection cf. the author's "The Resurrection Kerygma," *The Easter Message Today* (1964), pp. 59ff., esp. 101f.

[10] P. Tillich is aware of this dialectic; cf. his discussion of "experience of the spirit" and "ecstasy" in *Systematic Theology,* III (1963), pp. 111f.

identity on us. It probably could not be limited or challenged more severely than it is by this truth.

The identity of the prodigal is not to be sought in a demonstrable link between the various stages in his story. As noted, this could only produce biological identity, which is irrelevant to the story, to his reacceptance. The true secret of identity is not to be found, then, in a demonstrable link, for there is no such link. Possibly his self-alienation was indeed so great that the inhabitants of the village could no longer recognize him on his return; they could no longer "identify" him. The secret of identity is to be found, rather, not in himself, but in the mind of his father, in his father's love. Here and nowhere else it is preserved.

In this light we probably need to revise the usual concept of the divine likeness, which is constantly perceived, as in Thomism, in an indestructible continuity of human nature, so that it has to be insisted that man's nature is the same through the stages of innocence, fall, and redemption. If, however, man's real identity is hidden in the heart of God, this means that the divine likeness is not the sum total of man's demonstrable and persistent qualities. It is finally the image that God has of us.

This prepares the way for, and underlies, the christological concept that man's worth is not immanent; it is an alien dignity. What finally constitutes it is not demonstrable; it is an object of faith. Hence this dignity consists in what is done on and to us, not in us or anything we become. It consists in the fact that we are bought with a price, that Christ died for us (1 Corinthians 6:20; 8:11; Romans 14:15; cf. Deuteronomy 7:7; Proverbs 17:5; Malachi 2:11), and that our body is a temple of the Holy Spirit (1 Corinthians 3:16; 2 Corinthians 6:16; cf. ThE, I, § 817ff.; E.T. I, p. 165).

IX

Death of the Old Cartesian Self

1. INCORPORATION OF THE SELF INTO THE SALVATION EVENT INSTEAD OF THE REVERSE

We are confronted by the unique and paradoxical situation that we have to speak of the identity of the human self before and after faith, in birth and new birth, and yet this identity is not objectifiable and the question regarding it is continually erased. If, however, the self is relativized as a theme of theology, the self-consciousness is called in question as the place of theological orientation. Thus the whole Cartesian approach is challenged.

To the degree that this finding is in line with Reformation theology, as we shall try to show, Hegel is in error when he says that the Protestant principle establishes self-consciousness as an essential element in truth, and that Descartes is its true initiator. Hence we are forced to protest when a Roman Catholic interpreter speaks of Luther's pre-philosophical Cartesianism and of the central place of the ego in his theology (cf. Hegel's *Sämmtliche Werke,* 3rd ed. [1959], pp. 328 and 258ff.; P. Hacker, *Das Ich im Glauben bei M. Luther* [1966], p. 13). In fact Luther relativizes the self (cf. E. Schott, *Fleisch und Geist nach Luthers Lehre unter besonderer Berücksichtigung des Begriffs totus homo* [1928], esp. pp. 50ff.; R. Hermann, *Luthers These "Gerecht und Sünder zugleich"* [1930], esp. pp. 229ff.). This may be seen especially in his description of conscience and the subject of faith as a mathematical point (cf. WA, 40, I, 21, 12; WA, 40, II, 527, 9; WA, 40, III, 527, 33 and in exposition W. Elert, *Morphologie des Luthertums,* I [1931], p. 72; E.T. *The Structure of Lutheranism,* I [1962], pp. 81f.).

This banning of the question of the self and self-consciousness (or self-understanding) to the theological periphery confirms our criticism of more recent theology when it gives such prominence to the problem of appropriation. This criticism may be summarized as follows.

By making this problem central theology pushes epistemological and methodological matters to the forefront. These are necessarily oriented to the subject's structure of understanding, as classically illustrated in Kant's

Critiques. Discussing appropriation, they have to put the prior question of what is proper to man, of the self and its structure. We are thus trapped in permanent analysis of existence and introspective inquiry. This is what the Cartesian approach involves. Nor does it stop there. For this form of inquiry carries with it a filtering of the content of the kerygma. Only that which can become the content of my self-consciousness and which can be localized in the self and its categories is acceptable to my faith and understanding.

This fatal error can be avoided only if it is seriously admitted that the question of the self and self-consciousness can be relativized without dropping altogether the problem of identity. God's summons, the father's mercy, the work of the Holy Spirit, all reach back to my natural state. The miracle of the new birth is performed on those who have the first birth. Creative change takes hold of what is made. But being both "creative" and "change," it does not fit into the schemata of the old self nor submit to its conditions. It changes the schemata and the implied conditions.

"Who am I, and what can I thus appropriate in faith and understanding?" is not the real question. I learn who I am only from what happens to me and changes me. Not only does God's Word create the hearer. The hearer learns what he can hear only from this Word, not from preliminary self-analysis.[1] This puts the question of the self on the periphery where it ceases to be a real question and becomes a preliminary one in the true sense.

In this sense G. Bornkamm is right to take issue with Bultmann's attempt to present Paul's theology as anthropology, i.e., to expound it from the standpoint of self-understanding.[2] In opposition Bornkamm advances the cogent thesis that what Paul is concerned about is not a new self-understanding but a new history and existence in and through which I am taken up into the history of Christ.[3] "Christ in me" precedes "I in Christ." The self is determined by what has taken place, and does take place, on and to me, by what is thus before me and outside me. This is what Cullmann has in view when to the thesis that I must appropriate the salvation event he opposes the Pauline thesis that in faith I am integrated into the salvation history enacted preveniently outside me and before me.[4] H. Iwand expresses it most forcefully of all when, following Luther, he says that encounter with God's Word as a believer does not mean that I draw God and his Word into my existence but that I can break away from my self-enclosed being and through the Word be drawn into God and his power and possibilities, so that I am born again. Only the believer can stand over against himself in this way, whereas in the theology and philosophy of the nineteenth century history, facts, speech, thou, and person were all sucked into the self-consciousness.[5] This bold thesis of Iwand that the believer integrates his existence into God's

---

[1] Cf. Goethe's criticism of introspection (rather than action and experience) as a way to self-knowledge (ThE, II, 1, § 1386ff.).

[2] Cf. his article "Paulus," RGG².

[3] G. Bornkamm, "Mythos und Evangelium," ThEx, N.F. 26, p. 25.

[4] O. Cullmann, *Heil als Geschichte* (1965), pp. 100ff.; E.T. *Salvation in History* (1967), pp. 118ff.

[5] *Nachgelassene Werke,* I (1962), pp. 194f.

Word (not *vice versa*) and comes to confront the old, self-enclosed self sheds a new and unexpected light on the crisis of identity and on the theological status the question concerning it can claim.

2. POSSIBILITIES OF THE SALVATION EVENT INSTEAD OF POSSIBILITIES OF THE SELF

We are directed to the same crisis by another consideration to which the problem of appropriation necessarily gives rise.

If we venture to translate the term "appropriation" into the vocabulary of the NT we might say that it means hearing the voice of Christ as it applies to me (John 18:37). Now only he who *is* of the truth can hear this voice. What does it mean to *be* in the truth?

Of the many aspects of this being we shall select only one that is particularly pertinent here. It means to have dealings with the truth.[6] Now we have dealings only with persons. Persons cannot be manipulated. They are not at our disposal. They are not objects. I cannot take up any attitude I like to them. Persons with whom I have dealings advance a claim that can bring about a full subject-object interchange and incur commitment. I, too, am affected by these dealings. Thus to be in the truth is to let the truth work on us, to expose ourselves to it, to surrender to it, to let it shape our lives.[7] Only in this doing of the truth, which means surrendering to it and living with it, can it be manifested and have the chance to validate itself (John 7:17).

This confirms what we have been saying. Only if the validation of the truth takes place in dealings with it can appropriation cease to be a mere form of reflection which presupposes possibilities and methodological conditions in virtue of which the content of faith can be integrated into my self-consciousness. Now the possibilities are learned only in action, in dealings with the truth. The possibilities at issue here do not consist in potentialities of my own; they are the possibilities of the Word. For this reason we cannot calculate them. And since they are worked out on my own self by changing and regenerating it, the self, too, can no longer be calculated. Hence it cannot be a theme apart. The question of Nicodemus in John 3:4: "How can a man be born when he is old? Can he enter the second time into his mother's womb, and be born?" is falsely put, since it reckons only with possibilities enclosed in man's identity and produced by his entelechy. The further question: "How can these things be?" is tied to the same sphere. The answer of Jesus, however, presents the very different plane of events on which regeneration takes place, namely, the plane of God's possibilities. These cannot be calculated. They are like the wind; we do not know where it comes from or where it goes (3:8). In characteristic fashion we are then shown that incalculability applies not only to the moving of the Spirit, and hence to God's possibilities, but also to the one in whom these possibilities are worked out (the self): "So is every one that is born of the Spirit" (v. 8). The self

---

[6] Cf. K. Kerényi, *Umgang mit dem Göttlichen,* 2nd ed. (1961), pp. 4ff.

[7] Cf. G. Bernanos, *The Diary of a Country Priest* (1937), p. 109.

experiences itself, and therewith the possibility of new birth, as it claims God's possibilities and is thus "outside" itself, living God's history rather than its own, confronting itself. Identity can be stated now only in the confession that God's mercy has visited me. In this "me" the self has become the other confronting itself. This is important when we look back.

We do not look back on possibilities that the I realized or that were elicited from within (in Socratic fashion). The I was grasped by God's possibilities. Thus it ceased to be an independent theme. The question of identity between the old and the new self is thus pointless. In other words, when Nicodemus asks about continuity in his question: "How can these things be?" he is missing the real theme. The question which he puts fatefully affects the horizon of possible answers. In it regeneration can be thought of only as an evolution or mutation of the entelechy of the self. But if it is described as the experience of God's possibilities, which it really is, then the question of the identity and continuity of the self is transcended by the knowledge that the old self has to die, that it does die like the grain of wheat (John 12:24), and that we are buried with Christ by baptism into his death (Romans 6:4; Colossians 2:12). The one who is snatched from death and raised again is not interested in what was raised again; he is interested in him who raised it.

Adopting this view, faith is not saying something new about the old themes. It is presenting new themes. In relation to the themes, too, it is true that "old things are passed away."

3. IDENTITY OF THE FAITHFULNESS OF GOD INSTEAD OF OUR IDENTITY

A final aberration due to focusing on the self and self-consciousness must finally be described. We have said that this concentration leads to prior decisions about what God's Word can be. We now ask what kind of decisions these are. Thus far it has been said that they carry with them the postulate that the kerygma must be appropriated and that it must be subjected to the schema of self-understanding. What does this postulate mean for the understanding of God's Word? This is the crucial question these prior decisions raise.

To the degree that theological interest focuses on appropriation, faith becomes a matter of understanding.[8] Naturally it is a special type of understanding. Faith has its own niche in hermeneutics. Naturally, too, if faith is not to be a legalistic decree or implicit faith, it always involves understanding. The Spirit whose testimony leads to faith is a Spirit of understanding (cf. 1 Corinthians 2:9ff.). Hence faith and understanding are not to be sundered. The present problem is that they may be wrongly related, especially when the question of understanding, of understandability, and of the conditions of understanding is put under the rule of the Cartesian principle. For then it is assumed that what is to be understood is on the same plane as the one who is seeking to understand.

---

[8] Cf. Bultmann's title *Glauben und Verstehen* (*Faith and Understanding*).

It makes no difference in principle here whether the plane is the same because of a divinatory relation between the author and what is to be understood (as in Schleiermacher and Dilthey) or because of a thematic point of
comparison which orients the inquiry, as in Bultmann (GV, II, p. 216). Paul
Claudel uses the term "connaissance" for being on the same plane in this way.
He construes it as "con-naissance," being born together, living on the same
earth. When the question of understandability is integrated in this way into
the question of faith, all possible acts of appropriation are determined by it.
And since only the plane of the self is familiar, and thus constitutes the fixed
point of orientation, what can be understood and accepted as credible is
necessarily limited. It was perhaps because of this restriction of possibilities
that Goethe had a distaste for epistemological questions, or at least for their
primacy, complaining against Kant that he had gone too far; Goethe himself
never thought about thinking (cf. R. A. Schröder, ThLZ [1949], p. 532).

If the principles of understanding are the criterion of what can be appropriated in faith, then God's Word becomes at once an interpretation. For,
since understanding is a mode of interpretation, it seeks the Word of God
which is to be understood on its own level, and thus treats it as an interpretative Word.

Regarded thus, understanding itself blocks the way to what really counts.
For God's Word is not interpretative; it is creative. It brings forth being out
of nothing. It thus transcends all analogies and all supposedly common
planes. Unlike the Greek logos, God's Word is not related to a being which
it discloses; it calls what is not into being (Romans 4:17). It is active, not
interpretative. "He speaks and it is done; he commands and it stands fast"
(Psalm 33:9). Being an active rather than an interpretative or "apophantic"
word, God's Word changes the self rather than disclosing it. Hence it does not
permit of prior principles of understanding. As the existence which is being
understood is given up to death, so its principles of understanding are given
up to death.

This means, however, that continuity and identity in the change from death
to life are not to be sought in the principles of understanding which supposedly persist, nor in the human self as the Cartesian point of reference.
They are to be sought outside the self in the faithfulness of God, in the image
that he has of me, and in the tenacity with which he adheres to it. Identity is
riveted to God's Word, which remains the same both in our world of sin and
death and also in his world of life and righteousness (Iwand, *op. cit.*, pp.
200f.). Thus faith abandons the Cartesian approach and its axiom: "I am I."
It clings instead to the Word of him who proclaims himself as Yahweh: "I
am who I will be" (Exodus 3:14), the God of Abraham, Isaac, and Jacob.
Where the Word is active and creative, the only identity is ec-centric (*ibid.*,
p. 202).

Again, while an interpretative word can only speak in terms of validity,
the active and creative Word contains facticity. Regeneration takes place.
New being takes place. The prior facts of salvation history are posited thereby. Since the Word effected them, and the Word produces faith and relates

it to the facts, I cannot seek the mighty acts of God, the events and facts, outside the Word. Nothing is to be seen outside the Word and outside faith.

Hence faith does not have to reassure itself by first examining the facts which are its basis. It does not investigate before believing. If it does, it disparages the Word which posits the facts. It tries to establish a prior relation to reality on the basis of which it can prove that the Word has a real foundation and is in touch with reality. Faith can take this false path only if it grants normativity to the subject-object relation which underlies its "normal" understanding of reality. In this case the Cartesian I (the subject in the relation) again plays the part of a norm. Since, however, God's mighty acts are effected by the Word, I can have access to them only through the faith that this Word brings into being. Hence there can be no certainty concerning these acts apart from the Word and faith. One might also put it thus: The facts cannot be known by the old self; they are non-existent for its "mind" and "heart" (1 Corinthians 2:9).

This does not mean that faith discharges a kind of creative function by taking some of the raw material of history and giving it the religious significance of salvation history. If salvation history is not a datum for faith but the product of faith, deriving its significance from it, we are back in the sphere of Cartesian subjectivity, which can explain something that stands out from the raw state of facticity, that is laden with significance, only in terms of its own divinatory faculty, its interpretative power, or its charisma of investing with meaning. Indeed, it is only a nuance of the same thing, and not its opposite, when this kind of efficacious faith is understood, not as grounded in the constitution of the human self, but as imparted to the self as a gift of grace.[9] Many modern Cartesian theologians undoubtedly view it thus. But whereas Calvin says: "Take the word away and no faith is left" (Inst., III, 2), they reverse the saying: "Take faith away, and no word is left" (cf. Iwand, *op. cit.,* p. 207). When faith does not project meaning, all that remains is naked facticity which has no word or meaning. In Cartesian thought, then, the word, as an interpretative word, can only be the contribution of him who interprets even though he does not produce this on his own initiative but it is evoked by what is without, by the history that encounters it, unleashing its possibilities in the same Socratic manner.

In the face of all this one has to realize that the relation of Word and faith or salvation event and faith is irreversible. God's creative and active Word precedes both faith and the event which as the sphere of God's mighty acts is the content of faith. This Word is pre-existent in relation to all these things. It is this Word, not faith, which makes events significant, which constitutes them salvation history, and which thereby takes them out of the ordinary flow of events.

One might also say that this Word discloses itself to be God's Word, and to be relevant to me. Faith does not cooperate in this regard. If it did it would not be the opposite of good works. It would itself be a work. It would thus

---

[9] For a good nontheological example of this, cf. Theodor Lessing, *Geschichte als Sinngebung des Sinnlosen,* 4th ed. (1927).

lose its soteriological point.[10] In fact, however, it is the Spirit of God himself who confesses this Word, who bears witness to it as his own, and who causes the historical event to become preaching of God's mighty acts. Thus Peter's address at Pentecost makes it plain that the miracle of the Spirit unlocks the history. The history begins to preach. It points to the one who enacts it and causes it to be salvation history. Peter adduces known facts. But what they imply and express is not known. This is set forth when the Spirit validates them as the mighty acts of God.

When it is plain what the events contain as God's Word, they are marked off as a miracle from the rest of the historical nexus and they thus come to occupy a privileged position as salvation events, as the events of revelation and proclamation.

Ontically this separation entails the same breach of continuity as we have noted in the transition from the old man to the new. Hence there is no occasion to ask: "How can these things be?" in relation to salvation events from creation to the coming again. This question is possible only if a continuous nexus is illegitimately presupposed—a nexus whose continuity can be objectified. Identity and continuity are irrelevant as conditions of being if we have to do with a creative Word which summons being out of nothing and then destroys what has been summoned out of nothing, gives it up to death, and raises it up again.

The Word is the origin of being. Hence I cannot integrate it into the continuity of being or of an interpretative event. How can something be put in a system when it is the very basis of this system?

The problem that the natural orientation of our epistemological functions causes us to search the field of being, when what is at issue is its basis, is brought to our notice by the doctrine of the pre-existence of Christ (John 1:1; Colossians 1:16; Hebrews 1:2), i.e., the statement that everything in heaven and earth is created in Christ. This has the following implications.

If we remain within the framework of our epistemological functions, we seek Christ in history; we seek the historical Jesus. Now the Word was truly made flesh (John 1:14). He came into history. He can thus be documented historically. Even secular history comes up against the historicity of Jesus of Nazareth. Yet he cannot be explained by the continuity of historical occurrence or integrated into it. This is at least true of what is said about him, of what the witnesses proclaim concerning him.

Quite apart from possible accretions, we are thus faced with the question of this extra element which transcends historical continuity. The alternatives (already intimated) are as follows.

Either the extra element can be put to the account of faith, which finds

---

[10] From one angle Luther can call faith a good work (WA, 23, 29) and can even defend it as such against the papal view that it is a *habitus* (6, 206). Nevertheless, this has nothing to do with its real point, i.e., its function in justification. The justifying significance of faith does not derive from its reference to itself as a work but from its reference to its object; we are not to stay at ourselves or our faith but to crawl into Christ (10, I, 1, 126, 14).

significance in normal events. In this case continuity is re-established. It is the closed correspondence between a historical event and our self-consciousness. Salvation history is a history which is characterized by this correspondence. Take this away (take faith away) and ordinary facts remain.

Or—the second alternative—the extra element is due to the appearance of something qualitatively different in Christ which escapes the continuity of occurrence because it is its basis. In this case we have a creative Word which lies behind the world, which makes possible all human speech, and which cannot therefore be understood as a special instance of human speech. If the incarnate Word can be heard, if even the individual sayings of Jesus strike home to us, we come into contact with the origin, which is God's creative Word.

The same applies in relation to the resurrection message. Here again we are faced with the question of the extra element which does not fit into the continuity of the normal historical nexus. Is the witness to the resurrection just a commentary on Good Friday (Bultmann)? Is it a concept of faith rather than its basis (W. Herrmann)? Or do we have here the "Let there be" of the creative Word which leads down to death and up from it again (1 Samuel 2:6), so that the continuity of the historical nexus is broken?

This question arises everywhere. It is ultimately the question of the significance of the human self as a point of theological reference. Our findings are these.

1. The philosophical model of the categorical imperative and the biblical model of the parable of the Prodigal Son have shown us that the identity of the self (conscience, the younger son) has to be considered if the miracle of change is to be attested, but it cannot be objectified.

2. It cannot be objectified because what happens to me in the reconstructive Word cannot be fitted into my schema of understanding; it transcends this schema. As the philosophical model shows, my conscience is given new axioms.

3. Thus the Cartesian self cannot serve as the point of reference in theological thinking. It allows no place for death and resurrection. Faith relates me to what is outside me, and this is unreasonable to the concept of identity. In faith I confront myself. Old things have passed away.

4. In contrast, the Cartesian approach clings to the possibility which the interpretative structure of the human subject seems to offer.

5. Since the question of the recognizable identity and continuity of the self through death and resurrection falls to the ground, the two concepts are related to what is outside me. Identity and continuity consist in the faithfulness of God, who stands by his Word.

6. Since this Word is active and not interpretative, since it summons what is into life, it is prior to faith and understanding, "pre-existent." The correspondence of history and the believing self does not give significance to the salvation event; the creative Word establishes this correspondence.

The Cartesian I is thus given up to death. It ceases to be an independent theme or to tell me through its conditions of consciousness what the theme should be. It becomes a theme only in view of what has happened to me and of that from which I am rescued. It is relevant only as a point of reference for what takes place for me as death and resurrection, as the miracle of transformation. Nor is this its own history. It is the event of the Word (and Spirit) into which it is caught up: "I live, yet not I, but Christ lives in me," or "I am in Christ."

This is the paradoxical way in which the theme of my identity can be discussed.

4. EXCURSUS ON THEOLOGICAL DISCUSSION OF THESE QUESTIONS AND DEBATE WITH HERBERT BRAUN AS A TYPICAL REPRESENTATIVE OF CARTESIAN THEOLOGY

These findings mean that we have made some prior decisions about the question of God, i.e., the problem how we can speak about God's being and activity. At this stage of pre-decision we stand by the essential point that the creative Word alone has the initiative in positing the relation to the human self and therewith—for the self is this relation and experiences itself in it— in positing the self itself and self-consciousness. Thus far the dialog between Cartesian and non-Cartesian theology has concentrated on this theme. In conclusion we shall consider some typical positions in the debate.

When the young Barth made his famous remark that as theologians we have to speak about God but we are men and as such we cannot do so,[11] Barth's reason for the "cannot" differs from that of Kant, who dismissed the proofs of God and pointed out that God is not within the sphere of our experience. The real problem in speaking about God is that we do not control the God-man relation; it lies under the sovereign control of God. We are empowered to talk about him only as he turns to us and makes himself known to us. This means that our talk about him follows the fact that he speaks to us, and does so about himself. We have to recognize, then, both that we ought and also that we cannot, and we must give God the glory thereby. We give him the glory by not claiming that we have established the relation in which alone we can talk about him, but by leaving it to his sovereign freedom. (We are here applying what Barth says to our own problem.) If the impossible is thus possible, it is the miracle of his self-disclosure.

But does not Cartesian theology say the same? To be fair to it we must consider it in its earlier stages and not just its final upshot. Does it not have a concern for the sovereignty of God and his Word which its many champions have presented in many different ways? Where, then, does it break down? Although we have already put this question, along with the answers we think should be given, we might do well to illustrate and test it once again by considering the paradigmatic opposite of Barth's position, namely, that of Herbert Braun.

Now even in this very decided representative of Cartesian theology, theo-

---

[11] *Das Wort Gottes und die Theologie* (1929 ed.), p. 158; E.T. *The Word of God and the Word of Man* (1928), p. 186.

logical thinking does not begin with proclamation of the Cartesian self but with proclamation of the sovereignty of God's Word.

This sovereignty first manifests itself negatively in the fact that the believer does not produce of himself the self-understanding contained in his faith; this has come to him as an experience from outside the self and therefore he cannot control it.[12] This experience carries with it its uncontrollability and is thereby distinguished from the timeless truth of an idea.[13]

For, at least in principle, a timeless idea can be produced by me even if in the first instance it encounters me as an impartation from without. Lessing's truths of revelation show this. They are simply disguised truths of reason in mythical form. As such they can be controlled, in principle, by mankind. When they come by way of revelation from without, this is just a speeding up of access to them. Man does not have to discover them through a long process of inquiry. He has simply to grasp what he found earlier, or what was disclosed to him. Furthermore, once the truth of an idea is perceived, it is always ours. Braun distinguishes the kerygma of God's Word from the timeless idea in both respects.

First, I cannot find it myself; it is a contingent impartation. Even when it comes to me, it does not become my possession. It is always related to a new achievement of proclamation. It is always act and never habit. It thus retains sovereignty over me.

This means, second, that although what comes to me from without is connected with the history of Jesus of Nazareth, one may not infer that the continuity between the historical figure and the christological titles, or between the christological titles and my faith, is mediated historically. (There is demarcation from the historical as well as the timeless.) It is in believing self-understanding that I experience directly the evidence of what happens to me, so that conviction is determined, not by the mode of transmission, but by the cogency of what happens.

The self-understanding of faith thus belongs to a third category of phenomena. Relations to father, wife, or friends cannot be grouped under either idea or what is merely transmitted. They are phenomena that simply exist, and are valid and binding because they do so. Similarly, the self-understanding of faith as this is mediated by the NT is simply a happening, an event.[14]

In Braun's view the sovereignty of the Word of God expressed herein is remarkably close to the doctrine of justification in Paul and the Reformers. There is an element of "grace alone" here which rules out all cooperation on man's part. Braun's "precondition" in man corresponds to the Reformers' "cooperation." The sovereignty of God's Word is such that no precondition or prior achievement is required of man. The one addressed does not have to show his goodwill by philosophical adjustment to antiquity; he does not

---

[12] H. Braun, "Der Sinn der neutestamentlichen Christologie," *Gesammelte Studien zum NT und seiner Umwelt,* 2nd ed. (1967), pp. 243ff.

[13] *Ibid.,* pp. 275ff.

[14] *Ibid.,* pp. 276f. Cf. "Vom Verstehen des NT," *ibid.,* pp. 296ff.

have to show that he is addressable. The NT Word is certainly connected with ancient metaphysics, which it uses as a contemporary mode of expression. But it displays its sovereignty precisely by being its own proof, by relativizing ancient metaphysics as a purely historical instrument, and by thus holding aloof from it, so that we do not have to accept it as a condition of coming to faith.[15]

In this kind of approach, which stresses both the sovereignty of God's Word and also that of the self-understanding of faith to which it gives rise, it is not easy to see that the Cartesian starting-point is determinative, the transcendence of the I being reduced and theology becoming the self-consciousness of immanent fellow-humanity.

To grasp this, it is important to note that another concept corresponds to that of the sovereignty of God's Word and that the relation between them has not been clearly thought through. This is the concept of the sovereignty of the human self-consciousness.

We have seen that the sovereignty of the Word implies the rejection of any precondition or prior achievement on man's part. If we follow Braun and take the acceptance of ancient metaphysics as an example, a (justifiable) concession is made here to the sovereignty of the self-consciousness of faith. This is proclaimed as sovereign because it, too, can stand alone; the identity of its contemporaneity can be accepted. But the relation between the two sovereignties, that of the Word and that of the self, is not clarified. It simply insinuates itself as an axiom which directs reflection without being its theme.

There is not, of course, any cheating. It seems to be beyond question that the correspondence of the two sovereignties arises in relation to contemporaneity and identity. For here the two are surely interrelated. The sovereignty of self-consciousness is not grounded merely in the fact that justice must be done to the claim of modern man to maturity and autonomy. It is also grounded in the fact that God's Word is his Word that goes forth today, just as Christ is not just the historical Jesus but the exalted and present Lord. The very idea of the "addressing" of God's Word means that it comes to every time and situation, that it is contemporary, and that it makes the hearer contemporary to it. Yet even if the two sovereignties so obviously coincide at this point of the presence and identity of the self, at other points the position might be very different, and if so, the question at once arises which of the two takes precedence.

This is an acute question in Braun in relation to another precondition which raises far more problems than the obviously unnecessary acceptance of a metaphysics that the Bible simply uses as an instrumental mode of expression. We come up against this further example, for which the term precondition is far more doubtful, when we consider how far the circle of ancient philosophical expression extends, or, more precisely, where the boundary between God's Word and its conditioned form of expression is to be drawn. Are we to include in this relativized sphere the so-called "objectifying think-

---

[15] *Ibid.*, pp. 290f.

ing" which is for Braun a mode of theological deliberation which ignores man when it speaks about God? For this type of thought the world of God is a self-existent entity at a specific time and place.[16] Many parts of the NT, Braun thinks, treat God as self-existent and remote from man in this way. Thus faith in Hebrews 11:6 is believing that God is, and that he rewards those who seek him. This precondition that man has to satisfy is said to be a dominant theme in much of the NT.[17]

This precondition is simply the acceptance of Christian theism, which is regarded as one of the philosophical presuppositions that shape the form of expression in the NT and are thus irrelevant for faith. Theism and atheism are both adiaphora. No prior achievement is required of us here either. To be able to believe, we do not first have to move over from atheism to theism.[18]

Now there need be no debate, even with Braun, about whether a prior theism is demanded, as though we could believe only if we first accepted the existence of God in general. Obviously no such condition is imposed. We know of no serious theologian, at any rate in the Reformation tradition, who would hold such a view. It makes sense only if we accept the possibility of proofs of God, and this would make Christian faith no more than a special form of what admits of general proof.

There is also no point in advancing only epistemological arguments (e.g., those of Kant) against efforts in this direction, and doing so as though modern, post-Kantian man were particularly helpless in this regard. We are well aware that objections can be made to these theistic constructions from the standpoint of faith itself. The achievement of a supposed theistic standpoint, of a demonstrable existence of God, would make thought the instrument of direct certainty, and faith would simply become a secondary consequence, an indirect certainty. Sight in the form of the evidence of acts of thought would no longer follow faith but would go before it as a condition. One has only to see this to grasp the theological as well as the epistemological senselessness of a construction which would demand the precondition of a theistic standpoint.

The true question that we have to put to Braun lies elsewhere.

If it were simply a question of the prior acceptance of a self-existent God about whom objectifying statements can be made in abstraction from man, then we could quickly agree with Braun. But do we really have here a precondition or a prior achievement in his sense? Is this what is in mind in Hebrews 11:6. It certainly says that "he that cometh to God must believe that he is, and that he is a rewarder of them that diligently seek him." But this saying is part of a varied testimony to God's saving acts in history from Abel by way of Moses to contemporary witnesses. Faith in the active and self-attesting God of this passage naturally implies the fact that he is, and that the author of these events transcends what he does, that he is not imprisoned in it, that he stands behind it and above it, and therefore that he is. What

---

[16] "Die Problematik einer Theologie des NT," *ibid.*, p. 334.

[17] *Ibid.*

[18] Cf. "Vom Verstehen des NT," *ibid.*, p. 291.

is for Hebrews the implication of the witness of faith Braun interprets as its premise, and he then brings his accusation of objectifying thought which is based on contemporary metaphysics and which must be relativized, then, as a mere mode of expression.

The question which we have to raise is whether the (alleged) objectifying thought which posits a self-existent God apart from man is perhaps objectionable to Braun, not merely because it might imply a disposition prior to faith, but because it is always a general implication of faith. Is theism itself (irrespective of its philosophical variations and simply as the statement that "God is")—is theism itself to be rejected as a necessary implication of faith in God and hence of the self-understanding of faith? Braun would seem to be saying that it should be. This rejection is the real thrust of his theology.

But here the competition of the two sovereignties cannot be so smoothly settled as in the question of contemporaneity and the rejection of an ancient mode of expression. For the question is now urgent: Why does Braun reject the (allegedly theistic) thesis that a self-existent God exists, or, more precisely, why does he reject this altogether and not just as a precondition? The answer to this question necessarily shows that in him the sovereignty of self-consciousness is battling for primacy, and that a switch is made to Cartesian theology at this point.

The self-consciousness battles for primacy, for, on the pretext that in the name of the modern understanding of the world it cannot accept a transcendent reality, it is ready to think of God in terms of his affinity to man and hence to make him the partner in a relation whose conditions are laid down by the structure of the self-consciousness. The way that the self-consciousness attains to dominance is particularly serious because it is not according to any set purpose but arises latently and coincidentally. Its latency is favored by the fact that it seems to correspond to the sovereignty of God's Word when this Word comes to man as he now is, retains his identity, and peels off its own outmoded form of expression. At this stage it is still not clear that the next moment this man as he now is will be saying what corresponds to his self-consciousness and what, being theistic and objectifiable, is to be attributed to another situation of consciousness, so that it cannot be the experience of a materially binding statement which can claim the rank of kerygma. Here the very same arguments used to advance the sovereignty of the Word of God at the first stage can now violate this sovereignty. At any rate, this is true when the sovereignty of God's Word is taken to imply the sovereignty of a transcendent Author who is independent of the human consciousness.

How does Braun arrive at this priority of consciousness, at this rejection of any statement about God as the one who transcends consciousness and the world, whether this be meant as premise or conclusion?

First, as the example of contemporaneity shows, his concern is simply to offer a description of the modalities within which the encounter between text and hearer takes place. This is ordinary enough and hardly calls for criticism. One can indeed sympathize with his personal emphasis. There is nothing parrot-like here. Traditional formulae are not unthinkingly accepted. Every kerygmatic claim is tested critically to find out whether or how far it touches my existence and can really claim me. Thus we find in Braun the confession of very personal encounters with the text which bear witness to a desire for utter honesty and for the type of criticism that is ready to put the knife to the very roots. In setting forth his own hearing and understanding of the NT he is trying to discharge for his readers the same function as the fathers, as those who had a different and earlier understanding, namely, that of guiding them rather than laying down the law, that of making them independent and mature in their own understanding in a kind of Socratic release.[19]

The later domination of consciousness is not yet to be seen in this history of one's own self-consciousness in its encounter with the text. For the moment it is simply stated that this or that in the text may impress me, that the text itself speaks, that through all the critical questions and layers of historically conditioned modes of expression it shows itself to be alive, that it speaks to me and applies to me for all its difference from me.[20]

But what does it mean that something speaks to me? It can mean only that it is about me.[21] To be sure, not everything spoken about me is relevant (e.g., gossip or rumors). If the texts relating to Jesus Christ strike home, there is a particular reason for this. Even in the mythical code of the Christ-event I recognize an expression of self-judgment.[22] The imperative that comes to me here compels my conscience to agree, since I am not confronted with rigorist demands designed for moral heroes. Jesus fraternizes with the ethically and religiously disqualified. He thus takes from me the burden of perfection and lets me think critically about my good deeds. I learn from him that I use them to glorify myself, so that they are a source of hubris.

When we trust in Jesus, however, we can renounce this type of imperative. For life is based on what we do not do and do not have, on what we are given. A "thou mayest" encloses and sustains the "thou shalt."[23] My life is not built on successful action. I am sustained from outside myself. The "I should" and "I may" both come to me from the same external source.

It is here that the subtle switch to Cartesian thinking takes place. For while the "thou shalt" and the "thou mayest" are a legitimate reflection of the Christ-event in my consciousness, this reflection seems surreptitiously to be used and understood along the lines of a normativity of the factual. It becomes this to the degree that it seems to contain the definition of God, or rather the definition of what God is for me. He is the source of my being under impulsion,[24] of my "I should" and my "I may." Negatively one may see here once again a protest against the concept of a self-existing God abstracted from this relation to my consciousness and its impulsion.

The close relation of this thesis to Schleiermacher's introduction to *The Christian Faith* is astounding. For Schleiermacher God is the source of my

---

[19] Cf. "Vom Verstehen des NT," *ibid.*, p. 294.   [20] *Ibid.*, pp. 292ff.
[21] *Ibid.*, pp. 295f.   [22] *Ibid.*   [23] *Ibid.*, p. 296.
[24] "Die Problematik einer Theologie des NT," *ibid.*, p. 341.

feeling of absolute dependence. He is the source of a specific situation in the consciousness. The protest against a self-existent God as the possible starting-point of theology is a prototype of the arguments used by Braun. Schleier-macher is at great pains to show that the proper sequence is not to begin with a statement about God's existence and nature and then to show that we are absolutely dependent on this omnipotent being. The very opposite is the truth. In an analysis of the self-consciousness I find the feeling of absolute dependence. Since in the immanent sphere I see only mixed feelings of free-dom and dependence, I can postulate as the point of contact of this radical feeling of dependence only a transcendent factor which I call God.

The two systems converge, not in the transcendence of God, but in the definition of God in terms of consciousness and in the resultant principle that all statements of faith or statements about what is relevant to me must be capable of being presented as forms of my self-consciousness. Thus in Braun the starting-point is a specific situation in the consciousness, although now this is not a general aspect of existence but is caused by some-thing outside, by the reality which meets me in the text. God is the source of the impulsion by which this situation is determined in the form of the "thou shalt" and "thou mayest." In neither case, however, is a prior *Deus dixit* required. To say that God has spoken is simply to describe what I have ex-perienced in the way of command and upholding.

Braun's concern here is that there should be no preamble, no concession to a historically conditioned metaphysics of transcendence. This may be seen in the way in which the impulsion is worked out in detail. Any possible incur-sion of transcendence is guarded against. The situation, even if brought about from outside, is described as an immanent one. It also comes about through something immanent, namely, one's fellow-man. The sustaining "I may" and the imperative "I should" do not derive from the universe at large. They are set before me in concrete confrontations with my fellow-man. God is a spe-cific form of fellow-humanity. He is the source of the fact that I am both up-held and also committed in terms of my fellow-man. The climax of this line of thought is that man as man, man in his fellow-humanity, "implies God."

Since God crops up only in relation to the conditions of my existence (fellow-humanity) and to the reactions of my consciousness thereto (im-pulsion), he himself comes under the same condition. This may be seen from the fact that Christ, who represents what is without, submits to these con-ditions. In him the union of upholding and imperative, of "thou mayest" and "thou shalt," is grasped and stated for the first time (prototypically, Schleiermacher would say). This is the first cause which releases the possi-bility that the paradoxical unity of upholding and commitment may be be-lieved.[25] The relativizing of that which is without is undoubtedly implied.

For, first, this external element is, in Socratic fashion, only a trigger to release something that is already contained potentially in the self. Hence no miracle of new creation stands between the old creature and the new, between

---

[25] This is how E. Käsemann puts it in his essay "Blind Alleys in the 'Jesus of His-tory' Controversy," *NT Questions of Today* (E.T. 1969), p. 45.

the stage prior to hearing the Word and the stage after hearing it. The old creature and the new are related only as unawakened existence is related to awakened existence. They are simply variations within the one identity which remains at the vanishing point of all Cartesian perspectives.

Second, the external element is relativized in the sense that, as in Lessing, revelation comes down as a cause and impulse into the process of human consciousness,[26] but again it simply releases possibilities already present in man and is increasingly absorbed into the consciousness, so that it makes this autarchous and makes itself redundant. Once it has performed its task, it can go.

The objection that must be brought against Braun is precisely that he struggles in vain against the insinuation that he is making the content of the self-consciousness of faith an idea which can be reabsorbed into the consciousness. His argument is, as we have seen, that the gospel of "thou shalt" and "thou mayest" is a permanent and ever renewed address. But can he sustain this[27] when it is evident to what extent the external element of God or Christ is subject to the conditions of existence and its consciousness? Can the need for constant repetition and ever new proclamation mean more than that the self-consciousness is too pliable to retain what it has once grasped? Nowhere does he express more drastically and unequivocally the fact that God is enclosed in the conditions of existence than in the statement that anthropology is the constant element and Christology is the variable.[28] The Cartesian self is the foundation of this whole view.

In this unusually consistent paradigm of a doctrine of God within the framework of Cartesian theology—and it is as such that Braun's work is important—we see the direct opposite of our own affirmation of the significance of the creative Word in the relation of God to the self and the self-consciousness. We recall again the saying of Calvin: "Take the word away and no faith is left," and its converse: "Take faith away and no word is left." But on the latter view no divine author of the Word is left either, since apart from his implication in the self-consciousness he is only a self-existent and transcendent entity, a mere hypostasis of theistic metaphysics.

Braun as a Cartesian example has shown us how this fatal reversal comes about and how it carries with it in grotesque fashion a new and second-rank metaphysics, namely, an existentialism which swallows up God in the self as pantheism swallows him up in the world.

Now it is true that we cannot speak about God without also speaking about his relation to the world, the self, and self-consciousness. Thus talk about God is always secular. We cannot talk about God without the world being present in some way, not by unhappy necessity, but because talk about God is addressed to the world.[29] For the same reason talk about God is also existential talk. In a simple adjustment of Ebeling's statement, one cannot talk

---

[26] Cf. the author's *Offenbarung, Vernunft und Existenz,* 5th ed. (1966).
[27] Käsemann, *loc. cit.,* asks the same question.
[28] Cf. his essay in ZThK (1957), p. 368.
[29] G. Ebeling, *Word and Faith* (E.T. 1963), p. 359.

about God without existence and the self-consciousness being present in some way.

But why is this so? Everything depends on the answer to this question. It does not depend on the question whether one can speak about God only within these relations or not. For in fact the Bible does speak about God only within these relations. Nor can or does a theology based on the Reformation understanding of the Bible take any other view.[30]

If it is asked, then, why one can talk about God only relationally, the point is whether this is an epistemological question or a strictly theological one.

If it is the former, interest focuses on the conditions which the self provides to enable us to speak about God, e.g., the categories of pure reason or the postulates of practical reason (the conscience) in the Kantian tradition, or on the conditions which existence provides to enable us to speak about God in the existential tradition. These possibilities can understand God only as the point of reference for my impulsion, only as that which is relevant to me. The common point in the Kantian and the existentialist focus is that both interpret the concept of God as an implication of the self-consciousness.

A strictly theological understanding of the relations, however, is quite different. Ebeling hints at the essential point when he bases the necessity of secular talk about God on the fact that this talk is addressed to the world. The same may be said about the relation of God to the self or the self-consciousness. We can speak about God only within God's relation to these because God has resolved to move outwards, to disclose himself in his Word, and, in keeping with the very nature of words, to address this Word to someone. The person addressed is thus presupposed in God's Word. If it can be perceived by us as claim (*Anspruch*) and promise (*Zuspruch*)—Braun's "thou shalt" and "thou mayest"—this is because it has first been spoken (*gesprochen*).

It would be absurd, of course, to see in this fact of God's speaking a preamble on the basis of which we accept what the divine message says, believing it because it has been authoritatively validated and not because of the evidence of its content. At this point noetic and ontic statements are easily confused.

The ontic side is that the claim and promise of the gospel apply to me and find actualization within fellow-humanity only because God has spoken. He has not remained silent. His divine fiat has gone forth. To the man who was already summoned into life by his creative Word there has now come also the further Word of his revelation.

Noetically, however, I do not come to faith and to understanding of God's Word by following this sequence in my self-consciousness. Here the order is reversed. I begin with the result of God's speaking, of his leaving the silence

---

[30] This cannot be said so unequivocally about a Roman Catholic theology with its strongly ontological schema. Yet in view of the many nuances and complexities within Roman Catholicism, generalizations are hardly possible. Modern Roman Catholicism in particular (cf. Daniélou, de Lubac, Guardini, Steinbüchel and Rahner) seems to be breaking free from the monopoly of ontology and returning to personal categories.

of aseity. The result is that the Word comes to me, that it applies to me, that it is evident to me. Nor is it merely an interpretative word. It does not just explain my existence. It does not just mobilize its latent potentiality. It is a transforming, creative Word, a fiat. Only as it transforms me can it be perceived. Flesh and blood cannot help me here (Matthew 16:17). The eye of the old man does not see, nor his ear hear, nor does it enter his heart (1 Corinthians 2:9). The Word creates its own hearer. It does so by transforming him and making him capable of doing its will, so that he sees the validation of this Word as God's Word. The Word, however, refers him to God as one who is without, who works on him, who transcends his consciousness, who also transcends the world, and who enjoys a self-renounced aseity.

It may well be, then, that man, or fellow-humanity, implies God. But this is so only because God implies himself, the miracle of condescension is manifested, and the Word has been made flesh. This is precisely what we do not find in Braun. From the noetic path of faith—its beginning with the implication of God, with the relation of God to the self and self-consciousness—he has made an ontic deduction about God's nature, namely, that he is no more than the implication and relation, that he is absorbed by these, that he lives only in them. H. Gollwitzer[31] is surely right, then, when he argues against Braun that, while the encounter with God always implies a new self-understanding and new attitudes to one's fellows, this encounter as the first and basic thing should not be equated or confused with its consequences.

The real issue is what we understand by the Word of God. Is it simply a qualification of the impulsion or unconditional application that I note when the self and communication with my fellows are illumined by certain texts?[32] Is it a purely interpretative Word? Or by the miracle of the Spirit (John 3:6, 8) does it posit a new existence in creative power, namely, the existence of the hearer in which it can be received, the Spirit is given, I am impelled, and my fellow-humanity is newly qualified, so that I know my neighbor whom God seeks, for whom he mourns, whom he has bought with a price, and for whom Christ died?

This is the crucial question. The question of God himself depends on the answer. Along the lines of Luther's principle that a person does works, one might say that God's work in the form of his Word is characterized by the one who speaks it. Only because he is the Creator and Redeemer can his Word be creative and redemptive. The Word is qualified by the one whose Word it is. For he gives himself in it. He does not present himself in it as someone who in truth he is not. Nevertheless, he is more than his Word even and precisely when he pours out himself wholly and without reserve in it (Luther).

He is more in the sense that he decided to speak. The Word is one possibility, just as silence is another. His speaking is thus an expression of his

---

[31] Cf. his *Die Existenz Gottes im Bekenntnis des Glaubens,* 4th ed. (1964), esp. pp. 98ff.; E.T. 1965, pp. 81ff.

[32] The surprising affinity between Braun's thinking and Kant's transcendentalism should be noted in this regard.

freedom. The one who freely realizes a possibility is himself more than the possibility.[33] This thought is on the border of speculation, but it does not cross it. It is a thought that we have to think in order to interpret the creative element in God's Word and to differentiate it from a purely interpretative word. This element can be expressed only by saying that it is "his" Word; it reflects his omnipotence as Creator. But when we say "his" Word we have to characterize the "his" as distinct from the "Word," just as when we say "my God" we have to get back behind the "my" and to characterize it as freedom of choice, as the choice of grace in the strict sense, that God is "my God."

One element in the wonder of the gospel and the change it brings about is my wonderment that God wills to be "my God," that he turns to me in Christ, that he calls me by the Spirit, enlightens me with his gifts and keeps me in the true faith. This condescension cannot be taken for granted. It is hardly appropriate when I think of myself as an actual sinner. As such I stand before the imperious will of God who is the author of the law. His love is a miracle by which God overcomes his own law—the law of his imperious majesty.

Is it really speculation or mere metaphysics to recall this boundary of the divine majesty which surrounds Immanuel, God for me, God in relation to me, God in his relevance for me? (If so, then all that Luther said about the *Deus absconditus* should be challenged in principle as well as criticized in detail.)[34]

But why bother about this boundary? Because it is only by so doing that we can conceive of the historicity of God's condescension. For we have here the contingent miracle, which no one can postulate, that God wills to be my God, that what ultimately counts is that he is the author of the gospel and not of the law. If I do not grasp this as an act of God which he performed as distinct from other available acts or possibilities, if I do not grasp it as a resolve which sees the heart of God confronted with a choice, a decision, a question of self-overcoming (cf. God's "repenting" in Genesis 6:6; 1 Samuel 15:11, 35; Jeremiah 26:3, 13, 19; Amos 7:3, 6; Jonah 3:9; Romans 11:29), then the love of God becomes a mere idea. Along such lines we might arrive with Abelard at a principle of indifference which embraces good and evil. Or we might arrive at a self-evident principle in contrast to non-self-evident miracle or the facticity that has to be learned about.

The whole point of Luther's doctrine of law and gospel and his attempt to keep the two apart is to characterize the gospel as the miracle which transcends the logic of the law and its judgment. For Luther strict differentiation is a safeguard against any turning of God's condescension, or what Braun calls the paradoxical unity of "I should" and "I may," into a principle, a transpolar indifference. It sees to it that we are here confronted with

---

[33] The so-called *extra Calvinisticum,* to which we shall return later, expresses this truth.

[34] Cf. the survey in W. von Loewenich, *Theologia crucis,* 2nd ed. (1933), pp. 21ff.

an event, a contingent resolve, a merciful self-overcoming of God the Judge (cf. ThE, I, § 554ff.; E.T. I, pp. 95ff.).

There is need of the dark foil of the *Deus absconditus,* of God before his resolve, of the God of open possibilities, to make the resolve of God articulate and to help us to understand what happens as history, as the contingent event of the mighty acts of God. Only this can prevent theology from regarding what is recounted in the texts as the mere explication of an idea, from viewing the historical narration as mythical symbolism, and from allowing the self-declaration of God as my God to be sucked into the swamp of the possessive pronoun, so that God becomes a mere implication of my self-consciousness.

Hence I have to speak about God in himself, in his eternity and transcendence. I do not do this with speculative intent or out of metaphysical curiosity or epistemological naiveté. I consider God in himself in order to express in the form of praise the fact that God for me is a miracle of history which God has posited and which cuts right across my postulates. It is for this very reason that the eye cannot see it, nor the ear hear it, nor has it entered the heart of man.

If this is so, however, we have to face the statement which Braun finds so horrifying, namely, that "God is." Here if anywhere God's being is manifest with a facticity that transcends the consciousness and lies behind all its implications. The very sovereignty of the divine decision for encounter with man in an I-thou relation demands of man unequivocal and explicit declaration of the divine aseity. For this reason I-statements about God are part of this declaration.[35]

When we look back on the way which has led us to this position, it is clear that what we say about God's being in himself is not in any sense pre-theological, metaphysical theory. Ontically this dimension in God does precede his resolving upon the Word and his self-determination as my God. Noetically, however, this position is the final stage in reflection which begins with the actual encounter with God. It is thus a conclusion, not a preamble. It is the epilogue, not the prolegomena, to theology.

This is decisive. All theological statements are determined essentially by their place and rank in the whole system. Some are in the foreground, some in the background. Some belong to the prologue, some to the epilogue. To overlook this distinction is to level them all down and to give them the same emphasis, whether they are soteriological or cosmological.

The doctrine of predestination as Luther discusses it in the preface to Romans might serve as an example. Luther asks here why the doctrine is dealt with in Romans 9-11. He answers that the doctrine of justification has to be expounded first so that predestination can then follow at the right material place. For the experience of justification shows that mercy is granted to me without basis. There is no key to its distribution in the sense of distributive justice. When I then consider how it is that God wills to be my God,

---

[35] Cf. H. G. Geyer, "Gottes Sein als Thema der Theologie," *Verkündigung und Forschung,* 166, 2, p. 14.

how it is that he turns to me, I stumble across the fact of the incalculable, which is grounded in the divine resolve. This is predestination. Noetically, reflection on foreordination comes at a later stage. But this seems to contradict the ontic priority of foreordination to justification. A temptation thus arises to put predestination first, to make it a preamble. This, however, gives rise to speculation or metaphysics. I can reflect on predestination only when I know God's condescension in justification, only when I have met God as my God. I can reflect on it only in terms of God's heart, retrospectively. This is its right place if confusion is to be avoided. Luther's principle that everything has its measure, time and age is especially important here (cf. Preface to Romans, WA Bibel, VII, pp. 2ff.).

The situation is fundamentally the same in Calvin. Although efforts are made to portray him as the theologian of predestination, and to see in this doctrine the key to his system, it does not come first in his presentation. It comes under discussion only in soteriological connections which presuppose both God for me and also the church (cf. already the first edition of the *Institutes* in 1536 and P. Barth, "Die Erwählungslehre in Calvins Institutio von 1536," *Barth Festschrift* [1936], pp. 434f.).

The pre-existence of Christ is another instance. Ontically Christ is before all worlds, but this is no reason for putting his pre-existence first in the noetic process. It comes better at the end. It has to be asserted when we reflect christologically on our encounter with the message and person of Christ.

To sum up, the statement that "God is" means nothing very generally and in isolation. It takes on meaning from its context. The context shows whether it is a mere precondition that I must first accept, whether it is only on this assumption that the news that God has revealed himself and wills to be my God can be relevant. If so, it is simply speculative metaphysics. To a generation of practicing atheists who accept finitude or the death of God it means less than nothing. It will rightly be regarded as a historically conditioned postulate.

But the context might also show that the statement is made within an actual encounter with God, within his address to me. In this case it is a legitimate description of what takes place outside me and on and to me. God is not just the implication of my existence or the source of my impulsion. How can he be when the Word in which I am related to him does not come to my old existence but brings about a new birth and produces the new self (as a new creation)? Then I can say that God implies himself. In so doing, however, he transforms everything, so that the term "implication" is no more apposite than the term "point of contact," as we have shown above.

From various angles this encounter with the creative Word of God sets me before the transcendent. I encounter something over against me. Just as, regenerated, I encounter myself (cf. Romans 7:18-23), so I come up against God, who invades my existence in this way and creates a gulf between the old self and the new self. This experience of the other, of the transforming and regenerating Spirit, includes the reflective statement "God is." It includes it to such a degree that God's being has to be stated as something which transcends his speaking and turning to me, and his aseity becomes the horizon of faith. To those who take seriously the confession "my Lord and my God" and the relation of God to the self and self-consciousness, God's turning to them is a miracle. This is possible, however, only if God's being transcends his word and work, only if his word and work manifest the resolve in which God wills to confess me and to be my God.

Perhaps we may best indicate the proper place for the statement that God is by saying that it should not come first as a preamble (which would be metaphysics) but that it is a variation on the statement "thou art." This expression in the second person is the original form. But this form presupposes a completed encounter and the new existence. It shows thereby that the statement has its place within and not before the relation of God to the self and self-consciousness. Ontically, however—and this cannot be over-emphasized—"God is" precedes this relation, is independent of it, and would still be true even if the primal silence were to spread again, the eclipse of total obduracy were to come, and the relation of God to the self-consciousness were to be no more, so that only the stones would cry out (Luke 19:40).

X

New Creation by the Spirit: Anthropological Aspect. The Old and the New Self

1. SURVEY OF THE DISCUSSION

Although the doctrine of the Holy Spirit introduced in Chapter VII was not much in evidence in the preceding section, all aspects of the debate were thematically controlled by it. For the crux of the matter was the relation between God's creative Word and our identity. The problem of identity has emerged as the central point in the controversy between Theology A and Theology B.

Cartesian theology (A) finds the locus of continuing identity in the human self-consciousness. This is given "pushes" from outside (Lessing). But these are absorbed, reshaped and integrated by the self-consciousness. They thus modify the identity without removing it. Under the theme of the point of contact we then advanced in opposition to this view the thesis that God's creative Word does not work only within the existing carnal self but reconstructs this and introduces a new identity. The dialectic of this process may be seen in the fact that the ongoing identity of the old and the new self must be kept in view only to guarantee the thought that it is the I that undergoes the new creation, that it is the firstborn that is born a second time. Thus we do not have a creation out of nothing. We have a transformation of what is there. To this extent the old self that is there has to find a place in our thinking.

The ongoing identity which unites the old self and the new is thus an indispensable concept. Yet it is also a marginal one. As such, it cannot be expounded in this form, or become a theme of its own. Continuity between the old self and the new cannot be shown. Hence the schema of such identity cannot be sustained. It cannot even become the theme of an explicit question. For such a question would be equivalent to the mistaken query of Nicodemus how these things can be.

The identity of the old self and the new has only restricted actuality. It arises only when we look back on what has happened. Nor does this retrospective glance take a speculative form. It is interwoven into doxology; I am the one to whom this happened. The boast of Israel is that God's covenant, mercy, and transforming intervention did not come to a people that was greater than all others—quite the contrary. What was at work here was unmerited and to that extent creative love (Deuteronomy 7:7f.; cf. Luther at the Heidelberg Disputation [WA, 1, 354, 35]).

The true theme is determined by the whence of the new identity. The Word that comes to me and refashions me is not integrated into the self-consciousness. The self is integrated instead into the salvation event. The whence of the new identity is thus the faithfulness of God. The constancy of our identity is to be found in the image that God has of us. It is thus the object of faith, not sight. Hence it cannot be objectified. My identity is "invisible" (2 Corinthians 4:18). I have it only in sure confidence in what is hoped for, in not doubting what is not seen (Hebrews 11:1). For these reasons the Cartesian I dies. The common factor in all these deliberations is something that we are told in the story of Nicodemus. The Spirit brings new birth, new creation. To this extent he breaks the continuity with the old self.

Who am I, then, if the Cartesian self is dead? To whom do I say "I"? What do I mean by the spiritual I who is brought on the scene by the miracle of the Spirit? This question can no longer be directed to the marginal concept of the ongoing identity of the old self with the new. It relates to the source of the new identity. It is thus oriented to the Spirit who re-creates in the Word. It also involves the question how far this outside factor becomes mine, so that I can speak of "my" spiritual self.

We shall consider this theme from various angles, beginning with the anthropological aspect.

2. LETTER AND SPIRIT

The question as to the whence of the new existence confronts us first of all with the alternative of Spirit or letter. For the creative Word which brings transformation is distinctively Spirit rather than letter. What does this mean?

As presented by Paul (Romans 2:27ff.; 7:6; 2 Corinthians 3:6) the juxtaposition of letter and Spirit implies the antithesis of law and gospel. The law here is specifically the Mosaic law. But this represents the Old Testament as a whole to the degree that this is a stage of word and revelation prior to Christ.

The word as letter and the word as Spirit determine the human self in fundamentally different ways.

Reaching me as human letter, the word remains outside me. It is a self-declaration of God's imperious will, which is opposed to my will. When the word comes in this form, it affects the self as follows, according to Paul.

First, it stirs up the self-will that is opposed to God's will. In the protest against what is against it, self-will achieves awareness of itself and mobilizes itself (Romans 7:8, 11; 5:13; the preceding "death" of sin is not non-existence but a state of incubation).

Second, even if my inward man (Romans 7:22) accepts the will of God declared in the letter, even if the "spiritual" law (Romans 7:14) gains my inward consent, I do not escape the simultaneous intensification of my self-will. As the external imperative is a protest against my present state (expressed in its negative significance and form, as in the Mosaic law; cf. ThE, I, § 696ff., 2178ff.; E.T. I, pp. 149ff., 444ff.), so this aroused state, now identified as self-will, protests against the threat posed to it by the law. The law, then, divides man. It evokes partial affirmation and partial negation. As letter, the word wins half the heart, as Luther puts it. There thus arises the conflict described by Paul in Romans 7:20.

For this reason the letter does not give life; it slays. It nails me to the thesis: This is how I am. The force of this thesis can lead temporarily to mythological forms of expression. Since I cannot break free but become more and more entangled in the conflict, it seems for the moment that an alien power is at work in me, robbing me of my identity: I am no longer identical with what I will (cf. Romans 7:15). Hence I do not understand myself. Who am I if I cannot control my acts, if I do not do what I want to do, if I am no longer the subject of my acts? It is not I who am at work here. It is the sin that dwells in me (7:20). I am delivered up to the power of another law (7:23) which causes me to do what I do not want to do.

This mythical hypostatizing of sin as a possessing and seducing power apart from the self, however, can only be a brief interlude in a meditation which circles helplessly around the question who the "I" is that is surrounded by alien entities. For on the one side the will of God that comes to me in the law is alien and opposed to my own will; it is the letter of a text which is not "my" text. Yet I cannot reject it. Something in me (the inward man) has to assent to it. Then on the other side I am alien to myself. I no longer control my acts but am under another law. Yet I cannot remove myself from the scene as a mere object of deception. I must identify myself with the sin and self-will that momentarily seem to be an alien force. I must say: "O wretched man that I am!" (7:24). I cannot say: "Who will detach me from self-will, from indwelling sin?" I have to say: "Who will deliver me from the body of this death?" (7:24f.).

Third, the letter of the law is also characterized by the fact that it can only proclaim to the human self the claim of God without imparting a new being that will enable it to meet this claim. It confers no conformity to what it demands; it simply brings to light nonconformity. It does not create; it merely exposes. We learn from it the difference between what God wills and what we are; we see in it the bottomless abyss between God's being and ours.[1] By holding us to our old identity, the word as letter nails us to it.[2]

---

[1] Iwand, *Nachgelassene Werke,* IV, p. 156.

[2] All this is, of course, only one aspect of the law, the so-called *usus elenchticus.* We shall have to discuss the other aspects later. We shall also have to consider the Pauline interpretation of the law as that which nails and slays us in relation to the more positive exposition of modern OT scholars such as G. von Rad and H. J. Kraus. For bibliography cf. Zimmerli in ThLZ (1960), 7. For the doctrine cf. also G. Ebeling, "Erwägungen zur Lehre vom Gesetz," ZThK (1958), 3; R. Hermann, *Zum Streit um die Überwindung des Gesetzes* (1958); R. Bring, "Der Mittler und

This, then, is the background against which the gospel stands and which sets in relief the word as Spirit as distinct from the word as letter. In contrast to the word which tells us what we do not have is the new and creative word which gives us what we do not have. This breaks the chain which binds us to the old identity and gives us a new identity.

In the hearing of the gospel the Spirit confers the new birth. When Paul describes this transformation into a new identity, he echoes the ancient promises of the impartation of the Spirit (Ezekiel 11:19; 36:26; Jeremiah 31:31ff.). Here already in the OT we find the antithesis of letter and Spirit. The law will stop affecting man merely as an external law from outside. It will stop being just a signpost and not "power in the bones" (Luther). The Spirit of God will renew the heart and grant conformity with what we ought to do, so that we can will what we ought to do. The stony heart will be changed into a heart of flesh (Ezekiel 11:19). We not only *should* walk in the commandments; we *shall* walk in them (36:26f.). The renewed heart will do spontaneously what ought to be done. The will of God no longer comes to it as a letter from outside. It is engraved in the heart, so that the demand "Know the Lord" is superfluous; the knowledge is already there. God has established a bridgehead in the heart. The presence of his Spirit there—and with it his own presence—enables us to meet him. This presence is new creation.

The idea of presence expresses precisely what the new element in the new being is. I am transformed. My heart is freed for encounter, for conformity. The will of God is not written on stone tablets in alien letters. It is engraved on my heart as my own program (2 Corinthians 3:3). Yet the idea of presence also shows that there has been a coming from outside. I myself am just the place where the Spirit of God has alighted in order to reconstruct me from within (1 Corinthians 3:16ff.; 2 Corinthians 6:16).

This creative work of God on me is a process which has all the marks of growth. With God's victories we also see our own defeats—the quenching of the Spirit (1 Thessalonians 5:19).

There is increase in faith. Not for nothing is faith compared to a grain of mustard seed (Matthew 17:20). It can grow (2 Thessalonians 1:3; 2 Peter 3:18; 2 Corinthians 10:15). We can ripen in faith (Ephesians 4:13ff.). Faith can be strengthened (Luke 17:5).

The process also includes defeats in which we do not yield to the Spirit. The command "Quench not the Spirit" implies that we may resist his work. If we are to burn in the Spirit (Romans 12:11), we must also take into account the possibility of putting out the flame. The demand to be filled with the Spirit means that we might also be, or become, empty (Ephesians 5:18). If we are to be strong in the Spirit of God, the apostle also knows the possibility of weakness, of being destitute of the Spirit (Ephesians 3:16). If we are not to grieve the Spirit of God, this means that we might hold aloof from him, or indeed that he might hold aloof from us (Ephesians 4:30).

---

das Gesetz," KD (1966), 4, pp. 292ff.; R. Iwand, *Nachgelassene Werke,* IV, pp. 165ff.; W. Elert, *Zwischen Gnade und Ungnade* (1948), pp. 132ff.

The fact that there is a process in which God alights in us and inwardly transforms us by his Spirit means that I can never express the new being into which I am transformed in terms of a self-identifying "I am." To speak thus is to misunderstand the new being as a habitual state. This is a misunderstanding because it means that I look away from the Spirit's work on me, from the process, and consider instead the alleged result, myself. I look away from the "becoming" which is required of me to a supposed "having become." I mistakenly understand myself as the new man and regard myself as the visible fruit of the Spirit.

The very fact that "sight" enters in here should pull us up short, for this is a process of faith.

In fact the introversion to which the misunderstanding of the new being as a state leads is the real crisis into which the young Luther was plunged before his Reformation breakthrough (so that he became a lifelong opponent of the idea of a habit or state). For introspection means self-observation with a view to ascertaining spiritual growth and the rise of the level of infused grace. This curving in upon oneself in the form of unceasing self-analysis means that we are constantly aware of failure and are thus brought to despair. There is no doubt but that the doctrine of infused grace leads to introspection, since grace is no longer understood as the divine favor (a quality in God) but rather as a quality in me, an adapted holiness.[3] The principle of "by grace alone" cannot free us from introspection when grace itself is understood as a habitual quality. Thus the decisive breakthrough for the young Luther was not just that he perceived the truth of "by grace alone" but that he was led by Staupitz to the crucified Lord and hence to an experience of salvation effected on him from without.

Since the work of the Spirit is a process into which I am called, and since the self effected by it can never be a theme in its own right, we face a distinctive barrier if we want to say: "I have the Holy Spirit." This phrase is never used in the Bible, although we find it in some holiness movements. Why should we not say this? The reason is that this phrase would express the inversion already noted and focus attention on my "I am." The same difficulty does not arise if we are content to say: "Through the Holy Spirit I have a Father in heaven or a Savior." For in this case I look away from self to the one who reveals himself to me in fellowship.

There are two important reasons, the one biblical and the other dogmatic, why the Holy Spirit should be viewed in his work on me rather than in the qualities which result from this work.

(1) The biblical reason is that the Holy Spirit lays hold of me in the form of faith (Galatians 3:2, 5; 5:22) and that it is only thus that he produces the fruits of the Spirit (Ephesians 5:9; Philippians 1:11; cf. ThE, I, § 254ff.; E. T. I, pp. 56ff.). The new man manifested in these fruits is not the

---

[3] The same is true in holiness movements such as those of Osiander and O. S. von Bibra, which focus on the state of having become righteous (cf. ThE, I, § 494ff.; E.T. I, pp. 82ff.).

goal of the Spirit's work (which I should concentrate on) but a by-product.[4] I do not put this by-product in its proper place if I keep my eye fixed on it. This is clear when it is realized that the means by which the Spirit takes possession of me is not an infused habit but faith. Faith focuses on the one to whom it owes its very existence. It focuses on the one on whom it is set. It focuses on what has happened to it, or, better, on the one who has met it in this happening. It would be absurd for faith to believe in itself or to gaze upon itself as introversion implies. The believer has in the strict sense forgotten himself. The subject of faith is a mathematical point. When faith is seen as the way in which the Spirit lays hold of me, as the Spirit's surrogate in me, this immunizes us against viewing the new being in terms of a habitual quality.

It might be objected that the NT constantly speaks of the Holy Spirit entering into or filling a man (cf. Luke 1:41, 67; Luke 4:1 [Jesus himself]; Acts 2:41; 4:8, 31; 6:3, 5; 7:55; 11:24; Ephesians 5:18), so that we have here a gift which might seem to be characterized as a conferred quality (Luke 11:13). Again, however, the principle applies that a person does deeds. Now in a sense the Spirit is God's work (cf. the granting of spiritual gifts—1 Corinthians 12:8ff., 28ff.; Romans 12:6ff.). Nevertheless, it is striking that these gifts are never detached from the giver. They are always his qualities and not those of the man who supposedly has them. As it is the person of God who characterizes these works of the Spirit and is present and at work in them, so the gifts for their part bring into contact with God, set up the relation to him, and are actualized only within this relation.

The story of Simon Magus is instructive here (Acts 8:9ff.). He has magical qualities which in many respects are like the spiritual gifts of the disciples (cf. the Egyptian magicians and Moses in Exodus 7:11, 22). He is regarded by those around him as the great power of God (Acts 8:10). But as he regards his magical powers as his own, so he thinks the gifts of the apostles are an aptitude which can be acquired (at a price). Peter reacts by pointing him to the relation between the gifts and the Word which is at work in them. If a man does not hear and accept the Word and the one who speaks through it, he is outside the sphere of spiritual gifts. Gifts are bound up with the attitude of the heart toward God (Acts 8:21). If they are to be called qualities, they are not qualities of man in the sense of conferred powers, but qualities of this relation between God and the heart. They come and go with this relation. They cannot be kept any more than the manna of Exodus 16:16ff. They are received according to the measure of faith, i.e., of the turning of the heart to him who gives them.

The same point arises when Jesus is asked by what power he does his mighty works (Matthew 21:23ff.; Mark 11:28ff.; Luke 20:2ff.). The question is legitimate, for the works alone do not show whether what is doing them is God's Spirit or the black arts. Miracles can also be done with the help of Beelzebub (Matthew 12:24ff.; Luke 11:15ff.; Mark 3:22). Hence the question gives evidence of spiritual awareness. One has to know how the

---

[4] Cf. G. Dehn, "Der neue Mensch," *Theologia viatorum* (1939), p. 75.

one who does the works stands before God to be able to say whether one is dealing with spiritual gifts or demonic powers. Spiritual gifts are qualified by their giver: God or Beelzebub. Furthermore, this qualification cannot be detached from the attitude of the doer's heart to the giver, i.e., from what we have called above the relation between them.

In this light too much should not be read into the many metaphors which depict the Spirit as a gift or a power or symbolize him as fire or storm (Acts 2:2f.). These metaphors are misunderstood if they are regarded as depictions of psychological processes, even though these be induced or imparted from without. The work of the Spirit points to the one who is at work. It is simply his presence in an active rather than a static sense.

This implies (a) that the Spirit, as in the systematic formulation of the doctrine of the Trinity, is equated with God or Christ, so that in some soteriological contexts the terms are interchangeable. Thus when Christ says "I in you" and "the Spirit in you" in John 14:17, 20, the meaning is identical. Similarly the Lord is the Spirit (2 Corinthians 3:17). During Christ's absence the Spirit represents Christ until he comes again (John 14-16). As the second Adam Christ is the life-giving Spirit who brings about resurrection from the dead (1 Corinthians 15:45).

This understanding of the Spirit's work also implies (b) that God's presence in the Spirit is tied to its constitutive mode, namely, the Word. The presence of God is the presence of the Word.[5] The Word calls me out of myself. Its subjective correlate is faith focused, not on the self, but on the object of faith. Faith does not relate the salvation event to the self-consciousness but vice versa. In faith I am integrated into this event; I participate in being in Christ.

We thus maintain that spiritual gifts are not to be understood in isolation as a mere "being in" man or as the nature of the new man. They simply describe God's activity, his presence in the Word, to which self-forgetting faith responds and corresponds. The gift of the Spirit and the Spirit as the giver are one and the same. The relation between the two aspects of this identity is correctly maintained if priority is accorded to the giver, if the gifts are understood in the light of the giver. This alone rules out the misunderstanding that endowment with the Spirit, or the sanctification of the new man, is not just a result of the presence of God by the Spirit as faith perceives it, but that it is the goal and faith is simply a means to reach this goal of the new being.

Since God's activity is his presence in the Spirit, by the Word, and to faith, we do best to say that the Spirit is God in action. This makes it impossible to view the results of the action (e.g., spiritual gifts) in isolation from the action and the one who acts.

---

[5] The controversy with the radicals caused Luther to uphold the close connection between the Word and the Spirit: "God will give no one the Spirit without the Word and the preaching office. . ." (WA, 17, II, 135, 22); the Holy Spirit does not work "without the external office and the external use of the sacraments" (43, 187, 7). God's internal work (the Spirit) is thus brought into special relation to his external work (the Word and sacrament).

(2) The dogmatic reason is that, especially in the doctrine of the Trinity, the Spirit has constantly been related to the active presence of God. This is not the place to prove this in detail. We shall simply take a single instance, which is perhaps representative. The focus in the trinitarian formulations is on the unity of the Spirit with the Father and the Son. This in turn has two implications.

The first (a) is that the Holy Spirit is spoken of in personal terms. He is the third person of the Trinity. This rules out the "dynamic" misunderstanding which would lead to the error that the Spirit and his gifts are ours, or that the Spirit is a material entity (fire and storm) which enters into me. Since the Spirit is a person he can encounter me in the same way as God or Christ can.

From this we can see once more that the phrase "I have the Holy Spirit" is erroneous if it denotes possession. I have the Spirit only in the same way as I have the Father and the Son when in faith I can say "my God" or "my Savior." Since, however, there is the possibility of "dynamic" misunderstanding in the case of the Spirit, the phrase should be avoided. The personal concept introduced by trinitarian teaching into the doctrine of the Spirit is a formal aid to such avoidance.

The second implication (b) of the equating of the Spirit with the Father and the Son is that he is brought into juxtaposition to us. This is done polemically when he is described as not created or made.[6] There is thus an infinite qualitative distinction between him and created impulses in the creature,[7] i.e., spirit as psychological, if induced, dynamism.

To be sure, the Spirit does work as an imparted power. But the effect—and especially the by-product—is not to be confused with the being at work. This would be just as wide of the mark as confusion of the Word of God with an aggregate of letters and sounds. Naturally the Word does take the form of letters and sounds. But these are only a medium. They are only a mode of manifestation which helps it to be perceived. Its true essence lies in what it says, from whom it comes, and to whom it is directed. Similarly the Spirit is not to be defined in terms of his mode of manifestation (as power or gift) but in terms of who (not what) he is. As the third person of the Trinity he is the active Lord, or the Lord in action.

3. SPIRIT AND IDENTITY

To look back for a moment, we began by asking to whom do I say "I" and what do I mean by this "I" when regeneration and new creation have been effected by the miracle of the Spirit. How far is that which reaches me outside as a creative Word also my own in relation to which I can say "I"? Since this theme of the I also implies what determines the I, i.e., the transforming and re-creating Word, we have investigated this Word in regard to the alternative of letter and Spirit contained within it. The letter, representing the

---

[6] Cf. the Athanasian Creed: "Not made, nor created, nor begotten, but proceeding."
[7] Cf. CA, I, 6 (confessed in opposition to the Valentinians and the followers of Paul of Samosata).

law, is always another law. It sunders the I and drives it into a corner (Romans 7:17ff.). But the Spirit, in contrast, is the presence of God in my heart, God in action to create conformity, so that I will what I ought to do (Jeremiah 31:31ff.).

To this transformed heart I can say "I" and speak of my own heart. We have seen, however, that this is possible only in a specific way. I have to keep in view the one who transforms me with his Spirit. I have to see myself as the temple or tabernacle in which he dwells. Thus the "I am" is constantly crossed out, or, better, supplemented by "Yet not I, but Christ liveth in me," or "I live in Christ" (Galatians 2:20). For it is by God's grace that I am what I am. Hence I can say "I am" only in praise and thanksgiving. It is false, a false "I am," if said in boasting. In such a form it is folly (Romans 1:22; 1 Corinthians 3:18). Even when Paul hypothetically, pedagogically, and incidentally does boast and say "I am" swaggeringly, he confesses ironically that he has become a fool in so doing (2 Corinthians 12:11).

What this boasting means, and how it falsifies the "I am," may be seen clearly when we ask what happens if the Spirit is viewed only in his effects or gifts, i.e., as the one who imparts a material quality. This degeneration of the statement "I am" is opposed by the assertion of the personal nature of the Spirit in the doctrine of the Trinity. Since the Spirit stands over against me, I cannot simply say: "I have the Spirit." I must be content to say: "Come, Creator Spirit." "I am" now denotes the relation which constitutes my new being. By the Spirit I am in Christ. By the Spirit Christ is in me. I say this in praise and thanksgiving.

We must now undertake a final test by trying to define as precisely as possible how that which the Spirit does to me and in me is related to what the letter cannot do. Some antitheses will help here.

The letter, as we have seen, provokes the conflict of Romans 7:14ff. by coming to me as an alien law from without. On the one side self-will and self-assertion are brought to light. On the other I have to admit that the law is right. The whole self is unable to assent or to surrender. Two spheres of the I are left in wearisome dialog and mutual conflict.

The opposing correlate of the work of the Spirit is easily discerned, for the first of the fruits of the Spirit in Galatians 5:22 is love. Whereas the heteronomous letter does not enable me to fulfil the law, since it clarifies and intensifies but does not overcome the contradiction in my existence, the love which is produced by the Spirit is called the fulfilling of the law. Why is it a fulfilling?

In contrast to the conflict of the divided I which is the work of the letter, love is a total movement of the I.[8] When I love it is not because I have to

---

[8] In this sense it solves the conflict caused by every imperative (e.g., Kant's) and not just that of the law of Moses. The distinctive work of the law is to shed a negative light on this conflict (as opposed to an optimistic one like that of Schiller). Paul regards the conflict negatively because he sees man essentially in his relation to God, to whom he is both totally indebted and also totally guilty. The partial

but because I will to. Promptitude and spontaneity are of the essence of love. Commanded or forced love that is contrary to inclination is a self-contradiction.[9] My heart is undivided in love for God.[10] As Luther says, the man who is transformed by the Spirit wills and acts with a cheerful and willing heart, not in servile fear or childish cupidity but out of a free and adult heart (Commentary on Romans, ed. Ficker, II, 166, 3).

The Spirit accomplishes conformity to God by releasing love in me so that I will what God wills. What the I that is freed by love can do in this new situation is done from the heart and not against it, voluntarily and not under the compulsion of an alien law. For I do it to God (Colossians 3:23). Thus loving action does not have to be impelled by an imperative.[11] It is determined by the indicative of the miracle of the Spirit toward me.

Love as the fruit of the Spirit and fulfilling of the law raises a controlling question regarding the statement "I am" as we have interpreted it.

If I am whole in love, not subject to an alien command working through me and against me but willing the law myself, does this mean that here a point is reached where the ability to love might be called a quality, my quality? Does not the statement that I love, that I do so undividedly, and with a prompt and cheerful heart, have to imply that I am the subject of this love, and that it is thus my love?[12] If so, is not our polemic against the idea of habit, and against the erroneous meaning of the "I am" in the new man, called in question?

In truth, however, I cannot regard myself as the subject of love, or regard my ability to love as a quality of my own, even a quality imparted by grace. Here again my ability to love is always related to that by which it is released and on which it is founded, namely, that I am loved first, that my love is simply a reflection of this, and that it finds its life in it (1 John 4:19).[13]

Our own conduct toward God is under the law of the echo which governs human reactions. The law cannot command me to love God because the command of an alien law produces the opposite of love, i.e., irritation. To a God who seems hostile I am hostile. Only when I see God's mercy in Christ and accept it in faith does God become an object worthy of love. This is a precise description of the man who is renewed by the Spirit. I can be a loving

---

obedience that might be rendered in the conflict is, then, no real satisfaction of the divine claim. Not to fulfil the whole law is not to fulfil it at all (Galatians 5:3). Cf. ThE, I, § 1354ff., 1493ff.; E.T. I, pp. 281, 299ff.

[9]Thus the great commandment of Jesus (Matthew 5:44; 19:19; 22:39) does not order love. It demands insight into what neighbors and enemies are for me and what attitude I "automatically" take to them when I consider God's attitude to me (Matthew 18:32). Cf. ThE, II, 2, § 450.

[10] Cf. on this Holl, I (1932), p. 179.

[11] On the significance of imperatives in NT exhortation cf. ThE, I, § 465ff.; E.T. I, pp. 74ff.

[12] Augustine's well-known interrelating of love of self and love of God is the classical instance of this approach (cf. ThE, I, § 1712ff.; E.T. I, pp. 337ff.).

[13] For a fine statement of this truth cf. Apol. CA, III, 7ff. We shall simply develop this here.

subject only because God is a lovable object. The two statements are insepa-
rable correlates.

The correlation is so structured, of course, that the statements are irreversible. God's love is not a recognition and honoring of, nor a reaction to, the
fact that I love him and to this degree fulfil his law. My ability to love is the
reverse side of the fact that God is a lovable object for me.

The term "lovable object" makes it clear that my own love and my ability
to love are inadequately described if they are simply viewed as a mode of
reacting. For reacting suggests that I resolve to draw conclusions, to show
myself thankful, and hence to do something, i.e., to love God. The love of
God made possible by the miracle of the Spirit is not to be integrated into
a subsequent process of reaction. It is given to me at once and totally as the
reverse side of the fact that God is presented to me as a lovable object. I cannot say that he is this without being posited along with him as a loving subject. My ability to love is the reverse side, not the result, of God's loving me.
It is so, at any rate, when I see God's love in Christ and accept it for Christ's
sake by faith.

We thus have here a strict analogy to righteousness. My righteousness is
simply the reverse side of the fact that God is the one who makes righteous
(in an active righteousness rather than the distributive righteousness of the
law). Here again my own righteousness is not just a reaction to his, as
though I were purified for fulfilment of the law by justification. It is the correlate of God's righteousness on my side.

Thus, as I have to say: "I am the righteousness of Christ," or "My righteousness is that I am right with God, or he has made me right with him,"
so I must say: "My love for God is simply his love for me, its subjective
correlate."

This ultimate statement is the answer to our controlling question. Even
the statement "I am the one who loves" cannot describe my love, or my
ability to love, as a quality. It can be uttered only in thanksgiving and in
praise of the one who first loved me. The "I am" as a statement about what is
mine is also a statement about what I am not, about the relation into which
I am called when God is present with me by his Spirit and makes me his temple. In the strict sense "I am" on the lips of the new man can never denote
what is inward, only what is outward. This is the paradox of the new existence.

4. FLESH AND SPIRIT

The question what I mean by the spiritual I that is brought into being by
the miracle of the Spirit, what new identity is at issue, is still the point when
we inquire into the relation between the flesh and the Spirit. Both in different
ways determine the identity of the I. For this I is determined by either the
one or the other. As concerns flesh, this alternative arises only in a specific
area of meaning, namely, when flesh has for me normative rank, when it is
the orientation of my existence, when carnality is thus the sign of this
existence.

To avoid misunderstanding, we should not overlook the fact that the term has an innocuous sense with no normative rank, and that in this sense it is not an alternative to the Spirit. This is clear in Paul, even though the antithesis of flesh and Spirit is important for him. Flesh may simply be used to indicate the locus of man's empirical existence. "After the flesh" Christ was a shoot of David's house and of Israel (Romans 1:3; 9:5). "After the flesh" Abraham was the forefather of the Jews (Romans 4:1). Means of sustenance and support during the span of earthly life are carnal (Romans 15:27; 1 Corinthians 9:11). Like the body—the two terms are synonymous in such passages—the flesh is also afflicted by scars, wounds, and sicknesses (2 Corinthians 12:7; Galatians 4:19f.; 6:17).

The concept of flesh or fleshliness loses its indifferent character at once, however, when it is used to characterize a particular mode of conduct. Thus my walk may be "carnal" (2 Corinthians 10:2) when I boast (2 Corinthians 11:18) or list values in my empirical life to which I appeal. For in such a case I am building upon something external and corruptible which has been set aside and which can be no real foundation (Philippians 3:4; Galatians 3:3). Circumcision is an example. It affects only the periphery of a man, not his heart. It is thus an error to try to build on a fleshly thing like this.

This false mode of carnal conduct does not strictly *lead* to this false basis of existence; it *derives* from it. My flesh-dominated being gives rise to the appropriate conduct and causes me to "mind" (Romans 8:5) carnal things. Because what has its origin in the flesh is itself fleshly, its follows a fleshly course, i.e., it behaves carnally (cf. John 3:6) and is subject to death (Romans 8:13).

This does not mean that carnal conduct simply follows the impulses. It may do so, since this is one of the forms by which I bind myself to empirical values (Galatians 6:19-21; 1 Corinthians 6:9). But it may also be conduct which is grounded in such lofty values as secular wisdom (1 Corinthians 1:26), or legal perfectionism (Galatians 3:3), or privileges of birth (Philippians 3:4). Even intellectual and moral things can bear the mark of the carnal. Flesh here denotes what is corruptible, provisional, and transcended. This is why everything that belongs to its sphere of power must end in death (Romans 7:5).

In its normative aspect flesh is the opposite of Spirit. The two are mutually exclusive alternatives. When a man is touched by the creative power of God's Word and experiences the new birth, a change of dominion takes place as he passes from determination by the flesh to determination by the Spirit. Existence is given a new whence and a new whither. Hence the question of identity again arises.

Once more we cannot assert continuity between the two stages of determination. We are confronted by the break of the creative miracle of the Spirit which does not permit us to view the "how" of what we receive in faith.

Such a continuity could be demonstrated only if the spiritual man were a kind of second nature which might be given me by exercise or habit and which could thus be regarded as a variation on the original status. This continuity might be possible if the new being were an improved version of the old, distinguished from it only quantitatively (cf. Luther, WA, 18, 632, 3ff.). But this is not so. The Spirit of God slays, conquers, and subdues the old existence (Romans 6:3). That which is born of flesh, and can "mind" only the flesh, can only resist the Spirit. There is enmity between the two (Romans 8:5f.; Galatians 5:17). No transition between them is possible. Nor is the enmity merely a stage in a process which embraces both dominions.

The discontinuous transformation which separates the two dominions involves a complete reorientation of life. Existence based on the flesh brings forth quite different fruits from that controlled by the Spirit (Galatians 5:19ff.). There is a completely different self-understanding. To use a Kierkegaardian phrase, existence controlled by the flesh has an absolute attitude toward the relative. It bases the ultimate on the provisional. It thus achieves pseudo-spirituality. It uses the flesh for what only the Spirit can provide. The flesh is thus blind to its limitations. The spiritual man, when he looks back on his prior life in the flesh, alone can see the true relation between the two (cf. Luther, Romans, II, 170, 7f.). The Spirit renews me and destroys the identity with my past. Contemplating God, I am no longer the man I was (Isaiah 43:24f.; 44:22). Thus understanding of myself in terms of the flesh binds me to my empirical being, to determination by my past.

Involved here is a change in my relation to time. I am delivered from bondage to the past. This bondage means identification with the things in the past that burden me (Psalm 25:7). I cannot break free from what I have done, from what I have done amiss, from what I have made myself. It may be that guilt torments me. It may be that I boastingly exaggerate the past. It may be that I will not accept it and in Promethean fashion try to fling it from me. But I cannot break free from it. I am no less bound by the future too, since I move toward it in anxiety (Matthew 5:25), fear, and hope.[14]

For the spiritual man, this continuity with the past and the future is broken.

The continuity with the past is broken, for, in the forgiving mind of God, I am no longer the man I was. He does not remember my sins. I am Christ's righteousness. Being set over against himself, the believer is set over against his past. "I forget what is behind me," says Paul (Philippians 3:13). This forgetting is fitting praise of God's forgetting. To dwell on the past, to "rake about" in it, is to yield to the pseudo-spirituality of the flesh. It is to be more divine than God and to attribute to him things that he has long since put out of mind.

Continuity with the future is also broken, for, whereas the flesh concentrates on empirical existence and thus faces the empirical incalculability of the future with fear and hope, the spiritual man, having been transformed, knows the category of miracle, of God's possibilities, and of God's care which leaves no place for human care. The incalculability of the future has lost its terrors for the man who once regarded it as beyond control but now realizes that it is under the control of God.

---

[14] G. Ebeling, *Theologie und Verkündigung,* 2nd ed. (1963), pp. 86ff.; E.T. *Theology and Proclamation* (1966), pp. 86ff.

Thus the change from determination by the flesh to determination by the Spirit is in fact a radical change in lordship. The necessary renunciation of all attempts to establish or even to seek any continuity between the two lordships does not have to mean that the change is abrupt, that it is complete the moment it takes place or that it does not have the characteristics of growth. We find such concepts in some holiness movements which want to see certain infused qualities in empirical existence and which are thus at root still thinking in carnal fashion (cf. ThE, I, § 494ff.; E.T. I, pp. 82ff.). What they overlook is that the spiritual man not only believes what is invisible but is himself invisible and can only be believed. The new man determined by the Spirit is still in process of becoming. This becoming, however, is not to be understood as the continuous development of an abiding entelechy but as the warfare and controversy in which the Spirit gains ground over the resisting flesh and completes the work that has been begun (Philippians 1:6). Assurance of this completion does not rest on the fact that a seed has been given and will develop. It is grounded in the promise that it is the Spirit who gives life (2 Corinthians 3:6), that he will help our weakness (Romans 8:26), and that we already enjoy his first-fruits (Romans 8:23).

If we know that the work of the Spirit will continue and will be finished, we do so only in promise and hence only by faith with its ordering to what it does not see. There are, then, no continuities whose premises we know and which we can evaluate. In the sphere of the promise, however, we can speak of the growth or becoming of the new man.

In this sense my history is not the self-development of my entelechy. It is the history of the Spirit with me. It is the history of his increasing "occupation" which will end eschatologically with God as all in all (1 Corinthians 15:28). The work of the Spirit which has begun on and in me is a pledge (*arrabōn*), an instalment, and a seal of what is granted to me by promise (2 Corinthians 1:22; 5:5; Ephesians 1:14).

The nature of this history of the Spirit's increasing occupation might be misunderstood in two ways.

First, one might see it from the standpoint of specific, partial, and quantitative change. Now it is true that there is a quantitative warming of the stone which lies in the sun.[15] But this is not the real point at issue. The real point is that the goal of fleshly existence is set aside. Centering on oneself is over. The temptation remains. The possibility still confronts me. But it can no longer overpower me. It has lost authority over me. We have died to it (Romans 6:2; 7:6; 1 Peter 2:24). We live in another dimension. We are in another service and under another Lord (Romans 6:15ff.). Existence in the flesh still afflicts us. We still know anxiety, care, false hope, the impulse of

---

[15] Along with this metaphor for increase in sanctification Luther uses many other expressions (cf. Romans, II, 76, 30ff.; 101, 20; 267, 2ff.; cf. ThE, I, § 1097ff.; E.T. I, pp. 226ff.). To speak of being made increasingly righteous is perhaps legitimate as a confession that the Spirit's pledge is being fulfilled and that the empirical man is being brought into conformity with the new man. This is perhaps what Martin Kähler had in view on his deathbed when he said that now there was nothing more standing between God and him (Anna Kähler, *Martin Kähler, Theologe und Christ* [1926]).

nature and spirit. But we no longer fall into these hands that grasp after us. We do not assent to these things. We are no longer ready to live in their name. In that sense we no longer fulfil them.[16] This question of direction, of a new course, is always the urgent one. It thus pushes into the background the question of quantitative progress, at least as an independent theme.

The second misunderstanding is related to the first. If I focus on quantitative progress, the empirical man and his visibility are given a thematic rank which they should not have. The subject of faith then becomes, not a mathematical point, but an extended area which is brought under scrutiny. Faith itself then becomes a work whose intensity, constancy, and height are continually measured. Thus the new being is subjected to the same curving in upon itself which is a mark of carnal existence. In faith I now no longer believe in the Lord who works on me by the Spirit. I believe in faith itself, i.e., in faith as the manifestation of a new holiness. Thus faith becomes a psychological property rather than a spiritual property.[17]

The identity of the new man again lies outside man himself in the fact that God is faithful and that he acknowledges the pledge of the Spirit given to us in promise.

Thus the new existence does not depend on its own constancy or impregnability, and even less on the signs of progress it gives. The outward symptoms are those of feverish restlessness. The earthen vessel in which we have the treasure of the new being is always close to breaking (2 Corinthians 4:7). We have troubles and are afraid (4:8). We are given up to death. We are chastised. We are sorrowful and glad (2 Corinthians 6:9f.). We are sifted by trials (Luke 22:28; 1 Peter 1:6; James 1:2, 12).

The agitation of the struggle in which the spiritual man experiences his birth-pangs, the alternation of victory and defeat, of resistance and surrender, is encircled, however, by the constancy of a faithfulness which will never fail us and by a preservation which cannot be affected by that which makes the empirical manifestation so confused. Faith in Jesus Christ remains the same through all the alternations of doubt and trial and experiences of strength and weakness. It remains unchanged because it is not grounded in its psychological quality as experience or its ethical quality as a work. It is founded upon the One in whom it believes, in the Lord and his faithfulness.

There is thus constancy and steadfastness only because the essence of the spiritual man lies outside himself. His citizenship is in heaven (Philippians 3:20) where the fluctuations of fever cannot touch it. His name is registered in heaven where it is safe from the attack of all the powers that seek to expunge it (Luke 10:20).

This sounds Platonic, but is not meant that way. For in this context heaven

---

[16] Note in this regard Luther's characteristic distinction between "doing" and "fulfilling" (*facere* and *perficere;* Romans, II, 182, 6 and 28).

[17] Cf. Luther's distinction here between "spiritual" existence as my being before God and "psychic" existence as my being before myself (E. Schott, *Fleisch und Geist* . . . , p. 56).

is not a transcendent place. It means that God's heart is inclined to me. His being is open ("opened heaven").

But how can I express this in terms of the identity formula "I am"? Who am I? Am I subject to that fever? Am I the one whose name is written in heaven? Or am I both? We are thus confronted by the problem we have met many times before: that of identity and how it is to be formulated.

Here again, of course, the "I am" is controlled by the history which overtakes me and into which I am taken up. For I am the man I am before God. My form of being is thus expressed in a relation. I am the one who is taken up into this relation.

When I say that "I am taken up," I mean the "I am" of the feverish carnal existence which has been overtaken by the miracle of the Spirit. But when I say that as one who has thus been taken up I am in a new relation to God, I mean the "I am" of the heavenly citizenship with its rights and protection.

Thus I am both. I am the old man and I am also the new man, just as the prodigal who returns home from the far country is both the alienated son and also the one to whom as such the right of return and the attributes of sonship are granted. If, however, I have to say where is the true locus of what I am, then I can only answer that it is in the second "I am." I am the one who is apprehended (Philippians 3:12), for whom what has grasped me heretofore, with all the enslavements of carnal existence, is now past, and who is now oriented to the one who has apprehended him and whom he in turn apprehends.

Luther expounds the change in identity in terms of the judgment with its question of identity. When conscience accuses me, it forces me to say "I am" in identification with my carnal self. Thou art thy past, says conscience. Thou art what thou hast done, what thou hast behind thee. But the heart which sets its trust in Christ objects to this accusation of conscience: Christ died for me; he bought me with a price; he made satisfaction; he made my sins his own (identifying me with himself) and he made his righteousness mine (identifying himself with me). Hence I am righteous with the same righteousness as he is. My sin, however, did not affect him. It has been swallowed up in the depths of his infinite righteousness. For God's heart is greater than ours. Who, then, will accuse God's elect? Who dare identify them with themselves, with their carnal existence? A change of identity takes place which we might formulate as follows. I am not the one whom the accusation of conscience has in view when it identifies me with my past. I am the one whom God protects against the accusation of my conscience as an "associate" of Jesus Christ. I stand at his side in the judgment. I am covered by his name.

Always, then, I am the one I am for God. In my carnal existence I am the one he accuses in the law while my conscience defends me (God as prosecuting attorney and the heart as attorney for the defense). Then I am the one he defends while my conscience accuses me (the heart as prosecuting attorney and God as the attorney for the defense). The change of identity finds expression in this alternation of accusation and defense.

The unity in this change does not lie in me, or at any rate not in demonstrable fashion. It lies in God, although here again it cannot be demonstrated. For just as I cannot say what constitutes the unity of law and gospel (cf. ThE, I, § 604ff.; E.T. I, pp. 117ff.), so I cannot say how God seeks me while accusing me, or fetches me home while visiting me. If I were to try to show and establish this, I could do so only by means of a speculative teleology of the law which robs it of the unconditionality of its accusation. The unity of the change is grounded in God. The only basis of my ongoing identity lies in faith in his faithfulness. I cannot see or formulate the abiding "principles" of this faithfulness, for the term "principle" is only a necessary invention of the intellect which is meant to grasp the abiding element, and it not only fails to do this but threatens even by raising the question to be untrue to the theme of faith (cf. again Luther in Romans, II, 44, 3ff.).

Faith itself can only accept what it is by God's defense—a defense for which it can find no reason and which simply comes as miracle with no basis in divine principles. The believer "is" the one to whom the righteousness of God's Son is ascribed and from whom his old existence is taken away.

Luther is thus consistent when he describes this new identity as identification with Christ, or comes close to so doing. By faith in Christ we are so united to him that with him we become as it were one person that cannot be sundered. Hence I may say that I am like Christ, and similarly Christ says: I am like that sinner who depends on me. Faith unites to Christ in the same way as a husband is united to his wife (WA, 40, I, 285, 24). Thus God and we are in one and the same righteousness. When he says: "Thou art righteous," then I am righteous, for we are what he makes us, so that we are in him and his being is our being (WA, 5, 144).

When I say that I identify myself with Christ's righteousness, and hence with what God's creative Word makes of me, this is poles apart from the monistic ontology that the phrases might suggest. For I can make this identification only in faith, i.e., only as I believe the Word of God which promises me all this and tells me that I am now another man for God in Christ. Since my being is a being in relation, since it is only a being before God, this being another for God is in fact and (in the strict sense) ontologically another being. It "is" another being. As Iwand puts it, to have faith means not to seek our new life in ourselves but in Christ, yet in such a way that we regard this new life, not as his life, but as ours (Iwand, op. cit., IV, p. 155).

This casts further light on the development of the new man, on the process of his coming into being.

It has already been shown that this becoming is not the unfolding of infused habitual qualities. The spiritual man lives by what is assigned to him in the Word, by the alien righteousness of the Son of God. Any idea of self-development, however spiritual, is thus mistaken. On the other hand, the thought of becoming raises certain problems when we say that the spiritual man is determined from outside and that his becoming is the gradual victory of the Spirit or the increasing occupation of his carnal existence by the Spirit.

How can we conceive of this without falling back again into a quantitative and carnal mode of thought? Is not the attributing of the alien righteousness of the Son of God definitive? By God's grace I am what I am in virtue of the promise and pledge of the Spirit. I "am" it (1 Corinthians 15:10). How can I become it any "more" than I already am it? How can there be a comparative of this type of being? Is not such a comparative just as absurd here as in being married? How, then, are we to understand the "becoming" of the spiritual man? If the idea of becoming, of the conflict of the Spirit and the flesh, is implicit in the Pauline concept of the pledge, and if Luther also accepts it, even though he too is a theologian who stresses the givenness of the new existence and the creative promise, then this becoming must obviously be understood in a very specific way (cf. Luther, WA, 38, 568; 57, 102, 16; 17, II, 116, 32; 7, 336, 31).

In fact, it is. The assignment or impartation of a new being is definitive to the extent that God's Word: "Thou art righteous for me (in Jesus Christ)," can never be excelled. I am accepted and I cannot be more accepted. In this dimension of our spiritual existence there can thus be no becoming. But did we not say that it was the old carnal existence which experienced this divine address, and that its occurrence on the old I was important in the question of identity? At once, then, the problem arises how the definitiveness and absoluteness of the divine address works itself out on the old existence. If we are now servants of righteousness and therefore paradoxically free (Romans 6:18), this cannot be a matter of indifference for the fulfilment of my existence (Romans 6:1ff.). To put it more pointedly, the definitiveness with which this existence is re-established must work itself out in such a way that in its manifestations and fulfilments this existence grows into what it already is.

This is where Paul's interrelating of the indicative and imperative is theologically important (cf. ThE, I, § 465ff.; E.T. I, pp. 74ff.). For Paul's imperatives always refer back to what has already happened to me. They are not oriented to a future form of existence which is still to be achieved. They relate to a determination of existence which is already past, and they insist that I for my part now do what has already been done on me. You are risen with Christ—seek then those things which are above; you are dead with Christ—mortify then your members (Colossians 3:1ff.). There is at this point real growth into the new existence; there is real conflict in becoming.

But how? A plausible answer is that faith is just the initial act and that the real thing to which it leads is this growth, the final maturity, the ultimate congruence between the empirical man and the spiritual man. In this sense, the new form of life is an end in itself, while Christ and faith are merely means to this end. This is the answer which many theologians give.

There is certainly good reason to fear that in this we might still carnally cling to the empirical man and come under the fatal control of self-centeredness, of curving in upon oneself. The theological conceptions which regard Christ as a power that enables us to achieve what the categorical imperative alone is unable to bring about are there before us as a warning.[18] But can we escape their logic? How are we to prevent the spiritual form of the empirical man surreptitiously becoming the real theme again?

Luther offers the decisive insight which keeps us to the proper theme and prevents progress from filling the foreground of our vision. Progress is natural, he thinks, when we are like the stone which lies in the sun. But this progress is a continual new beginning, a return to him who establishes our existence, to the Word that brought us to faith, to the baptism in which we died to the old man. Progress, then, is not a form of self-development. It is a placing of myself under that which continually determines my life, under the Spirit who has taken up the battle against the flesh. When I place myself under that which establishes my existence, I give the Spirit room to work and let the imperative which is spoken over my life become strong. A return to the beginning which did not imply giving the Spirit room and the progress which results from this would be nonsensical. It would be *deficere* rather than *proficere*. Commencement without progress is regress (WA, 4, 350, 14ff.).

Progress is emphatically not an end in itself. It is not what I can do by way of cooperation when I develop as a result of the divine initiative. If I look on my new existence in this way, pseudo-spiritual self-centeredness is unavoidable. In fact progress is just a by-product of what God has begun in me. My own task, to which the imperatives point me, is simply to go, and continually to return, to the place where God is at work, i.e., where I am brought to faith by his Word and receive his Spirit as a pledge.

Faith never outgrows its beginning. It grows into this beginning. Its beginning is the creative Word of God which effects regeneration. This is where our becoming commences. This is where the battle between the Spirit and the flesh takes place. The demand that we should enter into this becoming, this conflict, is simply a demand that, faced with the alternatives that hang over our lives, we should take our place with the Spirit and let him be our advocate (Romans 8:26). When we accept his intercession and live by that alien righteousness in faith, we can no longer be so interested in our own empirical image that we are reflected in it, that we give it permanence, in short, that we allow it to become a theological theme of its own.

---

[18] The ethics of W. Herrmann are a good example. Here the commands of God do not materially demand anything different from what is also required by the categorical imperative. The specifically Christian side is simply that the Christian is given power to do the good, whereas the non-Christian, although he knows it equally well, is unable to achieve it. Without trust in Christ we cannot overcome guilt or the external limitations of the will (*Ethik*, 2nd ed. [1901], pp. 119, 129 and cf. the title of the section: "Christian Faith as the Power to Do the Good" [pp. 110ff.]).

XI

New Creation by the Spirit: Hermeneutical Aspect. A Theological Epistemology

We have seen that in Cartesian theology there is a shift of emphasis. The image of empirical man himself, as reflected in his self-understanding, is of interest and achieves thematic rank. We have conceded to this theology that it does not have to stop at empirical man. Although some polemical confessionalism refuses to admit this, its intentions include kerygmatic address from outside. Thus God's Spirit is usually differentiated clearly from man's spirit.

We have also tried to show in various ways and from very different angles why these intentions are not realized in Cartesian theology. In a sphere of understanding which is dominated by the question of appropriation it is impossible to think in terms of the creative Word which creates a new creature and thus transcends the old creature and its schema of understanding. Exclusive focus on the question of appropriation means that the identity or continuity of the human self is proclaimed or accepted as a condition of acceptance or appropriation of the Word.

In contrast we have spoken of the death of the Cartesian I. With the help of the antitheses of letter and Spirit and flesh and Spirit we have depicted the change that the creative Word brings about and its implication for my identity. The drift of our inquiry has been: What does "I am" mean in relation to the spiritual man when he is "outside himself," when he has an alien righteousness, and when he stands over against himself? How does what is proper to the regenerate man relate to what is alien to him? How far can he identify himself with the spiritual existence which is the work of the Spirit?

The question of the work of the Spirit, which we have so far considered anthropologically in relation to the problem of identity, is one which must now be tackled from the hermeneutical angle.

In connection with the question of appropriation we have already seen how important the hermeneutical problem is. One might put it as follows: Do I draw the creative Word into my self-consciousness so that it is integrated into this and can no longer be regarded as a creative Word but only as one that modifies this self-consciousness? Or does the creative Word draw me into its sphere of influence, so that I am integrated into the salvation event which works on me, and to that extent am referred to something outside myself?

This question has a new edge in relation to the knowledge of God, or to theological truth in general. It is thus a significant one hermeneutically. This is evident the moment we give it the new form: Is this truth the content of an interpretative Word or of a creative and active Word?

If the former, it conforms to our self-consciousness which also seeks truth and which in its pre-understanding already has questions that are designed to elicit it. Even if kerygmatically imparted truth modifies the prior consciousness of truth, it still remains within the sphere of the possibilities of modification intrinsic to this consciousness.

If, however, theological truth is the content of an active Word, the situation is fundamentally different. In this case the Word itself first creates the possibilities of my understanding and acceptance. The Fourth Gospel states this when it says that only he who is in the truth hears the voice (John 18:37) and that only he who does the will of God can know the truth that Jesus' teaching comes from God and is not invented by himself (John 7:17).

Negatively this means that in and of himself man does not have any possibility of accepting the truth. In Paul's phrase, it has not entered the heart of any man (1 Corinthians 2:9) and the natural man does not perceive the things of the Spirit of God (2:14). In the situation of his inauthentic existence he can only suppress the truth of God, holding it down in unrighteousness (Romans 1:18). The ontic state of man shatters his noetic possibilities. His knowledge, and with it his relation to the truth, can be corrected only as his being is corrected. Truth can disclose itself only when the darkness of existence (Romans 1:21) ends.

We have no control, however, over this background of existence on which the possibility of knowledge depends. It is not the object of either a theoretical (cognitive) or a practical (ethical) operation. Man cannot make himself different from what he is. Since, however, this being is relation to God, he has no control over the knowledge of God which is bound up with it. Knowledge of the truth is fundamentally closed to being in untruth. There is no breaking free from this circle.

The positive implication is that God's truth is revealed to me only when the Word which contains it is understood by me as an active Word, i.e., when it alters the conditions of existence itself, when it frees me for being in truth, when it effects the conformity of existence which opens up for it the way to the truth of God. If knowledge is possible only to the degree that there is an analogy between him who knows and what he is to know—we shall return to this later—then one might also say that the active Word of God must first create the analogy of my existence in order that the truth of his Word may be intelligible.

If, however, I regard God's Word as an active rather than an interpretative Word, then I am again confronted by the question of identity. For the Spirit whom the Word imparts to me and through whom it accomplishes my regeneration breaks continuity with my old existence, destroys it (2

Corinthians 5:17; cf. 1 John 2:8), and creatively summons up new possibilities that were not present in that existence. Without this breaking off of continuity with the old, the truth of God cannot be mediated. It would not be any the less true, of course, as the truth which is not imparted and not understood.

Truth may well be the same as that which discloses itself, which enlightens, and which is thus intelligible,[1] and we can accept this in relation to God's truth. It, too, is disclosure, being evident. But the question is: For whom is it disclosed, and to whom is it evident? The truth which is concealed from the natural man, or, paradoxically, the truth which conceals and "must" conceal itself from the natural man,[2] is true even apart from man. It is in this case evident only to God himself. It is restricted to the Logos who is as yet only with God (John 1:2). It is the wisdom which is with God before all self-disclosure (Proverbs 8:22; cf. Job 28:20ff.). Knowledge of God is self-knowledge here. Truth is God's knowledge of himself. If truth basically implies perceptibility, and if it thus presupposes transcendental apperception and hence a subject of perception, God himself is this subject. He alone is self-analogous.

This extreme concept of a truth which is truth only with and for God shows plainly what is meant by a creative and active Word and by the testimony of the Holy Spirit. They mean that with a new fiat God summons me out of my forgetfulness of existence and the truth and transforms me by giving me a share in himself and his self-knowledge. The Spirit who explores the depths of Godhead (1 Corinthians 2:10) is God's own Spirit. Only he is analogous to himself, so that he alone can grasp the truth of his own profundity. But this Spirit is imparted to me to give me a share in God's analogy and to grant me the conformity which finds enactment in love (1 John 4:12).

Since the issue here is God's relation to himself, i.e., the truth of God in his self-knowledge, trinitarian statements are in order. For the self-knowledge of God in virtue of his self-analogy is not just pneumatological ("the Spirit searches the depths of deity"); it is also christological: Christ as the Son or Word of God knows the truth in the immediacy of that self-knowledge. When we belong to him we also share in this truth to which we would otherwise be closed. "No man hath seen God at any time; the only begotten Son which is in the bosom of the Father, he hath declared him" (John 1:18). "Not that any man hath seen the Father, save he which is of God, he hath seen the Father" (6:46). Here in the form of the one existence of the Son of God is the full conformity which gives access to God's truth. Here is no longer the indirectness of a mirror with its distortion; here is "face to face" (1 Corinthians 13:12). In Christ we are ordered to this conformity

---

[1] Cf. Heidegger's analysis of truth as nonconcealment.

[2] This "must" is important in Luther's doctrine of the bondage of the will. The reference here is not to coercion from outside, which would destroy responsibility. It is to an inner necessity. I must accept this necessity and impute it to myself (cf. Cl, III, 125, 23ff.; III, 204, 30).

of the Son of God. As we can say: "We are his righteousness," so we can say: "We are his conformity with the Father." We have a share in the truth which he has—which he so has that he is it (John 14:6).

This brings us to the hermeneutical problem. I can understand the truth of God only through the Holy Spirit,[3] since the analogy which underlies this understanding is imparted through him. This analogy, however, is an analogy of being before it is one of understanding. The existence of this analogy points to the creative and active Word of God which renews this being in the miracle of the Spirit and causes it truly and authentically to "be."

To discuss this thoroughly we must first deal with some more preliminary questions.

1. RELATION OF PROCLAMATION AND THEOLOGY

If everything depends on whether we understand the Word to be interpretative or creative, the further problem at once arises: Where do we meet the decisive, active Word? A provisional answer to this question is that we meet it where it strikes us as an effectual Word in the sense that in the law and the gospel it breaks off the old existence and starts a new one, bringing sins to light and forgiving them, changing God's rejection into an acceptance which gives me a new future and makes me a new creature in the miracle of the Spirit.

This effectual Word is spoken in proclamation, preaching, and pastoral counseling. Theology as a reflective act can only be subsequent meditation on the faith that has arisen on this basis.[4] It thus has a part in the event of new creation. It considers what has happened, relates the event to the one to whom it occurs, and weighs the consequences for my understanding of self and the world, i.e., for the question of identity.

No matter what may belong to the sphere of theological reflection, it is always grounded in that which is the ground of the new existence itself. No matter how it goes in detail, its intention is always to describe the truth, God's truth. Since, however, disclosure of this truth is bound up with a specific state of existence, with being in the truth, theological reflection on the truth is also tied to this existential pre-condition. It can be pursued only on the basis of a state of existence which already has the break with the old existence behind it and which has been called to life by the active Word of the miracle of the Spirit.

This means that theology follows the proclamation of the Word; it cannot in principle precede it.

This is what Anselm has in mind in the prayer at the beginning of the *Proslogion*. Faith, which has its source in proclamation, takes precedence over theology (c. 1) so that we do not understand in order to believe; we believe

---

[3] The related christological statements show what was the theological concern of the western church when it adopted the double procession ("proceeding from the Father and the Son").

[4] For a similar Roman Catholic view cf. K. Rahner, *Schriften zur Theologie*, I (1954), p. 66; E.T. *Theological Investigations*, I (1961), p. 55.

in order to understand (cf. Augustine, In Joh. Tract., 40, 9). Knowledge only follows the faith which leads by way of hope to love.

The question arises here whether Cartesian theology has not in fact reversed this relation (although it does not have to do so). If theological inquiry is determined by analysis of pre-understanding and self-understanding, this surely decides what statements can be accepted as candidates for appropriation by this understanding. What can be called God's work is fixed in advance. What is set before me as God's word or work must be correlative to what my own consciousness has already indicated.

In other words, I do not first learn from God's active Word what his action is or can be and then go on to reflect on this experience of God's possibilities. I first reflect on what I can accept as the ostensible work of God. The order of precedence between theology and proclamation is thus reversed.

This raises the point whether our present plight is not due precisely to this reversal. We do not seek the rationale of proclamation after the event itself. In perverse fashion we first consult theological theory to find out what is the possibility of proclamation. This pre-vision is theological arrogance. Theology is here claiming a primacy for which it is quite unsuited. In the process it is terrorizing the community of those who are called to the miracle of the Spirit. It is bound to fail, for its whole enterprise is mistaken and it leaves out of its calculations the reality of the Spirit who precedes reflection. It is thus condemned to a permanent situation of preliminary inquiry.

This may be seen in the contemporary fixation on hermeneutical questions, i.e., on epistemology and methodology. All these are late disciplines which have their source in the scepticism to which the discovery and consolidation of the Cartesian I necessarily give rise.

Now obviously hermeneutics has a place. For scepticism must be acknowledged if it is to be overcome. It must not be repressed. Thus our reference to fixation on hermeneutics should not be construed as an attack on hermeneutics as such. There is certainly no need to be frightened by it. The real issue is its place in the total theological enterprise. This is where we have doubts. When the self-demonstration of the act of proclamation is not accepted, preliminary reflection on the possibility of proclamation, on addressability, and on the conditions of appropriation can go on forever. This means that we can never get away from hermeneutics.

A good illustration of the fact that method should be subordinate to fact is provided by the mistake that Schleiermacher made regarding the date of Plato's Phaedros. Under the influence of Schlegel Schleiermacher claimed that this was Plato's first work, his argument being that it deals with the methodological question why Plato uses dialog to expound his philosophy. We now know, of course, that the Phaedros was the last dialog. Only at the end does Plato consider methodology. He first exposes himself to being and on this basis "receives," as it were, his dialogical method. Encounter with being forces him, and at the end he asks why this is so, validating in reflection what he has done under the impulsion of being before any theorizing.

There is an analogy here to the relation between proclamation and theology. Theology puts its question on the basis of encounter with the proclaimed Word and exposure to it. Hermeneutics then investigates the question and its modalities and conditions. It is the epilogue in a process which is effected by the creative Word in the miracle of the Spirit. It is never a prologue.

Now it would be ungenerous to accuse even an extreme Cartesian theology of simply regarding hermeneutics as a prologue. One must obviously admit that its methodological deliberations are stimulated by problems that arise out of the summons of the kerygma. On the other hand the Cartesian I which is the abiding subject of appropriation seems to see to it that methodological questions are always at the forefront. In secondary authors these questions can easily become an intellectual exercise which never leaves any room for the real theme. The method of textual interpretation is learned—in case the text should ever be read.

Methodological questions are a transportation problem. Such a problem arises only when there is something to shift. To discuss it when there is nothing to move is absurd. But this height of absurdity seems to be common enough today.

It might well be, then, that God's Word is best preserved where we are simply exposed to it, where we are reached by its proclamation, and where methodological questions are naively, or unthinkingly, or perhaps even culpably ignored. If a secular example might help, the performance of Shakespeare's plays does not have to be postponed until a philological analysis has been completed. In fact, a good performance, which is quite possible without such an analysis, may ultimately contribute to it (cf. J. Kott, *Shakespeare heute* [1964]).

At this point we must pause and ask ourselves whether this order of proclamation and theology can actually be sustained. Can there actually be exposure to the proclamation of God's Word, and the work of the Word in the Spirit, without accompanying theological reflection? Indeed, is not God's Word itself theology as well as proclamation? If so, how can an order be established between the two?

If we are to see whether and how far God's Word is both theology and proclamation, and what this implies for the primacy of the active Word and the Spirit-event that is advocated here, we do best to start with the preaching situation and hence to investigate the problem as a concrete issue.

The Bible from which I take a text for expository proclamation is obviously intrinsic to preaching. But what if this book dissolves historically in my very hands? What if the *sola Scriptura* of the Reformation and the supposed self-interpretation of the Word by the Spirit prove to be so much waste paper? What if this Word is at best only a "witness" to which I for my part now bear witness? To be normative, does not this Word have to be God's Word and not just man's witness? To be God's Word, does it not have to have a unity—we use the term elastically and not in the sense of uniformity—which it is given by its divine author? Does not this mean that a canon which might contain a jumble of the authoritative and the non-authoritative, of God's active Word and man's interpretative word, of revelation and witness to revelation (or supposed revelation), would necessarily cease to be a canon? But does not the biblical canon, and with it its function as a text for my preaching, threaten to fall apart into widely differing elements? Do not the Gospels, let alone the Epistles, have different theological profiles? Have not the authors projected a distinct theological understanding into the traditional accounts of the historical Jesus, so that we often lose sight of the bond of union and have to ask ourselves which variant (that of Mark or that of Matthew) is to be decisive for us? Or should we allow the one to correct the other in our preaching?[5]

The reason why we find these different profiles is that the NT offers theology as well as proclamation. We have thus to ask what is the implication of this for our initial thesis that theology comes after proclamation, that before we can practice theology we have first to be reached by the Word of proclamation which renews our existence. If the kerygma as we have it in the NT manifests a combination of theology and proclamation, this seems to be a weighty indication that the material subordination of theology to proclamation does not have to find expression in a perceptible, chronological succession.

In fact there is no moment of pure proclamation just as there is no pure state of contemplation or feeling. As proclamation is appropriated and articulated and passed on, it is already caught up in reflection[6] and brought into relation to our stock of concepts, to the questions and states of our existence, to the situation of the hearers and much else.[7] This means that what is proclaimed and passed on—even and precisely when it takes the form of recorded facts that affect me directly like the history of Jesus—is always present in interpreted form. This process of interpretation is itself theology.

Thus Matthew in his account of the stilling of the storm accords only second rank to the miracle. It is not so much the basis of faith, as in Mark; it is rather an illustration of faith. Thus we have more than record and proclamation. A theological thesis about miracle is part of the record and proclamation.

Such theses vary. They introduce perspectives into the stories which, being different, threaten to destroy the unity of the stories. Does the unity of the kerygma remain behind this distinction in theological perspective? Is the canon still there when reflection has brought with it discursive deviation?

This has to be possible if we are to be able to preach the Bible in terms of the priority of the Word of proclamation and in so doing to tie it in with theological reflection. If it were not possible to find and invoke the underlying unity of the Word, then we should have to choose between the theologies offered in Scripture, e.g., in the NT. We should then be disciples of Paul, John, or Matthew, but not biblical Christians. We should have to abandon the *sola Scriptura*. For this makes sense only if it implies the "monopoly" of the

---

[5] Cf. the different accounts of the stilling of the storm in Matthew, Mark, and Luke.

[6] Thus Karl Rahner observes that even though the initial degree of reflection may be small, it is never wholly absent (*op. cit.*, p. 78; E.T. p. 66).

[7] Cf. Tillich's concept of "correlation," *Systematic Theology*, I, pp. 59ff.

active Word that comes to us, strikes us, and summons us to a new being.

In fact exegetes are always trying to find this kerygma which entails underlying unity, this address which stands behind the theologies of the synoptists and apostles and indeed the schemes of thought adopted from later Jewish apocalyptic, Gnosticism, and mythology. We need not discuss here the different ways in which the various schools of NT scholarship do this, whether by more conventional presupposition or by critical inquiry.

The crucial issue here—and it again leads on directly to the problem of proclamation—is that to a large extent, especially in Cartesian theology, the idea seems to be that kerygmatic unity must be found behind the many theologies and these must be interpreted in terms of the kerygmatic core. Now it may be granted that interpretation as a theoretical act is in fact one of various ways of fulfilling the task. It is no doubt the way that biblical scholarship should take. Our question is, however, whether it is not just one way of relating to the texts—a way which I cannot just decide to take but which depends on many conditions over which I have no control.

The decisive condition is that the texts have spoken to me. By the witness of the Spirit they have become for me an active and transforming Word. They have led me to the truth of being in which I can hear the voice. In short, faith is the decisive condition if interpretation is to be possible. Without it I cannot even begin to ask about the kerygmatic core, about what is unconditionally relevant to me. Before interpretation of the texts (according to their own meaning) can even begin, I must first come face to face with something over which I have no control, namely, that the texts interpret me, and that in so doing they transform me. It is only in this act of transformation that I learn that I am interpreted here, and that before God I have a completely different "image" from that held by my own prior self-consciousness.

The experience of being interpreted by the active Word of God presupposes that by the miracle of the Spirit this active Word changes the conditions of my being by bringing me into the truth of being. Only as I undergo its own interpretation can I myself interpret. Without this can I really relate scientifically to the texts, e.g., as an atheist or neutral religious scholar? To this question I can only reply in the negative if I espouse the thesis that I must approach the texts with a right relation, that I must have been addressed by them and transformed by the Spirit if I am to hear what is really said, that I must be in the truth to hear the voice. Only on this condition is scientific interpretation one of the possible ways of finding the kerygma behind the theologies.

Even then we must stress that it is only one possible way. We must not absolutize it as the only possibility. The normative way in the history of the church and its proclamation has in fact been a different one, namely, that of learning what God's Word is in the act of proclamation itself. In other words, qualification as the Word of God comes in practice.

To explain and defend this we should have to use many arguments that will come up later in the doctrine of the Word of God. Thus the relation of Word and Spirit plays a part here. In the present context it must suffice if we make only one reference, although this touches the nerve of the matter. We are speaking of the development of the canon.

The canon is the epitome of the unity of Holy Scripture and its focus on the active Word of the one God, the God of Abraham, Isaac, and Jacob, the Father of Jesus Christ. This canon did not come into being by theoretical interpretation of the available texts or by systematic investigation of their intention. No justification of the choice was offered in principle. The canon arose, and was then defined rather than constituted, as certain books established themselves in the practical proclamation of the church, while other candidates failed to do so.[8]

In the act or practice of proclamation canonical rank was brought to light. In other words, God acknowledged his Word. This means that in principle the canon is not closed on the Reformation view. We cannot say what might not prove to be canonical in the further course of proclamation.

From this it seems that only in the course of proclamation does it come to light what is in Scripture itself the proclamation behind the theologies. The crippling error which Cartesian tendencies have brought into theology obviously consists in the view that one has first to know what can count as proclamation, so that surreptitiously theological reflection takes precedence over proclamation.

In reality what we said about the subordination of interpretation to faith exposes the error. I can legitimately interpret the biblical texts in terms of the kerygmatic core only when I have been touched by this kerygma and have come to faith through the witness of the Spirit. But how can I believe without proclaiming? Is there faith without witness (Matthew 12:34; Acts 4:20)? Interpretation begins, then, as the counter-question of the man who is apprehended. Then everything is in order. Perversion arises when interpretation is not pursued as a counter-question into what empowers us for proclamation but takes on the rank of an *a priori* pre-construction which planes down proclamation and puts it under our own control. In this regard, something that our prior deliberations have already brought to light may be noted again. The program of interpretation in Cartesian theology was not proposed and planned. It simply arose on the basis of certain presuppositions. But having arisen, it makes the task of reflection a never ending one and by its failure to reach any conclusion it does permanent damage, achieving the very opposite of *parrhesia*.

At this point we may refer to an important distinction between the teacher and the student which works itself out in empirically discernible fashion too. In virtue of his practical and spiritual experience the teacher is in touch with kerygmatic realities. Even if this hermeneutical program may come very close to *a priori* pre-construction, there may always be seen in it an element of the counter-question, even if only in traces. This is not so in the student, who enters the hall of theology through the vestibule of hermeneutical and

---

[8]Cf. H. Diem, "Das Problem des Schriftkanons," *Theologische Studien*, 32 (1952) and "Die Einheit der Schrift," ETh (1953), 9, pp. 385ff.

methodological prolegomena. Here the counter-question yields to never ending reflection, and the perversion is complete.

The second generation is always the one that suffers in Cartesian schools. The homiletical efforts of students who are brought up in this theological climate, and who are frequently entangled in methodological and other pre-considerations, offer a good illustration. Students who are unsure of their matter always tend to take refuge in methodological questions. But here the material theological premises increase the tendency to such a degree that quantity is confused with quality and what we have called perversion results.

2. TRUTH INTENDED IN PROCLAMATION AND THEOLOGY. DISCUSSION OF THE CONCEPT OF TRUTH

a. Truth sui generis

The section on proclamation and theology developed a thesis which lies behind all our deliberations thus far. Our concern is with a particular style of truth. This is a truth that we cannot control, that has not entered the heart of man, that the natural man cannot perceive. It is a truth which leads me to being in truth and which thus transforms me. This transforming character of truth is what is brought to light by the active Word that mediates it. This Word is plainly the instrument of the miracle of the Spirit, bringing new birth and the new creation of the spiritual man.

This hermeneutics of the Holy Spirit means that the truth intended cannot possibly fall under the general categories which are the epistemological conditions for the usual definition of truth. We are thus confronted again by the familiar phenomenon in theology that when terms are transferred to theology they undergo a sharp modification of sense. Linguistically we still have the same word "truth," but it now denotes something very different.

The term still stands in analogy to what is usually called truth. Otherwise we should have to coin a new word and enter the hazy zone of glossolalia. Even after their "baptism" theological words still display their original meaning. We have here the same dialectic of identity and change as in the case of the person of the new and spiritual man. The new man is not a creation out of nothing. This is a miracle of change. He is made out of the existing material of the old man. Similarly the new terms are not a creation out of nothing. They are the old terms filled with new content.

There thus arises the unique dialectic in which we speak of Christian truth, not as a special form of truth, but as truth *sui generis* both by nature and origin. But this includes rather than excludes the fact that we can define the relation between the theological view of truth and what is usually understood by truth in the secular sphere.

In this sense there seem to be three forms of truth which might be characterized as follows: (1) a truth which we can know; (2) a truth which applies to us; and (3) a truth which understands us before we can understand it.

(1) What we can know and express in a generally valid synthetic judgment must be objectifiable. What is discovered thus has the character of what is

right. The right, as Martin Heidegger puts it,[9] says something suitable about an object. To be right it does not have to disclose its nature. When such disclosure takes place we have the true. The right is not yet the true. Only the true brings us into a free relation to what reaches us in terms of its nature.

This would bring us at once to a second form if we did not have to discuss, or at least to raise, an intermediate question. Does that which applies to us enter the picture only as we investigate the nature and significance of what is rightly known? Might it be that even that which is right can already reach us? A common view today is that it is our absolute right to collect knowledge, to extend indefinitely our knowledge of the right. As W. H. Auden points out, we agree that food and sex can be intolerable to excess, but we will not admit that intellectual curiosity is a desire like any other and that exact knowledge (the right) and truth are not identical. Perhaps we should be asking: What should I know? rather than: What can I know? Perhaps the only knowledge that can be true for us is that which we can measure up to in our lives. But this seems to us to be crack-brained and even immoral because it opposes the autonomy of the chain reaction of constant scientific inquiry.

Be that as it may, the question is whether even the question of the right as such (and not just that of nature and significance) does not have an existential reference, confronting us with the possibility that right knowledge and the technical use we make of it may be more than we can handle. In face of scientific knowledge it might well be that we are in the position of the sorcerer's apprentice. In face of possible space exploration it might well be that we are not by nature capable of exploiting the physical possibilities now open to us. It thus seems that there is no such thing as a neutral knowledge which does not affect our existence. Scholarship too, and even resolve upon it, provokes response and enforces the question of our attitude to it, of its significance for us, and of the way and end of our occupation with it.

Thus the transition from truth as knowledge to the second form of truth—truth as it applies to us—is a fluid one. The two forms are not sharply divided.

(2) This brings us to the second form, namely, truth as it applies to us.

This truth has to do with the meaning or nature of things, whether this denotes the meaning that sustains us or the meaninglessness that challenges us either by crushing us or by being so absurd that it provokes our powers of resistance and thus has a creative effect (cf. Camus and Benn).

Meaning and meaninglessness are always incarnate in persons. In the last resort being human describes the relation to the meaning or meaninglessness that either sustains me or threatens to crush me. Personal being is ontically characterized by concern in being for being itself.[10] There is in being a relation of being to being. One might almost say that being itself is such a relation. This relation is its truth. Plato saw this when he said that for him the question of truth is the question of authentic (as distinct from phenomenal)

---

[9] "Die Frage nach der Technik," *Vorträge und Aufsätze* (1954), 15.
[10] Cf. M. Heidegger, *Being and Time,* p. 32.

being and that the essence of a man results from the relation he either has or does not have to authentic being. On having or not having this relation depends his essential life or his subjection to confusion by appearance.

Since the relation of existence to being or meaning is not objectifiable, I can only understand personal life and not explain it. This distinction between scientific "explaining" and intellectual "understanding" was made by Dilthey.[11] In this context understanding as distinct from explaining means that insight into the life of another person demands a specific existential precondition, namely, that I represent in my own person the same structure of existence as that of the other person's life. Only because I myself have a relation of being and meaning can I see the other in the same relation. Only for this reason can I appreciate his boredom and emptiness, his anxiety, his defective being, or his fulness of being. Only for this reason can I understand that this other being, like myself, is summoned to grasp his destiny and risks missing it. Solidarity with the other under the same theme of existence makes understanding possible.

Dilthey in his work on the development of hermeneutics[12] works out psychologically the solidarity which makes understanding possible. It is the power of empathy, which is not unlike Schleiermacher's divinatory understanding. This ability rests on the kinship between expositor and author. It demands constant study enhanced by an empathetic life.[13] This ability, however, is only a psychological reflection of the ontological solidarity that exists between expositor and author as common bearers of personal life who share the same life and are in the same relation which constitutes the essence of existence. Bultmann is thus closer to the ontological secret of understanding when he describes it as a pre-condition that the expositor should have a living relation to what is directly or indirectly expressed in the text. In poetic, philosophical, and especially kerygmatic texts this is ultimate reality, to which both author and expositor stand related and which declares itself in intelligible fashion in the ciphers of the text. A certain "musicality" expressing the empathy of the receptive intellectual constitution may intensify and refine the process of understanding. But it can do so only within the ontic solidarity and can be no substitute for this. If there is no ontic solidarity, as may happen in face of an alien interpretation of existence, the "musicality" may produce aesthetic appreciation but will miss the heart of the matter. We see this in purely aesthetic interpretations and evaluations of Bach's religious works as these are found among those who enjoy them for purely secular reasons.

(3) Finally we must glance at the third form of truth. This is the truth that understands us before we understand it. In Pauline terms (1 Corinthians 13:12) it is the truth which we know as and after we are known by it. I can speak of the truth in this sense only when I see it incarnate in a person, in

---

[11] Der Aufbau der geschichtlichen Welt in den Geisteswissenschaften, Gesammelte Schriften, VII (1927; 3rd ed. 1961), pp. 71, 80ff., 86, 92, 141, etc.

[12] Gesammelte Schriften, V (1924; 3rd ed. 1961), pp. 317-331, esp. 326f.

[13] Ibid., pp. 326f.; cf. Bultmann, GV, II (1952), p. 215.

the king of truth (John 18:37f.). Apart from this I may well speak of a truth which discloses itself to me (cf. the literal sense of the Greek *alḗtheia*) or which applies to me. A truth which knows and sees me, however, can only be a living other that is resolved upon communication with me. This living other is not to be understood, of course, as one to whom I am related in the general solidarity of the same constitution of being. It is not, as I am, in a relation to meaning or to ultimate truth. If it were, I might say that this other *form* had known me before I knew it, just as my mother did. But I could not say that the *truth* which is at issue here had known me before I knew it.

Christ's relation to the truth is in fact stated in a unique way which rules out even an enhanced form of ordinary solidarity with me. The exceptional character of Christ according to the NT consists in the fact that he does not just represent a relation to meaning (logos); he is the Logos. Truth is incarnate in him and identical with him. Truth is what he is; the ultimate reality which gives meaning appears in him, namely, the faithfulness of God which constitutes his truth according to Romans 3:3, which endures, on which one may rely, and which as *dikaiosyne* is opposed to human *pseudos*.[14] Christ does not merely proclaim to us the truth of God's faithfulness which sustains our life and gives it stability and meaning. He is this truth in bodily form present among us. He is thus characterized by "am" and "is" judgments which articulate being and not just doing. "I am the way, the truth, and the life" (John 14:6). "He is our peace" (Ephesians 2:14).

b. Understanding and Calling

Naturally this concept of truth-in-person raises new problems of knowledge and appropriation, i.e., of epistemology. Whereas we could distinguish the understanding of personal life from the explaining of science, grounding it in the solidarity of the common situations of existence, a completely new mode of understanding arises in face of Christ who is the truth and who to this extent differentiates himself from our existential situation. I cannot understand Christ merely as I understand other men.

The different existential situation in which he does not simply relate to the truth but actually is the truth may also be seen in that which, following Dilthey, we have called the psychological reflection of this situation. One cannot speak meaningfully of the possibility of divinatory empathy with Christ's person, with his "inner life" (W. Herrmann).

Of the many epistemological problems that result when we try to speak of understanding Christ I will mention only two, and these only in outline.

(1) Understanding, as we have seen, implies a certain analogy between the one who understands and the one who is understood. But if I understand myself as one who has fallen away from the truth of God, I cannot understand the king of truth, for the analogy necessary thereto does not exist. In fact the synoptic stories are full of illustrations of the way in which Jesus

---

[14] Cf. R. Bultmann, Art. *alḗtheia*, TDNT, I, pp. 242f.

was continually misunderstood and not recognized. He was taken to be a rabbi, a wonder-worker, a fetish, a political messiah and so forth. He was simply evaluated according to available analogies when in fact he does not belong at all to the schema of such analogies. The parables of Jesus, which make so much use of familiar figures and familiar natural features, demonstrate as it were by experiment the fact that he transcends all possible parallels and that obduracy and incomprehension are greatest where one would expect them to be broken down (Matthew 13:13). He who is the truth cannot be understood by those who are not in the truth. Whether I can understand him depends on whether he first brings me to the truth, or, epistemologically, on whether he sets up an analogy with himself. To that degree I am the object of a calling. Whether Christ can be an object of understanding for me depends on prior calling. Only he who is of the truth, i.e., is brought into it, can hear his voice.

(2) With calling I and my existence are put under obligation. Not just my ears and my perceptive reason are engaged. In biblical terms, my heart, the core of my being, is also engaged. I am not just summoned to hear and ponder; I am called to discipleship and fellowship. This means existential participation to the utmost. The goal is not to grasp the truth but to be in it, i.e., to exist in the name of the faithfulness of God which confronts me bodily in Christ. Thus discipleship cuts deep. It means separation from what was there before. It means breaks and partings. I put my hand to the plow. I cannot look back. I am confronted by the transvaluation of all values. I am called out of the familiar world and its security. I must renounce even what I previously regarded as pious duties (Matthew 8:18-22).

c. Revelation and Accessibility

Calling by the one who knows me before I can understand him (John 1:48) is an event that I cannot control. The understanding of Christ is also grounded in presuppositions that I cannot control. This mode of understanding, then, lies right outside what is normal and familiar when we think of the universities and their faculties and the methods and concepts of scholarship. When we are faced with the task of theological understanding two conditions that make up the character of science (and scientific understanding) seem not to be fulfilled, namely, general validity and controllability. If the ability to understand is tied to calling and to certain related conditions of existence, namely, being in truth, then the constitutive criteria of scholarship seem to be missing. This raises in passing the serious question what a theological faculty is really doing in a university.

We must try to put the issue in sharper focus. The secular concept of science is rational in the sense that its axioms shed light directly. They are grounded in the *a priori* structure of the consciousness. The connection of the concepts and methods with these axioms is thus evident. All this makes it evident that the inclusion of theology in the academic structure raises profound problems.

Since theology implies the category of the *revelation* of a truth and hence an encounter with what Paul says no eye has seen or ear heard (1 Corinthians 2:9), so that it is not evident in principle and cannot even be the object of a postulate, the assumption understandably arises that theology, when defined in this way, is a foreign body in the system of rational disciplines; it is, as it were, a foreign body composed of interplanetary matter.

To appreciate the full scope of this distinction we need only recall the resoluteness with which Kierkegaard argued that the Christian reality of salvation is wholly other, i.e., it is a reality which is defined *totaliter-aliter.*

Kierkegaard's well-known assertion of the infinite qualitative distinction between time and eternity perhaps comes to its most forceful symbolical expression in the doctrine of the Holy Spirit. This doctrine does not merely say that the content of the Christian kerygma—salvation history—bursts through the continuity of the immanent historical process and rests on a unique and supernatural act of the Lord of history. The doctrine also says that this historical content is accessible only in the form of a supernatural self-disclosure. According to the older tradition the concept of revelation does not mean only that something special has happened in the objective sense. It also means that this event can be known only through a special form of illumination, namely, faith. The accessibility that cannot be controlled (i.e., the noetic side of the matter) has always been called "illumination by the Holy Spirit."

Paul described this rationally nonavailable accessibility as follows. As the nature of man is accessible only to a man, so God alone can know what is in God (1 Corinthians 2:11). Paul was thinking in terms of the necessary analogy between knower and known. We can know only that for which we are in some sense adequate. I could not grasp Plato's doctrine of the ideas if Plato did not address analogous elements in my own consciousness, e.g., the ability to form certain collective concepts. For God, however, there is no equal or adequate being outside himself. Hence he alone can know himself. His self-consciousness alone can have empathetic knowledge of himself.[15] This thesis of theological epistemology is plain to everybody.

In the working out of this thesis the term "revelation" means self-disclosure in the sense that God gives other beings a share in his self-consciousness, in the understanding of his true being. Thus the nature of revelation is more than the popular view of it is aware of; it does not refer only to certain forms of supernatural inspiration. Revelation denotes a fundamental relation between God and man, namely, that of qualitative distinction and hence of God's objective inaccessibility to man. It then denotes the epistemological block that results from this distinction. Finally, it stands for the miracle of the divine self-disclosure, the participation in God's self-knowledge, which alone removes the block.

We might put all this in terms of the thesis that the primary reference of revelation is not to certain events, or, to put it crassly, to the biblical stories. Revelation is epistemologically a category, a form of spiritual experience.

---

[15] Cf. Thomas Aquinas, *Summa Theologica,* I, q. 12, a. 4.

This form is characterized by the fact that it permits of knowledge only by participation in the divine self-knowledge.[16]

d. Place of the Methodological Question

Is it possible, then, that as man cannot see himself or know himself apart from revelation, so reason cannot see or investigate itself, but needs an external criterion by which to measure its ability and limitations? (Cf. ThE, II, 1, § 1321ff.).

Theology is in fact referring to a suprarational criterion of this kind when it speaks of the entanglement of reason in man's personal fate and when it has thus to speak of fallen or hybrid reason, which rationally legitimates man's fears and hopes, which sets up ideologies, and which allots to man world-views that are suitable to him. When theology speaks of this lost reason that is unaware of its own limitations, it also sees that the event of redemption extends to the sphere of reason too.

There arises, then, a theological critique of impure reason. This critique differs from Kant's epistemological theory, for it is made on another level. Kant's analysis brings to light the immanent structure of reason. The theological critique, however, begins with an investigation of the existence which enfolds reason. It speaks of the fall and rising again of this existence. For it, reason is only one of the dimensions of human existence which are totally and irrevocably subject to the destiny of man.

The secret of reason does not lie in itself or its functional structure. It lies in its humanity. Reason is human reason. There can thus be a redeemed reason which is restored to understanding and reintegrated into its order. Of this reason which is liberated for God and for itself one may thus say in truth that, while the peace of God is higher than all reason, "under" the peace of God reason stands highest.

Since both dimensions of the consciousness of truth—which are naturally to be distinguished from double truth—are obviously in personal union in those who as believers have both scientific consciousness and also a love of methodically purified knowledge, it should be possible, formally at least, to reach agreement on the methods of theological knowledge even with those who do not share its material presupposition, namely, Christian faith.

The methods used to get to know an object are related to this object. This can be shown easily enough when we think of objects that can be viewed from different angles. Thus suicide is a very different object for ethics on the one side and statistics on the other.

Ethically suicide is an object of philosophical decision. This embraces many issues derived from my understanding of existence. If I ask whether I should kill myself or not, I am faced with the problem of life and death, with responsibility to my Creator, with the nexus of sin and guilt which I want to escape, and so forth.

---

[16] In this position there is obvious divergence from the understanding of history in thinkers like, e.g., W. Pannenberg.

Statistically, however, suicide is merely a phenomenon of numbers. The individual instance is part of the series with its annual ebb and flow and yet at the same time the astonishing consistency which makes of the suicide rate almost a natural law. Statistically suicide is thus dehumanized and, one might almost say, dehistoricized. The elements of individual decision with all its ramifications play no part at this level.

We thus come to two conclusions. The first is that I may study suicide as either a human problem or a scientific problem, and the methods will vary according to the way in which the object of study is qualified.

The second is, conversely, that the methods adopted, whether those of ethics or those of statistics, will present me with radically different objects of study.

The dialectic which prevails here might be stated as follows. The object determines the method and the method fashions the object. If one separates the act of knowledge and the object, grotesque results follow. The girl who wants to drown herself for love must first ask whether there is a vacancy for her in the suicide rate. This is comical. But so, too, is the opposite. The comical aspect is that different objects—suicide understood statistically and suicide understood ethically—are confused with one another, and so too are our attitudes to them, i.e., the methods of knowledge that we employ.

The objects of knowledge are thus profoundly ambivalent. They can be the objects of very different inquiries and approaches. This ambivalence is particularly severe when we come to the object of theology. A phenomenon which is familiar in other spheres takes on a new acuteness here. This is quickly illustrated.

At the heart of the Christian message is the Christmas proclamation "The Word was made flesh." This means that when we now say "God" we cannot have in view world-transcendence that is accessible only to mystical ecstasy or soaring theory; what we are now speaking of is the God who moves history, who has entered into it, and who has accepted solidarity with man. This act of divine descent into flesh or history, this condescension, finds expression in the stories of Christ's temptation and passion. Here all transcendence is given up, and Luther's thesis makes sense when he says that God cannot be drawn deeply enough into the flesh.

If we take seriously this central point of the Christian message that God became incarnate and that the Lord of history became a figure in it, the question arises how and in what sense the miracle of Christmas can be an object of human knowledge. What methodological presuppositions are we to adopt to attain to knowledge of this reality?

The only possible answer is that the salvation event has basically two aspects, just as elemental processes can have two aspects in microphysics. The two aspects may be described as follows.

First, the salvation event is part of earthly history. It is also an element in the history of religion. It can be documented as such. It is thus an object of historical science. It takes place within the world. In this dimension the years A.D. 1-30 are a theme in secular history.[17]

Second, however, the true theme of this event, its character as salvation event, is not an object of ordinary historical study. We have here a process in which the Lord of history becomes a figure in history. Only faith, however, can see him as the Lord. Faith has thus the function of a category of knowledge in relation to this event.

Once it is admitted that this is really a salvation event, the self-disclosure of the personal God, this event demands the category of faith if it is to be the object of knowledge.

Even in human matters there are things that are perceptible only to the personal category of love. In them love has the same epistemological function as faith does here. Nobility of soul, or even charm, cannot be known in an objective, unprejudiced, and unloving way. This is surely what Goethe meant when he said one can understand only what one loves.

Now the salvation event is tied to the first beginnings of Christianity, to what took place between A.D. 1 and 30. There was a real birth, crucifixion, and resurrection of the Lord. These facts of the salvation event have ontic reality. But this does not mean that the salvation event is accessible in the same sense as the historical facts to which it is tied. Kierkegaard can even say that by entering history Christ evades ordinary perception. He is not immediately present. His very historicity is a kind of incognito. For by plunging into the stream of religious history Christ subjects himself to ambivalence. He can be regarded as an ordinary figure on the stage of history. He can be viewed as the founder of a religion or as a religious man.

The difference in the two approaches does not have to imply that mankind is divided into two groups, one of which has a historically objective outlook and the other the existential outlook of faith. Both aspects are present in the person of the believing Christian. For the Christian who has faith in the Kyrios Christ sees that Christ and the events surrounding him are embedded in the general history of religion. They are part of the history of thought. Analogies to other cults (e.g., that of Dionysus) are perceived. The juxtaposition of the two aspects has, indeed, theological significance. For the resultant ambivalence is intrinsic to faith. Faith is the opposite of sight, i.e., of something that may be perceived, that is available. The ambivalence shows that the object of faith is outside our control. It discloses itself only in the gift of faith.

Safeguarded here is the epistemological thesis that the object of knowledge determines the categories and methods by which we know it. The same fact, as in the case of suicide, takes on different qualities according to the approach, e.g., ethics or statistics. In formal analogy the same fact is on the one side a datable event in history and on the other side the irruption of eternity.

An axiom of knowledge which is especially worked out and used in epistemology and hermeneutics is that there has to be some analogy between the

---

[17] Cf., e.g., E. Norden, *Die Geburt des Kindes* (1924).

knowing subject and the known object. We have referred to this already and in elucidation we have referred to Dilthey and Bultmann.

The decisive problem in this context is whether the necessary analogy is available when we are trying to understand the divine realities and saving events which theology describes as its truth. This is the crucial point in the so-called conflict of the faculties. For theology says that in the natural course of things no such analogy is at hand. This is why there is no such thing as natural theology. No analogy exists because of man's fate, which the Christian message calls sin. Sin means man's alienation from the Lord of his life. It means breach of fellowship. Epistemologically this breach of communication means the loss of the analogy and therefore exclusion from the knowledge of God.

This gives us new insight on Paul's statement about no eye having seen or ear heard. We can now see the epistemological background of the verse. We stand in analogy to the historical facts of religious history, even the history of the Christian religion. But we do not stand in analogy to the divine truth manifested in these facts. This is why Christ is incognito within them.

We are thus led to an important conclusion. If there is to be any theological knowledge, any understanding of the salvation event, the analogy has to be re-established in an act of new creation. The divine Word must create its own hearer, the subject of understanding. The theological point at which to speak of this creative function of the Word, of this creation of the hearer, and hence of theological epistemology, is in the doctrine of the Holy Spirit. For this doctrine, as noted already, tells us that we are called to share in the divine self-knowledge and are thus set in a real analogy. In this sense the Spirit searches all things, even the deep things of God (1 Corinthians 2:10).

The doctrine also makes it clear why theology can never agree that its epistemological processes are heteronomous. There would be heteronomy only if the object of faith, and consequently of knowledge, were dictated from outside, so that we should have dogmas in the sense of compulsory teachings. For the man who is set in the new analogy there is no compulsion. Faith is free and spontaneous. Like love, it is not commanded. It is won by the power of the One who encounters us. What spontaneity is for faith is evidence within the epistemological act related to it. Since this evidence is not under our control, theological statements cannot have the character of proof or demonstration. They will always be proclamation, address, and appeal. They can be made, however, only in confidence in the awakening and creative and effectual power of the Word entrusted to them.

XII

Summary of the Relation between Cartesian Theology (A) and Non-Cartesian Theology (B)

The core of the distinction between the two theologies, which we have tried to make in various ways and from various angles, is to be sought (1) materially in a different definition of the relation between proclamation and theology, (2) methodologically in a different understanding of the appropriation of the kerygma, and (3) in the different relation to what is "new" which results from (1) and (2).

(1) The precedence of proclamation over theology which Theology B espouses is directed against the ever threatening possibility that theology will openly or surreptitiously gain the primacy, so that it will think that it can fix *a priori* the conditions of faith and of subsequent theological reflection. These conditions will be based on the consciousness of truth in a given age. In our own age they will include the secular elimination of the concept of transcendence in defining what is credible and what may therefore be said in theological statements. The theology of a Braun or van Buren has shown us where this can lead. God is simply the source of my own impulsion. Prayer is no longer made to a transcendent person. It is simply a reflection on the world and our fellow-men.

We remember how we came to assert the precedence of proclamation. This has as its content God's creative and active Word which not only discloses itself to the hearer but creates this hearer, bringing him to being in the truth. Proclamation of this kind, and not the theology which develops out of it, is the medium of the Spirit and his creative work. Theology is a reaction of the existence already smitten by this Word. It describes reflectively the basis and content of the assurance already appropriated to us.

This includes rather than excludes the fact that non-Cartesian theology (B) also accepts the consciousness of the age. It is trying to communicate with the age. It is not perennial theology aloof from the distinction of the epochs. The only point is that it assigns to the reference to the age, and to the resultant questions, a very different place. If the contemporary self-consciousness does not lay down the conditions of credibility, it cannot claim normative rank. Nevertheless, being addressed by proclamation, it is drawn into it and it does in this way become a theme of theological reflection. The contemporary with his self-consciousness is not just a target who later kindles a certain practical and pedagogic interest when it is a question of getting the message across. His being addressed, and hence he himself as well, belong to the essence of the message. This aims at the salvation of man. It accomplishes this salvation in the incarnation of the Logos. Thus God sets himself alongside man in the solidarity of love.

The Word can thus be received only as the recipient himself makes the movement of the Word to man along with it and after it. The Creator Spirit, who does the real work, refers us to our neighbors in the vehicle of the Word. To deny this movement of the Word to others would be to reject its pragmatic value and its supreme efficacy. It would also be to plunge the man who owes it to his neighbors into profound self-contradiction. He would be guilty of failure in relation to the Word. He would also go to pieces in himself, existentially. For Word and existence cannot be sundered; the Word renews existence in the power of the Spirit. To keep the Word to oneself is thus to fall into contradiction both against the Word and also against oneself by interrupting the ministry of the Creator to men. As the Word is other and more than mere impartation, as it is the fulfilling and refashioning Word, this interruption means more than the mere silencing and rejection of the Word. It means that the fulness of spiritual life set in motion by it is withheld at some point from one's neighbor.

As existence is multi-dimensional, and the Word works over a broad spectrum, this self-contradiction can have many aspects. A few may be mentioned by way of illustration.

The Word has to be passed on ("We cannot but speak" [Acts 4:20]) because there is only one name on which salvation depends. How can we withhold this from men (Acts 4:12)? The immanent imperative of the Word is so strong that Paul would have to call down a Woe upon himself if he did not obey it (1 Corinthians 9:16). Note that it is he who would do this, not the Word which he makes of none effect by his silence. He himself would set himself in contradiction with the Word and he would thus bring down the Woe upon himself. When the witness tries to be silent, the Word entrusted to him becomes a fire in his bones which has no outlet but rages and consumes within (Jeremiah 20:9).

A second dimension of the self-contradiction is that if a man receives forgiveness but will not pass on forgiveness, trying to keep out of the movement of the Word to others, he is a fool and a knave like the unforgiving servant, for he is harming himself (Matthew 18:21ff.).

Similarly if we ourselves are given food and drink and shelter and clothing, but do not recognize our Savior in the neighbor who is hungry and thirsty and homeless and naked, we place ourselves outside the process of life into which the new-creating Word has called us (Matthew 25:41ff.).

The aiming of the message at man, or, from our standpoint, at our neighbor, implies that inquiry into the neighbor, his mentality, the horizon of his questions and interests, his concepts, his orientation as a contemporary, is inherent to both the content and also the act of proclamation itself.

This is the place for existential analysis. We did not challenge existential analysis as such. We simply challenged the normative rank accorded to it as that which controls theological investigation and therewith the kerygmatic answer.

Theology B gives existential analysis another place and rank. Or, since it is Cartesian theology which is not conservative but makes a change, it restores to existential analysis its true place and rank. How does it do this?

The essential point is that it raises the question of the structure of existence and time in another climate and with another purpose. It is not trying to define what can be absorbed by the self-consciousness and hence what can be believed. Nor is it apologetically concerned to accommodate itself to contemporaries. If it were, man would be just as important and exalted in (normative) rank as in the introverted attempt at self-understanding and the associated perception of what seems to be acceptable as kerygma and imperative (as, e.g., in the Enlightenment).

In Theology B existential analysis arises out of the movement to our neighbors which is immanent in the kerygma itself. It thus arises out of love. When through the effective Word our eyes are opened to our neighbors and to what is at stake for them in encounter or non-encounter with the Word, we are extremely concerned about the question who our neighbors are, what bothers them, what are their questions and searchings and errors, and what concepts will be most useful in approaching them. It is here that existential analysis comes in. It is here that psychological, philosophical, sociological, and similar questions become urgent ones.

The movement toward the neighbor which is released by the Word-Spirit event is a love which, like all love, presses for understanding. At this point, however, the understanding of love is not in terms of the worthiness of the other to be loved. The exact opposite is true. The love awakened in the new existence is there first and it then calls for understanding. The one who is awakened for love sees in the neighbor someone he never saw before, namely, one whom God has mourned and sought and bought with a price. This refashions the task and theme of understanding.

Naturally the new question of love implies the question of myself and my self-understanding.[1] It does so, as we have seen, because the miracle of new creation raises the question of my identity. But love also makes the question of the self and the existential analysis of the self urgent for another reason.

Love presupposes solidarity and identification with my neighbor and contemporary. It also effects this. This is a "repetition" of the movement of God's active love. As condescension this love accepts solidarity with those who sit in darkness and the shadow of death. It sets itself under the pressures of history, temptation, and death. The man who loves suffers from the fact that he does not understand his neighbor. He seems to use a different frequency.

---

[1] The command "Thou shalt love thy neighbor as thyself" expresses already this reference to the self. Augustine found here a basis for his special theory of self-love (cf. Holl, III [1928], pp. 54ff.; ThE, I, § 1712ff.; E.T. I, pp. 337ff.).

The suffering of this type of love is due to one's own being. It thus implies the question of one's own being.

If, then, a man proclaims in love, he cannot simply explain the lack of understanding, the invincible indifference, or the opposition which he encounters by attributing it to the offense which is constitutively related to the message and which has to come (Luke 17:1; 1 Corinthians 1:23). He must ask whether his own lack of solidarity might be responsible for the lack of understanding. He must be ready to regard the latter as a personal objection. Perhaps he is behind the times. Perhaps he is clinging to a dead past. Perhaps he is an oddity whose strange tales are treated tolerantly but are not taken seriously.

Similarly, the church is perhaps regarded as a "drop-out" group in a pluralistic society. It is accepted as a kind of natural park or extraterritorial power but not as a vital institution which can be trusted in the modern age with its problems and situations. If lack of understanding is a provocation, the counter-question regarding ourselves is raised. We are asked whether we are real contemporaries. Do we truly belong to our own age?

Several examples might be given. It is a well-known fact that many businessmen are more open to witness from a successful colleague than from a pastor. This colleague knows the same pressures and problems as they do. The credibility of his faith is demonstrated and catches their attention. The pastor, on the other hand, is open to the objection that he lives in another world which blinds him to the realities of life that stand in the way of faith, e.g., the autonomy of economic life or the anonymity of corporations. The concept of the worker-priest in France was designed to meet this very problem. The idea was to demonstrate a solidarity which would illustrate the credibility of faith in the situation of the modern worker.

We find the same impact of the question of the self and its contemporaneity in many attempts which the church is now making to update itself and to display solidarity with the age. The use of beat and jazz in worship, of dialog in proclamation, and of slang in the pulpit are all obvious signs of this.

Although many of those who take part in them are not aware of this, these attempts carry with them the summons to make a decision between Cartesian and non-Cartesian theology.

The Cartesian alternative involves asking who the contemporary is that is alien to the message which we want to bring to him. It is not just a matter of accommodating ourselves to him or presenting the gospel in a suitable form. The question goes deeper. Realizing that we can gain a hearing only in solidarity and contemporaneity, we put the self-critical question whether and how far we are meeting these claims or doing all we can to satisfy them. We thus have to work on our own "image" to make it that of a modern man. We have to work on the conditions which seek to make faith credible. Indirectly and without thinking we adopt the approach which begins with self-understanding as this has been analyzed in our study of Cartesian theology. The sensitive hearer will soon spot this. More clearly than in the related theological and theoretical processes he will detect the manipulation of the Christian message for a practical end.

Non-Cartesian theology may adopt similar procedures and attempt modern forms of proclamation. If it is faithful to its intentions, however—and unfortunately, since we are sinners, this cannot be taken for granted—there will be a decisive difference in spite of the external similarity. This modernity will not be cultivated in order to make the gospel preachable. It will be a spontaneous and nonpragmatic expression of an existing contemporaneity. If contemporaneity is the subject of special inquiry and hence the content of the corresponding self-correction, this will be because love is compelling us to establish solidarity. These nuances are decisive—probably so even in practice. (On this cf. the author's *Leiden an der Kirche,* 2nd ed. 1965.)

It is love, then, which is both the basis and also the effective cause of contemporary solidarity. The love at issue here is the experienced love of him who first loved me (1 John 4:19). This love has triggered my own ability to love. Love is also the passing on of this love to others who are also embraced and purchased by it.

From this love springs the legitimate form of the question: Who is my neighbor? (Luke 10:29, 36). The legitimate form, unlike that of the scribe, does not try to avoid the neighbor. It wants to seek and to save him. Within this question of the neighbor practical interest is kindled in the way he is structured. Is he oppressed by guilt or afflicted by meaninglessness? Does he have a false sense of security? Does he need to be shaken by the law? Is he already shaken and does he need to be established by the gospel?[2]

Within this legitimate question as to the neighbor the question of the self is also legitimate: Who am I to be able to preach to my contemporaries? While this question implies the question of contemporaneity, self-critical existential analysis cannot be the final word here. Beyond the positive or negative things brought to light by this analysis, the promise stands that I *am* apprehended (Philippians 3:12), that I *have been* transformed into a new creature, and that if I put what has happened to me first, all other things, including solidarity with my contemporaries, will be added to me (Matthew 6:33; Luke 12:31). The man who loves cannot be a stranger in the world.

(2) As regards the problem of appropriation, which the two theologies solve in very different ways, we need only recall the decisive point. If this question, under the pressure of intellectual developments, is allowed to become the dominant problem, it leads to the primacy of existential analysis in theology. For this lays down the conditions of appropriation. Hence theology may well be swallowed up in anthropology.

In answer to this, we have pointed out in the name of non-Cartesian theology that God's Word cannot be appropriated by any present state of existence. By the miracle of the Holy Spirit it refashions the old creature and thus itself sets up the conditions under which it may be heard and received. It is active Word. We do not bring God and his Word into our existence. We

---

[2] These are Luther's questions to the Antinomians (cf. ThE, I, § 599, 641, 652; E.T. I, pp. 117, 130, 133).

ourselves are set over against ourselves in regeneration and we are integrated into God's history. Thus the self is not, as in Cartesian theology, an identity within which there are merely variations of self-understanding. This identity of the self can only be understood dialectically: I live, yet not I, but Christ lives in me.

The question of identity is still theologically significant to the degree that it is I on whom the miracle of the new birth is performed. The returning prodigal has the same identity as the one who broke free from his father. But this is identity in retrospect, in respect to the old self that has been overcome. It is not the identity of an entelechy which may vary within certain limits or which may be modified by a push from outside.

In Cartesian theology the entelechy can certainly be affected by the external kerygma. In the first instance the kerygma may be understood transcendentally. It is outside man, just as God's revelation and instruction in Lessing's *Education of the Human Race* is not just a symbol of self-development but stands for something outside man that acts upon him. The kerygma alters the self-consciousness. It gives it impulses which are not self-generated. Nevertheless, this theology is oriented to the self and its self-understanding. It is oriented to the identity of the self. Hence the ultimate interest here is in processes of integration, and consequently in the question how the message is appropriated. The ongoing entelechy is thus the true theme.

This is why theology is changed into anthropology. It is no wonder, then, that the final step in this direction is that the latent and unintended elements of Feuerbach's understanding of religion become open and virulent. In death of God theology the transcendent other (God) becomes a mere fantasy and man is summoned to consider and master his secularity. What Feuerbach formulated as an analytical thesis against Christianity is now made the program of dying Christianity itself. Theology is now anthropology; it can be nothing else but anthropology. This is the self-judgment of a theological approach which is carried through to the bitter end. We shall discuss this self-judgment in detail in the second half of the book.

(3) A final result of our deliberations may now be recalled. We began by discussing the validity of the alternative "modern" and "conservative" in theology. An analysis of the two terms showed that they are not in fact legitimate. The true issue is the difference between Cartesian and non-Cartesian theology (Theology A and Theology B). Now at the end, however, further light is shed on the alternative "modern" and "conservative" which we contested and, we hope, managed to overcome.

If we start with the creative Word-act of God which brings about transformation in the miracle of the Spirit, this implies that outside the new creation there is nothing "new" in the church in the sense of something "modern" which outdates the old.[3] An obvious reason why this is so is that the life of the church is not that of a self-grounded entelechy or institution. There is no autonomous growth of the church. There is no independent self-development.

---

[3] This is obviously not meant to be a defense of the establishment or as opposition to any possibility of new and better and modern things at this level.

Hence there is no phenomenon of the new. The church is the body of Christ. It shares his life. It is integrated into him. It confronts itself as an institution. Christ, however, is "the same forever" (Hebrews 13:8). We do not look for another (Luke 7:19, 20). We do not look for a new state of the world or existence in which this Lord, who is the same, is transcended or replaced. Faith may experience many surprises. To that degree it may experience many new things. But these will only be a new side of one and the same Lord.

What, then, is the meaning of "old" or "young" or "new" or "renewing" for the church on its pilgrim march? Can the church have an independent life if it is truly the body of the risen, living, and exalted Lord?[4]

In principle there is nothing new either on earth or indeed in heaven. This statement involves a crisis for the term "modern" when it is meant theologically. This in turn sheds light on what we have called the anthropological approach of Cartesian theology. So long as our gaze is fixed on the human self and on changes in the understanding of the self and the world, there will be self-development and hence there will always be new things which crowd out the old. The old creature is desirous of new things.

It is no surprise, then, that Calvin as well as Luther is very critical of novelty, or, as we should say, modernity (cf. E. Wolf, *op. cit.*, pp. 139ff.). Have we then set up a new church? asks Luther (*Hans Worst,* 1541; Cl, IV, 329, 20). The answer is: No, we stand by the true and old church (330, 18), whereas they—the Papists—are "the new and false church"—"the whore and school of the devil" (334, 3). The Reformation is a reestablishment of what is old, not an addition to it. The one who makes additions in the sense of modern improvements is the devil: The name of the devil is "in Hebrew Leviathan, one who adds, who makes a thing more than it should be" (*On Penance,* WA, 8, 141, 30).

---

[4] E. Wolf, "Erneuerung der Kirche im Licht der Reformation," *Peregrinatio,* II (1965), p. 141.

Part Two

THEOLOGY IN
SELF-GROUNDED SECULARITY

*Situation and Task of Theology
in the Generation
of the Supposed Death of God*

"The abyss has no cover."
—Job 26:6

XIII

Theme and Questionability of the Slogan Death of God

1. LINK BETWEEN DEATH OF GOD THEOLOGY AND SECULARIZATION

Thus far we have been noting how the world that is aware of its secularity engages in theological reflection. The problem of appropriation which dominates the modern period arose out of a sense that the world is a closed nexus of experience which does not include God as a perceptible object. Since God is not in this nexus but transcends it, the question is raised whether and how far he can have a place among the certainties which the world's nexus of experience imparts. Even if it is replied that the certainty of God is grounded in a unique experience (cf. the postulate of practical reason in Kant), the normative significance of what the nexus puts at our disposal as valid experience demands that the special certainty of God be brought into relation to other aspects of validity.

How this finds expression in the question of appropriation we have seen in very different forms of Cartesian theology. Whether the self-consciousness be that of reason, feeling, or existence, the self in its immanence or within the nexus of immanent experience has been the starting-point for every question. It is of no significance that the stress may differ in relation to the nexus, that the nexus may be viewed representatively as history, as environment, or as fellow-humanity. What matters is simply that the starting-point of all thinking, including theological thinking, is man as he is there in his givenness and in the givenness of his world.

Only at a later date has it come to light that in this form of inquiry there are certain tendencies which limit what may be said about God. In Cartesian theology this limitation is not the initial concern. The determinative question is how far and in what dimension of my being God reaches me. Where does he make himself noticeable? Where does he become the theme? When man begins with himself as a given, God is a problem. He is not self-evident. He is not a co-given. In this theological approach, then, we find reflected a self-resting finitude, namely, a finitude in which God is not also a given but in which man has to struggle to find a place for him in and above the world and within our own self-consciousness. Once the justification of the sinner was the primary question. Now there is a preparatory question. God must justify himself. Basically Cartesian theology centers on the question of theodicy.

Now that we have considered the reflection of the new understanding of the self and the world in theological thinking, we must turn directly to this understanding. In so doing we are following a dramatic law. The hero of the play does not appear in the first scenes. We learn about him through what others say. But now the time has come for the hero himself, the new understanding, to enter.

Our purpose in expounding the modern understanding of the world is not one of general diagnosis. It is still theological. Even if we are not taking this understanding as our starting-point, and hence as a prejudicial impulse, we and our message still confront the world and its self-understanding. Indeed, we do not merely confront it; we are part of it. Christians study physics in an "atheistic" way. They accept laws like the conservation of energy. They also do historical work in which they refrain from ideological or theological constructions in relation to the nexus of events, and stick to statements about facts and about what can be proved. They also can (and should) engage in politics, avoiding theocratic utopias and making what is real and attainable the object of their activity. Christians are pragmatists.[1] No matter what may be their theological starting-point, they too are summoned out of this "atheistic" attachment to the given and won for a new certainty. For them theology is and always will be an inner dialog between the spiritual man and the natural man.

We cannot ignore the fact that in our proclamation we go to a world which understands itself "atheistically" in the sense described. If "God so loved the world, that he gave his only begotten Son" (John 3:16), and if the gospel is thus addressed to the world, then our proclamation has to study the world and its self-understanding and to relate itself to it. The adult community with its Christian conventions does not pose the questions to which the answers and corrections of proclamation relate; the world poses them, namely, the world which today regards itself "atheistically."

In this regard, too, a saying that we quoted earlier from Luther can help us. Progress in faith does not lead us to a certain state of sanctification. It refers us back to continual recommencement, i.e., to the place where we are summoned out of ungodly attachments and won for faith.

The new man is always at the beginning. He does not grow out of, but into, this beginning. He does not leave the initiation of baptism behind him. He continually creeps back into it. The overcoming of the old Adam keeps taking place afresh. If the old Adam is the man who understands himself "atheistically" in the sense of secularity, the beginning of his new existence means a continual overcoming of this presupposition of his self-understanding.

---

[1] Cf. Harvey Cox, *The Secular City* (1965), pp. 60ff.

Thus Christian proclamation is missionary or it is nothing. The heart of being missionary is calling and remembering that we are called. If one of the essential criteria of the health of the church and its teaching (Titus 2:2) is that both contain within them the impulse of mission, this is not because of an urge for expansion as a sign of overflowing vitality but because of the understanding of faith as calling and as concentration on the beginning. This helps the church to resist the temptation to think in terms of the perfection of the spiritual life, of the institution, or of the standard of sanctification. The church does not think of itself as an adult community which is grounded in traditions and which then develops them. It is a community of the called, of those who are commanded to leave the old existence. The missionary community is the community which is ever young. It continually receives afresh the miracle of faith. It lives its day of baptism every day.

Proclamation, then, must be guided by the question: "What reason does anyone really have to believe in the Christian message if he does not believe out of conviction?" As a basis for this question we advance the thesis that the "atheistic" self-understanding of secular man, not the mature community, fixes the question which our proclamation answers and corrects. Paradoxically the unbeliever rather than the believer is the criterion for the credibility of a theology, i.e., for the rank of the arguments with which it relates to its basis and sets its goals.

In our earlier discussion of the relation between proclamation and theology we have seen that proclamation tries to avoid the imminent danger of letting the inquiry, in this case that of secular man, achieve normative rank or prejudicial significance.

We remember what it is that must block this. The question of the self-understanding of secular man must not become the starting-point of theological thinking. It must arise only as the retrospective question of the called concerning that out of which they are called. Furthermore the question as to the self-understanding of secular men must arise out of love. The gospel tells me to ask about my neighbor, my secular brother. It tells me that I must be in solidarity with him according to the model of the incarnation. The question of the place where and whence he exists is the same as the retrospective question of my own whence.

We insist that the question of the "atheistically" understood secular world is not just diagnostic. It has a theological aim. It is the retrospective question about the whence of my own being as one who is called.

Our concern, then, is with the nature of secularization. But before we tackle this phenomenon itself and the understanding of existence which it expresses, we must first consider another concept which expresses in acute form the proclamation of self-resting finitude and the implied rejection of transcendence and the supernatural. This is the strident concept of the "death of God" with which certain American theologians have provocatively summed up much of the theological thinking of the day.[2]

---

[2]Cf. T. J. J. Altizer and W. Hamilton, *Radical Theology and the Death of God* (1966); T. J. J. Altizer, *The Gospel of Christian Atheism* (1966); P. van Buren,

Although as a theologian one has reservations in discussing such a slogan, it has the merit of offering excellent opportunities to survey the interaction of the Christian message with the questions of the day. There are various reasons why we cannot take the concept as such seriously.

First, it has the stridency of a provocative slogan which, like demythologization, arouses emotions and reactions which do not arise out of discussion with belief itself. Second, the "death of God" is not intended seriously. It is used as a kind of bluff. A catchword of atheistic philosophy fashioned chiefly by Nietzsche is suddenly presented, not as the antithesis of faith, but as its starting-point. A distinctive solidarity of different fronts is thus apparently achieved.

The slogan cannot be meant literally since it involves a logical contradiction. Either the God who is now dead never really was God, so that his death is in fact only the death of an earlier illusion, or the death of God means simply that he is dead for us, that a certain experience of God has gone, that a prior certainty has been extinguished, that a recognized concept of God has been weakened or revised, so that God himself is not really dead, but only a form of our faith or of our view of God. If God *is* dead, he cannot die, for there has never been a God and Feuerbach is right. Only belief in God can die, and it can do so only if there is no God. For if God is, he will constantly find recognition and kindle new faith.[3]

Concepts of God may vary, but for all believers God himself is independent of the consciousness. It is he who constitutes the consciousness and not *vice versa* (Isaiah 43:11, 13). Hence he cannot die; he can only withdraw from the consciousness (cf. Matthew 13:13ff.; Isaiah 6:10; 48:4; 63:17; Jeremiah 5:3; Ezekiel 2:4; Zechariah 7:11f.). If he is non-existent in the sense of Feuerbach, and is thus the mere content of our own consciousness, he cannot die. That which does not exist cannot die. Its non-existence is simply unmasked when the consciousness stops manufacturing ideas of God.

We are thus justified in steering clear of an intrinsically absurd notion. Nevertheless, it can still help us in our theological analyses. It can do so only if we take the slogan symbolically to denote the loss of a certain experience of God or of the experience of God generally. On this understanding, discussion of the slogan can be helpful in various ways.

First, it expresses the fact that God has no part in the modern experience of reality. In our conceptual and pre-conceptual dealings with nature, history, and the environment we are confronted by a dedivinization of the world.

Second, the death of God theologians have shown that the non-existence or irrelevance of God means that a specific form of the experience of God has in fact come to an end, namely, the experience of God as a supernatural being who comes into the cosmic nexus from outside. This God of the theistic

The Secular Meaning of the Gospel (1963); K. Hamilton, God Is Dead: The Anatomy of a Slogan (1966); T. W. Ogletree, The Death of God Controversy (1966); G. Vahanian, The Death of God: The Culture of Our Post-Christian Era (1961).
[3] Cf. C. Schrempf's criticism of Nietzsche's idea of the death of God (Gesammelte Werke, Vol. IX, III, p. 278).

tradition cannot be brought into our scheme of categories according to Kant's analysis. He is thus an epistemological absurdity. Furthermore, he is at odds with every conceivable form of existential experience. This is defined by experience of self-resting finitude and the autarchy of the present world. The experience and mastering of reality as though there were no God expresses a methodological principle of science and technology. But it also implies a generally felt dogmatic principle, namely, that God is irrelevant to our experience of reality. God does not arise here either as heuristic principle, as stimulant, or as limitation.

If transcendence has no part to play, we are led to both a negative and a positive conclusion.

The negative conclusion is that the transcendent God is now present for us only as a precondition in Braun's sense. Since he is not experienced in our encounter with reality, he is simply proposed as an axiom which we must accept and believe. He is thus an authoritative premise. But this is unacceptable to the mind that has come of age. Thus theology can only ratify the rejection of the transcendent God by the secular mind.

The positive conclusion is that if we cannot seek God in transcendence we must investigate his earthly actuality. The question now is: "Where is God at work?" "Where is he relevant?" The transcendent God is dead, but what about the God immanent in the this-worldly nexus of experience? Has not God subjected himself to this world and entered into our sufferings in Christ? Has he not accepted weakness so that we can even put him to death now that he has delivered himself into our hands?

This provides new theological insights and directions which are surprising and even shocking, not merely to theologians, but also to the children of the world, because they change the usual problems in so distinctive a way.

It used to be that a general idea of God in the sense of natural theology was readily accepted and the real trouble began with Christ and Christology. But now the very opposite is true. The almighty God who abandoned history and let the innocent suffer without doing anything is challenged. Christ, however, is close to us, for in him we see the suffering and powerless God, and he represents this God as well as us in our sufferings. Because of this strange reversal a cabaret could present the "God is dead boys" as champions of the view that "there is no God and Jesus is his Son."

Third, the theological proponents of this thesis intentionally address the present situation by taking its secularism seriously. They do not just interpret it theologically. They make it a norm for interpretation of the gospel and for theology.

Surprise and confusion have been caused on all hands by the grotesque change of front that this implies. Christians are now seen contending against the transcendent God, against a theistic view of God. They are making common cause against Christian tradition with opponents, with the indifferent, and with other groups. Whether the surprise is due to shock at the advanced tactics or pleasure at the sensation is beside the point. The fact is that the slogan gets to the mind of contemporaries even when a christological implication is seen—Christ is the son of the dead God—which is usually overlooked because it is so odd.

At the heart of the thesis one can undoubtedly see solidarity with the contemporary world. As Christians we do not usually feel that we are members of a secular age either statistically or in living experience. We are not included "with you" in self-resting finitude. But our very message, so the thesis runs, affirms our secularity and forces us to abandon transcendence. This declaration of solidarity with the secular age seems to create initially a surprised readiness to hear. This readiness is transitory, for joy in the self-affirmation lasts no longer than surprise at the quarter from which it comes, and the fundamentally confused theology leads either to agnosticism or back again to the tradition.

Fourth, it is plain that this honest attempt at solidarity with the age and its questions can have a reverse effect and lead to a situation in which the gospel can only say what the age is well able to tell itself, representing an aspect of life which is already at the command of life. We are again tempted to invoke the shades of Lessing, who seems to have anticipated every conceivable position in Cartesian theology. Education, he says in his *Education of the Human Race,* cannot give a man anything that is not already there and that he cannot develop for himself. Lessing was accepting the educational theory of his age. But in applying it to the gospel he necessarily restricted what the gospel can say to what man can tell himself, to what is already stored up in his own truths of reason. Thus education is superfluous. It has only an interim task. For those who have come of age it is irrelevant.

The death of God theologians, restricted by the presuppositions of secular thought, can say in the gospel no more than what is already contained in these presuppositions. And now the processes are far shorter than Lessing believed. In Lessing's day men were only half-adult. The age of maturity, of the pure gospel of reason, was still ahead. Education could still bring something that was for a time new to the pre-adult age. The death of God theologians, however, see in the autarchy of this world the epochal sign of achieved adulthood beyond which there is nothing either to impart or to expect. They can certainly provide from the Christian tradition perspectives which briefly seem to offer surprising variations and developments of what is already sensed. But these are only changing forms which the imagination of one and the same consciousness itself creates.

If one is inclined to accept rather than to reject these aspects, they quickly become commonplace. They do not introduce anything which transcends man, which is alien to him. They are simply a part of himself. They are experienced as a kind of second nature. The most urgent question as to the actuality of God, or the possibility of a secular theology which will find God in the world, finally produces a God who is simply an event in world-occurrence (cf. van Buren's view of prayer [Chapter V. 5b]).

We may sum up our survey by saying that the death of God theologians make a virtue out of the "necessity" of secular man in relation to traditional ideas of God. This is an exaggeration, but it stresses the decisive point.

The "necessity" is that the transcendent God is not present to the empirical mentality of secular man. He is non-existent, dead. He is no longer in the picture. The "necessity" may be seen in man's epistemologically clarified concept of truth, for God is no longer regarded as a possible object of experience. It may also be seen in the pre-reflective immediacy of experience. Here man accepts only what is given and normal. He does not take into account transcendent interventions.

But the "necessity" is changed from an apparent loss of religious substance into a "virtue" if one accepts the view of the death of God theologians that Christianity itself carries within it the tendency toward this-worldly consolidation. God in Christ subjects himself to the sufferings of the world. Love for our neighbors is simply the Christian aspect of reflection on this-worldly concerns.

It would be unfair to suggest that the concept is governed by pragmatic considerations as though the only aim were to find a path to the secular world which has gone astray from the church and hardened itself against any religious kerygma. If we do not allow aversion to this theology to master us but try to find positive elements in it, we shall come to the very opposite conclusion, namely, that Christianity, which itself opened the door to secularization as we shall see later, is simply experiencing self-clarification in reaction to this secularization. In trying to interpret itself in secular terms, it is learning what Christianity really means, and what it has always meant with its transcendent symbols.

2. OVERESTIMATION OF THE SECULAR. ELIMINATION OF THE HISTORY OF FAITH AND TEMPTATION

The passionate concentration of death of God theologians on the secular situation causes them to overlook the fact that many of the problems that seem to demand re-orientation are not really new but very old.

Certainly the empirical mentality is new. Our knowledge and mastery of the world are now bound up with immanence as a closed nexus of experience. We cannot go back behind Kant even though new questions do arise in relation to him. We can no longer grasp God directly as the old proofs assumed. God is not one among other objects. To this degree epistemological theory documents his absence. Nor is experience of God's inaccessibility to experience confined to epistemology. It has become man's second nature. It controls his dealings with the world.

God's existentially experienced absence, however, is to be sharply distinguished from this originally noetic absence. Job's awareness that heaven is closed and that we are the playthings of fate is as old as the hills. It is the theme of myth and tragedy. Believers experience it too.

The death of God theologians do something momentous when they overlook this spiritual experience of the OT people of God and the NT community. If they had not done this, the gap between them and the Christian tradition would perhaps have been much less. But they do it because they are under the illusion that God's absence or supposed death is a specifically modern experience. This is what underlies the much publicized statement that after Auschwitz it is no longer possible to praise the God "who o'er all things so wondrously reigneth,"[4] as though it was any easier for the tortured and persecuted of any previous age to do so. Were the degrees of terror less in all other cases? And in any case, can differences of degree alter the structure of faith?

We have here representatives of a theological type which so focuses on the self-consciousness of the moment that it loses all sense of history. The Now is isolated and discontinuous in a historical movement which is not perceived. Solidarity with those who are in the same stream is unnoticed. The Cartesian I takes on a certain unreality. It is paradoxical that those whose driving motive is solidarity with their own age should lose their solidarity with history and endow the present with absolute significance.

One sees here the same Docetism which is to be found in many other aspects of existentialism and its intellectual background. Existence is isolated. Sky and forest, history and neighbor, all lose their light and significance. They are no longer a sphere of relations in which the self lives and moves and "is." They are simply the dark background against which the light of existence shines and which threatens to swallow up the light. In Sartre's words, the other is the one who "fixes" me, who threatens to withdraw from my self-being, who becomes "hell" for me. Society does not characterize me as a communicating being, as a social and sociable animal. It reduces me to mere "man" and robs me of my identity. It is no wonder that the relation between faith and history can only be distorted here.

We shall now sketch the history of this experience of the absent, silent, and apparently dead God in order that we may escape the clutch of an absolutized present and regain awareness of the solidarity of our situation of faith with that of the patriarchs, prophets, apostles, and fathers.

The absence and hiddenness of God are not just a modern problem. They are a problem in every age. Each age has its own experience of them. Fundamentally their history runs parallel to that of faith. It is its alter ego.

One may see this from the nature of faith itself. Faith is not just faith in God. It is also faith against reality. Reality always seems to stand opposed to God's rule and hence to God's existence. Long before the modern idea ever arose of self-resting finitude—and this idea is only a form of the experience of absence—what the believer could see always seemed to be determined by forces and laws that resisted God's control. How else could the wicked prosper unpunished while the righteous were plagued every day and had to watch them triumph (Psalm 73)? Is it not the strategy of Satan

---

[4] This is the religious counterpart of the idea that no poems or novels or comedies can ever again be written after Auschwitz. In fact, at the concentration camp in Ravensbrück a Roman Catholic priest, on awakening every morning, used to sing the Gloria in a loud voice which could be heard through much of the camp even though he was beaten and tortured brutally (cf. K. Zuckmayer, *Erinnerungen* [1966], p. 431, speaking of Friedrich von Erxleben).

in Job (1:6ff.; 2:1ff.) to cause Job to go astray from God precisely by bringing him under the contradiction of reality?

But what is this reality which seems to bear witness to God's absence? It is a sphere of experience which does not yield to a certain self-understanding like that of Job. This self-understanding is to the effect that Job is righteous and that the course of things must run accordingly. His righteousness must be honored. Positively as well as negatively world history must be world judgment. The question arises, then, whether the contradiction between reality and God, which seems to bear witness to God's absence, is not in fact a contradiction between reality and ideas of God rather than God himself. Hence what we experience as the nearby God might well be the golden calf, whereas the true God is the distant God whom Moses finds on Mt. Sinai (Exodus 32:1ff.).

Thus the contradiction between reality and God which brings us under the temptation of God's supposed absence arises ultimately from the fact that we have an idolatrous image of this reality and this image has to be shattered. Here again a specific self-understanding, on which the later Cartesian self-understanding is simply a variation, becomes the measure of reality and therewith a spur to idolatry. When temptations arise through the contradiction between reality and God, this is a sign that idols are threatening to take over and that the painful process of their deposition must be carried through.

In fact the temptation is overcome only with their deposition. The contradiction between reality and God is never overcome by perception. If it were, Psalm 73:23ff. would have to run: "Because thou hast thought thus, I see that the wicked may triumph and I must suffer. Therefore I am continually with thee." We do not find this solution, however, in either Psalm 73 or Job (except perhaps for hints of it in the speeches of the friends).

What enables us to overcome the temptation is first a recognition of the fact that we are postulating how God has to act and react and be. This idolatrous image has to be smashed. Then temptation is overcome secondly by the believer when he goes into the sanctuary (Psalm 73:17), contemplates the end of God's unseen ways, and remembers the majesty of God which does not have to explain itself, but whose higher thoughts (Isaiah 55:8) must be trusted by man (Job 42). Against all appearances, in protest against the idolatrous picture of reality, there thus arises the confession: "I am continually with thee. . . ." No longer on the basis of that picture is God treated like an idol who has to react in terms of the cosmic system which I have postulated and who can be dispensed with if he does not do so—like an idol who is perhaps on a journey or asleep (1 Kings 18:27), who has ears and hears not . . . and hands that feel not (Psalm 115:6f.; Isaiah 44:9-20), who is absent or dead. Job takes the first step out of his temptation when in face of the emptiness which he sees in reality he learns to praise God (26:7).

What the OT people of God experienced as God's absence, but were able to overcome in faith over against idols, reappears in acute form in the NT theology of the cross. The cross represents God's extreme absence. It is a scandal to the Jew and folly to the Greek (1 Corinthians 1:23; Romans 9:32). There is here no theology of glory which can depict God at the heart of reality. There is instead a theology of the cross in which God is concealed.[5] According to tradition one of the seven last words speaks of God's absence: "My God, my God, why hast thou forsaken me?" (Mark 15:34). The twelve legions of angels who could have displayed God's nearness and existence stay away. They are not summoned (Matthew 26:53). The (idolatrous) image which the Jews and Greeks have of reality and of God's role in it is confounded. For a moment, however, the Son of God accepts this image. In this respect, too, he bears the sin of the world (John 1:29; Isaiah 53:7). He goes down to this depth and despairs with the despairing.

The temptation of an absent God is overcome here in the same way as in Job and the Psalms. Faith breaks through the encircling reality which is bearing witness against God. Appeal is made to him who is not seen (Hebrews 11:1). The complaint of Jesus, his cry of dereliction, is not a shriek in the void. It does not proclaim the death of God. This confession of God's remoteness is an assurance of his nearness.

Jesus is not speaking *about* God and his absence. He addresses him as Thou. His confession of dereliction is thus a prayer to him who has forsaken him. In this confession he also adopts the formulated prayer of the OT community (Psalm 22:1). He uses the Word of God to cry to the remote and absent God. This brings nearness and peace. An impossible prayer is prayed. A prayer is ventured which, if God's absence is not ultimate, can only be a questioning of reality. In the praying of this prayer, and in the implied breakthrough of faith, the absence of God becomes a vanishing dream and the death of God becomes a vanquished illusion.

Thus it is not only in the supposedly special situation of modern man but throughout the ages that faith has wrestled with the absence and the apparent death of God. In this struggle and the attainment of a triumphant Nevertheless it has continually looked back and tried to see what led it, or seduced it, into this experience of God's absence. In this survey it has interpreted the experience along two lines.

1. It has seen the experience as an expression of judgment. We have already pointed out that a self-manufactured idol is toppled here. Thus idolatry is judged. In idolatry the silence of God is experienced, and this can easily be equated with his death. The idolater who does not see his own creatureliness, who does not praise God or thank him (Romans 1:21), is "given up to" (*parédōken,* Romans 1:24, 28) the desires of his own heart and left alone. God abandons the processes that man has set in motion and lets man bear the consequences of his own action, i.e., he subjects him to the immanent laws of the processes.

Here, too, we find a self-enclosed finitude. Man has locked himself in a prison and God is far away. This leads us to the second aspect.

2. Since we are dealing with God's judgment, the truth is that God absents

---

[5] Cf. Luther at the Heidelberg Disputation and W. von Loewenich, *Theologia crucis,* 2nd ed. (1933).

himself. This means, negatively, that man has not driven God out with his idolatry and his declarations of autonomy. God himself has withdrawn. He has pushed man into self-resting finitude. As Léon Bloy puts it, God retires. This is the result when he is abandoned (Pascal).

He does this even to the point of forbidding the prophet to pray for the people and thus to bring about his intervention. God wills to be silent and to leave man to his own devices (Jeremiah 7:16; 11:14; 14:11). This silence will harden man's sin by seeming to vindicate it. How can it be sin when the one against whom one sins is absent or non-existent? Thus the judgment of absence intensifies the situation of judgment (cf. ThE, II, 1, § 2084ff.).

Man himself, of course, cannot force God out of the world or cause him to be absent. It is God himself who withdraws when he takes away his breath (Psalm 104:29) and denies his Spirit, so that men hear and see but do not understand or perceive (Matthew 13:13f.). Since man cannot force God out, no intellectual situation can do it. The question thus arises whether the dogma of self-resting finitude is not an expression of this situation of judgment, of God's self-retirement. Might it be that rejection of the transcendence of heaven consists, not in a true perception of reality, but in the closing of this heaven and the delivering up of man to finitude? This is why there is need of a theological interpretation of secularization and of man's declaration that he has come of age.

The most important result of this section is that the experience underlying the slogan "God is dead" is inherent in faith itself. It is immanent to faith and is not, then, restricted to a secular situation. Faith looks back on the judgment which it has escaped, on the divine hiddenness which corresponds to, and is provoked by, man's obduracy. It looks back on the confusing of God with an idol which necessarily led to the overthrow of the idol and which deduced from the demonstrated silence and impotence of the idol that God himself is absent or non-existent. This temptation is always a dark possibility accompanying faith. Faith can never get beyond the Nevertheless which overcomes this temptation. As faith in God it is also faith against the reality which constantly threatens to obscure things.

It obscures things as the past, trying to link and identify faith with what is behind it (Psalm 25:7; Job 13:26). It does so as the present, apparently contradicting any meaningful divine governance and raising the question of theodicy. It does so finally as the future, giving rise to anxiety and therefore to lack of confidence in the one who has promised to care for us (Matthew 6:31ff.). The Nevertheless which faith continually opposes to these obfuscations may be seen also in theological reflection. This, too, is always an inner dialog between the spiritual man and the natural man.

XIV

History of the Idea of the Death of God

1. NEW FORM OF ATHEISM

Although the experience underlying the slogan "God is dead" is inherent in faith, it has become more intense and taken on richer nuances in modern secularism. For this slogan expresses more than the experience of the absence of God or the atheistic assurance that there is no God. It carries with it the confession that God has been put to death and that something monstrous has thus taken place. What is prefigured in Prometheus or the building of the tower of Babel is now a programmatic declaration. Man has made himself the lord of this world and will not tolerate any other God. This is why God has to be killed.

The purely atheistic thesis is an academic one. This can be seen in its classical representative Feuerbach. Reasons can be seen for explaining away faith in God as a mere projection of fear and hope, and consequently as an illusion. It thus evaporates as so much froth. False emotions are pacified and replaced by a calm look at reality.

In death of God circles, however, the sphere of mere reasoning is left. We now have drama and action. An attack is made on God, and on all that he implies for us as the basis of existence. Killing involves serious repercussions. Sin and guilt attach to those who do it. In this sense Nietzsche is a prototype of the dramatic self-assertion of secularism. He, too, speaks about the slaying of God by us and about the monstrous nature of the deed—and he has more in view than a banal thesis which simply verifies the end of an illusion.

The parable of the madman in Nietzsche's *Fröhliche Wissenschaft* (ed. K. Schlechta, II, pp. 126ff.) gives expression to this. In full daylight this man lit a lantern and cried out in the market: I am looking for God. The people mocked and laughed: Is he lost? The madman glared at them and said: I will tell you where God is. We have killed him. All of us! We are his murderers. God is dead. God will stay dead. We have killed him. He then rushed into several churches and intoned a requiem to the eternal God. When questioned, he replied: What are these churches but the tomb and monument of God?

Atheistic reasoning seems secure and respectable compared with this explosive vision. It simply claims that we are now enlightened. Where we thought there was something there is nothing. Life is robbed of all its drama. The curtain has fallen on the main action, namely, on judgment, questioning, condemnation, and salvation. There is an interval. Men are left to themselves.

In contrast the death of God which is proclaimed by the madman is highly dramatic. It is marked by fear, by a shock effect, by telluric trauma, and by lamentation for the one who is slain: "Do you hear the little bell ringing? Kneel—the sacraments are being offered to a dying God" (H. Heine, *Zur Religion und Philosophie in Deutschland,* ed. H. Haufmann, V, 2). "We have long since put on mourning attire. De profundis" (V, 3). Instead of the light expected by the trivial atheist Nietzsche perceives that the act brings gloom and darkness. He who has killed God is not simply freed for this world. He traverses godless wastes and his worshipping heart is broken. In the age without God the new masters must be men who can endure to believe and to question without God, and also make decisions with the same depth of responsibility as faith formerly produced.

Similarly the monks of atheism found in Dostoievski are not cheap rationalists but martyrs of atheism who adopt it with pain and terror. Atheism here is akin to faith. The absolute alternative presented is either a complete plunge into unbelief or a bold flight beyond it to the ground of faith (W. Rehm, *Experimentum medietatis* [1947], p. 63). These suffering atheists seem almost to enjoy the promise made to the poor in spirit in Matthew 5:3. They are perhaps closer to the kingdom than secure believers or those who in their security renounce God. From the empty nothingness of selfhood, from whose horizon God has been banished, only the manifestation of Christ can save. The ground floor of empty existence brings receptivity to the supreme condescension of God, to the cross and the descent into hell. For Dostoievski the choice was between the fulfilled mystery and atheism (*Der unbekannte Dostojewski* [Munich, 1926], pp. 464, 480f.). This almost reminds us of some statements in the death of God theologians when they see in Christ the one in whom God delivered himself up to death, so that there is a strange affinity between atheism and faith in Christ. The same phenomenon may be seen in modern writers like James Baldwin (*Another Country*) or Samuel Beckett, in whose *Waiting for Godot* the hours of empty talk manifest a strange nearness to the absent one. It is because Godot does not come that the words have no significance. Thus the characters, who are no saints, take Godot more seriously than the spectators, who are trying to get the point but do not realize why there is no point.

This is the new nuance in the experience of God's absence which is intrinsic to faith. In the pain and martyrdom of unbelief God's absence is now declared to be his death. This declaration does not bring the release of enlightenment. It is a step into darkness, fear, dereliction, and chaotic inversion. It is accompanied by emptiness and tedium. The putting of God to death and the announcement of his death involve pain and terror.

To be sure, this is only the first reaction. As one may see perhaps in

Albert Camus, release from theistic tutelage may bring accomplishments in the absurdity of existence and produce joy in an unconquerable summer. Different stages may be seen in the death of God theologians. In the Germans one still finds fear, but in the Americans real or apparent victory is more characteristic. The situation has been accepted.

2. IDEA OF THE DEATH OF GOD AS PROMETHEAN LOGIC

When we attempt to illustrate the death of God concept by some typical examples, the unavoidable question arises where to begin. Our interest is systematic rather than historical. If, then, we start with a thirteenth-century notion, this is not because of any right of antiquity. It is because certain basic outlines are prefigured here which will be filled in when we come to the age of secularism.

In a cabalistic pseudepigraphon ascribed to Judah ben Bathyra[1] we are told that the prophet Jeremiah studied only the book Jezirah. A heavenly voice told him to take a companion, so he went to his son Sirah and they studied the book for three years. They then learned to combine the alphabet according to cabalistic principles and there was created a man with JHWH Elohim Emeth on his forehead. He had a knife in his hand and with this he cut the aleph off emeth and left only meth. Jeremiah then rent his clothes at the implied blasphemy—God the Lord is dead—and asked the man why he had done it. The man answered in a parable. An architect built many houses, cities and squares, but no one could learn his art or match his skill until two people persuaded him to teach them. When they had learned it they quarreled with him and set up as architects themselves at lower prices. Then the people stopped admiring the original architect and gave their commissions to them. In the same way God has created you in his own image and likeness. But now that you, like him, have created a man, it will be said: There is no God in the world apart from these two.

There are two anticipatory features here. The first is the Promethean element which gives rise to the inscription "God is dead." This is based on an illegal imitation of the Creator, or, rather, on the attempt to usurp his powers and functions. Man himself undertakes to create in his own image. This implies a displacement of God. The *homunculus* by whose fashioning man arrogates to himself creative and godlike qualities naturally understands himself as a refutation of God.

This is an inversion of what we find in Nietzsche. In Nietzsche God is first slain and only then does the question arise whether one must draw the deduction that man has to become God in order to regard himself as worthy of the deed. Does he not have to occupy the empty throne of the universe now that he has overthrown the previous lord? In Judah ben Bathyra, however, man's rebellious and pseudo-sovereign self-elevation comes first and the death of God logically follows.

---

[1] Cf. Gershom Scholem, *Zur Kabbala und ihrer Symbolik* (1965), pp. 234f.

The question arises which view is right. Fundamentally perhaps, even in Nietzsche, the story of the slaying of God begins with the Promethean self-consciousness of man. It is in the arrogance of this cosmic role that he wipes the horizon clean with a sponge. The prelude to the story of the death of God is the story of hubris. This is latent even in Jeremiah and his son. They do not seek to play the part of Prometheus. They give themselves to pious cabalistic practices. Possibly we have here the common factor in the two versions. In this unintentional prologue to the story of the death of God, in this hubris which is not deliberate, into which one is simply drawn until one day it is there, the *homunculus* begins to stir and act and suddenly the madman has to rush to the marketplace.

The second feature which recurs in later variations of the death of God concept is that the powers revealed and practiced by man are learned from God and are simply the exercise of a gift which is received from God. In NT terms it is the father's capital which the prodigal squanders and with whose help he plays the lord (Luke 15:13). The goods and gifts of God are used without God. Thus God by his generosity makes rivals for himself and sets up the competition that ruins him. He is like the architect who lets the two men learn his skills and is then undercut by them.

What is expressed here metaphorically is to be found again in many modern interpretations of secularism and the related concept of the death of God. From Friedrich Gogarten to Harvey Cox, in a wide variety of statements, the thesis is advanced that Christianity prepared the way for secularization, making it possible and giving it a start. For Christianity with its doctrine of the image of God makes man the partner of God. It allows room for decision. It opens up for man the way to emancipation and the far country. It leads him out of paradise. It summons him through faith to adulthood. Finally, through its message of the divine transcendence it desacralizes and dedemonizes the world. It drives out the gods. It makes possible in this way the manipulation of matter. It opens the door to science and technology.

In this context we cannot consider all the implications of this Christian derivation of secularism. An important feature of the diagnosis, however, is its assertion of the extreme paradox that the gifts of the very God who is wiped off the horizon as though he had never been provide the means whereby God is slain and man becomes the master of a godless waste or a liberated world. Is this the source of his disquiet in the godless waste? Is man unable to forget what made his experiment possible? Is this why he can never say that God is dead without bellicosity? Is this why it can never be a mere commonplace? Is this why he always has to say it defensively, as though maintaining a position which is fundamentally a negation? Can we not catch this undertone of constant self-reassurance even in Camus when his never ending summer is supposedly beginning in the midst of absurdity? This melancholy, as Guardini puts it in his *Hölderlin* (1939), p. 318, is man's unsettlement by proximity to the eternal which he neither wants nor attains, but ought to do so. This home from which man comes, and from which he receives all he has, is a constant source of unease.

3. IDEA OF THE DEATH OF GOD AS HEURISTIC PREMISE

The first modern vision of the death of God is to be found in Jean Paul in his "Sermon of the Dead Christ from the Edifice of the World on the Theme That There Is No God." Here we still have only a kind of trial run or heuristic experiment initiated by the question what it would imply if we had to say that there is no God. The heuristic point is similar to that of Paul when he asks what it would mean if Christ were not risen (1 Corinthians 15:14ff.). We should then be exposed as false witnesses of God, our faith would be vain, and we should be the most wretched of all men. A chain reaction of apocalyptically dreadful consequences would be triggered.

Jean Paul makes a similar experiment. He has a vision of the wasteland that the earth would become if God did not shine on it as its sun and grant it warmth and life. It would relapse into chaos. Atheism or the death of God is thus studied in terms of its cosmic significance. This world is as it were a criterion for the rank, the significance, and finally the very reality of the world beyond.

The discussion of atheism—and this is the point of interest—is not conducted in the strictly religious sphere. The Trinity, the atonement, judgment, and grace are not at issue. Only the present world—matters of climate and common life and the various orders—is relevant. These alone make the question of God a pertinent one.

Here, then, atheism is opposed in terms of the very question which introduces it. This is the question of the specific importance of the question of God for a self-consolidating secular consciousness. It is this consciousness which calls in question the transcendent reality of God. Hence this consciousness must also be the place of rebuttal. The realities of earth rather than religion are the field of battle on which the question of God is decided. Only the finite can be the criterion of the infinite.

For this reason we should be on guard against viewing Jean Paul's dream as a reactionary conjuring back of what is slipping away or against seeing in the evening bells which the man who has the dreadful vision of ungodliness hears a mere idyllizing of a very non-idyllic problem. Even in the dream the concept of God is placed under secular control. Jean Paul stands on modern soil.

The more narrowly religious elements in the vision occur only at three points, and even here they do not have independent significance.

First, the setting is religious. Christ himself comes to the one who has fallen asleep in the churchyard and proclaims from the great building of the cosmos the death of God. When the dead cry out: Christ, is God dead? he replies: There is no God. Thus Christ himself is only the highest of finite creatures. The idea that he is the representative of the absent God, to which the dialectic of modern death of God theologians tries to lend plausibility, finds no place here. God's absence, the inability of Christ to locate him anywhere in the cosmos, is strictly interpreted as non-existence. In this regard Jean Paul is closer to Nietzsche than to the dialectic of death of God theology.

Another religious element in the vision is when the children who are awakened in the churchyard come into the temple, fall down before the lofty figure on the altar, and say: "Jesus, have we no father?" and he replies with streaming tears: "We are all orphans, I and you, we are without a father." The world no longer has a father on which to rest. Life knows no warmth or shelter. It is thrust out into the void.

The third religious element is the absurd gesture of a prayer which is without validity because the praying hands fall off. One of the dead awakes and stretches out his arms in prayer, folding his hands, but his arms get longer and longer until they are detached, and the folded hands break off. As a world without God falls apart, so the connection of praying hands with the body snaps. There is no longer any organic whole. The organs break away from their allotted place as in Picasso's paintings. Here we find a displaced eye and there a wandering knee. And as judgment begins in the house of God (1 Peter 4:17), so the great perversion, the dissolution of order, begins with the annihilation of the holy. The gesture of prayer is broken. The thought here is not at all that prayer can be saved by reinterpretation, as in van Buren. The feverish attempt to achieve salvation by secularization could have been depicted by Jean Paul in the form of falling hands if this is what he had had in mind.

The main emphasis in the vision is not on the religious aspect. This simply provides the starting-point for the decisive theme, namely, that of the confusion caused in this world when it is deprived of its basis and center by the death of God, so that it falls into chaos and anything is possible. Reality without God becomes incalculable. There are no barriers. Hence anxiety arises. If everything is possible, everything is to be feared. The claim that the universe has no soul, that it is empty and basically futile, cannot be limited to the metaphysical domain. It determines our existence and our world with elemental force.

This is why the emptiness of the universe is portrayed with apocalyptic horror. Christ's cosmic search for God is graphically described. The empty world is now the plaything of fate, of unlimited and torturing possibilities. Complaint is made against eternal necessity and capricious chance. The day when they will destroy the house of our existence is anticipated.

When this day will come is the decisive question. There is no stopping at the death of God. When the world above is cut away, business cannot go on as usual here below, and perhaps even a little more easily now that religious error has been dispelled and we can live more conformably with the present order and achieve our own individuality. No, the cosmic structure cannot achieve any emancipated glory or govern itself maturely as technopolis (as in Harvey Cox). The proclamation of the death of God means attack on this structure too. Its collapse also is expected. But what is this assault upon or undermining of being which the death of God entails?

It is both anthropological and cosmological. Contact with the world and one's fellows is broken, for the system of reference is eliminated. If the God of Descartes does not exist—a handy illustration—there is no path from the self to the outside world and the result is illusory caricature and deception. A docetic unreality lies over everything. Polar isolation like that expressed by Caspar David Friedrich drives the man who denies God into unsettling solitude. The whole intellectual world is broken by atheism and shatters into innumerable volatile selfs which glitter and run and rove and flow together and part again with no unity or consistency. No one is so alone as the man who denies God. With an orphaned heart that has lost its higher Father he mourns by the corpse of nature which is not ruled or held together by any soul but grows waxen in the grave. As Jean Paul puts it, he is alone in the broad burying ground of the universe. He is left on his own and has lost the infinite breast on which he used to recline.

One gets a hint here of the solipsism which is grotesquely developed in Jean Paul's younger contemporary Max Stirner (Caspar Schmidt) in his strange book *Der Einzige und sein Eigentum*. Here the icy waste of the vision becomes a speculative postulate or a precise affirmation of the waking consciousness.

A further chain reaction in the relation of man to the world and himself is set in motion by the death of God. The eternal midnight at which time halts because there is no Lord of the times robs me of the Creator. In place of the dependence which the Creator implies we do not find, as in modern secularization, the adulthood, or possible adulthood, of man. We find instead the usurper who necessarily occupies the throne of the deposed God. In visionary form the result of the building of the tower of Babel is thus portrayed. The head of him whose upper limit has been removed reaches like a Titan into the space from which God has been driven. Vacated heaven is or will be filled by the one who has emptied it, or who regards it as empty. Religion as well as physics can allow no vacuum. When the Creator is banished, man is his own creator. On whom can the dignity of origin be conferred but the lonely one who is now on his own and whose voice in imitation of a Thou comes back to himself like a foolish echo? But if each is his own father and creator, why should he not be also his own destroying angel?

In fact the self-creator who has no God does not attain to freedom. He comes under the curse of his own unlimited rule. Who is there outside the self-creator who can set a limit for him and say: Thus far and no further (cf. Job 38:11)? What can resist him? Nothing can have the cosmic commission or authority to do so if there is no one to confer it.

Death has always been a restraint of this kind which mocks at self-rule. It has the appearance of something absolutely beyond control. Can it still be this for the self-creator? Must not the self-creator be also the self-destroyer? Obviously the one who makes himself can also do away with himself.

What Jean Paul intimates Nietzsche works out in all its logic. The mad self-creator must also master death. As deicide he must also be suicide. He must do away with himself (*Werke,* ed. Kröner, 8, 144f.). Death as the grasp of finitude is only an irrational physiological fact which must be turned into a moral necessity (16, 315). This is done when one does not meekly submit to death but when one accomplishes it. In Zarathustra suicide is achieved death in contrast to that which is suffered naturally. In natural death man is defeated, while in suicide he conquers (6, 105-108). When the summit of the life we have planned is reached, then is the time to leave it. We must know how to say No as well as Yes. We must understand death as well as life (*loc. cit.*). To submit to death instead of mastering it is to fall victim to subhuman pity. There is among men nothing more banal than death (3, 233). To take it passively is unworthy of the self-creator. In natural death the body is a confining and often sick and stupid jailer and master who decides when his noble prisoner should die. Natural death is nature's suicide, the destroying of rational being by the irrational (3, 294; cf. the author's *Tod und Leben,* 2nd ed. [1946], pp. 34ff.).

Jean Paul does not take the new step which Nietzsche ventures, namely, that of making of the necessity of the death of God the virtue of a productive absurdity, so that life seems to be intensified instead of destroyed and driven to suicide.[2] Jean Paul merely hints at the necessity of self-destruction, at the unavoidable function of being one's own angel of destruction. What he regards with dread Nietzsche extols as the victory of the rational over the irrational. Finally in Camus life has come to terms with itself and seems to achieve enhanced intensity in the midst of the absurd.

Who is right, the one who while he still has faith has a vision of what it would mean if life were to lose its center, or the one who invents accommodating and consoling formulae like the slogans "the world come of age" and "liberated secularism"?

The dream closes in extreme stress and thus runs the gamut of anxiety from fear of empty space and fatherless infinity to the anguish of the extreme constriction of existence. This is expressed in the ancient myth of the Midgard serpent encircling and compressing and crushing the universe so that the infinite temple becomes a mere cemetery chapel. Then an infinitely extended clapper strikes the last hour of time and the cosmic structure cracks as the dreamer wakes up.

Anxiety is a this-worldly emotion. But its object cannot be localized in this world. It is not connected with one object among others. This is what distinguishes it from fear, which is fear of something. Since the feared object has a clear profile, I am not defenseless against it. I can react and take countermeasures. Fear, then, does not mean absolute subjection. It is mixed, like Schleiermacher's partial feeling of dependence and partial feeling of freedom (GL § 4). Anxiety, however, has no identifiable object. It is part of being in the world. Since I am in the world, and my activity relates, not to this as such, but to my attitude within it, anxiety is akin to the feeling of absolute dependence (*loc. cit.*). But it is a specific form of it. Since absolute dependence cannot relate to any immanent object, for in relation to these I enjoy a measure of freedom, Schleiermacher describes its point of reference

---

[2] Cf. Albert Camus on "Absurdity and Suicide" in *The Myth of Sisyphus* (E.T. 1955); H. J. Baden, *Literatur und Selbstmord* (1965).

as God. But for him God is related to the figure of Christ. Hence the feeling of absolute dependence does not mean metaphysical terror. It is another term for religious security. The point of reference for absolute dependence is also the object of my trust. Commitment to it thus means peace rather than the fear of fatalism.

This security is unconvincing, however, for the atheistic visionary. Here absolute dependence does not mean reclining on the infinite breast of the Father. It means abandonment to fixed and irrational nothingness, to cold and endless necessity, to capricious chance. Thus, instead of being sheltered on every side (Psalm 139:5), we are crushed by the Midgard serpent. Whether I fear or rejoice, whether I go to a funeral or a wedding, whether winter freezes me or spring intoxicates me: all these variations of immanence are under the same oppression. Ghosts lurk on the fringes of even the most beautiful celebrations.

On the fringes! This implies that terror is transcendent. This world, when detached from God, is not "self-resting." It is not closed to the outside. It is not autarchous. It poses the question of meaning that immanent ends cannot answer. It asks about the whence and whither of the whole system which encloses these ends and gives them their ranking. The man who used to find in the Father of the universe an answer to this question can now put it only with the uneasiness and terror of one who is abandoned. The earlier answer has been silenced with the death of God. But the question itself has not been silenced. It has an indelible character. This is why it causes fear. So far man has not been able to come to terms with it. He has not grasped its positive feature. He has not been able to transform this necessity into a productive virtue.

We again ask: Who is right? Who has truth on his side—the man who recognizes the situation with terror or the one who has psychologically integrated and sublimated his terror?

The subject of the terrible vision is that the death of God thrusts us out into the insecurity of infinite space or narrow constriction. Solipsistic solitude and unlimited self-rule gain ground. Anxiety prevails. One thinks of Pascal's analysis of the man who denies God. This man has the same existential experiences. He knows emptiness both as anxiety and also as tedium. The reason why this state cannot be overcome is as follows. The question of that which either gives transcendent meaning to me and my life or causes me to end in meaninglessness and nothingness cannot be suppressed. The melancholy of those who are assaulted by futility is classically illustrated by the monkish malady of *acedia*. As Kierkegaard has shown, this is rooted in the fact that the eternal is no longer desired unequivocally but it still declares its presence and is the theme of my question.[3] The purity of heart which seeks only one thing is no longer present. It has been replaced by multiple desire. There is a hysteria of the spirit, of which Nero is an example.[4]

---

[3] Kierkegaard, *Stages on Life's Way* (1945), pp. 171, 322f.; *Christian Discourses* (1971).
[4] Cf. W. Rehm, *Experimentum medietatis* (1947), pp. 185f.

Nero's split personality caused him to become a paradigm of melancholy in the century of the baroque, while for Pascal he represented loneliness and tedium and misery for all his imperial splendor. His tension is due to the fact that he will not face the question of the essential and yet cannot suppress it.[5] He thus satiates himself with lusts. He exhausts what this world can offer. He tastes its every refinement. Yet he cannot find rest even though he has everything. Why not? Because he cannot suppress the nagging question of basis, goal, and meaning, and yet he will not face it. This explains his melancholy. As Guardini says of Hölderlin, he is unsettled by the proximity of the eternal which he no longer wills or attains, but ought to do so. His unease derives from his indifference to a question from which he cannot free himself. It is a sin of the spirit.[6]

Some modern theologians like van Buren seem to regard this nexus of experience as non-existent when they argue that after the death of God secular man has lost all sense of the transcendent—obviously on the ground that it is not the object of an intellectual question. There seems to be no discussion of the origin of this deficiency or of other symptoms, like melancholy and tedium, which betray the impingement of transcendence. These symptoms are well attested in intellectual history and they show that we need to consider whether the elimination of the question of transcendence from the reflective consciousness is not perhaps due to Neronic suppression, to what Paul calls "holding down the truth in unrighteousness" (*katéchein en adikía*, Romans 1:18). Might it not be that the suggested irrelevance of every transcendent reference is not to be credited to the so-called modern consciousness, just as it is not to be credited to man's own activity and creative urge when these present themselves as a triumph, whereas in truth they might well be acts of flight and suppression?

It is odd to what extent the idea of suppression—along with other psychological categories—is used in interpretation of states of consciousness and modes of conduct, and yet it seldom seems to have occurred to anyone to investigate the element of suppression in the principle of self-resting finitude and the irrelevance of the transcendent. The reason is perhaps that melancholy and tedium and other symptoms of secularism are no longer interpreted existentially in terms of the unresolved question of the whence and whither which lies within them. Instead they are investigated psychologically and psychoanalytically. But psychology and psychoanalysis themselves are usually reflective forms of an existence based on suppression. In this sense psychoanalysis has itself been called a sickness in the ultimate sense.[7]

What we have here is simply the maturing of a lengthy process. Consideration of this should prevent us from seeing only modern states of consciousness at work. The renaissance in its understanding of *acedia* veers off

---

[5] *Ibid.*, p. 186.

[6] Cf. Kierkegaard's quotation from Gregory the Great in the entry in his *Journals* for July 20, 1839 (E.T. 1938, p. 75).

[7] Cf. J. Bodamer, "Die Krankheit der Psychoanalyse," *Wort und Wahrheit* (1955), 3, pp. 183ff.; Victor E. Frankl, "Kritik und Überwindung der Psychoanalyse," *Universitas* (1952), 7, p. 193; Gertrud von le Fort, *Schweisstuch der Veronika* (1935).

into psychology without really recognizing the cleavage of soul. How could it possibly achieve this recognition when the suppressing of transcendence removes from view the polarity which is indispensable if the cleavage is even to be perceived, let alone understood?

Thus, whereas the monastic athletes of sorrow regard *acedia* as a sin, in Petrarch it becomes a purely psychological and irrational feeling of lack of desire or overabundance. The reworking of the condition, its transformation into a virtue rather than a necessity, may already be seen here. Melancholy can, as it were, be enjoyed. It is estimated positively. It is regarded as an attitude which is related to genius and is thus the price that the creative man must pay for straining beyond the imposed limits and reaching after the divine sphere.[8]

Nevertheless, these attempts to ennoble melancholy, to see in it something heroic,[9] to relate it to creative genius, can hardly disguise the fact that theology is here being integrated into anthropology and man is being burdened with a usurped role which is really that of the God who is displaced from the upper world and who is consequently absent. The continual presence of the question of transcendence may thus be inferred once again.

The question now is whether the man who proclaims his secularity can pretend to believe in the pure secularity which he claims that he has attained and in which he alleges that he now abides. Is not Jean Paul's fear of this new situation far more honest? Does he not depict its original form prior to all the manipulations which suppress and sublimate and transform it? Just because this first declaration of the death of God touches only marginally on theological themes and describes instead the terror of the abandoned and chaotic world and the misery of the wasteland without God, it shows that this world is never merely this world, that its horizons cannot be ignored, and that the question of transcendence is ineluctably implied.

Yet in Jean Paul this is only a dream. It is a drill or exercise in the territory in which the death of God is only assumed. It is an "as if" experiment with a heuristic purpose. Atheism is studied in order to find out what God means. The exercise, however, very quickly becomes the real thing. It becomes the content of waking consciousness.

4. IDEA OF THE DEATH OF GOD AS THE CONTENT OF WAKING CONSCIOUSNESS

a. Wetzel

Ten years after Jean Paul's Sermon, and in obvious dependence upon it, there appeared *The Night Watches of Bonaventura*. This was published anonymously and contemporaries were puzzled by the question who wrote it. Jean Paul regarded it as a work of Schelling. Other names suggested were E. T. A. Hoffmann, Caroline Schlegel, and Clemens von Brentano. Modern authorities ascribe it to Gottlieb Wetzel.[10] The symbolical and stylistic similarities to

---

[8] Rehm, *op. cit.,* p. 190.

[9] Cf. E. Panofsky and F. Saxl, *Dürers Melancolia* (1923), pp. 30ff.; J. Huizinga, *Waning of the Middle Ages* (E.T. 1924), p. 25; Rehm, *loc. cit.*

[10] 1804; the references are to the 1946 edition of Renate Riemeck.

Jean Paul's work make the material differences all the more noticeable.

Thus Jean Paul only dreams of atheism, and then comes back to certainty of faith, but in Wetzel life itself has become an anxious dream. The death of God, an "as if" for Jean Paul, is a reality for Wetzel. The existence of God is now the content of a dream. The watcher of the night who has the vision is, with the wonderful porter who makes night into day, the only one awake in a world of dreamers. What he sees in his lonely vigil is the complete emptying out of being and its subjection to nothingness.

As in Jean Paul, although now in reality, man is nothing in the wasteland of a universe without God. In his infinite emptiness he is quantitatively null. He is not even given the distinction of being God's partner. He is not addressed by God and thereby granted creaturely nobility. Man is presented as this nihil in the monolog of the mad creator in the *Ninth Watch* (pp. 122f.).

Being relegated to nothingness, man asks for a mirror in order to see and identify himself. For out in the infinite, deprived of all relations, he is as it were a swimmer with no identity. The one who is no longer addressed as a Thou is in danger of losing his I-ness. This is why the question of identity arises. This is why the mirror is wanted. The lost I wants to reassure itself.[11] But after the death of God the attempt at identification fails. The I is only the thought of a thought and the dream of a dream. It faces nothingness (p. 140).

Man's abandonment without relations, which threatens to deprive him of identity, leads also in distinctive dialectic to arrogant titanism. After the death of God man alone remains. He can thus engage in demonic if despairing boasting. In the proximity of nothingness the I can see and hear only itself. In this extended nothingness, the only thing of significance is in a bracket behind the sign "insignificant" or "meaningless." This produces the dread of anxiety. When it feels called, as Samuel did in 1 Samuel 3:4, 6, in reality it hears only "myself in me" (p. 182). It hears the echo of its own voice. It is thus subject to the same solipsism as the dreamer in Jean Paul. It has lost this world as well as the world beyond. It is referred back to itself alone. It is worldless as well as godless. It lives in a ghostly and docetic world of appearance. Thus, as Hannah Arendt says,[12] man is set at a far greater distance from the earth and phenomenal reality than he ever could be by any Christian hope of the hereafter.

"Then I saw myself alone in nothingness. The last earth merely glimmered at a great distance like a dying spark. . . . A single note oscillated heavily and earnestly through the waste — it was departing time, and eternity now set in. I had now ceased to think of anything else; I thought only of myself. No object could be discerned but the great and terrible I which tore itself to pieces and constantly bore itself again in devouring itself. All change ended with time and there reigned only an eternally empty tedium. I tried to

---

[11] Cf. the varied symbolism in relation to the same question of identity in Max Frisch.

[12] *Vita activa oder Vom tätigen Leben* (1960), p. 312.

destroy myself—but I remained and felt myself immortal" (pp. 182f.).

Here, then, there is no joy in the consolidation of one's own emancipated humanity which has cast off all tutelage. There is only terror at the resultant expanded nothingness of the I which has to maintain itself and cannot break free. Man is not the lord of his new lordship. In a deeper sense, in spite of the achieved death of Zarathustra, man cannot be his own destroying angel even though he would like to. He cannot break free from his nothingness. He has to endure his immortality.

Immortality with no goal which makes it worthwhile is a burden. Immortality with no grace and with no one to give grace and meaning is a permanent and tormenting enclosure in nothingness. Against a different background we see the same thing in Marlowe's Faust. After twenty-four years of the pact with the devil Faust begins to dread his own immortality. He asks the mountains to fall on him, the earth to swallow him up, the cosmos to be dissolved in him. The torment and tedium of empty but ineluctable continuation is the same thing as *acedia*. It is the melancholy which carries with it assurance of destiny but has lost the one who destines, so that it is plunged into self-contradiction. Man wants to be I but is not addressed as Thou. He wants identity but he is in the absurd ambivalence of being both nothing and alone. Wakefully this time, there is again an involuntary cry for the transcendence which is indeed lost but which is intimated as an ongoing question even in the absurdity of nothingness.

Perhaps one may detect in Wetzel the first signs of accommodation to this plunge into nothingness. For full despair can last only for a moment. Then it leads logically either to the annihilating of nothingness and the destruction of the self-creator or to the making of a virtue of the necessity and the inauguration of new dreams in which the creative element is kindled by the confrontation with nothingness and emancipation becomes adulthood. In Wetzel man encourages himself: The stronger and more assured he is, the more childish are all things mysterious and miraculous (p. 202). He clings to this world like the dying freethinker who rejects the hell of his moralizing priest and looks at the three spring roses blooming at his bedside (p. 18). Yet he cannot banish altogether the comfortless boundary: The skeleton is always behind the ogling mask and life is only a robe of bells which nothingness has draped about itself so that it may ring out and then finally tear the robe with a grimace and fling it away.

The vision of the churchyard in the last watch is very close to the work of Jean Paul even in detail. The great difference is that the gigantic force of nature, the terrible mother who has given birth to herself and all things, and who has no heart in her breast but forms little ones for amusement (p. 212), appears now in a waking vision rather than in a dream. The watcher of the night sees the infinity of the cosmic night while others lull themselves in dreams and see the Lord God and his angels. We have here the same terrible cry as in Jean Paul: "I no longer see thee, Father—where art thou?" But the God of wish and longing is only a fabricated mask which crumbles at the slightest touch: "I scatter this handful of fatherly dust in the air, and it remains—nothing" (p. 214). This is the death of God. It is no help to hide the corpse's face with masks. Life cannot be simulated. The beautiful dream of the Father is over.

The following points seem to be theologically significant in this vision of the death of God.

First, the anxious dream of a godless waste is no longer a heuristically fruitful premise from which one can awake to the reality of God-filled being. The illusion now is the divine fatherhood, and we awake from this to real life as to an anxious dream.

Second, the real death of God does not mean only that the world to come is eliminated, so that by subtraction the solid world remains. It means also that this world itself becomes a mask, a robe of bells which has been put on. The merry sound and the glitter and the sparkle simply conceal the basic nothingness lurking behind all things. But they do so only for a time. The negation "God is dead" which is put before the bracket devalues all the positive quantities within the bracket and makes them an empty show.

Third, the pain and self-destructive passion with which the thesis is advanced show that it is inextricably bound up with a question that cannot be silenced, namely, that of the transcendent or of the meaninglessness and futility that its absence entails. This question is the secret theme underlying the vision of Jean Paul and the night watches of Wetzel. The postulate that there must be meaning is what gives force to the assertion of meaninglessness and to despair at the diagnosis that God is dead. The man who defends meaninglessness puts the knife to his own roots. This is true at least in the early stages when consoling reinterpretations have not yet been started. In fact, what Wetzel expresses in his work is a gigantic suicide. Or rather, it is an attempted suicide, for paradoxically nothingness can never become nothing. Notwithstanding all statements to the contrary, it has indestructible being. In a dreadful way it is immortal. And this raises afresh the question of transcendence which is implicit in all being.[13]

How does it come about that a thing is and is not nothing? This old philosophical question is particularly urgent here. It is not that the question points to the transcendent God or to the Father of Jesus Christ and thus forms a starting-point for the ontological proof. The question of the ground of being, however, cannot be detached from the question whether and how far being is meaningful. Radically meaningless being cannot be "thought." What is thinkable is only mere matter which has not yet been called into being.

Wetzel seems to see that there is no evading the question of transcendence when he asks why nothingness is not nothing but has the form of being. His answer is that we cannot have any concept of utter emptiness. In our experience even a vacuum is always between bodies. For Wetzel, then, there has to be a something to which emptiness relates. What is this something?

If we are not mistaken, it has two forms. When time vanishes (p. 183) and

---

[13] Cf. Paul Tillich's *The Courage to Be* (1952). The postulate that there is meaning is always the basis of despair at meaninglessness.

change and movement cease, there remains only the great and terrible I. This is itself null and wants to destroy itself. Its attempt to do this, even though it fails by reason of awful immortality, is the one real something. The something is thus the process of unsuccessful self-destruction. Wetzel also seems to believe, however, that the world remains, that it is in movement, and hence that "something" happens. But what is this something if it is not meaningful movement oriented to a goal? It cannot be this, however, if God is dead. Movement of formless matter is not thinkable. What can that which moves itself actually "be"?

Wetzel concocts the monstrous paradox that nothing devours itself as the man who is nothing is in the act of destroying himself. The conflict of nothing with itself gives the impression that "something" is happening. But it is a sham battle. The unreal is in conflict with itself. The only real thing is the act of conflict (pp. 114f.).

This is the point where transcendence comes in. For one cannot avoid asking why nothing is in conflict with itself. Are those who deny the death of God merely dissemblers when they see transcendence here, i.e., the prior awareness of meaning without which the absurdity of self-engulfing nothingness could not be perceived? Could that which comes from nothing see nothing, note its conflict with itself, and finally try to destroy itself because of its futility?

Wetzel, however, just fails to put the question which again makes the matter of the death of God an open one and brings back the one who has been supposedly discarded. For he does not ask why nothing is engaged in conflict with itself. He is more interested in what would happen should the conflict cease. Would the second world of eternity return? Would the supposedly dead God be all in all (1 Corinthians 15:28; cf. Romans 11:32)? That would be humbug, says Wetzel. No, in this case real nothing and absolute death would rule.

One could in fact say that nothing which is no longer in conflict with itself would no longer have even a whisper of something alongside it. It would be pure nothing. But we do not know it as such. This is why Wetzel's question is not properly put. In its absolute form nothing is a demonically eschatological "as if" notion which we have to manufacture if we are to form the concept of emptiness without movement. And to try to substitute eternity for this abstract vacuum would indeed be humbug.

Eternity cannot be saved by manipulations of extreme notions like this, nor can the Father be resurrected out of the "fatherly dust." But is this the real point? On his own level Wetzel's question should have been why we have to think in terms of this self-conflict when we think of nothing. If nothing exists, why does there have to be this civil war and this passion for self-destruction? Do we not get here the signal-flash of a very distant God which he wants us to regard as a sign of life? Do we not see here the indelible character of the question—it is only a question—of what transcends nothingness and gives it being through this conflict with itself?

b. Jens Peter Jacobsen

The basic pattern seems to have remained in Wetzel. There has simply been a change in the embellishing symbols. The death of God does not vanish with the dream as in Jean Paul. It is part of our waking relation to the world. Nevertheless, it is a waking *dream*. The relation to the world is thus tenuous and docetic. Reality has lost all hold.

Along the same lines a distinctive unreality pervades the work of Jacobsen. There is constant relapse here into illusion. Mogens,[14] who has seen his beloved Camilla perish in flames, goes mad. In this state he falls on his knees and beseeches God to reverse what has happened. Henning in *Der Schuss im Nebel* (1875) is beset by crazy notions. Frau Marie Grubbe in the work of this name (1876) dies in madness and the priest can neither pray with her nor give her the last rites. In *The Pest in Bergamo* (1881) madness stalks the ravaged city and joins forces with hell. Finally, the monk is on the edge of madness when he has a dreadful vision of Christ leaving the cross and in disgust at the human race returning to heaven.

The world depicted by Jacobsen is governed by experience of the death of God. God is a dream which is dispelled by the meaninglessness and futility of events. Mogens' prayer is not heard. Niels Lyhne implores heaven in vain that Edele Lyhne not die. When his petition is flung back from heaven's gates he stops praying and after a period of revolt becomes indifferent to his non-being. A despairing return to the dream that God exists and a cry of prayer when his little son dies are regarded by him as apostasy from and unfaithfulness to his atheistic beliefs. He finally resolves to accept life as it is. When he dies he will not see the priest and dies a bitter death.

Wetzel's concept of the death of God recurs in Jacobsen to the degree that as the life to come is abandoned increasing fulness is expected from this life. Only when God is dead and when disillusioned humanity is freed from churchly Christianity can life drop the burden of transcendence and achieve its true destiny. "On the day," says Niels Lyhne, "when mankind can freely rejoice: There is no God, on that day it will fashion at a stroke a new heaven and a new earth." The great things previously sought outside will then be found within. As heaven and hell lose their power, conscience will grow and come of age. Since there is no solution outside in judgment or grace, hopelessness must be conquered here and now. This world takes on fulness and significance. The earth becomes our country. It becomes "the home of our heart where we do not live a wretched hour as alien guests but forever." Life is intensified when everything is contained within it. "The great stream of love which flows to the God in whom there is faith will flow over the earth when heaven is empty." This is the atheistic hope which as a program of world renewal we find again in Marxist eschatology. It is the new dream of the life that has come to itself.

In fact, however, the expected paradise proves to be a godless wasteland. The emptiness of life intensifies when the dream of self-transcendence is set

---

[14] Mogens, 1872. The references are to the Jena edition, *Gesammelte Werke* (1905).

aside. The increased sensuality of self-inverted life leads to chaos and banality and finally to derangement. An empty and indifferent existence becomes an insupportable encumbrance. There is no home on earth or God in heaven or goal in the future. Expectations are disappointed. The earth without God is no home at all. The attempt to suck life to the full is a failure now that it is all the more evident that all acts and events are without direction. The attempt to find meaning in the desire for communication also founders. The bond snaps.

There thus opens up the abyss of this world encircled by nothing. This is depicted in *The Pest in Bergamo*. When penitential monks visit the vile and plague-stricken town they are met at first by scorn and derision. When they prove the seriousness of their message by self-flagellation, scorn gives way to awe and respect. They detect signs of grace. This is a collective state similar to the brief interim we find elsewhere in the spiritual histories of Jacobsen's characters. For recurring moments there is a backing off from the abyss of unbelief and ridicule, a sudden return to the lost God for refuge, a brief prayer, the passing breath of grace. But then at once, and recurrently, the attack of weakness and the relapse into dreaming are corrected. A monk leaves the circle of penitents to belie the terrors of judgment, hell, and purgatory. He calls to the shuddering crowd: There is no mediator between God and us; no Jesus died for us on the cross. After enduring the torment of nailing to the cross Jesus turned in anger from those who mocked him, told them that men were not worthy of him, tore his hands from the nails, cast his robe over his shoulders, and went back to heaven in regal indignation. The cross stood empty and the work of atonement was never finished. So the monk continues to cry: No Jesus died for us on the cross. Then with the praying and singing monks he goes to the city gate while the crowd watches them transfixed.

The dialectic of the death of God is encapsulated in this vision. Self-resting and self-enclosed finitude does not bring the hoped-for liberation. Usurpation of what formerly belonged to the next world does not carry with it the newly possible growth in fulness. Terror at the dream or perception of the loss of transcendence, as in Jean Paul and Wetzel, remains the last word. When there is no halting, one can only try to hold out. This fact, and the further fact that atheism is possible only as self-assertion and protest, is a sign that man's being has a point of reference into which he must inquire. To inquire into the self is to inquire into this point of reference. Man does inquire into himself. He is ordained to self-comprehension.

Even when man's search for answers fails, the question itself remains and is the source of unrest or madness. In face of this persistent question there can be no refuge in self-resting finitude. The statement that God is dead can never be made with relaxed indifference. It is always the despairing if honestly demanded negative report.

Were the question to be silenced—which never happens—humanity itself would be at an end. Responsibility and self-relation in it would be extinguished. The earth would be changed from the home of man into an abstract lunar landscape. The wretched hour in which he was a guest on earth would not become a protracted stay at home but banishment to an inhuman wilderness. The forsaken cross stands as a sign that the question as to the point of reference remains and that atheism can be espoused only in negation. The cross is indeed empty. Atonement is unfinished. The partnership to which it might be related does not exist. But the cross, even if empty, remains as a sign. It gives no answers, but it raises the question why there are no answers.

c. Nietzsche

For Nietzsche, as distinct from the previous authors mentioned, the experience of the death of God is not a violent emancipation of this-worldly reality from soothing dreams. For him the world above is not a prison from which, with the call to awake, we have to break out with force and cunning. Consciously at least—if we refrain from depth analysis—this is the position. Nietzsche confesses that he had no true religious difficulties. Hence he did not have to reject religious solutions with pain and effort. He says that he did not know the meaning of sinfulness and therefore had no criterion by which to recognize the sting of conscience. He claims that atheism was for him neither a result nor an event, but an instinct.[15]

Since he does not suffer the pain of having to break free, atheism is for him a pure transition to freedom and the winning through to a new atmosphere. For philosophers and freethinkers news of the death of the old God is like the dawn. It fills the heart with thankfulness, astonishment, and expectation. Even though the horizon is not clear, it is free. The sea is open for our ships.[16]

In view of this celebration one might ask why fear arises. Why is there talk of destruction, overthrow, and catastrophe? Why is the man who proclaims the death of God the prophet of a darkness such as the earth has never known?[17] Why do we no longer feel at home? Why is the ice thin beneath us?[18] Why does Nietzsche say that memory will connect his name with something terrible? Why does he say that he is not a man but dynamite?[19] Why does he speak of the wilderness extending?[20]

The solution to the apparent contradiction is that the pain is felt, not by the prophet himself, but by those in the grip of the traditions which surround him. He himself is the opposite of a spirit of negation. He is an incomparable bringer of good news.[21] His previously inexpressible message[22] is bad news and banishment only for those who are not atheists by instinct but who have fallen victim to the corruption of transcendence.

Thus the coming fulfilments which will shake off all the restrictions of transcendence presuppose an interim of breaking free, of nihilistic disruption.

---

[15] *Ecce homo,* Kröner, 15, p. 26.
[16] *Fröhliche Wissenschaft,* Kröner, 5, p. 272.
[17] *Ibid.,* pp. 271f.   [18] *Ibid.,* pp. 334f.
[19] Cf. *Ecce homo,* Kröner, 15, p. 116.
[20] *Zarathustra,* Kröner, 6, p. 444; E.T. 1908, IV, p. 419.
[21] Kröner, 15, p. 117.   [22] *Ibid.*

Nihilism is a pathological interlude[23] which must first be lived through before high and beautiful and daring things can be affirmed. Thus the nihilistic disruption is not really a negation. It is the destruction which makes possible a new form of existence.[24] Even now in the pangs of transition the hidden Yes in us is stronger than every No or Perhaps from which we and our age suffer.[25]

The position that Nietzsche is opposing is viewed too narrowly if we think that he is proclaiming only the death of the Christian God. He is attacking the whole Western tradition, whose metaphysics has been characterized since Plato by a distinction between the sensory and the supersensory world. He is thus deplatonizing rather than dechristianizing. He is putting the axe to the root of all norms, standards, values, and ideals that belong to the Greek-Christian tradition. He is thus aiming at a true uprooting, at a transvaluation of all values, as illustrated by his treatment of such basic values as the true, the good, and the beautiful.[26] He is not just attacking that which is of Christian origin.

His fundamental protest, which is directed against the illusion of a transcendently determined cosmic order, focuses on the point that this order interprets life incorrectly and thus subjects it to destructive perversion. This false interpretation is marked by two main features.

First, it deprives life in this world of its full significance and thus extinguishes true and real life.[27] This results from the fact that the ruling value judgments are decadent and lead men astray from their basic instincts.[28] We are thus trapped by the decadent instincts of antiquated races.[29] Preference for the suffering and decadent leads to a negative selection.[30]

This decadence, which in the form of Christianity poisoned young and fresh barbarian peoples,[31] did not merely result from a perverse interpretation of life. It was also fostered with cynical purpose in order to tame elemental life. To make sick is the only way to weaken brute energy. The church understood this. It corrupted and weakened man while claiming to improve him.[32]

Second, the idea of God and the world to come offers an easy escape when life and its burdens have to be endured and when puzzling questions are too hard for us. At this point Nietzsche follows Laplace in claiming that the hypothesis of God is not necessary. It is not necessary to explain what is obscure. Nor is it necessary to make tolerable what is intolerable. In this regard God is an invention of our own weakness. This weakness prevents us from standing on our own and affirming ourselves. Hence the poets dream up the incorruptible.

It should be noted in this regard that the diagnosis that God is dead results

---

23 *Willie zur Macht*, Kröner, 15, p. 152; E.T. *Will for Power* (1967), I, 13, p. 14.
24 Kröner, 12, p. 368.   25 Kröner, 5, p. 337.
26 Cf. M. Heidegger, "Nietzsches Wort 'Gott ist tot,'" *Holzwege* (1950), pp. 199ff.
27 Kröner, 15, p. 62.   28 *Ibid.*, p. 167; *Will for Power*, I, 39, p. 25.
29 *Ibid.*, p. 179; *Will for Power*, I, 53, p. 33.
30 *Ibid.*, p. 323; *Will for Power*, II, 246, pp. 141f. Cf. the end of *Ecce homo*, Kröner, 15, pp. 126f.
31 Kröner, 3, p. 123.   32 Kröner, 8, pp. 103f.

either (1) when God is seen as the correlate of human weakness, whether as a projection of this weakness[33] or as a stratagem to weaken or tame the human race, or (2) when God's transcendence is viewed as purely other-worldly rather than as the unconditioned in the conditioned, so that God is not in the conditions of being any more. In this case he can be supported only by authoritarian institutions, and the declaration of his death is thus a breaking through to one's own autonomy, will, and power.[34]

It must be conceded that the God of the Bible is hardly recognizable in this idea of God. The reference is rather to the offspring of a metaphysical or pragmatic theism which is designed to solve the unmastered problems of existence or thought and to help (or cause) our weakness, i.e., to a god of the gaps.[35] That there has been this abuse of God, his degrading to an ideology of human weakness, can hardly be contested. Christian advocates and institutions are responsible for it; it is they who have provoked the reaction of atheism, and put shovels in the hands of the gravediggers for the burial of God.

Thus Nietzsche is not just fighting decadence; he is also fighting a degenerate view of God. His arrogance in opposing God and proclaiming his death is not, to the best of our human judgment, guilty hubris but a prejudice induced by the empirical phenomenon of Christianity, its institutions, its theology, and its behavior. Strictly Nietzsche stands, not for apostasy, but for reaction against apostasy—reaction, not in the name of that from which there is apostasy, but of that to which there is apostasy, and hence in supposed protest against the name of the Lord whose discredited image is before him. Adapting Schiller's famous phrase, we might say that the church's history is the church's judgment and that Nietzsche is the agent of this judgment. Jesus Christ and Nietzsche are like two ships that pass in the night. When Nietzsche thinks that he is speaking of Christ, he is speaking only of an image of Christ distorted by the church. Nevertheless, he does have for Christ an ultimate respect; he says that fundamentally there was only one Christian, and he died on the cross.[36]

The mere fact that Nietzsche is the agent of a judgment that the church has brought down on itself, and that he strikes only the confused contemporary form of the church's Lord and not Christ himself, is enough to rule out any pharisaic apologetic against his atheism or any condemnation of Nietzsche himself as one of the "goats." Even the element of caricature in Nietzsche carries with it a call to repentance. If he wears the skin of the blond beast rather than soft clothing, he becomes unwillingly and unwittingly

---

[33] Although Nietzsche had no high view of Feuerbach, H. de Lubac (*Die Tragödie des Humanismus ohne Gott* [1950], pp. 39ff.) is right when he points out that in relation to religion he adopted the latter's theory of projection.
[34] Cf. on this G. Vahanian, *The Death of God. The Culture of Our Post-Christian Era* (1961), pp. 44ff.
[35] Cf. Charles du Bos, *Extraits d'un journal*, pp. 177ff., quoted in de Lubac, *op. cit.*, p. 47.
[36] *Antichrist,* No. 39, Kröner, 8, p. 265.

a preacher in the wilderness whose summons is not to be rejected apologetically but received and taken to heart.

If the real adversary is a mistaken tradition of values, a historical transposition, then the best way to fight the error is not to refute its decrees and results and thus to prove the non-existence of Platonic-Christian transcendence, i.e., the death of God. It is rather to unmask the rise of the perversion and the reason for the masquerade. Once the background is brought to light, there is no need to prove that there is no God. While the refutation of the older proofs of God can only be provisional and must await a better proof that will challenge the refutation, understanding of the rise of a metaphysical specter is definitive and helps to level the site on which the new, emancipated, Zarathustran man can live. This strategy of proof by genealogy is the up-to-date one from the time of Feuerbach, and it is adopted by Nietzsche.[37]

A basic question arises here: Can the attempt to establish the historical relativity of scales of value reach the goal of explaining the values themselves genealogically, i.e., in terms of the flux of history?[38] Or can the demonstration of historical influences on the scale of values mean only that a basic human situation is characterized by value references and that historical influences merely arise in relation to modifications of the understanding of the basic situation and its references?[39] This is a fundamental question whose importance can hardly be overestimated.

In the first case—we shall use conscience as an illustration—conscience itself is a product of evolution. To that extent the polarity of good and evil which determines its schema of values has no force of its own. It is to be understood merely as a function and result of the evolutionary process. In the second case, however, conscience denotes a basic human situation which is in principle nonderivable and which in fact regulates all attempts at derivation. For the question of truth stands always under an imperative and accepts it as an immanent principle of theoretical reason (cf. Kant's Preface to the *Critique of Pure Reason*).

Only the understanding of what is attested to be good or evil by the conscience is subject to historical modification, not the unconditioned understanding of the values themselves. Thus for some tribes it might be an ethical duty to kill and to scalp enemies. This might seem contrary to the Western view and to the so-called rights of man. But it still implies an unconditional ought and ought not. It rests on an invariable basic human situation.

On which side does Nietzsche stand? Is he just challenging a traditional understanding of the basic situation but accepting the axiomatic integrity of the latter, or is he dissolving the situation itself in the evolutionary stream? If the latter, a radical overthrow of values is entailed and, as in Stirner, we

---

[37] Cf. *Morgenröte*, No. 85 in Schlechta, I, 1073.
[38] Cf. Herbert Spencer on good and evil and the conscience as a kind of moral computer, and on this ThE, I, § 1465ff. and F. Loeser, *Deontik, Planung und Leitung der moralischen Entwicklung* (1966).
[39] Cf. Herbert Marcuse, *One-Dimensional Man* (1964).

have man in a state of pure nature with his elemental instincts and will for power. Truth in this case is merely an enhancement of the sense of power. Knowledge is a tool of force, and truth for its own sake is an empty phrase. The same applies to the good and the beautiful.[40]

Since man cannot escape values this means that pure nature itself becomes a value and the blond beast who lusts for prey and conquest is set up as a model. What qualifies a value is not its truth but whether or not it enhances life, so that I will it.

This seems in fact to be the drift of Nietzsche's thinking. He flings down a radical challenge. He offers a genealogical and evolutionary explanation. He is the Darwin of ethics. He does not investigate conscience in terms of the basic human situation. He is not interested in the orientation or relations of values. What he seeks is the source of this need for an orientation. What relations does the need create? Thus the category of the whence rather than the whither of existence (including its basic situation) controls all his questions. His analysis of conscience is an example. He does not relate it to the polarity of good and evil. He explains it in terms of its supposed source. In other words, he does not define it upwards in relation to the givenness of values (cf. ThE, I, § 1852ff.; E.T. I, pp. 383ff.) but downwards in relation to its point of evolutionary origin. Thus in the genealogy of morals—and the use of this phrase as a title[41] is characteristic—he describes conscience as a phenomenon of decadence. It is a substitute for organs now lost. Man used to live by instincts of aggression and self-preservation.[42] As he built the shelter of civilization, the situation of stress eased. The instincts atrophied. But, in psychological terms, they could not perish; they were thus repressed and in the process underwent a change of function. The fighting instinct was directed inwards rather than outwards. Man himself became the battleground of his instincts. He suffered inner disruption. He came to be fighting, not someone else, but himself. There thus arose the conflict between will and impulse, flesh and spirit, good and evil. Tension replaced man's original simplicity as a creature of instinct.

The fall from instinctual life is a point at which modern sociological anthropology comes close to Nietzsche.[43] The decisive difference is that the forfeiture of the instincts is not now viewed as a loss but as an opportunity for freedom and culture. Man can now press beyond his impulses to conscious acts. He has thus to seek norms by which to direct his otherwise chaotic and random action. With the loss of the natural order there has to arise a deliberately shaped order of civilization (Schelsky, *op. cit.*, p. 242).

One can hardly object against this understanding that it, too, views the values as surrogates for instincts and thus explains the ethical organ of conscience by a process of repression. For the basic human situation which is at

---

[40] *Antichrist*, No. 2, Kröner, 8, p. 218.
[41] *Genealogie der Moral;* cf. Kröner, 7, p. 375; cf. ThE, I, § 1484ff.
[42] Cf. K. Lorenz, *Das sogenannte Böse* (1963); E.T. *On Aggression* (1966).
[43] Cf. A. Gehlen, *Der Mensch. Seine Natur und seine Stellung in der Welt* (1950); H. Schelsky, "Die sozialen Formen der sexuellen Beziehungen" in H. Giese, *Die Sexualität des Menschen* (1955).

issue in the responsible ordering of values and norms is not derived nor is it merely a sign of declension. The loss of instincts is the decisive opportunity for the basic human situation. Hence the situation itself is not an object of deduction. It is seen from the standpoint of the factors which provide its opportunity. The process is thus a very different one from that in Nietzsche.

For Nietzsche the instinctual state is the model, humanizing is decadence, and the supposed basic situation is derivative. Here, however, the model is the basic human situation which is attained by release from the bondage of the instincts, whether this situation take a Christian, humanist, or any other form. If man is defective, as in Gehlen, this is not meant negatively but ironically. The defect is a chance for man to find his identity and to come to himself. The point in common with Nietzsche is that man's power of normative self-direction cannot be understood apart from his deprivation of the instincts.

This is also the point, however, where the difference in the real interpretation of man begins. For one has to ask here from what standpoint we want to see the nature of man. Is man to be seen in terms of the normativity of his point of departure as a creature of instinct or in terms of the normativity of his destiny with self-direction as the basic human situation. In the one case (Nietzsche) man is defined genealogically in terms of his whence; in the other he is defined teleologically in terms of his whither.

We thus maintain that in Nietzsche the normative and exemplary situation of man is the original one preceding the basic situation, which cannot, then, be regarded as basic at all. Man is not derived from mind or deity. He is set among the beasts. He is the strongest beast because he is the most cunning. A product of this is his intellectuality. For a paradigm of undivided and pre-divided man Nietzsche resorts to the bold concept of Descartes that man is to be regarded as a machine. Consciousness and spirit simply denote a relative imperfection of the organism, a testing, tasting, groping, and worrying which consume nervous energy. It is denied that anything perfect can be done so long as it is done consciously.[44]

We recall that what led Nietzsche to state that God is dead was the animal instinct which he says he still had and which made him a precursor and herald of the higher man whose second naiveté will replace his lost primal state. To clear the way for this new man the interim of Platonic-Christian traditions must be ended. This raises the question of what preceded the intervening stage. The evolutionary aspect is thus introduced. When this becomes dominant, there is a temptation to regard the interim merely as a period of error and declension. There are in it no positive signs of something trying to free itself from the animal stage and to come to itself.

This is why we ask whether Nietzsche, when he attacks the Western tradition with this goal and with these means, is really attacking the traditions and not denying altogether the basic human situation which presses up in the traditions and has—perhaps—been perverted and concealed. Simply to

---

[44] *Antichrist,* No. 14, Kröner, 8, p. 229.

say that the situation has been perverted and concealed is not to deny it as such. There might have been such perversion and concealment, and Nietzsche might have unmasked it, e.g., in the form of some concepts of abstract transcendence, or a supposedly theological metaphysics which robs this world of its content and thus gives rise to an illusion or a corruption of transcendence. Nietzsche's thesis might thus appeal with justice to examples from church history and the history of thought.

The argument, then, does not have to drag the basic situation itself into the swamp of such perversions or to prove that it is a product of error. Indeed, it might even be asked whether witness is not borne to the basic situation in the erroneous interpretations, so that the real issue is the perversion of this situation, not the derivation of the situation from perverted development.

Certainly we have a perversion in an abstract heaven and hell which are the object of a fear and hope that bear no relation to the world and existence. But has this perversion produced the values of the good, the true, and the beautiful? Or is it a perversion of these values, so that the perversion presupposes them? Even metaphysically misdirected ideas of heaven and hell appeal to the basic human situation to the degree that they seek to describe a good which is rewarded and an evil which is avenged. Such ideas would have no basis in reality at all if they did not contain an appeal to man's basic situation or could not count on having a bridgehead in man's consciousness and conscience.

Thus these metaphysical constructs do not produce the original polarity of good and evil. They simply exploit it in a perverted way. To some extent pragmatically and cynically they use the knowledge of good and evil to promote the good without immediate reward and to restrain the evil without immediate punishment. The books will be balanced in the next world. The passion for social justice can thus be blunted by the promise of pie in the sky. (Karl Marx had a correct insight here, but, like Nietzsche, he threw out the baby with the bath water.)

Thus Nietzsche, equating the perversions of the history of human consciousness with what we have called the basic human situation, mounted an attack on the very structure of human existence itself. He took on more than he had at first intended. He had originally had in mind the error of a tradition. But his genealogical inquiry into evolutionary origins led him to claim, not merely that there had been fateful manipulations of the ongoing basic situation, as he might well do, but that the situation itself is to be understood as a product of evolution and is thus to be denied.

If the premise of our own investigation of Nietzsche is true, namely, that the basic situation, as an orientation to normative obligations, is a constant element in humanity as such, then even in Nietzsche himself the indelible character of this situation will continually manifest itself. He will not be able to talk it away.

Nor does he, for the news of the death of God is not a mere bit of information which is passed on by an unaffected diagnostician who is oriented to the stage of the constitutionally a-religious new man. It does not arouse emotions merely among those to whom it comes. The madman himself, as well as the people on the market square, is shaken to the core by it. A cool diagnostician would never accuse himself of having murdered God. He would not have done anything; he would simply be reporting. A further sign that the madman cannot escape the God who is supposed to be dead is that he rushes into the churches and strikes up a requiem to God. Eternity is still there as the eternal rest of the dead God. The church is still his monument. In his aggressive headlong rush Nietzsche is caught from behind by the power he is fighting. It is not where he thinks it is. It is all around him. Even though the sun has gone down the heaven of life still glows with its light, and so it is in the *Genealogie der Moral:* Even we who understand, who are without God, who think nonmetaphysically, even we still take our fire from the conflagration which a thousand-year-old faith kindled, the Christian belief . . . that God is the truth and the truth is divine (Kröner, 7, p. 470).

Is this only a historical backwash, the drag of tradition which can still influence prophets of the new age and prevent them from abandoning the table of values that is now outdated? Or do we have evidence here of the basic human situation, of that which was at work in tradition and made it its (however perverted) witness, of that which will take care that there will always be new forms of its presence and manifestation? Does not Nietzsche himself offer confirmation of this?

Nihilism as the total destruction of traditional value systems is indeed a pathological interim (Kröner, 15, p. 152; *Will for Power,* I, 13, p. 14). It sets in when we have tried to find a non-existent meaning in things and have lost heart. The goal is not reached. There is no answer to the question of Why (15, pp. 145-148; *Will for Power,* I, pp. 9-11). As noted, however, this is only transitional. The night of wandering in the ruins will give place to a new day when new guiding stars will be visible in the heavens—new values and new goals. If the old values and norms and universals to which history was subjected have now lost touch with reality and all the rational categories which by projection brought into being a false world have been unmasked, then new scaffoldings with new scales of value will arise on the leveled site. If the old values are plainly pragmatic veilings of utility, what they serve, i.e., the assertion of the will for power. will become the new supreme value hanging at the top of the new scaffoldings.

The basic situation which drives man to self-comprehension, overthrows the rule of instinct, and makes him responsible for his values, naturally takes action against those who try to escape it. It makes its presence felt and necessitates new values when the old ones have been destroyed. But might we not have here a genuine perversion when the one who rejects values and that which controls them from without assumes the rank of a new indicator of values and becomes a superman? Does not historical experience of this perversion tell us that wherever the "superman" is proclaimed "non-man" takes the field?

Sartre is another example of the way in which the basic situation, after its

supposed overthrow, still exacts its tribute. He, too, in the name of total freedom opposes the dominion of universals and the givenness of basic norms.
His protest is against the view (cf. Aristotle) that "essence" as a normative
concept controls existence. The latter in its sheer facticity comes first. It is
a kind of empty sheet on which we write. Our freedom is not restricted to
the narrow space in which we decide whether or not we will obey the given
norms and commandments of God. Our freedom is total. Its posits the norms
and commandments. The determinative significance of the past is not recognized. Man breaks free from this too. He is not the object of what is given; he
is the subject of a future which is to be grasped in freedom.

This seems to have atheistic implications which Sartre accepts. For in this
system God represents the given past. He is the epitome of the essence that
dictates to man. He is thus declared to be dead when self-existence proclaims
that it alone is alive.

This implication is a stringent one, of course, only under one condition,
namely, that God is understood as a demiurge who heteronomously imposes
that essence and thereby forces on man the task of responsible self-comprehension, i.e., his basic situation. The God of the Bible, however, is far different. As the author of the law and the gospel he stands in correspondence to
this basic human situation but is not identical with it (cf. G. Ebeling, *Gott
und Wort* [1966], pp. 50ff.; E.T. *God and Word* [1967], pp. 42ff.). What
Sartre says may be true of the God of the Enlightenment but it is not true of
the Father of Jesus Christ (cf. L. Gabriel, *Existenzphilosophie* [1951], p. 271
and Sartre's *Situations* [1965]).

Once again does not the basic situation catch up with the one who denies
it? Is it not a blatant contradiction that he who denies the givenness of
essence feels compelled to sketch a new essence? The total freedom which he
proclaims is not an uncommitted libertinism. He is not championing whim
and caprice. His freedom is a committed freedom whose protest against
essence and the first cause is ethically motivated. But what imposes the obligation if it is not the essence that precedes existence? What forces us to make
binding decisions? Is not the basic human situation continued here in another
form? Do we not see here the indelible character of essence? Might it not be,
then, that only the traditional form of essence is contested and not essence
itself (cf. ThE, I, § 1965ff.)?

Nietzsche himself seems to be entangled in an insoluble self-contradiction
when proclamation of the death of the basic human situation conceals itself
behind proclamation of the death of God. He is encircled by the very thing
that he denies.

The evidence of this encirclement is underrated if it is treated as merely
the backwash of the tradition which is opposed and which gives rise to the
pathological interim for those trying to break free from it. He is not caught
by the past which is vanishing but by the present of the basic situation denied
by him.

Understandably this is not expressly stated. The situation of the higher
man with his extreme egocentricity cannot be explained. The absurd is inex-

plicable. Things would have been different if Nietzsche had had a system. Is it only on constitutional grounds—grounds of his entelechy—that he does not? Or did the final absurdity stand in his way, so that the only form of statement he could use was that of prophetic aphorism?

What is not expressly stated, however, may be seen in the self-contradiction of existence itself. It is no moralism—and certainly no pharisaic moralism—if this one who transvalues all values, this prophet of the new man, is measured by his self-demonstrated ability or inability to meet his demand on life or life itself.

In this demand the question arises whether what is demanded can be lived out apart from the basic situation which is denied. Is this life possible? In this biographical question—for that is what it is—we come up against the suspected self-contradiction. The advocate of the beast of prey and a war ethic is on the edge of sickness. He is unable to be even a medical orderly for a few weeks, let alone a soldier. The one who lives beyond good and evil has a very tender conscience and hides his rebellious visions from pious old English ladies in order to spare them. The prophet of unbroken Dionysiac life diligently avoids sexual eros, the sphere of supreme elemental vitality.

It would be unfair to use this biographical information merely to show that Nietzsche did not reach the ideal in his own life. Failure to reach it does not refute the principle proclaimed. If it did nearly every philosophy would be discredited. It is necessary, then, to show the bearing of the biographical material.

When we ask whether this teaching can be lived out, we are not concerned with a quantitatively perfect congruence between life and teaching but rather with the fundamental possibility of even intending to live out the teaching. The possibility of merely aiming at this life, quite apart from the degree of attainment, would be identical with the possibility of ignoring the basic human situation. There is, however, no such possibility. It is to show this, and to show it in relation to the life-theory of the new man, that we refer to the fact that the real Nietzsche was overtaken by the basic situation, that he himself lived in it, and that he thus confirmed it in his life.[45]

Only broken visions can express the absurdity of an existence which simply leaves the solipsistic ghost of a man who is detached from his origin and goal, robbed of his basic situation, and consequently deprived of all reality. Good examples may be found in the unpublished Dionysus dithyrambs.[46]

The hanged Zarathustra, the crucified Dionysus, who is surrounded by mirrors, who no longer looks out, who sees only himself, who is no longer in relation but is himself the goal and object of all relations, is a complete absurdity which cannot be sustained any longer, which cannot be lived out, which signifies the end. Zarathustra collapses because "beyond" good and

---

[45] Karl Schlechta draws attention to other contradictions, e.g., between laughter and a world in which there is nothing to laugh at (cf. *Fröhliche Wissenschaft*, Schlechta, II, 34, 269 and cf. also III, 1446f.).

[46] Cf. Schlechta, III, 1377 and cf. also the later Zarathustra, Kröner, 8, pp. 422f., 424; Schlechta, II, 1250f.

evil, if it is more than the devaluation of a specific form of good and evil, is also "beyond" the basic human situation and it reduces man to a docetic shadow. Man is indeed an open being. He is a being with many possibilities. But he does not have the possibility of transcending himself, or being more than man, superman. If he makes the foolish attempt to be this, he simply confronts himself as a shadow.

The madness of Nietzsche, although pathologically definable, seems in a kind of pre-established harmony to be the result of his taking this course. Trying to transcend himself, he is overtaken by the transcendence that he denies. He is struck by lightning from the supposedly false deities whose "underhand ways" he would not allow.[47] The God he declared to be dead did not leave an empty space and evacuated heaven did not become a vacuum. When transcendence is denied man must become his own transcendence. He must transcend himself. In extreme distortion the ongoing presence of the basic human situation is thus manifested.

It is the riddle of Nietzsche's madness that the curve of a physiologically explicable process and the curve of intellectual destiny converge. The result of his thinking, namely, the absurd, is achieved and it finds a response in physiology.

Thus we find in Nietzsche's own life the illusion of his first bright dreams and his later and darker visions—the superman that he himself sought to be. The illusion stretches from his dreadful belief that he will provoke a desperate war, and that he has the young emperor in his hands, to ideas of omnipresence and a trivial egocentricity.[48]

In Nietzsche one may see again, although in grandiose apocalyptic form, the same thing as we have found in other ways in the other prophets of the death of God, namely, that man cannot escape transcendence, that the act of slaying God is indeed too great for us as the madman testifies, and that the superhumanity which corresponds to the death of God means in the last resort self-destruction. Self-destruction implies the establishment of human existence apart from its basic situation. This experiment cannot succeed because there is no ground beyond good and evil but short of transcendence. Self-destruction means being overtaken by a transcendence which is not wanted and which thus takes the form of judgment. This judgment condemns to self-transcendence and hence to an absurd presence of transcendence.

d. Excursus on Hegel

As opposed to a common view in theological circles, Hegel's theses about the death of God do not belong to the present discussion. Whereas the authors already treated, whether in sorrow or in the intoxication of a triumphant breakthrough, regard themselves as atheists, and therefore use the phrase "death of God" to signify his non-existence, for Hegel the death of

---

[47] *Wille zur Macht,* Kröner, 15, p. 150; *Will for Power,* I, 12, p. 13.
[48] Cf. Schlechta, III, 1348, 1351, 1378f.

God is simply a "moment" in God which confirms him and merely denotes the transition in which he comes to himself.[49]

Hegel, then, is erroneously and rather frivolously press-ganged by theologians when they take him to be the initiator or at least a representative of the period after the death of God.[50]

The place of the concept in Hegel's total system can be fixed only if one keeps in view the central thought that the absolute posits itself only as it opposes itself and does not remain alone. If it remains alone we have a bad absoluteness, the abstractly general and eternal prior to its realization.[51] The fact that the absolute opposes itself and comes to itself in this way means that it limits and negates itself.

But this is only transitional. The process is completed by negation of this negation. Thus the infinite is infinite in the true sense, which includes this process, only through the finite which it opposes to itself and in which it unceasingly continues. The relative finite is not, then, the exclusive antithesis or contradiction of the absolute infinite; it is enveloped by this. The absolute needs the counterpart of the finite to be able to come to itself by negation of the negation.

Nor does the absolute spirit need the finite only in regard to its ontic coming to itself. It needs it also noetically in relation to its self-consciousness. Thus Hegel defines the essence of religion as the process whereby the absolute spirit knows itself in a finite way. Conversely, the finite spirit knows its knowing as the absolute spirit.[52]

At the end of his treatise on faith and knowledge[53] Hegel shows how far the pure concept is a bad infinity, the dreadful abyss of nothing. This is true even of God if he is without the counterpart of the finite. "The pure concept . . . infinity as the abyss of nothing in which all being sinks, necessarily describes the infinite pain which formerly was . . . only the feeling on which the religion of the new age rests, the feeling that God is dead, as purely a moment, but not more than a moment, of pure idea."[54]

Philosophical existence is thus given to the sacrifice of empirical being (Jesus Christ) in the form of a speculative Good Friday, which would otherwise be (only) historical. Through this severity alone can the supreme totality rise up in all its seriousness and from its deepest depth, all-encompassing, and achieving the clearest freedom of its form. The death of God thus repre-

---

[49] Cf. R. Garaudy, "Gott ist tot." Eine Einführung in das System und die Methode Hegels (1966); H. P. Schmidt, Verheissung und Schrecken der Freiheit (1964), esp. pp. 277ff.

[50] Cf. esp. Dorothee Sölle, Stellvertretung, Ein Kapitel Theologie nach dem "Tode Gottes" (1965); cf. p. 12.

[51] Philosophy of Religion (1895), I, pp. 205f.

[52] Philosophy of Religion; cf. Werke (1832), 11, p. 122.

[53] Sämtliche Werke, ed. Glockner, I, p. 433.

[54] Here Hegel quotes Pascal and a Lutheran chorale (Würzburg, 1628) whose original by Johann Rist spoke of God's death in the second stanza: "God himself is dead," though this was later made into a reference to the death of his Son: "The Son of God lies dead."

sents the Golgotha of the absolute spirit which at the end of the phenomenology serves to express conceptualized history.[55]

This history marks the transition in which the absolute spirit becomes conscious of itself in the finite spirit, in which its negation reaches its goal in the counterpart of the finite, and in which it thus comes to itself. This Golgotha, this speculative Good Friday, is, then, the turning-point when supreme totality rises up to the clearest freedom of its form and the negation of the negation takes place.

This brings to light the real meaning of Hegel's statement that God is dead. This death is a transition in which the counterpart of the finite reaches its deepest depth. In the historical self-manifestation of the absolute spirit this occurs with the crucifixion of Christ, as Hegel shows with his express reference to the Lutheran chorale (cf. n. 54) and its line: "God himself is dead." This expresses poetically his point that the extreme of antithetical finitude, the death of God, is only a moment in God himself. In intention, then, Hegel's statement is not atheistic. On the contrary, it is a self-affirmation of God after the manner of dialectical coming to himself.

The line in the chorale, "God himself is dead," tells us that the human, the finite, the frail, the weak, the negative is a "divine moment," i.e., it is in God and not outside him. Its otherness does not prevent unity with God. Supreme knowledge of the idea of spirit is contained in it. Death means that the human element is stripped off and the divine aspect is manifested. But death is also negative. It is the extreme form of that to which man as a natural being, and therefore God himself, is exposed (*Philosophy of Religion*, I, p. 210). The one to whom the dying finite is thus exposed, into whom it dies and in whom it suffers death in extreme opposition, has no death, which would mean his non-existence or absence; he simply goes through a process of self-development within which death occurs as a mere "moment."

It is, of course, a terrible thought that God is dead, that everything eternal and true is not, that there is negation even in God. Supreme pain, hopelessness, and surrender are involved in it (*ibid.*, p. 205). But the process does not stop here. There is a reversal. God maintains himself in the process so that this becomes the death of death. God rises to life again; he thus becomes the antithesis (*ibid.*).

What is first worked out as a pure concept is given direct and visible form in the death, resurrection, and exaltation of Christ to the right hand of God. As God's indirectness as abstract generality is removed in the first sphere (that of pure thought), so the abstraction of humanity, the indirectness of individuality, is removed in the second. This takes place through death. Christ's death is the death of death, the negation of the negation. But it is God who has put death to death by emerging from it. He is the one of whom it is said: "Thou dost not leave thy righteous one in the grave, thou dost not let thy holy one see corruption" (Psalm 16:10, quoted freely by Hegel).

Thus finitude, humanity, and humiliation are alien to Christ as the one who

---

55 Cf. H. P. Schmidt, *op. cit.*, p. 283.

is absolutely God. They belong to men. It is their finitude that Christ has assumed in all its forms even to the point of evil. This is defined as being for self over against God. But he has assumed it in order to put it to death through his death. His doing this, his uniting of absolute extremes, is the manifestation of infinite love (*loc. cit.*). The fact that God made himself identical with what is alien to him in order to put it to death is the speculative background of the statement that Christ bore the sin of the world and made reconciliation with God.

Since, then, God's death is only a negative transitional stage in the process of coming to himself, since it is only his departure from heaven and abstract generality, and since God's identity recognizes itself in non-identity, God's being is everywhere presupposed, and not only his being, but his being as infinite love as this is seen in the uniting of absolute extremes.

We thus see in the idea of the death of God, or the visible Christ-event, the basic thought of Hegel that the absolute posits itself only when it leaves a bad infinity, the abyss of nothing, and limits and negates itself. Only by negation of this negation is it the absolute. God as a unity without differentiation must die in order to give himself to the world: This is nothing without him, and he is nothing without it.

This is not the place for a radical theological criticism of Hegel. Our only concern is to show that this concept of the death of God is not a form of the atheistic schema which is usually expressed in it and which with the help of this slogan causes the horror that has necessarily resulted at certain periods in history. Hegel certainly refers to utter hopelessness as the religious situation of the new age (cf. *Glauben und Wissen, Sämtliche Werke,* ed. Glockner, I, p. 433), but this is not at all the same as what death of God theologians have in view. It does not characterize a complete departure from transcendence and the definitive entry of modern man into autarchous immanence. The terror of a lost God is interpreted as a moment in God and the fear of the corresponding experience is seen as a moment in the process of finite consciousness. No doubt the new age represents this stage in the process, but it is only a transition, not to what is historically past, but to a promised new moment which can already be present speculatively and which is given visible form in the exaltation of Christ.

Nothing is further from Hegel than the conclusion of Nietzsche, who absolutizes what is relative—a mere moment—in Hegel. There can be no question here of a proclamation of the autarchy of this world after the definitive death of God. This world is simply the finite which God has opposed to himself in order to be himself in the negation of the negation, to remain himself in it, to come forth from it.

Thus it is a radical misunderstanding of Hegel to enlist him as an atheist because of his notion of the death of God[56] and to understand him in terms of the content which this notion undoubtedly has in Nietzsche.

A theological criticism of Hegel cannot, then, begin at this point. It must

---

[56] Cf. on this point the sound conclusion of Garaudy, even though he is a Marxist philosopher (*op. cit.,* p. 430).

look at the schema of thought within which the statement occurs. It must study the monistic schema which views occurrence as the self-development of the idea.

Within this schema religion as a moment in this self-development is the knowledge of the divine spirit about himself through the mediation of the finite spirit (ed. Glockner, 15, p. 216). God needs this religion. For he is God only insofar as he knows himself. His self-knowledge . . . is his self-consciousness in man (as the finite spirit) and man's knowledge of God which moves on to man's self-knowledge in God.

In regard to this schema which views all occurrence merely as a necessary modification of the totality of the spirit, one may ask whether the finite here is really the radical opposition which it seems to be in its extreme form, in evil, in being for self over against God. If all this is a moment, is not the radical nature of the antithesis called in question? Is not the gulf between God and man a doubtful one if the absolute spirit knows himself in finite knowledge and if the finite spirit knows his knowing as the absolute spirit?

The question how far evil is a radical antithesis to God and yet not outside his control, but within his purpose and permission, is an ancient one in theology. Two things have to be avoided. The first is the Gnostic and Manichaean error which sets evil over against God in an abstract dualism so that finally there are two opposing gods. The second is the opposite error which robs evil of its antithetical character and makes it simply the dialectical counterpole of the good. Julius Müller (in his *Die christliche Lehre von der Sünde,* 2nd ed. [1844], I, pp. 41ff.) has collected some references in which evil is presented as a dialectical necessity, and he also quotes the hymn which refers to the fall as a *felix culpa* ("blessed fault") because it made possible the redemptive work of Christ (pp. 446f.).

Naturally this is not the place to try to work out a doctrine which avoids the two extremes. Theology's constant wrestling with them, however, keeps us alert to the danger of aberration on the one side or the other. Thus even in the most definite statements against Manichaeism, and even in Luther's most daring formulations of God's sovereignty in his *Bondage of the Will,* there is resistance to any kind of dialectic in which evil is necessary or merely transitional. Thus Christian theology already has the antidote to Hegel's poison. (On Luther cf. ThE, I, § 598ff.)

In Hegel himself evil is a necessary transition in the teleological process, and his polarity of good and evil does not allow natural things to be good. Only by separation does he overcome being in itself and its simple naturalness. Thus evil has a justifiable place in the process so long as things do not stop at being for self over against God and evil can thus be claimed as merely a transition or "moment."

God's identity in the non-identity mediated through the process of self-actualization, the fact that the human and finite spirit, even in the stages of extreme alienation, can also be a moment of the infinite and hence its attribute, necessarily carries with it the possibility of an inversion of the whole concept. This was carried through by the left-wing Hegelians, and God became simply an attribute of man and his consciousness. Here we undoubtedly have to face the question put by Garaudy, namely, whether the "ambivalent" philosophy of Hegel is finally "theology or humanism," so that we have to see an alternative where Hegel intended a synthesis.[57]

Thus, while it is undoubtedly an error to impute atheism to Hegel on the basis of his statement that God is dead, the humanist elements in his thought give ample support to the view "that the left-wing Hegelians, and later Feuerbach and Marx, found in him the methodological principles of a criticism of religion which necessarily led to atheism."[58]

[57] Garaudy, op. cit., p. 426.
[58] Ibid., p. 430.

XV

Theological Evaluation of the Idea of the Death of God. Basis of a Secular and Atheistic Knowledge of the World (Science) and Mastery over It (Technology)

1. KANT'S COPERNICAN REVOLUTION ACCORDING TO HEINRICH HEINE

The death of God idea as we found it programmatically, not in Hegel, but in the other authors and especially in Nietzsche, tries to express the emancipation of this world as it has come to consciousness of itself and is now ruled by man. It does this with strongly emotional accents, especially in the rejection of a traditional cosmic order which is grounded in the dictatorship of an imaginary world above. The hope of Prometheus and the despair of Sisyphus intermingle, as we have seen, in these emotions. Renounced transcendence still surrounds us. The cover of immanence still has holes. Evacuated heaven raises abhorrence of a vacuum, and man tries to fill the gap with a degree of self-evaluation which is not only a gigantic failure but which, in the question why the attempt must be made, bears witness to the presence of that which transcends man.

The rebellious feeling with which the death of God and the autonomous establishment of this world are proclaimed seems to leave Christian theologians—apart from a few eccentrics—no choice as to the way in which they react. Even if they accept the march of history toward the establishment of secularity and do not flinch from a post-religious age, they can only hold aloof from Promethean posturing, whether with or without recognition of their own partial guilt in provoking this attitude.

How does it come about, however, that they can accept at all the movement of history, the step into modern secularism, into the age of atheistic science, technology, and understanding of existence? Is the strand of Promethean revolt, of the superman and self-elevation, accompanied by a more modest strand which points in the same direction and which does not at once eliminate faith from the discussion, whether as subject or object, since the discussion thrives on the contesting of faith?

There is in fact such a strand, and its normative initiator and representative is Immanuel Kant. In a very non-Promethean way Kant effected a basic

Copernican revolution[1] which brought man into the subject-object correlation of immanent experience of the world. He also set off a theological earthquake to the degree that *via* Ritschl and Herrmann he stimulated theological conceptions which sought to put the Christian message in terms of secular man. The theological relevance of Kant right up to our own time has hardly been noticed or pondered.[2] Nevertheless, unless we take Kant into account we can hardly deal properly with secularization or the secular interpretation of the Christian message.

For reasons which will soon become evident we do best to start with the interpretation of Kant by Heinrich Heine. Heine forges the link between the death of God concept and the this-worldliness of general consciousness which Kant initiated.[3]

As one would expect, there is, of course, a good deal of irony in Heine's discussion. Thus he notes that the rational criticism which has pulverized the arguments for God's existence familiar to us from the time of Anselm has not put an end to the existence of God himself. Furthermore, fine-spun Berlin dialectic—he is probably referring to Hegel—cannot even kill a cat, let alone God. Heine himself has personal proof how little dangerous it is. It is always destroying people, and they always remain alive (*op. cit.,* p. 170; E.T. p. 12). As regards theology, he has a statement worth pondering by the death of God theologians: "There are in Germany theologians who want to put an end to the good Lord; it is always our friends who betray us" (*Nachlese-Gedanken und Einfälle, Sämtliche Werke,* Meyers Klassiker Ausgabe, 7, p. 409).

Heine blames Kant for the disconcerting news of God's death. Kant it was who stormed heaven, put the garrison to the sword, left the ruler of the world swimming in his own blood, and destroyed mercy, fatherly goodness, rewards for restraint in this world, and the immortality of the soul (*Zur Geschichte der Religion und Philosophie in Deutschland,* pp. 269f.; E.T. p. 119). The implicit if not explicit reason why Kant proclaimed God's death is that for Kant God was a noumenon. The transcendental being formerly called God was thus an invention or illusion (p. 266; E.T. p. 115). The kinship to Feuerbach here raises the question whether Heine's interpretation is correct. Since this is a very typical misunderstanding which has influenced modern views of secularization, including proclamation of the death of God, this question merits discussion.

Now Kant undoubtedly did not proclaim the death of God explicitly. Theologically, his epistemological analysis simply says that God transcends the sphere of our experience. Hence he is not present and not objectifiable in this sphere. He cannot possibly be the subject of a synthetic judgment *a priori*

---

[1] We use the comparison with Copernicus in a formal rather than a material sense to denote the intensity of the revolution.

[2] We have had occasion to note it at various points in our presentation of Cartesian theology.

[3] Cf. H. Heine, *Zur Geschichte der Religion und Philosophie in Deutschland, Werke und Briefe,* ed. Hans Kaufmann, V (1961); E.T. *Religion and Philosophy in Germany* (1959 ed.).

or *a posteriori*. To argue, however, that God is thus an illusion for Kant is to be guilty of a misinterpretation whose origin is easy to see. It consists in the ancient and modern substitution of an ontic statement (that God does not exist) for a noetic statement (that God cannot be known or proved). The mistake consists in a false deduction that what is not objectifiable is not objectively existent.

The basis, of course, is that the criterion of objectivity consists in the demonstration of the objectifiability of what is said to be objective. This applies to all objects in the world of experience and to all judgments about them. It is an open question, however, whether the concept of objectivity can be restricted to this sphere. Can it not also describe a fact or value which is independent of the knowing subject and which thus encounters this subject as something transsubjective?

This problem of the objectivity which transcends objectifiability is relevant in theology, although not in theology alone.

Thus it is of the nature of the saving event that as God's work it is grounded outside us, that it encounters us, and that it is not, then, produced by us or by our creative interpretative activity.

The doctrine of the Holy Spirit expresses the fact that it is grounded outside us. Quite apart from the fact that it is not produced by our divinatory creativity, we are also unable to reproduce it on our own interpretative initiative (cf. Matthew 13:13ff. and Luther on the third article of the Creed in SC). We cannot get access to it on our own at all. We are told that it discloses itself to us, that the Holy Spirit, not our spirit, bears witness to it. Here, then, we have objective facts and values, outside man and having their basis outside him, whose objectifiability is paradoxically displayed in the fact that they are not objectifiable and that they escape the grasp of our own experience. Objectifiability means noetic control. What we have here, however, is the uncontrollable which can be ours only by grace and whose objectivity is demonstrated in this very privilege.[4]

It is to be noted that the friction to which the concept of objectivity seems to be subject is particularly severe theologically in the resurrection kerygma.[5] Do the appearances of the risen Lord belong to the objectivity of the Easter event even though they may not be objectifiable? Or are they reproductions— we do not say products—of the imagination which were stimulated and stirred up by the kerygma? Is then the real event for the historian limited to that which can be objectified historically, and are the appearances merely an addition and commentary on the part of the men concerned, a reaction to the event and not the event itself, a product of the human sense of significance but not that which is significant?

We are undoubtedly faced here by a basic decision regarding the resur-

---

[4] Values like truth, goodness, and beauty offer something of a parallel in the non-theological world. They too—although some pragmatists would deny this—come to us with a claim from without and are thus objective but not under our control.

[5] Cf. the author's "The Resurrection Kerygma" in *The Easter Message Today* (New York, 1964), pp. 59ff.

rection kerygma which is of supreme strategic importance for theology, for the understanding of faith itself, and hence for the spiritual life. This key question, however, involves a decision about what we mean by objectivity. Is it limited to the objectifiable or does it include the transsubjective which is independent of man and encounters him from outside?

We sense the terminological difficulty which results when we extend the concept of objectivity to the sphere of the non-objectifiable. It is the terminological difficulty which lies behind all theological terms. As we have noted earlier, these are given new meanings, and in regard to their original content they can be adopted only in very broken analogies. Logos as used in John's Gospel is the example we used earlier. The term "history" gives rise to similar problems in theological thought.[6]

Objectivity belongs to the same category. From the time of Kant it has been used for objectifiable facts and values in the sphere of our experience. In this restricted sense it can be used only in a very limited way in theological statements.

In Kant, of course, the term does carry a transsubjective element. There is a distinction here from the total productivity of Fichte's ego, which posits the non-ego too. In Kant our creative consciousness does not produce the objects of the world of experience. We are affected by the *Dingen an sich*. They set in motion our forms of perception and our categories. The world of experience arises through the cooperation of the outer and inner factors. The outer or transsubjective factor is contained in what we experience.

Nevertheless Kant does not say that the originally transsubjective *Dingen an sich* are objective. They become objective, the objects of my experience, when through the forms of perception and the categories they are drawn into the subject-object relation and are thus objectifiable. The epistemological perspective which dominates the *Critique of Pure Reason* directs Kant's attention exclusively to the problem of transcendental perception. He wants to see how something becomes an object to me and for me, i.e., how the noetic relation arises between me and the object. Inevitably, then, objectivity is equated with objectifiability. To put it negatively, what is not objectifiable cannot be objective for me.

To the degree that this concept of objectivity forms the criterion whether a judgment has general validity, this form of general validity can no longer be predicated of the existence of God. But what is a God who can no longer claim this unlimited validity? Has he not ceased to be God? In competition with the validity of a mathematical or physical statement does he not fall hopelessly behind?

This seems to be what Heine has in mind when he says that Kant put the garrison of heaven to the sword. In summary form the argument is as fol-

---

[6] Cf. the distinctions made between "geschichtlich" and "historisch." The following works may be consulted: J. Schniewind, "A Reply to Bultmann," KM, pp. 51ff.; W. Pannenberg, "Heilgeschehen und Geschichte," KD (1959), 3, p. 222; H. Diem, *Der irdische Jesus und der Christus des Glaubens* (1957), pp. 9f.; G. Gloege, "Zur Versöhnungslehre K. Barths," ThLZ (1960), 3, p. 170.

lows. God is not objectifiable for Kant. Hence he is not objective. He cannot be predicated with the general validity of a synthetic judgment *a priori*. Consequently he does not exist.

Heine, however, makes the mistake of distorting Kant and doing something that Kant himself refused to do. He does not restrict Kant's criterion of objectifiability to the sphere of experience. He applies it to God himself and he thus interprets the non-appearance of God in the world of experience as his non-existence. (This is a simplification; we shall see later that the matter is a little more complicated.) He construes unknowability as non-existence. He thus takes the momentous step of reading a noetic and epistemological statement ontologically.

At this point we cannot resist commenting on modern theological usage. The terms objective and objectivity have now come under a theological ban. The subject-object relation is said to be of little help in understanding revelation and the kerygma. (This is the common view of the Bultmann school.) There are various reasons for this ban.

First, it is based on objections to the grounding of faith outside itself, i.e., in provable supernatural facts. Second, Kant's view of objectivity is accepted (even though Kant may not be quoted and his presuppositions are adopted only subconsciously). Thus objectifiability is made a condition of any statements about objectivity. This means that the independent facticity of the salvation event has to be reduced to the secular and nonsupernatural sphere and transcendent kerygmatic elements are relegated to inwardness, i.e., to the dimension in which an objectifiable event achieves significance for me and my self-understanding is affected and changed by it.

In other words, we have a more refined form of that which Heine does quite crudely. What Kant intended noetically is surreptitiously changed into ontology. There is no "being" in revelation, only "being aware" (cf. my essay "The Restatement of New Testament Mythology," KM, pp. 138ff.). In our view, however, theology should not restrict the objectivity of what it says about the facts and values of the salvation event by the postulate of objectifiability. It should not let itself be imprisoned in Kant's epistemological inquiry. At the very least it should ask itself whether and how far it has come under these influences. Why should not the concept of objectivity be "baptized" like other concepts when it is adopted into theological usage? Theology does not have to use the term in its given function, e.g., to support what it says about the facticity of the salvation event. It does not have to adopt it merely to express the transsubjectivity, the transcendence, which encounters man.

It can keep the concept only if it recognizes the problem of a controlling function and guards against misuse in terms of the original philosophical content (objectifiability), just as John's Gospel protects the Logos concept against Stoic misunderstanding. We should have such a functional misuse if with its help we tried to base faith on demonstrable (i.e., objectifiable) facts and therefore on realities outside faith. The attempt to show a historical symmetry between prophecy and fulfilment, or to use historical miracles as a ground of faith, or to argue, as in popular apologetics, that the resurrection of Christ is the best-attested event in all antiquity, might be quoted in this connection.

This kind of objective proof of faith actually destroys faith. For it gives it a foundation in something which is generally valid and in so doing makes two things unavoidable.

First, it degrades faith to the status of a purely moral phenomenon, to a practical obedience in which I actively confess demonstrable supernatural facts. Second, the wonder of the salvation event, of the mighty acts of God, is destroyed to the degree that God's action is restricted to purely historical facts when in reality it also embraces illumination by the Holy Spirit, i.e., the granting of access to these facts, the opening of the eyes and ears, and the overcoming of hardness of heart. (For a similar concept of objectivity cf. W. Joest in KD [1955], 1, p. 80, line 23.)

We now return to Heine's interpretation of Kant.

How is it that Heine did not notice his slipping over from the noetic sphere to the ontic? Ultimately the reason is not to be sought in what Kant says but in the mere fact that he is discussing the existence of God. As Heine himself observes, discussion of God's existence always excited him. For him doubt of God is doubt of life itself. It is death (*op. cit.,* p. 267; E.T. p. 116).

The discussion itself is the new and disturbing thing and not the actual handling of the traditional proofs or the negative judgment on their adequacy. In fact Anselm's proof, as we shall see later, is not a discussion in this sense. It is not an inquiry to which the proof which follows is an answer. It is simply a transposition of the certainty of faith into the certainty of thought, as the opening prayer in the *Proslogion* shows very clearly. To that degree there is in the strict sense no "proof" of God. A proof is polemical by nature. It is opposing another thesis or answering a question. It is thus moving from the uncertain to the certain, with the proof itself as the basis. In Anselm the two certainties are simply brought together. The certainty of faith, or existence in the truth, comes first and thought is required only to overcome the lag and to bring itself into line with the existential certainty.

In Kant and the moderns from the time of Descartes' systematic doubt, however, the inquiry no longer starts with a given certainty. Thought does not begin with a standard of existence. It is not trying to match up to this or to achieve it. Its question is a radical groping. It asks in uncertainty. It calls in question. To question God, however, is to "doubt life itself."

One might reverse Heine's statement: Doubt of life itself is doubt of God. Doubt of God does not affect only the upper and supernatural floor of the cosmic building. It affects the very foundations. When doubted, life itself is no longer secure. Life itself has no certainty when God becomes an object of discussion.

Priority belongs, however, to the original form. To doubt God is to undermine life. It is to make it a madhouse. There is an echo of Jean Paul here. There is also an anticipation of the hellish dereliction of Sartre. What is not willed, planned, or intended in Wetzel and Jacobsen has now emerged.

This world is not granted freedom with the death of God. The chaos of meaninglessness is unleashed and manifested.

Doubt of God is doubt of life itself. For God is not the distant inhabitant of a hereafter. He sustains life. Thus doubt of him is more than doubt of the religious sphere.

But the terrible questioning of God has already been uttered. His unknowability has been proclaimed. Does not this mean, Heine seems to be saying, that the very basis, goal, and meaning of life itself have also been pronounced inscrutable? Has not life become a perishing corpse?

What Kant stated epistemologically, as the tracing of a pure, nonmetaphysical, and God-free subject-object relation and the establishment of an empirical secular foreground, awakens in Heine ontological terror. For what does God mean if in the foreground of the world of experience, if in my world and your world, we not only may but must ignore him? Can this God be anything more than a squatter on the edge of the universe, an emigrant of the world to come, a representative of what only comes when it is all over? What kind of God is this who does not belong to the heart of this world, who is pushed out onto the periphery? Is not the unsuspecting calm with which Kant, presumably with no ontological dread, investigates the conditions of experience apart from God, itself extremely terrifying? Does he have no inkling of what is really at stake?

In these questions we have tried to work out the implications of Heine's questions to Kant, deliberately choosing formulations which form a bridge to what has been commonly said, especially since Gogarten and Bonhoeffer, about the secularity of God and his relation to the center of our existence.

Obviously Heine regards the epistemological approach of Kant as the critical point. Merely to question God's knowability is to announce his death. There is no need to defend the announcement by cutting away the next world or holding out hopes for this world. The mode of thought itself, the way of investigating the conditions of our existence here, is all that is needed. To abandon him at this point is to abandon him everywhere.

When Kant tries to reintroduce certainty of God by the way of practical reason, giving him a place within the postulate of the supreme good (*Critique of Practical Reason,* pp. 112, 114), Heine no longer believes him. Later postulates cannot alter the fact that God does not appear in the world. The God who has been murdered epistemologically cannot be brought to life again in this way. In the macabre attempt to revive him, Heine thinks, Kant's philanthropic purpose is only too evident. He describes the manipulations of thought with biting irony.

Kant sees his old servant Lampe, a faithful old soul whose last prop has been knocked away by the declaration of the death of God. Tears run down his face. Kant, who is a good man as well as a great philosopher, has pity on him. Half in kindness and half in irony he says that Lampe must have a God. Otherwise he cannot be happy. Practical reason says this. So practical reason will bring to light the existence of God. Kant thus revived the corpse of deism which theoretical reason had slain (Heine, *op. cit.,* p. 270; E.T. p. 119).

To have banished God from the empirical realm of theoretical reason is to have killed him and hence to have killed existence itself. To try to fetch God back by other forms of assurance, by the postulate of happiness, is a mere trick. For Heine, then, Kant is a prophet of the death of God.

At the end of the second book, Heine suggests that he has given Jehovah a decisive shove so that he must get ready to die (E.T. p. 103). Until this happens he must still wander about the world. First he becomes more and more spiritual. For example, he lives the peripheral life of a mere postulate. Without influence or concreteness, he then becomes a sentimental father, a general friend of man, an altruist. But he can do no real good, just as the tears of a senile old man are no help. Finally the bell rings. We should all kneel; they are bringing the sacraments to a dying God (loc. cit.; cf. Schopenhauer's similar description in a letter he wrote to Frauenstädt on August 21, 1852: O. Lindner, A. Schopenhauer, Von ihm und über ihn, 1863, p. 553).

In relation to the question whether Kant's transcendentalism did in fact result in the sacraments being brought to a dying God we may put the counter-question whether even implicitly Kant doubted God when banishing him from the empirical world. Indeed, did Descartes actually doubt him when at first the only remaining certainty was that of the I which executes the act of thought and doubt?

Certainly there are several weighty objections to an affirmative answer to this counter-question. In both Kant and Descartes doubt is methodological and not fundamental. Two things show this.

First, they are not surprised by doubt. They intentionally explore it. They are not subject to it. It is not existential for them, as Kierkegaard might say. They doubt only respecting the affinity to God of one definite dimension of their existence, namely, the noetic dimension.

Second, their doubt, even though sharp, is partial. It has an epistemological function. It is thus a planned and restricted doubt. As such it remains under control. It is prevented from spreading like a fire to all the stories and to the very foundations of the building.

This may be seen in detail in Kant's thoughts on God. A few of the more important aspects may be mentioned.

Kant neither denies the existence of God nor does he challenge in principle the existence of a God who reveals himself in history.[7] His only aim is to take from faith in God false supporting arguments. He accepts God's *ousia* but not the possibility of a *noesis* of God, or at least not a particular kind of *noesis*. What are the questioned or negated forms of the knowledge of God? If we are right there are two such forms.

First, Kant does not think we have a valid way of knowing God so long as we think that this knowledge of God and his will comes merely by historical mediation, by a positive "God says" which we have to accept. If we persist in this historical faith the will of God is a *heteros nomos* for us. The claims

---

[7] He can thus speak quite freely about revelation even in the historical sense, and with no suggestion of doubt (cf. *Religion within the Limits of Reason Alone,* pp. 142ff.).

of declarations of the divine will have to be tested by practical reason so that their validity may be proved and, if they pass the test, they may be made autonomously rather than heteronomously.[8]

What occupies Kant here is not the common idea[9] that historical certainty can only be fragmentary and approximate.[10] For him the problem of historical revelation is that it raises a claim from without and is thus a heteronomous decree. This is why he can speak disparagingly of a mere historical faith.[11] The God who proclaims himself only in history will not be appropriated but will remain outside. This is a critical problem once man understands himself in his autonomy, and hence as his own *autos*.

In principle, then, Kant does not deny revelation or the possibility of certainty regarding it. But he cannot let it remain an external authority. Its heteronomous externality can be overcome, however, only if revelation has a bridgehead in my autonomous consciousness from which its impulses can come to meet us and it can be validated by our autonomy. This takes place as, e.g., the will of God expressed in the Ten Commandments contains the same maxims as those advocated by the categorical imperative, so that these maxims are the content in that specific form.

The negative side is that in principle revelation cannot be something which transcends reason. Revealed faith as distinct from mere rational faith simply expresses a specific mode or history of the process of religious knowledge. Its presupposition is that we first have an impartation of what a divine commandment is.[12] This is first received, although not definitively, from history. In a revelation which does not harden into a historical dictate, but can be validated ethically, it can then be completely absorbed by my autonomous self-understanding.[13] If I do not accept this, the implication is that God is demanding from me special duties[14] which are not suggested by my civil conscience. This would be to degrade God, for accepting such special duties from him would imply that he could receive something from me and that I could affect him or do something for him.[15]

Second, reason is affronted and its integrity is destroyed when we assume that by theoretical knowledge it can assure us of the objective reality[16] of the idea of God, of which we are certain only in the moral consciousness.[17]

---

[8] Cf. ThE, I, § 102ff. and also Thielicke-Schrey, "Glaube und Handeln," *Sammlung Dieterich*, 130, pp. XLVIIIff.

[9] Cf. Lessing's distinction between the necessary truths of reason and the accidental truths of history, and on this the author's *Offenbarung, Vernunft und Existenz*, 5th ed. (1967).

[10] The only hint of this in Kant is that historical experience comes under synthetic judgments *a posteriori* and these are less stringent than synthetic judgments *a priori*.

[11] *Religion within the Limits of Reason Alone*, p. 166.

[12] *Ibid.*, pp. 142f.

[13] Cf. Lessing's idea that the truth of revelation can become the truth of reason in his *Education of the Human Race*.

[14] *Religion within the Limits of Reason Alone*, pp. 142ff.

[15] *Ibid.*   [16] *Ibid.*

[17] In the form of the postulate of the supreme good (*Critique of Practical Reason*, pp. 112, 114).

If it tries to do this, reason is not sufficiently self-critical. It inappropriately extends its radius of action beyond objective experience and thus exceeds its competence. It also violates the dignity of God by dragging him into the present world and making him one object among others. Although Kant is not thinking theologically in the strict sense, he is here adopting a theological concern which we emphasized above. Reason damages faith by trying to ground it objectively in a sphere outside itself.

In sum, Kant does not deny God; he denies a particular way of experiencing his existence. His gaze is directed primarily on the dignity of man; he is thus dominated by an anthropological concern. Man is "heteronomized" when his belief rests on a historical, clerical, or institutional authority or on a speculative demonstrability of God. The adult autonomous I cannot be bypassed as a control point. Understanding itself as an *autos,* it must "appropriate" to itself whatever comes to it with the claim to divine authority and hence with the claim to be God.

Yet Kant's concern in this line of argument is theological as well as anthropological. The dignity of God is at stake as well as that of man. Special duties which are not suggested by the ethical consciousness and which cannot be validated or appropriated by it are only "courtly duties." They make God into a despot. This role degrades him, for he comes to need our offerings, e.g., the sacrifice of the intellect, or specific religious achievements. Furthermore, by perceiving God speculatively, we make him a fetish, an objectifiable secular object.

It may be noted that at this point Kant opens up some theologically fruitful perspectives, though he himself would hardly have claimed them as such. This is why he has had such an effect on theology even to our own day, and why there have been and are many professed or secret Kantians in the schools of Ritschl and Bultmann. In this regard Kant is not unlike Heidegger, who did not intend certain deductions that existential theology made from his thought, and even had reservations regarding them, but who still prepared the way for them and set them in motion.

These matters are more clearly expressed by Kant in the practical sphere than the theoretical sphere. For him to force God into secular objectivity is to force reactions from him by earthly devices which I can use, e.g., formulae of invocation in a magical sense, or ecclesiastical observances.[18] This is to integrate God into a natural course of action which I can control.[19]

When I do this I degrade God (1) by making him part of the world, (2) by using him as a means to serve my own ends[20] so that he is no longer God, and (3) by not asking whether all this is well-pleasing to him, since he means nothing to me as a person and my only concern is with my own purposes.[21] To drag God into secularity in this way is to make him a "fetish."[22]

One might say, then, that Kant criticizes a falsely based belief in God not merely out of an epistemological concern but also out of a concern for the dignity of God. His criticism is thus "to the greater glory of God." This raises

---

[18] *Religion within the Limits of Reason Alone,* pp. 165f.
[19] *Ibid.*　　[20] *Ibid.*　　[21] *Ibid.*　　[22] *Ibid.*

the question whether one can really regard him as the initiator of the death of God concept.

Nevertheless, it is not just in a flight of fancy that Heine views him as such. For is not God pushed out onto the periphery here? Is he not removed from the center of life? Can this idea of God have any force? Can it revolutionize life? Is not God reduced in effect to the senile helplessness of Heine's depiction?

The God of Kant can indeed have no initiative or direct influence on our lives. If as the one who effects the supreme good by transcendentally uniting the imperative and happiness he were to be a motive of action, this action would be ethically devaluated and eudaemonism would reign. To make God's will an independent motive is to heteronomize the conscience and to do despite to man's dignity. It is also to make God a tyrant and to give me a eudaemonistic regard for his good pleasure or his favorable reactions. To be sure, the moral consciousness is only a criterion of faith in God. The voice from Sinai is not silenced. It has simply to be validated by this criterion. Nevertheless, does not the criterion of the final authority surreptitiously take on normative rank itself?

The history of theology shows plainly that criteria which are meant to serve norms constantly become their masters. We have already seen how this has come about in modern hermeneutics. The hermeneutical principle which has the role of a criterion finally prejudges what answers the text can give. It thus takes on normative rank and is no longer open to the incalculable things which the kerygma itself might impose. One can see the same process in Roman Catholic theology when we turn to the relation between Scripture and tradition or Scripture and the teaching office. Thus the teaching office sets out as a criterion but quietly and progressively achieves a dominant position. The relation between the teaching office and natural law offers another example. Here natural law begins as the authority and the teaching office as a criterion. But again the criterion increasingly becomes more important than the norm and (dialectically rather than directly) serves as a norm for it (cf. ThE, II, 2, § 3839ff.; E.T. II, pp. 544ff.).

Man, then, is finally autarchous. His world is controlled by his epistemological powers and the world of experience shaped by them. In the last resort he confronts only himself.[23] We thus have a self-enclosed finitude from whose walls the name of God comes only as a lost and empty echo, and only when man has first named it, since God himself has no voice, and the summons: "Adam, where art thou?" cannot be attributed to this God. We can thus appreciate what Heine has in mind.

We must now study the impression made on Heine more closely, not out of philosophical interest in Kant, but because Kant as understood in this way offers a decisive prototype for the modern "atheistic" understanding of reality which controls scientific and historical investigation.

---

[23] In this regard he is an initiator of modern developments (cf. Heisenberg's *The Physicist's Conception of Nature* [E.T. 1958], pp. 22ff.).

2. KANT AND ANSELM. REORIENTATION OF THE MODERN VIEW OF THE WORLD

To grasp the revolutionary nature of the new understanding of reality without God one must set it against the background of scholastic ontology, in relation to which modern Christianity seems like an emancipation and within which Anselm and Descartes advanced their proofs of God. Naturally what we call medieval ontology is a very complex and varied movement so that the use of a comprehensive term for it might seem to be lacking in seriousness. Our present concern, however, is merely with some tendencies in it, so that a simplified model might be permitted.

If we were to describe the contrast rather emotionally and rhetorically, we might say that a reality, whether of being or thought, has to be regarded as full of God if God can be proved or "disclosed" (cf. Heidegger, *Being and Time*, pp. 56f.) from it, if it is full of potential manifestations of God, and that a reality has to be regarded as empty of God if God has the significance only of an extended line of being, so that he can be argued away altogether by the logic of a Feuerbach.

It might be instructive to consider the proof of God advanced by Anselm and Descartes from this angle.[24]

As is known, in Descartes' *Meditations*[25] the thought of God is the bridge from thought to being which is not to be found in the form of an attempt to gain direct certainty of the existence of the external world. The I, which has complete certainty of itself as the subject of thought (*cogito—sum*), can see no possibility of attaining to similar certainty regarding the external world. But it finds in itself the idea of God as the greatest than which a greater cannot be thought. The idea of the infinite—this conclusion goes rather beyond Anselm—cannot be produced by the finite consciousness. It thus points to the existence of something outside it. With this reference coincides a similar deduction of Anselm, namely, that that than which a greater cannot be thought implies its existence, since what exists surpasses what does not exist, and therefore what does not exist cannot be the greatest than which a greater cannot be thought.

Evidence for this existing magnitude also guarantees the existence of the external world. For the sceptical suggestion that the supreme being simply presents the external world to me as a figment and fantasy would make God into a demon and would thus set him in opposition to the axiomatically certain magnitude than which a greater cannot be thought.

To this extent the proof of God occupies a strategic position in Descartes' attempt to establish the subject-object relation, to take the I out of the closed circle of mere self-certainty, and to give it certainty of the world and an objective reference. The proof of God is the vital link uniting being and

---

[24] For present purposes the distinctions between the two presentations are of no significance.

[25] Cf. A. Schlatter's important but little-known work *Die philosophische Arbeit seit Descartes*, 4th ed. (1959), pp. 28ff.; reference might also be made to K. Barth, *Anselm: Fides quaerens intellectum* (1931); E.T. 1960.

thought. Thought gives me certainty about the intrinsic being which sustains all being; and certainty of being, of my relation to the world, is imparted by evidence about intrinsic being.

Since a fundamental question of philosophy, namely, that of the relation between thought and being, is answered here with the help of the proof of God, the problem arises whether this step from thought to being is legitimate. This problem is identical with another question: How cogent is the ontological proof of God? In answering this question, we are not going to discuss the counter-arguments which have been mounted against it from Thomas to Kant. Kant's objections in particular do not concern us here since they apply only within an understanding of reality that is quite different from that of the ontological proof. Our interest focuses, in fact, on the presupposed understanding of reality which makes the proof either possible and even perhaps self-evident on the one side, or absurd on the other.

A specific understanding of reality underlies the ontological movement from thought to being. That which is later disclosed in the form of a proof is already presupposed. In other words, God is presupposed as the supreme good to which all things are oriented and in which they have their basis.

Consequently the nature of things can be expressed only as their order is perceived. Discovery of their truth rests on discovery of their "rightness." Their rightness is their place in the order. This order is a structure of ends which are related to one another and also oriented to a final end.

The truth of a thing is disclosed more fully—the possibility of comparatives and superlatives is characteristic—the more explicitly it is related not merely to the proximate ends but to the final end. The line of creaturely things extends as it were to the one at the end, and as they relate to this they come into the true relation to one another which corresponds to their order of being, and in so doing they achieve the truth which consists in this appropriateness, i.e., their rightness.

Things are thus true when they fully express their being, i.e., when they are what they ought to be. What they ought to be is known from their position and function within the order of being. An event is true insofar as it corresponds to this. Fire is true and right when it warms, for this is what it is supposed to do.[26] This means that quartz is "truer" as crystal than as pebble, since its potentialities are best realized and manifested in this form.

Truth, then, is not tied down to the way a deduction is made in thought, e.g., whether it involves a contradiction or not. Truth is a quality which belongs to the sphere of being. It relates to what things are according to their true nature, i.e., their order. That which occupies and fulfils its position in the totality of being is true.

Only in this light can one see how the concept of truth applies to thought and utterance. For Anselm these are true when they correspond to their place, i.e., when they "get" the rightness of things. To do this is to "get" the place of things in the totality of being, i.e., their conformity to the norm. Thought can achieve this only when it is itself within the order of being to

[26] Cf. R. Allers, *Anselm von Canterbury* (1936), p. 97.

which it relates, i.e., when it is oriented to the final end (Anselm, *Monologion,* cc. 1-10; *De veritate*). Its self-understanding is true when it understands itself thus. The truth of its self-understanding is thus grounded in its own position within the order of being. It does not contribute anything new which thought has discovered. The truth of being is simply reflected in my thought and makes it a kind of mode of itself.

The understanding of truth which holds sway in Anselm is thus characterized by a hierarchical gradation of being. At the head is the supreme existent truth which is the cause of all others. Subordinate to this is the truth of things which is caused by the supreme truth to the degree that this determines its rightness by orientation to the final end. The truth of things for its part determines the truth of thought. More precisely, the thinking being—seen here in analogy to creaturely things—takes part in the truth of things by accepting its right position within the order of being. The truth of the existence of things is the effect of the supreme truth and it is also the cause of the truth of knowledge or utterance. But these two truths are not the cause of any other truths (*De veritate,* x; cf. Allers, *op. cit.,* p. 41). Truth is not enlarged or extended by formal deductions, by what Kant calls synthetic judgments *a priori* or *a posteriori*. Truth is enlarged only as thought places itself at the disposal of the supreme truth as effect or reflection, and becomes, as it were, increasingly pure in this relation.

The rank and intention of Descartes' proof of God are wrongly appraised, and unsuitable epistemological arguments are used to demolish it, if we do not realize that Descartes thinks against the background of the order of being as thus characterized. Only thus does his movement from thought to being make sense. Only thus does it not seem absurd that the existence of that than which no greater can be thought should be deduced from the idea of it. A particular presupposition lies behind this conclusion.

Because God "is"—and is self-evidently presupposed in this "is"—every being achieves its true state of existence only as it is adequate to its end, and only as this end is a stage to the final end—quartz, for example, being a preliminary stage of crystal and finding its truth in this. Man achieves his state of existence only as he thinks, only as he is a thinking being. By thought the tradition of the ontological argument means the act in which thought relates to the final end and to its basis. As it does this it is itself in the truth (Anselm quotes John 3:21 in this connection; cf. Allers, *op. cit.,* p. 97) and it can thus perceive the truth or rightness of things.

Man, then, is related from the very first to that than which no greater can be thought. The reason why this is so, and why man must think of his final destiny, is that according to the ontological schema the final end—God—is at work in him, finding reflection in the thought of man. As the subject of thought relates to the final end, this thought "is" in the truth and consequently it also "thinks" the truth.

If, then, the idea of a greatest than which no greater can be thought carries with it the implication that this greatest exists, this is not strictly speaking a logical deduction any more than is the *Cogito—ergo sum*. It is simply the development of an implication. The act of thought as such is constitutively oriented to the final end; it draws its life from this relation. If it were to deny the final end, i.e., the magnitude than which can be no greater, it would deny itself. Thought which is detached from the order of being and from its final end is a distortion and an utter absurdity.

The statement about the greatest than which no greater can be thought is a statement about thought itself. The statement about its existence which it then has to make is a statement about its own existence. In relation to the act of thought I have to think of a subject, and therefore I have to say *sum* ("I am"). In exactly the same way I have to think the intentionality of the act and therefore to state its orientation to the final end.

I am not making a logical deduction when I do this. I am not offering a proof. I am simply stating and disclosing what I do when I think. I thus reflect the first and chief and existing truth which strikes me. In the last resort there is no real *ergo* here—this suggests a deduction. There is simply a statement: *Cogito—sum; cogito—summum ens.* As the *cogitare* is a reality, so the *esse* of the I and of the *summum ens* is a reality.

As we delineate this understanding of truth, which is also an understanding of thought, we attempt almost meditatively to place ourselves in the feeling of being which underlies it and is also released by it. This feeling is determined by the self-evident way in which being and the thought of being are basically related, so that the basis is also stated and present when I think and when in so doing I address things in their relation. This basis is the non-objective presupposition of every act of thought and every contact with things.

Only when an attempt has been made to penetrate into ontological thought to this point can doubts be raised as to the logical structure of the Cartesian proof, or, better, demonstration of God. In spite of, or perhaps because of, the closed nature of this schema, might it not be that we have here a logical trick, a begging of the question? Does not the demonstration presuppose the very thing which it supposedly proves?

To speak in terms of logical deduction, what we obviously seem to have here is an inversion of premise and consequence. Whereas Descartes actually says: "Because I must think God, he exists," he really ought to say: "Because God exists, I must think him." He thus seems to be operating with an understanding of reality, i.e., of the relation between thought and being, into which God has already been secretly smuggled. Like a conjurer, he can then produce the rabbit out of the hat.

Certainly all reality is here understood in the light of God as the *summum ens.* Is this then a vicious circle? Is Descartes speculatively taking out of the world what he has previously put in speculatively?

It is a mistake to talk of conjuring. This would apply only if the presupposition of the *summum ens* had been gained by a speculative trick, only if it were a product—or manipulation—of the thought, which then offers a demonstration of the *summum ens.* If, however, thought becomes aware of its own basis, then it is simply explicating a certainty whence it derives and by which it sees itself empowered to think. It is simply stating theoretically, i.e., in the form of acts of thought, what it already knows nontheoretically. Just because we have here explication of the self-certainty which does not derive from thought but which makes thought possible and promising, and places at its disposal the system of reference within which alone it can be thought, the concept of a proof is completely out of place. For a proof makes the transition from what is uncertain to what is certain. It gives birth to certainty. A speculatively achieved certainty in which the premise is speculatively smuggled in would be indeed a sham certainty. A proof achieved in this way would be a deceptive begging of the question.

But this is not at all the case here. The certainty which is brought to light as the self-certainty of thought is prior to all thought and comes from other sources. One may see this in the prayer with which Anselm opens his demonstration of God (*Proslogion,* c. II) and also in his preceding statement (c. I) that his aim is to understand the truth of God which his heart already believes and loves. He does not want to understand in order to believe, which would put understanding before belief. He believes in order to understand, so that the theme, the basis, and the scope of the ensuing understanding are determined by the certainty of belief.

Thus Anselm does not prove the existence of God in order to be able to pray to him. If he were offering a proof in the modern sense, intellectual honesty would demand that he adopt this order. Until the proof had led from the uncertain to the certain, properly grounded prayer would not be possible because there could be no certainty as to the existence of the one to whom prayer would be made. Anselm, however, prays before he "proves." He obviously does not expect the proof to offer him either the basis or an enhancement of certainty. The understanding simply has to catch up with what existence already knows. Believing and understanding do not synchronize. They are apart. Believing is ahead of understanding. In faith we know more than we do with reason. Reason cannot go further than faith or get ahead of it. Its task is to catch up with faith and to permeate the certainty of faith with understanding. Faith seeks understanding and wants it to repeat its own certainty. It wants this because without it the understanding would be silent when the believer prays; it could not share in the prayer. This would mean that my turning to God would not be total. I should not love him in all the dimensions of my being. I should not love him in the dimension of the understanding.

To prevent this, faith seeks to bring the understanding along with it, to impart to it its own certainty, and hence to transpose this into rationality. In relation to understanding the faith which is on ahead is thus the giver rather than the recipient. It does not seek either basis or confirmation from understanding. It does not expect any increase in the knowledge of God apart from a possible enlargement of the horizon of its certainty. Faith wants reason to repeat what it knows, so that it may then make its own confessional response.

The way in which reason confesses is by acknowledgment, by the Yea and

Amen of understanding. Faith is not enriched by this. It is not given a prop. It does not achieve greater certainty. Understanding does not add to its certainty.[27] But the totality of the I follows the lead of faith.

That there is this discrepancy between faith and understanding, and hence the need to overcome it, is due to the remoteness from God which sin has produced. On the one side man is bound by love for God and on the other side he is cast out of his sight.[28] Thus God's absence is constantly experienced even though he is omnipresent (*Proslogion*, c. I). Reason is particularly affected by this. The diminution of freedom which sin brings with it applies to reason too. Thus, before beginning an intellectual demonstration of God, man is summoned to shelter for a while from his restless thoughts, to set aside his cares, and to refrain from burdensome work (*ibid.*). The unquestionable reference here is to that which dominates us, and thus restricts the freedom of the understanding, in the fall from God. Light is thus shed on the discrepancy between the certainty of faith and the understanding which lags behind, being harassed by the "absence" of God.

Here, however, the crucial question arises: What does faith believe, and what does the understanding reflect when it transposes what is believed into its own sphere?[29]

When we today read that faith precedes understanding, we might easily and, as experience shows, we continually do fall into a twofold misunderstanding.

First, we are tempted to think in terms of Lessing's thesis that faith and the revelation in which it believes are a naive and mythical prelude to understanding, so that they will become superfluous once that which is accepted unreflectingly and on authority becomes our own autarchous insight.[30] Now it is surely obvious that Anselm does not have this kind of preceding but ultimately redundant faith in mind. Faith does not retire when its search has found understanding. It continues to believe. It has simply drawn the rational self into its worship. It does not bow out when what previously was only believed is now known and understood.

Second, we are tempted to assume that the logical argument is as follows. The premise is that faith believes in God as him than whom no greater can be thought. Reflection then shows that the object of faith exists. The cosmic system is then deduced from the thought of God. One descries a teleology of proximate and final ends. Finally, it is shown that this system for its part implies the thought of God and thus offers presuppositions for the initial proof that God must also exist. Strictly, however, these would not be presuppositions but post-suppositions, since cosmic teleology is deduced from

---

[27] In the language of seventeenth-century orthodoxy we have in Anselm an organic rather than a normative use of reason (cf. J. Gerhard, *Loci theol.*, II, 371; A. Calov, *Systema*, I, 358, etc.; cf. ThE, II, § 1321ff.).

[28] *Proslogion*, c. I; it is not by chance that Anselm quotes Psalm 51:11 here.

[29] We find a similar transposition in relation to the atonement in the *Cur deus homo?* Faith is not made possible by a preceding understanding of the necessity of Christ's atoning death; instead it precedes this understanding.

[30] Cf. the author's *Offenbarung, Vernunft und Existenz*, 5th ed. (1967), pp. 120ff.

prior conviction as to the existence of the supreme being. The dog is thus chasing its own tail. We seem to have a typical instance of begging the question.

But this again is undoubtedly a caricature of the ontological thought of Anselm. The *Proslogion* makes it plain that the procedure is not one of deduction from faith in God as though "conclusions" could bring knowledge that faith alone cannot do. Anselm is not a precursor of the group against which Laplace fulminates. He does not say that.we need the hypothesis "God" to explain the world and to perceive its design. All that Anselm does is to translate faith into the form of reflection. Understanding is restricted to this process of translation.

Anselm, then, does not make deductions from God to the structure of the world or *vice versa*. Faith is not led beyond itself speculatively. It is not given new knowledge in this way. It is not enlarged. Its certainty is not increased. As the opening prayer of the *Proslogion* puts it, we want to understand what we believe, namely, *that* thou art and *what* thou art. We believe among other things that thou art the Creator of the world (*Monologion*, c. XIV, XXXIff.). We thus believe that God's creative being is in all things, permeates all things, that from him and through him and in him are all things (*ibid.*, c. XIV). We believe in the world as a created world which is in analogy to God, which refers to him, and which is filled by him.

Statements about the world and its structure are not, then, deductions from faith's assertion that God is. Faith already believes in the world too. This has its place in faith. If Heine says that doubt of God is doubt of life itself (*op. cit.*, p. 267; E.T. p. 116), Anselm is saying that faith in God is faith in life itself.

The world is thus an implication of faith rather than a deduction from it. God as cause and the world as effect are correlative for faith and they are not to be separated. How can one say "God" seriously and not also express the fact that he is the Creator and that he thus stands in relation to what is created? God without the world is an absurd thought; a world without God also falls under the same verdict of absurdity.

When faith reflects, therefore, it states what it already contains. Theology and cosmology are thus faith's self-explication through thoughts; they are not a speculative preamble or expansion of faith with the help of thoughts.[31] If one might venture to express what takes place here in Kantian terms, the point would be that Anselm passes analytic rather than synthetic judgments.

The earthquake of Kant's thought is that he detaches the act of thought from the faith which underlies it. This affects much more than the thought of God and its significance. In view of the correlation between God and the world, Creator and creature, the understanding of the world is also altered. In addition to the theological revolution we have here a cosmological revolution of shattering proportions.

Kant begins with an abstraction similar to that which led Descartes to

---

[31] Karl Barth rightly says that seeking understanding is integral to faith (*op. cit.*, p. 6; E.T. 1960, p. 16).

the speculative product of the *homunculus* who is only a thinking being. This was the result of an artificial restriction entailed by methodological doubt. It is the incontestable ontic element which remains when doubt has destroyed all self-evident certainties. This element is the subject of thought. But it is only this. Hence it can be described neutrally or indifferently as something, as a thing. Any self-understanding of the thinking self which goes beyond it cannot have the integrity of what is free from doubt. If it describes itself as tasting and feeling, as a person, as one who has a conscience or the feeling of absolute dependence, all this might be an illusion. The only thing that cannot be doubted is the *homunculus* of the thinking being. Only when we are certain of this as the one thing that remains can we attempt on this basis to construct the profile of man and finally to recapture the horizon of his world.

Under the dominion of the Cartesian I, whose significance in theological history we have tried to show,[32] Kant reduces reality to the thinking thing and the acting thing (if one might use these as ciphers for the two great critiques) and he examines the structure and the radius of action of these. Like Descartes, although not in the form of an express program, he arrives at this remnant by methodological doubt. He shows how naive are our views and processes of thought. Especially in his doctrine of the antinomies he makes it plain that the results of our logical speculation are a mere illusion when reason exceeds its competence, i.e., the border of its possible experience, and pursues metaphysics.

The distinction from Descartes is that in this restriction he does not use the proof of God to mediate between thought and being. He arrives at a direct certainty of what is external, of the world.

For the thinking being[33] what is external is the world of experience which is objectified by sensory perception and the understanding. Without this the power of perception and knowledge is not thinkable. This power is activated and can thus be affirmed only when it is affected by things in themselves.[34] The ability to know, which is determined by phenomenal forms and the categories, is a mode of ruling and shaping. This implies something that can be ruled and shaped. The subject posits the object.[35]

For the acting being the world is the sphere for the application of the disposition and the material for the fulfilment of duties. It does not confront the I in values or as a teleological nexus.[36] Values are manifested in the acting being. They come to light as the content of a disposition which expresses itself externally in action.[37]

---

[32] This is an area that needs greater exploration, especially in relation to existentialism.

[33] Kant does not actually use the term *res cogitans*, but it seems to sum up what he has in view, namely, the subject that can acquire knowledge.

[34] Cf. Eugen Herrigel, *Urstoff und Urform* (*Heidelberger Abhandlungen zur Philosophie*) and also *Die metaphysische Form* (1929).

[35] This is the starting-point of Fichte's idealism (cf. ThE, I, § 416ff.).

[36] On this cf. especially the *Critique of Judgment*.

[37] For a diametrically opposite view of the basis of values cf. Max Scheler, *Der*

Since the thinking and acting I is the starting-point, faith is not needed as a basis of understanding and action. There is also no place for the teleology of the cosmic structure which results from what we have called faith in the world. Kant's epistemological interest focuses on the "pure act" of perceiving and knowing and on the underlying apparatus. He investigates the structural conditions under which this apparatus works without letting it be determined by anything outside itself—things in themselves—and without integrating it into any embracing entity. What might lie outside it, e.g., the idea of God as the guarantee of the supreme good, cannot throw light on the structural conditions and cannot be regarded as determining them (as in Anselm). What might be outside or above can be registered only insofar as it declares itself in the structure of knowledge or conscience. Thus the confluence of happiness and duty declares itself, e.g., as a relation that we have to postulate, as the postulate of the supreme good, in reason itself.

Behind Kant's epistemology lies the ontological premise that it is possible to see reality as self-enclosed finitude and to understand the cosmic nexus without believing in something that embraces it. The premise is that one can bring to light the reality of the world from within, i.e., that it is possible to get at the world of experience from the standpoint of the subject-object relation which lies within it.

This possibility, or the advocacy of this possibility, is the real landslide. An attempt is made to make the world the object of knowledge apart from the basis, meaning, and goal of the world as elemental causes and conditions of this knowledge and also as its ultimate goal. These are excluded because the world is approached from within the subject-object relation, from within experience itself, and because it is presented only in its objectifiable state.

This objectifiable state, however, is not the totality of the world. It is only one of its dimensions. The totality cannot be objectifiable because it embraces the subject-object relation. In religious terms, it establishes the miracle of this relation. It builds the bridge which Descartes found in his proof of God.

Kantian thought, then, does not offer us any noetic possibility of making all reality the theme of empirical statements. If it can be objected against Anselm that his demonstration of God rests on an understanding of reality and a schema of thought which contain a prior decision that God exists, the similar objection might be brought against Kant that with his restriction of the world to the mere sphere of objective experience, and with his reduction of man to the immanent counterpart of this sphere, he has chased God out of the world and broken the link to the totality of the cosmic nexus, and, moreover, that his epistemological conception forced him to do this. For, as we have seen, the totality of the world is not in fact objectifiable.

Existentially we constantly reckon with this totality. We do so when we put the question of meaning and thus relate ourselves to something comprehen-

---

Formalismus in der Ethik und die materiale Wertethik (Halle, 1927). On the debate between Kant and Scheler cf. the author's book, *Das Verhältnis zwischen dem Ethischen und dem Ästhetischen* (Leipzig, 1932), pp. 46-65.

sive. We are always doing existentially, then, what is said to be epistemologically impossible. The existence which seeks the totality, relates itself to it, and lives by it, transcends the I which is reduced by Kant to thinking and acting being. The experience of reality in life itself transcends the objectifiable sphere of being. But how is this transcendence to be expressed in our age? In the form of dotted lines and postulates on the outer margin of philosophy? Can this tardy recognition do justice to the existential experience of transcendence, especially as it has only regulative and not constitutive significance for the rise of knowledge?

Heine already spotted "something" when he spoke of the doubt which is doubt of life itself. The idea of God which is fetched back again at the end can no longer make up for the fact that the world and man himself have been taken up and made a theme of their own without it.

3. THE REAL END OF ANSELM'S WAY. THE CHRISTOLOGICAL BACKGROUND OF THIS END

What is the source of the new presupposition?

This question is important since the gap between once and now also denotes the principle which lies behind modern scientific and historical investigation and technology. For this principle means the understanding of the world as a self-enclosed system of forces which does not allow intervention from above, which runs its own course autonomously, although still leaving a limited area for human freedom. What we have here is the secular understanding of the world which finds expression in secularization or secularism.[38]

The secular mind does not simply deny God any more than Kant did. But it does not reckon with him as a magnitude that has a place in the world or in life (which is rather more than challenging him merely as a cosmic magnitude). He is thought to have no relevance for the understanding of secular relations or for modifications, whether technical or organizational, of secular processes.

In this sense Hugo Grotius could already argue at the beginning of the seventeenth century that law would be valid and sovereign even were there no God. He does not say that there is no God. He does say, however, that God has no influence on the norms and structures of law. If he is proclaimed to be the author of law, this does not mean that law has received impulses or contents from this author which it could not produce by its own sovereignty. The proclamation means that the sovereignty of law is expressed by a subsequent reference back to this author.[39] God is simply a cipher, or, in Zwingli's term, an *alloiosis,* an expression which denotes something that exists even without him. As the author of the law God symbolizes the rank and significance of moral and legal norms; he does not constitute them. The machinery of the world works very well without this symbol, for it draws on immanent forces and functions according to immanent laws.

---

[38] F. Gogarten makes this distinction. We shall discuss it later, along with the question whether secularization is to be regarded as a result of Christianity.
[39] Cf. Kant's imperative, which is a command as though it were a command of God.

There seems to be something in it—how much we have yet to see—when modern theologians from Gogarten to Harvey Cox agree that Christianity itself has opened the door to this secular understanding of the world. Through Christ as cosmocrator it demythologized the world. It banished the powers (*stoicheia*) and the gods. It thus enabled men to view the world as a sphere of things and forces and to approach it objectively. This understanding in turn is the presupposition of a scientific approach and of investigation and action according to the laws of physics and technology.

Now it may well be true that, cautiously expressed, the Christian faith has a certain affinity to this secular emancipation of the world. But even if it does, one may suspect that this is not an attack on God. What could arise only through the help of faith will show signs of openness to faith. Might it not be, then, that secularization is not the conclusion of a history with God, that it does not imply God's death, but that it is a colon rather than a period? The godless wasteland of self-resting finitude offers man a chance in the same way as the wilderness did to Israel when it was led by the pillar of fire (Exodus 13:21; Numbers 14:14; Nehemiah 9:12, 19). God is not dead but we are dead for him, and we must go the way of death to have the same opportunity as the grain of wheat which goes down into the earth (John 12:23). Might it not be that we are on this way? This suggestion has a certain plausibility when we think of the new developments in theology and proclamation which are grounded in this experience of secularity and which receive and mediate new and immeasurable impulses through mastery of this experience.

But we are jumping ahead. We must return to Anselm to put the true question. We have to consider whether the way of ontological thought—a fascinating and incomparably universal way—has not come to a legitimate end, and whether we have not been driven out into the wasteland to start afresh and to find the pillar of fire in the wilderness. It is conceivable, as we shall show, that the theological possibility indicated by Anselm has been worked out and that the faith which originally sought understanding has finally been dissolved in understanding. It might be that the judgment in this development must be accepted and that there can now be a new beginning, the purifying of the faith which has been absorbed and the resurrection of the God who has been buried in a secular grave.

But how could the possibilities of the ontological thought we find in Anselm be really exhausted? When we say "really" here, we mean, not that accidents overtook this thought from without and ruined it, but that the immanent logic of the process itself brought it to its end.

We note that all the things which were originally associated with faith can detach themselves from this and become free-floating ideas.

Thus the modern concept of humanity has its roots in the Christian understanding of man. This is so true that Greek traditions of thought can hardly be considered at all, or only peripherally, as a secondary source. In the unconditional assertion of human worth that we find in, e.g., secular theses about the rights of man, there is reflected the alien dignity which man has as one who was created by God, visited by him, bought with a price, and set under his protection. This reference was what made man sacred. God did not love him because of his independent dignity. It was because God loved him that he had this dignity and became sacred (cf. Deuteronomy 7:7f.). In modern secularization, however, the idea of the human increasingly breaks free from this basis. It holds fast to the rank conferred by it. But it regards itself as a self-proved idea. It claims the privilege of an axiom. It needs no external source. The same applies to such concepts as freedom and human brotherhood. We have here secularized theological concepts which have been detached from the basic reference to God and made into autonomous ideas.

J. Heckel (in his *Lex charitatis* [1953], p. 40) has shown how this kind of mutation took place when the French Revolution freed the ideas of liberty, equality, and fraternity from the Christian tradition. He points out that these concepts are prefigured in Luther and are then changed in the French Revolution. The change of order is itself significant. In Luther fraternity, as love of neighbor, comes first, and this is based on divine sonship. With this reference equality cannot denote abstract *égalité* but equal rank before a final court in spite of every distinction. The change that the concepts undergo when they are detached from their original basis and made into ideas may be seen from the giving of first place to liberty. This liberty is no longer controlled by the one who gives it and makes it possible. It thus threatens to become the liberty of the strong which diminishes the liberty of the weak (cf. E. Heimann, *Reason and Faith in Modern Society* (1961), pp. 39f., and the author's "Was heisst Freiheit?" in *Der Einzelne und der Apparat,* 2nd ed. [1966], pp. 51ff.). The way in which Vatican II re-related the terms to the Christian understanding is of interest.

In a basically similar way the world which Anselm believed *sub specie Dei* can become the symbol of a general teleology which holds good even apart from the faith which originally validated it. Thus the teleology becomes an emancipated secular principle. The result of the process of emancipation may be seen in deism, which advocates a self-contained fulness of meaning and the teleological order of all being, and which often tries to demonstrate this in fantastic ways.

To find something that has no meaning destroys this understanding. This is perhaps why there is such an attraction to the exotic. Thus Gottfried Ohnefurcht Richter in his comprehensive *Ichthyotheology* (1754), when he appeals to fish as a proof of God, is troubled by the question whether deep-sea fish can have any purpose since they do not provide food for man and have no other obvious value. A thing which is of no use has no meaning and contradicts the assumed teleology of all being. Richter solves the problem by arguing that such fish agitate the water by swimming and thus purify it; they have, then, a meaningful function in creation. Even that which does not serve man as the crown of creation directly, may serve him indirectly. Indirectly, then, it has meaning. Other examples from deism are legion. One may refer merely to B. H. Brockes, *Irdisches Vergnügen in Gott,* 9 vols. (1721 ff.); F. C. Lesser, *Lithotheology* (1735); *Testaceotheology* (1744); C. Bonnet, *Betrachtungen über die Natur* (1774). Cf. ThE, II, 1, § 831.

The aim of deism is to lead man, through contemplation of the wonderful teleological structure of the world, to admiration, fear, and love of the great and loving and wise Creator. But the meaning or purpose of the structure lies within itself, and only in respect to its origin and goal does it point to the Creator. God is thus pushed out onto the periphery. He is the clockmaker who makes the clock and sets it going, and then it runs by itself with no further intervention. This significant comparison shows that the mechanism of the world is regarded as independent in its functioning. It follows its own patterns and needs no external direction.

A more naive version of the same thought may be seen in the intellectual teleology of Hegel. Here the intellect does not perceive what faith believes. It perceives directly by viewing phenomena and seeing their teleological structure. It is forgotten that faith in God originally functioned as a heuristic principle in this perception. All that remains is the supposedly self-evident product of an understanding which once used that principle and even accorded it much higher rank than that of a purely heuristic principle.

Nor is this all. The intellect, once freed from faith, not only perceives phenomena directly; it also perceives faith. It interprets it—we remember Lessing—as a naive preliminary stage. But faith increasingly yields to logos and thus in the long run makes itself superfluous. Or else, as in Feuerbach and many forms of modern psychoanalysis, the intellect derives faith from spiritual powers and processes. It thus integrates faith into its own understanding rather than letting itself be guided by it. To use a familiar metaphor of Kant's, the question arises whether philosophy as the representative of the intellect, and the former handmaid of theology, is merely following the trail or throwing light upon it. And soon one does not have to ask which role the intellect is playing or whether it is finally maid or mistress.

The way in which certain concepts of the kerygma and faith have become free and autonomous ideas is typical of the first stage of secularization. One may see an example of the same process in the tendency for the law to free itself from the author of the law in post-exilic Judaism.

On the return from exile Judaism does not simply return to the covenant in order to cleanse from the roots up the shattered relation to God for which it had endured the punishment of the exile. Instead it tinkered around with the symptoms of the trouble, i.e., specific transgressions of the law. This led to concentration on its casuistic demands.

W. Gutbrod is right enough (TDNT, IV, p. 1043) when he points out that no basic repudiation of the covenant was intended. Theoretically it was still in force. But there was an unmistakable shift of accent. The law was no longer established by the covenant. It now brought into being the relation to God set up in the covenant. It thus gained independent stature and came to be regarded as a means whereby Israel could remain in God's grace (*ibid.*, p. 1043, lines 32ff.). Hints of this may be seen in, e.g., Ps. 19; 2 Chron. 27f. With this detaching of the law from its author the reason for the law is no longer appreciated. It is no longer seen as a means to bring Israel to the divine covenant of grace by obedience. Nor is it seen as an opportunity for offering a counter-signature to this. A twofold degeneration ensues.

First, the original link between covenant and law is lost to view. The emancipation of the law carries with it the temptation to regard God's action as a reaction to human initiatives. Formal observance of the law is the key to the relation between God and man.

Second, the law, being detached from its original point in love of God and neighbor, becomes formal and casuistic as in extreme forms of Rabbinic Judaism. The prophets had already protested against this; thus Amos showed that literal observance could mean refusal of true obedience and an actual lack of love (Amos 2:6; 8:4ff.; cf. Jeremiah 8:8).

Along these lines the law is separated from its function in salvation history and alienated from its original purpose. This emancipation is a prototype of the process which we have illustrated by the emancipation of the teleological principle. Since Anselm teleology, too, has become autonomous. It has become an idea which, freed from faith, stands at the disposal of the empirical consciousness. The similarity between the two processes is evident.

This is the process which we had in mind when we spoke of the end of Anselm's way of thought. This way seems to end at the point where what is seen in the light of faith—the teleology of the world—has become a free-floating idea which can be distilled by direct and independent perception from observation of secular phenomena.

Once this takes place, some fundamental results follow.

First, the relation to God naturally changes. Previously the relation to the world was determined by the preceding relation to God, by an I-Thou relation. Creation was interpreted in the light of the Creator, to whom I can pray, to whom I can say Thou, and who calls me by name. Now, however, the I-it relation to the world is the basic reference of existence. In this relation God does not arise as a Thou. He has to be added by additional operations of thought.

In this sense deism is the first step to the banishing of the Thou and of prayer from the remaining relation to God. The deist can still praise and give thanks. He can no longer ask. For what is perfect could only be disturbed by divine intervention.[40] But mere doxology without petition, the cry "Thy will be done" without the request "Give us this day our daily bread," makes of prayer a pious lyricism which can persist even though one's life is not changed. Doxology alone is Thou-less. It is controlled not by the one addressed, but by the one who is expressing himself here. The I-it relation to the world is no longer broken. The voice of man is the only personal element. Once again man is simply in encounter with himself.

---

[40] It seems to me that the history of the understanding of prayer needs to be analyzed from this angle. The basis of the concept of prayer as a monolog (van Buren, H. Braun, and cf. H. Zahrnt, *Die Sache mit Gott* [1966], p. 360) might well be found here.

Second, our relation to the world and the history of this relation are affected.

Anselm's way comes to an end when the teleological structure of the world is no longer seen in terms of its ultimate end, i.e., in terms of the God who underlies and governs it, but when we perceive only its immanent ends and the autonomy of its functions. If there is an initial reference to God, this soon drops away. The immediacy of our reference to the world begins within a theologically shaped cosmology. Existing things are seen in their essence. Faith in creation even posthumously raises the question of teleology. It leaves behind the forms and categories which are initially used in a direct approach to phenomena. Faith in the Creator still operates as a heuristic principle.

Once immediacy is accepted, however, it soon leads beyond the first religious stage. To commit oneself to empiricism and to focus on phenomena is an incalculable enterprise. One cannot follow the older ontology or deism in letting phenomena be pre-formed by given metaphysical ideas[41] and in thus formulating such maxims as "only what ought to be can be," or "only what must be is." There are no longer any essences by which to judge existences. The existent is approached directly, and it may surprise us or lead us in directions we did not intend.

The modern investigator of phenomena is always ready for surprises and he is basically informed by divine curiosity (as Einstein put it). He is also prepared for the fact that traditional teleology will intervene as a metaphysical principle to which is ascribed the function of an essence which precedes existence and which thus interferes with objective and presuppositionless observation of existents. Permanent conflict is thus demanded against the presuppositions that get in the way of simple access to the world. Kant's epistemology is motivated by this conflict.

If, however, teleology is viewed as a pre-judgment, the slender remaining link to the peripheral thought of God is broken. For this link consists in the fact that the encounter with phenomena offered references to God whether in the form of a teleological proof or of the need for the postulate of God to overcome contradictions which could not be reconciled in the immanent world of experience. The I-it relation to the world thus occupied a key position regarding what was still possible as a concept of God.

Once teleology is unmasked as pre-judgment, however, this concept is bound to change. The unmasking cannot be arrested. For the concern to view phenomena objectively leads to a confrontation with meaninglessness, first in individual events (the Lisbon earthquake) and then in the total impression.[42] Once the world ceases to be a totality of meaning which is divinely guaranteed and therefore believed even though it cannot be seen, it is no

---

[41] Cf. the way in which Aristotelian metaphysics hampered simple observation in medieval medicine. On this cf. W. Leibbrand, *Der göttliche Stab des Äskulap. Eine Metaphysik des Arztes* (1939), pp. 210ff., 260ff., 291ff.; G. Scherz, *Niels Stensen. Denker und Forscher im Barock* (1964).

[42] Cf. T. Lessing, *Geschichte als Sinngebung des Sinnlosen*, 4th ed. (1927).

longer possible to explain meaninglessness by saying that we can get only a limited and fragmentary view of the whole, as Leibniz argued in his theodicy. We can no longer be compared to the dog which howls when it hears a fugue by Bach (H. Pichler).

If God is seen in the light of the world rather than *vice versa*, then the concept of God is simply a function of our experience of the world. Paul Gerhardt, even though he went through the dreadful experience of the Thirty Years War, could still write his hymns of praise and joy precisely because his experience of the world did not play the part of a criterion which would determine the conditions for the possibility of faith. The hope for release when least expected can arise only when the Nevertheless of faith takes precedence over the experience of reality which seems to contradict it.

Nor do we need to go back to exceptional experiences to come up against the alternative of interpreting God in terms of experience or *vice versa*. The tyranny of autonomous processes, the controlling and manipulating of man, the degrading of man to be partial bearer of function,[43] and the depersonalized collectivism which is triggered thereby pose the same alternative. If the resultant social structure is the basis of our investigation of the totality of existence, the latter can only appear to be confused and restricted. To the degree that the personality of the I is destroyed, to that degree it ceases to be capable of a Thou and it thus invokes a collective in which is no communication. In the structure of being which is destroyed in this way, God can no longer call us by name or call us to him as a Thou. The I has to call itself by name in order to find itself. Only he who finds God, or is found by him, can also find himself. This, then, is the alternative. Instead of interpreting God in terms of our experience of the world, we need to interpret our experience of the world in terms of God. Dietrich Bonhoeffer expresses this in his poem *Who Am I?* (*Auf dem Wege zur Freiheit* [1947], p. 16; E.T. *Letters and Papers from Prison* [1971], pp. 347f.). He cannot establish his identity on the basis of secular experience, i.e., by deduction from his effect on others or by introspection. Only as he is called by name does he know who he is: "Whoever I am, thou knowest, O God, I am thine."

The "penultimate" basis of the false view that experience of the world can be the criterion of the concept of God is the fear of falling into an abstract dualism of this world and the world above. When God is relegated to a transcendence which is remote from immanence while man is tied to immanence, which he can enjoy directly as the object of knowledge and action, being is divided into a worldless God and a godless world. The worldless God who is not related to existence is irrelevant to me. Hence he can be explained only by past secular experiences, i.e., in terms of an outdated tradition. He is just as dead as the experiences which in their day produced the idea of God.

Whereas this God is irrelevant to me, the immediacy of experienced im-

---

[43] Cf. H. Freyer, *Theorie des gegenwärtigen Zeitalters,* 2nd ed. (1956), and "Die Idee der Freiheit im technischen Zeitalter," *Universitas* (1959), 3, pp. 225ff.; ThE, III, § 83ff.

manence is highly relevant. I am related to it empirically. I experience it daily. I can investigate it exactly. I can win freedom of action and control by perceiving its necessity, i.e., its orderly course. Since the hypothesis of God is superfluous within this understanding and mastery of the world, and does not actually occur within it, God is dead. The hypothesis is dead even though, as in Ernst Bloch, the unconditional and total content of hope which the hypothesis used to represent still remains.[44] In place of the God of hope we have the god Hope, i.e., deified hope, which is produced by the utopian fantasying and development of what is there potentially in present secular conditions.

Thus, as W. Hamilton declares, transcendence as a whole is lost and not just the God of theism. A transcendence distinct from the immanence of secular experience cannot be upheld. There can be no competing with the immediacy, the evidence, and the elemental character of our experience of reality. The idea of the death of God is demanded. Nor is it transitional in Hegel's sense. It is definitive and final.

The decisive switch to the false alternative is made for what we have called the penultimate reason, namely, the setting up of a polarity between immanence and transcendence. For the rise of this abstract dualism which automatically leads to the autarchy of this world and the death of God there is, however, an ultimate theological reason. What is this?

For Anselm there could be no split between this world and the next. The supreme being was not just transcendent. It was also present in the teleological nexus of being. It permeated this being. The direct relation between the believer and the omnipresent supreme being did not allow any portion of being to be viewed apart from the supreme being in immanent isolation as an emancipated portion.

The immanence of God in this world, which does not integrate him into it but lets him be God, and maintains his distinction from the world, is based on a theological presupposition which we have described as the ultimate basis. This is the incarnation, the answer to the question: Cur Deus homo? In the incarnation of the Word God and secular reality are brought together. In it we thus have the secularity of God. God surrenders his transcendence in favor of his condescension. He does it, however, without becoming identical with the world.

In various forms this problem has continually played a part in Christology. At the time of the Reformation we find it in the so-called Calvinistic *extra* which was held over against Luther even though Luther himself had some essential safeguards against the incarnation of the Word becoming a renunciation of God's deity, as though God were only immanent. The point of the Calvinistic *extra* was that Calvin, although he agreed with Luther in teaching the communication of the attributes, did not want to see the second person of the Trinity "exhausted" in the historical man Jesus. The Logos is not completely absorbed by the flesh which he assumes. For he is the subject of this assuming. He thus transcends it. Consequently he is out of the flesh

---

44 E. Bloch, *Das Prinzip Hoffnung* (1959), pp. 1415f.

(*eksarkos*) as well as in it (*ensarkos*). (Cf. Inst., II, 13, 4 and II, 14.)

A distinctive variation of the problem has cropped up in modern theological discussion within the conceptions (already discussed) of H. Braun and others. Here it is argued that God is the form of fellow-humanity for which love is made possible by encounter (H. Braun, "Gottes Existenz und meine Geschichtlichkeit," *Zeit und Geschichte*, p. 408). This necessarily raises the question, however, whether God is not a mere symbol for fellow-humanity, whether he is not absorbed in the world (if fellow-humanity is a *pars-pro-toto* for the world). Manfred Metzger resists the charge that God is swallowed up in man or that one's fellow-man is identified with God ("Redliche Predigt," *op. cit.*, p. 425). Locating is not identifying; its aim is simply to make concrete (p. 426). God is encountered only in this world and not anywhere else (p. 427). The question is simply where he is to be found. Only as our human reality can he be talked of (p. 425). But this original intention of speaking about God in relation to the world rather than in transcendent and docetic distance from it did not need to overthrow the thesis of the Calvinistic *extra* that God or the Logos is not absorbed in the finitude of this world nor equated with fellow-humanity. For, as we have seen, it is an implication of the incarnation that we can never speak of God in pure transcendence but only in his condenscension to man. Hence it is quite justifiable to focus theologically on the question where we meet with God in the world.

It is justifiable, however, only when the issue is that of knowing God and talking about him. Unwittingly, the authors in question seem to have done a switch here. They have allowed a noetic statement about God to become an ontic statement. Since God can be known only in his secularity, they argue, he is not transcendent (Metzger, pp. 423f.). He has no place at all outside this world (Braun, *op. cit.*, p. 411).

The fatal mistake which is made here, and which leads contrary to the original intention to an equation of God and the world, is the fusing of God's knowability with his being. A false deduction is drawn: God can be experienced only in his secularity, therefore he "is" secular.

The noetic and ontic dimensions are thus confused. For the condescension of God in the incarnation of the Word points to the reason why God becomes secular and makes himself knowable in the world. This reason is his love which impels him to empty himself. Subjection to finitude in this self-emptying, however, means that he comes into finitude from without, and to that degree he transcends it.

The point of the incarnation, of God's coming into the world, can be seen and told only when the motive of self-emptying love is expressed, of a love, that is, which did not need to empty itself, which incurred self-denial and self-alienation thereby. The only way to put this is to say that God is transcendent, that he is above the world, and that he leaves the "story of heaven."

God's knowability in the world is not identical, then, with his being. This being transcends his knowability because he makes himself knowable. He "is" more in his being than what he "does" in terms of it.

In "death of God" circles the incarnation is not understood. To understand it one has to listen to the critical question put by the Calvinistic *extra*. This indicates that the one who condescends is always more than the one he condescends to be. He is not just identical with this one. To put it mythically, God does not slam the door of heaven behind him when he comes down to earth. He is not locked out. He does not become a prisoner of this world whose border he has crossed. He is still the God of heaven and earth. It is just because he is above the world that the miracle of his love is his becoming "worldly."

One is tempted to put this in the form of the paradox that the miracle of God's secularity is his transcendence. This is only a paradox. It holds good only so long as we do not think of transcendence abstractly and fall into dualism between this world and the other world. God is not defined by a concept of transcendence. On the contrary, transcendence is defined by the God who is manifest in Christ, by the incarnation of the Logos. This transcendence means the heaven which is open above Bethlehem. It is a transcendence which graciously discloses itself even to the point of secularity.

Since the event of the incarnation we can in fact speak of God's transcendence only in secular terms. It is there in our lives. But the difference between God and the world must always remain if we are not to fall into pantheism or to allow theology to be dissolved in pure ethics.

We thus see the significance of Christology in defining the relation between God and the world or transcendence and immanence. We shall have to turn, then, to certain central points in Christology which are important to this relation.

In Christ God becomes subject to the pressure of history, its finitude, and its nexus of guilt, even to the death of the cross. As God's condescension reaches down to the lowest depth of historical existence, there is no secular sphere nor dimension of human existence in the world which is without affinity to God and consequently to transcendence. The resurrection of Christ is for faith a declaration that God remains himself and that he transcends his secularity in the way that one who loves transcends the act of his love, or that the track is more than the stations which it passes and which mark its direction and nature. Two things, then, are plainly and indeed ontologically grounded in Christology.

First, there is no separate transcendence which is simply above the world. God has left the "story of heaven." He has come down into the depths of history. He has become secular. His transcendence has become immanence.

Second, the secularity of God,[45] as the exaltation of Christ bears witness, does not mean that God has been absorbed into this world or that he has died into the world. If this were so, then the world would indeed be his heir and it would fill with deified hopes the vacuum left by the banishment of the hypothesis of God.[46] The resurrection of the flesh, of dust (the sign of the

---

[45] Secularity is not an exact term in relation to God since it tends to suggest a state rather than an act (cf. E. Jüngel, *Gottes Sein ist im Werden*, 2nd ed. [Tübingen, 1967]).

[46] E. Bloch, *op. cit.*, pp. 1415f.

finite), points, however, to the fact that this world is not self-grounded. It receives its ground, goal, and meaning from the one who transcends it.

This twofold truth overcomes the dualism of transcendence and immanence by ruling out a godless world and a worldless God and showing that God is oriented to the world and the world to God, or, better, that God is the one in whose positing both orientations are grounded.

To sum up provisionally, the way of Anselm's ontology, in which transcendence and immanence are related teleologically through the incarnation, has now come to an end for the following reasons.

First, teleology has emancipated itself from its theological basis and become an immanent principle.[47]

Second, the direct experience of reality implied therewith has become a criterion for what may be known about God. To some extent openly and to some extent tacitly, God has become a cipher for understanding the world under the assault of meaninglessness. The self-destruction of theology when it is changed into an idea implies necessarily the loss of God when he is integrated into the world, i.e., the death of God. Godlessness is thus a result of worldlessness just as worldlessness is a result of pushing God into mere transcendence.

Thus atheism does not begin with a Promethean gesture of defiance against heaven. It does not begin with a violent assassination of God. What Nietzsche's madman says and does is not an initiatory act in this sense. The slaying of God is the logical result of a process which we have called the decline of Anselm's ontology. When faith ceases to define, to interpret, and to control the experience of reality; when the emancipated experience of reality lays down the conditions on which one may believe, a process is set in motion which will necessarily lead in the long run to proclamation of the death of God.[48]

If God is not at the center of life, he will not be on the margin either. He can stay only briefly on the boundary where he was put, e.g., by deism. That which does not affect life has no life. The strategy of ideological dictatorships shows a diabolical grasp of this law. It allows theology only in a negative mode. An esoteric cultus is permitted in a sacral sphere, but it is shut out of life and prevented from affecting its center, the everyday world and its orders. The point is that if the experiment succeeds, God himself, the God of the cultus, will be put to death. The mausoleum in which he is locked has the function of the dagger which kills him. When God becomes worldless, when he is banished to a periphery of cultus and transcendence, he has no further place in life. He has no "form." Hence he no longer "is," since God's being is unthinkable apart from his activity as cosmocrator. Instead of a Promethean attack we have a poisoning of God in homeopathic doses. With songs of praise and doxological acclamations he is conducted to the frontier

---

[47] We use this term deliberately, for even in deism, which puts God at the beginning and the end, teleology is self-contained (cf. Christian Wolff, *Vernünftige Gedanken von Gott, der Welt und der Seele des Menschen* . . . [1773], esp. § 1, 553ff., 1037ff.).

[48] Cf. George Bernanos, *The Diary of a Country Priest* (1937), p. 109.

of the world and finally sent off into transcendence. At last he becomes an absurdity. Immanence fills the resultant vacuum with its utopian mythologoumena. It enthrones the god Hope which it has itself invented.

4. PROSPECTS FOR A NEW BEGINNING. REVISIONS OF THE QUESTION OF CERTAINTY

This brings us back to our starting-point, namely, to what we said about Kant as the modern representative of this process.

In Kant God does not figure in the world of experience, whether as that which causes the world of experience to arise in our consciousness or as that which determines our practical daily dealings with it. God vegetates as a regulative idea on the outermost periphery. He no longer initiates anything. If, as the eschatological magnitude which reconciles in the *summum bonum* the immanent contradiction between duty and happiness, he were to be a direct motive of action, he would radically pervert ethics and allow eudaemonism to rule.

Is not this the philosophical basis of the modern docetism which chokes Christian proclamation in the homeopathic manner described by making it otherworldly and reducing to nil the relevance of God for this world and our life in it?

a. Theological Openness of Kant's Philosophy as Seen in Wilhelm Herrmann

Perhaps one might speak of a death of God in Kant, as Heine does, if Kant had left only one way to union with God, namely, that of being able to think of God only as a postulate. This would indeed entail his death, not merely because no breath of life comes forth from the mausoleum of postulates, but also because in the very next step of thought this empty postulate can be revoked. Did not Heine himself point out ironically that this pitiful remnant of God was left in only for the sake of poor old Lampe? Are not the feet of those who will carry away this remnant already at the door? Do we not already see Feuerbach who will show that this last hazy picture of God is simply a projection of dream and longing?

The time has now come, however, when we must raise a decisive question which might point in a very different direction. Is it really true that the way of a mere postulate is the only access to certainty about God which Kant has left open for himself or for those who think along the same lines as he does?

There have been theologians, and there still are, who accept Kant's approach, who even build his philosophy into the basic structure of their theology, and who realize that we cannot jump back over the gulf to pre-Kantian thought.

They agree (1) that after Kant we can no longer give proof of God with the help of synthetic judgments *a priori* or with evidence from the objective empirical world. Noetic certainty about God is thus unattainable. Access to him by way of knowledge and sight is blocked. Faith has lost all props of this kind. It thus has to base its certainty on something else.

Theological schools which resolutely accept the removal of these props, however, do not usually see in this a restriction of the Christian faith. On the contrary, they see a new and unheard-of chance to view faith in its own autonomy and in the special form of its own objective reference. Kant's philosophy seems incidentally to give new access to the Reformation principle of "by faith alone," and along these lines it is often thought to have an affinity to Luther.

These theologians also agree (2) that after Kant one can no longer achieve certainty of faith by an appeal to history. Purely historical belief would be an import from outside. It would be an external authority for the man who has emerged from self-incurred tutelage to the light of rational and personal adulthood. A certainty induced from without is impossible after Kant. Certainty must have a bridgehead in one's own consciousness. The transcendental I has to have a part in it.

This consideration has been especially fruitful theologically. For it has forced us to ask how we can appropriate that which, as revelation, claims our faith. It has forced us to ask how we can take it seriously in the understanding. Here again there seems to be a link with the Reformation. When Luther sought a gracious God, did he not establish a bridgehead in the consciousness which comes to the claim of revelation with a question and appropriates it as an answer, so that the claim is not just a legal decree?

These theologians agree finally (3) that after Kant one cannot go back on the autonomy of the consciousness and play off a theonomous determination of man against it. Kant's declaration of man's autonomy, which seems at first to be simply the negative proclamation of the emancipation of mankind and the radical rejection of all theonomous traditions, is felt by some theologians, e.g., Wilhelm Herrmann (*Ethik,* 2nd ed. [1901]), to be a theological liberation and not in the least a liberation from theology.

Kant's proclamation of autonomy was indeed full of productive impulses, for (1) it made necessary a rethinking of the polarity of law and gospel in the light of autonomy. Was not theonomy, which could appeal only to a positivist "God says," a law which kills? Does not this law crush man's personality, whereas the gospel summons to freedom (John 8:36; 2 Corinthians 3:17; Galatians 5:1, 13)? But if it summons to freedom, what else can it be but a summons to man's self-determination in some form, to his autonomy? Here again there is an obvious link with certain axioms of Reformation theology.

Kant's proclamation of autonomy also made necessary (2) a self-critical consideration of the question what *autos* will lie behind the new autonomy which cannot be denied. Will it be the old self, the self of the rational man which remains identical with itself? Or will it be the self of the man who is renewed by the Holy Spirit, the new creature? When man crosses the threshold of faith and confronts himself, does he not get outside himself and win a new self? The unavoidable concept of autonomy forces theology, then, to think through the problem of the identity of the self which lies behind autonomy. It thus raises the question of the creative Word, the theme of the new creation which is effected by the Spirit. The primitive content of the tradition is brought to life in a new way.

The simple fact that there is a post-Kantian theology, and that it exists *with* Kant and not just *in spite of* him, raises the question whether there might not be in this system some different and perhaps completely new forms of certainty which are not at all grounded in the certainty of mere postulates and which are possibly independent of this type of certainty altogether. If this were the only certainty, then with Heine we could and should speak of the death of God in Kant. But how, then, could such diverse thinkers as Schleiermacher, Ritschl, Herrmann, Bultmann, and Emil Brunner achieve along Kantian lines wholly new grounds of certainty and a re-actualization of the traditional theological heritage? Might there not be even more and as yet undiscovered approaches along these lines?

In fact the thought of Kant contains some essential indications of this kind. If Kant is rightly seen to be a prototype of modern thought, in which the autarchy of this world is established, it is not without significance that these hints of new and different forms of the certainty of faith should be found in him. Two such indications may now be mentioned.

(1) The first is to be found in Kant's principle that rational belief is to be regarded as the criterion for the validity of biblical claims.[49] In a hyper-conservative theology this is usually viewed negatively. It is regarded as a vote of no confidence in the traditional deposit of faith. This is no longer to be accepted unreflectingly and point by point. It is to be discussed critically. There is thus involved an element of hubris to the degree that man makes his reason a superior court and himself becomes the master of God's Word.

Now one might allow that this is really the background music of Kant's philosophy. Nevertheless it is not the only way of understanding the critical function of reason, especially when this philosophy is made the basis of further inquiry and impulses are perceived in it which were not present in Kant's own mind. At this point we face a basic hermeneutical problem. Should one discuss a thinker (or even an OT prophet) only within the framework of his own explicit self-understanding, or is it possible to understand him better than he understood himself in his own time and place?

It is already a question whether one is not throttling the theological impulses in Kant if one views reason too narrowly as a criterion. Detached from the Enlightenment system, reason merely stands for man's adult responsibility, for the fact that he cannot be untrue to his nature and humanity but is summoned into the situation of a court which is pledged to response and responsibility. When man on intellectual grounds views his nature as that of a rational being he can express his personal responsibility only by proclaiming that the reason which determines his being is the criterion of all the truth-claims and the imperatives which come to him.

In this sense Lessing is misunderstood completely, and pressed into a historically conditioned system, if what he says about the superiority of the

---

[49] *Religion within the Limits of Reason Alone,* pp. 78, 94ff.

necessary truths of reason over the accidental truths of history is interpreted rationalistically and the concept "truth of reason" is taken to imply pure intellectuality. The situation here is much the same as in Kant. The essence of man for Lessing—he is historically conditioned here—lies in his possession of reason. If, therefore, he wants to say that man must respond to a truth-claim with his essence, that he has to be in dialog with the one who claims him, that he cannot be a servile recipient or play the part of a mere object, then within his particular terminology he has to say that reason must come into play as man's dominant attribute, and he gives it the function of a criterion. If one were to tie them down to their terminology, both Lessing and Kant would be outmoded for a consciousness which understands itself post-rationalistically and which is no longer convinced of the significance of reason as that which constitutes humanity.

This is, however, a complete misinterpretation. What Lessing and Kant are proclaiming is not reason itself but reason as the representative of the essence of man, or, as we should say today, of human existence. The point is not the role of reason itself but of what it represents.

It is right, then, to find in both Lessing and Kant an impulse which goes far beyond their own time. Both face the question how far the Christian kerygma and its reception can be responded to from the center of humanity, or, in other terms, how it is possible and thinkable that the kerygma should not overpower the *humanum* as a legal authority, but that there should be an analogy, i.e., an understanding and assenting reception of the kerygma.

This question, however, can be transposed into very different systems of thought. It can be relevant, e.g., in a system which views the essence of humanity in terms of existence or secularity rather than reason. If, then, one does not confine Kant to his own time and its concept of reason, but takes reason as a symbol for the essence of man, two things are plain.

First, Kant's thought contains impulses toward critical revision even for philosophies and theologies which espouse very different concepts of the essence of humanity. Second, we are to see in the proclamation of reason as a criterion more than malicious joy at finding in human rationality a means to escape the drag of religious traditions and to encounter both the starry heaven and also any other authority with the passion of adulthood. The real point is investigation of the kerygma with a view to finding out how far it stands in correlation to my consciousness, responsibility, existence, and secularity, and therefore how far it is a present reality.

Theological Kantians caught this note in the Königsberg philosopher. They could thus accept his philosophy and see in it a model which prefigures the correspondence of the kerygma and human existence and which above all raises the question of this correspondence. In keeping with this is the fact that theological Kantians like Herrmann were not controlled by the question: "What can I in good conscience reject?" (which would have accorded with the malicious form of emancipation), but rather by the question: "What can I in good conscience accept and keep?"

Schleiermacher moves in the same direction when in terms of a religious rather than a rationalistic definition of man he asks whether and how far Christian truth can be brought into correspondence with this definition, or whether and how far the religious system of categories can appropriate the claims of the kerygma. Indeed, we find an early form of this question in Melanchthon's *Loci* of 1521 when he asks whether the expressibility of christological doctrines is controlled and limited by what is said about Christ's benefits. For when I speak of benefits I have also to speak of their recipients. The human existence which receives them has thus to be taken into account too. Correspondence between the kerygma and the nature of man is thus brought into relief even though Melanchthon is separated by a wide gulf from the Cartesian approach which controls the correspondence between the kerygma and the nature of man in Kant and Kantian theologians. (The analogy between Melanchthon and Kant should not be overlooked for this reason.)

(2) It is obvious, then, that Kant's thought is open to the future and is not tied to the historically conditioned schema of his rationality. Once we realize that reason is for him simply a representative of the essence of man, and that other representatives of this can be substituted for it, Kant's philosophy is open in principle to other forms of certainty to which the essence of man has an affinity. These are at its disposal even though they lie outside rationality and objective experience.

Wilhelm Herrmann is again an important example here. A problem for him as a Kantian is how there can be the experience of the unconditioned which the biblical revelation requires of him when it claims to carry with it a presence of God in the historical form of Jesus of Nazareth. How can Kantian man respond to the experience of the unconditioned within the conditioned empirical sphere of history? How can this experience be valid for him? For the significance of Christ as the Savior, as a divine being (*The Communion of the Christian with God* [E.T., 2nd ed. 1906], p. 117f.), implies something transcendent which cannot be gathered from the objective experience of history. A synthetic judgment *a priori* or *a posteriori* can never lead to the exact conclusion: "Therefore" the divine predicate befits the figure of Christ; here the unconditioned is objectifiable within the conditions of history.

Herrmann, certain of this presence of the unconditioned in Jesus Christ, accounts for this certainty by tracing it to a mode of personal experience which lies outside rationality. This experience brings him into contact with the inner life of Jesus in which an overpowering and incontestable reality encounters us (*op. cit.*, p. 62). Our conviction that the person of Jesus can be the basis of our faith (p. 59) does not rest on a historical judgment. It rests on a personal experience, i.e., one grounded in personal communication. Herrmann can even speak (rather oddly) of objective grounds (p. 118) which on the basis of this experience lead us to see God himself in the human phenomenon of Jesus. First, we have known the historical fact of Jesus as part of our reality and felt its force. Then we experience the fact that in God, whose work upon us is nowhere so plain as in the power of the person of

Jesus over us, moral thoughts which impel us inwardly take on personal life (p. 85). We are thus aware that in the fact of his person God has dealings with us; we detect his work in the development of our own inner life (p. 103). Hence a kind of practical syllogism mediates to us the certainty of his nature and unconditionality through the effect that the fact of his person has on us.

We need not discuss here whether Herrmann's key concept of the inner life of Jesus is a possible one or whether psychological categories in general are suitable when it is a matter of certainty regarding his person.[50] Even if we think, as we do, that the concept is materially inappropriate, it still has the significance of a hint. It bears witness that I can have certainty apart from objectifiable experience or postulates. I can have it by personal encounter. Here one may have the experience of trust, which is a kind of certainty (cf. Herrmann, *Ethik*, 5th ed. [1913], p. 42). This experience occurs when we note that a man obeys an unconditional will and that the same will controls us. We then know where we are with him.

We can have this certainty of trust in relation to Jesus. For we not only see him obeying an unconditional will. This will has achieved personal life in him (*Verkehr*, p. 85). It is embodied and present in him. We can thus have the unconditional certainty of trust in an analogy to moral experience.

Kant's approach is obviously adopted here. Our own consciousness is the criterion of all truth even though it is controlled now, not by theoretical reason, but by human personality. Nor is personality meant in Kant's sense. For him it is essentially characterized by solipsistic practical reason. Here it is historical personality in an I-Thou relation.

Herrmann is still thinking along Kantian lines. Like Kant he is examining the conditions of certainty in the human subject. For him, however, this subject is not governed by theoretical and practical reason. It is not a rational being in Kant's sense. It is a being which through the mediation of unconditional norms (an unconditional will) is related to a Thou in whom it can trust.

What unites Herrmann and Kant is the question of correspondence or analogy between what is accorded final certainty and the structural conditions of the human subject. We might also say that it is the common question of appropriation, i.e., the question which cannot be avoided once man has discovered his own being, i.e., his autonomy in one or another form. The distinction between the two is that Herrmann attempts to locate the origin of certainty, and especially of certainty about the being of Jesus, at a different point in the subject.

In this context we need not go into the doubtful aspects of Herrmann's view. What we have already said about Cartesian theology should make them plain enough.

Here, too, the Cartesian I forms the constant and unchanging point of reference. What raises a claim to truth, e.g., in the fact of Christ's person,

---

[50] On this basic question cf. the important book of J. Rothert, *Gewissheit und Vergewisserung als theologisches Problem* (1963).

cannot shatter this I, cannot make it the old I, cannot give birth to a new creature; it can only confirm the moral self- and pre-understanding of this I. It adapts itself fully to the normative consciousness even when this consciousness is refined and developed by it within certain constant and abiding limits.

These objections, however, do not affect the present discussion. Our concern here is to show that theology can adopt Kant's approach without advancing the same basis for certainty (or uncertainty) of God, i.e., without pushing God over the horizon of secular experience and, in the form of transcendent postulates, consigning him to the furthermost periphery and therefore to complete ineffectiveness. Theological Kantians and their modern descendants in the school of Bultmann make it clear that Kant's philosophy still leaves open the theological possibility of finding very different sources of certainty outside reason.

As concerns Kant, his biography seems to indicate that he, too, knew more than the God of his postulates. The Christian tradition had already confronted him with the problem of God even before he began his career as a philosopher. The God of Scripture and the (orthodox or rational) proclamation of the church were for him a constant theme of debate, a claim, a continual summons to mobilize the criterion of his rational consciousness on the one side or the other. At all events, Kant knew more than the God of his philosophy, as Heine clearly failed to see when he confused what Kant thought he could account for noetically with what he believed *de facto*. Kant had to face the experience which others had of God and what they presented as revelation. He did not basically contest their claim nor did he deny that there might be sources of certainty outside reason. To find these, however, was not his problem. His problem was to test what I may accept as binding in my capacity as a rational creature. To discover this he invoked reason as a criterion of certainty of God, but only as a criterion and not as an exclusive source.

When, as in the *Critique of Practical Reason*, he makes reason a source of certainty as well through the postulates it produces, he does this only for heuristic reasons. In order to establish what reason can achieve as a criterion when faced with the claims of revelation, he has to present it in pure form and develop the potential theology enclosed in it. He must perform an act of doubt, reduction, and refusal to listen such as that which Descartes performed when he arrived at his *Cogito—sum*.

The experiment which Kant made heuristically on the philosophical drawing board, and which led to his postulate of God, was not, however, the whole of his own confession. To use the words of Pascal, Kant had dealings with the God of Abraham, Isaac, and Jacob as well as the God of the philosophers or of his own philosophy. Kant, too, knew the possibility of other sources of certainty apart from rational and moral sources. The only point is that he did not regard it as his own task to seek these sources or to commit himself to one of them as Herrmann did; instead he concerned himself exclusively with the noetic problem of certainty.

That Kant knew other truths apart from those whose certainty may be shown epistemologically is just as sure as that Lessing did. Could not Lessing confess on occasion that the heart knows more and different things than the head?

b. Schleiermacher and Kierkegaard as Further Examples

What we have tried to show in Herrmann, namely, that the Kantian approach leaves the way open for forms of certainty in relation to God which differ from what Kant's own teaching on pure and practical reason could offer, may also be seen in all the theologies which start in some manner with subjectivity. These theologies are all affected by the Kantian revolution. We shall consider two which lie at opposite extremes from one another, the theology of Schleiermacher on the one side and that of Kierkegaard on the other.

In Schleiermacher, too, the validity of religious experience is at issue. This cannot be established by history or metaphysics. It is not related, then, to any authority. If it were anchored in authority of any kind, it would be external and would not be appropriated by me. It is valid for me only when what is said in religious documents enters into correspondence with my religious categories and therefore with my subjectivity, which is analyzed in the introduction to the *Christian Faith*. (For all the differences in detail the basic approach is the same in the *Reden* too.)

Certainty about God cannot be based, then, on a "God says." Before the word God can mean anything, it must be shown to be prepared for in my subjectivity and to have a place in its structure. When this is done, statements about God from the Bible or other religious documents or teachings can be housed in my subjectivity and can thus be appropriated. This is why Schleiermacher opens the *Christian Faith*, not with the doctrine of God, but with an analysis of subjectivity, which is determined by a religious form of self-consciousness, namely, the feeling of absolute dependence. The source of the absolute dependence of our receptive and self-active existence is called God.

Schleiermacher does not begin with God and then say that we are absolutely dependent on God. This would be dogmatic metaphysics and intellectual fantasy. We begin with the feeling of absolute dependence, awareness of which embraces all partial feelings of dependence and freedom, and then we raise the question of its source and find the answer in God. If God then reveals himself as the God of the Bible does, the experience is like that of an astronomer when he finds a star which he had first calculated and located in theory. When it is then discovered empirically he is certain that it is not an optical illusion or projection. He is confronted with a reality.

In relation to this view similar questions arise as in relation to Kant's doctrine of God. In particular one has to ask whether the God of self-consciousness, who is not unlike Kant's postulated God in his peripheral externality and vagueness, is not an unreal and completely ineffectual specter. Would not Heine have to say of him that he is an expiring God, a pitiful shadow of himself? If this is all that we can find of him, God surely bears a suspiciously striking resemblance to this waning faith.

Even less so than in the case of Kant, however, should one call the God constructed out of subjectivity the only result of possible religious experience. Here again, as in Kant, we simply have the conditions and criteria which can act as a check on very different forms of experience and certainty.

These other forms may be found in what biblical history and the church's proclamation tell us about God. What comes forth from our subjectivity to meet these experiences serves the purpose of enabling us to appropriate them, so that they are not mere dogmas or compulsory beliefs. When it is a matter of saying what "I" believe instead of repeating in childish fashion what is believed by others, I must find a bridgehead in myself where the forces of revelation can land and find a footing. It was Schleiermacher's passionate contention in his letters to Lücke that the analysis of self-consciousness is simply the establishment of a bridgehead and not the deployment of the whole army of possible religious experience.

Christian religious experience does indeed come from outside. Its source is the salvation event in God's history which happens "to me" as well as "in me" and which I must come to know in its contingency. But it cannot remain outside me or merely "to me." It must be appropriated. Hence I must constantly relate it to what comes forth from my self-consciousness to meet it.

It is because appropriation is the guiding theme that Schleiermacher's *Christian Faith* looks like anthropology. Its focus is always on what happens to my "disposition" under the influence of what is without. It seems as though a history of the self-consciousness is being written. Doctrines are descriptions of pious states (§ 15). It makes no essential difference whether they are viewed thus or as concepts of divine attributes and modes of action, or indeed as statements about the characteristics of the world (§ 30). What they intend, e.g., in christological statements, has an affinity to my inwardness and to the cosmos. They may thus be presented from different angles. Faith can be described only in terms of that which in me and the world has affinity to it. In describing it thus, I am made immune from Docetism and blind authoritarianism. I am describing God in his actuality.

The limitation of this procedure may also be seen here. Revelation can only have a Socratic significance for me. It is simply a trigger to release and develop what is already in the psyche. It can only set going a history of the consciousness. It can only bring about a variation in it. It is limited by the potentialities of the consciousness. There can be no new creating by the Holy Spirit. There can only be variations within a permanent identity.

We see here the effect of the Cartesian approach which we have already studied right up to the existential theology of our own day.

Our present concern, however, is not with this aspect. We are simply trying to show that a (greatly modified) Kantian approach, which makes the subject the criterion of all possible certainties, is open to very different sources of certainty and that possible certainties are not at all restricted to that which emerges with investigation of the possibilities of the theoretical, practical, or religious consciousness, whether in the form of the postulate of the *summum bonum* (Kant) or in that of the source of the feeling of absolute dependence (Schleiermacher).

In both cases, though more clearly in Schleiermacher than Kant, actual religious experience points to something transcendent which does not arise out of a mere explication of the self-consciousness. This is particularly evident in Schleiermacher.

In the *Christian Faith* he strictly observes his principle of developing Christian doctrines only as they accord with subjectivity., with the dispositions of Christian piety. This is why there is little place for eschatology in his presentation.[51] As a preacher at Holy Trinity in Berlin, however, he displays great freedom. He is no longer a prisoner of his system. He can point uninhibitedly to the sources of certainty or experience even though he cannot locate them systematically. The preacher knows more than the theologian.

Heine spoke of the death of God in Kant because Kant pushed God out onto the periphery where he was effectual neither in the understanding nor in the mastering of life. If the charge is only partially true in relation to Kant, it is even less applicable to Schleiermacher. The charge would hold good only if the sole concern of these thinkers were with the concept of God within the system. But to assume this is to do justice to the intellectual significance of neither of them. If this had been their sole concern they could hardly have exerted the positive theological influence they did.

In both the way is left open for other forms of experience. Schleiermacher the preacher shows how intensively these other forms can be taken. For in him encounter with the biblical Christ bursts open all the schemata of thought and experience. This rather than the derivation of God from absolute dependence is the effectual force which shapes life and gives it form. One finds adequate proof of this, apart from all else, in Schleiermacher's ethics.

In a radically different way Kierkegaard also begins with subjectivity. What relates him to Schleiermacher, and both of them to Kant, is the idea that every form of appropriation is determined by the fact that the human subject has a part, and has to have a part, in what it must appropriate. The manner of participation and the nature of the subject are, of course, wholly and utterly different. Participation is described by Kierkegaard as the infinite passion of inwardness and the subject is characterized by the fact that it is existent rather than the bearer of a theoretical, practical, or religious consciousness.

Kierkegaard, too, begins with the impossibility of an objective certainty of revelation and hence of God himself. For him as for Schleiermacher, and later Martin Kähler, it is not possible that historical investigation should give us objective certainty, first, that Jesus lived, and second, that he is the Son of God who brings salvation. Objective study can bring only relative results

---

[51] E. Brunner refers to the "eschatological lacuna" in Schleiermacher (*Die Mystik und das Wort* [1924]).

which cannot be the basis of the absolute certainty which is essential to faith as a life-decision.

Thus we read in the *Philosophical Fragments* that Christianity is something historical, in relation to which the best knowledge we can achieve is only an approximation, and yet as such it purports to have decisive significance for my eternal salvation (E.T. 1942, p. 92). But mere approximation is not an adequate basis for eternal salvation. Thus history cannot give us objective certainty.

Along Kantian lines one might say that God does not figure in the zone of our experience, or at any rate that he does not do so in such a way that he is demonstrable in the strict sense and with general objective validity. It is thus a monstrous confusion to present the truth of Christianity with an appearance of objectifiability. This leads to the misunderstanding that truth is knowledge . . . whereas in primitive Christianity everything that is said points to the fact that truth is being.[52] The failure of the attempt to arrive at objective certainty makes it apparent that what is at issue here is being, a creatively effected new being.

Kierkegaard points out again and again that God cannot be reduced to objective thought, as in the conceivable link between the idea of deity and the idea of humanity. He conceals himself in extreme paradox. He becomes an individual man. Once I have understood objective truths I lose interest in them. They do not affect my existence. They call for no commitment. When I know, however, that my temporal and eternal destiny hangs on a truth, and when I realize that this truth is not objectifiable, the infinite passion of my inwardness is unleashed. The supreme truth of existence is objective uncertainty held in the most passionate inwardness.[53] God hides in an incognito so that he cannot be grasped objectively and can thus command the strongest possible commitment. Kierkegaard can even venture the bold metaphor that God practices the art of love. He is like a girl who leaves her lover uncertain whether she loves him in return and who thus stirs him to the most ardent passion.

Since I cannot have certainty of God as a theoretical subject or transcendental ego, I see that a specific being is required, that I have to be subject to the truth in my existence if it is to have relevance for me. The truth is not, then, a distant thing outside. It is the relation in which I stand to this thing outside. Thus truth is a being, a being in truth, a new and created being which I cannot control. The believer does not inquire into something that is objectively valid. He inquires into the relation in which he stands to the truth, into his being, into the state of his existence.

Unlike Kant and Schleiermacher, who, theoretically at least, count on the constancy of the Cartesian I, Kierkegaard makes a break with this tradition of thought. He begins with subjectivity and makes this the criterion of what may be unconditional certainty. But the subjectivity he has in mind is not the old self. It is the self which is enabled in faith to love God and which

---

[52] *Training in Christianity*, pp. 200ff.
[53] *Concluding Unscientific Postscript,* p. 182.

therefore understands easily that which a proof outside faith cannot give but is more likely to obscure.[54]

Thus Kierkegaard thinks along Kantian lines, even though his real philosophical opponent is Hegel. But the common starting in subjectivity is perhaps not the most important link with Kant. For they understand subjectivity very differently. The crucial link is that both of them, although again in very different directions, can see that objective attempts to achieve certainty within our experience lead nowhere when it is a matter of certainty of God.

This realization is not a declaration of theological bankruptcy, as Heine thought it was in Kant's case. It is not a funeral for God. It is the negative aspect of theology. It simply acknowledges that Christian truth, which is a truth of being and relation, cannot be sought or found in the sphere of the objectifiable. This discovery frees us for the insight that Christian truth draws on other sources.

Kant's thinking is open even in relation to this unexpected development.

c. Decisive Theological Alternatives in the Post-Kantian Age

We may sum up as follows. Kant's immanent view of the world, which is restricted to the horizon of experience, means that the traditional ontology, represented here by Anselm, degenerates into a teleologism. In this process God is depersonalized. He becomes no more than an efficient and final cause. Even the divine origin and goal of events, which the deists still retained as part of the chain of occurrence, is questioned by Kant and reduced to a mere postulate. Thus Kantian philosophy, as a turning-point to the modern age in the true sense, confronts us with a fundamental alternative.

(1) On the one side is the deduction which Heine feared and which Feuerbach drew (after the stages of high idealism and especially of Hegelianism had been traversed), namely, that God is robbed of all reality. The claim to happiness, and the coinciding of happiness and duty which God guarantees, is regarded as a dream by Feuerbach or a pragmatic supposition by Marx; it is explained in terms of psychology or political strategy. The next step is that of a self-resting immanence which is hermetically sealed against anything outside. Strictly the term immanence is no longer suitable here, since it still carries with it a reminiscence of the transcendent world. The self-enclosed world now regards itself as the totality. What was once regarded as transcendent, or as belonging to the future world, it takes over as its own utopian possibility. It seizes heaven and makes the god Hope its inherent principle. Here we have indeed a declaration of the death of God.

(2) On the other side post-Kantian man, seeing the possibility of being imprisoned in his world, looks for new forms of religious experience, for new and unique encounters. These may differ among themselves and may even be antithetical.

Thus Schleiermacher subjects the religious to genuine categories which

---

[54] Cf. *Edifying Discourses*, IV, pp. 30ff.

differ from the categories of theoretical and practical reason, of metaphysics and morality (*Reden,* 2). To these other categories there corresponds a specific form of experience which does not come under other intellectual categories. Later a specific religious *a priori* can be established and the modes of experience actualized here can be associated on equal terms with the forms in which theoretical reason knows truth and the conscience is aware of moral norms.[55]

The particularity of the religious mode of experience may be given a personal basis, as in Herrmann, in encounter with the inner life of Jesus. It may be regarded as validated by very specific spiritual reactions which I have in encounter with religious phenomena and their biblical documentation. They mediate to me an evidence of truth which makes me independent of the purely historical authority of its attestation. Thus Lessing in the *Demonstration of the Spirit and Power* can say that what matters is the experience and not the explanation of it. When a paralytic feels the benefit of an electric spark, what does he care whether Nollet or Franklin is right? Experience places at our disposal specific ways to religious truth which differ from other forms of rational certainty.

We also recall that in Kierkegaard the existence-transforming Word causes us to be in the truth and opens up access to it. Naturally the particularity of religious experience may also be simple and even naive. Appeal is simply made to the atmosphere of truth which pervades it. We are surely right to assume that this is the average situation in a Christian congregation.

At a certain stage of spiritual maturity this naive evidence for the truth of faith can no longer be regarded as adequate. Truth cannot be separated from the man who knows it. Hence the different statements about it have to be in mutual communication. This does not mean that they have to be in agreement or that they have to be harmonized. (The scandalous truth of the Christian faith can never be brought into this kind of harmony.) It does mean, however, that the place of Christian truth in the whole nexus of consciousness has to be defined and accounted for. Otherwise there would be a split in the consciousness and a consequent lack of intellectual honesty.

No matter how the particularity of the mode of religious experience may be defined, it is obvious at least that Kant's fundamental self-criticism of thought does not have to be merely destructive nor does it leave open only the way that finally leads to proclamation of the death of God. What is made necessary theologically by Kant is either that God becomes a marginal postulate and hence unreal or that unique modes of religious experience must be found. The necessity imposed can be fruitful and can offer opportunities in two ways, so that it is unfair to condemn it as merely destructive.

First and negatively it can overthrow false and incredible certainties of an objective kind. This can create problems in an age of historicism. Certainty

---

[55] Cf. E. Troeltsch, *Gesammelte Schriften,* II (1913), pp. 754ff.; A. Nygren, *Die Gültigkeit der religiösen Erfahrung* (1922); K. Bornhausen, "Das religiöse Apriori bei E. Troeltsch und R. Otto," *Zeitschrift für Philosophie und philosophische Kritik,* 139 (1910).

of God or Christ cannot rest on a study of the objective contents of history or in the illusion that history offers a proof of God and that faith may thus busy itself with a foundation that derives from sight.

The idea that this could be done was always contrary to faith. The NT itself is critical in this regard. It does not make a visible miracle the basis of faith and allows that such a miracle may be ambivalent (Matthew 21:23, 24, 27; Mark 11:28f.; Luke 20:2, 8; John 6:26). In the age of historicism, however, what faith already knew is unexpectedly confirmed from outside. Historical knowledge which demands objectification is necessarily relative. It cannot verify an event for which there is no analogy. Even the verifiable elements, e.g., in the story of Jesus, lead only to approximate certainty and cannot be the basis of the absolute certainty which faith needs.

Faith has always been tempted to seek the security of objective props. Since Kant, however, this is obviously contrary to knowledge as well as faith. Historicism, then, is not just a challenge to faith. It also summons faith to remember its own basis, to be true to itself, and not to seek aid from outside, or to subject itself to sight.

Even before the challenge of historicism to the basis of faith, Kant asserted the nonverifiability of this basis.[56] He showed the necessity of that which historicism has demonstrated empirically. Whereas historicism has made it clear that all attempts to square the circle fail, Kant showed *a priori* why they are bound to fail and why they will always do so.

Theologians who follow Kant, when under historical attack, will never think that they can beat historicism on its own ground, that they can oppose positive construction to its critical destruction, and that they can thus prop up faith historically.[57] They will seek a radically different basis for faith which is more appropriate to faith itself because it forswears objectifiability and accords to faith its own basis of certainty.

Kant has thus helped to clarify the theological doctrine of faith by strengthening from a philosophical angle its conviction that there is no certainty about God outside faith, no certainty on which the possibility of faith might stand as a logical deduction. God may be found only in faith and not outside it. This call to faith to remember its own unique certainty is implied in Kant's destructive work.

Second and positively Kant's criticism carries with it a summons, not, as in deism, to arrive at experience of God through experience of the world and thus to make natural theology the basis of faith, but rather to achieve awareness of God directly and thus to begin at the theological center. Directness here can only mean seeking experience of God where he bears witness to himself directly, i.e., in his Word, in his incarnate Word, in the person and message of Jesus Christ.

---

[56] Lessing and others like Semler and Reimarus show that the problem of historicism is not just post-Kantian. They are thus precursors of the movement of historicism. In Kant himself history and the historical play only a minor role.

[57] Many "positive" theologians at the turn of the century tried to do this, e.g., E. König in the OT field and T. von Zahn in the NT field.

Implicitly and indirectly, then, Kant shows that we must take a different path from that of natural theology. God is not to be understood in the light of the world but *vice versa*. An analogy of faith must replace the analogy of being.[58] In the name of Luther's principle that the person does the works, the world can be understood only in terms of its author and creation only in terms of the underlying Word and him who spoke it. To begin with God himself rather than the world does not mean a new step into worldless transcendence nor does it have to be linked to confession of a God who is not here in the world. It implies instead a new approach to the world if God is regarded as the Father of Jesus Christ and hence as the one who loved the world (John 3:16) and condescended to it.

All this is not in Kant nor can it be read out of his works. These possibilities and openings within Kant's approach come to light only later as appeal is made to Kant, both negatively and positively, for views of a very different provenance. Philosophers like Fichte and Schopenhauer developed different aspects of this thought and found new possibilities in it. Similarly Christian theologians had to try Kant's approach and to see what openings it still left, or even suggested, for their certainty of faith. In some sense Kant was like a prophet who could not see all the dimensions implicit in his prophecy and had to leave it to historical fulfilment to bring them to light. It is along these lines that we have perceived other possibilities implied in Kant's thought and studied the post-Kantians and their efforts to keep the certainties of faith in the fire of Kant's criticism and to let the foundations of these certainties be recast in the fire.

There is thus good reason to put Kant at the heart of this discussion. If only in relation to vocabulary and method, theology has always been in close communication with philosophy.[59] No philosopher has necessitated a revision of theological principles in so dominating a fashion as Kant. No philosopher has inaugurated the secularity of theological thinking as he has done. He is still secretly present in every theological discussion today even when many of those who participate do not realize that he is looking in whenever they speak about the subject-object relation, or existence, or pre-understanding, or the death of God, or hope.

We may proclaim as the result of this discussion that modern post-Kantian man has put to death a false and degenerate picture of God, so that the true God may again announce himself. Because it has been shown that God cannot be experienced objectively, the old truth may be seen afresh that only God can give experience of God and that only in his light do we see light (Psalm 36:9). A new way is thus opened up for the doctrine of the Holy

---

[58] We shall deal with the problem of analogy in the doctrine of creation. On the analogies of faith and being cf. H. G. Pöhlmann, *Analogia entis und fidei* (1965); H. Diem, *Theologie als kirchliche Wissenschaft,* I (1951), pp. 28ff.; G. Söhngen, *Die Einheit in der Theologie* (1952), pp. 235ff.; F. Flückiger in Stud. gen. (1955), 2, pp. 678ff.

[59] Cf. the role of Kant in relation to Ritschl, Herrmann, and Heim, or of the Neo-Kantians in relation to the early Barth, or of Grisebach in relation to Gogarten, or of Heidegger in relation to Bultmann.

Spirit and the being in the truth in which he sets us (1 Corinthians 2:9-11). Our concern in Chapters VII-XI was to claim this possibility and to pave the way to this doctrine.

The destroying of false certainties through Kant and since Kant was obviously not designed to offer new opportunities for the certainty of faith. Often it was purely critical and destructive. Often it was a step in the dark or the void. It was never the path to unequivocal certainty. The alternative developments of Kant show this clearly enough. The godless waste is a possibility as well as a new basis of certainty. A new coming of God may be looked for, but his death can also be proclaimed. The questions are all open. It is still a time of decision. Only the hands of the clock have moved. What seems to be a blank page from which the old inscriptions have been erased might well be a symbol of the spiritual poverty to which the promises are given.

XVI

Godless World and Worldless God
The Theological Problem of Secularization

1. CONCEPTUAL CLARIFICATION[1]

The change in thought of which we have been speaking, and in which we find a kind of experience and handling of the world as though there were no God, carries with it a trend toward the phenomenon which is usually known as secularization or secularism.

This raises several theological problems, some of which we have dealt with already. Is this process the development of a possibility in Christianity itself, perhaps even a product of it (Gogarten), or is it a negation of Christianity, an emancipation which rejects or is indifferent to the tradition from which it breaks free? Furthermore, how can we speak of God in a world in

---

[1] Bibliography: A. Auer in *Festgabe für Karl Rahner*, I (1964), pp. 333ff.; E. Benz, *Ideen zu einer Theologie der Religionsgeschichte* (1960); H. Blumenberg, *Die Legitimität der Neuzeit* (1966); D. Bonhoeffer, *Widerstand und Ergebung,* 8th ed. (1958); E.T. *Letters and Papers from Prison* (1973); R. Bultmann, "Der Gottesgedanke und der moderne Mensch," ZThK (1963), 3, pp. 353ff.; P. M. van Buren, *The Secular Meaning of the Gospel* (1963); H. Cox, *The Secular City* (1966); S. Daecke, *Die Weltlichkeit Gottes und die Weltlichkeit der Welt* (1967); F. Delekat, *Über den Begriff der Säkularisation* (1958); G. Ebeling, "Die nicht-religiöse Interpretation biblischer Begriffe," *Wort und Glaube,* 3rd ed. (1967), pp. 90ff.; E.T. *Word and Faith* (1963), pp. 98ff.; also "Weltliches Reden von Gott," *op. cit.,* pp. 372ff.; G. Gloege, *Heilsgeschehen und Welt,* I (1965), pp. 286ff.; F. Gogarten, *Verhängnis und Hoffnung der Neuzeit,* 2nd ed. (1958); also "Theologie und Geschichte," ZThK (1953), 3, esp. pp. 348ff.; also *Der Mensch zwischen Gott und Welt,* 3rd ed. (1962); E. Heimann, *Reason and Faith in Modern Society* (1961); A. Kempt, *Die Säkularisierung in universalhistorischer Auffassung* (1960); A. T. van Leeuwen, *Christentum und Weltgeschichte. Das Heil und der Säkularismus* (1966); A. E. Loen, *Säkularismus. Von der wahren Voraussetzung und angeblichen Gottlosigkeit der Wissenschaft* (1965); J. B. Metz, "Weltverständnis im Glauben," *Geist und Leben,* 35 (1962); C. H. Ratschow, Art. "Säkularismus" in RGG[3], V, pp. 1288ff.; R. G. Smith, "Christlicher Glaube und Säkularismus," ZThK (1966), 1; H. Thielicke, *Fragen des Christentums an die moderne Welt* (1947); G. Vahanian, *Wait without Idols* (1964); C. F. von Weizsäcker, *Die Tragweite der Wissenschaft* (1964); Van Austin Harvey, "Die Gottesfrage in der amerikanischen Theologie," ZThK (1967), 3.

which he is no longer present? Can we do so only as the church is called to depart from the godless world and live in a ghetto? Does it have to summon to repentance this world which has lost its center and demand that it reverse the movement of secularization? Or is secularization irreversible? Is it a necessary historical phase which faith itself has initiated and which is to be accepted in the name of the same faith? But how can it be accepted when the task of speaking about God remains? Are we to speak about him in secular terms? Are biblical terms to be interpreted in secular fashion? And what does this mean? Does it mean that God is to be deprived of his transcendence and reduced to his presence and action in the world?

Before tackling these thronging questions it might be well to define our terms.

The word secularization originally had a legal and an ecclesiastical sense.

Legally it referred to the taking over of sacral institutions by the state or some other secular authority and their alienation to a secular use. Thus monasteries might be secularized. The first use of the word in this sense is in the Peace of Westphalia in 1648. Ecclesiastically the word denotes the irrevocable releasing of persons in religious orders from their conventual obligations.

As used today, the term secularization has broken free from its original sense. It is used for the intellectual process which leads from a theonomous understanding of the world to an autonomous view and which thus forges the presuppositions that determine the methods and axioms of modern science, technology, and historicism (in the broad sense) as well as our naive dealings with the world.

The derivation of the word means that it still carries with it an idea of emancipation and hence a reference to the yoke from which one is emancipated. It does not contain a self-evident, thetic statement about the secularity of the world but implies a polemical anti-thetic position whether it be that the world protestingly breaks free from what it takes to be the threat of theonomy or that the champions of theonomy separate themselves from secular prodigals and thus use the word disparagingly and almost as an anathema.[2]

In fixing the sense, however, we need to consider the etymology as well as the legal and ecclesiastical derivation.

The word derives from the Latin *saeculum,* which means century and is used in a transferred sense for the Greek aeon.[3] In the NT the aeon is the time before the coming aeon, the secular age between the fall and judgment. Qualifying at the same time the state of the world, it comes to be differentiated from the Greek *kosmos* in the same way as *saeculum* then does from *mundus.*

The *kosmos* is the static order of the world. It is the world as a nexus

---

[2] For a more recent nonpolemical thetic use cf. Gogarten on the one side and Blumenberg on the other.

[3] Cf. H. Sasse, Art. *aiōn,* TDNT, I, pp. 197ff.; R. Löwe, *Kosmos und Aion* (1935); ThE, II, 1, § 110ff.; E.T. I, pp. 17f.

embracing men and things and controlling their movement. Hebrew faith, as Cox rightly observes (*op. cit.,* p. 22), adds the concept of time to the spatial view of the Greeks. History replaces a static web of relations. History is the sequence of events which God governs and which may thus be seen as a unity.[4] It is directed to a goal. Its structure is linear rather than cyclic. Hence the world can be described only in the categories of historical thought. It is moving to its end. It is the age of advent in which decisions are made which are important for the coming aeon which will begin with Christ's *parousia.* This time of the world, then, is qualified time, *kairos,* the epoch of salvation, the hour of decision (2 Corinthians 6:2; Luke 4:19-21).[5]

When this time which is oriented to its goal and fulfilment is detached from its reference and thus robbed of its point, a fundamental rift takes place. The world becomes a fragment and that from which it is detached remains only in the form of relics of transcendence. What was eternity, for which this age was only a preparation, is taken up into this age so that the age constantly transcends itself, whether in the form of utopias, or of the god Hope, or of ideologies, or of other forms of neo-humanism.

The concept of secularization is still gripped by fear of this rift since it carries with it a reference to the age that is robbed of its goal and hence cannot be neutral but is filled with resentment and remonstrance. One has only to put the term secularization back into Greek, and to speak of aeonization, to feel the apprehension which is invoked by a process which can hardly even begin without giving the impression of blasphemy and indeed of a perversion of being itself.

The emancipation might be seen, of course, from another angle. On this view it is not just a revolt against theonomous conditions. Secularization is implied in the conditions themselves. This might apply when the Christian faith represents the theonomous bond. In this case secularization might be viewed as the attainment of adulthood, of an independent and autonomous relation to the world, which faith itself initiates. The historical process of emancipation, then, is simply another form of Christianity.

If, as Gogarten and Cox seem to argue, this understanding is correct, then the secularization effected by faith carries with it a commitment to faith and the possibility of it, so that it need not lose the reference to what it apprehends as eternity and to what is set for it as a goal in the coming aeon. As Bonhoeffer says, we have to recognize that we must live in this world as though there were no God, but we recognize this before God; it is God himself who compels us to recognize it.[6]

---

[4] Cf. M. Eliade, *Der Mythos der ewigen Wiederkehr* (1953), pp. 152ff.; K. Löwith, *Weltgeschichte und Heilsgeschehen,* 2nd ed. (1953); H. W. Wolf, "Das Geschichtsverständnis der alttestamentlichen Prophetie," ETh (1960), 5, pp. 218ff.

[5] Although *kairos* can be used as a synonym of *chronos* (cf. Acts 1:7), there is the same difference between the two as between *aion* and *kosmos. Kairos* is time related to God and Christ, who are sometimes connected with it by a possessive genitive (e.g., Matthew 26:18; 2 Thessalonians 2:6); cf. also the use of the definite article (e.g., in Luke 21:8; Revelation 1:3; 22:10).

[6] *Widerstand und Ergebung,* p. 241; E.T. *Letters and Papers from Prison* (1971), p. 360.

How does God compel us when he is supposedly made an object of indifference in the act of secularization? He frees us to claim the world and to rule it. Pure rejection of God would make this impossible. In such rejection we could not claim the world; we would be subject to its claim. We should not see it objectively; we should people it with new gods and mythologoumena. We should ideologize it. The God who lets us live in the world without the working hypothesis of God is the same God before whom we constantly stand. If we did not do so, new hypotheses of God would arise; we should be the victims of ideologizing.

Along these lines secularization is open to God. The *saeculum* is not emancipated when it is investigated and mastered as though there were no God. It does not become a fragment. It is simply freed from idols; it always stands in the presence of the true God. We have been given hints of this in our analysis of Kant and of the secularization initiated by him. The reactions to him in theology have brought to light the transcendent elements immanent in his sense of immanence. What belongs to this world cannot be self-enclosed. It cannot be limited to the sphere of theoretical experience.

Nevertheless, many forms of secular consciousness flatly reject any connection with what seemed to trigger it. They do not regard themselves as the result of this consciousness. Indeed, they refuse to see in the modern secular consciousness an emancipation which stands in opposition to theonomy. It is only with reservations, then, that one can regard secularization as typical of the modern age. For secularization, as we have seen, does linguistically imply emancipation and protest. It does not, then, give clear manifestation of the autonomy of the world.

This is why H. Blumenberg (*op. cit.,* p. 50) will not define it theologically, i.e., as a movement of emancipation. As he sees it, the modern age is in conflict with theology and is thus secular. It is the age of secularism rather than secularization. It is not breaking free from theonomy as a norm and hence does not admit even a negative dependence. Secularism is positive self-discovery. It is triggered, but not produced, by the preceding theonomy. The definitive and absolute pronouncements of theonomy provoke it by suppressing the autonomous urge of the world for self-being and self-certainty. But self-reflection produces it.

Christianity, then, simply plays the role of a matchmaker in secularization. Secularization, however, belongs to a vocabulary whose significance depends on presuppositions which are no longer valid for the historian or philosopher. It is thus a meaningless concept (*op. cit.,* p. 11). Modern thinkers do not regard themselves as apostates but as those who have come to themselves even though this does involve a war of liberation. Modern secularism is not just a reaction. It is an action in its own right.

As we have noted, the proper term for this understanding is secularism rather than secularization.[7] The point here is not that man sees himself as a son who has come of age and who now takes over the running of the world as the steward of God. Instead, man detaches his autonomy and

---

[7] Cf. Gogarten, *Verhängnis und Hoffnung der Neuzeit,* pp. 45ff.

responsibility from any connection with sonship. He views them autarchously. He exercises them in full sovereignty.

This attitude, according to Gogarten, flies in the face of both God and the world. It flies in the face of God by making man the product of his own works and justifying him thereby. It flies in the face of the world by detaching it from God so that man can do with it as he sees fit, viewing himself as its master, whereas in truth he will necessarily come to know its power over him, since when the world is no longer regarded as God's possession man has to understand himself in terms of his dealings with it and has to try to establish his salvation and existence in terms of its realities and laws.

Naturally, secularism too can be understood theologically. On this view the secularist does not look the same as he does to himself. For he is now interpreted in terms of fatherhood and sonship and set in relations which he not only does not think apply to him but also does not see to be the thing whose rejection constitutes him in his secularism. Nevertheless, the phenomenon of secularism remains. Whether interpreted theologically or not, its mark is a self-grounded secularity which is merely provoked by the supposedly definitive kerygma of sonship.

Secularization, then, carries an open reference back to that which makes possible a free use of the world and its investigation and control as though there were no God. In contrast, secularism denies this reference, espousing the self-enclosed autarchy of the world and the self-grounded autarchy of reason.

2. UNDERSTANDING OF THE WORLD AS THOUGH THERE WERE NO GOD

Having defined our terms, we may now turn to some typical phenomena of emancipated secularity. In depicting these we need not for the moment say whether they are to be viewed in terms of secularization or secularism.

Science especially with its presuppositions, axioms, and methods represents the new kerygma of self-enclosed immanence. Some statements in physics, e.g., the law of the conservation of matter, or the second law of thermodynamics, would not be conceivable apart from a closed system and the presupposition that the world is finite. Similarly biology reckons on a structure of causes and ends. It cannot evade the teleological question of ends, but when it raises this question it is not interested in ultimate answers. If it were, it would have to deal with questions that transcend the horizon of experience. It would find itself in the uncontrollable sphere of speculation and metaphysics, and would thus be in opposition to its own epistemological presuppositions. Instead it sets itself the more modest task of giving simple answers in the realm of experience. Thus cats have sharp claws to preserve the species.[8]

The self-restriction of the teleological question to the immanent sphere of

---

[8] Cf. K. Lorenz, *Das sogenannte Böse. Zur Naturgeschichte der Aggression* (1963), pp. 19ff.; E.T. *On Aggression* (1966), pp. 12ff.

experience is even plainer when one studies the link between this kind of teleology and causality. This link, which is constantly claimed in biology, is more familiar to us in the historical world. When I act, I study ends. If I take out inflamed tonsils, two teleological questions arise: "Why are they there?" and "Why should they be taken out?" But to answer these questions one has also to examine the causal nexus, i.e., to raise the question of causes, in this case that of the sickness. The link betwen causality and teleology forms the truth in the Marxist statement, which goes back to Hegel, that our freedom consists of insight into necessity. I cannot discharge a function or make it serve the end I have in view unless I know the laws of its operation, its necessity, and take this into account in my discharging of it. One might even say that the question of causes arises out of the need to act purposefully, for in order to do this I have to know the nexus of events in which I am going to participate and I have to know its laws. If I do not, I cannot achieve the goals I have set, even though I can show they are right.

The relations to causes and ends are both characterized by the fact that they pertain only to the immanent and hence to a limited sphere. They are thus the theme of meaningful and answerable questions only if they are viewed as structural forms of a closed and self-resting system of being and functions. The analogy of being here, i.e., between man and animal behavior, can relate only to phenomena within the immanent nexus of being and not to the correspondence between the temporal and the eternal. Hence it can only be a further demonstration of the self-enclosed nexus concerning whose transcendental meaning it is epistemologically impossible and indeed unnecessary to ask.

There is indeed no further need for the hypothesis of God, which can only symbolize the epitome of total knowledge. This hypothesis has no ontic significance, since it does not alter the given nexus of events. Nor does it have any noetic value, for it contributes nothing to the gaining of partial knowledge, signifying only a retreat into the asylum of ignorance, nor can it offer any viewpoint which, e.g., as a statement about final ends, would extend the controllable sphere of immanent experience.

The question of transcendental meaning is thus crowded out by that of the nexus of immanent ends which can be discerned and controlled and which the I can influence in freedom. The sense of the knowability of all things—they can be grasped in principle in a closed and finite system—gives rise to a sense that they can also be manipulated. They are placed at my disposal. Human freedom thus experiences an unheard-of growth in its radius of action. This applies in every sphere of life, e.g., in the social and political realm as well as science and technology.

It is understandable that Christianity should always view secularization anthropologically as apostasy and theologically as divine judgment. Innumerable Christian critics of culture agree on this point.

Romans 1:18ff. is invoked either explicitly or implicitly to explain the pathological phenomena at the horizontal level, e.g., in culture, society, or sex. That is to say, there is seen first a vertical perversion, a confusion of

Creator and creature, a loss of the center.[9] In an application of Paul's vertical-horizontal relation to secularization, all the dubious features in the modern world, e.g., the revolt of means, the degeneration of man into a mere means of production, ideological despotism, and libertinism, are explained as results of apostasy from God. Paul's reference to "being delivered up" is also adduced in interpretation of the perversions of the modern world (Romans 1:24). When finitude proclaims its sovereignty, judgment upon it takes the form of the abandonment of the world to the laws immanent in it. The judgment is that the world has its will. Having emancipated itself, it is left to itself. Men are alone. As Léon Bloy puts it, God has retired.

This interpretation of secularization would seem to mean that the church should withdraw from the world. Getting mixed up in secular matters like politics is necessarily a denial of God, since in collective action one is forced to act under the sign of a declaration of the autarchy of this world which makes purely objective action impossible and involves participation in the denial and solidarity with the movement of apostasy.

It is well not to blunt the seriousness of this conclusion by speaking of a flight from the world, thus discrediting the whole approach at once, and perhaps mobilizing to this end the saying of Christ in John 17:15. For secularization is always confronted by the question—no matter how we answer it—whether the world which grasps itself in its immanence is what the NT understands by the world (in the sense of cosmos and especially of aeon). As we have seen already, world in the NT is the sphere in which the Logos became flesh, the sphere of God's condescension, of his mighty acts, and of human decision. It is the sphere of relation. It is the world only to the extent that it is ordered to what makes it the world, i.e., to the Creator, Judge, and Redeemer (cf. ThE, II, 1, § 113ff.; E.T. I, pp. 18ff.). When this reference which constitutes it is missing, in the strict sense it ceases to be the world. It becomes a surrogate for the kingdom of God. It takes over God's attributes and in its utopias proclaims itself to be the place of salvation.

This world of usurpation is presented in the visions of Revelation (cf. the interpretation of Revelation 13 in ThE, II, 2, § 342ff.).

The beast from the abyss assumes power and is honored in a pseudo-religious rite. It uses the binding power of faith to enslave men. It dematerializes all processes, e.g., buying and selling, and ideologizes them, marking them with the mark of the beast (Revelation 13:16f.), so that even everyday economic transactions are taken up into the cultus and demand ceremonial veneration. World power takes on the divine attribute of omnipresence by permeating all processes ideologically. There are no spheres outside the reach of the beast. Its grasp and presence cannot be evaded. There is no flight into pure objectivity or rational action. Whatever is done is confessional; it is part of the worship of the beast. The world becomes a blasphemous imitation of the temple of God. It becomes the site of demonic

---

[9] Cf. H. Sedlmayr, *Verlust der Mitte. Die bildende Kunst des 19. und 20. Jahrhunderts als Symbol der Zeit* (1948); H. de Lubac, *Die Tragödie des Humanismus ohne Gott* (1950).

praises. Doxologies that originally referred to God are transferred to the beast: "Who is like unto thee, O Lord, among the gods?" (Exodus 15:11). The emperor becomes the god.

This total concentration of all secular processes upon the beast unleashes a tremendous dynamic so that great things are done (13:13f.). These results validate the mission of the beast. Thus great vigilance, patience, steadfastness, and above all discernment are needed to keep the faith and not to fall victim to the perversion (13:9f.; 14:4f.). For externally the beast is very like the power of God. It even imitates the figure of Christ and takes on the appearance of the Lamb, although in truth the dragon speaks through it (3:11-14). This leads especially to a perversion in the field of the state, since the state is a prominent institutional expression of the world and hence the polarity of church and state is a particularly articulate expression of the antithesis between God's kingdom and the world. But now this antithesis comes to an end, so that the understanding of the world integral to the doctrine of the two kingdoms is no longer applicable to the concrete situation (cf. ThE, II, 1, § 2022ff.).

This process may be seen in ideological tyranny and the totalitarian state. The state centers all secular matters on itself. In demonic imitation of God it becomes the father of all. Its omnipresence is manifested in its leaving of no spheres outside its control. Not to confess what it represents and embodies in all areas means withdrawal from everything. To evade its ideology is to leave it, since its ideology is identical with itself. The rape of freedom organized by it relates also to freedom of movement. A sinister mark of ideological tyranny is that it leaves no place for withdrawal whether by retreat or by emigration. Here again there is an aping of divine attributes: "If I take the wings of the morning . . . even there shall thy hand lead me . . ." (Psalm 139:9).[10] If in the Marxist-Leninist sphere the church has constantly to choose between cooperation and aloofness, this is only a critical form of the question that necessarily arises in relation to a world which ceases in the strict sense to be merely world, which becomes pseudo-sacral, and which establishes itself as a definitive entity.

According to the definitions given above, what we have here is secularism rather than secularization. In the latter, as may be seen in Kant and his successors, the movement of emancipation would still have a backward reference. The self-understanding would be that of adult sonship. Theonomy and autonomy would still be linked. Here, however, these exits from immanence are blocked. The very concept of immanence is removed. For, when this loses transcendence as its correlate, it is meaningless. Whatever it meant earlier now becomes the epitome of the totality of reality, a description of being itself and not just the sum of what is.

Theologians who make use of the intrinsically meaningful distinction between secularization and secularism usually overlook one important aspect

---

[10] For the aping of divine attributes in literary depiction cf. the works of Solovaev, Lagerlöf, and Jung-Stilling. Examples may be found in H. Schlier, "Vom Antichrist," *Theologische Aufsätze für Karl Barth* (1936), pp. 110ff.

of the modern situations which bring these phenomena with them, namely, that the crucial question whether one accepts secularization or goes with secularism is not just set before Christians, so that, with the help of the Holy Spirit, they may now decide which way to take. In reality Christians are already in one of the two situations, the secularized or the secularist. They have been thrust into one of them by history. Thus they are already in a modern democracy with its pluralist society or in an ideological system marked by secularism.

In the former case the decision between two possibilities of the secular may still be open. Christians may be called upon to understand themselves in terms of adult sonship or the world may be called upon to view itself realistically and to withstand all lurking tendencies toward ideologizing. In the latter case, however, Christians are already in an ideologized situation. They are encircled by secularism as a historical fact. The soberness of a Christian understanding of the world is required of them but they have little opportunity of active response. They are excluded by their faith from holding key positions in which they might arrest the slide into secularism. The situation which makes this slide inevitable is already present. They can only confess symbolically and in a narrow sphere what the world really is and what is meant within it by a reason which is redeemed for realism and rendered immune to ideologies (cf. ThE, II, 1, § 1321ff.).

This symbolical confession entails constant decision between cooperation and aloofness. Even in ideological tyranny some action may be possible either in government or in social service. If it is, such action is a confession of faith in secular mode. It may be, however, that the ideological permeation of a sphere is so complete that cooperation involves co-confession. Whereas cooperation is possible in the former case, aloofness is demanded in the latter.

No theological interpretation of secularization is possible without a consideration of these borderline situations.

Such situations are characterized by the fact that the question is no longer one of prevention or acceptance. It is not a matter of resisting or acquiescing in the slide into secularism, into the declaration of the world's autarchy. The situation of secularism is already there. The only decision is between cooperation and aloofness.

There can be no general answer to the question which to choose. Such an answer would mean either strict conformity or consistent (and physically impossible) withdrawal. The question is a detailed one which is put afresh each day and in each situation.

To overlook this is to slip into the facile and theologically undifferentiated thesis that one may approve of secularization (perhaps as a product of Christianity) but that secularism is a parting from the father and a journey into the far country. This thesis may be apt when the Christian is the son who is still facing the question what to do with his inheritance and whether to seek emancipation abroad. But the situation is very different when the son is born in the far country and the people there know nothing about the father but have created their own cosmic structure.

Secularization and secularism are not just an alternative to Christianity. They are historical situations in which Christianity exists and concerning whose rise it is not even asked. In spite of all the alleged openness to the world of theologians who have made the *saeculum*, the secular interpretation of biblical texts and the secularity of Christians, their special concern, we still find the same theological sickness, namely, that of focusing on the Christian situation, of ignoring the theme of the world and its situation, and hence of ignoring the Christian situation in its implication in the world. This is why we so often find blanket endorsements of secularization which are theologically imprecise and undifferentiated and which are thus of little help to anyone.

The question of cooperation or aloofness can arise in democracy too, especially when there is an erroneous understanding of the redemption of reason for realism, as in some versions of the Lutheran doctrine of the two kingdoms. Here the secular sphere has been left to follow its own laws and not brought under the norm of the commandments of God. The church accepts no responsibility for secular matters and confines itself to preaching. The result is an abstract separation between time and eternity. This schizophrenia took very concrete form in the days of National Socialism when the church made no stand on matters of foreign or domestic policy, e.g., in such matters as education or the Jewish question, on the ground that these were purely political affairs. On this whole question cf. the pertinent criticisms of Karl Barth, *Die Evangelische Kirche Deutschlands nach dem Zusammenbruch des Dritten Reiches* (1946), the discussion of these in H. Diem, *K. Barths Kritik am deutschen Luthertum* (1947), and the general treatment of the doctrine of the two kingdoms in ThE, I, § 1783ff.; E.T. I, pp. 359ff.

3. SECULARIZATION AS A PRODUCT OF CHRISTIANITY?

a. Interpretations of Secularized Existence

We have seen that it will not do simply to confess the secular self-understanding of the world. The phenomena denoted by the terms secularization and secularism are too complex for this. The process of secularization is also too little within the competence or under the control of Christians.

Even if secularization is a product of Christianity itself—and this thesis is disputed, e.g., by Blumenberg—it has not in fact been initiated by the church or theology. Thus the Reformation doctrine of the two kingdoms gives the world a certain rational autonomy[11] but it still relates this to the theonomy of the kingdom of God (ThE, I, § 1824ff.; E.T. I, pp. 373ff.). Again the doctrine does not rest on a theologically initiated recommencement, on a product of faith itself. It may equally well be interpreted as a response of faith to a new consciousness of the world with which faith is already con-

---

[11] Cf. F. Lau, *"Äusserliche Ordnung"* . . . *in der Theologie Luthers* (1933).

fronted and which finds its expression in the Renaissance. The doctrine of the two kingdoms is a reaction rather than an initiatory action.

Even the theologians of the Enlightenment did not initiate the movement. In their battle for the principle of reason in theology they fought only in their own field, namely, that of theology and the church. In the history of thought they too were confronted and provoked. They thus reacted. Even in Lessing one may sometimes detect pain that the new questions disturb the peace of a theologically established world and cause unrest and division.

It is too simple again to say merely that faith necessarily led to secularization, that the latter is its legitimate offspring. What is right in this thesis, as distinct from the correctness of the thesis itself, will call for discussion later. The fact that it does not solve the whole theological mystery of secularization may be seen from the pertinent observation that Christian theology did not plan or initiate the process of secularization. It was overtaken by it and then had either to try to refute it apologetically or to accept it willy-nilly.

E. Troeltsch noted this in his famous lecture "Die Bedeutung des Protestantismus für die Entstehung der modernen Welt." The point here is that Protestantism contributed to the rise of the modern world but only as one factor among others. The creative forces are really to be found in movements outside and even hostile to the Reformation. Elements of antiquity which had amalgamated with Christianity broke free in the Renaissance, found expression in the sects, and finally promoted the Enlightenment understanding of the world. The Reformation played its part by breaking the hegemony of the medieval church, sapping the power of Christian culture, and thus freeing the way for the autonomy of the family, law, the state, social and economic life, science, and art. Thus Protestantism had a liberating rather than a creative influence. By its criticism it broke the monopoly of the clericalist theocracy and thus opened the gates to free revolutionary movements of another origin, providing religious sponsorship for them. Thus the modern ideas of personality and freedom have taken their religious and metaphysical foundation from Protestantism.

When one considers on the one hand the forces making for secularization in Christian theology and on the other hand the unintentional nature of the process, the fact that it presses in from without, a divided impression is left which might perhaps be formulated in the conclusion that Christian theology has attracted secularization to itself.

The point here is that Christian faith contains elements which make secularization possible. But it did not plan it. The idea that it did, which is most strongly and least critically advocated by Harvey Cox, is historically impossible. It would mean interpreting Christian resistance to secularization as inner apostasy. It does not take into account the ambivalent position which Christian faith has always adopted, and has probably had to adopt, toward secularization.[12]

---

[12] Cox's attempt to interpret all the phenomena of secularization as a fulfilment of biblical prophecies, and to see in the anonymity and mobility of modern society an unheard-of opportunity for Christian faith and freedom, can have grotesque con-

Secularization is not a child of the church. The church views it with alarm as a foundling. It has led on to widespread secularism. It has challenged the transcendental status of faith. Hence we have good cause not to speak too strongly of secularization as a product of Christianity, nor to grant it facile Christian approval, and especially not to welcome it with jubilation.

Historically the connection between secularization and the Christian faith is more complicated than has thus far appeared. Even Blumenberg with his massive historical data falls short by focusing on the intellectual history of the West and by treating the theonomous Middle Ages only as a kind of transitory interlude.

To see the full scope of the problem one needs to discuss and to interpret secularization in the non-Christian world as well. One finds the same emancipation from traditional religions in countries like Japan. It seems to be indissolubly bound up with empirical science and technical civilization. In other countries, too, one has to ask whether there are presuppositions in the various religions that trigger secularization or whether we merely have movements of emancipation that are to be explained on other grounds.

Discussions with representatives of other countries as well as Western theologians and philosophers seem to indicate that the thesis of a Christian origin still has much to commend it.

References to non-Christian manifestations are met by the counter-question as to the provenance of technical civilization and empirical science. Did these arise in each country separately or were they exported from Christian nations? Once introduced, they bring emancipation and lead on to secularism. Hence there is no point in trying to attribute each declaration of autarchy to impulses in the national religions. The trigger of the new understanding of the world is to be found in Christianity. This alone with its concept of redemption has defused myth and established an objective relation to the world which is the foundation of technical control over it. The process has thus been set in motion by Christianity and has then spread to the whole globe in a kind of chain reaction.

One must admit that to the best of our present knowledge this view is hard to refute even though instinct is against attributing a global phenomenon to so limited a cause. Blumenberg would probably argue that the world is engaged in the process of developing self-awareness and that Christianity interrupts the process rather than triggering it. This may not be very convincing, but it shows us that there is need to clarify the many open and unsolved questions that still confront us.

Our present thesis is that Christian faith has attracted secularization to itself. But to attract something one has to have elements in oneself, a disposition in one's own organism, that will be favorable. The term "attraction" thus brings to light the dialectic proper to the phenomenon of secularization. For on the one hand an objective relation to the world is the result of the

---

sequences. With typical American optimism every necessity is here a virtue and every mortgage a promise. One can only wish that the witty and dazzling style had been accompanied by a better theology.

Christian understanding of the world, while on the other hand it leads to its possible denial.

It is a result to the degree that it implies release from bondage (e.g., to myths) and is thus a mode of redemption. But denial is possible to the degree that absolute autarchy can be deduced from the idea of an immanence which forms a self-enclosed functioning mechanism. This autarchy is absolute because it rejects transcendence as irrelevant (as in heuristic atheism) and indeed excludes it. Transcendent elements can all be explained in terms of the totality of the world, whether as the inferences of poor logic (the proofs of God) or as psychological projections (the products of fear and hope as in Feuerbach).

We have said that this denial is possible. It is not necessary. For when the world is freed and becomes the theme of objective knowledge it may demand that we remember the ground of its emancipation. In seeking this ground reason may stumble across faith, i.e., the faith which is itself grounded in an act of redemption and which finds the emancipation of reason in the same event. This emancipation means liberation from the domination of myth and hence objectivity in the study and manipulation of the world.

Now it is beyond question that Christianity does contain elements that carry with them an objective relation to the world, so that it is no accident that modern science and technology arose in the Christian West. For, rightly understood, Christianity means a dedivinizing and hence a secularizing of the world, its purging of myth and magic (Metz, *op. cit.*, p. 175). In principle, then, secularization as the dedivinization of a world of gods is not at all anti-Christian. It is an implication of the gospel (Loen, *op. cit.*, p. 54).

The gospel, then, makes possible a rational and objective investigation of the world. It opens up the possibility of a scientific and technological relation to it.

In a sinister world of demonic domination man is a hapless object. He cannot play the part of a subject. He cannot freely objectify the world. Rational conduct is thus impossible. By dedemonizing the world Christian proclamation removes the decisive hindrance to science and technology (Loen, *op. cit.*, p. 225). For example, the Hindu cannot study the anatomy of the cow since the cow is sacred and has to be venerated. He cannot deal with it objectively.

It is well known that much time was needed in the Christian West before the objectivity of the relation to the world could be viewed as a possibility implicit in Christian faith. The individual acts of redemption were not synchronized. The lordship of Christ over the heart quickly manifested itself in the assurance of sins forgiven, but his lordship over the world and the defusing of its gods were not realized to the same degree. One may see the lack of synchronization in the weaker brethren who were afraid of idol-meats.

In our view the basic problem in the relation between justification and sanctification lies precisely here. Christ takes possession of the individual dimensions of our lives successively rather than simultaneously. The heart believes in him, but the new blood has not yet been pumped to all the members, so that they may still be numb. It is possible, then, that proclamation of the dominion of Christ might not yet have reached such areas as sex or economic relations or social obligations and that discipleship lags behind in these spheres. This is why the Christian can often seem schizophrenic. The fact that the individual acts of redemption do not synchronize explains this.

The resultant schizophrenia is called hypocrisy (*hypokriteia*) by Jesus. He does not have in mind an act of deliberate deception but rather an objective self-contradiction which arises when action is not in harmony with the faith underlying it. Thus we find this objective and perhaps unrealized self-contradiction in the man who offers his gift on the altar without first setting right his relation to his neighbor (Matthew 5:24f.) or again in the man who is secretly serving two masters (Matthew 6:24). I am guilty of the same self-contradiction if I do not claim the objectivity in relation to the world for which faith frees me, if the world still has tabu areas which are regarded as sacral and are occupied by forces that are not yet disarmed.

Thus the Christian West needed time before it could view the body objectively and study anatomy. The condemnation of early attempts at anatomy was due to the continued existence of tabu areas which did not permit of an objective relation to the world. Awareness of the dedivinization of the world did not come simultaneously with faith in the one who reduces all the gods to vanity. It came later. Thus the breakthrough to freedom, e.g., of anatomical research, did not really come in protest against the tutelage of faith or Christian prejudice. It came in the name of faith, with conscious appeal to it, and with the accusation against the victims of tabus that they were not claiming their faith, that they were weaker brothers.[13]

The free and objective contemplation of reality implied in the methodological axioms of modern science brings us up against the paradoxical fact that the dedivinization of the world does not involve God but takes place in his name (cf. Chapter V. 3). It is God's triumph over the gods. It is the overthrow of the world of myth by faith (1 John 5:4). It is the victory which makes objective knowledge possible.

If, then, we live in this world as though there were no God, we do so before God, since the dedivinization of the world has its source in him, and since the world is sustained in this dedivinization only as he is remembered as the normative power in it. If he is not, the world begins to fill itself with gods again. Redivinization begins.

This does not mean a return to the vanquished religions. It means post-religious ideologizing. The banished gods return as idols. If the world is not viewed before God, if its upper boundary is eliminated, immanence itself

---

[13] Cf. the baroque anatomist Niels Jensen, who became Roman Catholic bishop of Hamburg, but still pursued his anatomical research to testify to God's glory in the human organs and also to bear witness to the freedom for such investigation, as we read in the biography by G. Scherz, *Niels Jensen* (1964).

takes on religious and metaphysical proportions and the gods are back. The world is decked out in the attributes of God.

In this sense Marxist-Leninism can again speak of the infinity of the world. This ideologically controlled thesis is advanced in violent opposition to Einstein's theory of relativity and the implied finitude of the universe. The reason for the polemic is that the possibilities of matter will be restricted by the opposite view and that this restriction will leave a place for the idea of an infinite God and a Christian eternity. Thus the world has to be called infinite and matter eternal.[14]

The world, then, is redivinized under nonreligious auspices. It is ideologized. Although in a manner different from that of the mythical pre-Christian epoch, an ideological pre-judgment destroys the objective relation to the world and the freedom of investigation. The similarity between the two forms of interference is obvious. The ideological pre-judgment, too, ascribes a specific force to (material) reality, i.e., that of infinity. Knowledge of the exact data of physics is hampered by this *numen tremendum et fascinosum*.[15] We may thus conclude that contemplation of the world before God preserves as well as initiates an objective relation to it.

The most systematic development of the thesis that secularization is connected with an understanding of the world which faith made possible is to be found in Gogarten, especially in his book *Verhängnis und Hoffnung der Neuzeit* (quoted as VH) and his essay "Theologie und Geschichte" (quoted as TH). Gogarten's thesis is that secularization is a legitimate result of the Christian faith in its original form (in the NT and Paul) and in its rediscovery and dogmatic formulation at the Reformation.

His key concept in elucidating the relation of man to the world is sonship (VH, p. 49). Sonship implies (1) being under God and (2) personal independence over against the Father. This independence is also called adulthood and means freedom and supremacy in relation to the world, which is entrusted to the son as his inheritance (VH, pp. 31ff.).

Sonship and the relation to the world defined thereby can be lost through two forms of conduct vis-à-vis God. The one is pre-Christian and the other post-Christian.

(1) Pre-Christian conduct shows the heir to be immature. In this condition (cf. Galatians 4:1-7) he does not differ from a slave. His servile bondage is characterized by dependence on the law. By this Gogarten does not mean God's law in the Word but any order which is normative for men (VH, pp. 64ff.). Law as understood here is the epitome of the power which the world has for the immature, who worship it instead of God (TH, p. 353).

Hence man in the state of immaturity mythicizes the orders of the world.

---

[14] Cf. R. Havemann, *Dialektik ohne Dogma? Naturwissenschaft und Weltanschauung* (1964), esp. pp. 53ff.

[15] On the conflict between the ideas of a finite universe and an infinite universe cf. *Sowjetwissenschaft* (1949), 3, pp. 291ff.; A. Buchholz, "Das naturwissenschaftlich-ideologische Weltbild der Sowjetunion," *Osteuropa* (1957), 2, pp. 77f.; G. A. Wetter in *Universitas* (1958), pp. 461ff. On the whole problem of ideologizing cf. ThE, II, 2, § 154ff., esp. 235-347; E.T. II, pp. 26ff., esp. 39ff.

This means that he does not confront them as a personal subject but dependently fuses into them. It also means that he expects salvation from them, for the world expressed in the orders is worshipped instead of God and hence it also has to bring salvation—again in God's place.

This immaturity is ended by the work of salvation done in Christ (VH, pp. 49ff.). Here man experiences his sonship and hence his immediacy to God, which rescues him from bondage to the forces of the cosmos and therewith from the law. The mythical world into which man fuses now becomes a historical world within which man attains to free, adult and personal encounter and as a son rules over the inheritance of the world which is put in his hands. The world for whose form and mode of being man is responsible is the world of history (TH, p. 350).

The step from myth to history which the gospel effects brings into being a new relation to the world in which the world is transferred to the responsible rule of the son and hence objectified. The world is no longer sacral; it is the object of knowledge and action.

As regards their significance as law the orders now receive a new function. They take on their true function. Far from bringing salvation they simply have the task of preserving the world as God's creation. They thus lead now to rational worship, i.e., they summon man to know the will of God with his reason to the degree that this relates to the order and preservation of the world (VH, p. 79). In the measure that the world is desacralized and secularized for the son, a rational relation to it can come into being.

This process of desacralizing goes hand in hand with a removal of the place of salvation out of the world and its location in the word of the gospel. There thus arise two sharply differentiated relations, that between reason and world and that between faith and gospel.

(2) In addition to the pre-Christian loss of the proper relation to the world we also find a post-Christian one. Here man separates his independence and responsibility from the root which gives it meaning. He no longer sees it in constitutive relation to his sonship. He no longer views the world as an inheritance which is guaranteed by the fatherhood of God. He understands it autarchously. This leads to revolutionary changes.

For one thing, it brings with it a new version of the mythical world. In modified form the world is again the place of salvation, since man now justifies himself, his existence, and his role in the world by his own works. He finds salvation in his cosmic function. Furthermore, he views the world as a totality and seeks its meaning. He thus grasps at the stars. He mounts up into the zones which transcend reason and to which salvation is ordered.

Over against this, believing action (VH, pp. 98f., 131) is more modest and realistic. It refrains from grasping at the meaning, totality, and salvation of the world. It leaves such things to faith. It restricts action to a part, to what corresponds to secular reason, to the concrete. It is thus immune against world programs, world views, and utopian dreams of world renewal (VH, p. 131). When man emancipates himself from sonship and declares himself to be autonomous and autarchous, he loses this objective relation to the world.

Whereas secularization is a valid expression of the objective relation to the world which results from faith, the secondary mythical mode of relating to the world leads to secularism. This is apostasy from the world as well as from the Father. It is a betrayal of objectivity. When reason has been empowered by the Father to break free from a mythical relation to the world, the son who mistakenly thinks he is on his own enslaves reason again by his ideologies, i.e., by a secondary mythical resacralization of the world.

For Gogarten, then, secularization is a valid product of Christian faith. He rightly points to certain affinities between faith and a rational relation to the world. He is also correct when he connects the freedom of science to redemption from bondage, although he himself does not make this link explicitly. Nevertheless, certain objections arise to his view.

(1) Secularism is not just a temptation for the man who knows his sonship and may betray it. It is also a given historical state which is not set up by our decision but which has already established itself. The ideological world of secularism can exclude wide areas from objective use, from administration as an inheritance, even for the man who knows his sonship and wants to live in the corresponding relation to the world. The superpersonal character of secularism, its collective and institutional quality, cannot be ignored when, as in secularization, the historical relation to faith and its decisions is considered.

(2) Gogarten's definition of the relation to the world in valid secularization is mostly negative. To rule the world in terms of sonship means not seeking salvation therein, not understanding the rule in a purely secular way. Beyond this, faith has no positive directions. Believing action is not characterized by its Christian content but by the fact that it is purely secular and rational action which claims no sacramental reference. It is thus action which does not compete with faith nor strive after that which is the province of faith alone, i.e., salvation. Being only rational, it is marked negatively by the renunciation of sacral goals.

The question arises, then, whether faith and action, God and the world, are not sundered here in an intolerable manner which is quite contrary to what we find in the NT. It seems that at the heart of this theology of secularization and plea for secularity a sharp antithesis is set up between this world and the world above, with immanent action on the one side and salvation-related faith on the other. Neither has anything to do with the other except for the hairbreadth line of connection that faith makes objective action possible, since it is faith that brings about the transition from the world of myth to that of history.

But have God's commandments, and the faith which accepts them as his commandments, no affinity at all to our secular action? Is this action really referred exclusively to its own immanent objectivity?

Gogarten quotes 1 Corinthians 10:23 in favor of this indifference of faith to the content of action: "All things are lawful" (VH, pp. 93f.). When Paul

adds that all things are not expedient, Gogarten argues that secular rationality or rational judgment is the judge of what is expedient. But this will not
do. For Paul love is the criterion. The strong Christian can eat idol-meats
because he knows that idols are nothing and therefore the meat has been
demythologized (cf. ThE, I, § 1545ff.). But he is prevented from eating, and
finds it not to be expedient, because he is concerned about the weaker brother
who does not yet perceive the unreality of idols and thus regards eating as
a betrayal of the Kyrios. The test is not reason; it is loving concern.

Nor is this love just a secular or human emotion. It takes its point from
faith. It is grounded in what the other is for me in faith. In spite of his
immaturity, and quite apart from his secular worth, he is one for whom
Christ died (Romans 14:15; 1 Corinthians 8:11). He has been bought with
a price (1 Corinthians 6:20; 7:23). The basis of my love for him is not
his rational worth or worthiness of love, but his alien dignity, the character
conferred on him by his role in the salvation event.

Hence I can only believe that which makes the other the object of my
love. I have this one who was bought with a price only in faith. If, therefore,
I choose from the wide variety of things permissible only that which is expedient from the standpoint of concern for the weaker brother, this is not a
rational choice. I do not choose this concern after the manner of secular
humanism or pragmatism, e.g., because it does least to disrupt the social
machinery. I make a decision of faith—a decision which might be very different without faith.

Faith, then, is not irrelevant to the content of action. It affects it materially.
The border between faith and action, which Gogarten so firmly seals, is
an open one.

Naturally the directions of faith are not to be viewed as additional and
specifically Christian laws which go beyond reason. The category of law is
out of place here. What faith demands, it also gives. If it demands loving
concern for the weaker brother, this is not a higher requirement than that
of the categorical imperative. There is no question of anything "higher" or
"more." Faith simply shows me that the other has been bought with a price.
It attaches to the other the same love with which I am bound to the Kyrios.
It thus releases promptitude and spontaneity. These reactions are contrary
to the servile obedience of the law. Thus the category of law is unable to
express the specific thing which is demanded in faith and which goes beyond
reason. Does not the commandment of the Sermon on the Mount point in
the same direction? Does not the radicalizing of the Mosaic law contain
demands which a secular evaluation can never contain, which are indeed
contrary to it, and which bring tension between the eschatological requirement of God and the demands and self-understandings of this aeon which
is hastening to its end?

It seems, then, that Gogarten drives a wedge between faith and reason,
the gospel and the world, which is calculated to intensify the emancipation
of the *saeculum* in such a way as to lead to secularism. The son's remem-
brance of the Father is reduced to the one thought that he has received the

inheritance from his hands along with the power to control it. But when this recollection is linked to the negative aim of protecting the inheritance from myth, from resacralization, from new expectations of salvation, an exclusive I-world relation threatens to develop which will make faith irrelevant and push it out onto the periphery of the world. Faith will no longer pulse through the organism. In a grotesque way it will become as imaginary and unreal as in a theology of transcendence and we shall be left with a new and modern version of the ancient docetic heresy. (On the Sermon on the Mount cf. ThE, I, § 1691, 1754, 1843; E.T. I, pp. 332ff., 348, 379ff.; II, 2, § 1008, 2612; E.T. II, pp. 157f., 381.)

Loen's interpretation of secularization focuses on the point where Gogarten sunders the world and the salvation event. Although there is no express criticism, his concern for the coincidence of the I of reason and the I of faith stands in broad juxtaposition to Gogarten. It should also be noted that with his work in the technical and mathematical sciences he has practical knowledge of the tension between faith and thought which arises in secularization and is thus proof against abstraction and immune from Docetism.

Loen follows the general view in his definition of the valid side of secularization. The world is not divine. Secularization as the dedivinization of the world is implied in the gospel (p. 54). If dedivinization includes God instead of being carried out in his name, secularization is, of course, against the gospel. The attempt to view it as a legitimate product of Christian faith comes to a halt if the world can no longer be recognized as creation, if the idea of creation becomes inconceivable, and if secularization thus comes to represent a hermetically closed system instead of an open one as in Kant (p. 54).

Loen thus detects an ambivalence in secularization which corresponds to Gogarten's polarity between secularization and secularism. Dedivinization might be a valid proclamation of freedom from myth or it might be the secularism of a world which is closed against the Father of Jesus Christ (p. 13). Apposite here is Paul's warning (Romans 12:2; cf. Luke 16:8) against the confusion of Creator and creature and the absolutizing of the provisional.

The latter possibility, however, should not lead us to the conclusion that the whole process ought to be reversed and that desecularization is needed (p. 54). To attempt to see the world as open to God, to redivinize the cosmos, to restore the age of religion, is the worst thing we could possibly do (p. 54). The true theological task is so to define the new relation to the world that it can be thought of as the creation of God, of the real God, of the Father of Jesus Christ. Creation is not, as in Gogarten, detached as God's salvation event from the empirical encounter with reality. As this salvation event, creation has to be relevant for the secular way in which we know and shape reality.

How can this be achieved? How can theological perspectives be relevant in secular reality, in pure reason, in the field of experience?

Loen concedes that mathematical physics is in its own sphere "free of God," although this is doubtful when one also considers its ultimate presuppositions (p. 226). His point is that the knowledge of reality, e.g., the reality of physics, is always achieved in a specific framework in which it alone is valid. But this knowledge is falsified when it breaks out of its own framework, e.g., when physics encompasses the humanities and is under the illusion that this reality too can be put in terms of physics. It is nonsense to think that every branch of knowledge can be reduced to mathematical physics (p. 37).

Thus the validity of scientific terms and statements is limited to the specific spheres in which they apply. (This is an unacknowledged variation on Kant's epistemology and his teaching on the limits and competence of reason.) For the various spheres of competence Loen uses the technical term "cadre," which he defines as a conceptual system serving as a framework into which concrete data can finally be integrated in such a way that this "integrability" constitutes their reality (p. 36n.).

It is obvious why the terms and methods of mathematical physics cannot form a cadre embracing the totality of our knowledge of reality. Biology (pp. 27ff.), psychology (pp. 67ff., 226), and history (pp. 110ff.) make this impossible. A science cannot look beyond its own horizon (p. 42). It is thus incompetent in relation to the insights which constitute cadres in other disciplines. To try to force a dimension of reality into an inappropriate cadre is nonsensical.

Paradoxically, however, the limited competence of a discipline constantly leads to attempts to transcend the set framework. It does so because the sciences usually fail to see that their cadres lie within the sphere of being (p. 42). They have to see the sphere of being which transcends the cadres before they can grasp the fact that they are partial and that their cadres are limited. But they are too naive for this. They act as though they were alone in the world. The specialist finds it hard to think there is anything outside his own field (p. 42). He is thus tempted to regard the methods and conceptual tools of his own discipline as universally valid. If these are "free of God," as in mathematical physics, he argues that the same is true of the sphere of being in general.

The reason for this illusion is that the discipline does not contain its own subject, i.e., man (p. 43). Mathematics does not know the man who pursues it. Only in anthropology do subject and object meet (p. 43).

To the degree that the human subject is unimportant in a science, as in mathematics, this science can rightly adopt a conceptuality which is "free of God" in its cadre. But this is no longer true in disciplines which, like psychology, deal expressly with man. It would be strange indeed if anthropology and psychology could be "free of God" in their conceptuality (p. 226). If God is the one who presupposes himself for us (p. 224), human existence is inconceivable apart from this presupposition. Thus the question of God is relevant at once when we reflect on man, whether as the subject or object of his knowledge.

The task, then, is in a conscious movement of "discontinuity" (p. 130) to oppose the cadre of God's saving action to reality as a self-enclosed totality of effects (p. 130). This cadre embraces everything: creation, reconciliation, redemption, and consummation. It thus embraces, too, the cadres of individual disciplines (p. 38).

The problem here is whether the term cadre is an apt one, since in all other instances it is limited to a particular sphere. Loen himself seems to be aware of the difficulty, for his reference to traversed discontinuity shows that he is passing into a different order.

Apart from the linguistic problem, the main thesis is highly relevant, namely, that God's saving action is significant within the secular and rational relation to reality. It is not important for this relation merely because it opens the door to free rationality. It is also materially present within our rational dealings with reality.

To take an example which Loen himself offers, psychotherapy, which must reflect on man as both subject and object, has to know what it means by guilt. It has constantly to decide whether the sense of guilt is merely a complex (as in Freud) or whether it expresses an objective disruption of existence (as in Frankl). For these and other basic decisions it is not a matter of indifference how we construe God's saving work in the law and the gospel or whether we ignore this work.

Loen, although not explicitly, raises the key question in relation to Gogarten's view of secularization: How can the diastasis between God's salvation and God's world be overcome? How can we avoid restricting the presence of this saving work to the initiatory act which makes possible a rational and secular relation to reality? Loen halts the decline into secularism, into an understanding of reality which finds no place for God. He opens up a new investigation of fundamental significance.

Possibly his own answer is not adequate. The cadre he proposes might lead to desecularization, to a Christian and theocratic world-view. The book does not go far enough for us to judge. It is a question, a start. Only dogmatic development could show whether he is able to steer a middle course between Scylla and Charybdis without coming to grief.

b. Affinity of Faith to the Objectivity of the World-Relation

The question of the relation of secularization to faith, and of the degree to which it may be regarded as a product of faith, is thus a complex one. This is partly due to the ambivalence of the phenomenon itself (secularization or secularism). It is partly due to the dogmatic problem of the relation between salvation and reality or faith and reason. It is partly due to the existential problem whether secularism is an object of decision or a given historical state.

It is advisable, then, to tackle the relation between secularization and faith from a new angle and thus to make a distinctive contribution to the implicit dialog between Bonhoeffer, Gogarten, Loen, and Blumenberg.

We may begin by stating that in the rationality of the exact sciences—the sphere which especially comes under the sign of secularization—there are elements which suggest deplatonization as well as dedivinization. That is to say, there is departure not merely from myth but also from a specific philosophical tradition which for its part had already broken with myth. The Platonic tradition as well as the world of myth did not open up the way to modern rationality.

This thesis, which we shall have to prove, is a very important one in this context. For if Christianity was a kind of episode which temporarily held up the development of theoretical curiosity (as Blumenberg suggests), then secularization must be explained apart from Christianity. It arose in spite of Christianity. It had to shake off Christianity. At the very most Christianity stimulated and challenged it. Secularization survived the interlude and found its way back to the path which ancient philosophy had already marked out for it (though Blumenberg himself does not sponsor this view [p. 78]), namely, the path of free theoretical curiosity, of dealings with reality itself.

If, however, we can show that ancient philosophy did not have this curiosity, at least in the sense that it characterizes modern science, and if we can also show that the episode of Christianity actually released elements that were not there before and thus opened the door to modern rationality, we have an important historical argument for the view that secularization is a result of Christianity, at least in the form familiar to us in the West. Secularization is not a return to Plato by closing the Christian interlude. It is itself deplatonizing and not just demythicizing.

In fact exact science was hardly possible for Plato. This is not just because scientific development has now carried us far beyond the standards of Plato's time. It is because of ultimate presuppositions in the way the question of truth was put at that time.

For Plato the materials on which natural forces and natural laws worked could not be completely permeated by them; they were merely shaped in a limited way. The concrete depiction of a geometrical figure makes this plain. It can only approximately and symbolically express the figure in view, e.g., a circle or a triangle. In the strict sense, there is no mathematical circle in the empirical world. It is simply an object of thought. What we produce concretely in imitation of it is an inadequate copy of the idea of a circle.

Plato's cosmogony as developed in the Timaeus explains why idea and reality are never congruent and never can be. At creation God acts as a demiurge or artisan or worker in wax (74c). He shapes existent matter according to an ideal plan and the form laid down in the plan. He is not omnipotent. He is simply the architect of the cosmos[16] who finds the realm of the visible in an irregular state of movement and leads it out of disorder into order. In the process of cosmic ordering we thus find two elements over which the demiurge has only conditional control, namely, the reason which has the ideal plan in view on the one side and the blind necessity which is immanent in matter on the other. There can never be an ideal fusion of original (idea) and matter in the sense of a perfect impressing of the ideal form on matter.

Plato expressed the resistant elements in matter in a graphic anthropomor-

---

[16] H. Leisegang, Art. "Plato" in Pauly-Wissowa, *Real-Encyclopädie*, XX, 2507.

phism when he said that reason tries with the help of "persuasion" to bring the blind necessity of matter under its mastery. Its success in this regard is only approximate. The substratum of disorder which the demiurge finds sees to it that a remnant of incongruence remains. This remnant explains the existence of evil and guilt. In Attic tragedy this immanent legacy carries with it the nexus of guilt and fate (cf. ThE, I, § 1336ff.; E.T. I, pp. 147ff.). The demiurge can achieve only limited results with matter. He can conform to the original only to the degree that necessity yields to persuasion. Hence he cannot do more than matter permits.

We, too, are under the same conditions as the demiurge when we try to represent the idea of mathematical figures and have to wrestle with autonomous matter. Here again there is a remnant that defies integration, so that complete identity between idea and form cannot be attained.

Knowledge, however, is not content with what the senses teach. It turns to the world of thought which is beyond appearance. It thus fights against material falsification and tries to compensate for the failures of the demiurge in his creation of the world. It does not accept naively the world as he fashioned it. Like him, it looks at the ideal plan which he could only fragmentarily carry out.

Related to the falsifying effect of matter[17] is the fact that Plato puts physics below mathematics. Thus the Greek world, to which we owe so many later developments, never tackled the problems of physics which have had so revolutionary an effect in the modern age. Physics, unlike mathematics, deals thematically with the outworking of laws on matter. Hence it can never get at the original. It is tied to the material copy. That is, of course, astronomical physics. But since this does not come under the description of earthly physics, it can only describe the original detached from matter. Strictly, then, the physics of the heavenly bodies and their movements is for Plato mathematics. The heavenly bodies are divine beings who escape falsification by matter. They thus depict the mathematical laws by which they operate in pure form and not as a copy. They do not move hither and thither but describe pure figures on an optical track. They are thus to be understood mathematically.

Earthly sciences, however, come under the law that what is "necessary" in the mathematics of the ideal kingdom is only "probable" in the world of experience and hence also of physics. The form of certainty is reduced.

In terms of the ultimate presuppositions set forth in the Timaeus, then, Platonic thought cannot even strive after the rationality which is expressed in Kant's synthetic judgments *a priori* and which is the basis of modern science. Such rationality can arise only if the scepticism with which Plato viewed the empirical manifestation of reason yields to the hope or even the certainty of finding the rational in pure form, in immediacy.

This certainty, which was impossible for Plato, is implied in the Christian belief in creation. This belief not only dedivinizes the world and makes possible an objective relation to it. It also deplatonizes the world. It denies the autonomy of pre-existent matter. It replaces this with the idea of creation

---

[17] I owe this insight to C. F. von Weizsäcker in a conversation on the Timaeus.

out of nothing. It also replaces the demiurge, the architect who stands under the limitations of matter, with the almighty Creator of heaven and earth.[18]

This carries with it a radical change in the presuppositions for investigation of the world and presentation of the regularity of its processes. What was impossible for Plato, Galileo as a thinker in the Christian tradition could regard as axiomatic in his research, namely, that mathematical law applies strictly and without diminution in nature.[19] This means that it does not belong merely to the realm of the idea. It determines the phenomena of the real world. No natural phenomena are not subject to it. No phenomena can be traced back to the irrational whims of resistant matter. Because law is actualized in nature, it can be conceptualized later and even first, and then verified by experiment.

The complex nature of phenomena means, of course, that more than one law is at work and not just that to which we direct our immediate attention. Thus it might seem that the law we are studying can be disturbed; it does not seem to work out in pure and consistent fashion. Plato might have seen here a reason for assuming falsification by matter. But Galileo with his belief that all natural events are subject to law was not disconcerted. He knew that phenomena which break one law follow another. Concrete reality is a diffuse field of laws working together and against one another. That which seems to upset the calculability of one law, and thus to challenge it, can itself be calculated. If we persist in our analysis of nature, we can master it.[20]

One may see here the difference which the belief in creation caused between the thought of Plato and that of Galileo. In Plato the demiurge leaves us a world which is only a partial success. What is really divine in it, the original, is only fragmentarily actualized. If knowledge tries to find this element, which is surely its true object, it certainly cannot do so in the realm of present reality. Hence it must press beyond phenomena into the spiritual zone of ideas.

For Galileo, however, the world was created out of nothing (on creation cf. ThE, I, § 712-762, 1330-1353). This means that only God, not matter, precedes the emergence of created reality. Nothing else can be adduced either in explanation of reality or as a basis of its non-explicability. If God is the one author of the world, it is an unmarred copy. It stands in an analogy of being to him. (This must be qualified in relation to man, of course, since history, as his sphere as existence, has been disrupted by sin, and hence we can no longer speak of a pure copy.) Man himself as God's image is of the same origin. As a rational creature he is oriented to the reason in nature. The same thoughts of God are actualized in both man and nature. Hence man can understand created things. (For the reason already given, history and the human sphere have fallen out of this framework, so that this knowability is restricted to the realm of nature.)

---

[18] In contrast Neo-Platonism intensifies the difference between form and matter by theologizing the idea and demonizing matter (Blumenberg, *op. cit.*, p. 80).

[19] On what follows cf. C. F. von Weizsäcker, *op. cit.*, pp. 110f.

[20] *Ibid.*

The doctrine of redemption points in the same direction as that of creation. For in the incarnation of the Logos the world is an object of the love of God and of acceptance by him. What was not too little for God cannot be too little for illumination by our reason. This is why Galileo, when defending the Copernican system before the inquisition, stated emphatically that we should not read only in the book of words which God has given us for redemption but also in the book of nature which God has given us in creation.[21]

This analogy between redemption and creation, between the spoken word and the word implied in creation, is the basis of the expectation which is indispensable for exact research and therefore for the modern approach to the world, namely, the expectation that the reality of nature will be a full manifestation of the thoughts of God from which it derives and that human reason, having the same origin, can comprehend this manifestation.

Obviously it would be pure speculation to argue that the question of exact law in phenomenal nature cannot be put in any other way. We do not know this and there is no limit to the ideas that our imagination can produce. Nevertheless, two points are incontestable.

The first is that historically the approach to exact science has in fact been by way of the Christian faith. The belief in creation has been the condition which has made possible creative trust in reality. Only this trust could play the role of a heuristic motive which would never be at rest until natural law was discovered.

Second, the approach to exact science was not possible on Platonic (or Neo-Platonic) presuppositions. To make it possible, then, Christian faith had to do two things. It had to demythicize the cosmos and it had also to deplatonize it.

---

[21] *Ibid.*, p. 111.

XVII

Consequences for a Christian Secularism

1. FREEDOM FROM THE WORLD AND FOR THE WORLD

On the basis of the material affinity and historical relation between the Christian faith and secularization, we may now set forth systematically the connections between them. We shall do so by summarizing and developing our previous findings.

a. Creation. As we have seen, the concept of creation out of nothing provides the condition for an objective approach to the world. This makes possible both freedom in relation to the world and also noetic control over it.

It makes freedom possible insofar as the one Lord dedivinizes the world. This means that man ceases to have significance only as an object, only as an integral part of the cosmic process. He attains to the position of one who confronts the world. His relation to it becomes historical instead of mythical.

The concept of creation makes noetic control possible insofar as it banishes the disruptive factor of blind and incalculable necessity, which is to be found in Platonic cosmogony. The world derives from the divine Logos. Its material legacy does not alienate it from the Logos. Man, the knowing subject, is as a creature analogous to the Logos. A subject-object relation to the world is thus possible. So is the expectation, which underlies and expedites all knowledge, that that which holds the world together, its Logos structure, can be found in the form of law.

The way is thus opened up for the rationality which shapes the relation to the world in the exact science of our own age.[1]

b. Exodus. The freedom to use the world noetically is grounded in freedom or distance from it. Historical confrontation implies distance. When the world is dedivinized it is disarmed (John 12:31) and we are released from its grasp. We are in the world but not of it any more than Christ is of it (John 8:23; 17:16). Hence we cannot love the world or be loved by it

---

[1] A typical exaggeration in Cox is that, while he gives a good exposition of the biblical creation narrative, he describes it as atheistic propaganda (*The Secular City*, p. 23).

(John 15:19). The world regards us as a foreign body (John 15:18; 17:14). We have a different spirit from that of the world (1 Corinthians 1:12) and so we cannot be conformed to it (Romans 12:2).

In the rationality which is conferred by faith we have openness to the world and a relation to it. But these are not grounded in solidarity with it. They rest on distance and separation from it. That which transcends the world is what makes us free for it. This is why Christ is the most free of all men and yet also the most closely related to the world (2 Corinthians 3:17). Similarly the one whom he has bought with a price can no longer be the servant of any man (1 Corinthians 7:23) and yet he is there for all and is subject to every man (Luther). A direct relation to the world, a declaration of relentless solidarity with it, would lead to the exact opposite. It would rob us of our freedom and make us conformable to the world. It would deliver us up to a new bondage and make us dependent on the spirit of the world as a form of its divinity.

We can best observe this secondary myth of secularity in the *church* when it becomes unfaithful to itself and its mission. A prominent form of the church's disloyalty is when, in adopting the kerygma of openness to the world, it overlooks the very thing that makes this possible. The promise that "all things are yours" is grounded in the comprehensive statement that "you are Christ's" (1 Corinthians 3:22f.). The promise is falsely secularized if an indefinite notion of freedom is abstracted from it and a secondary implication of the original statement is treated as its main point. A church which displays too direct an openness and thinks it can commend its message as the latest thing is unfaithful to its commission. Accommodation, which is part of addressing the message, becomes assimilation. The welcome which the world usually gives to this "flesh of our flesh" in the first act of assimilation quickly yields to indifference when it is seen that the address is up to date but the expected contents are missing.

The freedom to turn to the world is not an act which Christian faith has made possible once but which has now become insignificant and irrelevant. The fact that it is to be repeated constitutes, as we have seen, the ambivalence of secularization and makes possible the secularist variation, i.e., a claiming of the freedom opened up by faith and a simultaneous rejection of its basis.[2]

Faith is the permanent condition as well as the source of modern freedom for the world. The moment it no longer accompanies the freedom released by it, the moment the prodigal leaves his father, freedom for the world becomes a new form of bondage. For that moment the world again becomes a place of salvation, whether in the banal sense that it dictates the laws of conduct and grants its own justification or in the metaphysical sense that it becomes the place of utopian expectations and fulfilments, the temple of the god Hope (cf. ThE, II, 2, § 696ff., 833ff.; E.T. II, pp. 117ff., 134ff.).

---

[2] This freedom which has no basis leads to self-destruction (cf. what the old negro slave says about freedom when her master tells her she is free in William Faulkner's *Life in August* [1932], p. 418).

Our decisive thesis, then, is that what gives freedom for the world is also what gives freedom from the world, since it—or rather he—is not of this world and to that extent transcends it.

The opposite shows this thesis to be true. To make freedom an end in itself is to corrupt it. As E. Heimann observes,[3] a system in which freedom is the main value will easily deteriorate into a dominion of freedom for strong individuals, classes, and races at the expense of the weak. The type of freedom which forgets its basis produces the tyrannical counterpart of itself which Marxism describes empirically, if not theologically, when it denounces the dictatorship of those who enjoy free control over the means of production and who thus make this growth in freedom into an enslaving monopoly.

It is hardly necessary, however, to use a macrocosmic law of history to illustrate the way in which freedom destroys itself when it breaks free from transcendence and becomes an end in itself. The microcosm of individual life offers an equally good example.

An uncommitted freedom that lets us do as we like and thus gives free rein to caprice is obviously no more than a mask for a real lack of freedom. For it delivers us up to the law of least resistance and hence to a law that deprives us of freedom. We are pushed around by the most powerful forces at work in us, e.g., the lust for power or the sex drive, and so we fall victim to an anonymous authority. The way into the far country which the prodigal takes in Jesus' parable is thus a way which leads from the obligation of the father's home to the noncommitment of boundless self-rule. But it ends at the swine's trough, which is a symbol of complete self-alienation and slavish compulsion. It ends in the opposite of fredom. It *is* its opposite.

Real freedom is the open possibility of self-realization. Freedom to become what I ought to be is to be defined only as a specific form of obligation, since what I ought to be represents a commitment. The chains of unfreedom are not primarily broken by liberation from bonds but by acceptance of the true commitment which sustains our being. Whereas penultimate obligations, e.g., to the state, the libido, or caprice, lead to bondage, commitment to the ultimate power confers the freedom of sovereignty. For this power is ultimate not merely because it binds the one who encounters those other forces but also because it binds those other forces themselves. It thus empowers both by permitting freedom in its name and also by depriving of their strength the forces which try to limit and take away my freedom. The ultimate power is absolute in the sense that it relativizes the authority of the penultimate power. That which has the right to authorize can also cancel authorization.

To give a historical illustration, this explains why Luther was free in relation to the penultimate authorities of the empire and emperor at the Diet of Worms. The "I can do no other" points to a restriction of freedom. It puts an end to the arbitrariness of self-rule. But because the limitation stems from the ultimate power it also empowers and establishes sovereignty. The ultimate which transcends the penultimate confers freedom from the penulti-

---

[3] *Reason and Faith in Modern Society* (1961), pp. 39f.

mate and also freedom for it. What frees me for the world cannot come from the world. If it did, it would exercise the tyranny of the flesh and deliver me up to the way of all flesh (Galatians 6:8).

The distinction between unfreedom and freedom is not the distinction between commitment and noncommitment; it is the distinction between false (penultimate) and true (ultimate) commitment. The latter commitment is a symbol of that which transcends me and is not at home in the objectifiable world. Kant had this in mind when he said that the consciousness of freedom is based on realization of the unconditional nature of the "ought" of the practical logos. Since the goal of human existence crowds us with an unconditional and categorical claim, we know that we are under obligation to accept this goal and therefore we know, too, that we are free to accept it. This is the point of Kant's axiom: "You can, for you should."

We may thus say that commitment to the goal of self-realization empowers me for freedom. An act of empowering underlies the power to be free.

That which empowers me to be free may vary philosophically, but it is always something that transcends both myself and the world around me.[4] In Kant it is the practical logos which rejects my excuse that as a causally bound creature I cannot follow it, so that, paradoxically, it impels me to freedom. For Christians freedom arises, in contrast to bondage under the law, when they are made capable of adult sonship and learn to will what God wills. Freedom is thus the promptitude and spontaneity of love.

Freedom, then, rests on an empowering which is identical with my predetermination. Since I can control neither, and since my own power rests on the empowering imparted to me, they both transcend me.

Aesthetics offers a parallel. The poet achieves freedom when he makes his point in limited speech. The sculptor does the same when he binds himself to some given material which restricts caprice. The painter has only so many colors and forms with which to work. Limitless materials would in fact dissipate freedom. Thus the maxim that the master reveals himself in limitation is really a statement about the relation of freedom to the obligating power which makes it possible.

In the biblical message the reference to that which empowers me for freedom is a reference to him who empowers me, who will not have me enslaved to the world created by him, who as the Creator entrusts it as an inheritance to his adult son. The conferring of this privilege on human (as distinct from animal) creaturehood involves distance from the world in a general or natural sense. In theological as distinct from philosophical terms, this distance is a creaturely differentiation.

---

[4] This is even true of Hegel's freedom as "insight into necessity." By this he does not mean *laissez-faire*, which would destroy freedom. Historical necessities represent the structure of the objective spirit whose self-actualization causes and explains the necessities. Thus the basis of this freedom is transcendent. The Marxist variation on Hegel's concept preserves the transcendent element even though dialectical materialism will not permit it to be put this way. For here, too, the dialectical structure of being which is the basis of necessity rests on a (metaphysical) positing which does not derive from the experience of reality but which lies behind it.

In the creation story the first mark of man's distance from the world is the fact that the breath of divine life is breathed into man so that he has a special portion in God (Genesis 2:16). Then in Genesis 1:28; 2:16f. man does not, like other creatures, owe his existence simply to the divine fiat. He is addressed by God in the second person as a Thou. He is thus summoned into partnership with God.

The distance from the world which is prophetically prefigured in the order of creation comes to fulfilment in the order of redemption. To the degree that God acts on my behalf (1 Corinthians 6:20; 7:23), this distance from the world is radicalized. Because of our destiny and God's concern we are much more than the sparrows or the lilies (Matthew 6:26, 30; 10:31). Paradoxically we are much more than these just because we are not worthy to be called sons (Luke 15:19, 21). The fact that we cannot be worthy shows negatively that we are privileged in a way that creatures which cannot incur guilt can never be. The order of redemption manifests itself in the fact that the distance from the world which is established at creation but forfeited by man is restored, so that we are freed again from and for the world.

It does this by characterizing the present world as transitory and by taking us out of it. I am free for it and for an objective relation to it because I do not have to take it with such unconditional seriousness as I would if it were ultimate for me, and if I were thus to invest it with mythical or ideological significance. The diminishing of the world's importance is particularly expressed in eschatological passages since these pose the demand that we should not be excessively preoccupied with what is transitory but should devote ourselves to that which abides forever (1 John 2:17; 1 Peter 1:25). This why we are exhorted to "have as though we had not" (1 Corinthians 7:29-31; cf. Matthew 8:22). For the fashion of this world passes away, and in the kingdom of God there is neither marrying nor being married (Matthew 22:30; Luke 20:35f.). He who gives up the penultimate for the ultimate has the promise that he will gain much more than he loses (Matthew 10:20f.; 19:28).

Paradoxically, then, I take the world seriously only when I do not take it too seriously. I am free for it only when I am free from it. I can be "worldly" only when I am seized by that which transcends the world. I can inquire into the world objectively only when I see it called in question.

2. DISENGAGEMENT FROM AND ORIENTATION TO THE WORLD IN THE SERMON ON THE MOUNT AND THE DECALOG

It is for this reason that the Sermon on the Mount represents so preeminently this freedom for and from the world. By calling in question the fashion and order of this world, by summoning us as though the original state still existed and the kingdom of God were already come, it does not let us fall into the clutches of this passing aeon, of its autonomy, whose imperative we make our own, nor its orders, which we ideologize and embody politically as the totalitarian state. The Sermon on the Mount with its eschatological thrust immunizes us against "isms" and against the absolutizing of individual spheres of life after the manner of myth. It is important, then, to learn from it both distance from the world and also the freedom for the world which is released thereby. To that extent it has great ethical significance (cf. ThE, I, § 1783ff.). In it free secularity is transcended secularity.

The Sermon on the Mount, of course, is simply radicalizing something that is clearly discernible already in the OT. For it is a radicalization of the Decalog. The Ten Commandments, which are a norm for action in the world and which are thus open to the world, represent an attitude of distance from the world in their negative form: "Thou shalt not. . . ."[5] There are two essential reasons for this negative formulation, and it has one essential implication for our relation to the world.

The first reason is that man is referred, not to himself in his ideal potentiality, but to God, who questions him from without. He is addressed, not in terms of his optimal possibilities, but in terms of his actual achievement. He has fallen away from the Lord of the first commandment and turned to other gods.

This is why the protest against false gods is indissolubly bound up with God's self-proclamation in the first commandment: "I am the Lord thy God." The protest is not against a potential bondage. It is no mere warning. It relates to an actual state. The fall is already behind man. Apostasy from God is the same as turning to the gods. The ethical disorder which is the theme of the second table is merely a symptom of this corrupt attachment.

Thus the negative character of the commandments directs us to this element of protest. We are to renounce the state which has necessarily arisen under the dominion of other gods. "Thou shalt do no murder, for thou art a murderer." "Thou shalt not commit adultery, for thou art an adulterer."

The second reason for the negative formulation is that the cultic and human exclusiveness of Israel has to be stressed. Thou shalt not be like others. Others are men who do not enjoy the election which has been granted to Israel without any merit or worth of its own (Deuteronomy 7:7). Hence the negative form of the statement reminds us that this exclusiveness is grounded in the Lord of the first commandment and his self-determination as the God of Israel. This decision, which transcends all worldly action and has been taken concerning men, must be respected before the gate is opened for the worldly action for which norms are given in the Decalog. That which opens the gate to the world is not itself of the world.

These reasons for the negative structure of the Decalog carry with them an implication for the relation to the world set forth therein. The decision concerning man which also transcends him, namely, that God wills to be his God, makes man free for the world and enables him to live in it in sovereign freedom.

---

[5] Even the fifth commandment is negative in Deuteronomy 17:16 and Exodus 21:17 (cf. G. von Rad, *Old Testament Theology,* I [1962], p. 191, n. 7; cf. ThE, I, § 1783, E.T. I, pp. 359ff.).

The decision which controls all that follows means, of course, that the commandments are not maximal demands.[6]

Maximal demands are usually positive moral injunctions. Such injunctions are oriented to the ideal. But they are impossible when man already has the fall behind him and imperatives are primarily, then, a protest against the kind of man he is.

Again, maximal demands usually have an ideological background. They radicalize in accordance with secular values and thus produce an ethical form of myth. As myth divinizes the world and makes it absolute, so maximal demands present secular values in superlative form and confer on them the dignity of the definitive. The Decalog, however, speaks of what is absolutely displeasing to Yahweh and in this negative way it exhibits the marks of those who belong to him.[7]

A broad sphere of freedom and choice is thus left in the zones between what is forbidden. No casuistic fences are erected on the path of action. The path is simply marked so that we can avoid the cliffs on both sides (cf. ThE, I, § 2178ff.; E.T. I, pp. 444ff.). What belongs to Yahweh does not belong to other gods.[8]

What we have here, then, is the possibility of free, selective, and to that degree adult action in the world. This freedom, however, is not conferred by the world. It is not grounded in secularity. It derives from an empowering which transcends the world and which is not therefore of the world.

Since freedom for the world arises when an empowering which is not of the world is imparted, the summons out of the world, i.e., exodus, plays an important role in the Bible. It runs through the whole of Scripture like a thread.

The creation story and the Christian understanding of creation are marked by it. This may be inferred indirectly from our previous observation that faith in the Creator of heaven and earth, who is not tied to any determinative matter, necessarily summons us to exodus out of the world of myth. This faith breaks the dominion of powers and absolutized orders. In place of Plato's eternal matter we have the transitory world which cannot give meaning to our existence. As we become subject to the Lord of the finite, we are taken out of the finite and given a historical relation to it. Exodus from the mythical world means that instead of being part of this world we become the nothing out of which God creates something.

The Pauline doctrine of justification carries this to its logical conclusion. We cannot appeal to any quality in our own being or action, to any righteousness of the law (Romans 3:28). We are pointed exclusively to the divine favor. Thus the new creation is under the same law as the old. God is not bound by presuppositions. As he was not bound by determinative matter at the first creation, so he is not bound by what we bring or make available for him at the second. Thus the principle of "by faith alone" is another form of "creation out of nothing." It transfers this to the order of redemp-

---

[6] Von Rad, *op. cit.*, pp. 193f.   [7] *Ibid.*, p. 194.   [8] *Loc. cit.*

tion.[9] It, too, is a summons out of the world. All the criteria of the world and all the things which count in it and on which it rests have to be given up.

Claiming none of the moral values of the world, but referring us to the one who claims a monopoly of all values, the Decalog denotes an exodus. The God to whom it refers us is not on the list of gods. He tears up this list. Similarly, the individual commandments cannot be reduced to values on the tables of other nations. The same exclusiveness then applies to those who belong to this God. They are separated, called out, and summoned to exodus.

To give some outstanding examples, Abraham was called away from his country, his friends, and his father's house and told to go to a land which "I will show thee" (Genesis 12:1). He was torn away from the roots of life. He was sent into the anonymity of an alien land, into the unknown. Without any ties, he was tied only to the one who gave him the promise, and even then he was given no hint at the worldly level of how the promise could ever be brought to fulfilment (Acts 7:3ff.; Hebrews 11:8ff.).

This exodus prefigures that of the whole people out of Egypt and its mythical world. Here again the movement is away from all that supports life into the desert, the waste, nothing. There is no prepared path. Direction is given only by Yahweh's pillar of cloud and fire (Exodus 12:34ff.; 13:21; 1 Corinthians 10:1).

Exodus is also a mark of the church. It is true that etymologically we cannot equate *ecclesia* and "called out" (K. Stendahl, RGG[3], III, p. 1298). Nevertheless, as the community which is called to fellowship with the exalted Lord, the church expresses renunciation of fellowship with the world (cf. Matthew 10:1ff.; John 17:16; 15:19). Just because it is not of the world the church is free for the world. It is in the world as Christ's body and it has a part in his work as king, priest, and prophet (R. Prenter, RGG[3], III, p. 1316).

It has a part in his kingly work (1) by proclaiming Christ's universal rule as cosmocrator, not in terms of theocracy (as in A. A. van Ruler, *The Christian Church and the Old Testament* [1955; E.T. 1971]; cf. ThE, II, 2, § 4275; E.T. II, pp. 604ff.), but (a) negatively in the protection of the world from myth and ideology, (b) positively in the forbearance which permits of physical existence and offers time and space for salvation (ThE, I, § 1825ff., 1852ff., 2144ff.; E.T. I, pp. 373ff., 383ff., 434ff.) and (c) in the claim that man is more than the means of life (Matthew 6:25) or than institutions (Mark 2:27), that he is bought with a price, that he must not be made a mere instrument, and that Christ is Lord even of the cosmos and its storms (Matthew 8:18ff.).

It has a part in his priestly work (2) by representing the world before God in solidarity with it, by offering thanksgiving and praise on behalf of those

---

[9] As Luther characteristically observes in WA, 1, 183, 38-184, 3, it is God's nature to make something out of nothing. Therefore the man who is not nothing, out of him God can make nothing. Men, however, make one thing out of another. This is vain and unprofitable work.

who do not recognize that they are God's (Romans 1:18) and who have fallen under the spell of the divinized world.

It has a part in his prophetic work (3) by proclamation of the will of God and his offer of grace.

The sustaining note throughout is that faith makes free for the world, and directs us into it, just because it does not get its mission from the world, but must renounce the world and proceed by the way of exodus from it. It is empowered for its mission solely by the one who transcends the world, who calls it forth out of nothing, and who comes into it and overcomes it (John 16:33). The very thing that is not of the world is what makes me free for it.

This world-transcending empowering has two implications. First, the question where God is to be found in our secularity is a valid one. God without or merely above the world would be a docetic shade. For he would be unreal for worldly men. He would be able to claim only tradition and not living faith. He would thus be God only for the immature. Again, his proclamation, Immanuel, the God who is for us, who loves the world, who wants to manifest himself to it (John 3:16), would be distorted. It is thus legitimate to ask where God is present in our secularity.

The second implication is that the God about whose presence in the world we ask is more than his presence. He is not absorbed into the world. He is not just a cipher for fellow-humanity or reason in history. His being in the world is not a swallowing up in the world. What applies to his people, namely, that they come into the world only by the way of exodus and distance, so that they do not conform to the world, is even more applicable to him. The one who calls forth the world out of nothing and who empowers for openness to the world is not just a part of the world or the epitome of it. As we have seen, the Calvinistic *extra* symbolically safeguards this truth.[10]

3. INDIFFERENCE AND ENGAGEMENT

The grounding of relationship to the world in that which transcends the world opens up a new and deeper range of problems in this area. The God who is integrated into the world and robbed of his transcendence entails, as we have seen, a fresh divinizing of the world and hence a kind of remythicizing. But what happens to the relationship to the world when that which makes it possible maintains its transcendence?

We have been at some pains to show how freedom for the world arises, and with it objectivity in our dealings with the world. But a final critical testing of our thesis is required. One might begin by asking whether the possibility of being for the world and taking it seriously really does come by the way of exodus. (I cannot be for it unless I take it seriously.) Does not the summons out of the world, for all the commitment it carries with it, leave always a remnant of indifference? Does not "having as though we had not" (1 Corinthians 7) pose an eschatological challenge to the world which does not allow us to take it seriously?

---

[10] For absorption of God into the world cf. R. Rothe, *Ethik* (1869ff.) and A. Deutelmoser, *Luther, Staat und Glaube* (1937).

This is the charge brought against certain tendencies in separation such as an exaggerated eschatology or theistic transcendence. The same charge might be brought, however, against some modern theologians whose concern is to construe God in secular terms, to break down the antithesis between God and the world, and to depict God in his immanent presence.

Harvey Cox is an example. Cox (*The Secular City,* pp. 38ff.) finds in the secular technopolis a sphere which allows little place for developed or stable human relations. Individual contacts can achieve personal depth but in the main they are casual and functional. The functions themselves are only partial and fleeting and do not lead to personal encounters in any fulness. There is little neighborliness in the conventional sense.

Anonymity and mobility are the marks of this life and life-style. We meet and part according to easily interchangeable and rapidly dissolving functions. Usually anonymity and mobility are criticized by Christians on the ground that they bring with them depersonalization and the degeneration of fellowship into mere collectivism. But Cox makes a virtue of this necessity and tries to find in them a kerygmatic significance.

For him the featureless mass man who is reduced to dots on a card and wanders through Eliot's "wasteland" is in fact free man. He is liberated from mythicized order. He is not tied down by his environment. He can freely choose the contacts he wants. He stands aloof from the world, unseen and unreached by it. He thus attains to the distance which the biblical God desires with his summons to exodus.

Mobility also means emancipation from enslaving orders. It is thus another form of exodus. The forms of life-style demanded by technics, the depersonalizing and collectivizing tendencies which are usually deplored as perversions of the forms of fellowship willed by the Creator, are prefigured in the biblical model and are thus a final implication of the biblical kerygma rather than a departure from it.

But this emphatic and relentless acceptance of the world is perhaps after all only a disguised form of flight from the world. It is not a flight in the classical sense. There is no retreat into eschatology. All the same, the world is not taken seriously. How can it be when its given structures are simply accepted? Does not a challenge which measures it by what it ought to be, which points it to its lost destiny, really take the world much more seriously?

For what does taking the world seriously mean? To take it seriously is to see it as God wills it and not as it wills itself. Hence it is not taken seriously either when it is placed under an eschatological rejection or when it is accepted as it is and forced willy-nilly into a kerygmatic schema. In neither case is it seen as what it is for God.

The most common and indeed the traditional way of not taking the world seriously is when we so focus on the ultimate that we are indifferent to the penultimate, i.e., to existence in the transitory aeon with its orders, values, and gifts.

This form of indifference usually takes an eschatological form. There is no doubt that the "having as though we had not" of 1 Corinthians 7 is intended eschatologically. But what does it mean when the *parousia* is delayed and we are in a situation which demands that we establish ourselves in the world, that we have dealings with it, and that we rule it responsibly as an inheritance, certainly recognizing that it will pass away when the Lord returns, but not treating it as a negligible quantity because this return is imminent (or even "realized")? Does not Paul's statement lose its relevance in such circumstances? If not, what is its point?

The answer to this question has already been given, although not yet fully tested. As we said earlier, "having as though we had not" implies a turning to the world and frees us for objective and non-ideological dealings with it. Exodus from the world entails a purified return to it.

But what is meant in detail by this return? This is our present question.

It is of some help to note that an "objective" relation to the world is made possible "by having as though we had not," and that this is how theology leads on to modern rationality. The ability to be objective demands distance or noninvolvement. But this is only one dimension of the relation to the world, and the main significance of this dimension is noetic. What about the emotional side of life then? No great deed or creative achievement is possible without passion, without sacrifice, without dreams and rapture. But are not these creative emotions subdued and crushed here? Is it worth lavishing them on the transitory? Do they not demand an absolutizing of the relative? Do they not prolong what is doomed to perish and confer on it the status of the definitive?

These are not just theoretical questions. Christians continually catch themselves in the act of considering them. Theologians are exceptions here, since their calling directs them to the kingdom of God and to that extent they have a diminished degree of secularity which blunts the full severity of the problem. But what about the Christian statesman and businessman and others on levels which demand responsibility, planning, and initiative and hence an investing of a good deal of passion and sacrifice?

There is posed here in a very basic and existential way the question whether so much devotion to the material is worthwhile, whether decisive human potential is not wasted hereby, whether that which belongs to one's eternal destiny is not subjected here to the temporal, whether it is not all a chasing of chimerae and a missing of the true mark.

On the other hand it is still true that if freedom for the world is to be taken seriously, it must include passionate and personal devotion, at least if we are are not to be forced to the conclusion that Christians are second-class citizens who proceed at half-throttle and leave the true shaping of the world to its unhampered children.

We are thus taking up again questions that have already been posed and provisionally answered and submitting them to the fire of renewed testing. The aim of this testing is to define more precisely the relation between indifference and engagement which we have set forth here as a problem.

In this modified and sharpened form the focal problem is the theological significance of the penultimate things of this aeon. We shall now address this problem.

4. ULTIMATE AND PENULTIMATE

The fact that we are called to salvation and eternal bliss as our ultimate destiny does not mean that penultimate being in the corruptible world is unimportant or may be ignored. If it did, then this life would have only pilgrim significance and this world would be only a vestibule to heaven. If we missed the bus, our wait here would be an absurdity. The vast numbers of men who never received or who fail to hear the summons would be delivered up to meaninglessness.

Though this would seem to be a ridiculous conclusion and can hardly rank as a theological objection, yet it is not insignificant that we have to consider it and that it raises the question whether this can really be the true situation. Can it really be in keeping with the universal salvation which God has promised that there might be an absolute zone bereft of either salvation or meaning?[11]

What basis is there, however, for the belief that life in this world has any independent worth? In this connection "independent" certainly cannot mean "apart from salvation." For the offer of salvation is to all (Romans 11:32). The world was created in Christ (Ephesians 3:9; Colossians 1:16). Hence creation was with a view to salvation.[12] We may thus infer that no element in created being stands unrelated to salvation. But this is not the question. The question is how we are to evaluate theologically the state in which a man finds himself when, even though unwittingly and unwillingly he is ontically enclosed within the relation to salvation, he does not appropriate this salvation in the form of a decision, i.e., a decision of faith. Is this state outside faith (but not outside salvation) a meaningless one? Does it not have any value of its own?

In Roman Catholic theology this question is fairly easy to answer. This theology accords a certain autonomy to nature. While nature is perfected by grace, it has its own validity; this is why natural law is said to be legitimated by God (on nature in Thomism cf. ThE, I, § 972, 1880; E.T. I, pp. 200, 888ff.; on natural law cf. ThE, I, § 1852, 2010; E.T. I, pp. 383f., 400; II, 2, § 3872; E.T. II, pp. 548ff.). To Protestantism, however, which makes Paul's principle that whatsoever is not of faith is sin (Romans 14:23) the criterion of being and action, it does not seem that this relative autonomy of nature can be used as a possible argument.

Faith here seems to be a sign which is set before the bracket of existence and which classifies as either positive or negative all the values within the bracket irrespective of their content. From this standpoint, how can one possibly speak of immanent independent worth apart from faith? How can

---

[11] Universalism, of course, is not the issue here. The point is simply whether life in this world has any meaning apart from the relation to salvation as this is appropriated in faith.

[12] *Geschichte und Existenz*, pp. 366ff.

we reach any other conclusion than that the world is a vestibule, a place which offers the opportunity of faith, so that the life which is lived apart from faith is completely futile? Is there any other possibility of valid work in the world than that of promoting salvation, i.e., of preaching and evangelizing? Has the creative activity of the artist or the social planning of the statesman any real value? Is not eros swallowed up in marriage and is not its only goal that the two who are in love should go to heaven together?

If these rhetorical questions embody real truth, then they nullify and revoke all that we have previously said about the way in which faith posits an objective relation to the world. For an objective relation to the world necessarily means that we do justice to its affairs. How can we do this, however, if from the very outset these affairs are ruled out as negative? This is to do them such strict justice as to disqualify them. The implication then is that the apparent closeness to the world which faith has initiated is really a flight from it, not in the sense of leaving the world (as in John 17:15), but in the sense of not taking it seriously, of not granting it any significance of its own, of treating it only as the time and place which offers opportunity for repentance and faith.

In contrast, part of the modern understanding of reality is to see, to note, and to experience the reality of the world in its own specific worth. It is a mistake, however, to think that this form of taking worldly things seriously can be produced only by the view that the world is self-reposing finitude, so that our only option is to posit the absoluteness of the values in this finitude, as though there were no transcendental court to relativize them.

Certainly this understanding of the world as self-resting finitude helps us to take the world seriously and supplies the attendant emotions. Nevertheless, the world can be taken seriously even in spheres which are not characterized by emancipation from transcendence. Historically, this form of taking the world seriously has not always been part of a declension from faith. It has also occurred within Christianity. The new understanding of reality has manifested itself among Christians.

Whereas from Augustine to Luther the state was regarded partly as the apocalyptic counterpart of the kingdom of God and partly as an emergency order of grace to prevent chaos, so that it had relevance only in relation to faith, in the modern period it has been given even by Christian statesmen and political philosophers the value of an order of peace and justice (cf. ThE, II, 2, § 20, 1924; E.T. II, pp. 7ff., 289ff.). Again, whereas marriage was for Luther an emergency order to channel the sex drive, and hence a refuge for the weak, from the days of the Renaissance, and especially the Romantic Movement, eros has been regarded as a vital gift which enjoys the divine blessing. Thus marriage is no longer viewed as a mere bulwark against an impulse which corrupts faith and hinders salvation; it is now regarded as an order of life-fulfilment which eros helps to develop (cf. ThE, III, § 2287f.). The same applies in other spheres of life such as art, pedagogics, psychology, and social development.

The insight—for it is an insight—that reality has its own significance means that the kerygma is now related to that which encounters us in reality. It either has something to say about this altered understanding of reality or it is to be rejected in the name of this understanding. If it is rejected, the reason given is that it is out of date, that it is out of touch with the new understanding, and that it is invalidated with the overthrow of the old view.

When the problem is put in this way, it is obvious that we have here only another form of the general relation between the kerygma and world-views. But this raises again the question whether the kerygma may be detached from world-views or whether it must share their fate. This is fully perceived in the classical instance of the movement out of myth, but it has not been so clearly understood in relation to the new experience of reality. Theological ethics is particularly involved in the reinterpretation of the kerygma, since it has to deal with the new understanding of the world and the new relation to it.

The rule again applies that theology can neither be reactionary nor merely attempt restoration. Once realities are broken, we cannot go back, whether it be behind Kant's Copernican revolution, the historico-critical investigation of Scripture, or the scientific replacement of an understanding of creation that is bound up with specific theogonies and anthropogonies. Nor can we go back behind the discovery that reality has a worth of its own, e.g., the discovery of individual eros.

The basic question in the so-called secular interpretation of the kerygma and in a secular theology is the question of the relation of the law and gospel to what has now emerged as the autonomous significance of reality.

What it all boils down to is this. Does the gospel view the world simply as the space-time continuum which offers the opportunity for repentance and faith, or does the gospel allow us to accord independent meaning to secular reality? In other words, is the modern understanding of reality negated or affirmed by it? This is the crucial question of theology so far as the encounter between the gospel and modern secularity is concerned.

In order to forestall any possible misunderstanding, a more precise definition of "independent meaning" must be given. The point is not that we have here an aspect of secular reality which is not related to the salvation event and which this event does not have in view. If this were so, then independence would mean emancipation and the new understanding of reality would replace what the gospel has to say about the cosmos and the aeon. What independence does mean is that the values which have been brought to light in the modern world have to the gospel an affinity which is that of "position" rather than "negation."

Certainly the order of these values is challenged by the gospel. When God's will is no longer recognized as a standard and ideologies take its place, the value-scale is perverted and stands in need of correction, so that we can know what is really little and what is really big. Nevertheless, that which might be perverted does not intrinsically need the sanction of the gospel. Thus the autonomy of eros as a secular value can be given a positive place in the biblical understanding of marriage quite apart from any assessment of it as a libido which has to be channeled (cf. ThE, III, § 2086-2630 for a more extended treatment).

In proclamation this means that I do not have to destroy secular values so that a site may be leveled on which to build the heavenly Jerusalem. I do not have to call the whole world a vale of tears in order to set the city of God in the brighter relief. I do not have to declare everything a desert to make the divine springs the more attractive (cf. Psalm 46:4; 65:9f.). Instead, the gospel searches out man in his newly discovered values. It gives these another reference but it does not negate them.

The independence of values, then, does not imply any rivalry with the gospel, let alone its dissolution. It is rather illumined by the gospel and given a new reference to the salvation event. We shall now have to establish and develop this point.

One might note in passing that this question is discussed by Luther in his doctrine of the two kingdoms. The relative autonomy of world events and the implied independence of values are recognized here. Thus the commandments of God are not a direct norm for these events. They have to be transposed into the schema of relatively autonomous occurrence. Hence they are not to be applied with casuistic directness to this sphere. Since this sphere has its own immanent laws, reason is called into play. A politician has to do what is rational and he must observe the immanent laws of political events.

This cannot mean, however, that the secular kingdom is completely separate from the kingdom of God. There is still a close connection between them. God's dominion extends to the secular realm. The Christian who is at work in the world also belongs to both kingdoms, so that there is in addition a personal link between them (cf. ThE, I, § 1825ff.; E.T. I, pp. 373ff.).

The doctrine of the two kingdoms anticipates the modern autonomy of secular values. Here, however, the autonomy is not viewed as emancipation. It is set in the light of the gospel.

5. AUTONOMY OF VALUES

We shall now try to illustrate the way in which the gospel gives us access to the autonomy of values. Humanity will serve as our model.

Many forms of neo-humanism, from W. von Humboldt to Marxism, regard this value as purely secular. For them it is the apex of the secular pyramid which is constructed from below. Nevertheless, the positive status which is accorded to this value by the gospel is incontestable. Man so obviously has a privileged position in creation, and consequently in the world, that no great elaboration of the theme is necessary here. Man is God's partner in a way that other creatures are not. He is of more value than the sparrows. He takes precedence over institutions (like the sabbath). He is bought with a price. God so loved him that he gave his old begotten Son.

This estimation of man does not depend on whether he has faith or not, or on whether he is the son before going into the far country, in the far country, or after his return from it. The infinite stress laid on his existence confers an indelible character which is neither won nor lost, and can neither be augmented nor diminished, in any of these positions. As Pascal puts it, the deposed and disgraced king still has the mark of majesty even when his purple is stained and his scepter is broken.

It is no error to see here an ontological statement about the nature of man as such. Christians who take the side of God are not the only ones to be loved by him and to enjoy the privilege of this love. Man as *such* is loved, and so is the world in which he lives, *his* world.

This estimation of man gives him independent and irrevocable rank. If the value were not autonomous, if it were merely a transferred quality, if he had his rank only as an expected recipient of salvation and candidate for faith, then he might still be more than institutions. He would not be made for the sabbath or the state, but these for him. But it is hard to see how an objective assessment of the institutions could then be made, e.g., why constitutional democracy is better than ideological tyranny, so that we should accept the one and reject the other. It is hard to see this because in relation to the attainment of salvation or the possibility of faith institutions would all be a matter of indifference. One can win salvation under ideological tyranny and one can go to hell in a constitutional democracy.

When penultimate secular values and their independence are set aside in favor of an exclusive relation to ultimate salvation, the result is absolute ethical indifference and the impossibility of any binding decision between values and the actions determined by them. For the organization of the world, be it democratic or tyrannical, is neutral as far as the attainment of salvation is concerned.

This was the ethical problem of the early Barth. The absolute disjunction between time and eternity placed all immanent possibilities and values under the sentence of death. The utter blackness of everything worldly after the fall allowed of no difference of shading, so that ethical decision was governed by the maxim "perhaps and perhaps not." The whole complex of life as it now is, things serious and frivolous, right and wrong, beliefs, atheism and scepticism, and even the "perhaps and perhaps not," all came under the ax that was laid to the root of the tree. God's freedom in relation to them was the freedom of indifference (*Epistle to the Romans* [1950], p. 292).

Beyond all question, however, the neutrality which blocks choice and prevents responsible decision is not in accordance with the gospel. The various exhortations in the NT epistles, e.g., the household tables, give evidence of structured secular orders whose temporal relation does not in any sense call them in question. Nor do these recognizable relationships, e.g., the relationship of master and servant, husband and wife, or parents and children, exist only to dispose for faith or not. They are institutional reflections of the will of God.

It should be noted, then, that responsible differentiation in the sphere of things and institutions, and the responsible decisions which they make possible and demand, are thinkable only if autonomous rank is accorded to the penultimate things of the world, to its order and values, so that man is not confronted only by things that are ultimate. God wills the penultimate—this is the point. He wills it as the Lord of the world which he has created and which he destines for salvation. If we take the world seriously we are simply doing what God does. The privileges which neo-humanism confers on humanity are prefigured in the humanity of God.

If, then, we take humanity as an example of the autonomy of secular values, we see that the secular insight into the privileged nature of man is not the same thing as emancipation from the gospel. No bridges are broken by it. When the neo-humanist is summoned by the gospel, he finds in it the same humanity that he espouses. He is not anathematized.

The dialog between the gospel and neo-humanism does not mean that the gospel merely respects and adopts the secular thesis of humanity, using it as a point of contact (cf. ThE, I, § 1643ff.; E.T. I, pp. 321ff.) and then going beyond it. When the gospel makes contact, it also makes revisions.

The questions put to Jesus do not remain unaltered. They are amended by counter-questions. They are not, of course, ignored or discredited. One may see this, on another level, in Jesus' dealings with the Pharisees. He does not contest their desire to serve God. But on this basis the question arises whether they are doing what they intend to do, whether they can do it in terms of the law, whether they are not very like the son who says "I go" but does not go (Matthew 21:28ff.).

The gospel makes contact with the position of the Pharisees but it also challenges it. The position is not simply condemned as erroneous or unreal. It is taken seriously. It is accepted as a basis. But new questions are then put and it is called in question. If there were no position and the gospel came into the gaping vacuum of indifference, its "But I say unto you" (Matthew 5:28, 34, 39, 44) would simply fall into the void.

The same applies to the dialog between the gospel and neo-humanism. Here, too, we find contact, counter-question, and revision vis-à-vis the concept of humanity. No bounds are thus imposed for possible discussion with Humboldt or Marx.

Humboldt might be asked whether his way of making the development of the human entelechy the chief maxim is really in accord with a serious attitude to secular things. Is not secular work, e.g., that of the statesman, subjected too exclusively to the criterion whether or not this work serves the development of the personality of him who performs it? Is there no place for service or sacrifice? Marx might be asked whether his evaluation of man according to his place in the process of production does not involuntarily make him a cog in the machine, so that even though he has a higher place as the controlling cog, he is still a means and is treated as such.[13] The question we might put to both, then, is whether the privileges they accord to man can be upheld on the intellectual ground they occupy, or whether their "I go" does not mean a *de facto* nongoing if man in sublime and introverted egoism is concerned only about self-realization, or if he has only the place of a chief functionary in the material hierarchy of means.

This leads on to the further and crucial question (and challenge) whether

---

[13] Cf. *Theologie der Anfechtung* (1949), pp. 217ff.

man's privileges can be sustained if man is understood in terms only of his immanent value, i.e., his personal entelechy or his function and productivity. Are not his privileges inviolable only when they share in God's inviolability, i.e., when they derive from the fact that man is loved and visited and bought with a price, God having made the destiny of man his own in the incarnation?

Here alone do we avoid the extreme possibility of worthless lives with all that this involves, whereas it is hard to see how a deranged person who is incapable of any development of personality, or an unproductive person, can still enjoy the dignity of humanity on neo-humanist views. One need hardly do more than point to certain events in ideological dictatorships to see how these neo-humanist concepts may work out in extreme cases.[14]

We thus maintain that the autonomous worth of man as it is proclaimed in secular neo-humanism is accepted and not negated by the gospel. The gospel, too, teaches that man is privileged compared to things, creatures, and institutions. The "adoption" of the secular-humanistic thesis goes hand in hand with a radicalizing and questioning "But I say unto you." It tackles the thesis at its very root. It challenges it in the light of the alien dignity of man which is championed in the gospel. Does an immanent basis for man's dignity prove adequate? Does the worth ascribed to man in humanism hold up in negative cases? The thesis that man must be taken seriously is thus set in the light of a final seriousness, namely, that of God. The counter-question is asked whether this thesis expresses the seriousness of human life at all.

This means that, while the thesis is adopted, it is also radicalized and revised. The gospel is not spoken in the void. It comes up against positions which it can adopt and radicalize with its "But I say unto you." The law of Moses is one such position. Humanism is another. Other "isms" are others.

Thus the gospel can address the newly discovered autonomy of values. It can find man here. It can do so in such a way that secular man recognizes his own questions and values in it. It does not demote or eliminate his values. It is ready to let these values be baptized and go through death and resurrection. The humanity which secular man desires meets him in the gospel as a new creation which does not deny all recollection of the old but constantly calls it to mind with its "But I say unto you" (cf. Chapter IX).

We also maintain that only because the gospel opens up this access to the autonomy of values (and indeed to all world-views and to the men who hold them) does it sanctify the penultimate and make possible a differentiation of values. In so doing it offers a safeguard against the Docetism of a worldlessness which sets its signs fanatically only on the ultimate, on salvation, which ignores the penultimate, which thus falls victim to indifference that saps the power to decide, and which consequently leaves the shaping of the world to others.

The penultimate, however, has significance not only because God is the Lord of the world and the world's values cannot be completely opposed to

---

[14] To avoid any blanket condemnation we only say "may." Not all forms of neo-humanism lead to the grisly events to which we allude.

him,[15] but also for other reasons. The soteriological and eschatological statements of the gospel also demand that we take the penultimate seriously. For the gospel is addressed to those who live in the world. If it is thought that its recipients are not under the law or do not come under earthly values, the transcending and radicalizing "But I say unto you" loses its point, whereas it is in fact a constitutive part of the gospel. It is this because God comes down into this world in the incarnation of the Logos. When this is remembered, the place of man's secular life, as we have noted already, is always posited in and with the gospel.

If, then, we call the salvation of man the ultimate thing in the gospel, this includes the penultimate by which man as he exists in the world is determined in the form of values, norms, and other marks of orientation. If this penultimate is ignored and orientation is only to the ultimate, the ultimate becomes for us a part of the world and takes the place of the penultimate. Oriented thus, man lives already in an illegitimate prolepsis of the kingdom of God. The heavenly Jerusalem is no longer something toward which we are marching. It is claimed as our present dwelling-place.

This form of existence is to be found among eschatological fanatics and some (though by no means all) types of pietists. The idea is that we are no longer living in this aeon. We have no part in shaping it. We leave this to those with dirty hands who make it their business. We leave it to the unredeemed. The heavenly Jerusalem is our world.

It is often said—and we too are saying this in our own way—that secularism creates a vacuum at the point where faith finds eternity or transcendence and then has to fill the vacuum with its own inflated ideologies. What is often forgotten, however, is that ignoring the penultimate also creates a vacuum. The world is now left empty. But nature's abhorrence of a vacuum still applies. This time it is the eternal that fills the vacuum. Transcendence becomes the world. The ultimate of the heavenly Jerusalem becomes the earthly city.

An odd point is that this absorbing of eternity into time or of transcendence into the world does not usually take place where one would expect, i.e., in the different forms of secular emancipation. It is to be found where the attitude is nonsecular or even anti-secular, where the stations on the pilgrim way are accorded no reality, and where the gaze is so set on the ultimate that it becomes the abode of present existence and thus constitutes a substitute world.

The result is distortion, not merely of the world that God has posited for us, but also of the gospel itself. For the point of the gospel is to give us within our secular tasks the assurance that while we are in the world we are not of the world, that we are in Christ and his death and resurrection, that we

---

15 We put this cautiously so as to avoid the direct analogy of natural theology. The orders of this aeon are an institutional expression of the will of God but they are also a self-objectivization of fallen man. They are thus the structural form of an aeon that has revolted against God (cf. ThE, I, § 2144; E.T. I, pp. 434ff. and also, in discussion with Brunner and Gogarten, *Geschichte und Existenz,* pp. 104ff., 120ff.).

are thus taken out of the world, but that we are also given back to it in a new life (Romans 6:4; Colossians 2:12; 3:12; 1 Peter 3:21). But can we seriously hear the message of dying and rising again with Christ if we no longer live where this dying and rising again take place, if we no longer love life and the earth in such a way that with them everything seems to be lost and to come to an end?[16] Can we receive the message in any other way than as news which proclaims the destroying of what we love and yet also the restoring of what we meant by this love, even though we saw it only in a distorted reflection?

Unless we have this living and loving relation to the sun and moon, animals and plants, friends and loved ones (cf. the hymn "Fairest Lord Jesus"), the message of the resurrection will cease to radicalize and transcend. It will proclaim a static and abstract eternity which encircles us in timeless fashion and is the abode of immortal life. He who no longer loves life, he who no longer fears death as the terrible end of life, he who expresses the wish to depart and to be with Christ (Philippians 1:23) with resignation and no pain of parting, and thus overlooks the penultimate, can no longer receive the message of the resurrection. He does not catch the Yes and the No which it contains. He does not hear the Nevertheless of the faithfulness of God who confesses us and who with transcending and renewing love meets us at the point of the things we love.

Thus with the ultimate of the promise appropriated to us in the gospel there is also given a reference to the penultimate at which it meets us and which is thus confirmed as the point of meeting.

It was the great merit of Bonhoeffer to bring out the theological relevance of the penultimate. He speaks more clearly and authoritatively about this than he does in his aphoristic and fragmentary words about secular interpretation, which offer free rein to the imagination of expositors. In *Widerstand und Ergebung* (*Letters and Papers from Prison*) he argues that taking the penultimate seriously is a condition of receiving and proclaiming the ultimate. Only when we know the ineffability of the name of God can we pronounce the name of Jesus Christ. Only when we so love life and the earth that with them everything seems to be lost can we believe in the resurrection of the dead and a new world. Only when we accept the validity of the law of God can we speak of grace. Only when we recognize that God's wrath and retribution on his enemies is a valid reality can something of forgiveness and love for our enemies touch our hearts. If we go too quickly and directly to the NT we are not really Christians. We cannot speak the ultimate word before the penultimate. We live in the penultimate and believe in the ultimate (pp. 112f.; E.T. p. 157). We should so love God and trust in him in our lives and the good things he gives us that when the time comes—but only then—we can go to him with love and confidence and joy (p. 123; E.T. p. 168).

---

[16] D. Bonhoeffer, *Widerstand und Ergebung* (1951), p. 112; E.T. *Letters and Papers from Prison* (1971), p. 157.

6. OPENNESS AND DISTANCE IN RELATION TO THE WORLD

Our final question is that of the limits of the penultimate. The prefix shows that it has an upward limit. It can never become the ultimate. It does so only when the autonomous values of the world are absolutized. This can happen in different ways.

(1) The first way is that a part may be made the whole. Thus "spirit" or "economic reality" may be accorded totalitarian significance and usurp the role of the Creator. Theologically this means confusion of Creator and creature (Romans 1:23). The perversion expressed therein has horizontal as well as vertical implications. Creation is inwardly perverted when a part assumes control over the whole. This part is in no position to bind the whole. It forces other spheres into revolt. The intellectual milieu of the NT gives evidence of this. Parts of creation are continually deified as new theogonies succeed one another. The same may be seen in world-views.

The world-view is an attempt to subsume all phenomena under one theme. High idealism makes spirit this theme, while Marxism accords thematic rank to the economic-material basis of history. A mark of the world-view is that normative and thematic position is given to something creaturely. We thus have the interchange of Creator and creature. A creature is given the rank that from the very outset belongs only to the Creator, i.e., the rank of that which gives meaning to the universe. A creature is not content to be one point on the line of the creaturely. It wants to represent the whole line and thus takes on transcendental significance.

The seeds of chaos and collapse are carried in this perversion. For the creaturely entity which is made the theme of the universe is not able to carry out its role. Itself finite, it cannot comprehend and control the totality of the finite.

"Spirit" offers an example. Inevitably when this is absolutized in rationalism, intellectualism, etc., it entails a one-sided attachment to the spirit-side of life which cannot repress the underlying and irrational forces in human life. The spirit becomes the adversary of the soul (cf. L. Klages, *Der Geist als Widersacher der Seele*, 3rd ed. [1954]). It is no wonder, then, that the powers of blood and instinct should be mobilized against this lopsided orientation to spirit, that the will for power should be proclaimed, that the vital gods should put in a claim for homage, and that Dionysus should demand his myth and cultus. The confusing world of the instincts and primal emotions presses for development and does not feel in any way obliged to accept the rule of the intellect. It thus revolts. Only along these lines can we understand the revolution associated with the name of Nietzsche.

It may be part of the swing of the pendulum that the rule of spirit should be broken by the vital forces. But these in turn leave the spirit unsatisfied. Creaturely forces are again unable to bind everything creaturely. For spirit is more, and wills to be more, than a mere emanation, superstructure, and reflection of some material basis of world-occurrence. Works like Goethe's *Faust* or Bach's *St. Matthew's Passion* represent a striving for ultimate truth and not just a reflection of the social situation. Nor does vitalism do justice to the fact that man is more than a living creature. He is a moral person, the image of God, with a dignity of his own, even when, biologically, he is old and useless and unable to function. Inevitably, then, the powers of the spirit and the person revolt against subjection to the vital forces.

The same process of suppression and revolt arises whenever one creaturely entity tries to dominate the whole and the world is subjected to one creaturely theme as in a world-view. Thus deification of the individual, his exaltation as an entelechy whose supreme law is that of self-realization, so that relationships and calling are seen only from the standpoint of this inherent right (W. von Humboldt), necessarily means oppression of the human powers of relationship and leads to revolt. The drive for fellowship, if one may use so unguarded a term, finds no possibilities of development if one partner thinks he is regarded merely as a means to the self-development of the other. Again, the dignity of material tasks threatens to become a mere farce on this view and is thus driven to protest. On the other hand, deification of society and the swallowing up of the individual in a collective initiates a new rise of individualism.

To sum up, whole spheres of life are left out and stage a revolt whenever one creaturely entity is given a normative position which is quite unfitting. If society is made the norm the individual is forced into revolt, and *vice versa*. Innumerable instances of this rule could be given.

A survey of the history of world-views shows how rapidly these views succeed one another. It is a veritable parade of dethroned idols. When seen in retrospect it has almost a macabre aspect.

If we were to reduce the whole process to a formula, we might advance the three propositions that follow.

(i) When the authority of God the Creator is challenged, when he is not recognized as the norm of life and the one who gives it meaning, then false gods arise in the form of absolutized creaturely forces.

(ii) When the gods are enthroned, rivalry and strife arise among them and we thus have a secular variant of polytheism.

(iii) The strife of the gods leads to their collapse. No deified creaturely power is able to bind the others. It simply forces them to revolt. Hence it can reign only for a short time. It then vacates its throne in favor of the usurper. But the usurper, too, can exercise sham-sovereignty only for a brief period.

Thus the penultimate compromises itself when it does not observe the upper limit but arrogates to itself the role of the ultimate.

(2) Autonomous values may also be absolutized when a theology of radical secularity is formed which in battle against certain theistic concepts of God renounces all transcendence and identifies God with immanent occurrence. In this way, too, the penultimate is illegitimately extended beyond its upper limit, as we have seen earlier.

In addition to the upward limit, however, the penultimate also has a downward limit. This limit is the break where the penultimate loses its rank, i.e., where it ceases to be a dimension of reality with its own rank and its power of normative self-orientation. This boundary, too, can be overstepped in two ways.

(1) It can be overstepped in the form of indifference to everything earthly. This indifference arises if we live only in the name of the eschatological ultimate, so that there can be no differentiation of values or commitment to these values. We have here a dark world in which all cats are gray.

(2) The boundary may also be overstepped when faith so dedivinizes this world that things are robbed of their seriousness as well as their sacral dignity. All sense of kinship with them is lost and another form of indifference arises.

This new form of indifference may again be subdivided. Cox represents one aspect of it and Gogarten another.

(i) The exodus from the world of myth, to which the kerygma summons us according to Cox, leads to the endorsement of mobility and anonymity as these arise for mass society in the secular city (technopolis). The freedom conferred by the gospel is thus construed as a lack of attachment. Things are important only functionally. Hence I have dealings with them only at this level. They do not concern me in other ways. Any attempt to accord them higher significance or seriousness involves ideologizing and remythologizing.

Here, then, the concern to prevent the penultimate from transgressing its upper limit and taking on a new sacral significance leads to overstepping the lower limit. The penultimate sinks into a frigid rationality which no longer touches us existentially. Only the mind and not the heart is engaged. I no longer love my vocation. This would be an illegitimate deification. I just regard it as a job. This unattached objectivity makes me mobile. It makes parting easy. When there are no bonds, there is no painful untying of bonds.

Once this downward limit of the penultimate is crossed and it becomes a mere function, then its seriousness is taken away from it. How can I take a thing seriously when I no longer love it (as Bonhoeffer would say), when it is simply a matter for the function-oriented mind and not the attachment-forming heart? Friendship, neighborliness, home, country—these involve an invalid enhancement of the penultimate. From this standpoint patriotism with its emotional overtones is merely nationalism and it involves a reversion to myth. In a legitimate form of the penultimate we ought to speak, not of our country, but of democracy as a rational structure for the orderly interplay of political forces.

What we have here then, in the alleged name of Christian freedom and our opening up to the world, is in fact a reduction of secular reality. Whereas Paul speaks of "having as though we had not," the negative statement now holds good that the world does not have me. I have escaped its grasp. On the other hand, I do not have it; at any rate I do not have it if having means not merely a partial contact with its functions but the deep commitment of love.

An icy breath of mere intellectualism wafts through this world. It is not just desentimentalized; that would be a good thing. It is stripped of all emotional value. I can no longer love it as creation. All songs are stilled. There is no place for the creation psalms of the Bible or the extolling of the Creator in his works.

Does not the task of taking the penultimate seriously demand emotional doxology? Do there not have to be songs of friendship and love of country? Do we not have to form attachments to the penultimate if it is to have any validity at all? We are surely betrayed into docetic futility if in the name of the gospel we address the world and yet at the same time we reduce the world to the equivalent of a *homunculus*, i.e., a *mundulus*.

Either we can love the penultimate or it is nothing. Either we can form attachments to it or it is nothing. Attachments mean risks. Patriotism can degenerate into nationalism. Friendship can mean the deification of eros. But is there any Christianity without risks? To try to live without risks is a mark of the legalist and his servile mind. Risks arise with the freedom of adult sonship.

When we love the things and values of earth, we are asked whether we honor in them the one who entrusted them to us and who glorifies himself in them, who comprises their beauty and who reduces them to the dust again (1 John 2:17), or whether we fail to see the Lord of the world behind them and thus make them gods with their own power. We are asked about the ground of this love. We are not told to avoid this ground or to amputate the heart because false gods might find a point of entry there. Christians, too, might have guiding ideals in which the penultimate so claims the heart's attachment that it comes close to mythicization. But what creative enterprise is possible without dreams? Does the kerygma merely set warning lights against straying into the mythical, the theocratic, and the sacralizing, as it so often seems to do in Gogarten? Is the light of the world (John 8:12; 9:5) no more than a red signal warning us against dealings with the world? (We shall take up again in the Appendix the question of ideals as a mark of the penultimate.)

(ii) We find a similar reduction of secular reality in Gogarten. The way in which he demythologizes the world offers another example of the subtraction which assigns our relation to the world exclusively to the sphere of rationality.

The attempt to find meaning in history, to make all history the subject of discussion in a philosophy of history, carries us beyond the sphere of rationality and in the form of utopian dreams invests the world with contents which give it mythical potency and which transcend the horizon of rational experience. In the objective relation to the world which faith has made possible I renounce any material attempt to grasp the meaning or totality within which I ought to act.

To inquire into the totality, according to Gogarten, is to inquire into salvation with inappropriate categories, namely, those of the reason which shapes the world. Hence the Christian cannot orient himself to a program— least of all a Christian program—of world development. He simply does the partial things which correspond to profane reason, which are possible for it, and which are its immediate task.

The Christian has no material knowledge of what will and what will not stand at the judgment of God (VH, p. 131). Any claim to know this would transcend the material foreground reference and would involve the vision of a Christian utopia. The only theological point in relation to the penultimate is that I have authority to engage in objective and rational dealings with it. Apart from this one can only say negatively that I am warned against abandoning even to the slightest degree pure objectivity and the partial nature of my understanding of the world. If I do this, if I form visionary, imaginary, or speculative constructs, if I devote myself to dreams or constructions of the totality, I exceed the competence that faith has conferred on reason, not merely in the epistemological sense, but also in the sense that I am trying to see with God's eyes and to push into a sphere of salvation which is barred as regards secularity.

The same critical questions arise here as in relation to Cox. How can I take the world seriously if I see it only fragmentarily, if I deal with it only point by point as the occasion arises? Do not things and functions become important for me and make a claim upon me only as I inquire into their relations both to one another and also to the final end or meaning? Does not this question necessarily involve others? The relations I meet within, e.g., political activity, open up new perspectives. I have to inquire into the role of power and interest in the world, into the position of my country in the family of nations, into the role of the nations in general, into the laws of historical movement as these are manifested in *virtù* and *fortuna* (Machiavelli; cf. ThE, II, 2, § 838; E.T. II, pp. 134ff.), or challenge and response (Toynbee), or racial and class conflict. Can one reject these questions? If not, where do they stop? Can I have a living relation to the penultimate, can I really be open to the world, if I will not face the disturbing questions it poses? But disturbing questions do not permit of adequate answers. They constantly raise new questions. They involve an element of Faustian discontent.

Here again the risk of dissatisfaction is plain to see. For the situation that Gogarten fears might well be reached. The mythical bogey that led him to a theology of warning signals might take on reality. I might want to package God by conjuring up a totality in my pursuit of relations. Hegel's world-spirit might suddenly triumph. The material superstructure or the dialectic of history might play the role of a substitute God. Utopian concepts of salvation would then be brought into play.

Concerning this risk we can only repeat that it is not interdicted by faith. Faith proves itself in the midst of risks. If the risk were interdicted, the penultimate could never be taken seriously. All living relationship to it would be denied. There could be only a minimal rational relation to it. But this would make a mockery of all that the gospel says about the freedom of a Christian man, about openness to the world, and about adult sonship.

What it says about these things sanctions the risk. Man himself is from the very outset God's risk. The fall makes this plain. Statements like "all things are yours, and ye are Christ's" (1 Corinthians 3:22f.), or "all things are lawful" (10:23), are full of risks. But they are no real risks for those who are anchored in the ultimate. For them the penultimate is naturally called to order and assigned its limits.

We live for the world because we have died to it and have been made open to it by dying and rising again with Christ. Hence there need be no fear of probing too deeply or thinking too generously. Such fear would merely be a form of servility and hence of the immaturity that wants legal guarantees. The risk of hubris is undoubtedly there when we ask such searching questions. But we also remember Luther's bold recommendation to the timorous Melanchthon: Sin boldly, but even more boldly believe and rejoice in Christ (Enders, pp. 208, 118ff.). Belief in Christ, and Paul's "But ye are Christ's," will see to it that we are protected when we enter the domain of freedom.

Against insurgent legalism there is obviously no assurance in the sense of a theology that is proof against it. The fall can affect theological work too. If not, then there would be one work by which we might be justified and which would not need forgiveness, namely, that of theology.

Instead, it is clear that legalism can invade theological thought even though it has locked the main gate against it. It manifests itself in the demanded purism of rationality or the constant fear of going beyond the competence of reason by dreaming dreams or raising the question of meaning. The sphere of salvation, which as the place of freedom and adult sonship differs from that of the law, is paradoxically provided with legal safeguards in this way.

But is not this a degrading of the penultimate and a sad minimizing of our understanding of the world? Where do we ever find a free and creative handling of the penultimate, or a decisive shaping of the world, without risk and vision and imagination? When has pure objectivity or rationality been enough? Is reason alone to be baptized while the emotions remain heathen? The NT demand "Be sober, be vigilant" (1 Peter 5:8) is surely not to be taken legalistically as a warning that we are never to dream and that we are to clip the wings of fantasy. It is telling us to be on the watch and to ride out temptation (1 Corinthians 10:13).

Our ventured questions and conceptions and constructive efforts are connected with a serious approach to the penultimate and with dedication to the world under the lordship of God. Otherwise we should simply have the uncommitted and unloving play of reason and a legalistic cult of soberness as a supreme value.

The soberness which is required of us in our dreams and constructions and bold questionings means philosophically that the world structure or the totality of the universe which we envisage has only heuristic and not dogmatic rank. It is a provisional and reformable means of orientation to the world. It can be abandoned like an experiment which addresses a question to nature, which anticipates the possible answer, and which can thus enlarge our knowledge, but which is also subject to revision.

Our philosophical systems, theological conceptions, interpretations of the penultimate, and even our metaphysics are all like this. They are provisional. Their purpose is purely heuristic. They aim at knowledge of the world. We build them like children playing with bricks. Sometimes, like children, we forget that we are playing and regard the buildings we put up as real ones. But then our Father comes and tells us to put them away and go to bed. Then it is time to realize that we have just been playing. The hour of soberness has come. The penultimate demands love and it also demands the end of love. For the world whose mark it is belongs to the Lord from the one end to the other (Psalm 50:12; 72:8; 93:1; 96:9f.). But it also perishes with its desires.

Our relation to it, then, is one of both seriousness and play. It is a "having as though we had not." Between the penultimate and us stands dying and rising again with Christ.

Thus tension has to be maintained between the ultimate and the penultimate. It must not be slackened by a puristic separation into this world and the next, into the sphere of the secular and the sphere of salvation. If the tension is not maintained, the cosmological result is that access to the world is restricted to the narrow area of reason, and it is thus reduced almost to nothing. Theologically the main attempt to reduce the tension takes place in eschatology. Here we are usually confronted with the following alternatives.

First, we may have a realized eschatology in which the world has reached its end.[17] It has been relativized by the ultimate. The only theological relevance of our relation to it is negative, as in Gogarten. The gospel as the word of salvation prevents us from making the world the agent of salvation and hence from relapse into myth. The world is set under sentence of death. Any material reference to it is theologically irrelevant. Such reference is restricted to objective and partial contact with its functions. Basically, then, the world is dissolved. The penultimate is docetically emptied of reality. Demythicizing of the world is carried to the point of depriving it of substance. We thus have a kind of sublime scorning of the world. Seen thus, it is not worthy to be the object of loving involvement or spirit-committed ventures.

Second, we may have an abstract futurist eschatology which with its imminent expectation regards the world only as a passing place of pilgrimage which is not to be taken seriously. Here material tasks can no longer be taken up with passion. To invest strength and love and spirit in long-term projects is pointless. Hands must not be soiled. There must be no meddling in secular affairs (cf. ThE, II, 2, § 618; E.T. II, p. 104 on Bismarck's arguments with his pietist friends over this matter). The world must be left to its children (Luke 16:8). These have the necessary passion but they do

---

[17] Cf. the thesis of Ernst Fuchs and Pannenberg's discussion of it in KD (1959), 3, p. 236.

not have the restraint of the eschatological challenge. They thus become guilty of a fanatical fixation on the penultimate (cf. the discussion of Bismarck and Hitler in ThE, II, 2, § 534ff.; E.T. II, pp. 92f.).

In the Christian life, then, secular passion and creative work at secular tasks have to traverse the narrow ridge between indifference to the world which views it merely as a place of pilgrimage and fanatical subjection to it which makes it an end in itself. The metaphor of the narrow ridge is perhaps misleading, however, inasmuch as it might suggest that there is a definite and knowable path between the two which is as it were the result of a parallelogram of forces, namely, on the one hand the force of the absolute demand which calls everything in question (e.g., the Sermon on the Mount), and on the other hand the force which resides in the independent weight of things and of secular functions.

If so, compromise would be the required result and we would have to rest content with it. The attainable measure of righteousness would be reached. The criterion of the law would be met.

The eschatological demand of the Sermon on the Mount, however, does not sanction this statistical result (cf. ThE, I, § 1847; E.T. I, p. 380). It represents the coming and already dawning aeon. It causes us to live in the zone where the aeons overlap. Because there is overlap and not just a boundary, I am not left to cross a narrow ridge unhindered. To think in terms of a ridge is the mistake of a legalism which wants guarantees.

In reality we have to cross the zone of eschatological cross-fire. We are under constant challenge. Even the most passionate commitment to the penultimate is subject to the mortification of "having as though we had not." The tension between the ultimate and the penultimate, with no chance of compromise, means that we cannot bring our action under the calculability of law. It is part of a living history with God. This permanently involves both sending into the world and also summoning out of it with decisions that may change daily and no possibility of long-distance legalistic calculation.

As we cannot provide for future days (Matthew 6:34), so there is no way of working out or safeguarding the decision between what we owe to the ultimate and what we owe to the penultimate. The question what is Caesar's and what is God's is an open one and cannot be solved by a legalistic separation of jurisdiction (Matthew 22:21). Nor can we solve it by not taking Caesar seriously. We have to cross the field of tension (cf. the Pauline relation between indicative and imperative in, e.g., Galatians 5:13-25; 1 Corinthians 6:9-11; Colossians 3:2f., and on this whole problem ThE, I, § 315ff.; E.T. I, pp. 83ff.). In the stormy areas, however, we are cared for (Matthew 6:8; 1 Peter 5:7) and protected against evil (John 17:15).

In considering the tension between the ultimate and the penultimate we have covered a good deal of ground. In granting to the world the rank of the penultimate two things should be borne in mind.

(1) We must not overlook this zone nor ignore it in the name of an

exclusive devotion to the ultimate. The autonomy of secular things is sanctioned by the gospel. It does, however, need this sanction.

(2) Freedom for the world rests on freedom from the world. Empowering for the penultimate is conferred by the ultimate. Openness to the world is possible only by "having as though we had not." It is ours only by dying and rising again with Christ. Its autonomy has a place in the salvation event. Hence it has no power to separate us from this event (Romans 8:38).

Freedom for the world is thus empowered freedom. It is grounded in what is not of the world, in what transcends it. Abandonment of the transcendent basis makes freedom a subjection to the world. Freedom thus changes into bondage. The emancipation of freedom from subjection to the ultimate means its subjection to the penultimate. This destroys it. The classical example of this is the story of the prodigal son (Luke 15:11ff.). Freedom for the world—to put it as sharply as possible—has a basis which is above the world.

It is worth noting that even theologies which seem to erase the transcendent and tie faith and its objects to the immanent consciousness may still have a transcendent basis.

Erasure of the transcendent has constantly been objected against a theologian like Schleiermacher. Sections like § 15 of *The Christian Faith* seem to give substance to the charge. Yet this work contains elements which apparently contradict the lack of transcendence, and Schleiermacher lays special stress on these in his letters to Lücke. It seems that the autonomy of his system prevents him at this point from expressing his faith fully within it. He becomes the prisoner of his own principles. This is why Schleiermacher the preacher makes a fuller confession than Schleiermacher the theologian. Even though the transcendent basis of his theology cannot be brought to light in the system, however, it is still there, and it shapes his theology even while it is not an explicit part of it. We need the preacher's commentary on the systematician. (Perhaps this is true of others such as Bultmann.) Thus Schleiermacher the preacher makes christological and eschatological statements which do not derive from his theology of consciousness and which are like erratic blocks on its systematically leveled plain. We see here the transcendent conditions for that which God's presence makes possible in our immanent consciousness. One may refer in particular to the address which Schleiermacher gave at the funeral of his son Nathanael and also to his advent sermon on Matthew 21:9 (*Predigten von F. Schleiermacher*, ed. G. Reimer, IV [1844], pp. 992f. and II [1843], pp. 5, 12f., 18ff.).

7. THEOLOGICAL CONCLUSION: CHRISTOLOGICAL BACKGROUND OF THE GOD-WORLD RELATION

The relation between God and the world, which is the premise behind all openness to the world and distance from it, is not itself objectifiable. That is to say, it cannot be demonstrated in such a way that a system can claim to embrace both transcendence and immanence and then relate them as two different strata of reality. When attempts are made in this direction and theology is changed into metaphysics, the resultant God-world relation always prevents the world from being expressed in its worldliness and God from being expressed in his divinity.

This elimination of the possibility of expression may take place in two ways.

God may become a part of worldly reality as its numinous aspect or as a cipher for viewing things from the eternal standpoint (as in pantheism or polytheism). In this case the world is mythicized. On the other hand God may be seen in remote transcendence. He may be allotted a special existence which has no contact at all with the rest of reality.

Whereas the first way unites God and the world monistically, the second implies a dualistic antithesis between transcendence and immanence. Either way, the world is no longer worldly and God is no longer divine.

This makes it plain that one cannot treat the relation between God and man as a systematic entity. In neither case can the schema of transcendence and immanence express the relation. Either God and the world are equated or they are completely separated. Both equation and separation, as in an abstract antithesis of time and eternity, are a product of systematization.

There is a theological reason why the relation between God and the world cannot be systematized with the help of the transcendence-immanence schema. The reality of God is brought into relation with that of the world in the incarnation, i.e., in the fact that God revealed himself to the world, came down into it, and thus manifested himself as its basis, goal, and meaning.

This has the following implications for the relation between God and the world.

(1) God cannot be grasped in the categories which we use in our knowledge of secular realities, whether in the field of nature or in that of history. For if God is the basis, goal, and meaning of reality, he cannot be an element of the reality which he establishes and fills with meaning. There is between the reality of God and that of the world an ontological distinction which does not permit us to understand them as dimensions of one and the same reality. The basis is distinguished ontologically from what is based on it. It is not absorbed into it when it imparts its transcendent quality to it.

The constant error of natural theology is to erase this distinction. To work back from that which is based to its basis, from the reality of the world to that of God, is to obliterate the ontological distinction even though, as in the classical proofs of God, a superlative, causal, or teleological difference is perceived. For even in this distinction secular categories of thought are used, so that God is an attribute or function of secular reality. This reality imposes the conditions under which we can think of him. Since reason as the organ of knowledge corresponds to this reality, it is reason that formulates the conditions and then summarizes them as the possibility of the concept of God. The very term "possibility" shows how God is here included within the functional sphere of worldly reality, so that the ontological distinction is expunged.

(2) God as the basis, goal, and meaning of the world, as its Creator, Redeemer, and Consummator, is not objectifiable because he himself embraces the subject-object relation and hence cannot be drawn into it. He is the basis of the being of the world which I know and into which I willingly and creatively enter. But he is also the basis of my own being as the one who knows and wills and acts. He makes possible my knowing, willing, and acting.[18] He knows me before I can know myself or the world (Psalm 139:1, 16; 1 Corinthians 13:12). He refers me to the world which I am to know and to shape (Genesis 1:28). He gives me the possibility of knowledge, not just knowledge of the world, but also of himself (Romans 1:19f.). He is the basis as well as the object of the knowledge of God.

This embracing of the subject-object relation is expressed in the doctrine of the Holy Spirit. For the testimony of the Spirit tells us that it is God himself who creates the possibility of his being known. He thus discloses himself to the one who has no way of finding him (1 Corinthians 2:9f.). He himself gives the light in which we see him (Psalm 36:9). Hence the knowledge of God does not stand under the conditions of our thinking capacity, as in the classical proofs or natural theology. God himself grants the capacity through the gift of the Spirit, through his self-impartation.

If, then, God is the basis, goal, and meaning of being, I myself am included in this sphere of being as the subject which knows, wills, and acts. In everyday dealings with being I am not clearly conscious of this. I distinguish myself from being, at any rate in the historical and post-mythical world. I am free in relation to the starry heaven. As Heidegger would put it, I am aware of an ontological difference between being and existence.

Before God, however, although in a way that differs from that of myth and in a kind of secondary identity, existence is part of being. For God is the basis, goal, and meaning of my existence and to that extent of my thinking, willing, and acting, of my capacity to think, and also of my freedom. I have the world only as God gives it to me and lets me see it. I have God only insofar as he condescends to me, enters my world, discloses himself to me, and gives me the light in which I can see him.

Thus the relation between God and the world can be described only in trinitarian terms. God the Creator establishes the world. God the Redeemer condescends to the world and comes into it in the incarnation. God the Holy Spirit provides the conditions and means by which God may be known. God is thus the basis as well as the object of the knowledge of God. He is not only the one I have the possibility of knowing; he is also the basis of the possibility. He embraces both the being of the objectifiable world and also the subject of objectifying.

(3) The relation between God and the world carries with it three basic propositions.

(a) I can speak of God only in terms of the world. For God dwells in

---

[18] Descartes' proof of God may be arguable, but he is surely right at a decisive point when he understands God as the one who transcends the subject-object relation, since it is he who establishes the connection between the ego and the outside world.

inaccessible light (1 Timothy 6:16). I can have him only as he makes me participant in this light. He is present for me only in his self-disclosure. In all that I say about him I can never forget that he has condescended to me, that in love he has set himself in relation to the world (John 3:16), and that he is present with us in the incarnation of the Logos (John 1:14).

This condescension to the world means not only that I have to speak about him in terms of the world but also that I cannot speak about the world apart from its relation to God. There is nothing in the world that is without theological significance. The methods of science and historicism may be "atheistic," as we have seen, but they still have a theological reference once we include in them the man who uses these methods. For this man is not just the subject of this activity. He also belongs to the total nexus of which it is a part. If, for example, he works at atomic physics, he has still to ask whether he is adult enough for his knowledge and ability, or what is the relation between his scientific and technical means of mastering the world and the ends which they serve, or whether there might not be a revolt of means and a contradiction of the ends. The question of the ultimate is always present in the sphere of the penultimate.

(b) God's condescension to the world and the incarnation of the Logos confer on our "carnal" concepts the ability to confess the glory of God. God's invasion of the world is an invasion of our concepts and ideas; it is the divine accommodation.

Thus both Greeks and Jews seek after God and speak about him in their different ways (1 Corinthians 1:22-24). Parthians, Medes, and Elamites hear of God's mighty works in their own tongues (Acts 2:8-11). If we despise this coming of God into our own speech and try to transcend the incarnation in glossolalia, the transition to Docetism is easy (1 Corinthians 14:4ff.). Esctasy and enthusiasm are a form of self-elevation which conflicts with the divine condescension.

Here again one sees that that which establishes is not absorbed in that which is established by it. There is no equation. Ontological distinction is maintained. God's Word is never so bound to man's word that it takes on once and for all a fixed and unalterable form. God is never the one who has definitively entered; he is the one who is always entering. He thus transcends the world to which he comes in self-disclosure.

This finds concrete expression in the fact that Greeks and Jews, magi and rationalists, idealists and existentialists, have always to proclaim God's acts afresh in their own tongues. They cannot just adopt a fixed form of speech. We cannot just believe in the confession of the fathers; we have to confess our own faith. To believe only in the confession of the fathers is to think erroneously that the mighty acts of God have been put in a definitive form of speech, whereas in truth they are always being put in new forms as the Spirit moves where he will. From another angle we thus come up against our earlier thesis that there can be no perennial theology, only a history of theology and proclamation.

We maintain, then, that part of the condescension of God to the world is that he comes into the worldly or carnal concepts with which I confess his praise according to the vocabulary at my disposal in a given age.

(c) Although God's relation to the world is constantly expressed in all that I say about divine and secular things, it is not objectifiable, as we have seen, in the sense that I can state the reality of God and that of the world in an ontology which embraces both. Thus far we have simply described the negative consequences of this impossibility. We must now give the reason for it.

The reason is that the God-world relation has not been seen by any eye, nor has it entered the heart of any man. In other words, it does not consist in an ontically given and hence demonstrable analogy between the two realities. It is posited by God and it is thus one of his mighty deeds, i.e., the deeds whose meaning is summed up in the event of the incarnation. God has set himself in relation. Hence this relation cannot be constructed *a priori*. Being historically posited, it can only be confirmed *a posteriori,* and this only to the degree that it is intrinsic to God's mighty acts to let themselves be confirmed in this way, to bear witness to themselves, and to enter the heart of man, through the Holy Spirit.

The God-world relation is thus grounded in an "accidental truth of history" and not a "necessary truth of reason," as Lessing would put it. This is true at least if by accidental truth of history we mean not only events outside me but also the event of disclosure to or in me and the creation of faith. The mighty acts of God are not just those which happened there and then. They are also the making of this present to me and in me here and now. Salvation history is not just the history of the patriarchs, prophets, and apostles with all that to which they bear witness. It is also the history which the Holy Spirit makes in me when he draws me into these events of the past and gives me true faith.

Thus the God-world relation, as God's putting himself in relation to the world, is itself the object of faith.

The attempt to state it in an ontology which embraces both realities rests on the false premise that it can be seen apart from faith and presented in, e.g., the form of a principle of analogy, i.e., as a timeless truth of reason.

The classical instance of such an attempt is to be found in the early Apologists. Here the philosophical concept of the logos, as a synonym for the reality of the world which is permeated by reason, is the principle which embraces both God and the world and which thus represents transcendent timeless reality. Christ the Logos, then, is no longer the climax of the mighty acts of God in which God establishes his relation to the world. He is an illustration, confirmation, and final culmination of the logos principle which embraces both God and the world. The salvation event is thus drawn into a given schema which can be perceived apart from faith. The procedure is apologetic in the sense that both pagans and Christians can thus contend for a common principle which claims them both.

The point that the God-world relation is established in such a way that it is a historical event, and does not rest on a principle of analogy, does not have to mean that no analogies may be discerned. If God discloses himself to the world, comes into it, and accommodates himself to it as described, then the question of analogy is raised by the very concept of accommodation. For this implies that God's self-disclosure lays claim to what is there in the world. This can only mean that God bears witness to himself in analogies. In fact the biblical salvation event makes full use of analogies. Historical disasters are anticipations of eschatological judgment (cf. ThE, II, 1, § 2177ff.). The destruction of the temple prefigures the end of the world (Matthew 24:2f.). The parables in particular are full of analogies.

Nevertheless, these analogies are not just a bridge from the reality of the world to the reality of God. They obviously do not have the function of constituting a comprehensive schema by which the two realities can be systematically related. On the contrary, the parables, which make special use of analogies, set up a boundary between the two realities rather than creating a bridge. Their effect is to harden (Matthew 13:13-15). The reason for this is that it is not the analogy that brings God's self-disclosure into the heart. The analogy cannot replace the testimony of the Spirit. Analogies can be appreciated only when the light is kindled in which we see light. The lilies of the field and the fowls of the air remain silent (Matthew 6:26, 28) and cannot of themselves proclaim to me the fact that I need not be anxious. Pagans see them too and are still anxious (6:32). Only when I know the one who adds other things to those who seek first the kingdom of God (6:33; Luke 12:30) do the lilies add their voice and the analogies begin to shine forth. Stained-glass windows glow only in the sanctuary.

Rightly, then, an analogy of being which can be demonstrated as a truth of reason has been rejected in favor of an analogy of faith,[19] which is disclosed only in faith. This mode of disclosure is a confirmation of our thesis that the God-world relation and the analogies which represent it are part of the mighty deeds of God and are present only for faith. Only when the heart of all things reveals itself to me can I see the relation of all things to this heart, or more precisely, since seeing might carry with it a wrong connotation, only then can I believe the relation of all things to this heart.

Analogies, however, are relativized not only to the degree that I cannot have them *a priori* but also to the degree that I cannot appeal to their help in finding my way from the world to the reality of God. Naturally it is no accident, but expresses an analogy, that the prodigal son stands in a son-father relation to God. He is not just any man whom the father pities. He is his son. We thus have a natural analogy. Nevertheless, the analogy, as we have seen, cannot carry with it the refinding of the lost son and the restoring of the broken relationship. This is why the returning prodigal does not appeal to it. On the contrary, he admits that it in no way helps him: "I am not worthy to be called thy son" (Luke 15:21). Only assurance of the fatherly heart and the "history" of compassion that this sets in train give force to the analogy of sonship.

---

[19] Cf. F. Flückiger, "Analogia entis und analogia fidei," Stud. gen. (1955), 11, pp. 678ff.; H. G. Pöhlmann, *Analogia entis und analogia fidei* (1965).

If we (rightly) see in the analogy a symbol of the relation between the reality of God and that of the world, then we can see in it all the marks of this relation, and especially the decisive feature that the relation cannot be systematized but discloses itself only to the faith which posits this relation. It is thus a christological secret. It is grounded in the incarnation. Here the relation between God and the world is achieved and expressed. But here again it cannot be systematized. In spite of Anselm, there is no necessity about the *Cur deus homo* or the *Cur relatio dei et mundi*. Such questions cannot be answered in terms of a principle that embraces both aspects.

An implication of the christological background of the God-world relation —and the reference to Anselm is a first indication of this—is that all the efforts to systematize the reference are prefigured in the history of Christology. We already find here the problems which now concern us in connection with the concept of secularity, the secular interpretation of biblical statements, and the implied relation between the reality of God and that of the world.

The ontological schema of thought which uses the idea of "natures," and which is the dominant one in christological discussion up to the Reformation and even beyond it, carries with it a temptation to systematize the mystery of the incarnation (and with it the coincidence of the realities of God and the world in Christ) and hence to bring the two realities together in a comprehensive schema. Unwittingly, then, that which only faith can grasp is put in a zone outside faith in which objectifiable reality is sought. The famous statement of Melanchthon in his 1521 *Loci* that to know Christ is to know his benefits is a first effort, not yet fully worked out and involving all kinds of risks, to break out of this schema and even in reflection to make the God-world relation that is present in Christ an object of faith.

Christology necessarily breaks in pieces once and so long as the relation is systematized ontologically. We might even say that in the failure of all efforts to do this, and in the fact that the Christ in whom we believe continually bursts through the schema of thought that imprisons him, self-attestation is given to the truth of that which, while it is sought in faith, is not stated with the methods of faith. Some illustrations might help to show what we have in view.

In their attempts to systematize ontologically the relation between God and the world in the incarnation, Luther thought of Logos and *sarx* together while Zwingli thought of them apart.

Luther thought of them together because of his soteriological concern. In faith we have to have the undivided Christ, the fulness of deity and humanity in their unbroken reality. Godhead apart is no help, for God is conceivable only in the flesh of Christ (EA, 45, 316ff.; 46, 37ff.). Although all creatures have dealings with God, we cannot say of any that this is God. But faith says of Christ, not just that God is in him, but that Christ is God himself (30, 63). Where God is, there man is; what God does, man does; what man does and suffers, God does and suffers (30, 62 and 67; 46, 332f.). Because we have here the real presence of God in grace, God and humanity cannot be sundered. By virtue of the inward unity of God and man we have even to say that God died; we have to speak of the blood of God and the death of God (25, 312).

The doctrine of the communication of the attributes expresses this ontological focus on the unity of the natures, or rather on God's unconditional condescension and gracious presence (cf. 30, 204; 47, 177). So does the doctrine of ubiquity, which supports the real presence of Christ at the Lord's Supper. The thesis that the finite is capable of the infinite is the ontological schema which as premise and conclusion formally embraces this unconditional unity of the two natures.

Now Zwingli has the same soteriological interest as Luther. The two theologians have the same goal. Again, Zwingli does not deny the unity of Christ's person. He affirms it for the same reason as Luther, namely, to bear witness to the condescension of God in his solidarity with sinners. The patristic premises are the same. But within the same basic presentation different emphases lead to sharp christological differences. Whereas Luther lays stress on the unity of the two natures, Zwingli does the very opposite (cf. his eucharistic writings from 1526 onward).

Possibly a deeper analysis would show that nontheological factors played some part here, e.g., the influence of humanism and also (by way of Pico della Mirandola) that of Platonism. But be that as it may, Zwingli's immediate concern was that Luther's radical concept of the unity of the natures might destroy the seriousness of the incarnation. For what remains of the divinity if the divine nature encloses itself in the finitude of the human nature and we thus get such absurdities as the death of God? And what remains of the humanity if it takes on omnipresence by the communication of the attributes and thus loses the mark of corporeality and limited form? Do we not have to oppose to the paradoxes of Luther the principle that the finite is not capable of the infinite?

Zwingli, then, is concerned for real incarnation, which in his view is threatened by the attempt on Luther's part to think in terms of a full entry of God into existence in the flesh. Within the limits of the unity of the person he thus contends for the full distinction of the natures. Christ is Lord of all according to his divine nature (Matthew 28:18) but subject to Caesar according to his human nature (Luke 2:1). He knows all things according to his divine nature (John 17:25) but does not know the day of his return according to his human nature (Mark 13:32). He is eternally with the Father and omnipresent in heaven and earth according to his divine nature and he hungers, thirsts, suffers, dies, and undergoes spatial limitation according to his human nature.

The biblical statements do not, of course, make these distinctions. They relate what belongs to his two natures to Christ as the one person. But this does not imply a real intermingling. We have here what is called *alloiosis*. In more precise differentiation one would have to say that Christ did this or that according to his nature as God or man. In this way the concepts of divinity and humanity retain their meaning, and it is thus possible to conceive of the incarnation within the ontological schema. It can be appropriated, as we might put it today. It is not a hazy construct completely remote from us.

For Luther, however, *alloiosis* is the devil's mask. With its assumption that only the humanity suffered it destroys the whole meaning of the work of redemption. If faith can rest only on the fact that a mere man died for me, and that only Christ's humanity suffered, Christ is a sorry Savior. Indeed, he himself needs a Savior.

This discussion of the disagreement between Luther and Zwingli on the incarnation illustrates the fact that the God-world relation cannot be systematized nor expressed with the help of a schema of transcendence and immanence. Our conclusion is that the God-world relation can only be an object of faith and that its mode is part of the same mystery as that of God's incarnation, so that we have the same self-reference of God to man as in the incarnation, and can only believe in it. This is why attempts to systematize the relation, i.e., to put it in a fixed schema of thought, all break down in the same way as similar attempts in relation to the incarnation. We have such an attempt when with the help of an ontological schema an effort is made to express the mystery of the incarnation within the doctrine of the two natures, whether the aim be to show that the incarnation is a possibility of thought (as in Zwingli) or to press the schema to the point of breakdown (as in Luther).

It seems to us that the greater truth is on Luther's side, since his self-destroying attempt at systematization is a sign that the truth in question resists systematization and cannot finally be imprisoned in a system. Nevertheless, the significance of the ontological schema within which Luther thinks is not disparaged to the point where it is relativized as a mere manner of speech, and interest can focus exclusively on Luther's soteriological concern. It should not be forgotten that the ontological schema was important enough for Luther to serve as a basis for his opposition to Zwingli.

If, however, the schema breaks down in Christology (as we shall try to show later), then the whole debate between the Lutherans and the Reformed will demand fresh examination from different angles. In their historic form the two positions can hardly be maintained today.

Luther suspected that there were more serious differences behind the contradiction which the schema of thought itself produced. It seemed that on Zwingli's view the incarnation fitted too easily into a humanist schema. Zwingli had a pre-understanding, *a priori* principles, which did not need to be revised. If this is so, then he anticipated the type of theology that we have called Cartesian. This is the point that needs to be explored today. But we cannot do it in this context.

The attempt to systematize the unity of God and man in Christ, and hence indirectly the unity of God and the world, fails in both Luther and Zwingli. It fails either because the schema breaks down (Luther) or because it triumphs (Zwingli) and this triumph entails intolerable reductionism in the soteriological statements. So long as the sphere of faith is not abandoned, and the unity of God and man in Christ is stated as an article of faith, there is relative unanimity. But the consensus is broken once an effort is made to think through this unity, i.e., to express it in terms of a given schema.

Thus Luther thinks that Zwingli's idea of *alloiosis* means disloyalty to the incarnation. It robs the incarnation event of its point. God no longer sacrifices himself. A blameless man dies as an offering. Zwingli, however, sees the same disloyalty in Luther. Luther's logical insistence that God integrates himself unconditionally into humanity and its destiny takes from the terms divine and human all their force. They are reduced to absurdity. A dying God is no longer God and a ubiquitous body is no longer a body.

The sharpness of the dispute is clear when one keeps in mind Luther's persistent stress on the humanity of Christ, on his concrete being in the flesh.[20] Zwingli's arguments cannot shift him here because the schema of thought which is used does not allow that to be stated which faith has to confess.

In this connection we must again discuss the Calvinistic *extra,* which is, as we have seen, of great symbolical importance at this point. It is so because it is a kind of safety valve when Luther presses the condescension of God to finitude so insistently. Is not the one who condescends greater than that to which he condescends in virtue of the very fact that he does condescend, and that he does so by his own free resolve? Is not he who wills to be a man different from what we are in virtue of the very fact that he does so will? Is there not, then, a transcendent element in him which means that the terms used (e.g., in Luther's doctrine of the communication of attributes) lose their sharp contours?

This is the question which Calvin puts to Luther and which leads him to the formulation known as the Calvinistic *extra.* The Logos which was made flesh transcends the flesh. He has an extra dimension in relation to it (cf. Inst. [1536], IV and Inst. [1559], II, 13, 4).

It would be a mistake to think that Calvin is here correcting Luther "from outside." Luther's own thought already contains the *extra.* It does so implicitly to the degree that the ontological schema within which he tries to think through God's condescension to finitude in the incarnation breaks in his hand. It also does so explicitly at certain points.

One of these is his conclusion that if Christ's humanity is subject to finite limitation on the one side, but on the other side it shares the divine omnipresence and omnipotence in virtue of its union with deity, then outside and above its earthly and limited form of being it necessarily has another and a freer mode of existence (Cl, III, pp. 389 and 396). It is God who posits the ubiquity of the body.

One has to say then, and this is the argument of the Calvinistic *extra,* that God is not absorbed into that which is posited by him. He remains the one who posits and to that extent he transcends that which is posited. Thus Luther too can formulate the Calvinistic *extra.* Christ has humbled and limited himself. But he took the form of a servant; he was not in this

---

[20] Cf. T. Harnack, *Luthers Theologie* (1927 ed.), I, pp. 111-114.

form. In contrast he did not take the form of God; he was in it. He gave up that which belonged to him, humbling himself and becoming obedient to the Father (WA, 17, II, 238ff.).

The decisive point is that Christ was the subject of self-emptying. He was not subjected to finitude against his will. He was not thrown into it as we are. As the subject of self-emptying he transcends that which it implies. He remains this subject throughout his life, as the Calvinistic *extra* maintains. His life is a continual self-humiliation. The emptying is not a once-and-for-all event; it continually takes place afresh throughout the whole earthly life of Christ (P. Althaus, *Die Theologie Martin Luthers* [1962], p. 172; E.T. p. 195), and there is thus a constant self-transcending. As Luther puts it, he gave that (divine) form back to God, emptied himself, would not use that title against us, would not be unlike us. Hence he assumed servanthood and became the servant of us all (WA, 2, 145-152).

He *did* all this. He was the *subject* of it. This is the transcendent element in his being in the world, in his incarnation. This element, which bursts through in Luther because the pressure is too strong, is what the Calvinistic *extra* expresses with the help of the Logos terminology.

We have thus presented the theological conclusion to which our analysis of the God-world relation has led, namely, its christological background. The incarnation is the exemplary union of the reality of God and that of the world. This accomplished union is preceded by its prophetic intimation from creation onward. In it God discloses himself to the world and addresses to it his Word which with its creative fiat summons the world to life. He then continually addresses himself to it in judgment and in grace.

Since the incarnation is the exemplary instance of the relation which God has established to the world, there is no possibility of expressing the coincidence between God's reality and that of the world in terms of ontological systematics. The very attempt to do this is tantamount to saying that the elements of the system, e.g., concepts like nature, person, or analogy, belong to an uncreated realm which has been there from all eternity, so that they can embrace both the reality of God and that of the world.

This necessarily leads, however, to noetic idolatry. For these elements which are given uncreated rank are plucked out of worldly reality and have the character of deified creatureliness. The ontological system therewith makes God himself an element of worldly reality. It is at root an indirect form of natural theology.

The same integrating of God into worldly reality which may be seen here in uncreated ontological concepts finds a parallel today in the integration of the consciousness of God into the Cartesian I. This too, with its pre-understanding, its categories of truth and understanding, and its system of categories, places at our disposal fixed, irreformable, and eternal forms into which the consciousness of God must be crushed if it is to be appropriated.

The process is basically the same in both cases. The realities of God and the world are related with the help of a continuum of concept, reality, or consciousness, and in this relation they are systematized and objectified. The attempt to do this itself forms a kind of heretical continuum which runs through the whole history of theology. It hews out the conceptual tombs in which Christ is continually buried afresh, and seals them with the stone of the closed system.

But Christ continually rises again out of these tombs. The pressure of his truth breaks the systems. Often he does not appear to the guards at the tomb, for the watchers are so sure that the tomb is well guarded, and that they have taken everything into account, that they are fast asleep. He appears to others, to those who come later, to the men of the third day.

Luther was certainly not a watcher. It is true that the ontological schemata which he inherited led him to try to systematize the relation between divinity and humanity or God and the world (cf. the way in which he uses Occam's definitions of existence in space and time to support his doctrine of ubiquity). Nevertheless, the system breaks down at once. He does not let his concepts gain the upper hand. These fall asleep, and in their dreams they lose their contours. They become unreal in the doctrine of the communication of the attributes.

Zwingli rightly perceived this. His only fault was not to sense the truth which caused this impotence and confusion of concepts. He did not see that theological necessity might well be a virtue in Luther, i.e., the virtue of not letting the elements of the ontological schema become uncreated, eternal, and irreformable entities, but of exposing them to demolition by the truth which they vainly try to grasp and which itself grasps them. No doubt the demolition was naive and involuntary. Luther certainly did not deliberate on the limits of ontological conceptuality. Nevertheless, it happened. It happened because faith in Christ took precedence over the powers of reflection. These powers were thus held in check and their revolt was prevented.

To sum up, we maintain (1) that the relation between the reality of God and that of the world cannot be fixed ontologically. It is an object of faith like the incarnation in which it finds exemplary fulfilment. The Word of God which establishes the world, and which manifests itself to it, is not linked to that which establishes, and to which it manifests itself, by any demonstrable continuum. The continuum is creatively posited by this Word. This positing does not take place within the continuum. It transcends it. To that extent the continuum is just as much an object of faith as the Word which posits it. The continuum is not the quintessence of a timeless nexus (no matter what the etymology of the term might suggest); it is posited. Hence it is a historical event. It lives and moves in the spoken Word which goes forth and calls non-being into being. It is identical with the event of Christ and is one of the mighty acts of God. It is not above time. Instead it is historical, and is indeed the basis of all history.

We maintain (2) that the discovery of analogies cannot offer a basis for the relation between the reality of God and that of the world. Analogies exist. Otherwise there could be no talk of God at all. In such talk we use the language that we use for present reality. The analogous elements, however, e.g., terms like "father," are obscure parables which we hear but do not understand. Contact with God can never be secured by appeal to these elements (cf. again the fact that the prodigal cannot appeal to the fact that he is a son). The analogies begin to operate only in the light of faith, i.e., as analogies of faith. The parable is clear only when the one who gives it is known. Creation, as the setting of the analogy, manifests itself only in the light of the Word which summons it to life.

We maintain (3) that since the relation between the reality of God and that of the world is not to be thought of ontologically as an overarching third thing, we have always to speak of it in such a way that God transcends the relation which he establishes. He is never merely the one who has condescended; he is always the one who condescends. He is not just the humiliated; he humiliates himself. He does not enter our freedom in such a way as to be a mere symbol of our relations, e.g., our fellow-humanity; he is always the one who empowers us for freedom. He lets the allotted freedom last only so long as he is recognized as the one who empowers us for it. Arbitrarily and autonomously snatched freedom becomes servitude in the far country (Luke 15:11; Romans 1:18ff.).

Similarly the Logos does not take flesh in the sense that Christ is just immanent and is completely abandoned to guilt and finitude; he is always the one who gives himself up and humbles himself. Because he is the subject of this condescension and remains so to the very end of his earthly existence, he transcends the act of condescension. The Logos is always outside the flesh (*eksarkos*) as well as in the flesh (*ensarkos*).

We cannot accept as a principle either that the finite is capable ot the infinite or that it is not, for if we were to do so the ontological schema would cease to be a servant, would no longer be prepared to be cast aside, but would be guilty of the usurpation of power to which we have referred. The Calvinistic *extra* is thus a warning marginal note whenever we try to think through the relation between divinity and humanity, between the reality of God and that of the world.

XVIII

Tasks of Christian Secularity
Outline of the Themes of Proclamation

The value of a dogmatics depends on whether it can be preached. We have been implicitly discussing this in all the previous chapters, especially the last. We have had to do so because we have defined theology as a process of reflection which arises out of faith, i.e., out of proclamation already heard. It is thus subordinate to proclamation and yet also continually related to it.

This abiding relation between theology and proclamation has determined our guiding question, namely, what it means to talk of God in a historical phase of self-conscious secularity, and what it means to understand this phase in relation to God.

We now know the framework within which what we can say about God must be put. It must be put in a dialectic which is determined by two statements at opposite poles.

The first is that God condescends to the world. His Word is an addressed Word. To talk of God is to speak of this relation.

The second is that God transcends the world. He is not a cipher for purely immanent occurrence. He cannot be exchanged, as a cipher might be, for some other concept. Prayer is for this reason something more than reflection on the world.

While it is right to ask where God is to be found in life, and while sheer and aloof transcendence is to be rejected, God can never be reduced to his presence in the world. The term "God" can never mean something other than God himself. If it could be a cipher for something else, e.g., fellow-humanity, this would imply the death, not of God, but of this concept of God. The cause of death would be interchangeability. What is interchangeable can be replaced. What can be replaced does not have the quality of uniqueness and certainly cannot be the basis, goal, and meaning of all being.

Within this dialectic we shall now try to indicate with the help of examples some themes of proclamation that arise against this background. Our use of models means that we can give only aphoristic pointers. (For a more systematic treatment cf. ThE.) In the form of proclamation, which carries with it a relation to the world, we shall be offering an interpretation of the totality of human reality from the standpoint of eternity, or, better, in the light of the Word of God.

What does this mean?

Obviously it does not mean that we shall be attempting to formulate a Christian world-view that will enable us to present, with the help of Christian norms and a claim to binding truth, a total view of reality that will place at our disposal a closed and eternally valid and hence irreformable interpretation of all the phenomena of nature and history. Attempts of this kind would contradict what redemption means for the emancipation of reason, namely, that it can relate materially and openly to a reality which has been dedivinized and robbed of its numinous force. This opening up of reason means its liberation from prejudice. It is no longer tied to specific premises as under the dominion of medieval Aristotelianism. Hence it is not tied to the implications of these premises. Christian premises which might lead to the erection of a closed nexus of life and meaning would have the character of an intellectual theocracy. They would contest the adulthood and openness of reason. They would thus involve a fundamental self-contradiction. Instead of opening up reason they would put it in ideological cement. Christianity, too, can be ideologized.

(1) Our first point, then, is that Christianity, unlike Marxism, Idealism, etc., does not carry with it a world-view which subsumes all conceivable phenomena under Christian axioms and assigns a fixed place to all natural and historical processes. God can never be understood as the first principle (whether as cause or substance) from which all phenomena can be deduced (as effects or accidents).

God is certainly the basis, goal, and meaning of all being and occurrence. But this meaning is not to be regarded and formulated as a principle. It is a believed meaning. Hence we cannot see it. We cannot pursue it in its manifestations. Thus we believe that God is righteous, that he is love, that he wills salvation. But we do not see the relation of manifested reality to this theme of righteousness, love, and salvation.[1] We believe in the one whose thoughts are higher than ours but we cannot think these thoughts after him. Our reality does not make these thoughts clear. What we see has no meaning; we believe, however, that there is meaning to it. We believe in the theme without seeing the relation between it and its execution. This execution is hidden under the veil of the cross. God appears to us in the form of his opposite. There are two quite different reasons for this.

(a) God does not correspond to our image of him. He is not, for example, the God of Job during Job's affliction. He is not a cipher for the correspondence between guilt and punishment or merit and reward. (b) God in love has assumed the form of lowliness, the "non-divinity" of the cross. If he cannot be demonstrated or presented ontically and historically, this is not for philosophical reasons, e.g., that transcendence cannot be objectified or that the ground of reality does not have the form of reality. No, the

---

[1] Cf. A. Flew in *New Essays in Philosophical Theology*, pp. 96-99.

reason why he cannot be demonstrated or seen is that in loving condescension he takes another form, and that in virtue of his solidarity with man he seems only too human, whether as a psychological phenomenon (Feuerbach) or as a phenomenon of religious history which like the incarnation is embedded in many analogies.

Because God, as meaning, cannot be grasped as a principle to which all phenomena can be related or from which they can be derived; because he is the one in whose higher thoughts we believe even though we cannot see them in their execution, a closed interpretation of the world is impossible. We are confronted by the openness of venture and by constant surprise. Every unexpected turn in knowledge, every experience which overtakes us and which apparently does not belong in the domain of faith, shatters the supposedly Christian systems which have been built up secretly in our heads and hearts.

The question of theodicy lurks everywhere at all times. The question why God permits this or does that, or whether he exists at all, shows that faith thrusts us out into open country. It challenges the definitiveness of secretly constructed principles. It rebels against their rule.

Hence we have always to confess with Job: "Yet will I trust in him" (Job 13:15). Faith bears witness here that God cannot be imprisoned in a world-view in which everything is easy. We can only believe in him whose thoughts are higher than ours; we cannot put these thoughts into systems. We are thus liberated from all systems. We are not imprisoned in a Christian world-view or in Christian ideologies. We are summoned to openness and to ventures of a higher order.

This is why there can be no Christian philosophy of history. God is the Lord of history. He has disclosed his purposes for mankind. This has led some people to speculate on the possibility of a Christian interpretation of history.[2] A mark of what faith says about history, however, is that it is never about history as a whole, just as a mark of what it says about creation is that it is not about the whole universe. Statements of this kind deal with details rather than the whole. They refer to the highly personal encounter of faith with the Thou of God.

It is thus very much to the point that Luther in his exposition of the first article of the Creed does not say that God created the world at large and then me among other things. He first says that God created me. The development of Israel's belief in God takes a similar course. Yahweh is first known in detail, in a small segment of life, as the God who brought Israel out of Egypt. Only then does the certainty arise that he is the Lord of the nations and the cosmos. He is first known in the immediacy of faith as the God of the covenant, our God. Only then is the implied insight that he is the Lord of the world and of history made explicit. The God of all eternity is first the God of David's house and people in the thanksgiving prayer of 2 Samuel 7:17ff. The eschatological expectation linked to the fulfilment of universal

---

[2] Cf. K. G. Steck, *Die Idee der Heilsgeschichte* (1959); M. Kähler, *Geschichte der protestantischen Dogmatik im 19. Jahrhundert* (1962), pp. 103ff.

history, namely, that all the nations will come up to Mount Zion (Matthew 8:11), arises out of the certainty of personal faith that Christ is risen, that he is risen for me.

This point that statements about the whole are always explications of a reality of faith experienced in detail has important implications for proclamation.

We can see that the secular way of putting questions of faith is to ask first about the totality. The question is always a general one: What is the meaning of history? How can God allow evil? What about predestination and free will or the omnipotence of God and opposition to him? How can the statistical fact that some are predestined and others are not be harmonized with the righteousness of God? The problem of pedagogical method which this poses is that speculatively illuminating answers cannot be given to such questions. For these broad questions focus on relations with which we are legitimately confronted only in the details of the personal experience of faith.

Luther drew attention to this in model fashion in his introduction to Romans (WA Bibel, 7, 2-27). We must not fly too high. We do this if in the matter of predestination we raise the general statistical question. This leads to confusion, cowardice, or libertinism. Like Paul in Romans, we should make Christ and the gospel our first concern so that we may know our sin and his grace. We must turn to the details of faith. Then the question of predestination arises, not as a speculative statistical problem, but as wonder at the fact that with no obvious merits I am justified out of free grace. No one can adequately handle the broad problem of predestination and free will or predestination and the righteousness of God. We must first be brought to the point of our own faith-encounter with the free grace of God if we are to approach this problem legitimately. Such problems, then, are not for beginners who have not yet come to the point of detailed experience. This wine is too heady for infants. Each doctrine has its own measure, time, and age.

The implied problem of proclamation arises when the church writes memoranda on general questions such as industrial relations.[3] These studies of great economic, political, or historical matters may be very objective. They may make effective use of statistics. They may embody information contributed by experts. But they do not stop at objective argument. The argument focuses on a point which has to do with the faith, the personal faith, of those who are here confessing in the medium of argument. For this is what they are doing.

If this element is not noted or the faith shared, such documents cannot be understood even though their arguments are accepted. If, however, an objective statement is in the last resort proclamation, then in spite of the armor of argument it shares the defenselessness of proclamation. It is defenseless because the faith which it proclaims cannot be demonstrated. It depends

---

[3] This does not apply to papal encyclicals, since they appeal in large part to natural law.

on the sovereignty of the inner witness of the Spirit. Hence even this way of tackling the great questions of history from the standpoint of faith reaches a point where argument ends and the issue is whether the one who is addressed in the arguments is ready to come, or is called, to the place of belief which is also the source of the arguments.

In exactly the same sense the believer can reason with interested parties about the relation between predestination and free will. He can use arguments, and his arguments may even leave an impression of intellectual cogency. In the last resort, however, the validity of what he says will demonstrate itself, not in the fact that he proves his point, but rather in the fact that he issues a summons to personal faith and makes it plain that only in the light of this do his arguments have a justifiable basis and goal.

(2) Interpretation of the world from the standpoint of eternity does not start, then, with the fixities of a world-view. At the same time it does have a criterion by which a hierarchy of values may be set up, even though this hierarchy is so general that it leaves plenty of room for modifications in detail. This criterion is the primacy of man over things and over the world of the material in general. Man is summoned by the Creator to subdue the world (Genesis 1:28). Hence even the world's orders are not ends in themselves. They are to serve man and to be the structure of his fellow-humanity (cf. the sabbath in Mark 2:27).

The basis of the fact that man is not to be reduced to the functional or degraded into a mere means to an end lies in a quality of the human which transcends man's being in the world. Man has an alien dignity. This consists in the fact that he has been loved and visited by God, that he has been bought with a price (1 Corinthians 6:20; 7:23), and that Christ died for him (Romans 14:15; 1 Corinthians 8:11). Hence a proclamation which relates to the orders of life, to social structures, to the role of sex, to economic relations, etc., must use the primacy of man as a criterion.

A proclamation of this type will not be afraid of being concrete. It will discuss given social structures. It will introduce biological data as arguments in the sphere of sex. But these concrete elements will not be ends in themselves. They will serve as illustrations of the criterion whether the alien dignity of man is being respected in the structures. Thus sex will be understood purely as a biological medium for the human relation between two sexual beings (cf. ThE, III, § 2020ff.). In the way in which the primacy of man is established, e.g., by alien dignity and not by immanent functional worth, proclamation will seek to show that God is present in the world even though he is more than this presence.

(3) Interpretation of the world from the standpoint of eternity teaches us to be objective and bold. If in opposition to the mythical view of the world it robs the world of its numinous force, in opposition to secularism it de-ideologizes the world and shatters the many pseudo-absolutes which are constantly being set up. To be soberly objective does not mean being ordered to the world of things. As the previous section has shown, it can only mean perceiving the true order of rank which is established under the primacy of

man's alien dignity. Hence the new objectivity is the objectivity of love and not a purely secular rationality (1 Corinthians 10:23). I receive the objectivity of love, however, only as I find in man something that transcends him and that I cannot "see" but only believe. Only that which transcends the world lets us be truly worldly, i.e., lets us turn to the world boldly and without reserve.

(4) Interpretation from the standpoint of eternity does not treat man as an abstract bearer of humanity or, as one would say today, of existence. It treats him as concrete man in the web of secular relations. The fact that theology, and especially Theology A, usually overlooks this axiom of Christian proclamation has given rise to a new form of the ancient heresy of Docetism.

In early church history[4] Docetism denoted a heretical version of Christology. On this view Christ's body was regarded as a mere appearance and the substance of the message of the incarnation was thus impaired. Christ was called exclusively the Son of God. The related divine predicates did not seem to permit us to ascribe to him such features of humanity as limitation, finitude, and the possibility of temptation or suffering. The result of such theological ideas was a more or less shadowy and unreal heavenly being lacking any solidarity of existence with other men.

Docetism recurs today in a modified but no less momentous form. The only thing is that it now arises at another place. It has as it were slipped over from Christology into anthropology. Now it is man who is spoken of in an abstractly general and shadowy way.

G. Ebeling has rightly pointed out[5] that the concept of reality is, ironically, one of the most abstract in human thought. The earnest statement that God is not an idea but a reality is misleading inasmuch as it makes God a potential abstraction by trying to do the very opposite.

The same is true when we speak about man, who does not really exist as this nominalistic concept. Yet the concept is bandied about both in the pulpit and on the rostrum. The result is that the word of proclamation loses the constitutive and integral element of address. The one who is addressed does not see that it is he who is meant and affected. He feels no compulsion to undertake the task that is left to him, namely, that of subsuming himself as an individual under the master-concept "man."

More precisely, this docetic misunderstanding of man means that he is dissected out of the reality of history which surrounds and engulfs him and isolated as a being apart. As Bultmann puts it,[6] the NT sees the monstrous power of this sphere, the world. It sees that its cares and desires distract man from authentic concern for himself, from the questions of God and the world to come. It sees that man, imprisoned by the world, worries about things that are subject to corruption. It thus sees that the world is passing away.

---

[4] A. von Harnack, *Dogmengeschichte,* 5th ed. (1931), I, pp. 212ff.; E.T. *History of Dogma* (1961). I, pp. 253ff.

[5] *Wort und Glaube,* 3rd ed. (1967), p. 201; E.T. *Word and Faith* (1963), pp. 199f.

[6] GV, II (1952), pp. 59ff., esp. p. 68.

Man is entangled in it, not to his salvation, but to his destruction. Now this is all true. Nevertheless, it is only part of the story. Is it not also true that the freedom of man is attested in this world of his? Is not the world shown to be the place where God wills to encounter him both in his works and in his fellow-men, his neighbors? Is it not the place of his gifts and tasks—a place which is opened up to him by the fact that he is called out of it and then sent back into it? Is not the world the sphere which God has loved and for which he gave his only begotten Son? Can we really understand the world, then, merely as the power which imprisons man?

If we do understand it thus, then real man is brought to light only when he is isolated from this alien power and seen in himself apart from this world which heteronomizes him. But then he becomes a mere appearance, a worldless abstraction. For this aeon is not just an "accident" of his being which can be abstracted away without loss of the substance, the result being the human as such. This world is part of the essence of man. He "is" his world. The structure of this world with its laws of constriction, its autonomous trends, and its pitiless severity is only a macrocosmic reflection of his heart. Conversely, the heart is only a microcosmic expression of this world of his. Babylon can only try to be as great and immoderate as our Babylonian heart (Francis Thompson "The Heart," Sonnet II in *Poems* [1937], p. 320; on the relation between the world and man cf. ThE, I, § 2144ff. and *Geschichte und Existenz,* 2nd ed. [1964], pp. 66ff.). Man is man in his world and not man apart from his world. He is the one who qualifies this world of his and who objectifies himself in its structures. If he detaches himself from this context, the human is reduced to unreality.

This anthropological Docetism has come into theology by the way of existentialism. Existentialism views the external world as hostile and its movement as restrictive.[7] The world involves man in self-alienation. It heteronomizes and "fixes" him.[8] It is simply there (Heidegger). It is the sphere of the technically useful. Strictly, it can be spoken of only as a meaningless reality.[9] No sphere of life, whether animal, vegetable, or cultural, has any meaning. In face of the unconditional radiance of authentic existence the whole world becomes a background without meaning.[10] It becomes the dark foil which sets in relief the burning light of existence. The focus on this unconditional radiance of authentic existence is what allows entry to Docetism. It leads us to speak of man in the abstract and hence introduces the supposedly authentic man who is detached from the world and whom it can no longer "fix."

When this idea of abstract man is adopted in theology it takes from the gospel message its legitimate recipient and thereby changes it essentially. The change may be seen in its effect. Its form is found to be dull and insipid. The hearer does not see its relevance. Preached in this way, the gospel does not reach him. It does not speak to the reality which concerns him. This reality

---

[7] O. F. Bollnow, "Existenzphilosophie," *Systematische Philosophie* (1942), p. 349.

[8] J. P. Sartre, *L'Etre et le Néant* (1943); E.T. *Being and Nothingness* (1956).

[9] Bollnow, *op. cit.,* p. 356. [10] *Loc. cit.*

is what gives rise to the ultimate questions, e.g., the question of possible freedom in the impulsion of autonomous processes, or the question of meaning in the perfection of actualized goals and the self-perfecting means of actualization, or the question of the possibility of love and fellow-humanity in an increasingly organized world which separates the I and the Thou from one another by its impersonal structures, or the question of the possibility of being oneself in the midst of social categorization, or the question of the possibility of faith in the closed and immanent functional nexus of all things and processes. What can it mean in this world of forces that man with his alien dignity has immediacy to God, that in virtue of this immediacy he is not enmeshed in this world of forces, that he is detached from it, that he encounters it, and that in the name of his commitment to the ultimate he is no longer subject to the penultimate?

If redemption does not relate to man in this connection of his with the world, then it does not relate to him at all.

Yet man is aware that he is more than his secular functions. He is the being which transcends itself. Beyond all the immanent goals that he might attain man asks about the meaning which he has possibly missed in so doing (cf. the question of the rich young ruler in Mark 10:17). He asks about the design of creation which he has discarded and the prescribed identity which he has failed to win.

Since these are relevant questions for man, not least for modern man, the gospel is also relevant when, in contrast to the law, it comes as a liberating word which seeks man in the midst of his relations and blesses him with the royal freedom of the children of God. Conversely, when the word of redemption bears no correlation to the hopeless self-interpretation of man which persuades him that he has been betrayed and sold out to the structures of immanence, then this word seems irrelevant to those who are hopeless and oppressed; it is like an alien visitor from remote antiquity and both Redeemer and those who are invited to redemption are docetic shades.

The message of redemption is secular or it is nothing. It presents God in the world or it is sound and smoke. But to present God in the world does not mean equating him with the world. For—if we may repeat the decisive statement which we have tried to develop in this book—only that which transcends the world can make us worldly. Or, even more directly, only he who did not think it robbery to be equal with God (Philippians 2:6) and who left his eternity can direct us to time. And only to him who overcomes the world in his name is the world given back as an inheritance in which he is to keep the faith and to prove his freedom.

Appendix: Further Discussion of the Concept of Secularity and the Penultimate as Illustrated by the Question Whether the Ideal and Utopian Is Possible

1. PROBLEM OF HOPE

In Chapter XVII. 3-6 we came up against the question what is meant by the secularity of the son who has come of age. In many theological analyses of secularization the answer is that free action in the world implies especially the autonomy of reason. Now that the world is dedivinized, the believer can have an objective relation to it. Modern science is made possible. The discovery of the objective world and of its objectifiability has exemplary significance when it is a matter of characterizing the freedom which faith has made possible in relation to the world. This relation is defined as one of pure rationality.

The scientist, the technician, and the political or economic analyst are typical representatives of this rational relation. Nevertheless, one may ask whether even they can properly be called "rational" in their relation to the world. At some level they, too, are driven by the passion of wanting to find or to shape. This passion in turn is unleashed by the ability to envisage higher connections or desired goals. So long as we do not endow the term with a mystical sense, one might almost speak of the power of vision in this regard.

Thus statesmanship cannot concern itself only with the immediate and the partial. Even if politics is defined as the art of the possible and is thus restricted in scope, the statesman has creative power if he can conjure up images of a possible constellation of powers or an organized social structure. More distant goals of this kind, as in the classical utopias, usually exert considerable fascination and can thus be a political force.

They can, of course, be misused. They can become new mythologies and destroy a sober and rational relation to the world. The question is whether abuse negates any valid use. Can our dealings with the world be constructive without ideals, without an imaginative element? Even when the scientist works at the detailed task, is not this part of a visionary whole, an assumed cosmic nexus? Is not the whole to be discovered in the parts? Or, theologically, do we not find God in details?

The mature scientist does not expect, however, that he will get the total picture only as a kind of ideological superstructure at the conclusion of the accurate work which now claims his prior attention. It already affects his work by stimulating him and imparting ideas and insights. Just because the whole is greater than the parts, it acts as a spur in the analysis and correlating of the parts.

The possibility of abuse threatens in the form of mere dreaming or the development of "isms." Nevertheless, proper use is possible if the total view does not become a dogmatic metaphysics but remains within heuristic principles. When it does this, it is simply the hypothesis which lies behind the experiment and which is either confirmed by it or has to be revised in the light of it.

Two points are decisive here in relation to the theological problem of secularity. First, constructive dealings with the world are possible only if we transcend the factual in a higher curiosity which seeks to penetrate to that which inwardly holds the world together. Second, these constructive dealings are impossible without the fascination and the release of passion that this higher vision brings with it in both research and technology. To put it simply, there is need of hope. The question whether it will be properly or improperly used can be faced when we already have it.

Our previous deliberations have shown that the gift of the Christian faith to science and technology is in fact the readiness to be provisional, to relativize eschatologically, and hence to be sober in the NT sense. If this is taken to mean, however, the prohibition of all vision, then our dealings with the world will be restricted or more properly reduced to pure rationality. But this in turn means that we cannot speak of real freedom in relation to the world. Man is now free in relation to it only as an abstract intellectual subject. His humanity is understood docetically. The world which is opened up to reason is withheld from man as such, since man is more than his mere rationality.

Even in secular theology a limited and reduced form of freedom for the world entails disparagement of the world and retreat from it not unlike what we find in many pietist circles. The Christian cannot be a constructive statesman, economic expert, or scientific discoverer. He must leave all significant achievements to the children of the world who are less restricted. For the visions of the remythicized world do not hamper objectification as those of the original mythical world did. The spirits that once inhabited things and events are now at work in science and technology themselves. What is "technically sweet" (Oppenheimer), what can be known and shaped, is irresistible. The modern Faust makes his own pacts with the devil.

We shall now try to think through this basic problem of the Christian relation to the world with the help of a model. The problem of the ideal will serve here. For we have in the ideal the transcending of reality to which we referred. The ideal describes, not what is, but what should be. This is regarded as attainable, at least approximately. It thus arises out of the world. It is a possibility and hence it poses a task.

If we want to take the penultimate seriously and not jump past it to the ultimate, we shall have to analyze theologically the concept of the ideal. Can the penultimate be taken seriously if it is not related to dreams, visions, and the powers of the imagination as well as reason? Is our relation to the world free if it does not carry with it creative possibilities and engage all our powers?

It is no accident that some secular theologians have a purely negative and not just a broken relation to the ideal. The reduction of secularity to which we have referred entails controversy with the ideal. Now it is obvious from our theological analysis of secularization that we are not recommending a positive relation to the ideal. Dying and rising again with Christ, the dialectic of distance and openness in relation to the world, will also be noticeable in our encounter with it. Nevertheless, along with our main purpose of using the ideal as a model of our relation to the world, we shall also be able to bring under critical scrutiny the pure intellectualism which under the guise of sobriety seems to be present in many theologies that are espoused today.

2. MAN IN THE LIGHT OF THE IDEAL

To have ideals is to be convinced that we and the reality around us are not congruent with our destiny. The ideal is an indication of failure. Before we mount the throne of theological judgment and condemn the arbitrariness and illusory character of ideals, we should first note that symbolically they carry with them a call to repentance. Indeed, this call may often be an open and aggressive one.

The modern youth movement, for instance, is an aggressive attack on the social and indeed the whole adult establishment. Here ideals and the criticism are of a piece. Similarly Kant's imperative triggers an attack on the indicative and to that degree it is a message of repentance. Good means abandoning evil (Wilhelm Busch). But I can leave only that which already is (at least potentially).

An *idea* serves as the criterion for distinguishing between the imperative and the indicative. The idea of humanity, as in Kant, Schleiermacher, or David Strauss, makes it clear that we do not measure up to what we should be. Similarly, the idea of the state lies behind all attempts to achieve it, even the best. The idea serves both as a critical principle by which our concrete being is judged and also as a goal of action. When it becomes a goal, the idea becomes the *ideal*.

Each of us has an image of what he should be. When I measure myself by my own self-image, I realize that I am not congruent with it. My image thus becomes a judgment which may plunge me into discontent or even into melancholy and despair. Yet this image also takes on the role of a normative ideal which I must try to actualize. Only when I do so do I attain to freedom and hence to peace.

When we analyze the ideal more closely, however, we find that it may be either an abstract norm or that it may go beyond abstraction and become a specific vision, e.g., the vision of a world in which mankind is organized according to the laws of virtue or the principles of love, with no more poverty, hunger, or sickness. When the ideal becomes concrete in this way, we have a *utopia*. The utopia is the content of a collective hope.

The utopia, then, is an ideal which is given concrete shape, related to a suprapersonal—collective or cosmic—state, made the subject of hope, and held to be attainable. We move on an elevated plain when we start with the idea and go on by way of the ideal to the utopia.

There is a precipitous drop off this plateau, however, when the ideal and the utopia are not held in honor because of the truth of their inner content but because of their psychological attractiveness and the possibility of mobilizing their political force. In this case we have *ideology*. Ideology may be defined as a pragmatized ideal.

In our discussion we shall be speaking of this fall into ideology under the heading of the self-jeopardizing of the ideal. But very quickly we shall reach the subsection on the jeopardizing of the ideal by us. It will thus be seen that there is an element of irony in the main title. Strictly speaking, one cannot speak of the self-jeopardizing of the ideal. It is always we ourselves who destroy the ideal.

3. SELF-JEOPARDIZING OF THE IDEAL

We shall first describe the fall from the utopia into ideology, since this runs right through the process of the self-jeopardizing of the ideal as a critical symbol of hope. To this end we must first examine the nature of utopias rather more precisely.

a. Utopia

If we are correct, there are three entirely different types of utopia: (i) a specific plan for the world; (ii) a purely visionary utopia; and (iii) a utopia which transcends history.

(i) More's utopia is a good instance of a specific plan for the world, especially in its antithesis to Machiavelli (cf. ThE, II, 2, § 833-886).

Machiavelli describes history as a neutral interplay of forces without either meaning or goal. Princes must be taught how to take part in this interplay and not to be swamped by it. We have in history a kind of storm which unleashes natural forces and meteorological research is needed if we are not only to survive the storm but also to harness it, e.g., by using the run-off as water power.

In contrast, More regards man as a being with a destiny who must try to achieve his creaturely *telos* in all areas of life, and especially in the state. The aim of man's existence comes to its fullest expression in the order, peace, and prosperity of the state. Hence the utopian state objectifies and institutionalizes the nature of man.

One may detect here a basic difference in approach. But the difference is not that Machiavelli has a pessimistic and realistic view of man, whereas

More is an idealistic and optimistic dreamer. Realism and utopianism cannot be distinguished as simply as that. More knows very well how questionable man is. He is fully acquainted with his passions, his greed, and his egotism. His ideal state is designed to check human passion and to offer vents for it. A breath of scepticism runs through it. Man is not going to be any different from what he is. Institutions can curb him only to a degree. His greed can be quenched in part by prosperity and social equality. That is all.

The question arises how so sober and realistic a thinker could ever describe a utopia. The answer seems to be that More views man from two angles. He sees him as he is (greedy, egotistical, and sensual). He also sees him as he is destined to be and as he really is, i.e., as the being in whom spirit triumphs over impulse, righteousness over egotism, and God's peace over force.

If this is perceived, we shall not dismiss More's utopia as mere fantasy. What More presents is a social structure in which man's essential being is objectified in antithesis to his empirical being. Man is thus confronted here with his true being even though it does not correspond to his present reality and is concealed behind self-alienation. A statement is made about man which is wholly realistic in the sense that it is aware of his sin and corruption. In antithesis to Machiavelli, man is not just a natural force which can be plotted and predicted. He is a being which transcends itself and which has a destiny.

In this kind of utopia which wants to show what man really is, it would be a mistake to describe him empirically as a murderer, thief, or adulterer. More knows that man is these things *de facto*. But he cannot allow that we have here a definition of the true nature of man. The Christian, too, must be on guard lest in his realistic interpretation of man he regards fallen man as "real" man. Real man is man as God created him in his own image and as we see him in the face of Jesus Christ.

It is Machiavelli who equates the true nature of man with his *de facto* state. In contrast, More sees the true nature of man apart from his *de facto* state. For him man is man as he ought to be. This man is in conflict with man as he is. Man, then, is in contradiction, in non-identity. The same applies to the state. More does not describe the state as it is and then try to distil out of the best qualities the most efficient possible state. He offers a vision of the state which corresponds to the true destiny of man and which thereby brings the empirical state under judgment. To sum it all up, Machiavelli presents the indicative content of man and the state, while More presents the imperative content.

Christians will recognize one of their own main contentions here, namely, that men are to be described essentially and not just empirically. Thus the publicans and harlots of the NT are not defined by the fact that they are publicans and harlots but by their true being which transcends their present condition, namely, the fact that they are lost children whom the heavenly Father mourns and seeks. The love with which Jesus searches them out and which shapes his dealings with them is simply the charisma of seeing through the state of lostness to this true being of theirs.

Only when we appreciate this can we understand the tremendous mobilizing power of utopias in the rise of revolutionary movements. Man's yearning to find himself and his true nature is a political force of the first rank and hence an element in the shaping of the world. It is not true, as Machiavelli supposes, that only primitive impulses like the hunger for happiness or power, for bread and circuses, are basic factors. The longing to find one's destiny, even though it be suppressed and inarticulate, is also a historical force. This is why the political significance of utopias has often been perceived, as in Marxism. Ideas of peace, justice, and equality can trigger fanaticism. They are thus the high horse-powered motors of historical progress.

Utopias after the manner of Thomas More are not fairy tales. Fairy tales do not come under the restraint of reality and hence their main effect is only on children who cannot distinguish between the inner and the outer world. Adults can make this distinction and hence they dismiss fairy tales as mere dreaming which may produce either indolence or a relapse into childish sentimentality. The political force of utopias would be inexplicable if there were no more to them than this.

The reason for their force is that utopias bear a correlation to the actual nature and potential of man, so that man sees what he should be in them. Utopias have all the appeal of man's potential and destiny. They are, in Nietzsche's phrase, "monumental history" projected into the future. The kingdom of peace or the classless society is not just an antithesis to the present state. It represents the fully grown and fruit-bearing tree which is already contained as a seed in man's present condition.

(ii) The second form of utopia is the purely visionary one. A negative feature of this is that its ideals do not correspond to even the ultimate possibilities of history, so that the antithesis between the essential and the empirical image of man is lost to view. Absolute goals are now set. From the Christian standpoint this would mean applying the laws of God's transcendent kingdom unchanged to the present aeon, as the sixteenth-century radicals did or as Tolstoy tried to do in another way with his proclamation of a state without any army or police force.

This utopian dream founders for two reasons. (a) The kingdom of God is no longer here an object of expectation and faith. It is forced into the present aeon. History between the fall and the last judgment is thus left behind. Faith illegitimately tries to be sight. It erases the boundary between Now and One Day. It abandons the category of the Nevertheless. It wants to "have" in immediacy.

(b) The violent way in which the interim of this aeon is abandoned shows that the kingdom of God is no longer viewed here as an eschatological act of God. Instead it is made a goal of human acts. It becomes a work of man.

Faith is thus betrayed in two ways: (a) an attempt is made to press on from faith to sight, and (b) faith becomes a work. This form of utopia rests, then, on an illusion which is usually followed very quickly by disillusionment, at the very latest in the second generation.

(iii) We turn to the third form of utopia, that which transcends history, with a measure of trepidation and with a definite linguistic problem. For it is evident that this form cannot really be grouped with the others. It is in the strict sense a judgment on utopias. Yet it is by associating it with the others—in the same way as one might temporarily call Christianity a religion—that its distinction from the others is brought out.

This third form of utopia is what the Bible calls the eschaton, paradise, the kingdom of God, the absolutes behind the Sermon on the Mount. Here, too, the true nature of man, what he ought to be, is presented. One has only to consider the way in which the law of Moses is radicalized in the Sermon on the Mount to realize that man's final destiny is in view and that his present state is transcended. Man is challenged here as though he had just come from the hands of God or as though he already lived in the consummation of the kingdom. He is addressed in terms of his created and his eschatological nature.

In the relevant passages the Bible does not, of course, relate this authentic man to the present aeon or find any actual achievement of perfection. This man is non-existent man and yet he is also man as he will be after the resurrection. He is the man who does not yet know what he shall be (1 John 3:2) when in his kingdom God makes us congruent again with what he meant us to be. By addressing us as though we still were what we ought to be, or already were what we shall be, the Sermon on the Mount is a judgment on our interim state.

One should not conclude from this, of course, that the absolutes of the Sermon on the Mount are beyond the horizon of this world and do not strictly apply to us. Bismarck once said that we cannot rule the world by the Sermon on the Mount. It belongs to another dimension and statecraft demands opportunism and lack of scruple. Nevertheless, a comparison between Bismarck and Hitler shows that the Sermon on the Mount does cast some glimmer of light on the present world (cf. ThE, II, 2, § 520-650; E.T. II, pp. 92ff.).

Bismarck knew the Sermon on the Mount. This is why he knew how dubious politics is. Often enough he had to put might before right. But the challenge of the Sermon on the Mount kept him sane. It did not let him fall into the illusion that all is well with the present world. This explains perhaps his moderation.

Hitler, however, did not know the Sermon on the Mount. He felt no challenge to his political calculations. The state of the world as he diagnosed it gave him his imperatives. He believed that it was shaped by man's bestial nature. He believed that might usually triumphs over right. He was thus prepared to break treaties and to subject rights to the interest of power. His world was not called in question by any eschaton. It was a healthy body. Its condition gave him his laws. He knew no dualism of state and nature. He thus fell victim to an animal lack of restraint.

To return to the problem of the utopia, the eschaton of the kingdom of God shares with the utopia the one thought that the authenticity of man, his destiny and eschatological nature, comes to expression in it. It differs from it, however, to the degree that it is neither detached from transcendence and proclaimed as the goal of an autonomous possibility (as in the second form) nor is it understood as the historical possibility of a relative ideality (as in the first form).

Nevertheless the kingdom of God does call, as we have seen, for symbolical actualization and for a secret presence as judgment and grace. Thus only the first two forms are utopias in the strict sense. They both break down either (a) by demanding more than man can do, believing that man's nature can triumph over his state, or (b) by trying to bring the kingdom of God into the present, and thus replacing faith by sight and work.

We may thus advance a first conclusion. The utopia can be a first step toward the self-jeopardizing of the ideal (to use our ironical form of expression). It can refute the ideal as a dream, albeit a dream with many elements of truth, especially in its protests against the present state. It can unmask it as alien, disobedient, or unrealistic, and thus destroy it.

The utopian protest of man against his state, and his general revolt against the temporality of his existence, can take two forms in particular.

The one form is an illegitimate prolongation of the world, whether as mere continuation or as infinite progress. The individual thus becomes a drop in an endless river. He loses his immediacy to God. The stress on unconditionality and uniqueness which is laid on his existence before God is forfeited. In this regard Christians who look forward to the second coming are in the right of it, even though they may go astray in their dating.

The second form of protest against temporality is a premature termination of the world. The signal is given for this by those who make God's kingdom into a utopia, e.g., by doctrinaire pacifists who desire that even today lambs and wolves should lie down together (Isaiah 11:6) and the lion should eat straw like the ox (11:7; 65:25). The result is unwillingness to endure the fallen state of the world and to be content with the grace that shines as a light in our darkness.

The attempt to transcend this fallen world in a utopia which has the message of the kingdom of God as its Magna Carta is thus hubris and idolatry. Even though there are many questionable things in Luther's doctrine of the two kingdoms, its basic intention is clearly a good one, namely, to do everything it can to show the secularity of the world and to prevent the kingdom of God from becoming a utopia.

A final note about utopias is in order.

It might seem that the utopia is a kind of Christian vision, especially when, as in More, it distinguishes between what man is essentially and what he is empirically. The real drift of utopian desire, however, soon dispels this illusion. The utopia is based on the postulate that the essence and ideal of man can be realized. This human self-confidence which is the final error in utopias is shown to be false when man goes astray and reveals his bestiality.

Even in times of bestiality Christians can still praise God. Their petition "Thy kingdom come" is not negated by the night and by lack of response. It simply becomes the more fervent. For this kingdom is not a utopia which depends on human self-confidence. It is kept in the hand of the one whose help and comfort we need to pray for all the more, the more conscious we are of our own failure. When the last utopian illusion is dispelled, the dying Christian prays: "Father, into thy hands I commend my spirit."

The utopian, however, suffers a terrible shock when human bestiality destroys his confidence in man. His utopias then become apocalyptic nightmares like those of Aldous Huxley, Orwell, or Jack Williamson.

The ideal which is now self-jeopardized is shown to be ambivalent in its very core. It has (1) an aspect of truth, namely, that man is not congruent with his destiny but must seek himself, and (2) a demonic side, since it is confident that man can either reach his goal or at least approximate to it.

In this light we can see the decisive reason why God's kingdom is not to be understood as a utopia. God, not man, is the Lord of this kingdom. But the Lord is more than his kingdom. To make the kingdom a utopia is to set it over its Lord. More store is set by the state of peace and plenty than by the one who gives it and whose hand is mightier than what he gives (cf. John 6:26). The gift is sought as an end in itself, not as a way to the giver. Redemption is sought rather than the Redeemer, as when a cry to God is uttered in an emergency but once the emergency has passed God is again forgotten. Eyes which want only bread cannot wait. Only the one who sees the hand can say: "The eyes of all wait upon thee, and thou givest them their meat in due season" (Psalm 145:15). The one who sees the meat without the hand has no sense of the due season. He snatches it all at once.

The utopian wants the kingdom and not the Lord. Hence he cannot wait. He views himself as the savior. The time is not in God's hands; it is a date on the calendar. If this proves to be mistaken (as it will), then the utopia becomes an apocalypse, the prophet an existentialist, and the vision of hope a vision of anxiety. This is how the ideal is self-jeopardized.

b. Ideology

The collapse of the utopia is not the final stage in self-jeopardization. At the bottom of the precipice is ideology. The term really demands deeper and fuller historical analysis. In the present context we shall use it in a more restricted sense (cf. ThE, II, 2, § 154ff.; E.T. II, pp. 26ff.).

The ideal and the utopia contain elements of truth. They express a truth. Ideology, however, has another basis. The elements of truth and scientific reasoning in it are only a secondary intellectual alibi which it fashions for itself.

Two considerations lie behind ideology, especially in totalitarian or ideological states.

The first is acceptance of the fascination of utopias. Power can be gained through exploitation of this fascination. The myth of a Third Reich or a classless society is forged because of its power as an ideal and its ability to harness human passions and the human will. The point, then, is not whether the visions are true but what can be done to see that they are thought to be true, so that they can then mobilize fanaticism and fabricate illusions. The ensuing constructs are ideologies.

The second consideration is that the totalitarian state commands unlimited physical and organizational power. It can set up the terror of a dictatorship. No spheres of human life are outside its control. Hence there is no wilderness to which the inhabitants of this state can flee or even be sent. (This lack of any place of retreat is perhaps the most gloomy aspect of the totalitarian picture.)

Nevertheless, the power of the totalitarian state is in fact limited. The inhabitant of this state can take refuge within himself in a kind of inward emigration. This opposition of the uncontrollable element in man can be checked only by an attack on the personal core of man. Ideologies are the bacteria which can get through a man's skin to his inner being. Their job is to overcome his reason. This is why they use arguments and set up a scientific façade. The conscience must also be overpowered, for ethical action means decision and decision might mean opposition: Here I stand; I can do no other. This type of attitude is like sand in the well-oiled machinery.

Conscience cannot be overcome, however, merely by winning it over. Even when won over, it is still a questionable factor so long as it is vigilant. It must thus be overpowered. The impulses directed on man have to aim at another place instead of the personal core of conscience. This other place is the nervous system. The means of getting at this is propaganda, which does not try to convince—this would be an appeal to conscience—but which offers nervous stimulation by means of slogans, background noise, capture of the eye, and monotonous and concentrated repetition.

Ideologies are inseparably related to propaganda. They are thus pragmatic. They are intellectual weapons. They do not contain any authoritative truth, at least for the esoteric group which holds power. They are cynically exploited means of exercising power.

The distinction between ideologies and the ideal is that ideologies absolutize a by-product of the ideal. This by-product is the ability of ideals and utopias to mobilize human potential and to stimulate the kind of activism which the ideological hierarchy wants to harness. For the hierarchy it makes little difference whether the ideologies are true. Function rather than truth is what counts. The suggestion of truth is needed, however, if the ideology is to function. Pragmatism thus seeks the adornment and the validation of serious scholarship. In a kind of trick the pragmatic commitment of science to the party is thus conjoined with its supposed objectivity (cf. ThE, II, 2, § 196ff.; E.T. II, pp. 33ff.).

c. Way from the Ideal to Ideology

The question arises whether degeneration from the ideal to ideology is a necessary process? Is there no stopping this fall? Is nihilism, the nihilism of the esoteric initiates, the only logical end?

The process itself is easily illustrated. The saying of Kaiser Wilhelm I that the people need religion, while not intended ideologically, can mean that I personally have no time for religion but the masses need it because it makes them good subjects and we have to have it as an inner restraint and a means of uniting the nation psychologically.

We have here an ideological misuse of religion. While it is personally rejected and even perhaps scorned by rulers, its pragmatic by-product, i.e., its power to bind and unite men, is exploited. To keep men afraid of the last judgment is good psychological strategy even if one makes light of this judgment personally.

Humanity can also degenerate into an ideology, e.g., under the slogan of human relations. The process is the same. Perhaps my aim is to make money or to win social prestige. The people who help me to do this are a matter of indifference to me. I may even despise them. But I cannot let this show through or production would suffer, for there are irrational elements in economics too. I know that joy in work increases production and that good treatment can augment this. Hence I have to foster my social image. I must manifest concern, ask about the wife and children, show a pleasant face when in the factory—this is just as important as maintenance of the machinery. While humanity as such means nothing to me, I naturally mobilize the economic potential of good techniques in handling men.

Human relations can, of course, be more than this. We have here a possible but not a necessary degeneration into ideology. The form of degeneration is the same as in the case of religion. A by-product is used to tap human potential and to trigger joy, enthusiasm, and willingness. The thing itself is shunned. Men may even be despised, but the power which concern for men can unleash is used.

Many of the phenomena of modern secularism might well be traced back to unmasking the purpose behind ideological religion. Has it not been used sometimes as the opium of the people? Is not the adjective "Christian" simply a cover-up? May it not be that a good deal of social mistrust is due (in part at least) to the fact that a purely economic social concern is unconvincing, so that the ultimate cause of this mistrust is ideological?

4. JEOPARDIZING OF THE IDEAL BY ME

D. F. Strauss once said that the history of dogma is its judgment, since it leads to absurdity. One might say similarly that the history of the ideal is its judgment, since it is identical with the fall into ideology. Yet to say this is to fall victim to an optical illusion. For the ideal as such has no history. Only our relation to it has a history.

We are inclined in mythicizing fashion to ascribe a history to things and forces, especially when our own history is really at issue. Thus Jacob Burckhardt says that power is evil and he describes its insatiability and its lust for expansion. We also speak of the demonism of technology as though this were a being of its own and the subject of a history in which we men are involuntarily enmeshed. The ideal, too, is regarded as a temptress which entices us with its siren song and then finally dashes us against the cliffs.

Power, technology, and the ideal are favorite objects for the mythicization which deflects us away from our own history, i.e., from the history of powerful, technical, and idealistic man, and which thus offers us an excuse, as though these other things were really to blame for what happens, and we ourselves, I and Thou, were deceived and dragged along as tragic victims.

When the world is seen in this way, it takes on an apocalyptic hue. Secret forces lurk on every hand. Everything is dangerous. There is a dagger in every garment, suicidal power in science, falsehood in speech, aestheticism in art, night life in cities, clericalism and theocracy in the church. The mythical projections which in truth are only man's attempt to deflect attention from himself celebrate veritable orgies.

If we carry out the necessary demythologization—and it is much more profitable and relevant than that of the NT—we shall have to say, not that power is dangerous or evil, but that only the use of power can come under this verdict. The ideal itself is not a temptation; I myself am shown to be prone to temptation in my dealings with it. The ideal does not degenerate into ideology; I myself make it ideology.

The demythologizing of things and forces means that the apparently autonomous process becomes a piece of autobiography. I abandon the sentimental illusion that I am the victim of forces that have previously been mythicized and personified and come to see that this is simply an artifice of the old Adam who will not beat his own breast but tries to fashion a conductor for the lightning flash of judgment.

5. HEALING OF IDEALS

What therapy are we to seek here? In general terms the obvious answer is that if the fault arises through our use of ideals, this will also be the place of healing power for them.

Wrong attitudes to the ideal share a common feature. A material and impersonal perfection is envisaged. As noted, the utopian world dreams up a perfect order and sets it in the place of the Lord of world order. The order crowds out the person. Or again, in an ideological use of human relations, the economic apparatus crowds out the human person. Indeed, even when man makes himself the ideal in the form of a mythical leader or hero, he depersonalizes himself. He becomes the abstract and docetic bearer of qualities which are unreal and in distinction from which—in supreme irony—it is amusing to see him in private life.

The depersonalization which a wrong attitude to the ideal produces gives us an important clue to the right therapy. What is needed is an attitude which will remain human and personal and which will thus prevent an apparatus being put between us and our neighbors. The ideal can be valid, i.e., it will not entail a rejection of God, only if it keeps the neighbor before us and concern for him is not transferred to a perfect system.

The criterion whether the neighbor is still before us is whether we can love him. Jean Paul once said that love is the power to idealize. The interconnecting of love and the ideal can be fruitful so long as idealizing is not a trivial glorification but a process in which I understand and relate to the idea, or, better, the nature of the other. If there can be a form of idealizing which arises out of love rather than pragmatism or human hubris, this may show us how to seek theologically valid ideals, i.e., ideals which can be set in the sphere of the penultimate.

Now ideals can in fact arise out of love or personal relations. Thus love for one's mother can produce an idealized picture. Love of country can also lead us to speak in superlatives. To understand these idealized pictures as objective statements of reality is stupid. To call one's mother the most beautiful in the world or one's country the most glorious is not to compare them with other mothers or countries. Understood thus, for example, the ideal of one's country would be an ideological stimulus to nationalism. If we want to purify the ideal, to take from it the appearance and effects of hubris and idolatry, we have to fill out the idealization personally, or, better, to discover it in its possible personality. This can be done, however, not by equating it with mere goals or perfections, but only by seeking in the idealization the act through which we move toward men.

Concretely this means that such things as the state or democracy cannot be ideals in the strict sense. They are orders or structures which we cannot really "love." Although we cannot do this, we constantly do it, just as we worship idols even though basically this is not possible. Practice of such impossibilities avenges itself through the perversion to which we fall victim thereby. Objects which cannot be loved, and yet are loved, drive us into "isms."

In contrast, one's country can be the content of an ideal because it can be loved. It is the land of one's father and forefathers. It is filled with the image of one's neighbor. As home, it is the place in which I am related to men whom I meet on the way and who have a share in my destiny.

It may be noted, then, that questionable and erroneous ideals cannot be healed by demythologization alone but only by valid ideals that arise out of love. A demythologizing enlightenment affects only rationality and cannot trigger the dynamic historical action which is present when every dimension of the personality—will and imagination as well as reason—is affected. This is why Marxist-Leninism is strong enough to resist rational opposition, the unmasking of its ideal of classless society as ideology. It is not disturbed by mere demythicizing. To try to overthrow ideological bewitchment with the intellectualism of a purely negative enlightenment is absurd.

We can drive out the ideologized ideal only with the valid ideal. This is the image which love gives rise to: wives and children who are not enslaved; living societies which are not just collectives; freedom which does not become bondage to the functionary.

In relation to the personal nature of the true ideal it is significant that Jesus never speaks about the structure of the kingdom of God. He does not even hint at its material perfection. He relates it concretely to the neighbor. It is there when the lame walk, the blind see, and the poor have the gospel preached to them (Matthew 11:5). Albert Schweitzer is a good example of how this works out in practice. He could easily have dreamed up a utopia embodying his principle of reverence for life. Instead he went to Lambaréné and lived out the principle in the limited form of acts of concrete love. Similarly, the work of agencies like the Peace Corps in undeveloped lands is more important than conjuring up an ideal of planetary society, since it arises out of love for specific men to which other specific men are directed.

6. LOVE AS GUIDING IMAGE

Love for an ideal can be sober and healthy only when the ideal arises out of love. The excess of a false ideal can be checked, not by rational criticism, but only by the power of idealizing which love gives. Hence we do not decide in isolation from the ideal. The ideal contains within itself the question whether we will deify and absolutize it or whether we will expect from it the heuristic function of a guiding image.

Thus the teacher is bound to present ideals to his children and may even try to be an ideal. If he is a Christian, part of his witness will be to make it plain some day that he stands in solidarity with even the worst of them as a fallible and guilty man. But the point is that the child needs to go through the interim period of idealizing and should not say *a priori* that his teacher is no better than the rest. In contrast, if a teenager writes in an essay that Goethe is the greatest German poet, this is sad to read even though it may be true. The teenager should not be the one to write it.

Similarly the theological student who plays about with truths that the great ones in God's kingdom have arrived at only after a lifetime of intellectual struggle is like a boy whose mother has made his clothes so big that he has to grow into them. Both the ideal and its relativization have their proper age and time and hour.

Christian pedagogics can help us as we try to think through the basic problems that arise here. For it differs from humanistic pedagogics by not being oriented to the model of ideal man. It realizes that the development of man's impulses involves not only his creation and destiny but also demonic aspects, i.e., the tares which the adversary of God has also sown (Matthew 13:24ff.). The power of Christian education does not rest on ideal images which man has in front of him but on the events of creation and justification which he has behind him.

But just as the law corresponds to the gospel and God's Word is always two words and not just one, i.e., the word of judgment as well as the word of grace, so we do not have this truth only in retrospect. We also need interim images which we try to attain as goals. I have an imaginative side too, and I have to construct images if the divine gift of imagination is not to degenerate.

These images or ideals have primarily the role of the law since they bring me under judgment, as utopias do, until at a certain stage of experience and by existential action I bring them under judgment. When I do, however, this scepticism of spiritual sorrow differs at this point from a scepticism which thinks it knows it all without experience. It is better to begin with enthusiastic commitment, and then to run into the questions, than to be pessimistic from the very first and to try to avoid the idealistic detour. The prodigal son and his elder brother both realize that the far country is no ideal, but the former knows it through the suffering he has gone through while the latter stayed "nonhistorically" at home. This is why the angels of heaven rejoice over the knowledge of the prodigal; no one rejoices over the snobbism of the elder brother.

Can we ever get to the real thing, then, by premature scepticism and demythologization? We want things too directly, too cheaply, nonhistorically. The new form of fanaticism is not an illegal snatching at the eschaton but an illegal and nonhistorical judgment of the ideal which ought to come only through experience. The provisional is thus ignored and love, dedication, and passion are scorned. Christianity can become so wise that it also becomes sterile. The main thing is to keep step with God, not to run on ahead (D. Bonhoeffer). But we want to run on ahead. We want to be sceptical in order to spare ourselves the trouble of giving up ideals. We are afraid of the burden of detours. The statement that a straight line is the shortest distance between two points may be true in mathematics. It is not necessarily true in every other area.

7. PURPOSE OF DREAMS

Are we then to anathematize ideals because they stand in constant need of revision and restriction and because they present such a temptation? Does not this mean throwing out the baby with the bath water?

Creative passion in life depends on the ability to dream, no matter whether the dream be of a society or of a great man. A teacher who does not know how to teach us to dream, to conjure up ideal visions, is not worthy of the name. What would the world be without the dreams of fourteen-year-olds (Albert Schweitzer)? The dream is a glorification of the provisional. It is the passionate relation to it which engages the imagination. Can there be no place for this in Christian theology? This seems to be the common view today. We must now examine this view.

Only when we can dream and when our dreams can become a drive in active life does the critical question arise whether with the ideal I should be able to give disciplined thanks that there is something for us to admire, that God has given it authority and credibility in the shadow of sin and death, or whether I am merely setting up a false god. Only when I have a vision of the social state can I genuinely decide whether I am following an illusion of perfection which will finally perish of boredom or whether I realize that at the very best perfection can be only a basis for considering the real theme of human existence, namely, its achievement of meaning.

How can I know, however, whether it is obedience or idolatry, thankful admiration or illegitimate deification, if I evade the question by not venturing any ideals at all but taking refuge in a zone of ethical security which is not a place of obedience but a place beyond the decision between obedience and disobedience?

If we will not venture an ideal we are not asked whether we are prepared for sobriety. But the sobriety we think we have is really sterility. *A priori* chastity of this kind is simply impotence. One might also say that heady ideals must be ventured if we are to achieve true sobriety. To try to have the calm of age without going through the storms involves the penalty of not being wise at the right time. Premature cleverness gives way to senility.

The over-early scepticism which renounces all ideals is simply a triumph of worldly anxiety and not a triumph of the Kyrios who has overcome the world's anxiety. When this scepticism says that it is based on faith it is self-deception and a self-chosen idolatry. What is really at work is little faith rather than faith. This little faith is harassed by the vision of permanent failure. It does not trust the power of God to make something out of the spiritually poor, out of rich young rulers, out of intellectual sceptics, and out of over-imaginative idealists. It does not believe that God can gather people out of the lands of vision as well as the highways and hedges. Again, we have here a self-chosen idolatry to the extent that the illusion is cherished that one form of thought and feeling (namely, that of sceptical realism) is wholly congruent with the will of God and does not need grace, since it is constitutively in the truth.

The command to watch and be sober must not be made an end in itself, a virtue, a quality, a work. It has to be an attribute of faith, a readiness to be sober, a wakefulness, which allows us to dream even though we must be ready to wake up from our dreams. Otherwise we shall suffer from an endless tedium which will make the Lord of Christianity a caricature and which will cause the children of the world to flee from him before they have even heard a single word that he speaks.

8. GREATNESS AND MISERY OF THE IDEAL

Ideals are the visionary concentration of goals. They touch the imagination as well as abstract thought. When we follow them—as already suggested—we are like children playing with bricks and thinking they are living in the real world. Can we not really build in earnest because we know that the evening will come and we shall have to pack the bricks away? Is it not the greatness and gift of childhood that we can play and dream under our Father's eyes even though we are always ready to stop and pack up? Did not even Nietzsche realize that play is the best way of accomplishing great tasks?

Grace does not forbid playing and dreaming. The greatness of the ideal is precisely that we can play under the eyes of our Father. Its misery is that this is only play and that it has to stop when evening comes.

There is no place, of course, for absolutization. When we have to unpack our bricks in the morning and put them away again at night, this means that the ideal, insofar as it relates to Christian freedom, is always mobile and not fixed or static. Its status is heuristic. It is a trigger. It is penultimate and must be treated as such; it must not be rated higher than this. To take it seriously by not overrating it is to enter into a living and not just a static relation to it. A living relation is impossible, however, without will and imagination. The venture of interim idealization has thus to be made.

Even if the ideal can easily prove to be a confusing and fascinating bubble, we have to launch it into the air and not keep it on the ground. We have to learn to distinguish between what is true in it and what is false. The idea that we can preserve and domesticate ideals is a macabre one. If we are too afraid of tares we can never sow in hope.

Any man who is devoted to great goals has to dream about them. We can have visions without being mere visionaries. To be committed is to be committed in imagination too. The man who wills to do great things does not just will; he is also driven by emotions and inspired by ideals. Dreams are only anxious frenzy, however, if they are under constant control and are bombarded with orders instead of enjoying free course.

To make a goal of the penultimate, of ideals of state and society, of the visions of saints and heroes, is to take from them the radiance of creation and to rob them of dignity and authority. To live only in the name of the ultimate and to ignore the penultimate is to sin against this world by despising it pragmatically, by merely exploiting and harnessing such divinely given entities as country and friendship and authority, by refusing to become existentially involved.

It is also to lose the ultimate whose name is invoked for this relativization. If this world no longer shines and its dreams are extinguished, so that the world is empty and void as it was before creation, we can no longer hear the world-overcoming message of the miracle of death and resurrection and our ears are closed to the fact that the gospel transcends everything we love. How can there be anything of faith or of the defiance of the Nevertheless in a man who imagines that the resurrection and eternal life have to compete with earthly dreams? We do not have to break everything down in order to hear the consolation of the gospel, as in sermons which first show how terrible and meaningless everything is, and then point to faith as the way of deliverance.

Rivalry between God's kingdom and the wasteland of the world is too cheap. God's transcendence is better portrayed in the hymn: "Fair is the sunshine, Fairer still the moonlight, And all the twinkling, starry host; Jesus shines brighter, Jesus shines purer, Than all the angels heaven can boast." Firmaments and ideals pale before his greatness, but they do shine. To think that the light of eternity can shine only by making the earth dark and quenching ideals does little glory to God. It surrenders earth in order to honor heaven. It betrays the penultimate and in so doing makes the ultimate a docetic shadow.

It is sad to see how many contemporaries make the gospel a mere safeguard against playing with other fires. Christians are putting up warning lights everywhere, whether it be against ideals, or art, or secular wisdom. The world of flashing red lights—is that the world which redemption is meant for? Was the outpouring of Golgotha necessary for this sorry display? Can we really take the penultimate seriously if we view the world only as the product of our demythicizing?

From the broken walls of this perishing world the praise of Christians sounds forth, and only in praise and worship of the ultimate do they find sure and certain rest. They have this where God watches over them, where they weep and laugh, where they are sober and enthusiastic, where they are serious and yet engage in play. But self-selected stages and artificial sobrieties are not entrance halls to the kingdom of God. The world raves and leaps, and the ideal is dangerous. The Christian, however, stands in the shadow of the divine protection and knows something of the art of indulging in ideals and scorning the tempter.

Indexes

1. NAMES

405

2. SUBJECTS

3. SCRIPTURE REFERENCES

181 - Revelation ≠ Bible
140 - Kant's ethical system = Paul's